Currencies and Politics in the United States, Germany, and Japan

C. RANDALL HENNING

Currencies and Politics in the United States, Germany, and Japan

Institute for International Economics
Washington, DC
September 1994

C. Randall Henning, Research Associate, is coeditor of *Reviving the European Union* (1994), coauthor of *Dollar Politics: Exchange Rate Policymaking in the United States* (1989) and *Can Nations Agree? Issues in International Economic Cooperation* (1989), and author of and *Macroeconomic Diplomacy in the 1980s: Domestic Politics and International Conflict Among the United States, Japan, and Europe* (1987). He has written several articles on the politics of economic policymaking and international economic relations and has taught international political economy at American University.

INSTITUTE FOR INTERNATIONAL
ECONOMICS
11 Dupont Circle, NW
Washington, DC 20036-1207
(202) 328-9000   FAX: (202) 328-5432

C. Fred Bergsten, *Director*
Christine F. Lowry, *Director of Publications*

Cover design by Naylor Design, Inc.
Typesetting by Sandra F. Watts
Printing by Victor Graphics, Inc.

Printed in the United States of America
97 96 95 94   8 7 6 5 4 3 2

Library of Congress Cataloging-in-Publication Data

Henning, C. Randall.
    Currencies and Politics in the United States, Germany, and Japan / C. Randall Henning.
        p. cm.
    Includes bibliographical references and index.
    1. International finance. 2. Monetary policy—United States. 3. Foreign exchange—United States. 4. Monetary policy—Germany. 5. Foreign exchange—Germany. 6. Monetary policy—Japan. 7. Foreign exchange—Japan. I. Title.
    HG3881.H4269 1994
    332′.042—dc20   93-36895
                                                CIP

ISBN 0-88132-127-3

Marketed and Distributed outside the USA and Canada by Longman Group UK Limited, London

The views expressed in this publication are those of the author. This publication is part of the overall program of the Institute, as endorsed by its Board of Directors, but does not necessarily reflect the views of individual members of the Board or the Advisory Committee.

To my parents,
with love and appreciation

Contents

Preface

The Institute for International Economics has conducted ongoing research on the economics of international cooperation, especially among the major industrialized countries. We have published two important proposals for increasing the scope of policy coordination by John Williamson, *The Exchange Rate System* (1983, revised 1985) and *Targets and Indicators: A Blueprint for the International Coordination of Economic Policy* (1987, with Marcus H. Miller). The topic is addressed explicitly by Wendy Dobson in *Economic Policy Coordination: Requiem or Prologue?* (1991). It plays an important part in a number of our broader analyses, including *Deficits and the Dollar: The World Economy at Risk* by Stephen Marris (1985, revised 1987) and my *America in the World Economy: A Strategy for the 1990s* (1988).

In addition, the Institute has continually tried to assess the political foundations of international economic cooperation and the practical possibilities for implementing new designs. In the trade area, I. M. Destler's *American Trade Politics* (1986, revised 1992) has become a classic. On monetary issues, Yoichi Funabashi's *Managing the Dollar: From the Plaza to the Louvre* (1988, revised 1989) became the second leading nonfiction bestseller in Japan. John Williamson's *The Political Economy of Policy Reform* (1994) addressed the political underpinnings of the economic reforms that have been implanted successfully around the world in recent years.

Of most direct relevance to this volume, I. M. Destler and C. Randall Henning published *Dollar Politics: Exchange Rate Policymaking in the United States* in 1989. This was the first analysis of the domestic politics and procedures through which exchange rate policy is made in the United States. In this new book, Dr. Henning conducts a similar study of the other most important national economies, Germany and Japan, and extends his earlier analysis of the United States. The objectives are two-fold: to suggest improved policies and procedures in each of these three key countries, and especially to derive lessons for how they can cooperate more effectively on economic issues in the real world. Effective international economic cooperation must of course be grounded in realistic and sustainable political conditions in the countries that are most central to the cooperation process, and this book proposes new ways to link the politics and economics that could improve the prospects for such action.

The Institute for International Economics is a private nonprofit institution for the study and discussion of international economic policy. Its purpose is to analyze important issues in that area, and to develop and communicate practical new approaches for dealing with them. The Institute is completely nonpartisan.

The Institute is funded largely by philanthropic foundations. Major institutional grants are now being received from the German Marshall Fund of the United States, which created the Institute with a generous commitment of funds in 1981, and from the Ford Foundation, the William and Flora Hewlett Foundation, the William M. Keck, Jr. Foundation, the C. V. Starr Foundation, and the United States–Japan Foundation. A number of other foundations and private corporations also contribute to the highly diversified financial resources of the Institute. The Centre for Global Partnership provided partial support for this study. About 16 percent of the Institute's resources in our latest fiscal year were provided by contributors outside the United States, including about 7 percent from Japan.

The Board of Directors bears overall responsibility for the Institute and gives general guidance and approval to its research program—including identification of topics that are likely to become important to international economic policymakers over the medium run (generally, one to three years), and which thus should be addressed by the Institute. The Director, working closely with the staff and outside Advisory Committee, is responsible for the development of particular projects and makes the final decision to publish an individual study.

The Institute hopes that its studies and other activities will contribute to building a stronger foundation for international economic policy around the world. We invite readers of these publications to let us know how they think we can best accomplish this objective.

C. FRED BERGSTEN
Director
July 1994

x

Acknowledgments

I want to acknowledge at the outset all of the people who have contributed in numerous ways in the preparation of this book. I am somewhat awed by the length of this list and therefore the size of the debt that I have accumulated. Not only has the study benefited greatly from the contribution of colleagues and friends, but I have benefited intellectually and personally as well. My heartfelt thanks goes out to all of them.

I wish first to acknowledge C. Fred Bergsten and my colleagues at the Institute for International Economics for their support and critical review of this study. I cannot imagine a more stimulating intellectual environment for research in international economics and economic policymaking. The Institute has served as an ideal base for conducting this research project.

The second group that I wish to thank are the officials and former officials of governments, central banks, and political parties, and the executives of private banks, corporations, and representative associations in the United States, Germany, and Japan who consented to be interviewed in the course of my study. Most of them have requested anonymity and are therefore not cited in the text. Some of them also have commented on portions of the manuscript. This book would have been very different had it not been for knowledge of the first-hand experience of policymakers and private executives. I am very grateful for their generous sharing of time and information.

The third group to which I owe thanks are those people who have commented on drafts of all or part of the study. Peter Gourevitch, Stephan Haggard, Wilhelm Nölling, and Shijuro Ogata read and commented on virtually the entire manuscript, as did my wife, Heidi Ebel Henning. Many other people gave me helpful comments on chapter drafts or seminar presentations. Their advice and guidance were essential to this book. These people include James Ammerman, David M. Andrews, John M. Balder, Benjamin J. Cohen, Stephen Cooney, Wendy K. Dobson, Claudia Dziobek, Kimberly A. Elliott, Jessica Einhorn, Elena Folkerts-Landau, Jeffry A. Frieden, Hans-Peter Fröhlich, William Helkie, Keisuke Iida, Reimut Jochimsen, Karl Kaltenthaler, Ethan Kapstein, Peter B. Kenen, Michael

Kriele, Roger M. Kubarych, James Lister, Paul R. Masson, Andrew Moravcsik, Henry R. Nau, Marcus Noland, John S. Odell, Takeshi Ohta, Gumersindo Oliveros, Kenneth A. Oye, Scott Pardee, Louis W. Pauly, Jacques J. Polak, Detlev Rahmsdorff, Beate Reszat, J. David Richardson, Wolfgang Rieke, Jeremiah M. Riemer, W. R. Smyser, Robert Solomon, Edwin Truman, Niels Thygesen, Paul J. J. Welfens, John C. Wiecking, John Williamson, Paul Wonnacott, John T. Woolley, and Robert Zoellick. Over the course of the study I received constructive comments from many other people at a number of seminars at which I presented my findings, including a study group meeting held at the Institute for International Economics, the MIT/Harvard Seminar on International Institutions, a panel of an annual meeting of the American Political Science Association, and the International Business seminar at the Georgetown University School of Business.

I am also indebted to people who have written on policymaking in the countries treated here. Although these people are cited in the chapters that follow, I wish also to acknowledge a couple of them here. The chapter on the United States draws on a previous book and thus on the insights and contributions of my coauthor in that project, I. M. Destler, who also commented extensively on drafts for this book. The chapters on central banks and Germany benefited from an excellent book on the politics of central banking by John B. Goodman, who commented on this manuscript as well. I want to extend special thanks to him and Lou Pauly for their constructive criticism and encouragement throughout the study. Several conversations with Jerry Riemer also helped me to clarify my treatment of Germany.

I wish to acknowledge a number of research assistants who have worked with me, some of them on a volunteer basis, including Jason Lorber, Farah L. Press, Daniel Rosen, Regina Rüpke, Aaron Tam, Heinz Waechli, Christopher Wendel, and Michelle Wilkes. Naoko Anzai, Johanna Buurman, John Fowler, and Jeffrey Yost also contributed to the project. Their help has been invaluable, as has that of Anthony Stancil, who has assisted in preparing the manuscript.

I very much appreciate, as well, the help and expertise of Brigitte Coulton, Christine Lowry, and Valerie Norville in shepherding the manuscript to final publication.

Finally, the project was sustained not only by the Institute for International Economics but also by the logistical support provided by other organizations during my research trips to Germany and Japan. Those are principally the Deutsche Gesellschaft für Auswärtige Politik in Bonn, the Deutsche Bank Research Department in Frankfurt, and the Japan Center for International Finance in Tokyo.

Needless to say, these people and institutions do not necessarily share the conclusions reached here. None of these people or institutions are in any way responsible for flaws or omissions of any kind that might remain in the book.

Currencies and Politics in the United States, Germany, and Japan

1

Introduction

The three countries that are, at present and for the foreseeable future, most important to the management of international trade, finance, and macroeconomic affairs are the United States, Germany, and Japan. The relationships between the US dollar, on the one hand, and the German mark and the Japanese yen, on the other, dominate the international monetary system. American, German, and Japanese policies toward the foreign value of their currencies and the international monetary regime determine the macroeconomic "face" of each national economy toward the world economy. The external monetary policies of each of these three countries also determine the degree of cooperation among them, both bilaterally and multilaterally within the Group of Seven (G-7).

These three countries, though, have pursued very different external monetary policies since World War II. Japan and Germany adopted external monetary policies sensitive to the competitiveness of their national industries during most of this period. They maintained competitively valued currencies, using the full panoply of instruments available to manage the exchange rate directly. These two countries, furthermore, targeted domestic monetary policy toward stabilizing the exchange rate, Japan to a significantly greater extent than Germany.

The United States, on the other hand, often neglected the impact of exchange rates on the competitiveness of its traded goods sectors altogether. American authorities used foreign exchange intervention less often than did their counterparts in Japan and Germany. The United States adjusted domestic monetary policy for external reasons only rarely, and in those cases to support, not to depress, the value of the dollar. These differences in the patterns of external monetary policy among the three countries were entrenched, and they recurred over these decades.

This book is about the politics, institutions, and processes relating to external and internal monetary policymaking in the United States, Germany, and Japan. Previous studies of international monetary policymaking have been written on each of these countries separately. Despite the central importance of these countries to the world economy and their respective regions, however, no systematic comparison of external monetary policymaking within the three over a long period has been published.[1] In addition, the literature's coverage of these countries has been uneven: much more has been written (in all languages) about US external monetary policymaking than about German and Japanese policymaking. This book seeks to fill these gaps.

The specific analytical objective of this study is to explain the *differences* in the external monetary policies pursued by the three countries over the postwar period. In what ways did the United States, Germany, and Japan differ so as to generate contrasting policies? What was the source of the sensitivity of policy to competitiveness in Germany and Japan? Why did American policy periodically lapse into neglect of the exchange rate? This study seeks to identify the causes of the differences in the behavior of governments toward exchange rate problems.

The study is motivated by a desire to develop a better understanding of the fundamental determinants of policy outcomes as part of a search for improvement and advancement of policy performance. Between the triumphs and successes in exchange rate policy and international macroeconomic cooperation, there have also been grave errors and failures. The belief that governments and central banks can do better at stabilizing exchange rates and managing the world economy underlies this study. Some of the recommendations made at the end of this book hinge on this normative assessment of the potential for better international cooperation. The conclusions that emerge from the positive analysis of what causes the differences in policy outcomes among these three countries, however, are independent of this judgment.

Insufficient Explanations

A number of explanations are often used, casually, to explain the policy differences exhibited by the United States, Germany, Japan, and other countries in external monetary matters. One approach, a structural realist explanation, looks to the status of each country in the international economic system, in particular its location in the global hierarchy of economic power. A second simply looks to the openness of each country's

---

1. See the country chapters in this study for references to single-country studies and studies that compare two of the three countries considered here.

economy, in terms of the size of international trade flows in relation to national output. A third explanation stresses the domestic position of the state, particularly its strength relative to private actors and its activism in pursuit of industrial and economic development.

These explanations bring fundamental insights to bear on the comparative analysis of external monetary policymaking. Unfortunately, each for different reasons, these approaches do not specify policy outcomes in a fully satisfactory manner. Rather, they circumscribe only weakly the range of possible policy choices, leaving a great deal of policy variation unexplained. None of these theories is sufficient to explain the differences in policies exhibited by the United States, Germany, and Japan over the postwar period.

Consider the explanatory value of the international structure of economic power with reference to the United States. Structural realism predicts that a hegemonic power will bear a disproportionate share of the costs associated with creating and maintaining international regimes from which it also derives offsetting benefits. Because it held economic and political predominance during the two decades following World War II, according to this reasoning, the United States had the greatest interest in maintaining a smoothly functioning international monetary regime.

Superior economic power does help to explain US policy during the early postwar period. Under the Bretton Woods regime, the United States adopted a passive stance toward the valuation of the dollar and the balance of payments, thus enabling other countries to meet their own objectives. The costs of maintaining the regime, in terms of the progressive appreciation of the dollar and the vulnerability associated with the widespread use of the dollar as an international currency, were manageable given the size of the US economy. The supreme technological and competitive position of American producers, on which hegemony rested, enabled private corporations to countenance the progressive appreciation of the dollar in real terms and its overvaluation during the 1960s.

However, structural realism falls short of a complete explanation of national policies in a number of ways. First, power considerations do not explain the persistence of periodic neglect of the exchange rate and periodic acceptance of overvaluation on the part of US policymakers after the downfall of Bretton Woods in the early 1970s. Even after Europe and Japan mounted fierce competition against American producers, and after the switch to flexible exchange rates, US policy often exhibited a passivity with respect to international monetary affairs similar to that shown during the 1950s and 1960s. Second, this theoretical approach does not explain policy differences between countries similarly situated in the international structure of economic power. The substantial differences between Germany and Japan, as well as Britain and France, are not explained by their relative power status.

National power, fundamentally, tells us little about how governments select the objectives toward which they direct the influence at their disposal. American administrations in the 1960s, for example, might have taken preventive measures, such as a devaluation of the dollar, or could have redoubled their attempts to secure adjustment on the part of foreign partners to preserve the Bretton Woods regime, but chose not to. Hegemonic position alone cannot explain US choices in these matters, and policy outcomes were not preordained by American strength. Germany's experience since the late 1970s within the European Monetary System (EMS) demonstrates that countries with regional dominance can adopt very different roles within the monetary regimes centered upon them. Structural realism is notoriously poor at specifying national preferences in international economic relations, and in monetary relations in particular.

The next approach, focusing on the relative openness of each country's economy, explains part of the variation in policy outcomes among the United States, Germany, and Japan. Openness—as measured by the size of imports and exports in relation to GNP—increases the importance of the exchange rate to the domestic economy. Countries that are open are more likely to adjust domestic macroeconomic policies for the sake of external targets such as the balance of payments and the exchange rate. A more closed economy increases the value of monetary autonomy. Thus, the relative closure of the US economy limited both the costs of mistakes and the benefits of success in international trade and monetary affairs. American policymakers could afford to neglect the exchange rate from time to time while German and Japanese policymakers could not.

However, like structural realism, openness is not a sufficient explanation. First, the differences in external monetary policy do not correlate with differences in openness across countries. The Japanese economy, like the US economy, is far more closed than the German economy. Yet, in several ways, Japanese exchange rate policy has been as activist and conscious of competitiveness as Germany's, if not more so.[2] Second, changes in external monetary policies over time are not correlated with changes in openness. Both Germany and Japan experienced an increase in openness over the postwar period, a dramatic change in the case of Germany. Yet the priority these governments attached to a competitively valued currency has declined somewhat since the early postwar years.

---

2. The absence of a correlation between openness and policy outcomes is accentuated when we broaden our scope to the Group of Five (G-5) countries. Britain's economy is more open than either France's or Japan's, yet its external monetary policy bears strong similarities to American policy. France, on the other hand, pursued a set of competitiveness-conscious policies oriented toward exchange rate stability, much more like Japan's and Germany's than Britain's.

Fundamentally, openness restructures the choices available to policy-makers by creating additional opportunities as well as constraints on economic policies. Factors other than openness determine how governments take advantage of the opportunities and make trade-offs imposed by constraints. Openness makes the economy more sensitive to the exchange rate, but this reasoning cannot specify whether an open country will favor a low- or high-valued currency.

Finally, the role of the state provides a similarly incomplete explanation. The pursuit of export competitiveness by Japan is often attributed to the presence of a developmental, neomercantilist state, dominated by powerful and autonomous ministerial bureaucrats. The persistent undervaluation of the yen, this approach would suggest, was a product of this strategy of the state. But the priority attached to competitiveness in exchange rate policy remained high in Japan even after the decline of the developmental role of the state. Moreover, the pattern of Japanese exchange rate policymaking during the 1970s and 1980s, as described in subsequent chapters, does not suggest ministerial autonomy from private actors in the face of appreciation of the yen. Germany also pursued export competitiveness despite the very different structure and role of the German state. As for the United States, the American state is often described as porous and weak vis-à-vis societal actors but is, in fact, relatively autonomous in the area of exchange rate and monetary policy. The autonomy of the American state in this area, as discussed below, is very much a function of the structure of the private sector.

A state-centered approach falls short of a complete explanation on several grounds. First, precisely how states adopt a developmental role is often left unexamined. The state and society evolve together, and the role of the state, even if it is autonomous, is defined with reference to the economic and regulatory needs of the private sector. Second, the specification of state preferences in external monetary policy is ambiguous. The strength of the state and its autonomy from societal actors offer little guide as to whether the state will pursue a low-valued or a high-valued currency. Third, the state is not a unitary actor. Rather, the state is comprised of ministries and executive agencies, each with their own missions and objectives. The stronger the ministries are relative to the private sector, the stronger and more intense the competition among them is likely to be.

Highlighting the role of the state reminds us that the interests of government decision makers are separate from the interests of private actors. But, for the purposes of this study, the analysis of government institutions is best done by disaggregating the state into its agencies and ministries, specifically the central bank and, in most instances, the ministry of finance. The actions of government policymakers should be placed within the context of the private sector and the institutions that structure private-sector inputs to decision makers and thus determine their freedom of maneuver. This is the approach taken in the present study.

The Main Argument

This study argues that private-sector preferences and government institutions jointly determine the disposition of the United States, Germany,
and Japan toward international monetary matters. The relationship between private banks and industry within the countries studied fundamentally determines private-sector preferences on external currency valuation and the private-sector's ability to influence exchange rate policy.
Where banks are close to industry, specifically, private preferences tend
to favor a competitively valued, stable currency. Where banks are distant from industry, private preferences are weak and often discordant.
The degree to which private-sector preferences are translated into policy
outcomes depends on the organization of government institutions. The
independence of the central bank in setting domestic monetary policy,
primarily, and the relationship between the central bank and finance
ministry in setting external monetary policy, secondarily, determine whether
private preferences are served and, if so, which groups and sectors are
favored.

Analysis of the politics of exchange rate policy often emphasizes state
actors and institutions—principally central banks, finance ministries, and
other government ministries—and intergovernmental bargaining, to the
exclusion of societal preferences. Private-sector preferences, this study
argues, should be the starting point of the analysis, particularly of comparative analysis. A clear conception of societal preferences and how
they are formed is fundamental. This study develops the conceptual links
between the relationship between banks and industry, on the one hand,
and preferences regarding currency valuation and stability, on the other.

There are three principal causal connections between bank-industry
relations and external monetary policy: commonality of interests, interest
aggregation and expression, and channels of access to policymakers. First,
in countries where private banks and industry are close, the banks develop a strong interest in the international competitiveness of industrial
firms. In countries where banks and industry are relatively distant, banks
are far less concerned about firm competitiveness. Second, close ties between banks and industry facilitate the building of a consensus within
the private sector and its coherent articulation to official policymakers.
Third, strong relations with banking institutions open channels of access
for industry to the exchange rate policymaking process. Competitiveness-conscious and stability-oriented exchange rate policies are therefore
likely to be more effectively promoted by the private sector in countries
with close ties between banks and industry than in those with distant
ties. (These connections are treated in detail in chapter 2.)

Private preferences do not themselves produce policy, of course. The
institutions and agencies of the state make policy, specifically the government ministries, usually the ministry of finance, and the central bank.

Private preferences contribute substantially to policymaking, but are "refracted" or distorted by government institutions during their translation into policy outcomes. An independent central bank is likely to set limits on the extent to which a low-valued currency and corresponding inflation will be tolerated, and those limits might conflict with private preferences. The structures of both private preference formation and public institutions, therefore, are necessary to explain policy outcomes.

The organization of the private sector and the organization of the state are variables that have been stressed in the field of comparative political economy. The comparative analysis of the role of banks and financial systems has a venerable tradition going back as far as Alfred Marshall and, after World War II, Alexander Gerschenkron and Andrew Shonfield.[3] That tradition has been modernized by authors such as John Zysman, who stresses the bank-industry relationship in his exploration of industrial policy in France and Britain, and Peter Gourevitch.[4]

Peter Katzenstein and others compared foreign economic policies of advanced industrial states in the mid-1970s, in a study that incorporated private-sector organization and central bank independence in two composite variables, the degree of centralization of the state and society.[5] Peter Hall emphasized the financial system, central bank status, and international financial linkages in an institutional explanation of British and French macroeconomic and exchange rate policies, which includes illuminating comparisons to Germany.[6] In stressing the importance of the organization of the private sector and government institutions, the argument developed in this study also has much in common with a broader branch of political science that views institutions as crucial determinants of policy.[7]

---

3. Alfred Marshall, *Industry and Trade* (London: Macmillan, 1919); Alexander Gerschenkron, *Economic Backwardness in Historical Perspective: A Book of Essays* (Cambridge, MA: Harvard University Press, 1962); Andrew Shonfield, *Modern Capitalism: The Changing Balance of Public & Private Power* (London: Oxford University Press, 1969).

4. Peter Gourevitch, *Politics in Hard Times: Comparative Responses to International Economic Crises* (Ithaca, NY: Cornell University Press, 1986); John Zysman, *Governments, Markets, and Growth: Financial Systems and the Politics of Industrial Change* (Ithaca, NY: Cornell University Press, 1983).

5. Peter J. Katzenstein, ed., *Between Power and Plenty: Foreign Economic Policies of Advanced Industrial States* (Madison: Wisconsin University Press, 1978).

6. Peter Hall, *Governing the Economy: The Politics of State Intervention in Britain and France* (New York: Oxford University Press, 1986). See in particular chapter 9.

7. For examples of the approach labeled "new institutionalism," see James G. March and Johan P. Olsen, *Rediscovering Institutions: The Organizational Basis of Politics* (New York: Free Press, 1989); Douglass C. North, *Institutions, Institutional Change and Economic Performance* (Cambridge, UK: Cambridge University Press, 1990).

The present study builds on this earlier work first by explicating the ramifications of the relationship between banks and industry for the formation of external monetary preferences. Second, the study specifies how private preferences interact with central bank independence in the policymaking process. Third, the study reviews the postwar history of external monetary policymaking arrangements in each country, with emphasis on the floating-rate period. Finally, the study applies these concepts for the first time to a comparison of US, German, and Japanese external monetary policymaking.

External Monetary Policy

A word about the dependent variable, external monetary policy, is in order. By this term, I mean *state action to affect the external value and the international use of the national currency and the state's stance toward the international monetary regime.* The emphasis of this study is on what determines the behavior of the state (comprising ministries, central banks, and senior executive decision makers) and how the state responds to the challenges and opportunities that confront it in the international monetary realm.

Note that this study is not an attempt to explain exchange rate *market* outcomes, the particular levels at which markets value national currencies. This study is not an effort to develop a political economy model of exchange rate determination. The book explains *policy* outcomes: what governments and central banks do to manage the exchange rate, the role of the currency, and the regime. Exchange market outcomes are produced jointly by government policy and private activity, under flexible rate regimes. Because this study explains state action, not private activity, the market exchange rate would not be an appropriate proxy for government policy behavior.

The distinction between government action and exchange market outcomes is fundamentally important to the analysis conducted here. For example, both the German mark (hereafter referred to as the D-mark) and Japanese yen appreciated in nominal terms over the flexible-rate period. This fact alone tells us little about external monetary policy per se, however. The key question for this study is, did the German and Japanese governments resist, encourage, or take a neutral stance toward the appreciation of their currencies? The actions of the government and central bank in Germany and Japan describe the policy outcomes for the two countries. Thus, while the study will refer to market exchange rates frequently, they are not themselves the dependent variable.

In studying some economic policy areas, it is sufficient to look at simple measures to determine the policy stance of the state. Fiscal policy can be measured by the budget deficit. Trade policy can be measured by

Table 1.1 Elements of external monetary policy

1. Adjustments of domestic monetary policy to influence the exchange rate
2. Foreign exchange intervention
3. Capital controls
4. Stance toward the international role of the currency
5. Consistency of policy over time

the tariff or quota imposed. Monetary policy can be measured by the short-term interest rate, which the central bank controls. In the study of exchange rate policymaking, however, simple measures can be misleading. Under a fixed exchange rate regime, the exchange rate parity is a clear policy responsibility of the government. Under a flexible exchange rate regime, however, the exchange rate is not directly controlled by governments and is thus not an appropriate proxy for policy per se.

To assess policy outcomes, therefore, we must examine the use of the instruments that governments and central banks control directly. Because governments and central banks can use several tools to manage the external value of their currencies, assessing policy outcomes requires a broad survey of the use of these various instruments. The present study surveys five aspects of government and central bank management of exchange rates, listed in table 1.1. When combined, they present a comprehensive portrait, sketched in summary form at the end of the study, of external monetary policy in the three countries over the decades.

First, *domestic monetary policy* strongly affects the nominal exchange rate and is therefore a powerful tool of exchange rate management. Particularly as it is applied to the pursuit of exchange rate objectives, domestic monetary policy (interest rates and money growth) is thus part of external monetary policy under the broad definition adopted here. Because it affects the exchange rate by making financial assets more or less attractive to international investors, domestic monetary policy is as much a part of this study as the other tools of currency management.

Because the targeting of domestic monetary policy toward the exchange rate can compromise domestic objectives, however, governments and central banks often buy and sell foreign currency on the exchange markets directly. Governments and central banks have also used taxes and administrative controls on capital flows to manage the value of the currency. Thus, *foreign exchange intervention* and *capital controls* are the second and third elements of external monetary policy reviewed here. As tools that can separate domestic and external monetary conditions, these instruments are "wedging" techniques. Because the international use of a currency affects the range of options available to the issuing central bank and its government, fourth, the *role of the currency* in international trade, private financial portfolios, and official reserves is also an object of policy.

Finally, the study examines the continuity of government policy behavior over time. Are policymakers consistent and steady in their pursuit of exchange rate goals? Or does their attention to external monetary issues wax and wane over time? Policy continuity in itself is not an instrument of exchange rate management, strictly speaking. However, it indicates the degree of importance authorities attach to sending consistent price and policy signals to private actors engaged in international trade and investment. *Policy consistency* is thus the fifth element of policy considered in the country histories.

The dependent variable, encompassing these five elements, is intentionally defined in this study in comprehensive terms. This is necessary for a complete analysis of external monetary policymaking, because these tools are close substitutes for one another in exchange rate management. Examining only one tool, such as intervention or capital controls, while neglecting others, such as domestic monetary policy, would give a misleadingly incomplete picture of policy outcomes. Therefore, although the definition imposes a requirement that the country histories survey the use of several instruments for currency management—a considerable challenge for the case histories—the broad rather than narrow construction was selected as a more complete description of policy outcomes.

A country that pursues competitiveness-conscious and stability-oriented external monetary policies—as the previous section argued would be the tendency of a country with close relations between banks and industry—would tend to adjust domestic monetary policy to influence the exchange rate, intervene in foreign exchange markets, and impose capital controls, or some combination of these tools more often or with greater intensity than a country that does not pursue such policies. Such a country also is more likely to discourage an international role for the currency and to maintain consistency in policy over time. Note that a policy oriented toward "competitiveness," in the sense that the term is used here, seeks an exchange rate consistent with expanding or maintaining market share in tradeable goods. The term does not mean "competitive devaluation" and is consistent with either a depreciating or stable currency.

The treatment of domestic monetary policy in this study deserves an additional comment. Under some circumstances, governments can drive wedges between domestic and external monetary policy successfully. But, with the high degree of capital mobility that prevailed during the 1980s, external monetary policy must be broadly consistent with domestic monetary policy. Often, that consistency is achieved by adjusting exchange rate targets to conform to domestic monetary objectives. That is not always the case, however; sometimes domestic monetary policy is adjusted to conform to exchange rate objectives. For this reason among others, the use of domestic monetary policy as an exchange rate instrument lies at the center of the process of policymaking examined here.

Examining this use of domestic monetary policy raises the methodologically delicate problem of ascertaining the counterfactual monetary policy—the policy that would have been pursued in the absence of an exchange rate target or currency crisis. Would domestic monetary policy have remained unchanged in the absence of an undesirable depreciation of the currency, for example, or would the central bank have lowered interest rates for internal reasons in any event? The counterfactual monetary policy cannot be known for certain, of course, but, equally, constructing the probable counterfactual is indispensable to the task of reviewing the full range of government action to affect the exchange rate. Because an overview of domestic monetary policy, and the domestic and international considerations weighing upon it, is necessary to identify the probable counterfactual path, a discussion of domestic monetary policymaking figures prominently in the country case studies that follow.

There is a vigorous debate among economists over the relationship between government policy and exchange rates, as well as between exchange rates and the ultimate objectives of policy, output, and employment. Economists generally accept that changes in domestic monetary policy affect the nominal exchange rate, and therefore the real exchange rate over the short and medium term. Whether domestic monetary policy affects the real exchange rate over the long term is a more controversial issue. A second controversial issue is whether foreign exchange intervention affects the exchange rate if it does not also change domestic monetary conditions. During the 1980s, the majority of international economists were skeptical of the power of such "sterilized" intervention.[8] The failure of massive intervention to prevent the European currency crises of 1992–93 has reinforced general skepticism. However, two recent studies, based on daily intervention data previously unavailable to academic researchers, could well revise this conventional wisdom. Three researchers from the Bank of Italy conclude that internationally concerted interventions in the market for US dollars were effective during each of the 17 episodes in which they were conducted during 1985–91.[9] Dominguez and Frankel conclude that intervention was effective when

---

8. Hali J. Edison, *The Effectiveness of Central-Bank Intervention: A Survey of the Literature After 1982*, Special Papers in International Economics, No. 18 (Princeton: Princeton University, July 1993); Edison, "Foreign Currency Operations: An Annotated Bibliography," International Finance Discussion Papers, No. 380 (Washington: Federal Reserve Board of Governors, May 1990). For a nontechnical review, see Peter B. Kenen, *Managing Exchange Rates* (London: Royal Institute for International Affairs, 1988). Central banks "sterilize" intervention when they conduct open market operations to offset the effects of intervention on the money supply.

9. Pietro Catte, Giampaolo Galli, and Salvatore Rebecchini, "Concerted Interventions and the Dollar: An Analysis of Daily Data," paper prepared for the Ossola Memorial Conference, Perugia, July 1992, table 2, p. 5.

it was publicly announced or otherwise known to currency traders.[10] Although these economic links between government policy and exchange market outcomes are not examined in this study, there is more than sufficient evidence of the economic importance of policy to justify a study of policy determination that uses the tools of political economy.

Note, as well, that it is the broad pattern of policy outcomes over time, not dramatic shifts and specific policy announcements, that is important to this study. The formal cessation of gold convertibility in August 1971, the dollar rescue package of November 1978, the Plaza Agreement of 1985, and the Louvre Accord of 1987, for example, represent dramatic changes in American policy. These events are important as tiles in a mosaic that presents a larger picture of US policy—the degree of engagement of the government on currency matters, the cycles of neglect and activism, and periodic toleration of overvaluation. The independent variables selected in this study, private and government organization, generally change rarely or gradually over time and thus could not explain sharp or temporary changes in the dependent variable. The differences in the general patterns of policy outcomes of the three countries are the main interest of this study.

Study Design

The United States, Germany, and Japan were selected for this study for two main reasons. First, as noted above, these countries possess the three economies that are the most important to international commerce and finance. Second, each country has a distinct combination of the two main independent variables described above, private-sector organization and central bank status. The matrix in figure 1.1 displays these combinations for each country. As shown, the United States has weak connections between private banks and industry and a relatively independent central bank. Germany has strong ties between banks and industry and an independent central bank. Japan also has close bank-industry connections but a much less independent central bank. Examining different combinations of the independent variables gives the study explanatory leverage. As the case studies reveal, each combination of private-sector structure and central bank status produces a different set of policy outcomes.

To broaden the generalizability of the conclusions reached in this study, the experience of Britain and France will also be considered. Britain occupies the remaining quadrant in figure 1.1: it has weak ties between

---

10. Kathryn Dominguez and Jeffrey A. Frankel, *Does Foreign Exchange Intervention Work?* (Washington: Institute for International Economics, 1993).

Figure 1.1 Countries and independent variables

Central bank status

	Subordinate	Independent
Weak	(Britain)	United States
Strong	Japan (France)	Germany

Connection between banks and industry

Britain and France are listed here for comparative purposes, although they are not the subject of case studies in this book. Reforms in early 1994 granted a degree of independence to the Bank of France, and this could change the classification of France in the future.

banks and industry and a subordinate central bank. France, with close connections between banks and industry and a subordinate central bank throughout the period under review, occupies the same quadrant as Japan. Although Britain and France will not be examined in as much depth as the United States, Germany, and Japan, incorporating their experience increases the degrees of freedom of the study.

As its research method, this study employs a structured comparison of case histories of policymaking.[11] The following chapters review in detail monetary and exchange rate policies in the United States, Germany, and Japan, with special emphasis on the institutions, processes, and politics by which these policies were made. Each country chapter, which

11. In language more familiar to political scientists, this is the method of structured, focused comparison of disciplined-configurative case studies. Alexander L. George, "Case Studies and Theory Development: The Method of Structured, Focused Comparison," in *Diplomacy*, ed. Paul Lauren (New York: Free Press, 1979), pp. 43–68; Harry Eckstein, "Case Study and Theory in Political Science," in *Handbook of Political Science*, vol. 7, Fred Greenstein and Nelson Polsby, eds. (Reading, MA: Addison-Wesley, 1975), pp. 79–137. See as well Gary King, Robert O. Keohane, and Sidney Verba, *Designing Social Inquiry: Scientific Inference in Qualitative Research* (Princeton: Princeton University Press, 1994).

reviews policymaking during the whole postwar period but emphasizes the 1980s and early 1990s, is configured to facilitate a comparison among the three countries. The information on which these country case studies are based comes from multiple sources: government and central bank documents; official statistics; interviews of officials and former officials in governments and central banks and of politicians, businessmen, and bankers; newspaper and wire service reports; and the existing literature. Because many of the interviews were granted on the condition that the source not be identified, interviews are not specifically cited in most instances. Other sources are conventionally cited.

Policymaking in the United States, Germany, and Japan over the postwar period has been subject to a common backdrop of international economic relations and events. These three countries together faced the teetering and then collapse of the Bretton Woods regime in the 1960s and early 1970s. Together they faced the simultaneous rise of inflation and unemployment during the 1960s and 1970s and the wrenching effects of sudden changes in the price of oil. For the first time under flexible exchange rates, the advanced industrial countries promoted and contributed to international macroeconomic policy coordination in the late 1970s. After a hiatus during the first half of the 1980s, the United States, Germany, and Japan again pursued exchange rate and macroeconomic coordination in the second half of the decade.

Policymaking in each of these countries was thus linked in a sense to policymaking in the others by common experience. This raises questions as to whether national policy outcomes might be the product of changes in the world economy and international economic regimes that the cases hold in common rather than of institutions and processes at the domestic level and thus whether these cases are sufficiently independent of one another. The answer is that the cases can indeed be analyzed separately despite their sharing the same global economic system.

Cooperation and conflict at the international level are fundamentally the product of the outcomes of policymaking at the national level. With some exceptions, the international monetary regime has exercised only weak constraints over national policymaking in the postwar period. The interpretation and observance of the rules and norms of the regime are themselves elements of national policy. The maintenance of the Bretton Woods regime, its downfall, and the ebb and flow of international monetary cooperation over the 1970s, 1980s, and early 1990s depended crucially on the policy choices of the three most important countries in the system. National policies have thus exerted a far stronger influence over the international regime than vice versa.

This study therefore examines these cases independently. The common challenges presented to the United States, Germany, and Japan by the international economic system are a crucial part of the history of national policymaking. Against this common systemic backdrop, interestingly, the governments and central banks of the three countries responded differently.[12] Those differences in policy outcomes are what this book explains.

Organization of This Book

The next two chapters present the independent variables of the study in greater detail. Chapter 2 discusses the character of the national financial systems and the relationships between banks and industry within each of the three countries. That chapter also explains how and why close bank-industry relations should produce revealed preferences on the part of the private sector for competitive and stable valuation of the exchange rate and why distant bank-industry relations do not.

Chapter 3 identifies and describes the public sector institutions of monetary and exchange rate policymaking within each country. Comparing the relationships between the government and the central bank, that chapter concludes that the German Bundesbank is the most independent on domestic monetary matters, the US Federal Reserve ranks a close second, and the Bank of Japan is a distant third. On external monetary policy also, the Bundesbank and the Federal Reserve have considerably more latitude than has the Bank of Japan.

The three following chapters present the country case studies for Japan, Germany, and the United States, in that order. Chapter 4 reviews the evolution of Japanese monetary and exchange rate policy from the Bretton Woods period through four upward "realignments" of the yen during the 1970s and 1980s up through the early 1990s. The Ministry of Finance and the Bank of Japan acted frequently to stabilize the nominal value of the yen during its ups and downs. But Japanese industrial productivity increased much faster than productivity abroad, keeping the trend in the real value of the yen flat through 1985 and creating large and growing trade surpluses. By seeking to stabilize the nominal exchange rate when market forces tended to push the yen upward, government policy contributed to this result. In the late 1980s and early 1990s, though, private preferences and government policy changed more in Japan than in the other countries; Japanese authorities accepted unprecedentedly high values for the yen in real terms.

German monetary and exchange rate policymaking is discussed in chapter 5. Under both fixed and flexible exchange rates, German monetary policy frequently confronted a dilemma between internal and exter-

---

12. In this respect, the methodological approaches adopted by Katzenstein, ed., *Between Power and Plenty*, and Gourevitch, *Politics in Hard Times*, among several other researchers, are similar to this study.

nal monetary stability. The fact that this was considered a dilemma, however, underscores the importance Germany attached to the external stability of the D-mark. After the Bretton Woods period, Germany pursued a consistent two-track strategy of exchange rate stabilization toward other European currencies and flexibility toward the dollar. Because Germany had a lower rate of inflation than its neighbors during most of this period, nominal exchange rate stabilization provided Germany with substantial competitiveness benefits within Europe. In the early 1990s, economic policy decisions surrounding the unification of Germany undercut this extraordinarily competitive position and stimulated a series of speculative crises within the EMS. Consistent with its historical pursuit of exchange rate stability, however, Germany committed itself in principle to form a monetary union with its partners within the European Union.

Chapter 6 reviews the unfolding of external monetary policy outcomes in the United States since the Bretton Woods era. The chapter highlights the cyclical pattern of policy neglect and activism with respect to the exchange rate for the dollar. While US administrations have become engaged in exchange rate matters from time to time, that engagement has typically been followed by a period of prolonged neglect during which overvaluation of the dollar has often been tolerated. In the face of huge and growing trade deficits, American policy actively promoted dollar depreciation against all major currencies under the second Reagan administration and against the yen at the outset of the Clinton administration. Although this activism continues, there is little reason to expect that, should the trade deficit fall, the cyclical tendency to revert to neglect will not reassert itself in US policy.

Chapter 7 compares and explains the patterns of policy outcomes observed in the country chapters. The first part of the chapter compares the deployment by each country of the five elements of external monetary policy outlined above. The second section shows how these patterns of policy outcomes are caused by the particular combination of bank-industry relations and central bank independence within each country. This explanation is extended, in a brief discussion, to Britain and France as well. A look at the relationship between central banks and governments in external monetary policymaking supplements this analysis. The chapter concludes by relating this explanation to the change and continuity of policy in the three countries over the last several years.

The final part of the study, chapter 8, presents the major lessons and observations that bear on the design of policymaking institutions and discusses how such institutions relate to private interests. Here the study departs from positive analysis, the task of explaining outcomes, to prescribe institutions, policy processes, and reforms to improve policy outcomes. Each country's existing policymaking institutions have both strengths and weaknesses. The recommendations made here for the United States,

Japan, Germany, and the European Union, which in some cases are far-reaching, are designed to correct the weaknesses and reinforce the strengths. The objective of these prescriptions is to improve policy for the benefit of each country and to make national-level institutions "safe" for international monetary cooperation.

2

Banks, Industry, and Private Preferences

I would rather see Finance less proud and Industry more content.
—Winston Churchill, chancellor of the exchequer, 1925.[1]

The argument developed in this study emphasizes the importance of private-sector preferences in external monetary policymaking. The ways those preferences are formed and expressed within each country are structured by the relationship between the banking and industrial sectors. This chapter examines the differences in bank-industry relations within Germany, Japan, and the United States, and explains why we should expect those differences to affect policymaking and policy outcomes.

These three countries differ greatly in their pattern of bank financing for industrial development and expansion. Industrial corporations in the United States rely heavily for financing on the capital markets—for corporate bonds, equity, commercial paper, and other instruments—and comparatively little on American commercial banks. Germany and Japan, on the other hand, have financial systems in which banking institutions have been the primary conduit for channeling savings to industrial firms. The character of domestic financial systems affects the degree to which banks have interests in the international competitiveness of industrial firms and thus conditions the formation of private-sector preferences.[2]

---

1. Cited by D. E. Moggridge, *The Return to Gold 1925: The Formulation of Economic Policy and Its Critics* (London: Cambridge University Press, 1969), p. 54.

2. This analysis draws on the work of economists and political scientists discussed in chapter 1, namely, Marshall, *Industry and Trade*; Gerschenkron, *Economic Backwardness in Historical Perspective*; Shonfield, *Modern Capitalism*; Gourevitch, *Politics in Hard Times*; Zysman, *Governments, Markets, and Growth*; Katzenstein, ed., *Between Power and Plenty*; Hall, *Governing the Economy*.

Deregulation, liberalization, and technological innovation have brought substantial changes to the financial systems of the three countries considered here, particularly during the 1980s and early 1990s. For the reasons explained below, however, the convergence of these financial systems over time has been limited. Most of the fundamental differences among these financial systems that have been identified by previous authors persist today.

The first section of this chapter presents the theoretical reasoning linking bank-industry relations to external monetary policy outcomes. It explains how the status of banks affects the organization and expression of interests regarding the level and flexibility of the currency. The second section describes the financial systems and bank-industry relations in the three countries.

Framework for Analyzing Private Preferences

The character of the national financial system determines fundamentally the relationship among key sectors of the private economy. The financial system is thus a crucial institutional variable that structures the organization, aggregation, and articulation of private interests. Upon the financial system hinges the relationship between the banking and industrial sectors. Other sectors of the economy also are potentially important, but, for the reasons discussed below, banking and industry are emphasized.

This section begins with a review of the different types of finance and financial systems. The preferences of banks and industry regarding the level and flexibility of the exchange rate and the international role of the currency are then discussed. Three primary causal links between bank-industry relations and policy outcomes are outlined. The connection between financial structure and the international role of the currency and their impact on policymaking are examined. Finally, the section anticipates some of the potential challenges to the thesis.

National Financial Systems

To understand the importance of the institutional organization of finance to the politics of economic policy, consider first the channels through which funds flow from savers to ultimate borrowers within an economy. When savers invest directly with the users of capital, through the purchases of securities such as stocks or bonds issued by a nonfinancial company, *direct finance* is performed. *Indirect finance* is conducted through financial firms that intermediate the flow of savings between the saver and ultimate borrower. Banks, for example, receive savings in the form of deposits and issue loans to ultimate borrowers. Although financial innovation has blurred the distinction between direct and indirect finance, the distinction remains.

Direct finance takes place in *capital markets*, such as bond, stock, and commercial paper markets, in which securities can be bought and sold. (The underwriting of the issuance of corporate securities, done by securities firms or investment banks, is sometimes referred to, paradoxically, as *indirect intermediation*.) The efficient operation of these securities markets requires the support of a legal, informational, and institutional infrastructure. The market in equity shares requires a stock exchange in which trading can be conducted, freely available information that allows investors to assess risk, and laws and regulations that provide supervision and disclosure.

Indirect finance requires a different legal and institutional infrastructure. Financial intermediaries such as banks require prudential supervision and a lender of last resort in times of crisis, but they thrive on the lack of public availability of information. When making loans, for example, they perform the function of risk analysis performed by stock analysts, bond-rating agencies, and individual investors in capital markets. Intermediaries also pool risk when they diversify their asset portfolios.

Financial intermediaries are diverse and include banks, insurance companies, pension funds, social security systems, and credit unions. Banks are typically, though not always, the most important intermediaries in the amount of funds that flow through them and their level of activism with respect to borrowing corporations. Banks, like other intermediaries, usually engage in *maturity transformation*; that is, they hold short-term liabilities and long-term assets. In most cases, banks fund their own lending with short-term deposits by retail customers or money-market liabilities; in some cases, banks fund lending by issuing bonds. *Disintermediation* takes place when savers withdraw deposits from banks and invest directly in securities.

The prevalence or absence of financial intermediation in a national economy structures the institutional relationships within the private sector: the patterns of ownership, the control of corporations, the flow of information, and the exchange of personnel. The three countries considered here differ substantially in the mix of direct and indirect finance that characterizes their financial systems. Banks and other financial intermediaries have been more important in Germany and Japan than in the United States. Germany and Japan, in other words, have had *bank credit–based* financial systems while the United States has had a *capital market–based* financial system during the postwar period.[3]

Bank credit–based and capital market–based systems also differ in two other important respects that stem from the role of banks in inter-

---

3. The terminology is borrowed from Zysman, *Governments, Markets, and Growth*.

mediation. First, in addition to extending loans to industrial corporations, banks in credit-based systems own substantial quantities of corporate securities, both bonds and, more important, equity shares. To the extent that corporations do have access to capital markets within credit-based systems, that access is often governed by the banks themselves. Second, by virtue of their stock holdings, banks in credit-based systems also participate on the boards of directors and in the senior executive ranks of industrial firms. Security ownership and management participation is much less prevalent among banks in capital market–based financial systems.[4]

Preferences of Banks and Industry

In the analysis of private preferences for external monetary policy, it is fundamental to distinguish between preferences regarding the *external value* of the currency, the exchange rate, on the one hand, and preferences regarding the *flexibility* of currency values and the exchange rate regime on the other. The level of the exchange rate bears on the competitiveness of manufacturing and other tradeable goods and the country's terms of trade in international commerce. Changes in currency values affect the rate of domestic inflation through the price of tradeable goods. The degree of flexibility of the exchange rate determines the short-term volatility of currencies, risk and uncertainty about future prices, and the potential for sustained exchange rate misalignments. Limiting exchange rate flexibility, with a regional or international monetary regime that pegs currencies, might also require the surrender of domestic monetary autonomy, particularly under conditions of high capital mobility.

This section examines the preferences of *separate* banking and indus-

---

4. There is a growing literature on the efficacy of different financial systems for industrial development and competitiveness. The debate hinges, among other things, on whether institutional ties help overcome asymmetric information endemic to the relationship between lenders and borrowers and enable firms to adopt long-term planning and investment horizons. See, for example, R. Glenn Hubbard, *Asymmetric Information, Corporate Finance, and Investment*, National Bureau for Economic Research Project Report (Chicago: University of Chicago Press, 1990). For an application of this literature to the problem of US competitiveness, see Michael E. Porter, *Capital Choices: Changing the Way America Invests in Industry*, a research report presented to the Council on Competitiveness (Washington: Council on Competitiveness, 1992); US General Accounting Office, *Competitiveness Issues: The Business Environment in the United States, Japan, and Germany* (Washington: GAO, August 1993); Mark Roe, "Some Differences in Corporate Structure in Germany, Japan, and the United States," *Yale Law Journal* 102 (June 1993), 1927–2003. This discussion, however, is tangential to our concern in this chapter, which focuses on the effect of institutional and financial ties on preference identification and political activity rather than the efficiency of financial flows per se.

trial sectors in principle regarding both the level and flexibility of the exchange rate.[5] We consider first the preferences of banks and the financial sector, which depend on basic interests of the banking sector and international outreach of banks. Second, we examine industrial preferences, which differ from bank preferences in both direction and intensity. The next section of this chapter examines the effect on preference formation of combining banks and industry together.

Banking

Consider first the preferences of banks regarding the level of the exchange rate where they do not have international business or a substantial foreign-asset portfolio. Banks in their simplest form have a basic interest in low inflation. The key ingredient for bank profitability is a positive spread between the cost of funds and the return on assets. That spread is threatened when inflation rises, because the central bank may tighten monetary policy or because the market expects inflation to fall for other reasons. Because they prefer low inflation, banks prefer a stable or gradually appreciating currency to a depreciating currency. For such a bank, however, the exchange rate level is unlikely to be high on the agenda because domestic business conditions, financial regulation, and banking legislation are by far more important to bank profitability.

When banks branch out into international business, though, they develop additional reasons, actual and perceived, to prefer a strongly valued currency.[6] International bankers perceive a strong business interest in wide acceptance of their national currency.[7] That acceptance favors

---

5. For other examples of preference mapping, see I. M. Destler and C. Randall Henning, *Dollar Politics: Exchange Rate Policymaking in the United States* (Washington: Institute for International Economics, 1989), pp. 117–41; Sylvia Maxfield, *Governing Capital: International Finance and Mexican Politics* (Ithaca, NY: Cornell University Press, 1990), pp. 17–28; Jeffry A. Frieden, "Invested Interests: The Politics of National Economic Policies in a World of Global Finance," *International Organization* 45 (Autumn 1991): 425–52; Alberto Giovannini, "Exploring the Political Dimension of Optimum Currency Areas," in *The Monetary Future of Europe* (London: Centre for Economic Policy Research, 1993).

6. International banking activities include the financing of international transactions such as trade, accepting assets and liabilities in foreign currency, and foreign exchange trading services.

7. The magnitude, however, of the competitive advantage conferred on banks by the international use of the currency is unclear. See a study issued by the Federal Reserve Bank of New York in two volumes, *The International Competitiveness of U.S. Financial Firms: Products, Markets, and Conventional Performance Measures* (1991); *The International Competitiveness of U.S. Financial Firms: The Dynamics of Financial Industry Change* (1992).
    The competitive advantage has declined as the development of national and international financial markets has permitted the "unbundling" of previously bundled transactions. The use of swaps, forward contracts, futures and options, and other instruments

not only their individual banks but their national financial center, such as London or New York, as an international financial center. A gentle appreciation of the currency, in addition to limiting domestic inflation, favors such an international role for the currency. Because the value of the currency provides and symbolizes confidence—a fragile but essential business advantage—bankers judge a strongly valued currency to be much more attractive than a depreciating currency.[8]

Nonetheless, the intensity of the general preference for a strongly valued currency tends to be muted by the conflicting preferences of different departments within each bank. The departments responsible for foreign currency trading operations, fixed-income advisory services, domestic corporate lending, the international credit department, and the bank's own finance department have contrasting and conflicting preferences regarding the level of the exchange rate. The chief executive officer is typically unwilling and unable to reconcile the conflicting interests of the departments within his or her institution, and therefore generally takes an agnostic stance toward currency valuation.[9]

Banks have a different set of considerations when facing the choice between flexible and fixed exchange rates. Banks, especially those without international business, might value national autonomy in monetary policymaking.[10] They might well fear that exchange rate stabilization could threaten the independence of the central bank—the banks' patron within the state apparatus and the guardian of price stability—and provoke greater domestic interest rate volatility. But, in practice, banks' attitudes toward the exchange rate regime will depend not on abstract considerations but on the foreseeable ramifications of regime participation on domestic monetary policies. The expected direction of domestic mone-

---

can separate the choice of the currency of denomination of financial transactions from the choice of the provider of funds. Thus British banks in the late 19th century reaped greater benefits from the role of the pound sterling than American banks have reaped from the role of the dollar in the late 20th century. Nonetheless, not all transactions can be unbundled, and the use of hedging instruments carries some cost. Financial institutions thus continue to believe that a competitiveness advantage is indeed conferred by acceptance of the national currency as the denomination of international assets and liabilities.

8. In the rare cases when American banks have become politically active on exchange rate policy, for example, the dollar has been weak, not strong. The ramifications for confidence of the pace of depreciation was a particular source of concern during those few cases. British banks have opposed devaluation of the pound sterling in each of the par value regimes in which Britain has participated.

9. For analysis of the experience of American banks in the 1980s, see Destler and Henning, *Dollar Politics*, pp. 131–33.

10. Frieden stresses autonomy considerations in determining preferences regarding exchange rate flexibility. "Invested Interests," pp. 444–46.

tary policy under flexible and fixed exchange rates will determine the posture of banks toward the regime. Whether regime participation causes the national central bank to tighten or ease monetary policy depends on the policy tendencies of the other regime participants and the historical pattern of national monetary policy outcomes. If, for example, the national central bank has pursued inflationary monetary policy over previous decades, banks might well support participation in a regime that binds the hands of policymakers. Where national monetary autonomy has been abused by governments, it will not be valued by banks.

Banks engaged in international business are generally better able than corporate manufacturers to profit and protect themselves from volatile exchange rate fluctuations. Banks can cover their foreign-currency exposures more easily than can corporations, which have long-term commitments in fixed assets whose values are affected by exchange rates. Nonetheless, exchange rate volatility has inflicted large losses on banks and exposed weaknesses in management control. In a couple of instances, volatility has rendered banks completely insolvent and threatened associated creditor banks.[11]

For banks engaged in international business, the profits from foreign exchange trading depend directly on exchange rate volatility. Foreign exchange trading has been a growing and profitable business niche for banks. But the importance of this business niche should not be exaggerated as a source of bank preferences regarding currency flexibility. First, exchange rate stabilization does not eliminate all volatility in currency rates. The bands within the European Monetary System (EMS) and the Group of Seven (G-7) reference ranges of the late 1980s, for example, leave substantial room for exchange rate movements, opportunities for speculation, and need for hedging. Second, even when exchange rate regimes reduce volatility, banks, when speculating, can simply place larger bets on smaller exchange rate changes. Third, when volatility is suppressed in the currency market, it tends to reemerge elsewhere, providing the opportunity for speculation and hedging in those markets as well.[12] As volatility shifts from the foreign exchange market to the domestic money market, for example, a fall in the volume of foreign cur-

---

11. The failures of Bankhaus I. D. Herstatt and Franklin National Bank of New York are two examples from the 1970s. See Joan E. Spero, *The Failure of the Franklin National Bank: Challenge to the International Banking System* (New York: Columbia University Press, 1980).

12. The exchanges for foreign currency futures and options, such as the Chicago Mercantile Exchange, have an unambiguous interest in volatility that is not offset by these other considerations. These markets, discussed below, have been promoted under capital market–based financial systems and suppressed under bank credit–based financial systems.

rency swaps could be offset by an increase in the volume of interest rate swaps. Banks have similar opportunities to make money under either fixed or flexible exchange rate regimes.[13] Thus, foreign exchange trading hardly dominates bank preferences regarding the international monetary regime.[14]

Banks might fear that any shift toward managed exchange rates could eventually usher in capital controls, which would threaten international lines of business.[15] But it is equally true that banks might perceive the stability of the currency to be essential to international business and regime participation to be essential to the survival or promotion of the national financial center, such as New York or the City of London, as an international financial center.

Banks have clear interests in low inflation, minimizing government interference, and freedom from domestic and international capital controls. But these core interests of banks leave their preferences toward the level and flexibility of the exchange rate underdetermined. Those more precise preferences regarding external monetary affairs hinge on additional and multifaceted considerations.

Some specific preferences regarding external monetary policy can be ascertained. Banks dislike precipitously depreciating currencies, owing to the effects on inflation and international confidence, and favor stable or gradually appreciating currencies. By the same token, however, banks dislike rapidly appreciating currencies, because an appreciation that goes too far threatens domestic monetary control and will have to be corrected.

But bank preferences in general are variable, highly situationally dependent, and typically not held with high intensity. This is particularly true with respect to exchange rate flexibility, but applies with respect to the exchange rate level as well. There is simply no constant relationship between the core interests of banks and the external monetary regime. That relationship itself depends on how the context defines the opportunity cost associated with participation in an exchange rate stabilization regime.

---

13. Although individual banking institutions are not equally positioned to benefit from the new opportunities.

14. Note that banks in Europe have supported Economic and Monetary Union (EMU) despite the fact that a common currency would eliminate foreign exchange trading among separate European currencies. Note as well that American banks declined to join a short-lived lobbying campaign in favor of flexible exchange rates in the mid-1980s (discussed in chapter 6).

15. Even here, however, international capital controls might be essential to the protection of segmented, compartmentalized domestic financial systems and thus have the support of banking institutions resistant to change.

Industry

The industrial sector, by contrast, has an *un*ambiguous interest in a competitively valued currency, that is, a currency valuation that expands or maintains global market share. A high proportion of industrial output is tradeable, and industrial corporations are thus subject to price competition from foreign producers in both the home and export markets. Competitiveness in the global market determines the prosperity of the producers of tradeable industrial goods. A firm or industry need not be specifically export oriented to be concerned about the exchange rate. Low currency valuation raises the competitiveness of home producers at home and abroad.

It is true that many industrial producers use imported inputs and benefit from lower input costs associated with a highly valued currency. But the key determinant of competitiveness is the pricing of the domestic value added in the production process, which is determined by among other things the exchange rate. Individual corporations exhibit unique preferences depending on their mix of tradeable and nontradeable inputs and the degree of competition in the markets for their outputs. As a whole, however, the industrial sector favors a competitive, low external valuation of the currency.

Industrial corporations can limit their vulnerability to exchange rate fluctuations by using hedging instruments and by shifting production facilities abroad. However, the use of hedging instruments bears some cost and is not available for some types of exposures. Production shifting is a costly strategy, particularly as it often involves creating redundant capacity, and is thus available for only large, well-capitalized corporations. Small and medium-sized enterprises, and those with sunk investments in assets that are not mobile, cannot shift production abroad. Finally, exchange rate fluctuations and realignments often occur much more quickly than productive facilities can be shifted abroad.[16]

As investors, multinational corporations have an interest in a high-valued currency, which will improve their terms of trade when they buy foreign assets. After the investment is made, however, these corporations have an interest in a low-valued currency, which will raise the home-currency value of the income stream from those assets.

Strategies to cover exposure, shift facilities abroad, and invest in foreign assets, therefore, do not offset the interest of domestic industrial producers in low, competitive currency valuation. Most producers also prefer stable to unstable rates from the standpoint of certainty and long-

---

16. For example, as an alternative to lobbying against the strong dollar in the first half of the 1980s, Caterpillar Inc. considered shifting all or most operations overseas, but decided that it could not do so before the company went bankrupt. Accordingly, the company pressed for dollar realignment instead.

term planning. The senior executives of producing corporations, who usually regard themselves as practical businesspeople, production and marketing managers, engineers, or scientists, generally feel less confident on financial terrain and do not like to "play" the foreign exchange markets.[17]

The argument developed here stresses the importance of industry because industry is especially important to the national economy and constitutes the largest share by value of international trade. Owing to economies of scale, scope, and learning, the industrial sector has been the area of fastest productivity increases and is essential for growth in the standard of living. Industry has positive externalities to the rest of the economy that make it more important than its share in GNP reflects.

The industrial sector merits special attention, finally, because it places stronger emphasis on external monetary remedies to competitiveness problems, relative to alternative remedies such as trade protection and special subsidy programs, than do some other sectors of the economy. This is a matter of both primary preferences and the availability of alternative remedies to foreign competition. First, the exchange rate remedy confers competitiveness advantages not only in the home market but in the markets of foreign producers and in third markets as well. Trade protection, by contrast, works in the home market alone. Second, currency depreciation carries a smaller risk of foreign retaliation than does trade protection. Because access to the world market is relatively important for industrial companies, which must achieve economies of scale to compete successfully, such companies have weaker preferences for alternative remedies for foreign competition. Because government intervention and traditional protection is low for the industrial sector compared to agriculture, for example, industrial firms tend to have less access to alternative remedies.

Bank-Industry Relations and External Monetary Policy

The relationship between banks and industry affects the derivation and aggregation of private-sector preferences on external monetary policy,

---

17. Though more forcefully stated than most, the comments of Akio Morita, the chairman of Sony Corporation, are illustrative. He writes, "Money trading has a tendency to distort reality: this cannot be denied. The volume of currency entering the market for speculative purposes is many times larger than the volume of funds changing hands in settlement of tangible international trade. For industrialists, the value of money is a measuring stick that enables us to make sense of the firm's activities and operations. Therefore a system in which the value of money constantly fluctuates is unsatisfactory." *International Economic Insights*, March/April 1993, p. 26.

like other policies, through several channels. The present section focuses on three causal connections: the commonality of interest, interest aggregation and expression, and new channels of access to policymakers.

Solidarity of Interests

The previous section concluded that banks had a mild preference for a gently appreciating currency and a variable and ambiguous preference with respect to the international monetary regime. Industrial corporations, on the other hand, have an unambiguous interest in a competitively valued and stable currency. Strong ties to industry, therefore, transform the interests of banks in international competitiveness and exchange rate policy.

Heavy bank lending to industry naturally increases banks' direct business interest in the success of industry. The quality of the loan portfolio of banking institutions could be seriously impaired by corporate failures spawned by an overvalued currency. Bank holdings of corporate equity mean not only that bank income depends directly on corporate profitability but also that the assets and capital base of banks, and thus their ability to expand, vary with the fortunes of industry. Participation on the executive and supervisory boards of corporations and in the ranks of corporate management gives banks hands-on control over corporate decisions, high-quality information on the condition of the industry and the competitive challenges that it faces, and a reputational stake in the success of the firm.

Thus, direct stakes in industry transform the agnostic or high-valuation preferences of banks regarding the exchange rate into a strong interest in a valuation at which industry can successfully compete and in stability by which firms can plan and invest. Bank intermediation creates a private sector with views more unified on external monetary matters. It broadens the private-sector coalition in favor of a competitive and stable exchange rate.

In addition, close ties between banking and industry limit the size and intensity of the constituency for an international role for the currency. Banks that have a large share of their assets committed to industrial finance are less interested in developing international business and less able to take advantage of international opportunities. Banks that have been disintermediated from corporate finance have looked to the international arena as an alternative source of income.[18] Maintaining international confidence in the currency, however, may require restrictive monetary policy inimical to industry. Banks in countries with capital

---

18. Until late in the postwar period, for example, American banks were drawn toward international banking to a far greater extent than were German and Japanese banks.

market–based financial systems, therefore, tend to become stronger advocates for creating or maintaining international status for their currencies than do banks in credit-based financial systems.

Consensus Building

Bank-industry ties ease the task of interest aggregation and preference articulation in the private sector on international economic issues generally. When banks have large stakes in industry, and personnel and information flow more smoothly between them as a consequence, the interests of the two sectors are far less likely to be defined separately during the process of building business coalitions. Consensus building in the private sector is greatly facilitated by existing channels of routinized communication that derive from the long-standing institutional connections between banks and firms. When banks have few connections to industry, personnel and communications flow less naturally between the two sectors. Coalition building must establish cross-sectoral communication anew and must often overcome a sometimes deep cultural division between bankers and industrialists.

Bank-industry ties also facilitate the coherent articulation of those preferences to responsible officials in the government. Business organizations are likely to speak with fewer voices when banks and corporations are closely tied and thus coordinate their representation. When banks and industrial corporations have only weak connections between them, the private sector will speak with many voices and will therefore be less coordinated and less effective.

Reducing the cost of coalition building is particularly important in the case of exchange rate and external monetary policy. Because exchange rate effects are diffused across many sectors and companies, the benefits of a successful campaign for currency realignment are nonexcludable and nonappropriable. Private-sector lobbying on exchange rate matters is therefore subject to dilemmas of collective action.[19] Financial ties that help corporations and banks overcome incentives to free ride on the influence attempts of others facilitate interest group mobilization on external monetary policy.[20]

Channels of Access

Most important, close ties to the banking community create new channels of access for industry to the exchange rate policymaking process.

---

19. Joanne Gowa, "Public Goods and Political Institutions: Trade and Monetary Policy Processes in the United States," *International Organization* 42 (Winter 1988): 15–32.

20. Building a consensus in the private sector is also facilitated by high concentration among firms in the banking and traded-goods sectors, as in Germany and Japan.

The banking community is the natural client of finance ministries and central banks. In turn, ministries and central banks rely on banking institutions in numerous ways: as the channel through which monetary policy affects the real economy, as financiers and distributors of government debt, and as a bureaucratic raison d'être for regulation and supervision. Finance ministries and central banks, for all these reasons, must be sensitive to the health and needs of banking institutions. Owing to clientelism, therefore, finance ministries and central banks are typically more responsive to policy advocacy by banks and senior bank executives than from other sectors of the economy.[21]

Second, private banks and official financial institutions share many basic economic objectives and a professional ethos. Owing to institutional interests and professional acculturation, both tend to place higher value on fiscal rectitude and low inflation, for example, than their production-oriented counterparts in the private sector and government. Moreover, the private and official financial sectors exchange personnel at the senior and working levels.

When industry combines with banking, therefore, producer firms gain access to precisely those government institutions responsible for setting exchange rate policies. Corporate CEOs have greater entrée to exactly those policy processes to which access for corporate interests is otherwise typically denied. This is not to say that powerful industrial firms have no access to the finance minister in the absence of connections with banks; they often do. But, *ceteris paribus*, industries without bank ties possess fewer points of access to government policymaking, and those they do have tend to be with ministries and regulators, such as the ministry of industry or trade, which are isolated from monetary and exchange rate policymaking.

Financial Structure and International Use of the Currency

The character of the national financial system also affects external monetary policy through a separate channel from the effect of bank-industry relations on private preference formation. Through its effect on the attractiveness of the home currency for international uses, the domestic financial system creates the market context that defines not only the interests of financial institutions but also the set of choices available to policymakers.

---

21. See, for example, Rudolph Goldsheid, "A Sociological Approach to Problems of Public Finance," in Richard A. Musgrave and Alan Peacock, eds., *Classics in the Theory of Public Finance* (New York: Macmillan, 1958); Margaret Levi, *Of Rule and Revenue* (Berkeley: University of California Press, 1988), cited in Maxfield, *Governing Capital*, p. 23, n. 44.

Specifically, countries with credit-based systems have currencies that are, *ceteris paribus*, less attractive for international uses than countries with capital market–based systems. The more liquid and diverse the national capital markets, including the short-term money markets, the more attractive is the national currency as a store of value and transactions medium. When domestic financial and money markets are less developed, as they typically are in credit-based systems, the use of the currency is less convenient.

The international role for the currency is important for two reasons. First, a prominent international role for the currency creates the possibility of liability financing for current account deficits. Accepting external deficits is therefore less costly than it otherwise would be. Second, large international holdings of assets and liabilities denominated in the home currency can undermine, and at minimum complicate, exchange rate management and monetary control in the home country. Owing to their natural advantage as providers of an international currency, countries with market-based financial systems have less independent control over the external value of their exchange rates than countries with credit-based systems. The need to maintain confidence in the currency can constrain economic policy options. Therefore, an international role for the currency reshapes the policy choices available to governments, by both broadening and restricting the choice set, in ways that reinforce the effect of the character of the financial system on preference formation.

In addition, heavier reliance among banks on international business, typical of capital market–based financial systems, strongly predisposes them against government use of capital controls to manage the currency or the balance of payments. National banking communities that are relatively more committed to industrial finance than international lending or trade finance, for example, are not enthusiastic about capital controls, to be sure, but the intensity of their opposition to international controls is reduced on the margin. Such preferences render the use of controls more politically costly for governments with market-based financial systems than for those with credit-based financial systems.

Large international holdings of a currency, finally, also create *foreign* constituencies perpetuating its use and favoring a high valuation. Under the Bretton Woods regime, for example, the members of the British Commonwealth holding sterling balances and the American partners holding dollars had direct interests in avoiding sterling and dollar devaluations. Foreign central banks, in particular, lobbied heavily against devaluations and for adjustment through restrictive macroeconomic policies instead. That interest was shared by private holders of those currencies abroad.

These foreign constituencies can ally with domestic constituencies of countries with capital market–based financial systems, principally banks, to create a formidable transnational coalition against devaluation or depreciation. Connections between banks and industry in countries with credit-based systems, on the other hand, provide a domestic political antidote for any nascent transnational coalition favoring an exchange rate level that is overvalued from the standpoint of producer interests.

Challenges to the Thesis

This argument has stressed the importance of the relationship between banks and industry in structuring the preferences of the private sector and determining the effectiveness of their advocacy vis-à-vis government policymakers. The importance of this link to the political economy of external monetary policy might be questioned. Let me anticipate these objections.

First, why should a connection between banks and industry dominate the concerns of other sectors in the formation of private preferences? Several other sectors in the economy have potential interests in external monetary affairs. In addition to industry, the tradeable sector also includes agricultural goods, other primary goods, and a growing number of services. The combined share of these other sectors in total trade, however, remains much smaller than the share of industrial manufactures for the advanced countries. Agricultural interests occasionally weigh in on external monetary policy, but their activity on this set of issues is sporadic and halting.[22]

In principle, the *non*tradeable sector has an interest in the exchange rate that is equal in magnitude but opposite in direction to that of the tradeable sector. The real exchange rate, after all, is the relative price of tradeable and nontradeable goods. For example, whereas the producers of tradeable goods in Japan have benefited from competitive valuation of the yen during most of the postwar period, the nontradeable goods sector, a net purchaser of tradeable goods, has suffered.

In practice, however, the nontradeable sector is rarely mobilized politically on external monetary issues. Because the tradeable goods sector typically is much smaller than the nontradeable goods sector, the consequences of an exchange rate change are more highly concentrated in the tradeable sector. In the broad nontradeable sector, the effects of an exchange rate change are diffused. The exchange rate is thus far more salient for producers of tradeable goods than for producers of nontradeables and thus a more important item on their political agenda. Owing to dilemmas of collective action in lobbying, extraordinary (though not impossible) conditions are necessary to mobilize the dispersed interests of the nontradeable sector.

As an internationally immobile factor of production, labor in traded

---

22. In earlier stages of economic development, agricultural interests are more important to exchange rate policy. This applies to the advanced industrial countries earlier in this century and to developing countries today.

goods industries in principle also has a strong interest in low currency valuation. But in practice labor unions are much less active on exchange rate policy than are industrial firms and associations. Trade union organizations often aggregate their memberships in tradeable and nontradeable sectors and thereby dilute and disperse, if not fully offset, the interests of union members working in tradeable sectors in low currency valuation and exchange rate stability. Exchange rates tend to be low on the political action agenda of trade unions, particularly because unions are nearly constantly engaged in a number of other domestic struggles affecting their core interests. When they confront competitiveness problems, trade unions are more likely than corporations to prefer remedies other than exchange rate realignments, such as protectionist or quantitative trade measures.

In sum, having a comprehensive map of the external monetary preferences of all the sectors in the economy would be ideal. But for several reasons the argument advanced here does not emphasize their role. Typically, these other sectors have interests which are either (1) ambiguous or weak on external monetary issues, (2) diffused and therefore effectively immobilized, or (3) shielded by alternative remedies such as trade protection and subsidy programs. Banking and industry, when unified, constitute the most powerful institutional nexus in the political economy of advanced countries. Thus, there is diminishing value to mapping the preferences of additional sectors and, as argued in subsequent chapters, doing so is not necessary to explain the broad pattern of policy outcomes.

Second, why should we expect intimate bank-industry relations to promote industrial preferences and not bank preferences in policymaking? There are two compelling reasons. The first has to do with the intensity of the preferences of the two sides, the second with the interposition of banks between industry and policymakers. Bank preferences on external monetary matters are often ambivalent, weakly subscribed, and situationally dependent. But the preferences of industrial firms are unambiguous, held with greater intensity, and not nearly as situationally dependent. Thus, when combined, the relatively intense preferences of industry dominate the weak and ambivalent preferences of banks on exchange rate matters.

Further, the banks are strategically located between industry and policymakers. By and large, they have greater access to the decision makers in external monetary policy, mainly the finance ministry and central bank, than do industrial firms. Bank preferences will tend to have greater influence over policy, therefore, whether or not banks are close to industry. So it is more important that banks redefine their own interests, in light of close ties to industry, than that industrial firms become more sensitive to the preferences of banks.

A third objection to the thesis regarding bank-industry relations might be the argument that different national financial structures simply re-shuffle the domestic constituency for international competitiveness. Whereas banks are more interested in competitiveness in credit-based systems than they are in market-based systems, all the other nonbank suppliers of capital in credit-based systems, such as bondholders and equity share-holders, are correspondingly less interested in competitiveness, and less numerous, than they would be in capital market–based systems. Should not the total domestic constituency for producer competitiveness be the same with both systems?

The answer reveals the essential organizational and institutional character of the argument presented here. In the aggregate, the total stakes in competitiveness are indeed the same. The *specific form* of organization of those competitiveness interests, however, is fundamentally important. When banks have direct stakes in industrial performance internationally, that interest is concentrated in (sometimes large) established financial organizations with direct connections to government agencies with direct responsibility for exchange rate policy. When the financing of traded goods producers is conducted through capital markets, the interest in maintaining competitiveness is dispersed among unorganized stakeholders. Individual share- and bondholders have virtually no cross-communication, except through the market itself, and are not organized as a group. Institutional investors may be more highly organized than individuals but are far less likely than banks to be active toward corporate management and government policymakers. Rather than being concentrated, individual and institutional investors are atomized; rather than similar, they are heterogenous; rather than committed, they are able to exit by selling their shares or bonds; rather than connected to the key policymakers, they are distant. Each of these organizational differences lowers the cost of organizing to influence policy in credit-based systems and raises the cost in capital market–based systems.

Financial Market Structure of Germany, Japan, and the United States

The previous section has argued that the character of the national financial system will affect the derivation and aggregation of private preferences. The present section reviews the similarities and differences among the domestic financial structures of the three countries considered in this study. Those differences have been great historically, and they remain substantial notwithstanding the innovation and deregulation that have changed all three financial systems in recent years.

The present section compares the three national systems along three key distinguishing criteria: (1) the importance of banks as financial intermediaries; (2) bank holdings of corporate securities, particularly equities; (3) and bank participation on the boards of directors and in the ranks of senior-level management of firms.

We first review the basic organizational features of the three financial systems as they existed during most of the postwar period. Our purpose here is not to render a comprehensive description of these systems—which would require a book-length treatment itself—but to evaluate them as they affect bank-industry relations in particular. We then compare these systems quantitatively, within the limits of the comparability of national financial statistics, referring to tables 2.1–2.6 and figure 2.1. Finally, we assess the direction and magnitude of the changes in bank-industry relations that have resulted from changes in these financial systems. The section concludes that innovation and deregulation during the 1980s and early 1990s have not brought financial convergence.

Germany

The German financial system is the classic example of a highly bank-intermediated structure in which universal banks nurtured industrial development and remain close to industry. The central and powerful role of private banks in the German economy has been examined extensively in comparative political economy. Indeed, the German financial structure has served as the model for this system archetype.[23]

Germany's development in the late 19th century was financed by a banking system designed to facilitate the rapid mobilization and concentration of funds for catch-up industrialization.[24] Three large private banks dominated industrial finance and remain Germany's most important even today—Deutsche Bank, Dresdner Bank, and Commerzbank. These banks combined the full range of financial functions, including lending and securities flotation, in single financial institutions—thus the term "universal bank"—whose roles extended beyond the provision of funds to long-term planning and enterprise management. Bank loans were the primary financial vehicle for industrial expansion. This credit-based financial system was reestablished for reconstruction after World War II.[25]

Germany's banking system is compartmentalized like the US and Jap-

23. See Shonfield, *Modern Capitalism*; Zysman, *Governments, Markets, and Growth*. See also Alfred Steinherr and Christian Huveneers, *Universal Banks: The Prototype of Successful Banks in the Integrated European Market?* Centre for European Policy Studies, Research Report No. 2 (Brussels, 1989), pp. 22–27.

24. Marshall, *Industry and Trade*; Gerschenkron, *Economic Backwardness in Historical Perspective*; Shonfield, *Modern Capitalism*.

25. Allied occupation authorities originally disassembled the large banking institutions but permitted their recombination to facilitate recovery from the postwar economic depression.

anese banking systems. Germany has a three-group banking system composed of private, state-owned, and locally organized cooperative banks, among whom competition has been regulated and organized.[26] Cooperative banks, whose members are mostly small businesses and farmers, limit their operations to localities. The state banks are owned by the Länder governments and satisfy some of the public-sector capital requirements within the Land.[27] The private banks, led by the Big Three, are not geographically confined and are legally permitted to engage in the "universal" range of banking functions. Thus the compartmentalization of the German system, unlike the Japanese and American systems, does not separate lending and securities issuance for industrial and other enterprises.

Conducting both indirect and direct finance, therefore, the German private banks have made the capital markets largely endogenous to the banking system. Securities markets have evolved in Germany, to be sure. But German banks laid claim to this source of long-term finance for themselves first of all, after the government. To the extent that industrial corporations have tapped the German securities market, their access has been governed by the banks. The three large banks collectively own 30 percent of Deutsche Börse, the new consolidating entity for the eight regional stock exchanges, and control its operation. In the candid words of the Bundesbank, "Considering that the banks also play a central part in the securities markets, the German financial system as a whole is very largely identical with the banking system in its most important structural and functional features."[28]

Bank stakes in the nonfinancial sector, and industry in particular, were strengthened by substantial holdings of corporate stocks. In Germany, there are no legal limits to the share of equity of a single company a bank can own. Banks are forbidden only to invest more than 100 percent of their own capital in the stock of a single company. Of all shares outstanding, German banks own about 12 percent.[29] The most celebrated example is the 28 percent stake of Germany's largest bank, Deutsche Bank, in Germany's largest company, Daimler-Benz. Moreover, German

26. Claudia Dziobek, "The German Banking System and Financial Market Reforms," paper presented at Brookings Institution, Washington, 18 November 1992.

27. The state sector is somewhat larger than the private banking sector, comprising more than 40 percent of total bank assets in Germany until the early 1990s. Five of the top 10 banks are in the state sector. Dziobek, "German Banking System," tables 1 and 3.

28. Deutsche Bundesbank, *The Deutsche Bundesbank: Its Monetary Policy Instruments and Functions*, 3rd edition, Deutsche Bundesbank Special Series, no. 7 (Frankfurt, 1989), p. 40.

29. J. S. S. Edwards and Klaus Fischer, "Banks, Finance, and Investment in West Germany since 1970," Discussion Paper 497, Centre for Economic Policy Research (London, January 1991), cited in Frankel and Montgomery, "Financial Structure," p. 285, n. 18.

banks control a much larger proportion of corporate stock than they own outright, through individuals' deposits of shares, which the banks effectively vote by proxy under German law.[30]

Dependent on industrial performance, German banks have asserted influence and control over corporate decision making. Those banks at the center of corporate groupings, in particular, are deeply involved in the management of their affiliated industrial clients. The German pattern of interlocking corporate directorships is highly concentrated and centered substantially on the banks.[31] Deutsche Bank alone controls roughly 400 seats on the supervisory boards of large German companies. Among the 100 largest companies in Germany, the big three banks held 102 supervisory board seats and 21 board chairmanships in 1975.[32] This position has made German banks, in the words of one pair of observers, veritable "arbiters of corporate control."[33]

German banks are also relatively stable shareholders. They, like Japanese banks, have held substantial blocs of shares for decades, and report them on bank balance sheets at cost, far below market value. These equity holdings represent large hidden reserves, which supplement their financial power. By the same token, German banks are more sensitive than American banks to the market valuation of equity shares.

Several other elements of German law, in addition to accounting conventions, stack the deck in favor of bank intermediation over direct finance. Financial disclosure is permissive, enabling corporations to hide profits and assets from shareholders and the public, complicating securi-

---

30. Arno Gottschelk, "Stimmrechtseinfluss der Banken in den Aktionärversammlungen von Grossunternehmen," *WSI Mitteilungen*, May 1988. Note that control of only 25 percent of the voting shares gives banks veto rights under German law.

31. Rolf Ziegler, Donald Bender, and Hermann Biehler, "Industry and Banking in the German Corporate Network," and Ziegler, "Conclusion," in Frans N. Stokman, Rolf Ziegler, and John Scott, eds., *Networks of Corporate Power: A Comparative Analysis of Ten Countries* (Oxford: Polity Press, 1985), pp. 91–111 and pp. 267–87 respectively. See especially figure 15.1, p. 176.

32. According to the Monopolies Commission and Gessler Commission reports. Kenneth Dyson, "The State, Banks and Industry: The West German Case," in *State, Finance and Industry: A Comparative Analysis of Post-War Trends in Six Advanced Industrial Economies* (New York: St. Martin's Press, 1986), Andrew Cox, ed., pp. 118–41, esp. p. 129.

33. Frankel and Montgomery, "Financial Structures," p. 285. There is an extensive debate in Germany over the power of the banks vis-à-vis German corporations and the economy in general. For a review of this debate, see Christopher S. Allen, *Democratic Politics and Private Investment: Financial Regulation in the Federal Republic of Germany and the United States*, Research Report No. 2, American Institute for Contemporary German Studies (Washington, November 1990). While interesting, the debate is somewhat tangential to the argument presented here. To this study, the connections of banks and industry are more important than the direction of influence between them.

ties valuation. Bankruptcy law encourages close cooperation between corporations and their creditors, giving banks better opportunities than some other shareholders to protect their interests in workouts. Insider trading is not illegal, though the government intends to introduce legislation banning it, and has been routine until recently. The possibility of insider trading creates distrust of the markets and dampens demand for corporate equities. The prevalence of bank finance is changing, as examined in the later section, but still has a long way to go before even approaching the American system.[34]

Japan

Japanese banks, like German banks, have held a central position in the financing of national economic expansion. The pre–World War II *zaibatsu* was the primary organizational form for industrial development and wartime economic mobilization. Each *zaibatsu*, the holding company for the interests of powerful families, created its own bank. The postwar occupation, while dismantling the rest of the *zaibatsu*, left these banks virtually intact. Capital markets being underdeveloped, postwar economic revitalization was financed through bank credit, supported in turn by direct lending to the private banks from the Bank of Japan. Under this bank credit–based system, characterized variously as "overloan" or "overborrowing," indirect finance supplied over 90 percent of funds through the early 1970s.[35] The degree of bank financing for industry was thus much higher during the postwar high-growth period than even before the war.

---

34. Some scholars are reassessing the position of German banks in industry and the German economy in general. See, for example, J. S. S. Edwards and K. Fischer, "An Overview of the German Financial System," paper prepared for the Centre for Economic Policy Research, London (undated); Josef Esser, "Bank Power in West Germany Revised," *West European Politics* 13 (1990): 17–32; Christian Harm, "The Relationship between German Banks and Large German Firms," World Bank Country Economics Department, Working Papers, May 1992; Richard E. Deeg, "The State, Banks, and Economic Governance in Germany," paper presented to the APSA annual meeting, 3–6 September 1992. These essays, by my reading, amount to a useful qualification of the conventional view of the German system as one of organized capitalism, a view that remains essentially valid, particularly in comparative perspective.

35. Yoshio Suzuki, ed., *The Japanese Financial System* (Oxford: Clarendon Press, 1987); Eisuke Sakakibara and Yukio Noguchi, "Dissecting the Finance Ministry–Bank of Japan Dynasty: End of the Wartime System for Total Economic Mobilization," *Japan Echo* 4, no. 4 (Autumn, 1977): 88–124; M. Therese Flaherty and Itami Hiroyuki, "The Banking-Industrial Complex," and Edward J. Lincoln, "Japanese Bond and Stock Markets," in *Inside the Japanese System: Readings on Contemporary Society and Political Economy*, Daniel I. Okimoto and Thomas P. Rohlen, eds. (Stanford: Stanford University Press, 1988), pp. 54–63; Takatoshi Ito, *The Japanese Economy* (Cambridge: MIT Press, 1992); Robert A. Feldman, *Japanese Financial Markets: Deficits, Dilemmas, and Deregulation* (Cambridge: MIT Press, 1986); Bernard Eccleston, "State, Finance, and Industry in Japan," in *State, Finance, and Industry*, Andrew Cox, ed. (New York: St. Martin's Press, 1986), pp. 60–79.

Japan inherited from the occupation a system of compartmentalized financial institutions. Each set of financial institutions was designed to meet a specific set of financial needs in the economy. Firms could compete within each niche but not across different niches. This segmentation was enforced with tight controls on deposit interest rates and protected by controls on international capital movements. In particular, the Glass-Steagall separation of deposit-taking from securities issuance in American law was reproduced in postwar Japan via Article 65 of the Securities and Exchange Law of 1947.

The array of private financial institutions is headed by the 12 so-called "city banks," banks based in large cities with nationwide networks of deposit-taking branches. As of the mid-1980s, these city banks held 20 percent of the deposits of all financial institutions, 60 percent of the deposits of all banks, and provided 20 percent of the credit needs of private corporations.[36] Long-term credit banks, such as the Industrial Bank of Japan, are also heavy lenders to industry. Though they take deposits, the long-term credit banks raise funds mainly through bond issuance. The other depository institutions in the Japanese system include regional banks, trust banks, a specialized foreign exchange bank, plus an array of credit institutions for small business, agriculture, forestry, and fisheries. Of these other banks, the trust banks in particular are important sources of long-term financing for industry in the form of loans and securities holdings. In 1985, about 50 percent of their total lending financed investment in industrial equipment, generally by the largest corporations.[37]

The presence of securities companies, protected by Article 65, distinguishes the Japanese from the German financial system. These firms, dominated by the big four (Nomura, Daiwa, Yamaichi, and Nikko), play the central role in the securities market. In addition to trading and underwriting, their core businesses, the securities firms also manage securities investment trusts and issue short-term money market instruments (*gensaki* bills). In contrast to American investment banks, the Japanese securities firms have grown and become highly capitalized. Nomura Securities was Japan's most profitable company in the late 1980s.

Japanese banks retained their central position in industrial finance, however, despite the activity of the securities firms. First, the banks controlled the vast bulk of funds and directed them toward industrial purposes. Second, the city banks and long-term credit banks developed a significant position for themselves in the securities sector, through their control of loan financing, equity holdings in securities companies, and personnel transfers. These banks control four of the second-tier securities firms as well as a number of smaller ones. Third, while none of the

---

36. Suzuki, *Japanese Financial System*, p. 171.

37. Suzuki, *Japanese Financial System*, pp. 210–11.

big four securities firms are members of *keiretsu*, Daiwa, Nikko, and Yamaichi have paired up with Sumitomo, Mitsubishi, and Fuji banks in their *keiretsu* relations.[38] Thus, corporate groupings provide a mechanism for overcoming the functional segmentation of the financial markets. Fourth, the banks have had a different relationship to the securities markets than American banks have had. Like German banks, Japanese banks have had a substantial role in the securities markets themselves, as holders or indirect intermediaries of bonds and shares.[39] Fifth, while the Japanese equity market has grown, the market in corporate bonds is stunted. Government regulations make it expensive to issue such bonds and nearly impossible to trade them.[40]

Immediately after World War II, the city banks reinforced their position as the leading sources of capital within their corporate groupings. The grouping of industrial firms around major banks, the six financial *keiretsu*, elevated bank influence considerably above that within the pre-World War II *zaibatsu*.[41] All five of Japan's largest commercial banks are at the center of their own groups, which include the five leading trust banks, the five leading casualty insurance companies, and four of the five leading life insurance companies.[42]

---

38. Samuel L. Hayes and Philip M. Hubbard, *Investment Banking: A Tale of Three Cities* (Boston: Harvard Business School Press, 1990), chapter 7, pp. 169–92, esp. 170–71, 184–85.

39. The long-term credit banks, as mentioned above, are interposed between industrial firms and bond purchasers. During the early postwar decades, banks were obligated to purchase industrial bonds. During the 1970s and 1980s, they were forced to absorb government bonds as well. During the 1960s, banks, like other *keiretsu* members, were required to purchase equity in related firms to ward off foreign acquisitions after liberalization of the foreign direct investment law. Examples of the intimacy of banks and the securities markets abound.

40. *New York Times*, 16 May 1993.

41. Michael L. Gerlach, *Alliance Capitalism: The Social Organization of Japanese Business* (Berkeley: University of California Press, 1992), pp. 118–25. Masahiko Aoki, "Aspects of the Japanese Firm," and Iwao Nakatani, "The Economic Role of Financial Corporate Grouping," in *The Economic Analysis of the Japanese Firm*, Aoki, ed. (New York/Amsterdam: North-Holland, 1984); Michael Gerlach, "*Keiretsu* Organization in the Japanese Economy: Analysis and Trade Implications," in *Politics and Productivity: The Real Story of Why Japan Works*, Chalmers Johnson, Laura D'Andrea Tyson, and John Zysman, eds.(Cambridge, MA: Ballinger, 1989), pp. 141–74. See, too, Hugh Patrick and Henry Rosovsky, *Asia's New Giant: How the Japanese Economy Works* (Washington: Brookings Institution, 1976); Richard E. Caves and Masu Uekusa, *Industrial Organization in Japan* (Washington: Brookings Institution, 1976).

42. *Industrial Groupings in Japan* (Tokyo: Dodwell Marketing Consultants, 1982), pp. 380–85, cited in Gerlach, "*Keiretsu* Organization in the Japanese Economy," p. 145. Of the 1,612 companies listed on the Tokyo Stock Exchange, 1,100 belong to *keiretsu*, of which 846 belong to bank-centered *keiretsu*. Those companies represent exactly half of all companies listed and constitute 61 percent of total Exchange capitalization. *Euromoney*, November 1990, p. 16.

Like the German *Hausbank* relationship, Japanese banks developed "main bank" relationships with other members within their corporate groupings. As the main bank, a city bank provides a substantial proportion of firm capital, encourages other banks to lend to the firm, monitors the firm on behalf of all its creditors, and spearheads the rescue in times of financial distress.[43] The main bank relationship is cemented by cross-holdings of equity shares typical of *keiretsu*.

In Japan, a 10 percent limit on the proportion of stock of a single corporation that a bank was permitted to own was in place for most of the postwar period. That limit was tightened to 5 percent at the end of 1987. Despite these restrictions, Japanese banks owned roughly 20 percent of outstanding equity shares, compared with less than 1 percent in the United States. In 1980, the so-called main bank was one of the five largest shareholders for 72 percent of the firms listed on the first section of the Tokyo Stock Exchange.[44] In every sixth firm, a City bank or long-term credit bank was the largest share-holder.[45]

Japanese banks are stable, long-term shareholders, moreover. Like German banks, they disguise the true value of their equity holdings by valuing them at cost rather than market value. Under the rules of the Basel Accord on capital adequacy, Japanese banks are allowed to count part of unrealized gain on these holdings as tier 2 capital. In this way, Japanese banks are directly dependent on the valuation of their industrial equities and the prosperity of these firms.[46]

Japanese banks' own shares, furthermore, are held largely by their corporate borrowers, an arrangement that cements the relationship with the bank and acts as insurance.[47] In the past, corporations have

---

43. See Masahiko Aoki and Hugh Patrick, "The Japanese Main Bank System: An Introductory Overview"; John Y. Campbell and Yasushi Hamao, "Changing Patterns of Corporate Financing and the Main Bank System"; and Paul Sheard, "The Role of the Main Bank When Borrowing Firms Are in Financial Distress"; papers presented to the EDI/World Bank Workshop on the Japanese Main Bank System, 29 July–1 August 1992, Washington.

44. Paul Sheard, "Main Banks and Structural Adjustment in Japan," Australia-Japan Research Centre, Research Paper No. 129, December 1985, cited by Bisignano, "Structures of Financial Intermediation," p. 57.

45. The survey was conducted in 1979 and reported in *Japan Economic Journal*, 8 May 1979, as cited in Spindler, *Politics of International Credit*, p. 112.

46. Robert Zielinski and Nigel Holloway, *Unequal Equities: Power and Risk in Japan's Stock Market* (Japan: Kodansha International Ltd., 1991), pp. 41–46, 179–88.

47. Corporate equity holdings in the bank can serve as collateral for bank loans. David D. Hale, "Economic Consequences of the Tokyo Stock Market Crash," paper prepared for the US-Japan Consultative Committee on Monetary Policy, Washington, 23–24 July 1990, p. 9.

subsidized banks by redepositing funds raised by loans from them. Over 30 percent of corporate financial assets have been held in the form of bank deposits during most of the postwar period, substantially above their liquidity needs. The bank-company relationship extends to employee accounts as well.[48] Japanese banks therefore have a long-term commitment to their corporate clients—like German banks and unlike American banks—and will extend credits to corporations in financial difficulty.

The equity holdings of Japanese banks do not formally entitle them to board seats, as they do in Germany. Nonetheless, banks dispatch directors to a wide range of companies and are more likely than nonfinancial corporations to send directors to large firms.[49] Senior bank officers appoint corporate executives, develop corporate investment strategies, participate in long-term planning, help to coordinate corporate activities within their grouping, and frequently lead in developing workout strategies for bankrupt firms.[50] Therefore, while Japanese banks are less intrusive in strategic decision making within the firm than German banks, they are very active during periods of corporate financial distress. Compared with their counterparts in the United States, Japanese banks have remarkably detailed information about corporate activities and financial status.

Japanese insurance companies invest roughly half as much as the banks in corporate equities and have substantial bond holdings.[51] They and other institutional investors influence the stock market and securities business, more than do American institutional investors, and maintain ties to corporations.[52] Japanese banks therefore do not exercise as much influence over companies as German banks. Rather, they share power and influence with other group members, including institutional investors. But, though Japanese banks lie at the center of a more collective influence over corporate decision making, nonetheless they have been equally wedded to the fortunes of industry.

The state played different roles in postwar bank-industry relations in

---

48. Gerlach, *Alliance Capitalism*, p. 118.

49. Only one-third of directors come from outside the firm in Japan. But of the outside directors of large firms, more than one-half come from banks. Gerlach, *Alliance Capitalism*, pp. 134–35.

50. Jay W. Lorsch and Elizabeth A. MacIver, "Corporate Governance and Investment Time Horizons," manuscript, May 1991; J. Andrew Spindler, *The Politics of International Credit: Private Finance and Foreign Policy in Germany and Japan* (Washington: Brookings Institution, 1984), p. 112.

51. Zielinski and Holloway, *Unequal Equities*, pp. 46–55.

52. Insurance companies are less influential vis-à-vis the Ministry of Finance than the city banks, importantly. Hayes and Hubbard, *Investment Banking*, chapter 7.

Japan and Germany. The Japanese state itself, through the Bank of Japan, allocated capital among competing uses, favoring export-oriented industrial projects.[53] In Germany, industrial development was state sponsored rather than "state led." Taking responsibility for macroeconomic stabilization, including in the external monetary realm, the German state relied on the banks to allocate credit among competing industrial uses.[54]

Financial systems and bank-industry relations in Japan, to summarize, differ from those of Germany in notable ways: the existence of securities firms, the development of the equity markets, the power of the banks vis à vis nonfinancial corporations, and the role of the state. Despite these differences, however, the relationship between banks and industry in the two countries is very similar in the respects that concern this study. Banks historically have dominated the system of industrial finance in both countries. During most of the postwar period, banks supplied the bulk of the external funds of Japanese and German industrial enterprises. In both countries, equity holdings and corporate involvement are consistently much higher than in the United States. (See table 2.1 for a comparison.) The banks in both Germany and Japan, therefore, are much more closely tied to industry along each of these measures than they are in the United States.

United States

In the 19th century, American banking developed very much like banking in continental Europe, with a strong position in industrial finance. However, the US financial system evolved under historical circumstances very different from those of Germany and Japan. The organization of the banking system had been a contentious issue in American politics from the beginning,[55] and there was great popular suspicion of the concentration of economic power in the financial trusts, such as J. P.

---

53. Works stressing the central role of the Japanese state include T. J. Pempel, "Japanese Foreign Economic Policy: The Domestic Bases for International Behavior," in Katzenstein, ed., *Between Power and Plenty*, ch. 5; Chalmers Johnson, *MITI and the Japanese Miracle* (Stanford: Stanford University Press, 1982). Other relevant works include Kent E. Calder, *Crisis and Compensation: Public Policy and Political Stability in Japan, 1949–1986* (Princeton: Princeton University Press, 1988); Chalmers Johnson, Laura D'Andrea Tyson, and John Zysman, eds., *Politics and Productivity: The Real Story of Why Japan Works* (Cambridge, MA: Ballinger, 1989).

54. Zysman, *Governments, Markets, and Growth.*

55. "Banks are more dangerous than standing armies," Thomas Jefferson once said. Quoted in Beth Mintz and Michael Schwartz, *The Power Structure of American Business* (Chicago: University of Chicago Press, 1985), p. 1. Jefferson would not have been at all pleased with the 20th-century German and Japanese banking systems.

Table 2.1 Postwar bank-industry relations

Indicator	Japan	Germany	United States
Bank lending to industry[a]	High; recently fallen	Moderate-high; falling gradually	Low; falling
Bank ownership of corporate equity[b]	High (18–20%)	Moderate (11–12%)	None (less than 1%)
Bank influence over corporate decision making	Moderate (not dominant, but intimately involved)	High[c]	Low

a. As a percentage of total bank loans.
b. Bank ownership as a percentage of shares outstanding.
c. Including proxy voting of shares held in trust.

Morgan.[56] When the banking crisis of the Great Depression struck, the opponents of financial concentration prevailed in congressional legislation to reconstruct the banking system. That legislation included the Banking Act of 1933 (the Glass-Steagall Act) that, among other things, required commercial banks to divest themselves of investment banking units.[57] Thereafter, the functions of direct and indirect finance were no longer combined within the same banking institutions.

Corporate access to US capital markets thus bypassed the commercial banks through nonbank securities firms, "investment banks." These investment banks did not themselves control large sums of capital—the assets of commercial banks dwarfed theirs—nor did they hold large stakes in the companies issuing stocks and bonds. They underwrote corporate securities and thereby regulated corporate access to the bond and stock markets. The term "investment bank" is something of a misnomer, though. Firms such as Salomon Brothers and Goldman Sachs were more accurately described as primarily brokerage houses with arms specializing in securities underwriting.[58]

American commercial banks were forbidden to own stock in nonfinancial

---

56. John E. Owens, "The State Regulation and Deregulation of Financial Institutions and Services in the United States," in *State, Finance, and Industry*, Cox, ed., pp. 172–230; Michael Moran, "Politics, Banks, and Markets: An Anglo-American Comparison," *Political Studies* 32 (1984): 173–89.

57. In combination with the McFadden Act of 1927, the 1933 act established the geographic segmentation of the banking industry along state lines. This restriction persists today despite erosion and challenges from the competitive, money-center banks. The 1933 act also created federal deposit insurance, and the Banking Act of 1935 strengthened and reformed the Federal Reserve System.

58. *New York Times*, 25 May 1975, p. F1, cited by Mintz and Schwartz, *Power Structure of American Business*, p. 67.

corporations. Though this prohibition has since been relaxed—a 5 percent interest is now permissible through a bank holding company—American banks still do not own significant corporate equities. While banks have significant holdings of government securities, corporate bonds represent less than 4 percent of bank assets.

Bank officials often serve on the boards of directors of American corporations. But the outside directors from banks control no equity holdings and their purpose appears to be to meet the informational needs of banks and companies.[59] The US pattern of interlocking directorates is relatively decentralized. In that pattern, banks tend to be grouped by industrial firms rather than vice versa. Directorships are not a mechanism of bank control or intervention in corporate management.[60]

Nonfinancial firms have a much more arm's-length relationship with the major banks and borrow from them for relatively limited purposes of short- to medium-term financing. American bankruptcy laws reinforce the arm's-length character of bank-firm relations, while German and Japanese bankruptcy procedures encourage intermingling of bank financing and corporate control.[61] Corporate financial disclosure requirements reinforce the efficiency of the stock and bond markets by providing crucial information to independent analysts and credit agencies. Thorough disclosure undercuts the banks, which depend on information scarcity, in their roles as financial intermediaries.

Institutional investors, such as insurance companies, pension funds, and mutual funds, are correspondingly larger and more influential with-

---

59. US banks manage a very large share of trusts and pension funds as fiduciary agents. In the mid-1970s, banks managed 80 percent of pension fund assets. *Fortune*, 31 July 1978, cited by Mintz and Schwartz, p. 48. The stockholdings of these trusts and pension funds represent something on the order of one-quarter of total voting shares. Laws on fiduciary responsibility, however, require the banks to maintain a Chinese Wall between the trust and other businesses of the bank and to vote these shares in the interests of the holder. US Senate, Committee on Governmental Affairs, *Voting Rights in Major Corporations* (Washington: GPO, 1978); Aoki, "Aspects of the Japanese Firm," pp. 10–11.

60. Mintz and Schwartz, *The Power Structure of American Business*. Mintz and Schwartz search for evidence of bank dominance over US corporations and resort to an abstract concept of financial hegemony to conclude that the interests of financial institutions dominate. They are quick to qualify that conclusion by stating that the direct power over and involvement in industry that American banks exhibit is limited, a particularly significant qualification given their predilection to the opposite point of view (see pp. 249–50). These qualifications become the distinguishing feature of US business relations in comparative perspective. See Frans N. Stokman, Rolf Ziegler, and John Scott, eds., *Networks of Corporate Power: A Comparative Analysis of Ten Countries* (Oxford: Polity Press, 1985).

61. Allen B. Frankel and John D. Montgomery, "Financial Structure: An International Perspective," *Brookings Papers on Economic Activity* 1 (1991): 288–91.

in the United States compared with Germany and Japan. These institutional investors have commanded an increasing percentage of gross household financial assets over the postwar period, rising from about 13 percent in 1952 to 30 percent in 1990.[62] Pension funds and insurance companies, in turn, invested mainly in portfolios of government and corporate bonds and corporate stock. Mutual funds invested in short-term debt instruments as well.[63] Some institutional investors, particularly insurance companies, also hold seats on corporate boards and, like Japanese insurance companies, exercise some influence there. Nonetheless, by and large, these financial intermediaries have traditionally been and largely continue to be relatively passive investors. They do not take nearly as active an interest in the fortunes and management of industrial enterprises as do, for example, the universal banks in Germany.

In addition to the stock and bond markets, the banks have been further disintermediated in the market for short-term financing by the growth in the market for commercial paper issued directly by nonfinancial corporations.[64] The ability of corporations to bypass the commercial banks in this way was facilitated by the growth in money market mutual funds, large purchasers of corporate short-term paper. The growth of the short-term money market is symptomatic of the market-based system of finance in the United States; these markets have been constrained in Germany and Japan.

The institutional and regulatory choices made in the 1930s and after World War II, therefore, made it increasingly possible for savers and borrowers to circumvent the commercial banks. The share of financial assets intermediated by banks fell rapidly from 57.3 percent of total assets in 1946 to 38.2 percent in 1960, then quite gradually to 33.3 percent

---

62. Christine M. Cumming, Bonnie E. Loopesko, and Charles M. Lucas, "The U.S. Financial System at the Crossroads: Financial Stability and Financial Reform," and Richard Cantor, "The Institutionalization of Wealth Management and Competition in Wholesale Investor Services," in *International Competitiveness of U.S. Financial Firms: The Dynamics of Financial Industry Change*, Federal Reserve Bank of New York, pp. 1–36, 11–636, respectively.

63. The assets of US institutional investors were more than twice as large, as a percentage of total claims on the nonfinancial sector, as the assets of German and Japanese institutional investors in the mid-1970s. See table 2.4 below. Further, the most important institutional investors in Germany, life insurance companies, and Japan, trust banks and life insurance companies, invest a substantial share of their assets in bank deposits. Cumming, Loopesko, and Lucas, "U.S. Financial System at the Crossroads," p. 6, n. 5.

64. See, for example, Arturo Estrella, "Domestic Banks and Their Competitors in the Prime Commercial Loan Market," in Federal Reserve Bank of New York, *Recent Trends in Commercial Bank Profitability* (New York: Federal Reserve Bank of New York, September 1986), pp. 159–77. The penetration of foreign banks also contributed to the squeezing of US banks from corporate lending.

in 1985.[65] Bank loans to industry in particular, constituting only a minority of bank assets, followed a similar pattern of decline.

Comparative Overview

These differences in the financial systems of the three countries appear in the statistical comparison. Consider first the most aggregated measure, the degree of intermediation of financial assets taken as a whole. Financial assets that have been intermediated by financial institutions represent a consistently lower proportion of total domestic financial assets in the United States than in Japan and Germany. During the 1980s, 65.8 percent of all financial assets were intermediated in the United States, compared to 80.0 percent in Japan and an extraordinary 92.0 percent in Germany.[66]

The structure of the financial liabilities of corporations in the three countries gives a similar picture. Nonfinancial companies have been consistently more highly leveraged in Japan and Germany than in the United States.[67] German and Japanese firms raise far more funds through banks than through the securities markets. Since 1965, banks have consistently provided over half of net external finance in both countries, but only between 20 and 30 percent in the United States.[68] Figure 2.1 shows that bank credits represent roughly 90 percent of corporate liabilities in Germany and about 80 percent in Japan over this period, compared with less than 40 percent in the United States.

Consider next the overall status of the capital markets in the three countries. Table 2.2 illustrates the size of these markets for selected years since 1970. The capitalization of the bond and stock markets of the United States was a substantially higher share of GDP than that for Germany and Japan during most of this period. The large differences between the United States and Germany persisted in 1990.

The volume of Japanese stocks outstanding appears to have surpassed that in the United States in that year. However, the Japanese figure is

65. Board of Governors of the Federal Reserve System, Flow of Funds Accounts, as reported in Paul Starobin, "Bypassing Banks," *National Journal*, 9 March 1991, p. 559.

66. Joseph Bisignano, "Structures of Financial Intermediation, Corporate Finance and Central Banking," manuscript, Bank for International Settlements, December 1990, table 4.

67. C. E. V. Borio, *Leverage and Financing of Non-Financial Companies: An International Perspective*, Bank for International Settlements Economic Papers, No. 27 (May 1990), tables 1–7.

68. Frankel and Montgomery, "Financial Structure," fig. 6, p. 267; Joseph R. Bisignano, "Corporate Control and Financial Information," *Finance and International Economy*, vol. 5 (Oxford: Oxford University Press, 1992), pp. 107–21.

Figure 2.1a **Germany: composition of nonfinancial corporate liabilities,
1965–90**

percentage share of selected liabilities, at intervals of five fiscal years

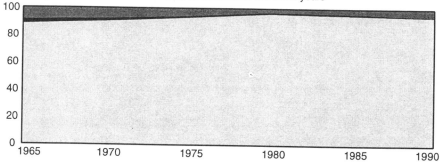

Figure 2.1b Japan: composition of nonfinancial corporate liabilities, 1965–90

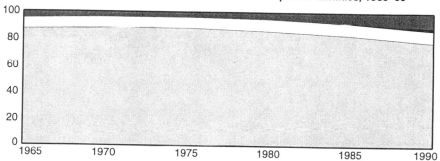

Figure 2.1c United States: composition of nonfinancial corporate liabilities, 1965–90

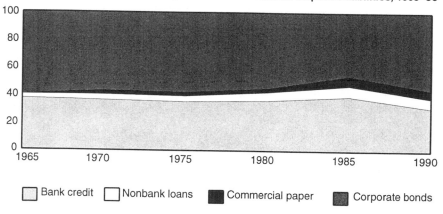

☐ Bank credit   ☐ Nonbank loans   ■ Commercial paper   ▨ Corporate bonds

German nonbank loans are not available. Japanese commercial paper market began in 1987.

Sources: *Monthly Report of the Deutsche Bundesbank*; Bank of Japan, *Economic Statistics Monthly*; Board of Governors of the Federal Reserve System, *Flow of Funds Accounts*. Reproduced from Federal Reserve Bank of New York, *International Competitiveness of US Financial Firms: The Dynamics of Financial Industry Change* (1992).

Table 2.2 Size of domestic securities markets, 1970–92

Year	Bonds as percentage of GDP	Equities as percentage of GDP	Total securities as percentage of GDP
1970			
United States	66.9	85.2	152.2
Germany	23.4	15.8	39.2
Japan	25.5	22.9	48.5
1980			
United States	65.2	58.6	123.8
Germany	37.1	9.5	46.6
Japan	60.3	33.2	93.5
1990			
United States	113.5	63.5	177.0
Germany	60.3	21.5	81.8
Japan	75.6	92.7	168.3
1992			
United States	129.6	86.2	215.8
Germany	71.8	18.8	90.6
Japan	76.5	64.4	140.9

Sources: Federal Reserve System, *Flow of Funds Accounts,* various issues; Deutsche Bundesbank, *Monthly Report* and *Statistical Supplement on Capital Markets,* various issues; Bank of Japan, *Economic Statistical Annual,* various issues.

substantially inflated and should be discounted for three reasons. First, Japanese banks themselves own a substantial proportion of stocks and bonds issued by companies. Second, eliminating the double counting of cross-holdings would reduce the valuation of the Japanese stock market by approximately 24 percent.[69] Third, the figure for this particular year is inflated by the "bubble economy" of the late 1980s. By the end of 1992, as the table also shows, the figure had fallen to 64 percent, while the valuation of US stocks outstanding rose sharply. While the growth of the Japanese stock market over the postwar period does not alter the rankings of the three countries considered here, these figures suggest that Japan is the country whose capital markets and financial system have changed the most (discussed below).

Most of the securities outstanding in the German and Japanese capital markets, furthermore, are issued not by corporations but by either the governments or the banks themselves. German and Japanese banks retain privileged access to the national bond market and issue vastly greater quantities of bonds than corporations are permitted to issue directly. Table 2.3 displays the relative size of issues by nonfinancial corporations alone. The US corporate sector relies the most heavily on bond issuance,

69. Jack McDonald, "The Mochiai Effect: Japanese Corporate Cross-Holdings," *The Journal of Portfolio Management,* fall 1989, cited by Franklin R. Edwards and Robert A. Eisenbeis, "Financial Institutions and Corporate Investment Horizons: An International Perspective," manuscript, 9 April 1991, p. 19.

Table 2.3 Bonds issued by nonfinancial institutions, 1970–90

Year	Bonds as percentage of GDP
1970	
United States	16.5
Germany	1.2
Japan	4.1
1980	
United States	13.6
Germany	0.3
Japan	3.8
1990	
United States	17.6
Germany	0.1
Japan	2.8

Sources: Federal Reserve System, *Flow of Funds Accounts,* various issues; Deutsche Bundesbank, *Monthly Report* and *Statistical Supplement on Capital Markets,* various issues; Bank of Japan, *Economic Statistics Annual,* various issues.

Japan ranks second, and, with only trivial amounts of corporate bond issuance, Germany ranks last. (Internationally issued bonds have been excluded from table 2.3. American issuers have been the most active in the foreign and Eurobond markets, followed by German and Japanese issuers.)

The role of banks among the institutions that intermediate credit to the nonfinancial sector in the three systems can be seen for the mid-1970s in table 2.4. Note that the share of deposit-taking institutions in liabilities to and claims on the nonfinancial sector as a whole was significantly higher for Germany and Japan than for the United States. The shares of long-term credit banks in claims on the nonfinancial sector were substantially higher for Japan and Germany than for the United States as well. Adding the shares of long-term credit and deposit-taking institutions together, Japanese and German institutions ranked closely with 80.9 and 83.6 percent of claims, and the US institutions ranked third with 59.7 percent. Insurance companies, pension funds, mutual funds, and trust banks (investing institutions) played a correspondingly much larger role in the United States, where the capital markets are well developed, than in Japan and Germany.

Finally, consider a measure of the direct exposure of the banking system to the manufacturing sector specifically. National data on the composition of loan portfolios of banks are not strictly comparable. The data that are available on loans outstanding to the manufacturing sector are assembled in table 2.5. Note that German banks' exposure to the manufacturing sector was roughly twice that of American banks during most

Table 2.4 Financial sectors' shares in intermediaries' total liabilities to and claims on the nonfinancial sector, end 1975 (percentages)

Intermediaries	United States	Japan	West Germany
Deposit-taking institutions			
Liabilities	57.3	68.7	61.5
Claims	51.8	58.1	60.1
Long-term credit institutions[a]			
Liabilities	5.5	11.0	12.8
Claims	7.9	22.8	23.5
Investing institutions			
Liabilities	32.3	16.0	20.0
Claims	31.2	15.0	13.0
Central bank			
Liabilities	4.2	4.3	5.4
Claims	4.2	4.1	2.3
Other financial institutions			
Liabilities	0.7	n.a.	0.3
Claims	4.9	n.a.	1.1

n.a. = not available.

a. Including public-sector agencies.

Source: Dimitri Vittas, ed., *Banking Systems Abroad* (London: Inter-Bank Research Organisation, 1978), p. 5.

of the postwar period, with one measure dropping to levels similar to the American ratio in the 1980s. Japanese banks' exposure was several multiples of American banks' exposure until 1990. The remarkable decline in the German and Japanese figures is discussed in the next section. Remember that the loan portfolio is one of several connections between banks and industry.

Change and Continuity in Financial Systems

The sources of change in bank-industry relations come from both within and outside the financial sector. Within the financial sector, two common trends apply: technological advance in the provision of financial services and the accumulation of wealth managed by nonbank financial intermediaries.[70] From outside the financial sector, two important

---

70. Cumming, Loopesko, and Lucas, "The U.S. Financial System at the Crossroads"; Lawrence M. Sweet, "Competition in Wholesale Credit Services," in *International Competitiveness of U.S. Financial Firms: The Dynamics of Financial Industry Change*, Federal Reserve Bank of New York, pp. 95–111. Cumming, Loopesko, and Lucas, pp. 5–8, and Sweet, pp. 106–8, also conduct brief comparisons of changes in these three countries.

Table 2.5a Japan: bank loans to manufacturing, 1960–90 (percentages)

	1960	1965	1970	1975	1980	1985	1990
As a percentage of total bank loans	49.3	47.9	44.3	37.5	31.5	24.5	13.4

Sources: Bank of Japan, *Economic Statistics Annual*, various issues; Bank of Japan, *Economic Statistics Monthly*.

Table 2.5b Germany: bank loans to manufacturing, 1960–90 (percentages)

	1960	1965	1970	1975	1980	1985	1990
As a percentage of loans to enterprises	28.7	32.2	35.3	29.0	24.1	20.4	18.4
As a percentage of total bank loans	23.4	22.4	19.4	14.6	12.7	10.4	9.3

Sources: Deutsche Bundesbank, *Monthly Reports*; *Capital Market Statistics*; and *Banking Statistics*, various issues.

Table 2.5c United States: bank loans to manufacturing, 1960–90 (percentages)

	1960	1965	1970	1975	1980	1985	1990
As a percentage of total bank loans	11.4	10.7	16.9	10.5	10.0	9.7	13.0

Sources: Federal Reserve Board, *Federal Reserve Bulletin*, various issues; Department of Commerce, *Quarterly Financial Report*, various issues.

Table 2.6 Financial sectors' shares in intermediaries' total liabilities to and claims on the nonfinancial sector, end 1990 (percentages)

Intermediaries	United States	Japan	Germany
Deposit-taking institutions			
Liabilities	33.2	46.3	59.1
Claims	36.4	46.8	65.0
Long-term credit institutions			
Liabilities	15.2	24.0	10.2
Claims	13.8	28.3	19.8
Investing institutions			
Liabilities	43.9	26.9	23.6
Claims	36.2	21.7	14.3
Central bank			
Liabilities	2.4	2.8	7.1
Claims	2.2	3.2	0.9
Other financial institutions			
Liabilities	5.3	n.a.	n.a.
Claims	11.5	n.a.	n.a.

n.a. = not available.

Sources: Bank of Japan, *Economic Statistics Annual,* various issues; Deutsche Bundesbank, *Monthly Reports, Statistical Supplement on Banking* and *Statistical Supplement on Capital Markets,* various issues; Federal Reserve Board, *Federal Reserve Bulletin,* various issues, and *Flow of Funds Accounts,* 1946–69, 1963–86 and Fourth Quarter 1992. Methodology adopted from Dimitri Vittas, ed., *Banking Systems Abroad* (London: Inter-Bank Research Organisation, 1978).

sources of change are corporations' borrowing in the international capital markets and domestic liberalization and deregulation.

These developments have produced disintermediation of the banks in all three countries. However, the trend is exhibited by countries from very different starting positions, as explained in the previous section, and the strength of each source of change differs across the three countries. While the general trend toward internationalization and globalization of financial markets might lead one to conclude that the different national financial systems will converge over time, a more careful examination suggests that convergence is very gradual at best.

Table 2.6 updates the statistics on the share of banks in intermediation on the same basis as table 2.4. Compare the combined share of deposit-taking institutions and the long-term credit banks. In Germany, their share had actually risen slightly from 83.6 percent to 84.8 percent by 1990. In Japan, their share had fallen modestly from 80.9 percent to 75.1 percent. The drop in the share of American banks and long-term credit institutions from 59.7 percent to 50.2 percent was more, not less, pronounced. The table focuses only on assets that are intermediated. But on this measure at least, the three countries are not converging.

The trend toward disintermediation of American banks, which had continued gradually since 1960, quickened in the second half of the 1980s. Their role in direct financing of American corporations declined as short-term loans were replaced by commercial paper and medium-term notes (and foreign short-term bank loans).[71] The wave of leveraged buy-outs during the 1980s raised corporate indebtedness substantially, largely through the issuance of "junk" bonds. American companies nonetheless remain far less indebted than their counterparts in Japan and Germany.

There is widespread recognition that the US banking industry suffers from unnecessary segmentation and regionalization and is in need of thorough reform. Pressure from financial institutions for banking reform arose in the early 1980s and was accentuated by the savings and loan scandals and crisis in the late 1980s. The Bush administration proposed substantial reforms that failed in Congress primarily because of the political fractionalization of the financial services industry. There has been no political consensus on banking reform and, as of this writing, no consensus is in sight.

US banks have responded to political paralysis by proceeding to develop "hub financial firms" that cut across product and industry lines separated by regulation.[72] A certain erosion notwithstanding, however, the separation between investment and commercial banking and the barriers to interregional consolidation remain in place. US banks continue to have virtually no equity stake and very limited management participation in American industry.

Germany has experienced several sources of financial change over the last decade.[73] Large corporations have sought more desirable terms for financing by going to the international financial markets, a trend common to Japanese firms as well. The *Hausbank* system is loosening, as firms seek to reduce dependence on single banks by borrowing from a

---

71. On changes in the US banking and financial system, see as well William S. Haraf and Rose Marie Kushmeider, eds., *Restructuring Banking and Financial Services in America* (Washington: American Enterprise Institute, 1988); Starobin, "Bypassing Banks"; David D. Hale, "Will the Weakness of the US Financial System Prevent an Economic Recovery in 1991?" paper prepared for the US-Japan Economic Policy Group, Tokyo, April 1991.

72. Cumming, Loopesko, and Lucas, "U.S. Financial System at the Crossroads," pp. 14–29.

73. On technological sources of change, see Herbert Oberbeck and Martin Baethge, "Computer and Pinstripes: Financial Institutions," in *Industry and Politics in West Germany: Toward the Third Republic*, Peter J. Katzenstein, ed. (Ithaca, NY: Cornell University Press, 1989), pp. 275–306.

greater number of them. With growth, a greater number of private banks are graduating to "universal bank" status. With German unification, the banks have been reluctant to assume risk in the industrial sector in the new Länder.[74] Finally, anticipating greater competition in financial services under the single market from other European financial centers, the federal government has launched the project *Finanzplatz Deutschland*. The project has unshackled the markets in securities and other financial instruments from government restraints and promises the consolidation of the eight regional stock markets.[75]

However, most German firms still do not have access to the international capital markets, and those who have loosened their ties to the *Hausbank* have not freed themselves from banks in general. *Finanzplatz Deutschland* faces obstacles in both the government and private sectors and will take years to live up to its promise.[76] The capital market continues to be endogenous to the banking system, and German banks maintain their equity position in industry and their supervisory role in management. Therefore, these trends have brought changes on the margin but have not fundamentally transformed the basic postwar relationship between banks and industry in Germany. Of the three countries, the German financial system has experienced the least change.

In Japan, by contrast, several waves of financial deregulation, beginning in the late 1970s and early 1980s, spawned a substantial increase in the use of capital markets, foreign and domestic, by large corporations.[77] The issuance of shares was particularly heavy during the spectacular "bubble economy" of 1987–89. Banks joined the speculation by, among other things, an excessive expansion of credits for the purchase of real estate.

The financing of Japanese manufacturing corporations in particular relied less on the banks. The ratio of loans to manufacturing industries to total loans by banks has declined over the decades as displayed in table 2.5. That ratio was nearly 50 percent in 1960 and declined to just over 30 percent in 1980. By 1985 it had declined to about 25 percent and by 1990 it had fallen to almost 13 per-

74. Deeg, "The State, Banks, and Economic Governance in Germany."

75. Federation of German Stock Exchanges, *Annual Report 1991* (Frankfurt, 1992).

76. Wendy Cooper, "The Finanzplatz Fairy Tale," *Institutional Investor*, May 1992, pp. 29–36.

77. On changes in Japan during the 1980s, see Frances McCall Rosenbluth, *Financial Politics in Contemporary Japan* (Ithaca, NY: Cornell University Press, 1989); Jeffrey A. Frankel, "Japanese Finance in the 1980s: A Survey," in *Trade with Japan: Has the Door Opened Wider?*, Paul Krugman, ed. (Chicago: University of Chicago Press, for NBER, 1991), Japan Economic Institute, "*Keiretsu* and Other Large Corporate Groups in Japan," Report No. 2A, 12 January 1990 (Washington); Gerlach, "*Keiretsu* Organization in the Japanese Economy."

cent.[78] Those changes reduced Japanese banks' stakes in manufacturing in this particular category.

Note, though, that the decline in Japanese bank exposure to industry in the loan portfolio represents only one of three measures of bank-industry relations. Despite the possibility that banks might sell shares to restructure their balance sheets during the current "growth recession," bank ownership of corporate equity does not appear to have greatly changed. Bank involvement in corporate management, if anything, is likely to increase under the financial distress presented by the current Japanese "recession." Banks can be expected to continue to play crucial roles within their *keiretsu*.[79]

Therefore, while bank-industry relations have changed more in Japan than in Germany and the United States, the recent important changes have not revolutionized these connections. The direct purchase of securities by individuals remains small, these investors having taken large losses with the fall in stock prices in the early 1990s.[80] Companies still raised substantially more than 80 percent of their financial needs from banks through 1986. In the second half of the 1980s, a large portion (in some cases a large majority) of bonds issued by Japanese corporations were effectively guaranteed by those firms' leading banks.[81] A significant portion of corporate bonds, issued inside and outside Japan, and equity shares are purchased by Japanese banks.[82] In addition, by one estimate, 30 to 40 percent of nonfinancial firms' new capital was used to purchase bank stocks to maintain *keiretsu* cross-holdings.[83] So, while the form of the credit may have changed in the late 1980s, the debtor-creditor commitment may not have shifted proportionately.[84] The trend toward financial market liberalization, moreover, has slowed and even gone into reverse in the early 1990s.[85]

---

78. See also Takeo Hoshi, Anil Kashyap, and David Scharfstein, "Bank Monitoring and Investment: Evidence from the Changing Structure of Japanese Corporate Banking Relationships," in *Asymmetric Information, Corporate Finance, and Investment*, Hubbard, ed., pp. 105–26.

79. Gerlach, *Alliance Capitalism*, pp. 125–32.

80. This includes funds passing through investment trusts. Gerlach, *Alliance Capitalism*, table 4.3, p. 130. See also *Wall Street Journal*, 18 May 1993.

81. A. Horiuchi, "Informational Properties of the Japanese Financial System," *Japan and the World Economy* 1, no. 3 (1989), cited by Bisignano, "Structures of Financial Intermediation," p.45, n. 84.

82. The commercial paper market, established in 1987, remains off-limits to nonbank financial companies. Sweet, "Competition in Wholesale Credit Services," p. 108.

83. *Nihon Keizai Shimbun*, 28 October 1989, cited by Gerlach, *Alliance Capitalism*, p. 131.

84. Bisignano, "Structures of Financial Intermediation," p. 45.

85. *New York Times*, 16 May 1993.

It is conceivable that financial institutions in Europe, Japan, and the United States might gradually converge toward a common model. In preparing for the single market in financial services, European financial firms are taking on pan-European, cross-industry business structures broadly resembling those of the emerging hub financial firms in the United States.[86] The links among financial firms within the financial *keiretsu* in Japan are a similar response to the problem of achieving economies of scope in a regulation-segmented system. However, it is unlikely that these three financial systems will converge without further, fundamental changes in the laws, regulations, and private practices that differentiate them.[87]

In summary, the German financial system has changed the least, the American system somewhat more, and the Japanese system the most. German banks experienced some erosion of their role as financial intermediaries during the late 1980s and early 1990s, but remain the dominant conduit through which external capital flows to industrial enterprises. Technical change and the institutionalization of wealth made the US financial system even more capital market–based than it had been in previous decades. The Japanese financial system has been more heavily influenced by deregulation and corporate borrowing abroad. While it has by no means reached the capital market–based model, the Japanese financial system shifted much further than Germany in the direction of the American financial system. The effects of this shift on external monetary policy outcomes will be discussed in later chapters.

Conclusion

This chapter has concluded that bank-industry relations have differed systematically in the United States, Germany, and Japan over the postwar period. Despite important changes in financial systems, these basic differences persist in the early 1990s. The observations of earlier authors with respect to financial differentiation remain substantially valid today. The changes should not be dismissed; Japan in particular has undergone notable financial liberalization and maturation. But financial convergence among these economies, if it occurs at all, is still a long way in the future.

The first section developed the argument that the relationship between banks and industry, a function of the character of the national financial system, structures the aggregation and expression of private

---

86. Cummings, Loopesko, and Lucas, "U.S. Financial System at the Crossroads," p. 30.

87. Similar conclusions are reached by, for example, GAO, *Competitiveness Issues*; Roe, "Some Differences in Corporate Structures in Germany, Japan, and the United States."

preferences on exchange rate matters. Those preferences will affect, though not solely determine, external monetary policy outcomes. As a corollary, we would expect that the country whose bank-industry relations have undergone the most dramatic change, Japan, will exhibit the greatest change in external monetary policy, *ceteris paribus*. As we will see in the comparison of policy outcomes conducted in later chapters, this is exactly what has happened.

In closing this discussion, consider the role of the state in financial systems and economic policy. Conceivably, close ties between banks and industry on the one hand and competitiveness-oriented external monetary policy on the other could be the twin products of a state that takes a strong role in the development of industry and the economy in general. According to this hypothesis, a strong state uses the financial system to impose its strategy on industrial producers and markets.[88] If this developmental state also pursues export growth through an undervalued currency, the correlation between bank-industry ties and external monetary policy could be spurious rather than causal.

The argument advanced in this study, by contrast, places bank-industry relations and private preferences, not the role of the state, at the beginning of the causal chain for three reasons. First and most important, the role of the state itself is the result of contentious politics that hinge substantially on bank-industry relations. In his analysis of the political economy of the energy sector in Japan, for example, Richard J. Samuels contends that the involvement and posture of the banks determine the timing and character of state regulation and control.[89] Second, even when the state has affected the development of the relationship between the financial sector and industrial firms, this is a financial structure the state cannot change readily and whose preferences it cannot ignore.[90] Kent E. Calder argues that the dramatic success of Japanese postwar capitalism resides not so much in the developmental state "but

---

88. Zysman in particular has stressed the importance of the character of the national financial system as an instrument of the state. *Governments, Markets, and Growth*.

89. Richard J. Samuels, *The Business of the Japanese State: Energy Markets in Comparative and Historical Perspective* (Ithaca, NY: Cornell University Press, 1987), pp. 273–77. He concludes: "Cartels and collusive arrangements involving state, industry, and financial institutions are therefore linked to the evolving norms of reciprocal consent; private banks are disproportionately important in shaping the way the state intervenes in markets. The pervasive role of the state in Japanese development, we observe, was usually preceded by extensive accommodation to private interests, especially banks" (p. 275). While advocating or consenting to state involvement with industry, the banks themselves were shielded from competition from the state by the compartmentalized financial system that limited the activities of the government financial institutions.

90. Andrew Cox emphasizes that states do not structure their financial systems as they please, and that societal consensus on state intervention in the industrial arena is fundamental.

most importantly in a formidable and distinctive set of private-sector institutions, including long-term credit banks and industrial groups in combination with the state."[91]

Third, the state is not unitary; it comprises ministries, bureaucracies, and political organs that in turn have very different missions, priorities, and objectives. Among the agencies of the state, central banks tend to be most attentive to the interests and preferences of the banking sector. The politicians and finance and economics ministries have a much broader set of objectives and concerns. Because authority over external monetary policy is shared between central banks and finance ministries, the state itself is less likely to pursue a coherent, consistent policy unless societal preferences are united by close ties between banks and industry. The "state," therefore, should be disaggregated into its constituent organs, specifically central banks and finance ministries. These bureaucracies and the relationships between them are described for the three countries in chapter 3.

---

91. Kent E. Calder, *Strategic Capitalism: Private Business and Public Purpose in Japanese Industrial Finance* (Princeton: Princeton University Press, 1993), p. 16.

3

Central Banks, Governments, and Policy Processes

The preceding chapter dealt with the organization of the private sector and the derivation of private preferences with respect to exchange rate policy. This chapter focuses on public institutions in Japan, Germany, and the United States and their respective roles in monetary and exchange rate policy formation and execution. This study argues, as previewed in chapter 1, that these institutions differ systematically across the three countries in ways that bear strongly on policy outcomes.

Specifically, this chapter identifies the similarities and differences among the three countries in the degree of central bank independence in the formation of domestic monetary policy and the balance of authority over external monetary policy between the central bank and the government. Central bank independence is a principal independent variable in this study; external monetary policy institutions are a secondary independent variable. The two are considered together in this chapter because of the strong functional connection between domestic and external monetary policy. Because domestic interest rates bear so heavily on the exchange rate, the respective roles of the central bank and government in external monetary policymaking can be contentious and should be carefully specified, particularly when the central bank is independent.

The section that follows discusses the conceptual framework of this comparison, defining the notion of central bank independence narrowly and specifically. The chapter then proceeds to three sections, devoted to Japan, Germany, and the United States, that discuss central bank independence. Each of these country sections also discusses the institutional organization of external monetary policymaking. The final section integrates these treatments into a structured comparison of policymaking institutions in the three countries.

Framework for Evaluation

The political economy of monetary policy formation in each country can be conceptualized in concentric circles of actors. The central bank and finance ministry, directly responsible for monetary and exchange rate policy, are at the core. In the first circle around the core are the head of government, the other economic policy ministries, and the legislature. The broader political and economic environment, including the private financial institutions, corporations, trade unions, and public attitudes in the society at large, form the second concentric circle. The international context, including the international monetary regime in particular, forms the third circle enveloping national policymaking. This chapter focuses primarily on the central bank and the government, the core and first circle around it.

Domestic Monetary Policy

Whether central banks should be independent from or subordinate to the rest of the government has been a crucial question in the design of economic institutions since the advent of central banking. One rationale for central bank independence revolves around the desirability of insulating monetary policy from political influences. Placing the responsibility for monetary policy in the hands of an independent, technocratic authority removes the instrument from electoral or partisan manipulation.[1]

The problem of time inconsistency provides a second rationale for independence. Private actors will raise wages and prices, thus perpetuating inflation, unless the monetary authority is credibly bound to a restrictive monetary policy in the future. That credibility can be bolstered by the institution of central bank independence.[2] Several empirical studies of industrial countries demonstrate that central bank independence is strongly correlated with low inflation but unrelated to growth and em-

1. Alberto Alesina, "Macroeconomics and Politics," in *NBER Macroeconomics Annual 1988*, Stanley Fischer, ed. (Cambridge, MA: MIT Press, 1988), pp. 13–69; Alberto Alesina and Guido Tabellini, "Credibility and Politics," *European Economic Review* 32 (1988): 542–50; Alberto Alesina, "Politics and Business Cycles in Industrial Democracies," *Economic Policy*, April 1989, pp. 57–98.

2. Finn E. Kydland and Edward C. Prescott, "Rules Rather Than Discretion: The Inconsistency of Optimal Plans," *Journal of Political Economy* 85 (June 1977): 473–91; Robert J. Barro and David B. Gordon, "Rules, Discretion and Reputation in a Model of Monetary Policy," *Journal of Monetary Economics* 12 (July 1983): 101–21; Susanne Lohmann, "Optimal Commitment in Monetary Policy: Credibility versus Flexibility," *American Economic Review* 82 (March 1992): 273–86.

ployment.[3] One study finds a significant positive relationship between central bank independence and economic growth.[4]

A word about the meaning of the term "independence," as applied to central banks, is in order at the outset. *Independence refers to the ability of the central bank to use the instruments of monetary control without instruction, guidance, or interference from the government.* The reader should note three aspects of this definition.

First, independence refers to the central bank's freedom of action in the sphere of monetary policy specifically. Only in the monetary realm is a discussion about independence meaningful. In virtually all other areas—financial market regulation, banking supervision, information gathering and statistics, and economic analysis, to name a few—central banks share power and authority with other organs of government.

Second, independence by this definition also extends only to domestic monetary policy; it does not include exchange rate policy and controls over international capital movements. In these external spheres, all central banks share authority with their governments, although the degree of authority sharing varies from country to country, as discussed below.

Third, note also that this notion of independence refers specifically to the relationship to the government, not to the host of financial, economic, and societal factors that also limit the policy options of central banks. The influence of the government over monetary policy is both a legal and a political matter. National legislation often defines the objectives and prerogatives of central banks ambiguously and frequently fails to specify how conflicts between them and governments are to be resolved. Thus, when such conflicts occur, the broader political environment becomes highly relevant as a court of appeal to dispute settlement.

The country sections that follow in this chapter assess the status of each of the three central banks considered here—the Bank of Japan, Bundesbank, and Federal Reserve—vis-à-vis their governments. Although the depth of the comparison among the central banks of Japan, Ger-

---

3. Robin Bade and Michael Parkin, "Central Bank Laws and Monetary Policy," manuscript, University of Western Ontario, 1985; Alberto Alesina and Lawrence H. Summers, "Central Bank Independence and Macroeconomic Performance: Some Comparative Evidence," Harvard International Economic Research Discussion Paper 1496, May 1990; Vittorio Grilli, Donato Masciandaro, and Guido Tabellini, "Political and Monetary Institutions and Public Financial Policies in the Industrial Countries," *Economic Policy*, October 1991, pp. 342–92. Grilli, Masciandaro, and Tabellini write that "having an independent central bank is almost like having a free lunch; there are benefits but no apparent costs in terms of macroeconomic performance" (p. 375). A later study argues, however, that this correlation is not causal: Adam S. Posen, "Why Central Bank Independence Does Not Cause Low Inflation: There Is No Institutional Fix for Politics," in *Finance and the International Economy: 7*, Richard O'Brien, ed. (Oxford: Oxford University Press, 1993), pp. 40–65.

4. J. Bradford DeLong and Lawrence H. Summers, "Macroeconomic Policy and Long-Run Growth," in *Policies for Long-Run Economic Growth* (Kansas City, MO: Federal Reserve Bank of Kansas City, 1993), pp. 93–128.

many, and the United States is unique to this study, a number of previous studies also have ranked central bank independence.[5] This chapter applies five basic criteria, which have been borrowed from earlier work and modified, in conducting this assessment of central bank status.[6]

First, to be completely independent, a central bank must have control over each of the main instruments of monetary policy: the official discount rate, open market operations, and minimum reserve requirements. Second, the ability of a central bank to pursue price stability exclusively is affected by the formal, and possibly competing, objectives that it might be directed to pursue in legislation. Third, the procedures of appointment, length of term, and dismissibility of senior officers in the central bank affect their willingness to resist government pressure. Fourth, any obligation to finance government deficits or a portion thereof compromises central bank independence. Fifth, central banks that are subject to strong oversight—including governmental or legislative review of bank policy, control over the bank budget, and audits of bank operations—have less latitude than those subject to weak oversight.

Before proceeding with this comparative exercise, it is useful to note

---

5. In addition to the works cited above, see John B. Goodman, *Monetary Sovereignty: The Politics of Central Banking in Western Europe* (Ithaca, NY: Cornell University Press, 1992); Goodman, *Central Bank–Government Relations in Major OECD Countries*, prepared for the US Congress, Joint Economic Committee, 102nd Cong., 1st sess. (Washington: GPO, 1991); Thomas F. Cargill and Michael M. Hutchison, "Monetary Policy and Political Economy: The Federal Reserve and Bank of Japan," in *Political Economy of American Monetary Policy*, Mayer, ed., pp. 165–80; Johnson, *Unpopular Measures: Translating Monetarism into Monetary Policy in Germany and the United States*, Ph.D. dissertation, Cornell University, 1991; King Binaian, Leroy O. Laney, and Thomas D. Willett, "Central Bank Independence: An International Comparison," in *Central Bankers, Bureaucratic Incentives, and Monetary Policy*, E. F. Toma and M. Toma, eds. (Dordrecht/Boston: Kluwer, 1986), pp. 199–218; John T. Woolley, "Central Banks and Inflation," in *The Politics of Inflation and Economic Stagnation*, Leon N. Lindberg and Charles S. Maier, eds. (Washington: Brookings Institution, 1985), pp. 318–48; Donald R. Hodgman, ed., *The Political Economy of Monetary Policy: National and International Aspects* (Boston: Federal Reserve Bank of Boston, 1983).

6. This study produces an ordinal ranking of central bank status, on a continuum between independent and subordinate, rather than an index number representing the degree of independence. Some other studies, such as Bade and Parkin, "Central Bank Laws and Monetary Policy," Alesina, "Macroeconomics and Politics," and Grilli, Masciandaro, and Tabellini, "Political and Monetary Institutions and Public Financial Policies," have calculated index measures for central bank independence. These procedures are useful for studies involving large numbers of countries that regress bank status on variables of economic performance. But they oversimplify the determinants of central bank status for the sake of quantification. In particular, the importance of the criteria used in calculating index values varies according to additional political and economic conditions. The importance of a requirement that the central bank finance government budget deficits depends, for example, on the fiscal profligacy of the government concerned. The importance of the length of the term of the central bank governor depends on the scope of his powers and the continuity of party control of the government. These more complex relationships are better captured in the in-depth, nonquantitative, case research approach suitable for studies of a small number of countries, such as this one.

that natural bureaucratic and practical factors impose limits to the de facto subordination of even the least independent of central banks. All central banks hold control over monetary policy at the operational level, which confers a minimal measure of bureaucratic influence. Operational control places central banks closer to the commercial banks than are government ministries. Operations also gives them access to more current and detailed information about banking institutions and market conditions, including the money and foreign exchange markets, than ministerial bureaucrats possess. Through their nationwide branch systems and direct contacts with financial institutions, central banks can conduct surveys of economic and business conditions. Research staffs, if they have them, provide central banks with the capacity to analyze this information, to which governmental ministries do not have direct access.

External Monetary Policy

Although external monetary policy and domestic monetary policy are functionally linked, the connection between them varies over time and across countries. Often wedges are driven between them, through capital and exchange controls or through other means. Thus, while related, domestic and external monetary policy are separate and distinct. The two sets of policy are determined by different institutions, or at least different subbureaucracies, and through different decision-making processes in which actors have different weights and prerogatives than those that determine domestic monetary policy. Thus, the institutions and processes of external monetary policy require separate specification and examination.

In external monetary policy, as in the domestic sphere, the institutional interests of central banks differ systematically from those of governments. Central banks' interests in the exchange rate and international role of the currency tend to be narrower than those of governments. As a rule, central banks are most concerned about the impact of the external value of the currency on domestic prices and financial markets and of the role of the currency on domestic monetary control. Governments, with broader responsibilities, tend to have correspondingly broader concerns. Their interests in exchange rates extend to competitiveness in international trade, politics of trade policy, maintenance of international economic regimes, foreign policy generally, and the effects of currency fluctuation on national spending and revenues, among other things. Governments' concerns about competitiveness are consistent with their desire for monetary ease in that these interests, respectively, argue for and contribute to a low-valued currency. Many of these considerations are shared, of course; central banks are also concerned to avoid protectionism and maintain international regimes, from which the leading central bank might derive great prestige. But central banks and governments share these interests with substantially different intensities.

Because the priorities of central banks and governments differ, there-fore, the balance of authority between them has important ramifications for external monetary policy outcomes. Identifying that balance of author-ity within each country requires careful scrutiny, however, because many standardized policymaking procedures are informal conventions agreed between the agencies rather than formal, legislatively mandated process-es. The legal framework for external monetary policymaking defines the division of labor between the central bank and finance ministry in these countries even more ambiguously than in the domestic monetary sphere. Particularly in Germany and the United States, these bureaucracies bar-gain and rebargain over their respective responsibilities and prerogatives within a very loose statutory framework. The balance of the prerogatives between the central bank and finance ministry also depends on the inter-national monetary regime to which the country subscribes.

In the country sections below, several criteria will be used to mea-sure the balance of authority between the central bank and finance ministry in external monetary policymaking.[7] Which bureaucracy owns foreign exchange reserves? Which bureaucracy makes decisions re-garding foreign exchange intervention? Who decides whether to enter a par value exchange rate regime? Who possesses authority to impose capital controls? And finally, who decides whether exchange rate con-siderations are effectively incorporated into domestic monetary policy decisions?

Japan

The description of the independence of the central bank of Japan is the most controversial, of the three central banks considered here, in the existing literature. Some analysts rank the independence of the Bank of Japan (BOJ) as low.[8] Other analysts rank its independence as high, com-parable to that of the Federal Reserve System in the United States.[9] This

---

7. See, as well, Wendy Dobson, *Economic Policy Coordination: Requiem or Prologue?* Policy Analyses in International Economics, No. 30 (Washington: Institute for International Eco-nomics, 1991), pp. 26–32.

8. Grilli, Masciandaro, and Tabellini, "Political and Monetary Institutions and Public Fi-nancial Policies."

9. Michael Parkin, "Domestic Monetary Institutions and Deficits," in *Deficits*, James M. Buchanan, Charles K. Rowley, and Robert D. Tollison, eds. (New York: Blackwell, 1986), pp. 310–37; Sylvester Eijffinger and Eric Schaling, "Central Bank Independence: Search-ing for the Philosophers' Stone," in *The New Europe: Evolving Economic and Financial Systems in East and West*, Donald E. Fair and Robert J. Raymond, eds. (Dordrecht/Boston: Kluwer, 1993). Parkin acknowledges that the Federal Reserve has more budgetary inde-pendence than does the Bank of Japan.

section concludes that the Bank of Japan is greatly constrained. The relative dominance of the Ministry of Finance (MOF) distinguishes domestic and external monetary policymaking in Japan from that in the United States and Germany. The Bank of Japan is, in fact, substantially less independent than its American and German counterparts.

Domestic Monetary Policy

The central bank's place in the structure of state institutions and the economy in Japan was established at the beginning of the period of industrialization. The Bank of Japan was created in 1882 as part of a flurry of institutional innovation and economic mobilization under the Meiji Restoration. The Bank of Japan Act established the new central bank under the control of the Ministry of Finance, along the lines of the National Bank of Belgium. Subsequent legislation on note issuance granted the bank, at the ministry's direction, great discretionary power over the supply of paper currency, following the German model. Whereas the Bank of England was a private bank given an official role, and the Federal Reserve System was established with the cooperation and support of the private banking sector, the Bank of Japan was an instrument that the state used to stabilize, unify, and dominate the financial system and to spur industrial and economic development.[10]

The central bank was harnessed to the World War II aims of Imperial Japan in 1942 by an amendment, modeled on the Nazi Reichsbank, that replaced the decision-making power of the directors with absolute authority of the bank governor, himself again responsible to the government.[11] This was reversed in 1949 under the American occupation, which also inserted a more democratic Policy Board into the structure of the bank.[12] But the delegation of monetary policy responsibility to the Policy Board conflicted with other, unchanged articles in the law that had clearly subordinated the bank to the ministry.

The subordination of BOJ to the Ministry of Finance was ordained by the leading role of the state in Japanese economic development at that time and by the central position of financial policy in the strategy of

---

10. Toshihiko Yoshino, "The Creation of the Bank of Japan: Its Western Origin and Adaptation," *The Developing Economies* 15 (December 1977): 381–401.

11. Eisuke Sakakibara and Yukio Noguchi, "Dissecting the Finance Ministry–Bank of Japan Dynasty: End of the Wartime System for Total Economic Mobilization," *Japan Echo* 4, no. 4 (autumn 1977): 100.

12. Kazumasa Iwata, "Political Process of Monetary Policy Making in Japan," Working Paper 13, Department of Social and International Relations, University of Tokyo, October 1989, pp. 7–8; Tomohiro Kinoshita, "The Federal Reserve System and the Bank of Japan," manuscript, May 1990, pp. 5–8; Bank of Japan, *Nihonginko Hyakunenshi* [*The One Hundred Year History of the Bank of Japan*] (Tokyo: The Bank of Japan, 1984).

industrialization.[13] The Japanese state provided the organizational leadership for the modernization of the economy in the early postwar period, as it had since the Meiji Restoration. The Ministry of Finance was responsible for mobilizing the financial resources of the country for the purpose of applying them to industrialization, and closely regulated a segmented, cartelized, protected system of private and public financial institutions. Presiding over the banking sector, in this heavily bank-intermediated financial system, was the Bank of Japan.

After World War II, BOJ remained at the pinnacle of Japanese finance, which basically retained its wartime structure, and MOF continued to dominate the central bank. The state-driven, hierarchical financial system that had been mobilized for war was redirected toward reconstruction and development, with the central bank fundamentally subordinated.[14] Because private sources of liquidity were scarce in early postwar Japan, the Bank of Japan became a crucial source of finance itself.[15] BOJ dominance of the banking system was central to the system of selective credit allocation applied to foster industrial development and export sectors.

In the late 1950s, after the end of the American occupation, the granting of greater independence to the Bank of Japan was debated during a wholesale reassessment of the Japanese financial system. Defenders of MOF dominance over BOJ cited the status of the Bank of England in Britain. Proponents of central bank independence cited the newly created Deutsche Bundesbank, noting that the postwar economic condition of Japan and Germany was similar. The official committee responsible for issuing a recommendation failed to reach a consensus, and changes in the central bank statute were rejected by the Ministry of Finance and the government.[16]

---

13. Chalmers Johnson, *MITI and the Japanese Miracle: The Growth of Industrial Policy, 1925–1975* (Stanford: Stanford University Press, 1982), is the classic treatise on the developmental role of the Japanese state. John Zysman, *Governments, Markets, and Growth: Financial Systems and the Politics of Industrial Change* (Ithaca, NY: Cornell University Press, 1983) treats the role of financial policy in industrial state strategy.

14. Sakakibara and Noguchi, "Dissecting the Finance Ministry–Bank of Japan Dynasty," p. 100.

15. Andrea Boltho describes BOJ as not simply a lender of last resort, like most central banks, but "virtually the sole lender" in Japan at that time. Boltho, *Japan: Economic Survey, 1953–1973* (London: Oxford University Press, 1975), p. 120.

16. Ministry of Finance, *Chuo Ginko Seido: Kinyu Seido Chosakai Toshin Narabi Kankei Shiryo* [*Central Banking System: Report of the Committee of Financial System Research and Related Materials*] (Tokyo, December 1960). For English-language treatments, see Yoshio Suzuki, ed., *The Japanese Financial System* (Oxford: Clarendon Press, 1987), pp. 314–15; Hugh T. Patrick, *Monetary Policy and Central Banking in Contemporary Japan* (Bombay: Bombay University Press, 1962), pp. 34–35; Frank C. Langdon, "Big Business Lobbying in Japan: The Case of Central Bank Reform," *American Political Science Review* 55 (September 1961): 527–38.

The Bank of Japan was much more important to the Japanese economy and development strategy, in the early postwar period, than the Federal Reserve and the Bundesbank were to their respective economies. The importance of government control over the central bank was accentuated by the breadth of BOJ's powers vis-à-vis the banking sector and its central position in the nation's economic strategy. Granting autonomy to BOJ would have surrendered not only control over monetary policy, which was important enough, but also control over the financial system and credit allocation, central instruments in the overall economic strategy of the state. As the developmental role of the state in industrial policy has declined over the postwar period,[17] the costs to state strategy of granting greater independence to BOJ have declined accordingly.

Organization of the Bank of Japan

The Bank of Japan has a unitary, centralized organizational structure. The central bank has a nationwide system of 33 branches that conduct financial business directly with private and government-owned banks. In contrast with the Federal Reserve and Bundesbank, BOJ is not subdivided into separate regional or district banks that dispatch representatives to the central board. All the central decision makers within BOJ are based in the headquarters offices in downtown Tokyo.

The authority on domestic monetary policy *formally* resides in the Policy Board of the central bank. The Policy Board consists of the governor of BOJ plus four additional members with voting privileges, one from each of four business sectors (city banks, regional banks, commerce and industry, and agriculture). Two additional members without voting privileges represent MOF and the Economic Planning Agency (EPA) on the Policy Board. The governor customarily serves as the chairman of the Policy Board. The body in theory decides the basic policies of the bank, including interest and discount rates.[18]

However, although the body had some real influence shortly after its introduction in 1949, the Policy Board failed to take root as the locus of real monetary decision making. The body became something of a sideshow to the actual policymaking process, earning it the derogatory appellation the "sleeping board." The Policy Board is substantially depen-

---

17. Kozo Yamamura and Yasukichi Yasuba, eds., *The Political Economy of Japan*, vol. 1, *The Domestic Transformation* (Stanford: Stanford University Press, 1987); Kent E. Calder, *Crisis and Compensation: Public Policy and Political Stability in Japan, 1949–1986* (Princeton: Princeton University Press, 1988); Leon Hollerman, *Japan, Disincorporated: The Economic Liberalization Process* (Stanford: Hoover Institution Press, 1988); Edward J. Lincoln, *Japan: Facing Economic Maturity* (Washington: Brookings Institution, 1988).

18. The Bank of Japan Law, Article 13, reprinted in Hans Aufricht, *Central Banking Legislation: A Collection of Central Bank, Monetary and Banking Laws*, vol. 2 (Washington: International Monetary Fund, 1961), pp. 426–29.

dent on the leadership of the governor and the technical analyses of the bank staff, who formulate the agenda, policy alternatives, and proposals brought to the board for consideration.[19]

The actual position of the BOJ bureaucracy on monetary policy is determined principally in an informal group of senior bank executives referred to as *marutaku*—that is, the "roundtable" or "executive committee."[20] Roundtable meetings include the governor, vice governor, and seven executive directors, of which the deputy governor for international relations is (usually the senior) one.[21] The group meets every business day except Wednesday to keep these officials informed of financial and exchange market developments and to discuss policy options.

The directors of the departments of the bank also participate in roundtable meetings, those from the departments of policy planning, credit and market management, and research and statistics being the most central to domestic monetary policy. Frequent meetings of the roundtable develop the bank consensus on, for example, the need for changes in the discount rate and the call money rate, and the targets for money growth. On the basis of these deliberations, BOJ will execute open market operations and approach MOF on discount rate changes.

Subordination of the Bank of Japan

It has become established practice that when BOJ wants to increase the discount rate, the central bank consults with MOF, the finance minister, and the prime minister. Their consent is necessary; BOJ will not change the discount rate if they do not agree.[22] If the top levels of the MOF

---

19. The Supreme Commander for the Allied Powers (SCAP) had originally proposed that the Policy Board be independent from the rest of the central bank, as the Federal Reserve Board of Governors is from the rest of the Federal Reserve System. Naoto Ichimada, the first postwar governor of BOJ, successfully persuaded SCAP to create the Policy Board as an appendage to the existing organizational structure of the bank, a form in which the body could be controlled more easily. Kent E. Calder, *Strategic Capitalism: Private Business and Public Purpose in Japanese Industrial Finance* (Princeton: Princeton University Press, 1993), pp. 43 and 300, n. 56.

20. The more formal name of this body is *yakuin shuukai*, meaning "executive directors' meeting."

21. The BOJ statute requires that at least three executive directors be appointed. It does not separately establish the position of deputy governor for international relations. He and the vice minister for international affairs at MOF have English titles that are often misunderstood abroad to be equivalent in rank to the vice governor and the vice minister for administration. They are in fact one rank less senior.

22. Descriptive confusion surrounding the role of BOJ in discount rate decisions is perpetuated by misleading statements on the part of Japanese politicians and bureaucrats in both MOF and BOJ who are anxious to maintain the fiction of BOJ independence. In 1990 Finance Minister Ryutaro Hashimoto stated baldly that discount rate matters are

bureaucracy support the move and the finance minister agrees, he in turn speaks with others in the Cabinet, in a consensus-building process described by the Japanese term *nemawashi*.

Although he is not always the first to be consulted, the prime minister is foremost in this consensus-building process. The prime minister generally does not insist on hands-on management of monetary policy, and he cannot hold out indefinitely against a consensus among MOF and BOJ officials in favor of a rate increase. But the prime minister's agreement is essential and his sole opposition can substantially delay a discount rate increase. The Bank of Japan governor might consult the prime minister directly with the knowledge of the finance minister. Prime ministers adopt different roles in the process, as do finance ministers. Prime Ministers Ikeda and Tanaka dominated monetary policy setting. Other prime ministers, such as Sato, Takeshita, and Kaifu, did not pressure the central bank. Prime Minister Nakasone gave free rein to Governor Maekawa but firm guidance to Governor Sumita.

The finance minister, who plays the central role in the *nemawashi* process, must reconcile conflicting considerations. As a politician, he is generally skeptical of warnings about inflation coming from BOJ. One senior politician characterizes the BOJ staff as "chronic alarmists": "They are always against reducing the rates and always for increasing the rates." But as a minister presiding over the MOF bureaucracy, he must be cautious. MOF typically stands between politicians and BOJ on monetary policy, and the minister cannot ignore the views of his officials.[23]

The minister of post and telecommunications also plays an important

---

under "the exclusive control of the Bank of Japan." Shinzo Oshima, "Interview with Finance Minister Ryutaro Hashimoto," *Seiron*, October 1990, translated and reprinted in U.S. Embassy Tokyo, "Summaries of Selected Japanese Magazines," November 1990, p. 28. The existence of a limited freedom of maneuver in monetary policy lends some plausibility to this public image for BOJ. However, as this section argues, objective evidence, unbiased sources, and reliable interviews indicate that statements such as Hashimoto's greatly exaggerate BOJ independence.

The fiction of BOJ independence serves several purposes. First, with respect to the private financial markets, the government benefits from portraying monetary policy as managed by the highly competent technocrats in BOJ and insulated from political pressures. Second, the finance minister can use BOJ as a scapegoat for high interest rates—a pattern commonly seen in the United States and Germany as well—only if he can convincingly argue that BOJ is outside his influence. Third, portraying BOJ as independent serves to downplay "Japanese exceptionalism" among its country peers, combating the international image of "Japan Inc." Finally, the fiction of central bank independence can help to deflect foreign pressure for an easing of monetary policy that the government and politicians oppose.

23. Interviews, Tokyo, January–February 1991. One former finance minister observes, "When a politician becomes a finance minister, he ceases to be a politician. He is 'domesticated' by the MOF bureaucracy. Otherwise he would not be called a good minister."

role. He administers the postal savings system, whose deposit rates must be adjusted with changes in the discount rate if large flows into and out of the postal savings accounts are to be avoided.[24] The other ministers—in particular of the Ministry of International Trade and Industry (MITI), the EPA, and the Ministry of Health and Welfare, which administers the public pension fund—also have policy interests in the discount rate decision. The finance minister must also consult with them to varying degrees.

Senior Japanese politicians differ as to the role the finance minister ought to play on monetary policy. One former finance minister interviewed for this study suggests that the person in the post should respect the central bank's role as the "policeman of the currency" and should act as a wall between political pressures and monetary policy. But another former finance minister acknowledges that in practice the minister acts more often as a conduit for political pressures.[25] Even if he chooses to act as a conduit, however, the finance minister is likely to express monetary preferences more conservative than those of other members of the cabinet, influenced as he is by MOF, and indeed more conservative than his own before he became minister.

The relationship among these institutions in making monetary policy depends in substantial measure, as it does in other countries, on the caliber of the individuals in office. For example, the prime minister's authority vis-à-vis the Bank of Japan and the minister of finance during the era of Liberal Democratic Party (LDP) rule depended on the strength of his LDP faction and his position within the faction. Ryutaro Hashimoto as finance minister played a stronger role vis-à-vis BOJ than did Kaifu as prime minister, because Hashimoto was a prominent member of a strong faction whereas Kaifu was not. Under the coalition governments since the downfall of the LDP in 1993, the prime minister's authority depends on the strength of his coalition government, and his relationship to the finance minister depends on coalition politics.

Authority over Monetary Instruments. The law empowers BOJ to conduct the full range of central banking activities and states that the central bank "shall determine" the discount and bank interest rates (Articles 20 and 21). As discussed above, however, in practice BOJ does not act on the discount rate without the explicit prior approval of MOF behind the scenes. Changes in minimum reserve requirements also require MOF

---

24. For a discussion of the consequences of dissonance between officially regulated postal deposit rates and market interest rates for the system of government finance, see Kent E. Calder, "Linking Welfare and the Developmental States: Postal Savings in Japan," *Journal of Japanese Studies* 16 (winter 1990): 52–57.

25. Interviews, Tokyo, January–February 1991.

approval. Open market operations, though, are conducted wholly at the discretion of BOJ.

Price Stability Objective.   BOJ has no legal mandate to pursue domestic price stability. The Bank of Japan Law defines the purpose of the central bank to be the regulation of currency and credit "in order that the general economic activities of the nation might adequately be enhanced." The BOJ is to be "managed solely for achievement of national aims," which are ultimately defined by the government (Articles 1 and 2).

Appointments.   The governor of the Bank of Japan is appointed by the cabinet for a five-year term. On the advice of the finance minister, the cabinet appoints the vice governor (sometimes referred to as the "senior deputy governor") to a five-year term as well. The finance minister alone appoints the rest of the senior executive BOJ personnel.[26] He appoints the executive directors to four-year terms, from among nominees recommended by the governor, and the bank auditors for three-year terms. One executive director comes from the ranks of MOF, by convention, while the remainder are promoted from among the BOJ staff.[27]

These appointments are not subject to the approval of the Diet. The senior staff officers can be dismissed by the cabinet and the finance minister if they "contravene the laws and ordinances, the By-Laws, or orders of the competent Minister, or prejudice public interests, or whenever it is deemed particularly necessary for the attainment of the object of the Bank" (Article 47). The Ministry of Finance exercised this authority, with the concurrence of the cabinet, when it dismissed Governor Toyotaro Yuki in 1944.[28] Although the cabinet and finance minister have not exercised this dismissal authority during the postwar period,[29] the ability to do so nonetheless is a source of leverage over BOJ.

By the convention that has evolved over the past two decades, the

---

26. The four voting members of the Policy Board are appointed by the cabinet and approved by the Diet for four-year terms. The two nonvoting members of the Policy Board, representing MOF and EPA, serve terms that are not fixed.

27. The executive director from MOF never has direct responsibility over any of the departments central to monetary policymaking. His responsibilities, expanded after the 1990 reorganization of BOJ, historically have been confined to government bond auctions and related matters. However, he participates in all the discussions of the roundtable.

28. Governor Yuki had opposed granting to the munitions minister the authority to approve lending to munitions companies without clearance from BOJ. Jerome B. Cohen, *Japan's Economy in War and Reconstruction*, (New York: Columbia University Press, 1950), p. 92, cited by Calder, *Strategic Capitalism*, p. 40.

29. Masaaki Nakao and Akinari Horii, "The Process of Decision-Making and Implementation of Monetary Policy in Japan," *Bank of Japan Special Paper 198* (Tokyo, March 1991), p. 31.

Table 3.1   Governors of the Bank of Japan, 1945–93

Governor	Tenure	Background
Shibusawa, Keizo	3/44–10/45	Yokohama Specie Bank, Dai Ichi Bank; minister of finance subsequently
Araki, Eikichi	10/45–6/46	Bank of Japan; purged; depurged, 1950
Ichimada, Naoto	6/46–12/54	Bank of Japan; later minister of finance in Hatoyama and Kishi cabinets
Araki, Eikichi	12/54–11/56	See above
Yamagiwa, Masamichi	11/56–12/64	Ministry of Finance, vice minister; Export-Import Bank
Usami, Makoto	12/64–12/69	Mitsubishi Bank
Sasaki, Tadashi	12/69–12/74	Bank of Japan
Morinaga, Teiichiro	12/74–12/79	Ministry of Finance, vice minister; Export-Import Bank
Maekawa, Haruo	12/79–12/84	Bank of Japan
Sumita, Satoshi	12/84–12/89	Ministry of Finance, vice minister; Export-Import Bank
Mieno, Yasushi	12/89–present	Bank of Japan

Source: Chalmers Johnson, *MITI and the Japanese Miracle: The Growth of Industrial Policy, 1925–1975* (Stanford: Stanford University Press, 1982), p. 201, table 14; Bank of Japan, *Annual Review*, 1992.

governorship has alternated between MOF and BOJ personnel. The deputy governorship goes to whichever bureaucracy does not occupy the governorship. Thus, when the governor is a MOF man, the deputy governor will be from BOJ. At the end of the five-year term, the deputy governor often becomes governor and his new deputy is selected from the senior MOF staff. Over the 1980s, for example, Haruo Maekawa, from BOJ, was served by Satoshi Sumita, the deputy from MOF, until Sumita became governor in December 1984. At that time, Yasushi Mieno from BOJ was appointed deputy governor; he subsequently became governor in December 1989 (table 3.1).

Financing the Government. The Bank of Japan Law sets no limit on the extension of credit to the government. The Finance Law of 1947 prohibits BOJ from underwriting government bonds and extending loans to the government of terms greater than one year. BOJ thus routinely provides credit in the form of underwriting short-term government bills.[30] Between 1973 and 1988, when the Japanese government ran substantial

---

30. Suzuki, *The Japanese Financial System*, p. 311. The central bank is formally required to purchase only the balance of bills remaining after public offering. The rate of interest on these government bills, however, is considerably below market rates, and there are in practice no private bids. Goodman, *Central Bank–Government Relations in Major OECD Countries*, p. 32.

budget deficits, moreover, BOJ also purchased government bonds to re-finance outstanding paper reaching maturity, which is permitted up to an amount authorized by the Diet.[31] But, although BOJ is vulnerable to demands to monetize deficits, large budget deficits have been the exception rather than the rule over the postwar period.

Oversight, Budget, and Audit.   The subordination of the central bank is sealed by the broad supervisory authority over it given to the government and, in particular, the Ministry of Finance. "The Bank of Japan," reads the law, "shall be under the supervision of the competent Minister," who may "order the Bank to undertake any necessary business, or order alterations in the By-Laws as well as other necessary actions." The finance minister may require reports, inspect the bank's affairs, and appoint a comptroller empowered to inspect and report on all bank activities (Articles 42–46). Finally, the finance minister approves the budget of the Bank of Japan in detail, a crucially important provision that crowns MOF dominance over the bank.

LDP-MOF-BOJ Triangle

Japanese politicians, bureaucrats, and central bankers have a unique triangular relationship. Ministerial bureaucrats possess an unusually high degree of autonomy from politicians in Japan. Thus, when politicians, the other economics ministries, and private business and financial institutions clamor for an easing of monetary policy, the position of MOF bureaucrats can be decisive. The MOF bureaucracy tends to be more conservative on monetary questions than most of the other relevant actors. A broad coincidence of views between MOF and BOJ thus enables them often to take a common position in the face of political and societal pressures.

The bureaucrats in MOF, therefore, often act as a buffer between BOJ and political pressures on domestic monetary questions. For this reason, the subordination of BOJ to MOF is not tantamount to exposing the central bank to political pressures. During the 1950s and 1960s, BOJ officials resented being characterized pejoratively as a mere "office within MOF's Banking Bureau." But in later decades, when MOF was persuaded that fighting inflation was a priority, the ministry's protection vis-à-vis LDP politicians was useful to the central bank.

When MOF and BOJ agree on the policy setting, they are usually powerful enough collectively to resist pressures for easing. When, on the other hand, MOF and BOJ disagree over the appropriate course of monetary policy, politicians, the other economics ministries, and private officials can have substantial influence. When the bureaucrats are

---

29. Nakao and Horii, "Monetary Policy in Japan," p. 31.

divided, the broader political and economic environment becomes particularly important to policymaking. Although LDP politicians gained influence relative to ministerial bureaucrats in a number of policy sectors over the postwar period, this trend does not describe the monetary policy area.

The potential alliance with MOF bureaucrats does not give BOJ effective freedom of maneuver equal to that of the Federal Reserve or Bundesbank, however. Although the two agencies share many differences with other parts of the government over economic policy, MOF nonetheless has a broader set of objectives than does the Bank of Japan. Those broader interests include domestic financial reorganization, exchange rate stability, economic growth, and budget deficit consolidation, to name a few, with which domestic price stability must compete for priority. Thus, while ministerial autonomy shields BOJ from politicians, it does not shield BOJ from pressures from the ministry itself to use monetary policy to help achieve these objectives. As chapter 4 recounts, for example, monetary stimulus was substituted for fiscal stimulus throughout the 1980s to protect MOF's primary objective of budget-deficit reduction. The relative autonomy of MOF bureaucrats, compared to foreign counterparts, therefore, does *not* provide the functional equivalent of central bank independence in Japan.

Although they might stand apart from politicians and the other ministries, the Ministry of Finance and BOJ seldom agree completely over the appropriate direction for monetary policy. As one senior Liberal Democratic Party politician contends, "It is a continuation of a small wrangling quarrel that keeps the system working."[32] MOF bureaucrats communicate their views on monetary policy to BOJ, and vice versa, through several channels of cross-deliberation among middle- and upper-level officials. A few words about that coordinating mechanism are in order.

Each month, the second-ranking officials in each organization, the administrative vice minister of finance and the deputy governor, and their senior subordinates confer as a group. Another crucial connection is that between the director general of the Banking Bureau and the director of the Department of Policy Planning, who consult, for example, on changes in the official discount rate (ODR). The chief of the minister's secretariat might also be consulted. When they differ, over the need for a discount rate increase, for example, the conflict is appealed to the higher officials within each organization. Conversations between the minister of finance and the governor, based on the deliberations of their staffs, ultimately determine whether the discount rate will be changed.[33]

While discount rate decisions are shared between the Bank of Japan

---

32. Interviews, Tokyo, January–February 1991.

33. Interviews, Tokyo, January–February 1991.

and the Ministry of Finance, the announcement of rate changes is generally made by the central bank. When interest rates are falling or will remain low, though, the finance minister is tempted to take credit—particularly when he has initiated a discount rate decrease—at the expense of the cultivated myth of BOJ independence. In August 1987, for example, Finance Minister Kiichi Miyazawa declared that Japan would not follow the United States and Germany in raising its discount rate.[34]

"Leaks," the unauthorized disclosure of policy deliberations, are a perennial feature of monetary policy formulation in Japan.[35] When ministries and BOJ disagree, one or the other might seek advantage in behind-the-scenes bargaining by disclosing the policy move to the press—one mechanism by which BOJ compensates for its institutional subordination.[36] The broad political process of consensus building on rate changes makes advance notice all the more difficult to suppress.

Evolution of Central Bank Status

Contention among the Liberal Democratic Party politicians, MOF bureaucrats, and central bankers for control of monetary policy was suppressed by the constraints imposed by the Bretton Woods regime during the 1950s and 1960s. The yen was pegged at 360 to the dollar in 1949 and was not altered, as were the major European currencies, over the lifetime of the fixed-rate regime. Japanese monetary policy in general accommodated rapid growth during these years. But when international payments imbalances threatened to unhinge the exchange rate parity, monetary policy was used to bring about international adjustment.

The collapse of the Bretton Woods regime in the early 1970s, however, eliminated the formal parity constraint on Japanese monetary policy. Domestic conflict over who within Japan would reap the discretionary benefit of this newfound policy latitude therefore reemerged. Politicians successfully seized on the opportunity to inflate the Japanese economy that the change in regime presented. In 1972, Prime Minister Kakuei Tanaka firmly directed the Bank of Japan to loosen monetary policy, against the advice of the central bank to do precisely the opposite.[37]

---

34. Henny Sender, "The Bank of Japan under Siege," *Institutional Investor*, November 1988, p. 59.

35. Though leaks are a standard, if unauthorized, way of conducting political business in the US federal government, American monetary policymaking has generally avoided this syndrome owing to central bank independence. The Bundesbank has also successfully kept forthcoming policy changes secret.

36. To lend more order to the policy process, MOF and BOJ reportedly agreed in the autumn of 1989 not to leak pending changes in the discount rate. That agreement proved to be very short-lived.

37. Takatoshi Ito, *The Japanese Economy* (Cambridge, MA: MIT Press, 1992), pp. 112, 127.

Tanaka was the leader of the largest faction within the LDP, the king-maker in Japanese politics. Although some prime ministers could be resisted, pressure from Tanaka could not. To the chagrin of both BOJ and some MOF officials, monetary policy was eased.

The results of Tanaka's easy money policy, reinforced by the first oil shock, were traumatic. The inflation rate rose to 12 percent in 1973 and 23 percent in 1974, accompanied by rumors of commodity shortages and consumer hoarding. This chastening experience effectively compromised politicians' influence over monetary policy thereafter. MOF deeply resented Tanaka's expansionary fiscal policy—which set in train large budget deficits that took the ministry a decade and a half to eliminate—and was as unhappy as BOJ with the results of the Tanaka reflation.[38] The ministry was opposed in principle to the interference of politicians in monetary policy, as this threatened MOF's own monetary prerogatives. The experience strengthened the resolve of both MOF and BOJ to block political intervention in the future, jolted the self-confidence of politicians in the monetary field, and solidified a societal consensus that politicians and monetary policy constituted a dangerous mixture. The institution of the practice of monetary targeting in late 1977, vaguely formulated as "forecasts" of money growth, symbolized BOJ's determination to resist political pressures for a renewed expansion.[39]

At the time of the second oil shock, accordingly, BOJ moved quickly to head off inflation and effectively used the experience of the early 1970s to support its intellectual case. In December 1979, Governor Teiichiro Morinaga, a career MOF man, was replaced by Haruo Maekawa, a career BOJ bureaucrat. In an episode that BOJ officials recount with pride, Governor Maekawa immediately petitioned Finance Minister Noboru Takeshita and Prime Minister Masayoshi Ohira for a further tightening of monetary policy. In February and March 1980, the discount rate was raised 1.0 and 1.75 percent respectively, to a peak of 9.0 percent. The victory was particularly sweet for BOJ because it broke the convention against raising the discount rate during Diet consideration of the government's budget. BOJ's policy shift solidified a decisive change in the conduct of Japanese monetary policy.[40]

As Japan entered the 1980s, the central bank had established a substantial precedent for independent monetary control that would be use-

---

38. Interviews, Tokyo, January–February 1991.

39. Akiyoshi Horiuchi, "Monetary Policies: Japan," in *The Politics of Economic Change in Postwar Japan and West Germany*, Haruo Fukui, Peter H. Merkl, Hubertus Müller-Groeling and Akio Watanabe, eds. (New York: St. Martin's Press, 1993), pp. 113–14.

40. After the mid-1970s, the growth of the money supply and the fluctuation in money growth declined substantially. As a result, inflation and the variability of growth also declined. See Yoshio Suzuki, *Japan's Economic Performance and International Role* (Tokyo: University of Tokyo Press, 1989).

Table 3.2 Prime ministers and ministers of finance of Japan, 1978-93

Inauguration date	Prime minister	Finance minister
November 1978	Masayoshi Ohira	Noboru Takeshita
July 1980	Zenko Suzuki	Michio Watanabe
November 1982 July 1986	Yasuhiro Nakasone	Noboru Takeshita Kiichi Miyazawa
November 1987 December 1988	Noboru Takeshita	Kiichi Miyazawa Tatsuo Murayama
June 1989	Sosuke Uno	
August 1989	Toshiki Kaifu	Ryutaro Hashimoto
November 1991 December 1992	Kiichi Miyazawa	Tsutomu Hata Yoshiro Hayashi
August 1993	Morihiro Hosokawa	Hirohisa Fujii

ful in its future conflicts with MOF and LDP politicians. (Prime ministers and finance ministers are listed in table 3.2.) BOJ was subjected to multiple political pressures during the 1980s, as the review of policymaking in chapter 4 shows. But BOJ's subjugation to MOF and the politicians was no longer as clear-cut. From the late 1970s onward, BOJ's effective freedom of maneuver varied with political and economic conditions.

In addition, BOJ's standing has benefited over the postwar decades from domestic financial market liberalization. In contrast to the other instruments of monetary control, the discount rate and minimum reserve requirements, open market operations is an instrument over which BOJ has full discretion. Deregulation of the financial markets and the money market has increased both the scope for and the effectiveness of open market operations in regulating aggregate demand. To the extent that open market operations have become increasingly important, BOJ has wrested greater freedom of maneuver from the Ministry of Finance.

Financial deregulation, however, has provided only limited comfort for the Bank of Japan. The discount rate retains an important role as the signal of the general stance of policymakers for private expectations. The practical scope for open market operations (OMOs) remains constrained by the relative narrowness and shallowness of these markets in Japan. Japan could liberalize and modernize the market in government securities, thereby providing a broader, deeper market in which BOJ might conduct open market operations. But the process of financial liberalization is closely controlled by MOF, and the deregulation of the government securities market has been slow and contentious because, among other reasons, it would increase the effective independence of the central bank. Securing greater independence for BOJ in the future will depend in large measure on further financial reforms.

The granting of greater independence to BOJ over the postwar period has been limited by an additional political condition. Continuous single-party control of the government between 1955 and 1993 distinguishes Japan from the United States, Germany, and its other large foreign partners. The political dominance of the Liberal Democratic Party perpetuated the institutional subordination of BOJ. With little prospect of losing effective control of the government over most of this period, the LDP had no incentive to grant independence to BOJ to bind the hands of future governments.[41] Because Japan's economic management was so closely associated with LDP economic policy in the postwar period, the party had all the more reason to secure policy control commensurate with its accountability. Now that the LDP has lost control of the government to a coalition of newly formed and former opposition parties, however, the political calculus of central bank independence is likely to change.

External Monetary Policy

The minister of finance leads the Japanese government in setting international financial and exchange rate policies. His policy primacy covers the exchange rate, capital controls and administrative guidance, the international role of the yen, and Japanese policy within the international financial institutions and toward the international monetary system. The finance minister is the principal Japanese policymaker with authority to make public statements about the yen/dollar exchange rate, supervise foreign exchange intervention, and commit the ministry and government to international bargains reached, for example, in the Group of Seven (G-7). The governor of the Bank of Japan also makes statements about exchange rates but has no independent authority to act or to commit the government to an international agreement.

The prime minister, when he decides to become involved in this policy domain, can be the most important member of the government on exchange rate matters. Japanese prime ministers have involved themselves in exchange rate issues more frequently than American presidents, as did Fukuda and Ohira in the 1970s and Nakasone in the mid-1980s. Nonetheless, the prime minister's involvement is the exception rather than the rule. The ministers of the Economic Planning Agency and the Ministry of International Trade and Industry, although they have some

---

41. John B. Goodman argues that binding the hands of successors has acted as a strong incentive for European politicians to create independent central banks. See "The Politics of Central Bank Independence," *Comparative Politics*, April 1991, pp. 329–49.

influence over general policy directions via their participation in the cabinet, are rarely involved in short-term or crisis intervention decisions.

Foreign Exchange Intervention

The Foreign Exchange Fund Special Account Law of 1951 establishes the legal framework for foreign currency operations. The law provides for the government's foreign currency fund and places it under the exclusive control of the minister of finance. The budget of the special account is to be prepared by the cabinet and approved by the Diet with the regular general account budget. The cabinet and finance minister also submit to the Diet statements of revenues and expenditures and of profits and losses of the account. Japan's contributions to the Bretton Woods institutions are covered by the account, and any operating profits from it can be transferred to the Trust Fund Bureau.[42]

The finance minister is empowered to direct the Bank of Japan, which was explicitly authorized to buy and sell foreign exchange, to administer the transactions of the account.[43] BOJ is obliged to purchase "financial bills," issued by MOF, to provide the account with funds with which to purchase foreign currency. When foreign exchange is sold from the account, the yen proceeds can be, but are not necessarily, used to retire these bills. As the amount of financial bills held by BOJ far exceeds Japan's foreign currency reserves, this mechanism has effectively monetized additional debt issued by MOF.

The law also enables the minister of finance to enlist the banking sector in support of his foreign exchange objectives by authorizing him, when he deems it necessary, to deposit with, loan to, and borrow from authorized foreign exchange banks (and foreign banks located abroad) the foreign exchange and assets belonging to the fund. The Special Account Law, importantly, does not require MOF to report the account's assets and liabilities, which would reveal these transactions.[44] These "hidden reserves" are partly disclosed in the reports on the condition of the banking system.[45]

The vice minister for international affairs and the executive director of BOJ in charge of foreign affairs oversee the exchange rate and interven-

---

42. "Foreign Exchange Fund Special Account Law (Law 56, 30 March 1951)," *EHS Law Bulletin Series: Series of Japanese Laws in English Version* (Tokyo, Eibun-Horei-sha, Inc.) vol. 5, CA, 5400.

43. See Articles 1, 5, and 6 of the Foreign Exchange Fund Special Account Law of 1951.

44. Foreign Exchange and Special Account Law of 1951.

45. Dean Taylor, "The Mismanaged Float: Official Intervention by the Industrialized Countries," in *The International Monetary System: Choices for the Future*, Michael B. Connolly, ed. (New York: Praeger, 1982), pp. 49–84, especially pp. 70–72.

tion policy. The day-to-day management of the foreign exchange special account is conducted by their subordinates, the director general of the International Finance Bureau within MOF and the director of the Foreign Department within BOJ. These officials and their immediate subordinates are responsible for policy guidelines and implementation, respectively.

MOF's International Finance Bureau itself is divided into several divisions—general affairs, coordination, banking, international capital, and international organizations, among others, each headed by a division director. Officials in the Foreign Exchange Funds Management Division work closely with those in the section of the Bank of Japan Foreign Department responsible for executing foreign currency operations. The main authority for intervention rests with the director general for the International Finance Bureau. He and the vice minister for international affairs determine the level and amount of intervention that will be conducted from the foreign exchange special account. In exercising this authority, they are ultimately responsible to the finance minister.

Because BOJ has operational autonomy in domestic open market operations, it can sterilize the effects of foreign exchange operations on domestic money markets. BOJ officials report that such sterilization is now routine, although it was not always conducted in earlier decades. Therefore, the MOF cannot use foreign exchange intervention to extract a more expansionary or domestic monetary policy from BOJ. When the ministry wants to target domestic monetary policy toward the exchange rate, it must pressure BOJ on interest rates and money growth directly.

Administrative Guidance

In addition to foreign exchange intervention, the Ministry of Finance can administer informal guidance over the investment and currency-hedging practices of the banks and nonbank financial institutions that it regulates in Japan. The effectiveness of administrative guidance, which is the legacy of the formal postwar capital controls, has diminished over time. But, because this policy instrument continues to be used and is distinct from American and German capital control mechanisms, a few words about it are in order here.

The Foreign Exchange and Foreign Trade Control Law of 1949 (FECL), which Japan adopted with the encouragement of the American occupation authorities, prohibited all capital transactions except those specifically approved by MITI or MOF.[46] That law set in place the capital controls that persisted, with some changes, for more than 30 years. The Foreign Exchange and Foreign Trade Control Law of 1979 finally, in

---

46. Johnson, *MITI and the Japanese Miracle*, pp. 25, 194–95.

principle, liberalized those transactions that were not specifically prohibited. In practice, however, the same transactions that were regulated under the old law remained regulated under the new law through administrative guidance.[47] Liberalization proceeded slowly throughout the 1980s.

To trade foreign exchange, under the new as well as the old FECL, a bank must be licensed by MOF as an authorized foreign exchange bank (AFEB). Virtually all foreign exchange transactions are routed through the AFEBs, which number about 330. AFEBs in turn report to MOF on their current and recent foreign exchange business; the larger banks report more frequently than the smaller banks. On the basis of the information provided to MOF, the ministry can exercise administrative guidance.

At the industry level, moreover, MOF coordinates banking policy through the national bank organization, *Zenginkyo*, with which officials have formal meetings once a month. Ministry-bank relations were further tightened by the *amakudari* system.[48] These control mechanisms rendered the AFEBs, as one commentator described them, a virtual "enforcement branch of MOF with oversight at the payment level" during much of the postwar period.[49]

In particular, MOF sets limits on the foreign exchange exposure of the banks. In the 1980s, Japanese banks engaged extensively in maturity transformation of mainly dollar assets and liabilities. Their combined (spot plus forward) net foreign exchange exposure could not exceed $1 million (positively or negatively) at the close of each business day.[50] Numerous exceptions were made, though not disclosed, by MOF that raised exposures in practice far above these levels.[51]

MOF also regulated the international business of the securities companies, issuing yen bonds for foreign corporations in the Japanese capital

---

47. Allan D. Smith, "The Japanese Foreign Exchange and Foreign Trade Control Law and Administrative Guidance: The Labyrinth and the Castle," *Law and Policy in International Business* 16, no. 2 (1984), 417–76. However, because MOF and MITI could no longer hold up a transaction by inaction, the changes in fact weakened administrative guidance. See pp. 422–24 and nn. 18 and 19. See also C. Johnson, *MITI and the Japanese Miracle*, p. 302.

48. On this system, whereby retired government officials are placed in the private sector, see Kent E. Calder, "Elites in an Equalizing Role? Ex-Bureaucrats as Coordinators and Intermediaries in the Government-Business Relationship," *Comparative Politics*, July 1989, pp. 379–403.

49. Smith, "The Japanese Foreign Exchange and Foreign Trade Control Law," pp. 440–46. The quotation appears on p. 441.

50. George S. Tavlas and Yuzuru Ozeki, "The Japanese Yen as an International Currency," *International Monetary Fund Working Paper*, January 1991, pp. 25–30.

51. Thus the real exposure limits for the banks are unknown publicly. See also Robert A. Feldman, *Japanese Financial Markets: Deficits, Dilemmas, and Deregulation* (Cambridge: MIT Press, 1986), pp. 156–57.

market and foreign-currency denominated securities for Japanese companies in markets abroad. To regulate long-term capital flows once they were formally liberalized, MOF coordinated all underwriting of nonresident issues in the bond market, setting the overall amount to be issued quarterly.[52] These procedures were liberalized substantially during the mid- and late 1980s.

Nonbank financial institutions, on the other hand, have developed very large foreign currency exposures. The insurance companies, pension funds, trust banks, and securities investment trusts (mutual funds administered by the subsidiaries of securities companies) hold foreign, dollar-denominated assets to back domestic, yen-denominated liabilities. These institutions match the long-term maturity structure of their liabilities with their assets, largely ignoring short-term exchange rate prospects. Neither the trust banks nor the life insurance companies are subject to prudential limitations on this exposure.[53] However, they have been subject to varying limits on the proportion of foreign assets in their portfolios.

Financial deregulation during the 1980s weakened the grip of the ministries over capital transactions. But liberalization did not eliminate MOF's capacity for administrative guidance over currency trading and international investment completely. The ministry's continuing powers of guidance reside in formal emergency powers under FECL and remaining general regulatory authority over financial institutions. MOF's vestigial powers of administrative guidance on currency matters vary across financial sectors depending on the ministry's domestic regulatory relationship to the sector. The commercial banks, with extensive international operations, are less regulated and less amenable to guidance. Insurance companies, on the other hand, are still heavily regulated and thus much more amenable to guidance on currency and international investment matters as well. This administrative influence, weakened though it might have been, remains far more extensive, detailed, and precise than the instruments available to MOF's American and German counterparts. MOF drew on these powers to manage international capital flows and exchange rates at several points during the 1980s.

Germany

The independence of the Deutsche Bundesbank is the single most important distinguishing feature of macroeconomic policymaking in Ger-

---

52. Smith, "The Japanese Foreign Exchange and Foreign Trade Control Law," pp. 454–55 and n. 149.

53. IMF, "Capital Account Developments in Japan and the Federal Republic of Germany: Institutional Influences and Structural Changes," *World Economic Outlook*, April 1989, Supp. Note 5, pp. 84–89.

many. Among the three countries examined in this study, Germany has the most independent central bank. That status derives only in part from the formal, legal relationship between the Bundesbank and the federal government. The broad political consensus in Germany that monetary stability is highly desirable, and that an independent central bank is necessary to safeguard stability, buttresses the Bundesbank's domestic status. The Bundesbank is also strong on matters of external monetary policy. But, because exchange rate policy is embedded in foreign policy and foreign trade relations, the Bundesbank faces greater competition from the government in external monetary policymaking than in the domestic monetary arena. The German central bank also must be cognizant of strong preferences for exchange rate stability on the part of the private sector and must weigh this goal judiciously against that of internal price stability.

The reader should note that monetary policymaking in Germany, more than in other countries, is undergoing institutional transformation. Two particular developments are producing these changes.

First, the economic, monetary, and political unification of Germany in 1990 necessitated a reorganization of the Bundesbank, which was completed in autumn 1992. That reform, discussed below, reduced the size of the governing body of the central bank and altered its composition on the margin, but did not fundamentally change the Bundesbank's independence vis-à-vis the government.

Second, the Maastricht Treaty, which entered into force in November 1993, obligates the member states to form a monetary union, in principle by the end of the decade, that would subordinate each of the central banks of the participating countries to the European System of Central Banks. Creation of a European monetary union—an uncertain prospect as of this writing—would therefore relegate the Bundesbank to the status of a district reserve bank. The bargaining between the Bundesbank, the German federal government, and their European counterparts over the institutional architecture of Economic and Monetary Union (EMU) is reviewed in chapter 5.

Domestic Monetary Policy

The Deutsche Bundesbank is the descendant of numerous previous incarnations of the German central bank.[54] The original Reichsbank was

---

54. Histories of German central banking include Goodman, *Monetary Sovereignty*, pp. 30–40; Carl-Ludwig Holtfrerich, "Relations between Monetary Authorities and Governmental Institutions: The Case of Germany from the 19th Century to the Present," in *Central Banks' Independence in Historical Perspective*, Gianni Toniolo, ed. (Berlin/New York: de Gruyter, 1988), pp. 105–60; David Marsh, *The Bundesbank: The Bank That Rules Europe* (London: Heinemann, 1992), pp. 91–167.

established in 1876 as the crowning act, in financial and monetary terms, of the founding of the German Reich in 1871. French reparations from the Franco-Prussian War of 1870–71, paid in gold bullion, provided the backing for the currency, the mark. The central bank, substantially dependent on the chancellor, played a strong role in national industrialization and later in economic mobilization for World War I.

After Germany's defeat in that war, as German inflation rose the victorious allies insisted the central bank be made independent in 1922. Formal independence alone proved to be no safeguard against financial disaster and hyperinflation, however. The Reichsbank made no use of its formal independence and chose to monetize the horrendous fiscal deficits of the Weimar Republic. Once hyperinflation ensued, the Dawes Commission asserted allied control over German monetary policy, eliminating the influence of the Weimar government over the Reichsbank.[55]

With changes in the central bank's legal charter in the late 1930s, the National Socialist Party completely subjugated the bank, now the Deutsche Reichsbank, and directed it toward the financial challenge posed by prosecuting World War II. During the post–World War II occupation, the Western allies reorganized the German financial system themselves. They were thus more successful than during the interwar period in imposing a truly independent central bank upon Germany. In 1948, the occupation authorities created the Bank deutscher Länder (BdL) with the currency reform that introduced the German mark (D-mark). On the theory that decentralization favored a liberal postwar political order in Germany, the new central bank was a loose collection of regional central banks established within the Western allied occupation zones. It was patterned on the Federal Reserve System in the United States. After the occupation, the Federal Republic created the Deutsche Bundesbank from the Bank deutscher Länder in 1957.

Organization of the Deutsche Bundesbank

The Deutsche Bundesbank is organized as a federal institution that closely parallels the political structure of the Federal Republic.[56] At the most

---

55. Carl-Ludwig Holtfrerich, *The German Inflation 1914-1923: Causes and Effects in International Perspective* (Berlin/New York: de Gruyter, 1986), chapter 5, pp. 105–194; Wilhelm Nölling, *Monetary Policy in Europe after Maastricht* (New York: St. Martin's Press, 1993), pp. 17–19.

56. There are a number of excellent reviews of the structure and functions of the Bundesbank and its role in German economic policymaking. See, in reverse chronological order, Hans-Eckart Scharrer, "West Germany," in *Politics of Economic Change*, Fukui, ed., pp. 115–44; Goodman, *Monetary Sovereignty*, chapters 2 and 3; Ellen Kennedy, *The Bundesbank: Germany's Central Bank in the International Monetary System* (London: Royal Institute for International Affairs, 1991); Heidemarie C. Sherman, "Central Banking in Germany and the Process of European Monetary Integration," *Tokyo Club Papers No. 3, 1990* (Tokyo:

senior level sits the Directorate. At the regional level sit the Land central banks, with the operational responsibility of serving private banks and local and regional governments. The members of the Directorate and the presidents of the Land central banks sit together in the Central Bank Council, which among other things determines monetary policy.

The federal character of the German central bank has been gradually reduced over the postwar period. The creation of the Bundesbank represented a partial recentralization of the central banking system.[57] The federal character of the Bundesbank was further reduced after German unification in the reorganization of 1992. The Deutsche Bundesbank Act of 1957, however, applied for most of the period under review in this study. As a federally organized institution, the Bundesbank is similar to the Federal Reserve System and distinct from the Bank of Japan.

The Directorate. The Directorate (*Direktorium*) is the central executive organ of the bank, seated in Frankfurt. The federal government nominates and the president of the Federal Republic appoints each member of the Directorate. Before 1993, the president of the Bundesbank, the vice president, and up to eight other members constituted the body. The reorganization of late 1992 now limits the size of the Directorate to eight members in total, rather than ten. As the federal government has generally appointed only seven members to the Directorate and is expected to continue to do so, however, the new, lower limit is not binding. The Directorate carries out the policy decisions of the Central Bank Council and wields great influence within it.

This executive body is responsible for the administration of the central bank. Each member of the Directorate has executive responsibility for one or more of the major operational divisions of the central bank. The president, at his option, has responsibility for press and public relations, legal affairs, and the audit department; another member for the research and statistics department; other members for the money and credit department, the international department, and so on. Transactions with the federal government, transactions with nationwide banks, foreign transactions and foreign exchange operations, and the conduct of open market operations are specifically reserved for the Directorate.

Tokyo Club Foundation for Global Studies, 1989), pp. 147–78; Deutsche Bundesbank, *The Deutsche Bundesbank: Its Monetary Policy Instruments and Functions*, 3rd ed., Deutsche Bundesbank Special Series No. 7 (Frankfurt: Deutsche Bundesbank, 1989). The following sections draw heavily from these accounts. For a good overview of the management of German economic policy in general, see Peter J. Katzenstein, *Policy and Politics in West Germany: The Growth of a Semisovereign State* (Philadelphia: Temple University Press, 1987), chapter 2.

57. For a discussion of the 1957 reorganization of the central bank, see *30 Jahre Deutsche Bundesbank: Die Entstehung des Bundesbankgesetzes vom 26. Juli 1957* (Frankfurt: Deutsche Bundesbank, 1988); Goodman, *Monetary Sovereignty*, pp. 30–40.

The president of the Bundesbank chairs the meetings of both the Directorate and the Central Bank Council. Although all the members of the Directorate speak publicly on bank policy, the president, like the chairman of the Federal Reserve and the governor of the Bank of Japan, is the primary representative of the central bank to the outside world. He delivers the after-meeting press conferences where changes in interest rate policy are announced.[58] He has the right to attend cabinet meetings when questions affecting the Bundesbank are considered.[59] The president attends international meetings of the International Monetary Fund (IMF) and Bank for International Settlements. He also attended and sometimes chaired the Committee of Central Bank Governors of the European Community and now sits on the council of its successor, the European Monetary Institute. These prerogatives do not guarantee that the president will dominate the Bundesbank internally. His personal stature depends on his skill in managing coalitions within the bank on policy. But by virtue of these roles the presidency carries greater weight than the other positions on the Directorate. The president and the member of the Directorate in charge of international affairs, moreover, are generally more likely than their colleagues to inject international considerations into monetary policymaking.

The Central Bank Council.   The Central Bank Council (*Zentralbankrat*) is the highest policymaking body of the Bundesbank. The members of the Directorate plus the presidents of the Land central banks compose the council. Because the Land central bank presidents outnumber the members of the Directorate, those members appointed by the Land governments outnumber those appointed by the federal government. During most of the postwar period, the Land central bank presidents outnumbered the Directorate by eleven to seven. With the 1992 reorganization, the ratio has fallen to nine to seven—a marginal shift in favor of central government appointees—as the federal government continues to decline to appoint more than seven members to the Directorate out of deference to the Länder.

The Central Bank Council establishes the monetary and credit policy of the Bundesbank, as well as basic guidelines for rules for the administration of the central bank. The president of the Bundesbank, and in his absence the vice president, chairs the meetings of the council. The

---

58. Central banking has proved to be impervious to gender diversity in Germany and the rest of the world. A woman has never been appointed to head either the Bundesbank, Federal Reserve, or Bank of Japan. Nor has a woman ever served on the Directorate of the Bundesbank or Policy Board of the Bank of Japan. A few women have served, however, on the Federal Reserve Board, and one has served as a Federal Reserve bank president. One woman has served as a Land central bank president.

59. The vice president also attends cabinet meetings on occasion.

council makes decisions by a simple majority vote, which is kept confidential. On matters of monetary policy, the council issues binding guidelines for the Directorate to follow in open market operations, for example, during intermeeting periods. Meeting frequently, every two weeks, the council can issue, and then adjust, relatively restrictive instructions.

The council generally does not become involved in the details of foreign exchange policy and leaves daily decisions on intervention to the Directorate. But when foreign exchange intervention threatens the successful targeting of money supply growth, the council's view becomes crucial to the conduct of external policy. Moreover, the council retains the right to issue specific instructions to the Directorate, including in the area of foreign exchange intervention.

Land Central Banks. Before German unification, the Bundesbank maintained one regional headquarters in each of the 11 Länder, the federal states, of West Germany. Since the reorganization of 1992, the Bundesbank maintains one regional bank for each of nine groupings of Länder. These Land central banks are responsible for transactions with the Länder governments, the other public authorities, such as Land-owned banks, and the private banks in their regions. They each operate a network of branch offices of the Bundesbank, numbering more than two hundred throughout the country.

The Land central banks are headed by a president, vice president, and in the larger banks one additional senior officer, who together constitute their managing boards. The presidents are effectively nominated by their Land governments, through the Bundesrat (the second chamber of the German parliament), in which the Länder are represented. On receipt of the nomination, the president of the Federal Republic makes the final appointment. The Central Bank Council is consulted on the nomination, but its objection has been overruled on several occasions. The vice presidents and other senior officials of each Land central bank are appointed by the Bundesbank itself; they are nominated by the Central Bank Council and appointed by the president of the Bundesbank.

When voting in the Central Bank Council, the Land central bank presidents have tended to be more conservative and more focused on domestic price stability than some of their Directorate colleagues. Thus the council as a whole has often favored giving less weight than the Directorate would give to exchange rate stability in domestic monetary policy in recent years. This generalization does not apply to all members of the council, of course. But, when domestic inflation prompted the Bundesbank to raise interest rates in the late 1980s and early 1990s, the Land central bank presidents were frequently behind the move toward tightening.[60]

---

60. Interviews, Bonn and Frankfurt, May–July 1990.

When high German interest rates created chaos within the European Monetary System (EMS), to the consternation of foreign governments and officials in Bonn, many of the Land central bank presidents were the most reluctant to ease.[61]

Independence of the Bundesbank

The independence of the Bundesbank, contrary to popular myth, was not constitutionally enshrined in the German Basic Law during most of the postwar period. The Bundesbank's autonomy was defined by statute in the Bundesbank Act of 1957. As such, it could be amended by a simple majority of the Bundestag, the German federal parliament. To accommodate the Maastricht Treaty, the article of the German Basic Law that dealt with the Bundesbank was changed in 1992. The new Article 88 stated that note-issuing authority was to be vested in a European central bank only if it is independent, implicitly conferring this status on the Bundesbank itself.[62]

Nevertheless, owing to broad political support for central bank independence among political parties, interest groups, and the public at large, the Bundesbank's free status has always had quasi-constitutional standing in Germany. Irrespective of their relationship to their governments, all central banks are firmly embedded in their national political systems. The German political system has endowed the Bundesbank with greater independence from the federal government than any other central bank within the G-7. The Bundesbank is not passive in the political process, moreover, and being independent should not be equated with being apolitical. The Bundesbank is highly political and its activism helps to safeguard its independence.

Authority over Monetary Instruments. The Bundesbank firmly controls the three primary means of regulating monetary conditions in Germany. The discount and the Lombard rates set the lower and upper boundaries, typically, for interest rates under the Bundesbank's repurchase agreements, its principal vehicle of open market operations. The Bundesbank can adjust the minimum reserve requirement as well, although its use of

---

61. The Land central bank presidents and their role within the Bundesbank have therefore become controversial. As former Chancellor Helmut Schmidt complains, "Do you need to have a president of a Land central bank in the Saarland or in Kiel? What is his job? He has to discount one bill and travel to Frankfurt every other week to raise his finger and say no. . . . The federalization of the Bundesbank mechanism was an understandable policy in the 1950s when the Bundesbank was created, to counter the fear of too much centralization. But it should be revised now." Quoted in Marsh, *The Bundesbank*, pp. 57 and 77.

62. "Gesetz zur Änderung des Grundgesetzes," *Bundesgesetzblatt*, no. 58 (24 December 1992), 2087.

this instrument is now rare. Changes in the central bank law have been required periodically to allow the Bundesbank to trade new types of monetary obligations to modernize open market operations.

The federal government is barred from instructing the Bundesbank in its regulation of monetary conditions. Members of the federal government have the right to attend Central Bank Council meetings and propose changes in monetary policy, although they cannot vote. The government can also defer an interest rate decision of the council for a two-week period, a right that has never been exercised.

Price Stability Objective. The founding law of the Bundesbank specifically gives it the responsibility of "safeguarding the currency" and explicitly addresses its relationship to the federal government:[63]

> Without prejudice to the performance of its functions, the Deutsche Bundesbank is required to support the general economic policy of the Federal Government. In exercising the powers conferred on it by this Act, it is independent of instructions from the Federal Government.

The statute therefore gives potentially conflicting guidelines to the central bank. Whether the Bundesbank has actually supported the general policies of the government has occasionally been the subject of vigorous debate. But the Bundesbank has successfully argued that the monetary-stability objective overrides any responsibility to the government.[64] Importantly, the central bank has been supported in that interpretation by powerful parties, interests, and the general public. That interpretation has been reinforced recently by the proviso, inserted into the German Basic Law at the time of the ratification of the Maastricht Treaty, that monetary policy should not be transferred to a European central bank unless that bank adheres to the objective of price stability.[65]

Appointments. The appointment procedures for members of the Directorate and the presidents of Land central banks differ, as discussed above. Members of the Directorate are nominated by the federal government and formally appointed by the federal president. In practice, the president has always deferred to the nomination of the government, which

---

63. *Deutsche Bundesbank Act*, Articles 3 and 12, as reprinted in Deutsche Bundesbank, *The Deutsche Bundesbank*, pp. 111 and 115.

64. Kennedy, *The Bundesbank*, pp. 21–28. For the Bundesbank's own statement of the meaning of the law, see *The Deutsche Bundesbank*, pp. 9–13. For a less sympathetic view, see Wilhelm Hankel, "Monetary Stability and the Welfare State," *German Tribune*, 6 June 1976, pp. 6–7, reproduced in Katzenstein, *Policy and Politics in West Germany*, pp. 115–17.

65. "Gesetz zur Änderung des Grundgesetzes," p. 2087.

**Table 3.3   Presidents and vice presidents
of the Deutsche Bundesbank**

President	Vice president	Beginning of tenure
Karl Blessing	Dr. Heinrich Tröger	1 January 1958
Dr. Karl Klasen	Dr. Otmar Emminger	1 January 1970
Dr. Otmar Emminger	Karl Otto Pöhl	1 June 1977
Karl Otto Pöhl	Prof. Helmut Schlesinger	1 January 1980
Prof. Helmut Schlesinger	Dr. Hans Tietmeyer	8 August 1991
Dr. Hans Tietmeyer	Johann W. Gaddum	1 October 1993

has in turn been agreed among the leaders of the coalition parties. Presidents of the Land central banks are formally nominated by the Bundesrat, in which the Land governments are represented, and appointed by the federal president. When making its nomination, the Bundesrat defers to the government(s) of the Land (Länder) in which the appointee would serve.

Both the members of the Directorate and the Land central bank presidents are appointed for eight years. In exceptional cases, such as when the appointee is approaching the mandatory retirement age of 68, the government can make an appointment for a period of not less than two years. Otmar Emminger served a two-and-a-half-year term during 1977–79; Helmut Schlesinger served a two-year term during 1991–93. Short terms, though, have indeed been the exception (table 3.3).

Because these terms are renewable, moreover, and the positions are well compensated, the typical length of service for council members has been almost 13 years. That is almost four years longer than the average tenure of coalition governments in Bonn and five years longer than the average tenure of chancellors under the Federal Republic. Appointees cannot be dismissed over policy conflicts with the government. They are not subject to instruction from the government.

There is a general consensus that federal appointments to the Directorate must not constitute an effort to manipulate the bank. The Bundesbank is, in the words of one senior German politician, a "Supreme Court for the currency." Public support for its independence strongly discourages governments from trying to "pack the Court."

The federal and Land governments nonetheless scrutinize party affiliation when making appointments to the Directorate and Central Bank Council. In theory, those appointments must be of qualified experts with independent professional standing who will act on that expertise rather than party membership. Land governments usually appoint presidents from among the ranks of former Land ministers and politicians of the governing party or coalition. In practice, therefore, their appointments are usually but not always highly qualified.

The federal government has in the past made appointments that maintain a political balance on the Directorate. Before Karl Otto Pöhl's resignation as president in 1991, there had been a tradition of selecting the president and the vice president from opposite political affiliations.[66] People with conservative affiliations have held both senior posts since then. Both the current president, Hans Tietmeyer, and vice president, Johann Wilhelm Gaddum, are members of the Christian Democratic Union (CDU). As partial compensation for these appointments, a Social Democrat was added to the Directorate.

Financing the Government. Until recently, the Bundesbank could extend short-term credits to federal and Land governments and government entities at its, not the government's, discretion. Those credits were capped for each category of borrower at specific, low levels that were established, in the case of the Land governments, on the basis of population size. The government was therefore not able to exploit these facilities to affect monetary conditions. Since January 1994, all such credits have been banned by the Maastricht Treaty provisions governing the transition to monetary union.

Originally, the Bundesbank provided funds for the membership payments to the International Monetary Fund and World Bank through loans to the government for that purpose. That authorization was repealed by legislation at the end of 1970, since which time contributions to the international financial institutions have been the responsibility of the Bundesbank directly.[67]

Oversight, Budget, and Audit. The federal government possesses no formal oversight authority vis-à-vis the Bundesbank. Members of the Directorate appear before committees of the Bundestag with some regularity to explain the Bundesbank's policies. Bundesbank officials, however, are not required to report to the Bundestag; and in fact Helmut Schlesinger rebuffed requests from Bundestag committees for his testimony. The central bank manages its own budget, which is neither subject to outside approval nor publicly released for external scrutiny. An audit of the bank's accounts is conducted by the Federal Court of Audit, itself independent from the government and legislature.[68]

---

66. David Marsh, *The Germans: A People at the Crossroads* (New York: St. Martin's Press, 1989), pp. 191–92, esp. n. 11. Karl Otto Pöhl has been a member of the Social Democratic Party (SPD) since 1948, while Helmut Schlesinger, though not a party member, is affiliated with the Christian Social Union (CSU). The tradition favored Pöhl's reappointment in 1987 despite the objections of CSU leader Franz-Josef Strauss. To give the Free Democratic Party (FDP) representation, Günter Storch was appointed to the Directorate in 1987.

67. *Deutsche Bundesbank Act of 1957*, Article 20, as amended and reproduced in *The Deutsche Bundesbank*, p. 120.

68. Goodman, *Central Bank–Government Relations in Major OECD Countries*, pp. 20–21.

The profits of the Bundesbank are transferred to the federal government, as in other countries. These transfers have become a significant source of revenue for Bonn, amounting to well over DM10 billion in some years. They are not in and of themselves a source of leverage over the Bundesbank, of course. But, because these payments rise and fall with gains and losses on foreign exchange, whether realized or not, exchange rate fluctuations affect government revenues.

Three aspects of the broader political and economic environment reinforce the independence of the Bundesbank in German economic policymaking. First, government budget deficits have been relatively restrained in Germany during most of the postwar period, thus reducing pressures on the central bank for monetization. (As a result of unification, however, Germany will experience large public-sector deficits, including the accounts of public-sector enterprises, throughout the decade of the 1990s.) Second, the German trade union structure is centralized and the wage rounds are highly organized. This relatively disciplined wage-setting process reduces competition among trade unions themselves for high wage settlements. Third, political and business elites, the press, and the public at large support the objective of price stability and perceive the independence of the Bundesbank to be vital to achieving this goal.

External Monetary Policymaking

In contrast to the Bundesbank's independence in the domestic sphere, the German central bank must share authority with the federal government in external monetary policymaking. The government retains the authority to commit Germany to any international currency-stabilization agreement and to establish the par value of the D-mark within such an arrangement. Meanwhile, the Bundesbank is responsible for conducting foreign exchange operations. The government's authority on the external side is fundamentally important, not only to exchange rate policy but to the Bundesbank's room for maneuver on the domestic side as well, owing to the dilemma that arises at times between maintaining internal price stability or exchange rate stability.

Foreign Exchange Intervention

No legal document explicitly specifies the role of the federal government in establishing the exchange rate regime and the role of the Bundesbank in managing it with intervention. As in the United States, the government and the central bank have agreed on their division of labor in international monetary affairs largely on their own. Their bargaining has taken place within a loose legal framework that has left a great deal of latitude for mutual agreement. The legality and appropriateness of their division of responsibility have been generally accepted within Germany.

Similarly, regarding foreign exchange intervention, neither the Basic Law nor statutes define the roles of the government or ministries. But the Bundesbank Act issues a clear grant of authority to the central bank to conduct foreign exchange operations. The statute defines the bank's scope of business in the international field broadly, including transactions with banks, corporations, and individuals in instruments denominated in foreign currency and precious metals (Articles 19 and 22). As a result, the Bundesbank owns all of Germany's international reserves and has complete operational control over intervention.

The Choice of Regime

When exercising its authority to establish or abandon a parity for the D-mark against foreign currencies in a formal stabilization agreement, the federal government must listen to the Bundesbank's advice. Nonetheless, the government alone decides whether to enter into such agreements with foreign capitals. The senior politicians in Bonn thus hold the legal authority to obligate the Bundesbank to defend specific exchange rate levels—even if those obligations impinge on Frankfurt's domestic monetary objectives.

The government's decision on the international regime determines the balance of authority over external monetary policy between it and the Bundesbank on an ongoing basis. In the absence of a formal exchange rate stabilization agreement, the Bundesbank retains full discretion over foreign exchange intervention. Under an exchange rate stabilization agreement, the government retains authority over realignments or abandonment of the regime.[69]

The postwar Bretton Woods regime was concluded among the governments, not the central banks, of participating countries. The governments, for example, are members of the International Monetary Fund and World Bank. The regime imposed upon the Bundesbank the obligation to intervene in the foreign exchange markets to prevent the D-mark from moving significantly against the dollar. Because the purchase of dollars required under the regime increased the German money supply, the Bundesbank increasingly lost control of domestic monetary conditions over the 1950s and 1960s.[70]

---

69. After the revaluation of the D-mark in 1961, some members of the Bundestag challenged the government's authority to change the external value of the currency. The government, in response, referred to the legislative history of the Bundesbank Act and inferred from the 1957 discussion that the Bundestag had intended that the government possess responsibility for the par value. This interpretation was accepted and never again questioned.

70. Otmar Emminger, *The D-mark and the Conflict between Internal and External Equilibrium*, Essays in International Finance 122 (Princeton: Princeton University, International Finance Section, June 1977).

Pressures to expand the money supply originating from the external sector were partly alleviated by revaluations of the D-mark. Those decisions, however, were entirely in the hands of the government and subject to its willingness to initiate realignment negotiations with partner governments. The political leaders who constituted the government, furthermore, were often more concerned with export growth and foreign relations, for example, than with domestic monetary conditions.

The demise of the Bretton Woods regime in the early 1970s, in which German policy played a significant role, liberated the Bundesbank from these constraints. The German central bank could thereafter take greater advantage of the domestic independence nominally inscribed in the Bundesbank law. The Bundesbank exercised this newfound freedom by tightening monetary policy in March 1973.

In place of the Bretton Woods regime, however, European governments constructed a regional exchange rate stabilization scheme. First the European Narrower Margins Arrangement, the "Snake," and then the European Monetary System, the EMS, were created to provide a European "island of stability" in a world of flexible rates. Since the early 1970s, therefore, the exchange rate policymaking system in Germany has been bifurcated along currency lines. Two different sets of institutional prerogatives coexist, one that applies to EMS currencies, the other that applies to the dollar and other non-EMS currencies.

European Monetary System.   The European Monetary System was established by a decision of the European Council, the heads of government of the member states of the European Community, in December 1978. Within the EMS was created the Exchange Rate Mechanism (ERM) that stabilized currency relationships among those countries, including Germany, that elected to participate. The framework for operational cooperation was established separately by a supplementary agreement among the central banks alone.[71]

Under the formal rules of the ERM, the Bundesbank has an unlimited obligation to intervene in the foreign exchange markets when the D-mark reaches the maximum permitted divergence from the central rate against the other currencies participating in the system. For most of the life of the EMS, the maximum divergence was 2¼ percent against most of the other currencies. The permitted divergence against the Italian lira, Spanish peseta, Portuguese escudo, and British pound was, at various times, 6 percent.[72] In August 1993, after a year of intense currency spec-

---

71. These documents are reproduced in Jacques van Ypersele and Jean-Claude Koeune, *The European Monetary System: Origins, Operations and Outlook* (Luxembourg: Office for Official Publications of the European Communities, 1985), annex 2, pp. 122–25, 129–33.

72. Members of the Community that do not participate in the ERM are nonetheless formal members of the EMS.

ulation that had driven the pound and lira from the ERM and threatened the link between the D-mark and French franc, these bands were drastically widened to 15 percent for all currencies except the Dutch guilder (discussed in chapter 5). The shift to wide bands made it unlikely that the Bundesbank would be formally obliged to intervene at the margin. There remains the distinct possibility, however, that European governments will reestablish narrow bands to implement their commitment under the Maastricht Treaty to form a monetary union.[73]

When intervening within the EMS framework, and assuming that the D-mark is in the strong position, the Bundesbank can extend short-term credits to the central bank of a weak currency to sell on the open market. Under some circumstances, specified in a 1987 agreement, the Bundesbank must lend D-marks to its counterparts even when their currencies have not yet reached the margins. Both measures, direct intervention and credit extension, affect the German money supply.

When the EMS was created, however, the Bundesbank extracted from the German government the informal right to "opt out" of the system should its obligations under the scheme lead to an increase of German liquidity that threatened domestic monetary stability. This important proviso was publicly discussed and sanctioned by key politicians (see chapter 5). It was also discussed with Germany's EMS partners in the European committees at the time. Importantly, however, the ultimate decision as to whether an increase in German liquidity would threaten domestic monetary stability rests with the German government, not the Bundesbank. Procedurally, the Bundesbank would have to request that the government release it from intervention obligations under the EMS when these conditions obtain.

At the European level, political responsibility for the management of the EMS resides in the Ecofin Council,[74] the council of the ministers of finance and economics of the member countries of the EC, now the European Union.[75] As long as exchange rates remain stable within the

---

73. Niels Thygesen, "Deepening the European Union: Monetary Arrangements," in *Reviving the European Union*, C. Randall Henning, Eduard Hochreiter, and Gary Clyde Hufbauer, eds. (Washington: Institute for International Economics, 1994), pp. 43–66.

74. Technically, these ministers do not meet as the Ecofin Council when addressing EMS matters. It is nonetheless the same group of officials meeting in the same location.

75. Ecofin is assisted by the Monetary Committee, a group that combines the deputies to the finance ministers and central bank governors in each country. The Committee of Central Bank Governors of the EC, meeting on the margin of meetings at the Bank for International Settlements in Basel, Switzerland, coordinated the central bank position and oversaw the EMS operationally during 1979–93. In 1994, the Committee of Central Bank Governors was replaced by the European Monetary Institute, with a similar membership, created under the Maastricht Treaty to supervise the transition to monetary union and seated in Frankfurt. The central banks manage the system primarily through coordination of domestic monetary policies, a process that the Bundesbank has effectively dominated heretofore.

ERM, there is very little involvement of the finance ministry officials. However, when currency rates within the ERM become unstable, the stance of the finance ministries becomes crucial.

When the Bundesbank's exchange rate commitments in the EMS come into conflict with its restraint of the growth of the domestic money supply, it will petition the German finance ministry to initiate negotiations with the EMS partners for a realignment within the system.[76] The finance ministry conducts these negotiations for Germany and the minister's approval is necessary for any decision. The Bundesbank can offer its advice on the necessity, size, and timing of a realignment, and usually does so vigorously, but is ultimately reliant on the finance ministry to act. For its part, the finance ministry cannot ignore the wishes of the Bundesbank, and consultation between the two on EMS matters is intensive.

When the finance ministry refuses to grant a realignment—which happened in the late 1980s, for example—the German central bank has no practical recourse. Theoretically, the Bundesbank could opt out of the system by refusing to honor the obligation to intervene at the margin of the ERM bands. This step, however, would trigger dire political consequences for the German central bank. The Bundesbank could consider such a move only if ERM participation produced a monetary expansion that was widely deplored within Germany by politically powerful groups. Even then, the Bundesbank would have to assess their political support carefully; the European Monetary System has been a central pillar of German economic policy. The Bundesbank knows that it would be risky to ignore private preferences for exchange rate stability.

The dilemmas for the Bundesbank have been moderated, though, by the fact that Frankfurt's monetary policy has generally dominated the ERM. Monetary policies of the participating countries have converged toward the Bundesbank's monetary standard, rather than toward a European average. To the surprise of many observers, during the 1980s Germany's partners accepted the D-mark as the "nominal anchor" of the system. Because countries such as France and Italy were strongly committed to existing parities, the ERM became, effectively, a D-mark zone.[77] The area of this zone was extended to Switzerland, Austria, and the

---

76. Alternatively, partner governments might initiate such negotiations themselves in the Monetary Committee and Ecofin.

77. Francesco Giavazzi and Alberto Giovannini, *Limiting Exchange Rate Flexibility: The European Monetary System* (Cambridge: MIT Press, 1989), especially chapter 4. For assessments of the German-dominance thesis, see Daniel Gros and Niels Thygesen, *The EMS: Achievements, Current Issues and Directions for the Future*, Centre for European Policy Studies Paper 35 (Brussels, 1988); Francesco Giavazzi, Stefano Micossi, and Marcus Miller, *The European Monetary System* (Cambridge, UK: Cambridge University Press, 1988); Paul De Grauwe and Lucas Papademos, eds., *The European Monetary System in the 1990s* (London/New York: Longman, 1990).

Nordic countries, which, with varying degrees of commitment, linked their currencies to the D-mark, or to the ECU, by shadowing the Bundesbank's monetary policies. The dominance of the D-mark persisted even after the unraveling of the ERM during 1992–93, as most partner countries continued to match German monetary policy despite the shift to wide bands. From the German standpoint, the ability to pursue German monetary preferences was and remains the fundamental difference between the EMS and the old Bretton Woods regime.

International Monetary System. Since the breakdown of the Bretton Woods regime, no formal, public exchange rate regime has governed the relationship of the D-mark to the currencies outside Europe. The D-mark has been allowed to fluctuate against the dollar and the yen, the first and second most important currency relationships outside Europe. The D-mark also has fluctuated against the European currencies not participating in the ERM, which have included the pound sterling for most of the life of the EMS and the Italian lira, as of this writing. Under the flexible exchange rate regime, the Bundesbank has much greater latitude than under fixed rates. In the absence of complicating agreements, such as the Louvre Accord within the G-7, the Bundesbank alone decides on intervention policy with regard to these non-EMS currencies.

When the German finance minister discusses exchange rates with American and Japanese counterparts, however, a potential conflict arises between his legitimate role in external monetary policy and the Bundesbank's domestic independence. Agreements within the G-7, in particular, are likely to engender this conflict. The Louvre Accord, for example, established confidential target ranges for currency fluctuation. This G-7 communiqué did not disclose the agreement in any detail, however. In contrast with a formal regime, the Louvre Accord was not codified in a document to be signed by the participants and ratified by national legislatures. The Bundesbank was effectively constrained by the agreement politically, but it was not formally bound by it legally. To seek his voluntary accession to such agreements, the president of the Bundesbank is invited to all G-7 meetings, as are his counterparts.

The government represents Germany in the International Monetary Fund, the World Bank, and the other multilateral development banks. The Bundesbank also represents Germany at the IMF, where it has had a role from the beginning. Germany's quota subscription to the IMF is provided directly from the Bundesbank. The Bundesbank therefore codetermines German policy positions in the IMF on matters that affect the reserve position and thus the central bank's financial status. Those matters include most routine lending decisions of the IMF Executive Board as well as decisions of the Board of Governors to increase quotas. On IMF matters that do not affect the financial position of the Bundesbank, the German finance ministry informs Frankfurt but can technically act without the Bundesbank's formal approval. The German executive director at the IMF is appointed alternately from the finance ministry and the Bundesbank. When the executive director is from the finance ministry, his deputy is chosen from the Bundesbank, and vice versa.

The Federal Government

Within the federal government, the major actors on external monetary policy are four: the chancellor, the finance ministry, economics ministry, and the foreign ministry. The chancellor and the ministers are always senior members of the political parties of the governing coalition. Under Chancellors Helmut Schmidt (SPD) and Helmut Kohl (CDU), the Free Democratic Party (FDP) controlled both the economics and foreign ministries. The control of the finance ministry shifted from the SPD to the CDU in 1982, and from the CDU to the Christian Social Union (CSU) in 1989.

During the 1950s and 1960s, international monetary questions, particularly revaluations of the D-mark, commanded great political attention, involved the chancellor personally, and required decisions of the full cabinet. During the 1970s and 1980s, under flexible exchange rates, the cabinet as a whole took a very low profile. As today, the chancellor and foreign minister became involved in exchange rate matters only on an exceptional basis. Those exceptions were fundamentally important, however, and usually involved wider political commitments to the European Community or the United States. The creation of the EMS and the launching of EMU, for example, were inspired by Schmidt, Kohl, and Foreign Minister Hans-Dietrich Genscher.

The Ministry of Economics and Ministry of Finance have had primary policy responsibility in international monetary affairs for the government. During the 1950s and 1960s, the Ministry of Economics took the lead on exchange rate matters. After the early 1970s, however, the Ministry of Finance came to speak for the government on international monetary matters. The shift was due to the relocation of the Department of Money and Credit from the economics to the finance ministry.

The Department of Money and Credit is responsible for international as well as domestic monetary affairs. Located in the Ministry of Economics in the 1950s, the department became prominent in the 1960s and early 1970s, as international monetary questions became hotly disputed domestically and internationally. The department thus became a politically important part of the economics minister's portfolio, contributing to the clout of ministers such as Ludwig Erhard and Karl Schiller.

When in 1972 Helmut Schmidt, then minister for economics and finance, surrendered the Ministry of Economics from his portfolio to the FDP at the beginning of the second Social-Liberal coalition, he insisted on retaining the Department of Money and Credit by transferring it to the Ministry of Finance.[78] The transfer has been a sore point ever since for both the Ministry of Economics and the FDP, which has controlled the ministry—a bureaucratic "Alsace-Lorraine," in the words of one senior former official.[79] In spite of the loss of direct policy responsibility, the Ministry of Economics and the FDP have through various devices succeeded in weighing in on external monetary issues.

United States

The Federal Reserve System, the central bank for the United States, is relatively independent from the administration and the Congress in setting domestic monetary policy. However, owing to the weaker political standing of the central bank among the public at large, the Federal Reserve's independent status is not as secure as that of the Bundesbank. On matters of external monetary policy, specifically foreign exchange intervention, authority is divided between the Federal Reserve and the Department of the Treasury. Divided authority exists in other countries as well, but occurs in the United States in the absence of a clear societal or governmental consensus on exchange rate objectives and guidelines.

Domestic Monetary Policymaking

The Federal Reserve System was created in 1914 after a century of bitter political conflict over the nation's banking system. The gradual loss of oligopolistic control by the elite New York financial community at the turn of the century was accompanied by successive financial panics. This turbulence, culminating in the crash of 1907, softened the opposition, largely within the banking community, to a limited role for government in finance.[80]

---

78. Schmidt's historic personal friendship with Valéry Giscard d'Estaing, which led to the creation of the EMS among other things, was forged in the negotiations over international monetary reform in the early and mid-1970s. Control over the Department of Money and Credit gave Schmidt standing to conduct these negotiations on Germany's behalf.

79. Count Otto Lambsdorff as minister of economics hoped to reclaim the department after the 1980 election. Although the FDP presented its best showing since 1961, in that election, the electoral outcome proved to be insufficient to extract this concession from the SPD in the intracoalition negotiations.

80. On the history of the Federal Reserve System, see John T. Woolley, *Monetary Politics: The Federal Reserve and the Politics of Monetary Policy* (Cambridge, UK: Cambridge University Press, 1984); Thomas Havrilesky, *The Pressures on American Monetary Policy* (Boston/ Dordrecht: Kluwer, 1993), chapters 1–3; William Greider, *Secrets of the Temple: How the Federal Reserve Runs the Country* (New York: Simon and Schuster, 1987); Milton Friedman and Anna J. Schwartz, *A Monetary History of the United States, 1867–1960* (Princeton: Princeton University Press, 1963); Richard H. Timberlake, *The Origins of Central Banking in the United States* (Cambridge, MA: Harvard University Press, 1978).

Establishment of the central banking system thus followed, not preceded, American industrialization. Rather than being created for the purpose of mobilizing capital for national development, as were central banks in some late-industrializing countries, the Federal Reserve System was created to provide stability to the banking and financial system. The Federal Reserve was created at a time when the country was abandoning laissez-faire economics, as part of the reaction to the excesses of the previous period that also produced antimonopoly legislation.

Modern-day concerns of macroeconomic stabilization, inflation control, and central bank independence were not the most important issues at the time of the Federal Reserve's creation. The provision of financial stability was the primary goal and the relative dominance of government and the private banks within the system was the most hard-fought issue. The Federal Reserve Act of 1913 contained no direct pronouncement that the central bank should be independent from the government, though there was wide consensus that the bank should be nonpolitical in its actions. Federal Reserve independence has varied substantially over its 80-year lifespan.

Since the Federal Reserve's establishment, several bouts of legislative reform have amended the system, its internal structure, and its relationship to the government and member banks. The New Deal reforms of the 1930s transferred power within the system from the regional district banks to the Board of Governors in Washington, DC. They also removed the secretary of the treasury as an ex officio member of the Federal Reserve Board. During and immediately after World War II the Federal Reserve fully accommodated the financial needs of the US government.

The independence of the Federal Reserve was not established until later, at the onset of the Korean War, when the Federal Reserve refused to purchase government bonds. That independence was established not by law but rather by an accord between the Truman administration and the Fed, with the support and approval of the Congress.[81] The modern-day Federal Reserve operates within a highly political environment in which its independence is underpinned by convention and consensus, rather than guaranteed by statute, and in which its freedom of maneuver cannot be taken for granted.

Organization of the Federal Reserve System

The present-day Federal Reserve has a two-tiered, federal organization. The system is composed of 12 geographic districts centered on Federal Reserve banks, which maintain direct contact with member private banking

---

81. Havrilesky, *Pressures on American Monetary Policy*, pp. 52–53, 104–06; Friedman and Schwartz, *Monetary History of the United States*, pp. 610–14, 623–32; Woolley, *Monetary Politics*, pp. 44–46.

institutions. The Board of Governors, seated in Washington, oversees this system. In these respects, the organization of the American central bank resembles the Bundesbank, which was broadly modeled upon it. On closer examination, however, there are substantial differences.

Board of Governors. The Board of Governors is the supreme body within the Federal Reserve System. The Board of Governors determines monetary policy, in cooperation with the presidents of the Federal Reserve banks, and supervises the Federal Reserve banks. It also regulates private banking institutions, in cooperation with other regulators, and oversees the payments and settlements system. The board alone is responsible for setting two of the three primary instruments of monetary policy, the discount rate and reserve requirements. The district Federal Reserve banks, which operate the discount window, must petition the board for changes in the discount rate. The board holds a voting majority in determining the third major instrument of monetary policy, open market operations.[82]

The board consists of seven governors, each serving a 14-year term. The terms are staggered in such a way that one expires on every even-numbered year. The governors are generally appointed from among the ranks of private bankers and economists, with some attention given to regional balance within the board. Once on the board, the governors develop substantive specialties and interests but, in contrast to the members of the Bundesbank's Directorate, do not themselves exercise executive responsibility over departments of the board or system. The Board of Governors—like the Bank of Japan and unlike the Directorate of the Bundesbank—sits at the federal capital, Washington, DC.

The board is led by the chairman, who serves a four-year term concurrently with a full fourteen-year term as a governor. Like his counterparts in other central banks, the chairman acts as the spokesman and chief representative of the Fed vis-à-vis the executive branch, Congress, the banking community, and the public at large.[83] The chairman's ability to form and develop consensus within the board and the Federal Open Market Committee (FOMC) on monetary policy is a crucial determinant of his success in that position. The loss by the chairman of a crucial vote within these bodies—which is rare—would bring his leadership into question and therefore become a resignation issue.

The chairman is also the chief international representative for the Fed as, for example, the alternate governor for the United States at the IMF

---

82. Board of Governors of the Federal Reserve System, *The Federal Reserve System: Purposes & Functions* (Washington: Board of Governors, 1984), pp. 4–6. See also Federal Reserve Act, as amended, in Board of Governors of the Federal Reserve System, *Federal Reserve Act and Other Statutory Provisions Affecting the Federal Reserve System* (Washington: Board of Governors, 1990).

83. Donald F. Kettl, *Leadership at the Fed* (New Haven: Yale University Press, 1986).

and World Bank and, more importantly, in the G-7 and the Bank for International Settlements (BIS) meetings. Because he conducts international negotiations for the Fed, the chairman will tend to present international considerations before the Board of Governors and FOMC. As present Chairman Alan Greenspan has remarked, the chairman must be an expert not only on banking and monetary policy but on foreign affairs as well.[84]

Federal Open Market Committee.   The Federal Open Market Committee (FOMC) has jurisdiction over the System Open Market Account, from which all open market operations are conducted. Under the leadership of the chairman of the Board of Governors, the FOMC issues the basic directives that guide the operations of the open market desk in New York. On these instructions, the manager of the account will augment or drain reserves from the banking system to maintain or adjust the federal funds rate, the overnight interbank interest rate on reserves. The FOMC may also grant permission for the chairman to employ open market operations to adjust the federal funds rates at his discretion within specific ranges during intermeeting periods. The FOMC, which meets eight times each year, also establishes the annual growth targets for the money supply as required by law.

The FOMC comprises both the Board of Governors and the presidents of the Federal Reserve banks in the 12 districts of the system. However, in contrast to the organization of the Bundesbank, not all 12 presidents vote in the FOMC. While all 12 district presidents attend FOMC meetings and participate in policy discussions, their voting strength is restricted to five votes. The president of the Federal Reserve Bank of New York has permanent voting rights. The remaining four voting privileges rotate annually among the remaining 11 presidents.[85] The seven members of the Board of Governors have a permanent right to vote in the FOMC and therefore always represent a majority.

The FOMC also has ultimate jurisdiction over foreign currency operations conducted on the System Open Market Account. The FOMC delegates specific intervention decisions and strategies—to the extent that Fed rather than Treasury officials determine them—to a subcommittee consisting of the chairman, vice chairman, and president of the Federal Reserve Bank of New York. The FOMC as a whole, however, will object to intervention policy if the intended effects on the exchange rate for the dollar are inconsistent with the committee's price and inflation pref-

---

84. Manuel Johnson, "Monetary Policy Outlook," speech sponsored by Washington Analysis Corporation, Washington, 24 October 1990.

85. *Federal Reserve Act*, Sections 12A and 14, reproduced in Board of Governors, *Federal Reserve Act*.

erences. It is the FOMC's policy to routinely sterilize the effects of foreign exchange operations on the reserve position of banks.

Federal Reserve Banks. The system is distinctly federal in that it comprises 12 Federal Reserve banks, each responsible for relationships with commercial banks in its geographic district. The Federal Reserve banks extend credits to their member banks through the discount window, hold banks' reserve balances, furnish coin and paper currency, conduct bank examinations, operate interbank clearance and settlements mechanisms, and act as fiscal agent for the Treasury, among other functions.[86]

The Federal Reserve Bank of New York is the most important of these banks, owing to the prominence of the banking institutions and financial markets that it oversees. The New York Fed was once the center of the Federal Reserve System. Its president was the leader of the system and retains permanent voting privileges on the FOMC. Tensions can arise between the New York Fed and the board in Washington on market-related matters, including foreign exchange intervention.

Reserve bank presidents as a group have tended to vote distinctly more conservatively on monetary policy than the governors on the board.[87] This tendency has prompted the Congress to give them special scrutiny, with some important members going so far as to propose eliminating the voting rights of the reserve bank presidents.[88] In the past, the governors have borne the brunt of congressional testimony and oversight for the Fed. But in March 1993, in an extraordinary session, the Senate Banking Committee instituted oversight hearings with all 12 reserve bank presidents.[89]

Federal Reserve Independence

The Federal Reserve Act does not mention or discuss the matter of institutional independence. Because the Federal Reserve was created by an

---

86. *Federal Reserve Act*, Section 4, reproduced in Board of Governors, *Federal Reserve Act*.

87. Woolley, *Monetary Politics*, table 3.6, p. 64; *Wall Street Journal*, 1 August 1991. Woolley attributes this tendency to the fact that the presidents have closer continuing links to private finance and business on a day-to-day basis than have members of the board in Washington. His argument is supported by a comparison with the Bundesbank. In Germany, the Land central bank presidents are appointed by Land governments, usually have strong party affiliations, and often have been former Land government officials. They have nonetheless, in recent historical experience, also voted more conservatively as a group than their counterparts on the Directorate.

88. See the proposal of Rep. Lee Hamilton (D-IN) and Sen. Paul Sarbanes (D-MD) in US House of Representatives, Committee on Banking, *The Monetary Policy Reform Act of 1991*, 102nd Cong., 1st sess., hearing on 13 November 1991 (Washington: GPO, 1992).

89. *Washington Post, New York Times*, 11 March 1993. Senators pressed them to accommodate the Clinton economic program, in light of the deficit reductions then proposed, and said they would be asked to return for another set of hearings.

act of Congress, and because Congress can change the law, with the signature of the president, the Fed reports to the legislative branch. Fed officials emphasize this as their connection to the democratic process. "[B]ecause the Federal Reserve works within the framework of the over-all objectives of economic and financial policy established by the govern-ment," the Fed writes, "it is more accurate to characterize the System as 'independent within the government.'"[90] This is indeed an accurate de-scription.[91]

Authority over Monetary Instruments. The Federal Reserve controls each of the three instruments necessary to effectively regulate monetary conditions in the United States. The Board of Governors in Washington sets the official discount rate and minimum reserve requirements. The FOMC directs open market operations with the aim of governing mone-tary aggregates and the federal funds rate, and thus short-term interest rates in general. The existence of a broad and liquid market in govern-ment bonds has made efficient open market operations possible; they are the Fed's primary tool of monetary control.

Price Stability Objective. The Federal Reserve law gives the central bank greater powers than clear guidelines on what objectives to pursue. Original legislation did not stipulate price stability as a primary purpose of the Fed. The Employment Act of 1946 and the Full Employment and Balanced Growth Act of 1978 specified that inflation control was an ob-jective of the federal government, but set potentially conflicting objec-tives for employment and growth as well.[92] Thus, the Federal Reserve has largely been able to define its own objectives in practice, giving

---

90. Board of Governors, *The Federal Reserve System*, p. 2.

91. The literature on the independence of the Federal Reserve is extensive. In addition to items previously cited, important works include Havrilesky, *Pressures on American Monetary Policy*, esp. chapters 4 and 7; Michael C. Munger and Brian E. Roberts, "The Federal Reserve and Its Institutional Environment: A Review," in *The Political Economy of American Monetary Policy*, Thomas Mayer, ed. (Cambridge/New York: Cambridge University Press, 1990), pp. 83–98; John T. Woolley, "Partisan Manipulation of the Econ-omy," *Journal of Politics* 50, no. 2 (1988): 335–60; Nathaniel Beck, "Domestic Political Sources of American Monetary Policy: 1955–82," *Journal of Politics* 46 (1984): 786–817; Edward J. Kane, "External Pressure and the Operations of the Fed," in *Political Economy of International and Domestic Monetary Relations*, Raymond E. Lombra and Willard E. Witte, eds. (Ames: Iowa State University Press, 1982), pp. 211–32; Richard Sylla, "The Autonomy of Monetary Authorities: The Case of the US Federal Reserve System," in *Central Banks' Independence in Historical Perspective*, Toniolo, ed., pp. 17–38; Richard E. Wagner, "Central Banking at the Fed: A Public Choice Perspective," *The Cato Journal* 6 (fall 1986): 519–38.

92. Board of Governors, *Federal Reserve Act*, pp. 389–90.

Table 3.4 Chairmen of the Board of Governors of the Federal Reserve System, 1948–94

Chairman	Beginning of term
Thomas McCabe	15 April 1948
William McC. Martin Jr.	2 April 1951
Arthur F. Burns	1 February 1970
G. William Miller	8 March 1978
Paul A. Volcker	6 August 1979
Alan Greenspan	11 August 1987

priority to price stability although not exclusively. But, in contrast to the Bundesbank, the Fed receives no support from statutes in pursuing price stability as a first priority.

Appointments. The president of the United States nominates the governors and the Senate confirms their appointment to the board. Both the president, who often defers to the Treasury secretary in these appointments, and the Senate use the process to impress upon the Fed and the nominees their monetary policy preferences. In the area of economic policy, the appointment of the chairman is second only to the selection of the Treasury secretary in importance to both the president and the Congress.

Owing to the relative shortness of his tenure, the chairman is appointed or reappointed once every presidential term. Since 1948, six different people have held the post of chairman. Excluding the incumbent, Alan Greenspan, their average tenure has been almost eight years, roughly equal to the average length of party control of the White House (table 3.4).

A member may not be reappointed after having served a full term, but may be reappointed to a full term after having served part of a term. Present-day governors generally do not serve out their full terms of 14 years. Though a number of governors have served for more than 14 years in the past, long tenure is the exception. The tenure of governors has been limited by voluntary resignations prompted by private-sector salaries that exceed board pay by several multiples. Thus, the average tenure for board members since World War II is less than seven years.[93] The average length of service of the members of the Board of Governors as of mid-1993 was about 4.1 years.

The district Federal Reserve bank presidents are elected by their local boards and approved by the Board of Governors, which can thereby

---

93. Calculated excluding the currently serving members.

exercise a veto. The chairman can exercise particular influence in the choice of presidents, a matter that vitally affects the composition of the FOMC and his ability to manage policy coalitions. Regional private banks control the majority of the seats on the district board, however, which selects presidents who vote more conservatively on average than members of the Board of Governors.[94] The presidents serve renewable terms of five years.

Financing the Government. While the Federal Reserve acts as the fiscal agent for the federal government, the central bank does not extend credit directly to it. This is a matter of modern practice; current US law neither requires the Federal Reserve to extend nor prohibits it from extending credit to the Treasury.[95] Indeed, during the 1930s and 1940s the Federal Reserve bought US government bonds on the primary market. When inflation became a primary threat at the outset of the Korean War, the Federal Reserve began to depart from a self-imposed practice of stabilizing government bond prices. This fundamentally important policy shift was negotiated with the Truman administration and in the full light of congressional hearings and a special commission on the subject.[96] Since that time, the Federal Reserve has limited its purchases of government bonds to reserve management operations in the secondary market.

Oversight, Budget, and Audit. The monetary policy of the Federal Reserve is subject to oversight by the banking committees of the Congress. The Full Employment and Balanced Growth Act of 1978 requires the Board of Governors to report in February and July of each year on recent economic trends, the targets for growth in the monetary aggregates, and the relationship of monetary policy to short-run objectives articulated by the president and the Congress. Since 1988, this analysis includes a statement on the impact of the exchange rate of the dollar on

---

94. Banking Committee Chairman Henry B. Gonzalez (D-TX) has proposed legislation that would subject district bank presidents to the same appointment procedure as the governors. See 103rd Cong., 1st sess., H.R. 28.

95. Until 1980, however, the Treasury had the right to instruct the Fed to purchase a limited amount of Treasury bonds, $3 billion, above and beyond prior Fed holdings. That right, granted under the Johnson Amendment to the Agricultural Reform Act of 1933, was eliminated by the Monetary Control Act of 1980. The Treasury may also borrow for the Exchange Stabilization Fund through a mechanism called "warehousing," elaborated below. This facility is exercised, however, at the Fed's, not solely the Treasury's, discretion.

96. Woolley, *Monetary Politics*, pp. 44–46; Milton Friedman and Anna J. Schwartz, *A Monetary History of the United States, 1867–1960* (Princeton: Princeton University Press, 1963), pp. 620–32; Kettl, *Leadership at the Fed*, pp. 59–81.

meeting economic objectives. The chairman of the Board of Governors presents the report to the committees in public hearings in which he is questioned intensively about the forecasts on which monetary policy has been predicated. Members of the banking committees use these hearings as an opportunity to communicate their preferences, usually but not always for expansion, to the chairman.

The expenses of the Federal Reserve System are paid from the earnings of the Federal Reserve banks. The budgets for the Board of Governors and the banks are not subject to approval by the administration or Congress. The budget of the Board of Governors only is published in the US government budget. A somewhat inaccessible budget for the system as a whole is released by the Federal Reserve for the current and preceding years. The profits of the system, which now amount to roughly $20 billion per year, are transferred annually to the Treasury.

The Board of Governors conducts regular audits and reviews of the Federal Reserve banks that are kept confidential from the administration, Congress, and public. Price Waterhouse, a public accounting firm, and the General Accounting Office (GAO), the oversight arm of the Congress, conduct an audit of the Federal Reserve annually. The scope of that audit is restricted to the nonmonetary policy aspects of Fed business. Transactions made under the direction of the FOMC and with foreign central banks and governments, for example, are outside the purview of these outside auditors. The Federal Reserve's budget procedures and audits are the subject of repeated assaults by individual members of Congress.[97]

External Monetary Policy

Over the postwar decades, the Treasury Department and Federal Reserve have dominated the management of international monetary policy. The two bureaucracies have generally been left alone in doing so, receiving only weak guidance from the broader political system. The Treasury possesses formal leadership on exchange rate policy, as it does on international financial matters generally. Although the president has become involved in exchange rate matters, his interest has been rare, episodic, and passing. Exchange rate matters have rarely been brought to the cabinet as a whole or to cabinet-level economic councils.

The Treasury, like finance ministries abroad, has guarded its prerogatives and has effectively dominated the rest of the executive branch in this policy area. The secretary typically proscribes other cabinet members from making statements about the dollar. Although the Fed chair-

---

97. See, for example, Lee H. Hamilton (D-IN), statement before the Subcommittee on Domestic Monetary Policy, Committee on Banking, Housing, and Urban Affairs, 9 November 1989.

man serves as alternate US governor at the International Monetary Fund, the secretary serves as the governor and Treasury officials represent the US government at the working level and at the multilateral development banks. In emergencies, the Treasury Department, not other executive agencies or the Fed, holds the authority to impose capital controls.

The Treasury can negotiate agreements with foreign finance ministries to stabilize currencies. When those accords are submitted to Congress and embodied in US law, as were the Bretton Woods agreements, the Federal Reserve is bound to defend the parties. However, in cases where those accords remain informal, as was the Louvre Accord of 1987, the obligation of the Federal Reserve to defend the agreement is ambiguous. The Fed's obligation to use domestic monetary policy to defend an agreement to which it is not a party is particularly unclear.

On matters of foreign exchange intervention, furthermore, the Treasury is sometimes beholden to the Federal Reserve to provide funds for the operations. Control over large blocks of potentially available intervention funds makes the Fed an equal partner with the Treasury. This control plus the Fed's supremacy over domestic monetary policy makes cooperation between the two bureaucracies essential. To a greater extent than in Germany and Japan, effective control over the instruments of external monetary policy is shared in the United States.

The mutual agreement of the Treasury and the Fed is virtually a necessary precondition for substantial foreign exchange operations. While the Treasury and the Fed agree most of the time, fortunately, they do not always concur and disagreement can arise at particularly important junctures. Because conflicts between the two powerful agencies seriously impair the effectiveness of foreign exchange operations, little intervention actually occurs when the two bureaucracies disagree. A bias toward inaction therefore resides within the institutional structure of US intervention decision making.[98] Difficulties in reaching a consensus among the Treasury and the Fed have sometimes been a source of frustration for foreign governments and central banks seeking American participation in concerted intervention.

The prerogatives of the Treasury and Federal Reserve in foreign exchange intervention are established by an informal understanding between the two agencies. US law underpins parts of this agreement, but the

---

98. For a more extensive review of the relationship between the Treasury and the Fed on exchange rate policy, including a discussion of the legal basis for their authorities, see I. M. Destler and C. Randall Henning, *Dollar Politics: Exchange Rate Policymaking in the United States* (Washington: Institute for International Economics, 1989), chapter 5; Paul A. Volcker and Toyoo Gyohten, *Changing Fortunes: The World's Money and the Threat to American Leadership* (New York: Times Books, 1992), pp. 232–35. The most recent official treatment of this subject is David C. Mulford, "Statement before the Committee on Banking, Finance, and Urban Affairs, US House of Representatives," 14 August 1990, Washington, US Department of the Treasury.

Fed and Treasury have had to arrange a modus vivendi to cover the many points on which the statutes are ambiguous. The Treasury has the lead in making decisions regarding intervention, by the terms of this bureaucratic bargain. The legal justification for this role stems from the secretary's status as the chief financial officer of the government and the official representative to the Bretton Woods institutions, as well as from the president's constitutional role in foreign policy. In addition, importantly, the secretary was granted exclusive control over the Exchange Stabilization Fund (ESF) that was created by the Gold Reserve Act of 1934.

Accordingly, the Federal Reserve seeks Treasury approval before intervening in the foreign exchange market. That interagency understanding was established when the United States resumed foreign currency operations in the early 1960s and was affirmed in a letter sent from Chairman Arthur F. Burns to Secretary George P. Shultz to clarify the responsibilities of the two agencies at the outset of the flexible rate regime. Because the Fed is the fiscal agent of the Treasury, furthermore, the New York Federal Reserve Bank conducts foreign exchange operations with ESF funds at the secretary's instruction.

The Federal Reserve is not by any means passive on matters of foreign exchange intervention, though. The funds available to the Treasury for intervention in the ESF, amounting to reserves of dollars and foreign currency worth about $21 billion at the end of fiscal 1991, are limited relative to potential needs. Equally important, the composition of its assets can constrain the capacity of the ESF to conduct foreign currency operations. Thus, the Treasury regularly asks the Federal Reserve to contribute its own funds to the intervention effort. By mutual agreement, the burden of intervention is usually split evenly between the Fed and the Treasury. This convention reinforces the unit-veto nature of intervention decisionmaking in the United States.

When the Treasury asks the Federal Reserve to commit system funds to the intervention effort, the potential for conflict arises. The Treasury does not have the legal authority to instruct the Fed to buy or sell foreign currency on the Fed's *own* account.[99] When the situation arises, Fed officials must judge the merits and likely effectiveness of the intervention effort. When the quantities involved are large, the FOMC, which has ultimate authority for the Fed on intervention operations, will take the final decision.[100]

---

99. The Treasury acknowledges that it does not have this right. See Mulford, "Statement to the Committee on Banking, Housing, and Urban Affairs," p. 5.

100. The legal basis for Federal Reserve intervention authority is interpretive. See Howard H. Hackley, "Memorandum to the Federal Open Market Committee on Legal Aspects of a Proposed Plan for Federal Reserve Operations in Foreign Currencies," 22 November 1961; Robert H. Knight, "Memorandum to the Secretary of the Treasury," 6 January 1962, reproduced in US Congress, House, Committee on Banking, *Report on the General*

When the dollar is appreciating, and the resources of the ESF are fully converted into foreign currency, the Fed must effectively carry the full burden of intervention. (This happened for example in the late 1980s.) If the Fed and Treasury agree that further intervention is necessary, they choose among several ways to finance the operation.[101] First, the Fed can intervene directly, selling dollars and purchasing D-marks or yen, for example, on its own account. Second, the Fed can effectively lend dollars to the ESF in exchange for the foreign currency held there. By "warehousing," as this transaction is called, its foreign currency with the Fed, the Treasury can raise more dollars with which to intervene in the markets on the account of the ESF directly.[102] During large interventions, the amount of warehousing can be substantial, and the FOMC places limits on this facility.[103]

When the problem is insufficient foreign exchange in the ESF to sell to support the dollar—rather than insufficient dollars to sell to limit its rise—the Treasury might turn to the Fed to activate its swap lines with foreign central banks. Those facilities amount to over $30 billion. The Treasury has some swap facilities of its own with foreign countries, but again these are limited. Owing to Fed control over these facilities, the Treasury is reliant on the Fed to support administration exchange rate and intervention policy, when that policy requires more resources than are at the disposal of the ESF.

The special role of the Federal Reserve Bank of New York further

---

Agreements to Borrow, 87th Cong., 2nd sess. (Washington: GPO, 1962), pp. 353–66. These legal opinions have been challenged occasionally by outside observers and isolated members of Congress. However, 30 years of precedent and practice, in the full view and with the passive consent of the Congress, would seem to effectively confer the legal right on the Fed to intervene. That interpretation is reinforced by a statute passed by Congress governing the disposition of the proceeds of intervention by the Fed.

101. In addition to the two mechanisms listed below, the ESF can "monetize" its Special Drawing Right (SDR) holdings by issuing SDR certificates to the Fed in exchange for dollars. This conversion is made at the option of the secretary.

102. A warehousing transaction consists of the sale of foreign currency from the ESF to the Fed and an agreement to repurchase it in the future. The sale is made at the prevailing spot exchange rate and the repurchase at the three-month forward rate at the time of sale. See US Department of the Treasury, *Exchange Stabilization Fund Annual Report, 1991*, October 1992, pp. 20–21. The exchange rate risk is therefore carried by the ESF. At times, the Fed has extended this privilege to the Treasury's general account.

103. Warehousing has been criticized as evading the budgetary prerogatives of the Congress and threatening stability-oriented monetary policies of the Fed. See, for example, US House of Representatives, Committee on Banking, Finance, and Urban Affairs, *Review of Treasury Department's Conduct of International Financial Policy*, hearings 14 August 1990, 101st Cong., 2nd sess. (Washington: GPO, 1990); Walker F. Todd, "Disorderly Markets: The Law, History, and Economics of the Exchange Stabilization Fund and U.S. Foreign Exchange Market Intervention," in *Research in Financial Markets: Private and Public Policy*, vol. 4, George Kaufman, ed. (Greenwich, CT: JAI Press, 1992).

complicates the process of exchange rate policy formation. Close to the markets, and possessing operational capabilities, the New York Fed has often been more disposed to intervene than the Board of Governors in Washington. When the board has been especially reticent, the New York Fed has sometimes found common cause with the Treasury on conducting operations. The fact that all intervention, whether on the account of the Fed or the ESF, is actually conducted by the trading desk in New York prevents gross failures of coordination. But reconciling the various and conflicting views of the Treasury, the Board of Governors, and his own reserve bank is a formidable task for the New York–based manager of foreign operations of the System Open Market Account.[104]

Fulfilling the external monetary objectives of the US Treasury depends centrally, of course, on the domestic monetary policy of the central bank, a more powerful determinant of exchange rates than foreign currency operations. Importantly, all foreign exchange operations conducted on the Fed's account, which thus affect bank reserves, are routinely sterilized by the Fed. (Operations conducted on the account of the ESF do not affect monetary conditions.) In this way, the FOMC isolates intervention decisions from decisions to inject exchange rate considerations into the determination of the target rate for federal funds. The inexorable link between domestic and external monetary policy compels interagency cooperation, particularly in countries with independent central banks.[105]

Although the Treasury and Fed have dominated international monetary policymaking, the Congress asserted formal oversight authority over exchange rate policy in 1988 and has exercised it since then. The Omnibus Trade and Competitiveness Act of that year requires the Treasury to report to the banking committees on exchange rate and international economic policy once each year followed by a six-month update. In addition to its report on the dollar and its ramifications for the trade balance and international capital flows, the Treasury must identify foreign governments that manipulate their currencies to obtain an unfair competitive advantage in international trade. The secretary of the Treasury is called upon to present the report, if asked, to hearings of the banking committees of the House and Senate.[106]

The reporting process has proved to be a useful innovation in exchange rate policymaking. The Treasury has cited newly industrializing economies (NIEs) for currency manipulation and the banking commit-

---

104. See, for example, Charles A. Coombs, *The Arena of International Finance* (New York: Wiley, 1976); Volcker and Gyohten, *Changing Fortunes*, pp. 234–35.

105. Volcker writes: "[A]t the end of the day, monetary policy will be a more powerful influence on exchange rates than intervention, which tells you where the final balance of power lies." Volcker and Gyohten, *Changing Fortunes*, p. 233.

106. *Omnibus Trade and Competitiveness Act of 1988*, sections 3001–3005, reprinted in *Congressional Record* (vol. 134, no. 51), 20 April 1988, pp. H1948–49.

tees have effectively reinforced the Treasury in its subsequent negotiations with these governments. But the Treasury has effectively avoided subjecting exchange rate policy, particularly vis-à-vis the G-7 partners, more broadly to congressional scrutiny, and the intensity of the attention of the banking committees has varied. Except in extreme circumstances, therefore, the Congress does not provide policy guidance on central exchange rate relationships that is sufficiently strong to adjudicate differences between the Fed and Treasury over policy.

Generally, therefore, cooperation between the Treasury and Federal Reserve on exchange rate matters does not have the benefit of guidelines based on a broad definition of American economic interests. Neither a societal consensus, a governmentwide agreement, nor statutory directives provide an anchor for external monetary decision making. These proud agencies are among the most professional in the US government but are nonetheless sometimes subject to bureaucratic tunnel vision and disagreements with one another. Higher objectives or principles that might arbitrate exchange rate policy disputes between the Federal Reserve and the Treasury generally do not exist in the American policymaking apparatus. The political explosion in the Congress over the trade deficit in the mid-1980s, which threatened rash protectionism, dictated cooperation between the Fed and Treasury at that time. But that period has proved to be exceptional indeed.

Comparison of Institutions, Processes, and Politics

The preceding sections have reviewed the public policymaking institutions for each country individually. The present section conducts a structured comparison of the policymaking institutions and processes in the three countries together. We consider first domestic monetary policymaking, and second external monetary policymaking.

Domestic Monetary Policy

The survey conducted here ranks the independence of the three central banks as follows: the Bundesbank is the most independent; the Federal Reserve is a close second; and the Bank of Japan is a distant third. The Bank of Japan is nonetheless more independent than the Bank of England and the Bank of France—at least until the Bank of France was granted significant independence in early 1994—which have implemented policies decided largely by their governments.[107] Compared with a

---

107. Alec Cairncross, "The Bank of England: Relationships with the Government, the Civil Service, and Parliament," and Jean Bouvier, "The Banque de France and the State from 1850 to the Present Day," in *Central Banks' Independence in Historical Perspective,* Toniolo, ed., pp. 39–72, 73–104; Goodman, *Monetary Sovereignty,* pp. 40–50, 103–41.

Table 3.5 Comparison of central bank independence in Japan, Germany, and the United States

	Bank of Japan	Bundesbank	Federal Reserve
Control over instruments	Partial	Complete	Complete
Legal priority to price stability	No	Yes	No
Appointments			
Term of board appointments	5 years	8 years	14 years
Dismissible by government	Yes	No	No
Subject to instructions	Yes	No	No
Requirement to finance government	Some	Prohibited	No
Oversight, budget, audit			
Government approval of budget	Yes	No	No
Oversight	Yes (Finance Ministry)	Very little	Yes (Congress)
Auditor	Finance Ministry	Independent	Independent

very broad set of central banks, the independence of the Bank of Japan would run in the middle of the pack.[108] The measures of central bank independence, or subordination, examined in the preceding country sections are summarized in table 3.5.

To review this survey briefly, the Bundesbank and Federal Reserve each control the three main instruments of their monetary policies. The Bank of Japan fully controls only one instrument, open market operations. The official discount rate is effectively set jointly with MOF, which also approves changes in the minimum reserve requirement. In terms of legal sanction for fighting inflation, the Bundesbank receives more support from its founding legislation than the Federal Reserve and Bank of Japan receive from theirs.

The criteria of appointments to bank positions indicate, again, that the Bank of Japan is at a substantial disadvantage compared with the Federal Reserve and the Bundesbank. The short, five-year terms of BOJ governors are partly mitigated by the fact that every other governor, the vice governor and the executive directors, are career employees of the central bank. But, technically, they remain dismissible by the government and subject to its instructions.

---

108. Alesina and Summers, "Central Bank Independence and Macroeconomic Performance."

The length of the term of governors would seem, on its face, to suggest greater independence of the Fed compared with the Bundesbank. Because Fed governors are poorly compensated in comparison to private-sector salaries, however, they typically resign before their terms are completed. These resignations reduce the average term of service of Fed governors substantially below that of members of the Bundesbank's Directorate. Also, Fed governors are subject to Senate confirmation whereas members of the Directorate are not subject to any similar process of approval by the Bundestag.

Concerning government financing, the Bank of Japan is again less independent that its institutional counterparts. The Bank of Japan has absorbed a larger proportion of government debt, for example, than have the Federal Reserve or the Bundesbank.[109] The Federal Reserve's independence on this score is secured by a nonstatutory accord. The Bundesbank's freedom from direct deficit financing is fully secured by legislation.

In the categories of oversight, budget, and audit, the Bank of Japan again appears weak relative to the Federal Reserve and Bundesbank in each category. The Bank of Japan is the only central bank in the Group of Ten that is dependent on government approval of its budget.[110] Note that congressional oversight distinguishes the Federal Reserve from the Bundesbank. That oversight is strengthened by the fact that it is conducted by the same congressional committee, the Senate Banking Committee, along with other committees, that is principally responsible for approving the president's nominees to the Board of Governors.

This rank ordering of the independence of the Bundesbank, Federal Reserve, and Bank of Japan is reinforced by the internal organizational structures of these central banks, which affect their ability to operate independently from the government. Central bank independence, all other things being equal, is inversely related to the degree of concentration of authority on monetary policy on the part of the central board, particularly its chairman.[111] The more concentrated the power, the sharper and more easily isolated is the point of access for influence attempts on the

---

109. With combined holdings of financial bills and bonds amounting to 32.9 trillion yen at the end of 1990, BOJ held almost 15 percent of the total central government debt outstanding of ¥222 trillion. Calculated from Bank of Japan, *Economic Statistics Monthly,* August 1991, table 82, pp. 117–18. By contrast, the holdings by the Federal Reserve amounted to 7.7 percent of total US Treasury debt at the end of 1990. *Federal Reserve Bulletin,* July 1991, table 1.14. Bundesbank lending to German public authorities was very small. *Monthly Report of the Deutsche Bundesbank* 43 (March 1991): table II.1.

110. Goodman, *Central Bank–Government Relations,* p. 32.

111. Within the United States over time, Havrilesky argues, the politicization of monetary policy parallels the movement toward an increasingly powerful Federal Reserve Board. See Havrilesky, *Pressures on American Monetary Policy,* especially pp. 340–44.

part of the government. Of these three central banks, the Bank of Japan is the most highly centralized. The Bundesbank, though it has become somewhat more centralized over time, remains quite decentralized relative to its foreign counterparts. The Federal Reserve, owing to the lesser role of the reserve bank presidents compared to the Land central bank presidents, is not as decentralized as the Bundesbank.

Finally, central banks and governments do not, of course, contend for control over monetary policy in a vacuum. Rather, they compete within a broader political environment that affects the outcome of conflicts between them. This environment, in each country, further reinforces the ranking of central bank independence established above. The level of public support for price stability and central bank independence, for example, is greatest by far in Germany, divided in the United States, and smallest in Japan. That support is reflected in the willingness of politicians to publicly criticize the central bank. Whereas German politicians are generally deeply reluctant to do so, American politicians criticize the Fed more frequently and expect the public to respond favorably. Japanese politicians almost view criticism of the Bank of Japan to be a legitimate part of the process of building consensus on monetary policy.

External Monetary Policy

In all three countries, the finance ministry leads in the establishment of exchange rate parities, declarations on the appropriate level of the exchange rate, negotiations with partner governments on exchange rate issues and representation to formal and informal international institutions. The finance ministry also possesses the authority to impose or rescind administrative controls on private capital movements in all three countries.

On matters of disposition of international reserves and foreign exchange intervention, in contrast, the central banks have greater power. However, their standing relative to their respective finance ministries differs in the three countries (table 3.6). In Japan, MOF controls the disposition of international reserves and dominates BOJ on foreign exchange intervention. In Germany, the Bundesbank owns all the international reserves and has sole operational discretion over their disposition. Within the confines of international agreements among governments, such as the EMS, on which the German central bank is consulted, the Bundesbank exercises its intervention authority freely.

In the United States, the Treasury has the formal intervention authority, but the Federal Reserve controls the largest share of funds available for such operations. The resources of the Exchange Stabilization Fund, controlled by the Treasury, can be depleted or otherwise committed. Foreign currency operations therefore require the cooperation of both bureaucracies, even when domestic monetary policy is not marshaled in

Table 3.6 Comparison of external monetary policymaking (locus of authority)

	Japan	Germany	United States
Control of international reserves	MOF	Bundesbank	Treasury and Fed own separate reserves
Operational decision on intervention	MOF, with BOJ	Bundesbank	Treasury and Fed
Exchange rate target setting	MOF	Ministry of Finance	Treasury
Clarity of agreement between central bank and finance ministry	Clear	Clear re EMS, ambiguous re G7	Ambiguous

support of exchange rate objectives. That cooperation, however, does not have the benefit of guidelines based on societal consensus or governmentwide agreement, much less statutory directives. With the temporary exception of the mid-1980s, when trade-deficit reduction became a top priority of the Congress, no overarching conception of national interest in exchange rate valuation or stability has existed in the United States to enforce cooperation between these agencies. Intervention decision making is thus a unit-veto system; little or no intervention takes place when there is substantial disagreement. There is a bias toward inaction as a result. (For a further discussion, see chapter 7).

The cooperative arrangement that has emerged between the Federal Reserve and the Treasury differs in significant ways from that between the Bundesbank and the German finance ministry. First, regarding G-7 exchange rate stabilization arrangements, these central bank-ministry agreements are similar in their ambiguity. However, the understanding between the Federal Reserve and the Treasury is more ambiguous than the agreement between their German counterparts concerning Germany's participation in the EMS specifically. Second, the Fed-Treasury agreement is less widely discussed or understood in the United States than is the division of responsibility between the Bundesbank and finance ministry in Germany.[112] Thus, third, the Bundesbank–finance ministry understanding has the implied consent of a broader spectrum of the political system within Germany than underpins the Fed-Treasury arrangement in the

---

112. The letters exchanged between the Bundesbank and finance ministry at the creation of the EMS have not been published, but their essential contents have been revealed and discussed, not only in Germany but within the Ecofin Council of the European Community. By contrast, the Burns-Shultz letter, for example, has no comparable exposure.

United States.[113] These differences have arisen partly because Germany has persistently practiced exchange rate stabilization within the EMS while the United States has practiced stabilization only episodically.

Finally, the relationship between the Bundesbank and finance ministry on EMS matters is more symmetrical than the Fed-Treasury relationship. The Fed seeks Treasury approval before intervening but does not necessarily intervene at Treasury's behest. The German finance ministry does not instruct the Bundesbank on intervention in the dollar market either. But, within the EMS, the German government has bound the Bundesbank, with its assent, to obligatory intervention to defend the ERM margins. Even though the Bundesbank-government agreement limits the central bank's obligation, the accord commits the resources of the Bundesbank in a way that the Fed's resources are not committed.

The degree to which the government could use its prerogatives in external monetary policymaking as leverage over the central bank's domestic monetary policy differs in the three countries accordingly. In Japan, where the Bank of Japan is subordinate to MOF on domestic monetary matters, the ministry's prerogatives in exchange rate policy seals its dominance of monetary policy overall. In the United States, the independence of the Federal Reserve and the sharing of exchange rate policymaking authority prevent the administration from imposing exchange rate considerations on the Fed's domestic monetary policy. In Germany, the independence of the Bundesbank confronts the authority of the federal government in setting exchange rate parities from time to time.

The following chapters review the policy experience of the three countries to illuminate the relationships among these institutions and describe how they have structured the choices of policymakers in action. The final chapters of this study will return to the subject of central bank–government relationships and their connection to international monetary cooperation.

---

113. Some members of Congress have questioned the role of the Fed and Treasury in intervention, illustrating that the political acceptance of these arrangements is less than unanimous. In Germany and Japan, though the wisdom of intervention might be called into question, the legitimacy of the institutions to carry out foreign exchange operations is not challenged, despite the fact that the purely legal basis for the division of labor on intervention is even more obscure in Germany than it is in the United States.

4

Monetary and Exchange Rate Policymaking in Japan

Japanese exchange rate and monetary policy has always been far more conscious of competitiveness in traded goods than has American policy. Japanese policy has also been more consistent and stable than American external monetary policy over the years. The foreign exchange markets have sometimes overwhelmed the efforts of the Ministry of Finance (MOF) and Bank of Japan (BOJ) to restrain or, less often, to support the yen. But exchange rate policy has consistently been an element of overall economic strategy in Japan. Policymakers in Tokyo have generally had more clearly articulated external monetary preferences than have officials in Washington.

The explanation presented in this book, as reviewed in the previous chapters, focuses on two distinguishing features of Japanese policymaking in the postwar period. Private-sector preferences favoring a competitive valuation of the yen have been underpinned by close relations between banks and industry. The subordination of the central bank by the government has given those preferences effective access to the instruments of monetary policy. I argue that this combination explains the competitiveness orientation of exchange rate policy during the postwar period, with the exception of the last few years, and the mix of monetary and fiscal policies during the 1980s.

The present chapter is the first of three that review monetary and exchange rate policymaking in Japan, Germany, and the United States, respectively. Each chapter assembles the case history from which a structured comparison of policy outcomes is derived and explained in chapter 7. We consider the history of Japanese policy first, reviewing the early postwar decades briefly, then examining the 1980s in greater depth.

The history of Japanese exchange rate policymaking is punctuated by four major realignments[1] of the yen since the beginning of the 1970s. The first realignment occurred during 1971–73, at the time of the breakdown of the Bretton Woods regime. The second realignment occurred during 1977–78, in the midst of conflict with the United States over macroeconomic and trade policies. The third realignment occurred during the second half of the 1980s. The appreciation of the yen during 1993 represents the fourth realignment, although the permanence of the current strength of the Japanese currency is unclear.

In this chapter, the first and second yen realignments are discussed in the next section, on the Bretton Woods era and the 1970s. The third realignment and the circumstances surrounding it are discussed in the second section, devoted primarily to policymaking during the 1980s. The defense of the yen at the end of the 1980s and its restabilization prior to the fourth realignment in 1993 are discussed in the second section as well. The final section concludes the chapter by summarizing the pattern of outcomes of external monetary and domestic macroeconomic policymaking.

Two words about exchange rate measures are in order before proceeding to the case history. First, the nominal value of the Japanese yen against the dollar will be quoted in yen per dollar, just as the value of the D-mark in the chapters on Germany and the United States is quoted in D-marks per dollar. As the dollar falls in value, the exchange rate also falls. This convention, however, introduces a descriptive oddity when presenting the story from the Japanese (and German) perspective: as the *value* of the Japanese (or German) currency rises, the quoted exchange *rate* falls.

Second, and more important, the distinction between *nominal* and *real* exchange rates is fundamental in this interpretive history of policymaking in Japan. The nominal exchange rate is the familiar yen-per-dollar rate quoted daily and is generally the focus of official statements and international agreements concerning currencies. The real exchange rate adjusts the nominal exchange rate for differences in domestic costs or price inflation and is presented in index form. The distinction is fundamental because Japanese productivity in tradeable goods rose dramatically over the postwar period. While the nominal value of the yen increased over the decades, its real value remained far more stable and even declined in some crucial instances. This fact is important to policymaking and to US-Japanese monetary relations because the real exchange rate, not the nominal rate, determines the international competitiveness of companies and the trade balance and thus affects growth and employment.

---

1. "Realignments" is used in this chapter to refer to a change in the range of fluctuation of the yen under the flexible-rate regime rather than in the formal sense of a change of parity under a fixed-rate regime.

Bretton Woods Era and 1970s

Bretton Woods Era

Japan entered the international monetary regime established at Bretton Woods while under occupation administration. A single exchange rate of 360 yen per US dollar was set in April 1949. Japan became a member of the International Monetary Fund in 1952.[2] In contrast to the major European countries, Japan's exchange rate parity remained unchanged for 22 years under the Bretton Woods regime.

The country's current account surplus did not emerge immediately; Japan was typically in current account deficit through the early 1960s. The yen was, if anything, overvalued during the early postwar years, and Japan along with other countries suffered a "dollar shortage."[3] When balance of payments constraints were reached, Japanese authorities tightened their typically highly expansionary domestic monetary policy in order to bring about international adjustment.

But the rate of domestic investment and the increase in productivity in the traded goods sector was spectacular. Thus, in real terms, the exchange rate of the yen declined by 27 percent over the fixed-rate period.[4] When Japan entered its period of chronic external surplus in the second half of the 1960s (figure 4.1), private industry and business had come to take the nominal exchange rate for granted. When speculation grew in favor of the yen, the government solemnly declared its dedication to maintaining the 360 yen-to-dollar exchange rate and developed elaborate packages of emergency measures to correct the payments imbalance.[5]

First Yen Realignment, 1971–73

Japanese officials were informed of President Richard M. Nixon and US Treasury Secretary John B. Connally's decision to float the dollar only shortly before the president made his 15 August 1971 speech to the

---

2. Takashi Shiraishi, *Japan's Trade Policies: 1945 to the Present Day* (London/Atlantic Highlands, NJ: Athlone Press, 1989), pp. 37–41, 68–69.

3. Ryutaro Komiya and Motoshige Itoh, "Japan's International Trade and Trade Policy," in *The Political Economy of Japan*, vol. 2, *The Changing International Context*, Takashi Inoguchi and Daniel I. Okimoto, eds. (Stanford: Stanford University Press, 1988), pp. 176–77. The 360 exchange rate was a compromise between officials in Washington, who had recommended a rate around 300, and the Japanese business community and SCAP, which lobbied for and recommended a lower yen. Robert C. Angel, *Explaining Economic Policy Failure: Japan in the 1969–1971 International Monetary Crisis* (New York: Columbia University Press, 1991), p. 38.

4. Over the 1950s, the real effective exchange rate of the yen declined by 35 percent (calculated by the author using unit labor cost in manufacturing).

5. For a review of these efforts to avoid revaluing the yen, see Angel, *Explaining Policy Failure.*

Figure 4.1 Japan: trade and current account balances, 1956–93

percentage of GDP

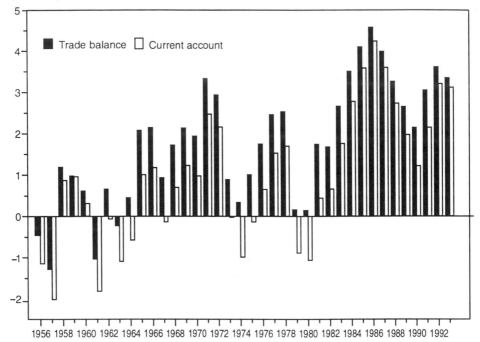

Source: Bank of Japan, *Economic Statistics Monthly*.

nation. The Ministry of Finance and the Bank of Japan had advised their banks and corporations that a revaluation of the yen was not imminent. Indeed, because of the government's stress on export promotion during the previous years, both industry and the commercial banks had accumulated sizable, uncovered dollar exposures. Because Japan was running a surplus at the time, industry held cash and accounts payable in dollars. BOJ had encouraged the banks to finance exports by discounting export bills at favorable interest rates for them. In these transactions with BOJ, however, the banks retained the foreign exchange risk (which had been negligible in previous years).

Both industry and banks had followed Japanese government guidance on managing foreign exchange exposure, and the government incurred a corresponding (moral) obligation. On 16 August, therefore, the MOF and BOJ decided to keep the foreign exchange markets open and buy dollars at the 360 yen parity. BOJ encouraged the exposed banks to cover their positions and used administrative guidance to try to prevent abuses of the crisis policy. Some financial firms nonetheless succeeded in borrowing dollars abroad and converting them to yen at the favorable exchange rate. The Bank of Japan purchased about $4.0 billion during the following 10 business days, until the decision to float the yen for the first time was announced.[6] The episode illustrates the tenacity with which the Japanese government clung to the Bretton Woods parity. It also reveals the close relationship between the Japanese state, exporting firms, and banks in the matter of exchange rate policy. Other governments closed their exchanges and prepared for the revaluation of their currencies against the dollar at this time. MOF and BOJ, however, maintained open exchanges, at officially supported rates that could be maintained only in the short run, to assist banks and trading companies caught by surprise by the "Nixon shock."

The yen was repegged at 308 to the dollar at the Smithsonian Agreement of December 1971, a revaluation of just under 17 percent. Prime Minister Kakuei Tanaka declared that the Smithsonian parity would be kept unchanged at any cost. This commitment, and the fear of deflationary effects of the prior yen revaluation, prompted an extraordinary expansion of the Japanese money supply. Monetary ease in turn sparked a price explosion that was unprecedented for Japan in the postwar period[7] (table 4.1).

The new Smithsonian exchange arrangements nonetheless proved to be unsustainable by early 1973. American authorities announced in February of that year that the dollar would be devalued by 10 percent. The February realignment also proved to be insufficient to save the fixed-rate system, and renewed speculation ushered in the flexible-rate regime a few weeks later, in March 1973. With the advent of flexible rates, the Japanese yen settled into a relatively narrow trading range of 260–65 (figure 4.2).

The next movement of the yen was downward, for a change, in response to the first oil shock. Confronted with skyrocketing domestic inflation, and believing that they were in a structural trade surplus, Japanese authorities intervened heavily to support the currency in November and December 1973 and January 1974. MOF also revised capital controls to favor inflows and discourage outflows.[8]

When the Japanese external surplus recovered from the oil shock at

---

6. Volcker and Gyohten, *Changing Fortunes*, pp. 93–94. A domestic political and international academic controversy erupted over the effective subsidy to firms and banks provided by the continued purchase of dollars at the unrealistic 360 exchange rate. Angel, *Explaining Policy Failure*, pp. 198–202.

7. Akiyoshi Horiuchi, "Monetary Policies: Japan," and Yutaka Kosai, "Anti-inflation Policy: Japan," in *The Politics of Economic Change in Postwar Japan and West Germany*, Haru Fukui, Peter H. Merkl, Hubertus Müller-Groeling, and Akio Watanabe, eds. (New York: Sto. Martin's Press 1993), pp. 101–15, 145–66; Takatoshi Ito, *The Japanese Economy* (Cambridge: MIT Press, 1992), p. 127.

8. Ryutaro Komiya and Miyako Suda, *Japan's Foreign Exchange Policy: 1971–82* [an English translation of *Gendai Kokusai Kin'yuron: Rekishi Seisakuhen* (Tokyo: Nihon Keizai Shinbunsha, 1983)] (Canberra, Australia: Australian National University, Australia-Japan Research Centre, 1991), p. 126 and table 3.3; Volcker and Gyohten, *Changing Fortunes*, p. 131; Horiuchi, "Monetary Policies: Japan," pp. 110–13.

Table 4.1 Japan: inflation, 1970–93 (percentages)

Year	Consumer prices	Wholesale prices
1970	7.93	3.62
1971	6.50	−0.62
1972	4.83	0.62
1973	11.65	15.84
1974	23.26	31.44
1975	11.64	3.11
1976	9.48	4.98
1977	8.08	1.87
1978	4.27	−2.57
1979	3.71	7.30
1980	7.65	17.82
1981	5.05	1.39
1982	2.73	1.77
1983	1.81	−2.22
1984	2.30	−0.20
1985	2.04	−1.19
1986	0.60	−9.10
1987	0.10	−3.74
1988	0.70	−1.03
1989	2.27	2.54
1990	3.09	2.03
1991	3.27	0.22
1992	1.70	−1.43
1993	1.25	−3.80

Source: Organization for Economic Cooperation and Development.

the end of 1975 and the yen rebounded, however, MOF intervened to limit the currency's rise. The yen was below 300 when that intervention began—levels comparable to the Smithsonian parity despite improved relative productivity in the interim. A US-Japanese debate thus erupted over whether this intervention, lasting into the middle of 1976, was "dirty," depressing the value of the yen unfairly, or "clean." C. Fred Bergsten, who later became assistant secretary of the Treasury for international affairs in the Carter administration, accused Japanese authorities of maintaining an inappropriately competitive rate and disguising the true extent of their operations by depositing the dollar proceeds in private banks.[9] MOF has in fact used the private banks as an unofficial extension of its foreign exchange account at various points during the fixed-rate regime and early flexible-rate period[10]—a practice now acknowledged by former MOF officials to have taken place.

---

9. C. Fred Bergsten, testimony to US Congress, House Banking Committee, 3 June 1976, and Joint Economic Committee, 18 October 1976, reprinted in *Managing International Economic Interdependence: Selected Papers of C. Fred Bergsten, 1975–1976* (Lexington, MA: D. C. Heath, 1977).

10. Dean Taylor, "The Mismanaged Float," pp. 70–72. Several authoritative studies conducted in the early 1980s concluded that the Japanese government no longer "manipulated" the yen through intervention to achieve unfair trade advantage.

Figure 4.2 Yen-dollar exchange rates, 1971–93

Yen-dollar exchange rate (monthly average); logarithmic scale

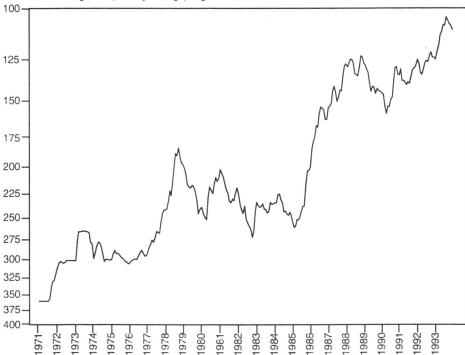

Source: International Monetary Fund, *International Financial Statistics.*

Limiting the rise of the yen contributed to the resurgence of the Japanese current account surplus in the second half of the 1970s. Japanese
commentators acknowledge that, in hindsight, intervention to cap the
yen occurred at levels that were "underestimated."[11] The Bretton Woods
regime had passed into history definitively; yet the Japanese government continued to actively manage the external value of the currency
with the various instruments at its disposal, principally capital and exchange controls and intervention.

Second Yen Realignment, 1977–78

Like the other major realignments of the yen, the second yen realignment became a dramatic domestic political issue. It accompanied open
conflict between the American and Japanese authorities on exchange rates
and macroeconomic management. The Carter administration declared its
intention to stimulate domestic demand when it assumed office in early

11. Komiya and Suda, *Japan's Foreign Exchange Policy*, p. 141.

1977. This would entail an appreciation of the yen, Tokyo was told, unless the Japanese government stimulated demand as well.[12] American desire for an appreciation of the yen became all the more evident when subsequent statements in 1978 designed to support the dollar specifically mentioned the D-mark but conspicuously omitted any reference to the Japanese currency.

The ensuing rise of the yen alarmed Japanese business and government officials, despite a trade surplus that would amount to 1.6 and 1.7 percent of GNP in 1977 and 1978. In late 1977, the Bank of Japan concluded that Japanese export industry across the board would suffer losses if the yen rose above 240.[13]

The Japanese government responded to the appreciation in several ways. First, MOF and BOJ intervened heavily in the dollar-yen market and encouraged the American authorities to do the same. During 1977 and the first 10 months of 1978, Japanese intervention to restrain the rise of the yen amounted to roughly $13 billion. Securing American cooperation in halting the rise of the yen against the dollar was the object of repeated attempts by the vice minister for international affairs, Michiya Matsukawa; his successor, Takehiro Sagami; the finance minister, Hideo Bo; and Prime Minister Takeo Fukuda in a meeting with President Jimmy Carter in early May 1978 and at the Bonn Summit meeting in July.[14]

Second, to satisfy foreign pressure to expand domestic demand, limit the appreciation of the yen, and offset the depressive impact of currency appreciation that had already occurred, the government adopted stimulative monetary and fiscal policies. Japanese authorities reduced the discount rate to an all-time low of 3.5 percent in March 1978. (The previous low had been 4.25 percent in 1972–73, during the first yen realignment.) After rising 8.2 percent in 1977, therefore, the narrow money supply (M1) rose 13.4 percent in 1978, and the broad money supply (M2+CDs) by about 12 percent.[15]

Foreign and domestic pressures overpowered MOF objections to ex-

12. Robert D. Putnam and C. Randall Henning, "The Bonn Summit of 1978: A Case of Coordination," in *Can Nations Agree? Issues in International Economic Cooperation*, Richard N. Cooper, Barry Eichengreen, Gerald Holtman, Robert D. Putnam, and C. Randall Henning (Washington: Brookings Institution, 1989), pp. 12–140. This section is also indebted to Keisuke Iida, "The Theory and Practice of International Economic Policy Coordination," (Ph.D. diss., Harvard University, May 1990), ch. 5; and Komiya and Suda, *Japan's Foreign Exchange Policy*, chapter 7.

13. Cited by Iida, *International Economic Policy Coordination*, p. 225. The sole exception was the color television industry.

14. Iida, *International Economic Policy Coordination*, pp. 220 and 228.

15. The Bank of Japan cited the strength of the yen specifically as a reason for this move. Nakao and Horii, "Monetary Policy in Japan," p. 37, table 4. Nonetheless, Japanese authorities kept money supply growth to about half the 20–25 percent levels reached during 1971–73.

pansionary fiscal policy. The Ministry of International Trade and Industry (MITI) instituted an interest-subsidized loan program for small and medium-sized exporting firms and an import enhancement program. Prime Minister Fukuda agreed at the July 1978 G-7 summit meeting in Bonn to present a supplemental budget to the Japanese Diet to attempt to achieve a 7 percent growth target, agreed upon during the previous winter and reiterated in the summit communiqué.[16] These measures raised the general government deficit in Japan to the postwar high of 5.5 percent of GNP in 1978.

In contrast to Japanese authorities, American officials were complacent about the appreciation of the yen (though by 1978 they had stopped encouraging this trend). Japanese unilateral efforts, as strong as they were, did not stem the movement. The yen reached a new all-time high against the dollar of 175.50 on 31 October.[17]

Japanese authorities gladly cooperated with the United States when the Carter administration and the Fed decided to halt the dollar slide the next day. As part of the dollar rescue package,[18] US authorities stated for the first time that the Japanese yen was indeed one of the currencies, in addition to the German mark and the Swiss franc, that had risen too far against the dollar. Japanese authorities considered this to be a great victory.[19] BOJ participated in concerted purchases of the dollar by the central banks around the world.

Yen Retreat, 1979–80

Concerted action on the exchange rate was successful in preventing further appreciation. The yen returned to the 200 vicinity at the end of

---

16. See, I. M. Destler and Hisao Mitsuyu, "Locomotives on Different Tracks: Macroeconomic Diplomacy, 1977–1979," in *Coping with U.S.-Japanese Economic Conflicts* (Lexington, MA: D. C. Heath, 1982), pp. 243–70, in addition to works cited above.

17. At this point the vice minister of MITI declared, "[The present yen rate] below 180 does not reflect the fundamental economic conditions and is clearly overvalued." *Nihon Keizai Shimbun*, 27 October 1978, cited by Ichiro Otani, "Exchange Rate Instability and Capital Controls: The Japanese Experience, 1978–81," in *Exchange Rate and Trade Instability: Causes, Consequences, and Remedies*, David Bigman and Teizo Taya, eds. (Cambridge, UK: Ballinger, 1983), p. 333, n. 1.

18. See chapter 6. Japanese officials declined a US request to ease monetary policy further, beyond the historically low discount rate already achieved, offering instead to intervene in large quantities and to establish exchange rate rules. Masaru Hayami, *Kaizu Naki Kokai: Hendo Sobasei Ju-nen* [The Voyage in Uncharted Waters: Ten Years of the Floating Exchange Rate System] (Tokyo: Toyo Keizai Shimposha, 1982), pp. 189–90, cited in Iida, *International Economic Policy Coordination*, p. 236.

19. However, Treasury spurned Japanese pleas to issue yen-denominated bonds, while it issued these so-called Carter bonds in both D-marks and Swiss francs.

Figure 4.3 Japan: monthly exchange rates, 1975–93

1985 average = 100; logarithmic scale

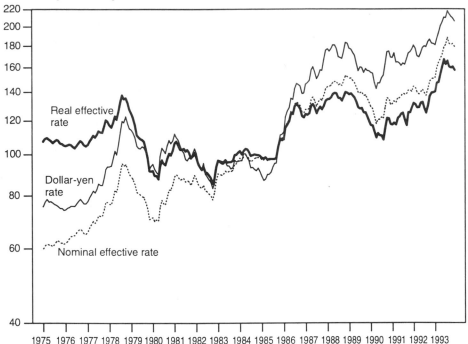

Source: International Monetary Fund, *International Financial Statistics*.

1978 and bounced between that level and 250 during 1979–80[20] (figure 4.2). This was the first episode in a sustained period of yen weakness that supported Japanese competitiveness into the mid-1980s.

Japanese business was greatly relieved by the yen's retreat. Had the currency remained above 200 to the dollar, competitiveness certainly would have been impaired. Owing to efforts to adapt to the higher yen through investment, moreover, the real effective value of the yen actually fell 15 percent below the 1975–77 average (figure 4.3).

The second yen realignment, therefore, hardly fazed the Japanese economy, which continued to register strong growth in 1979 and 1980 (after 6 and 5 percent growth in 1977 and 1978 respectively), sustained by strong domestic demand. Japan's current account ran a deficit in the neighborhood of 1 percent of GNP in 1979 and 1980, but the trade account never

---

20. The yen depreciated to the 240–250 level at the end of 1979, bounced back up to around 200 at the end of 1980, and then began a two-year decline. The new 200–250 range was substantially above the 285–305 range of winter 1974 through winter 1977, but also substantially below the 1978 peak.

fell into deficit and detracted from growth only in 1979. Moreover, inflation, fueled by the second oil shock, was on the rise (table 4.1).

Japan thus received more relief in the way of yen depreciation than MOF and BOJ preferred. They supported the yen, accordingly, with intervention, capital controls, and tightening of monetary policy. Japanese intervention began to resist the depreciation of the yen in March 1979, as the yen moved below the 220 level. The MOF and BOJ continued to intervene throughout the yen's depreciation until the turnaround, at 264, in early April 1980.[21] Between February 1979 and April 1980 Japanese authorities sold about $21 billion, not counting sales conducted by other central banks on the Bank of Japan's account.[22] In May and November 1979 and March 1980, MOF eased restrictions on capital inflows, to facilitate financing of the current account deficit.[23] Official dollar selling continued through the summer of 1980.

But in September 1980, when the yen had rebounded to about 210, Japanese authorities began to purchase dollars to hold the yen down. The effort to cap the yen continued through the turn of the year, when the rate broke the 200 barrier. At that level, BOJ Governor Maekawa declared that the "excessive appreciation" of the yen was undesirable.[24] The 210–230 range, therefore, appears to roughly define Japanese official exchange rate preferences at that time.

The Bank of Japan was anxious to avoid a repeat of the inflation that accompanied the first oil shock, and sought to tighten monetary policy as soon as the strong yen subsided in 1979. Japanese monetary policy had been caught in a dilemma between restraining inflation and restraining the yen during 1977–78. The second oil shock extracted BOJ from that dilemma, by simultaneously nearly eliminating the trade surplus and accelerating inflation. Authorities began to tighten monetary policy in April 1979—just after the OPEC announcement of price increases and a drop in the yen to around 220 to the dollar—with the first of three increases that brought the discount rate to 6.25 percent at the close of the year.[25]

---

21. In early March 1980, as the yen rate fell to 250, BOJ Governor Haruo Maekawa said, "The present depreciation of the yen is excessive because economic conditions do not justify the depreciation by 10 or 11 yen within a one-month period." *Nihon Keizai Shimbun*, 3 March 1980, cited by Otani, "Exchange Rate Instability," p. 333, n. 1.

22. As estimated by Komiya and Suda, *Japan's Foreign Exchange Policy*, pp. 268–70 and table 8.2.

23. The third package, announced by Finance Minister Noboru Takeshita, consisted of tightened reserve requirements, central bank credits, and eased restrictions on capital inflows. *Wall Street Journal*, 27 February 1980; *New York Times* and *Wall Street Journal*, 3 March 1980.

24. *New York Times*, 7 January 1980.

25. Koji Nakagawa, *Taikenteki Kinyu-seisaku-ron: Nichigin no mado kara* [*Personal Experiences in Financial Policy: From the Window of the Bank of Japan*] (Tokyo: Nihon Keizai Shimbunsha, 1981), chapter 3.

Figure 4.4 Japan: monthly interest rates, 1980–93

percentage

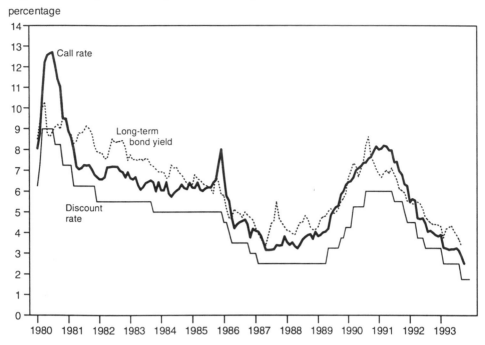

Source: International Monetary Fund, *International Financial Statistics*.

The Bank of Japan, however, was not satisfied with this tightening. When Haruo Maekawa replaced Teiichiro Morinaga as governor in December 1979, BOJ pressed firmly for additional interest rate increases (chapter 3). In February and March 1980, the discount rate was raised 1.0 and 1.75 percent, respectively, to a peak of 9.0 percent (figure 4.4).

Again, the external sector figured prominently in the decision making surrounding monetary tightening. The yen continued to be weak, between 240 and 250 during early 1980. Each rate increase was preceded by a similar tightening by the US Federal Reserve. When the yen strengthened in mid-1980, furthermore, Japan took this opportunity to ease monetary policy.[26] BOJ cited the exchange rate as either a policy objective or an important consideration when introducing these changes in domestic policy.[27]

---

26. Although inflation remained strong, MOF and BOJ reduced the discount rate in August 1980, as the yen rose above 220 and again in November when it neared 200.

27. See the summary of the statements by the BOJ Governor reproduced in Ralph C. Bryant, "Model Representations of Japanese Monetary Policy," *Monetary and Economic Studies* (9 September 1991), p. 20, table 1.

Selective Liberalization of Capital Controls

Pressures from business and politicians for the liberalization of the restrictions on international capital flows—essential to maintaining the rigid and highly regulated system of domestic finance created by the state as a tool of industrial development—mounted during the 1970s. The ministries and financial institutions conceded a gradual (some would say glacial) process of financial opening.

During the second realignment of the yen and subsequent retreat, MOF used its power to liberalize the controls on inflows and outflows at different speeds to manage the currency and the balance of payments. Progress toward liberalization was accelerated or stopped, even reversed, depending on the market pressures on the exchange rate and external balance. At the beginning of the decade, controls on outflows had been eased when the yen was strong, and controls on inflows had been eased when the yen weakened at the onset of the first oil shock. Similarly, during 1977–78, MOF restricted inflows and encouraged outflows to suppress the appreciation of the yen. MOF encouraged net capital inflow as the yen weakened during 1979–80.[28]

The new Foreign Exchange and Trade Control Law came into effect on 1 December 1980. This reform led eventually to the weakening of informal directives, and capital liberalization became one of the distinctive characteristics of the 1980s. In the early part of the 1980s, however, administrative guidance remained strong and MOF controlled in practice the private transactions that had been liberalized in principle by the new law. Formal and informal controls remained a recourse, furthermore, should MOF want to draw on them for exchange rate and international monetary purposes, and MOF used these powers during crises in the 1980s.

Summary

The change in international monetary regime at the beginning of the 1970s, a product of the Nixon administration, did not reflect a change in *Japanese* exchange rate preferences. After the switch to flexible exchange rates, the Japanese government continued to manage the yen's relationship to the dollar. To this end, MOF and BOJ applied the same arsenal that they had employed under fixed exchange rates: adjustments in macroeconomic policies, capital controls, import enhancement programs,

---

28. Mitsuhiro Fukao, "Liberalization of Japan's Foreign Exchange Controls and Structural Changes in the Balance of Payments," *Monetary and Economic Studies* 8 (September 1990): 101–65; Otani, "Exchange Rate Instability," appendix 13A, pp. 331–33. Covered interest parity had been strongly negative until 1979, reflecting the constraints on capital inflows until that year, and slightly positive thereafter, reflecting constraints on capital outflows until 1982. For a discussion, see Robert Alan Feldman, *Japanese Financial Markets: Deficits, Dilemmas, and Deregulation* (Cambridge: MIT Press, 1986), pp. 181–86.

and foreign exchange intervention. Capital and exchange controls were particularly important and lightened the burden on the other instruments such as intervention and domestic monetary policy. Japanese authorities also implored their American counterparts to take a more activist approach to the management of their bilateral exchange rate, with only temporary success.

Japanese activism was not completely one-sided; authorities sought to support as well as to depress the yen. But the dominant market trend was appreciation, not depreciation, of the currency. Authorities acted to limit the yen's rise despite enormous improvements in productivity in tradeable goods sectors. Although the nominal value of the yen rose during the first decade of the flexible-rate regime, there was no appreciation of the real effective exchange rate on any prolonged basis. The competitiveness of Japanese industry was preserved.

Policymaking since 1980

Japanese exchange rate and monetary policy has undergone five distinct phases since 1980. The first phase was dominated by the Reagan policy mix and noninterventionist attitude toward the strong dollar. Japan responded to US pressure to liberalize financial markets and increase the international role of the yen. But the overall Japanese economic strategy, and the role of the exchange rate in that strategy, remained fundamentally unchanged through this period. The yen remained weak, the current account remained in surplus, and growth remained strong.

Once American policy neglect unleashed protectionist forces in the United States, a concerted effort to realign currency rates and to coordinate macroeconomic policy marked the second phase, beginning with the Plaza Agreement. The active support of the Japanese government for yen appreciation was genuine, but exceptional and short-lived.

The third phase began with the Japanese decision to attempt to cap the appreciation of the yen and to stabilize the currency against the dollar. Japanese authorities first acted unilaterally, in the face of American official statements talking the dollar down, and then multilaterally by operating a covert, loose, and ad hoc regime of target ranges.

The Japanese government strongly resisted the depreciation of the yen from the levels reached in 1987–88 during the fourth phase, in 1989–90. This represented a significant change in exchange rate preferences and an adaptation to the strong yen. Japanese monetary authorities were nonetheless slow to raise interest rates in the face of rampant inflation in asset prices.

The fifth and final phase of external monetary policymaking, during 1991–92, coincided with the popping of the asset price bubble and a dramatic slowdown in economic growth. The strength of the yen was restored and the currency remained fairly stable. The earlier weakness of the yen and the economic slowdown, however, spurred the renewed growth of the trade surplus, which set the stage for conflict with the Clinton administration in 1993–94.

Phase 1: Yen Weakness and Export Boom, 1981–85

The Japanese economy emerged from the second oil shock and the whip-sawing of the yen during 1978–81 relatively unscathed. During the first half of the 1980s the yen was persistently weak, a product of both Japanese and American macroeconomic policy. The laissez-faire approach of the first Reagan administration toward the exchange market limited Japanese capabilities in managing the rate. The low yen and high dollar set the stage for later trade conflicts. But in general businessmen, politicians, and bureaucrats—with the exception of some officials at BOJ and MOF— were not alarmed by the weakness of the yen during 1981–85 and did not advocate sacrifices to counter it.

Macroeconomic Background

Japan alone among the G-7 countries avoided a recession in the early 1980s. The current account deficits of 1979 and 1980 were turned into modest surpluses in 1981 and 1982, while the trade surplus in those years registered just under 2 percent of GNP. The political problem of bilateral US-Japan trade imbalances was limited to specific sectors, and was effectively contained with the voluntary restraint agreement on Japanese exports of automobiles established in 1981.

Overall economic growth, while avoiding recession, had fallen from an average of 5.5 percent during 1977–80 to 2.9 and 2.0 percent in 1980 and 1981—substantially below potential. (The average annual growth rate during 1970–90 was 4.3 percent.) Wholesale price inflation was reduced from 17.8 percent in 1980 to 1.4 percent in 1981 and 1.8 percent in 1982. Consumer price inflation was reduced from 7.7 percent in 1980 to 5.1 percent in 1981 and 2.7 percent in 1982.

The government nonetheless was preoccupied with the size of the national debt, which grew to nearly 60 percent of GNP in 1982, on a gross basis, and would rise to 68 percent later in the mid-1980s.[29] Prime Minister Zenko Suzuki pledged not to solve the deficit problem by raising taxes and, at the insistence of the business community, sought to reduce expenditures. So important did he consider this program of "administrative reform" that Suzuki declared that he staked his "political life" on its success.[30] Yasuhiro Nakasone reaffirmed this basic stance shortly

---

29. When measured in net terms, including the favorable position of the social security account, Japanese public debt was considerably smaller.

30. *International Herald Tribune*, 13 September 1982.

after he became prime minister in November 1982.[31] With fiscal policy immobilized as a countercyclical instrument—as it has been during most of the postwar period—monetary policy carried the brunt of the burden of restimulating the Japanese economy.

US interest rates, which had been volatile since a fundamental change in Federal Reserve policy in October 1979, rose dramatically in the second half of 1980. But, even as US interest rates were setting postwar records, Japan managed to ease domestic monetary policy. MOF and BOJ reduced interest rates beginning in August 1980, the first of a progressive loosening that would continue throughout the decade[32] (figure 4.4). Unlike Germany (discussed in chapter 5), Japan was willing to countenance continued weakness of the external value of the currency.

The combination of American and Japanese policy mixes yielded a substantial interest rate differential in favor of the United States, to which capital flows predictably responded. The Japanese currency depreciated to 278 to the dollar in November 1982—causing howls of protest in the US Congress—rebounded to the vicinity of 230–240, at the beginning of 1983, and then depreciated gradually from that range over the following two years. The period from early 1983 through mid-1985 saw relative stability in interest and exchange rates.

Exchange Rate Policy

Japanese external monetary policy confronted an uncooperative partner in the first Reagan administration. Within a few months of the inauguration, the US Treasury, under the leadership of Secretary Donald T. Regan and his undersecretary for monetary affairs, Beryl W. Sprinkel, announced that it would no longer intervene in the foreign exchange markets, except under extraordinary circumstances such as the shooting of the president. Japanese authorities privately responded with dismay at this announcement, as did the Europeans. It had taken years of conflict to

---

31. Speaking at the beginning of 1983, Nakasone said, "We have to set various antirecessionary measures in motion and we must try to expand the economy gradually, but state finances are now at a standstill and the government can't spend much. . . . As a result, we have to depend on monetary policy and private-sector demand this year." *Wall Street Journal*, 3 January 1983.

32. The behind-the-scenes negotiations over the August rate cut provides a good illustration of MOF-BOJ bargaining on monetary policy. Finance Minister Michio Watanabe directed BOJ to reduce the discount rate by 1 percent. BOJ held out for a half-point reduction only. They compromised on a reduction of 0.75 percent.

The rate cuts were generally timed for moments of yen strength. The first two discount rate cuts were made as the yen was strengthening in the second half of 1980. The third rate cut of 1.0 percent in March 1981 occurred as inflation fell and the yen was in the neighborhood of 220. Weakness of the yen delayed the fourth discount rate cut until December 1981, despite continued decline in inflation, after the yen had begun to strengthen again.

engage the American authorities cooperatively in foreign exchange intervention, achieved in autumn 1978. The Regan-Sprinkel nonintervention policy harkened back to earlier days of exchange rate neglect by the United States.

After the Reagan administration's nonintervention announcement, the yen weakened to around 220. MOF and BOJ, acting unilaterally again, intervened repeatedly to support it during the remainder of the year and throughout 1982[33] (figure 4.5). The direction of intervention, moreover, was consistent throughout phase 1. Between the end of 1980 and the end 1985, all Japanese operations supported the yen; there were no significant dollar purchases.

Aware that unilateral intervention would have limited effectiveness, however, MOF reduced the frequency and quantity of intervention. From the beginning of 1983 through autumn 1985, including the dollar spike of early 1985, reported foreign exchange reserves changed by little more than estimated interest receipts.[34] In contrast to the period from autumn 1977 through winter 1980–81, therefore, intervention from spring 1981 through autumn 1985, and especially after the beginning of 1983, was substantially reduced.

MOF demonstrated little desire for a stronger yen, in any case, and certainly much less than the BOJ. To the contrary, as the yen fell to a five-year low of 270 in late September 1982, Finance Minister Michio Watanabe declared, in a matter-of-fact tone, that "there were no signs whatever" that the yen's weakness would end soon.[35]

Bank of Japan officials made their preferences for a stronger yen quite clear through declarations. In April 1983, Governor Maekawa called for "international concerted action" in foreign exchange markets and a "systematic investigation" of ways to achieve exchange rate stability. The performance of the floating-rate system in the 10 years since the demise of the Bretton Woods agreement, he stated, "hasn't come up to our expectations."[36] In May, Maekawa said that the yen's trading range, then around 236 to the dollar, was "still too low," and that Japan "must aim

---

33. They sold dollars during 14 out of 23 business days in July 1981, when the yen fell to 240, from 200 at the beginning of the year. *JEI Report*, 7 August 1981, pp. 1–2. They sold dollars in substantial quantities again in December. Between May 1981 and December 1982 Japanese authorities sold $11.8 billion, not counting official sales though foreign central banks. Komiya and Suda, *Japan's Foreign Exchange Policy*, table 8.3. During February–October 1982, when the yen dropped to 278 to the dollar, Japanese authorities sold roughly $8 billion. During the month of June, they intervened on all but two business days. *JEI Report*, 9 July 1982, p. 1.

34. See also David Jay Green, "Exchange Rate Policy and Intervention in Japan," *Keizai-Shirin* [The Hosei University Economic Review] 57, no. 3 (1989), p. 135, figure 1.

35. *New York Times*, 29 September 1982.

36. *Wall Street Journal*, 22 April 1983.

Figure 4.5 Japan: monthly change in foreign exchange reserves, 1980–93

billions of dollars

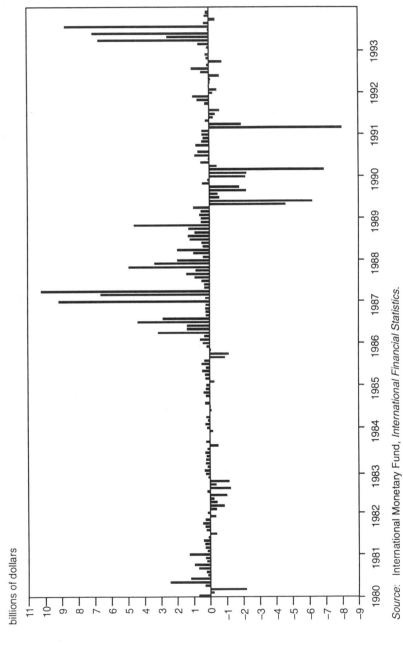

Source: International Monetary Fund, *International Financial Statistics.*

for a higher yen."[37] In spring 1984, when the yen was slightly stronger but weakening (and in the midst of the yen-dollar negotiations), BOJ issued a report urging a strengthening of the yen to promote imports over the long term. The bank also endorsed continued efforts to open Japan's markets and expand domestic demand but promoted a strong and stable yen as the primary objective.[38]

Monetary Policy

These declaratory differences between MOF and BOJ vis-à-vis the yen derived from their contrasting views on the Japanese policy mix during 1982 and 1983, and how monetary policy should respond to the dilemma of simultaneous weakness of the yen and slack domestic demand. In his complacency about the weakness of the yen in September 1982, Minister Watanabe seemed to signal his unwillingness to endorse a tightening of monetary policy to defend the currency.[39] During a reaffirmation of the policy of fiscal consolidation, Prime Minister Nakasone stated in early 1983 that growth would have to be provided by monetary policy. In April 1983, the government approved a stimulative economic package frontloading public works spending and calling for "flexible" monetary policy (though at this time the weakness of the yen was cited as a reason not to reduce the official discount rate).[40]

BOJ Governor Maekawa seemed to urge a change in the policy mix, by contrast, when he expressed his doubts in early 1983 about a significant increase in growth in the absence of stimulative policies by the government while at the same time holding out no hope for a cut in the discount rate.[41] While calling for a reexamination of the international monetary regime, Governor Maekawa several times expressed his desire for a stronger yen during this period. Because of the yen's weakness in spring 1983, he concluded, BOJ's ability to lower interest rates was "severely constricted."[42] The government secured its discount rate cut, one-half point to 5.0 percent, in October 1983, as part of a broader package of measures to stimulate domestic demand to promote imports.[43]

---

37. *Wall Street Journal*, 27 May 1983.

38. *New York Times*, 8 May 1984.

39. *New York Times*, 29 September 1982.

40. *Wall Street Journal*, 6 April 1983.

41. *JEI Report*, 4 February 1983, p. 6.

42. *Wall Street Journal*, 27 May 1983.

43. The package included a $5.2 billion tax cut and a speedup in public works spending. *JEI Report*, 21 October 1983, p. 33.

From the standpoint of management of the overall economy, in retrospect, monetary policy appears to have been adeptly managed during phase 1. Despite suggestions at the time that credit was restrained to prevent depreciation of the yen in the face of high interest rates in the United States,[44] growth was sustained at its long-term rate of increase at the same time that inflation was decisively reduced. Clearly, substantial economic sacrifices were not made for the sake of sustaining the yen's value. Monetary policy permitted the exchange rate to respond to the shift in the savings-investment balance, wrought in turn by the reduction in the budget deficit, and in that respect appears decidedly neutral.

Financial Liberalization

During 1982 and 1983, members of Congress and business leaders in the United States accused Japan of manipulating the yen to keep it artificially low. To counter these charges, in part, the Japanese government continued the pattern of selective liberalization of private transactions and altered government borrowing practices to support the yen. MOF issued small amounts of bonds in foreign currencies in foreign markets to promote capital flow into Japan and demonstrate its faith that the yen would rise in the long term.[45]

Treasury Secretary Regan and Undersecretary Sprinkel broadened the agenda of capital market liberalization through what came to be called the yen-dollar negotiations. Their publicly stated purpose for a long list of proposals to liberalize external and internal controls on capital in Japan was to promote the yen as an international currency and thereby increase its value. Officials at MOF did not share Regan and Sprinkel's view that the yen would appreciate as a result of the measures they negotiated. But the weakness of the yen and the flood of Japanese exports to the United States had created a political problem in Congress. Japanese officials deferred to the mistaken Treasury view that the yen-dollar talks were an appropriate strategy to deal with the budding political crisis in US-Japanese relations.

The Yen-Dollar Agreement was signed by Secretary Regan and Finance Minister Takeshita in April 1984. The product of domestic as well as external pressures for liberalization, the agreement provided for the liberalization of domestic markets and international transactions, to be

---

44. See, for example, Bank of Japan, Research and Statistics Department, "The Recent Development of the Japanese Economy and Macroeconomic Policy Objectives," Special Paper 133 (Tokyo, March 1986).

45. Robert V. Roosa, *The United States and Japan in the International Monetary System 1946–1985*, Group of Thirty Occasional Papers 21 (New York: Group of Thirty, 1986), pp. 49–52.

phased over the following years.[46] The immediate response of the yen, contrary to the forecasts of American officials during the negotiations, was to plunge against the dollar, to about 263 in February 1985.

Liberalization and Macroeconomic Policymaking

The Yen-Dollar Agreement was the latest round in an ongoing process of financial market liberalization that had largely integrated Japanese with world capital markets during the first half of the 1980s. The increase in international capital mobility for Japan produced a fundamental transformation in Japan's external macroeconomic relations. Through its effects on the exchange rate, international capital mobility also transformed the domestic politics of macroeconomic policy in Japan. These changes are best understood with reference to the well-known economic model articulated by Robert Mundell and Marcus Fleming separately.[47]

Liberalization, first of all, permitted Japanese savings to flow abroad more freely at precisely the moment at which that savings pool was growing. As the Japanese budget deficit declined, the US budget deficit was increasing. Without external capital liberalization, the extra savings would have been bottled up in the Japanese economy, unable to flow toward the higher interest rates in the United States. Restrictive fiscal policy would have increased the Japanese surplus by restricting domestic demand for tradeable goods. With financial flows stymied, the yen would have *risen* to offset the rise in the trade surplus.

However, with capital liberalization, the fiscal contraction would stimulate the outflow of capital needed to sustain the trade surplus. With perfect capital mobility, this capital outflow could exceed the financing requirement, *depressing* the yen further. The exchange rate would thereby accommodate or enhance, rather than offset, the increase in the current account surplus brought on by income effects through the trade account. With this additional source of demand, the fiscal consolidation could be achieved without as great a sacrifice in national income. Under

---

46. On the negotiation of this accord, see Francis Rosenbluth, *Financial Politics in Contemporary Japan* (Ithaca, NY: Cornell University Press, 1989); Louis W. Pauly, *Opening Financial Markets: Banking Politics on the Pacific Rim* (Ithaca, NY: Cornell University Press, 1988). For an evaluation of the agreement itself, see Jeffrey A. Frankel, *The Yen-Dollar Agreement*, POLICY ANALYSES IN INTERNATIONAL ECONOMICS 9 (Washington: Institute for International Economics, 1984); Stephen E. Haynes, Michael M. Hutchison, and Raymond F. Mikesell, *Japanese Financial Policies and the U.S. Trade Deficit*, Essays in International Finance 162 (Princeton: International Finance Section, Princeton University, April 1986), pp. 15–17.

47. J. M. Fleming, "Domestic Financial Policies under Fixed and under Floating Exchange Rates," *IMF Staff Papers* 9 (1962): 369–79; Robert Mundell, "Capital Mobility and Stabilization Policy under Fixed and Flexible Exchange Rates," *Canadian Journal of Economics and Political Science* (November 1963): 117–97. For a textbook treatment of this model, see Richard E. Caves, Jeffrey A. Frankel, and Ronald W. Jones, *World Trade and Payments: An Introduction*, 5th ed. (Glenview, IL: Scott Foresman, 1990), chapter 21.

flexible exchange rates, the effect of capital liberalization is to reverse the impact of fiscal policy on the exchange rate, amplify its impact on the external balance, and reduce its effect on overall output.[48]

Private sector preferences with respect to fiscal policy changed as the mechanisms through which it worked were altered by capital liberalization. Because a fiscal stimulus would tend to push the yen upward, Japanese business had far less incentive to lobby for budgetary expansion than it did during the 1970s. And, given the fiscal contraction underway in Japan, business could promote or accept with equanimity the liberalization of capital controls that weakened the currency and improved their international competitiveness. Had capital liberalization instead produced a surge of capital inflows, raising the yen and reducing net exports, industrial corporations and the banks close to them would have had to reconsider, at minimum, their position on the pace and terms of liberalization.

The effectiveness of monetary policy on both the exchange rate and output is enhanced by capital mobility. A monetary expansion will raise domestic demand and push the trade account toward deficit. With capital mobility, the fall in interest rates stimulates capital outflow, depressing the currency and thus favoring net exports.

Officials at the Bank of Japan clearly understood the Mundell-Fleming view of the relationship between the policy mix and the external balance. Yoshio Suzuki, then director of BOJ's research institute, explained:[49]

> [M]onetary relaxation alone cannot be a solution for international disequilibrium between Japan and the U.S. A policy mix change towards relatively tighter monetary policy together with an easier fiscal stance could be a solution for the international imbalance. Decrease in monetary growth or the constant monetary growth, accompanied by the expanding public sector deficit, will raise interest rates and lead to yen appreciation with a result of decline in the current account surplus, which will be also caused by the fact that the easier fiscal policy will absorb excess domestic savings at the same time.

In spite of the clarity of this argument, the Japanese government notably pursued precisely the opposite policy mix, with only temporary exceptions, throughout the 1980s.

---

48. These elements of the Mundell-Fleming model are applied to Japan in Naoko Ishii, Warwick McKibbin, and Jeffrey Sachs, "The Economic Policy Mix, Policy Cooperation, and Protectionism: Some Aspects of Macroeconomic Interdependence among the United States, Japan, and Other OECD Countries," *Journal of Policy Modeling* 7, no. 4: 533–72.

49. Yoshio Suzuki, "Japan's Monetary Policy over the Past 10 Years," *Bank of Japan Monetary and Economic Studies* 3, no. 2 (September 1985), p. 8. Suzuki went on to argue that the most appropriate prescription was a reduction in the American budget deficit.

Overview

In 1985, on a real effective basis, the yen stood at the same level as at the advent of flexible exchange rates (figure 4.3). During 1980–85, Japan's domestic demand increased 2.5 percent per year on average. Accommodated by American fiscal deficits, the burgeoning external surpluses raised the overall Japanese growth rate to 4.0 percent. More than one-third of Japan's growth during 1980–85, therefore, was supplied by the external sector. (During that period alone, Japanese domestic demand increased 3.1 percent and GNP increased 4.3 percent on average.)[50]

Increased net exports therefore enabled Japan to meet two potentially conflicting goals simultaneously. Budget deficit reduction was pursued with vigor. The general government deficit fell from 4.4 percent of GNP in 1980 to 0.8 percent in 1985. The reduction in the deficit of the central government was more moderate but substantial, falling from 6.0 percent of GNP in 1980 to 3.6 percent in 1985 (table 4.2). Normally this would have caused the economy to contract, particularly because the private savings surplus also increased during the first half of the 1980s.[51] But the external source of growth enabled Japan to reach, or very nearly reach, its long-term potential rate, 4.3 percent, nevertheless. This, during a period when the rest of the advanced industrialized countries experienced their deepest recession of the postwar period!

At the middle of the decade of the 1980s, indeed, it was difficult to detect fundamental change in the overall economic strategy of Japan. The country had undergone substantial changes in the wake of the two oil shocks: growth and investment had both fallen dramatically compared to the pre-oil shock period. The oil shocks had raised the price level, and inflation was conquered in the early 1980s. Capital controls were progressively eased. Outward foreign direct investment had begun to grow.

But the basic postwar strategy of achieving growth through industrial investment (still high by international standards) and exports remained very much intact. The high yen of the late 1970s and the current account deficits of 1979 and 1980 had been fully reversed. Importers, consumers, savers, and the beneficiaries of government spending and investment in public infrastructure were disadvantaged by the strategy of fiscal consolidation and export expansion. But, in the Japanese policy-

---

50. IMF, *World Economic Outlook*, April 1986, table A2, p. 180.

51. For an analysis of Japanese savings and investment behavior, see Stephen N. Marris, *Deficits and the Dollar: The World Economy at Risk*, POLICY ANALYSES IN INTERNATIONAL ECONOMICS 14 (Washington: Institute for International Economics, December 1985); Bela Balassa and Marcus Noland, *Japan and the World Economy* (Washington: Institute for International Economics, 1988).

making process, their concerns were subordinated to the objectives of investment, productivity, exports, and growth.

There were no effective domestic constraints on this strategy in Japan. General complacency over the weakness of the yen prevailed. Pockets of concern, such as those within BOJ, were greatly outnumbered by contentment with prevailing exchange rates. Any attempt during phase 1 to raise the value of the yen to reduce the external surplus would have foundered on the absence of any substantial, committed political force behind the effort.

Phase 2: Yen Appreciation, 1985–86

The primary constraint on the Japanese strategy of investment, export, and growth was the willingness of other countries, the United States in particular, to absorb Japanese production. That limit was reached in the mid-1980s, as the bilateral trade surplus with the United States soared. To compound the problem for the Japanese government, the Reagan administration was not handling its own domestic trade politics either skillfully or successfully. The explosion of protectionist sentiment on Capitol Hill in summer 1985 changed the political calculus of Japanese business, bureaucrats, and politicians. Rather than stand by as the Congress restricted Japanese access to US markets, Japanese officials preferred to undertake currency adjustment. The Japanese government thus backed, initially, a third major realignment of the yen.

Genesis of Policy Change

The principal proponents of the shift to yen appreciation, *endaka* as it was called in Japanese, were those people and bureaucracies that were most directly exposed to foreign pressures and whose constituencies would be most harmed by protectionist trade policies abroad. Export-oriented business and the Ministry of International Trade and Industry had become alarmed with protectionist sentiment in the United States. Politicians, such as Nakasone and Takeshita, who had dealt with American officials sensed the need for policy change. The Ministry of Foreign Affairs was concerned for the health of the political relationship between the two countries. MOF, though, responded reactively rather than proactively to the pressures from these concerned interests.[52]

The government's first response was the usual set of measures designed to appease disgruntled foreign countries. MITI engaged the Unit-

---

52. The best account of the change in Japanese policy at the time of the Plaza is Yoichi Funabashi, *Managing the Dollar: From the Plaza to the Louvre* (Washington: Institute for International Economics, 1988), chapter 4. For a Japanese participant's account, see Volcker and Gyohten, *Changing Fortunes*, pp. 248–58.

ed States in the Market-Oriented Sector Specific (MOSS) talks early in 1985. The cabinet recommended an "action program" of tariff cuts in June to reduce the trade surplus.[53] In July, BOJ Governor Sumita said the yen should be strengthened because expanding domestic demand would have only limited results in reducing the current account position.[54] An advisory group to Prime Minister Nakasone seriously considered imposing controls on capital outflows to strengthen the yen. But MOF had continued to liberalize capital controls during 1985 and thus rejected this proposal.[55]

The second Reagan administration, however, offered Japan an opportunity to engage the Americans constructively in exchange rate cooperation. As Yoichi Funabashi reports, Treasury Secretary James Baker, Finance Minister Takeshita, and officials in both ministries negotiated secretly during the summer of 1985 for an exchange rate remedy to the trade imbalance.[56]

The Plaza Agreement

Japanese politicians and officials who initiated the strong yen policy vastly underestimated the size of the correction that was in store. They also underestimated the realignment that was necessary to achieve adjustment and to mute protectionist pressure in the US Congress. Their privately held exchange rate target at the time of the Plaza meeting on 22 September 1985 was 210 yen to the dollar. This target later was reduced to 200.[57] The largest portion of the exchange rate adjustment that took place after the Plaza meeting, therefore, occurred against the wishes of the Japanese government, the BOJ, the politicians, and the private sector. Six months after the initiation of the new policy at the Plaza, the government would be fighting a rear guard action to resist yen appreciation.

On the day of the Plaza Agreement, the yen stood at 242 to the dollar. As part of the collective program to achieve "some further orderly appreciation of the main non-dollar currencies against the dollar," Japan agreed to intervene to strengthen the yen, and did so to the tune of $3 billion during the six weeks after the meeting. Japan also agreed to "flexible management of monetary policy," financial market liberaliza-

---

53. *New York Times*, 24 June 1985.

54. *Wall Street Journal*, 9 July.

55. *Washington Post*, 11 September 1985. Vice Minister for International Affairs Tomomitsu Oba called on Nakasone to state that such controls were impossible.

56. Funabashi, *Managing the Dollar*, chapter 1.

57. Funabashi, *Managing the Dollar*, p. 24; Volcker and Gyohten, *Changing Fortunes*, p. 254.

tion, and internationalization of the yen with the aim of strengthening the Japanese currency. Notably, stimulation of domestic demand was to rest on private consumption and investment; Japanese fiscal policy was expressly directed toward reducing the budget deficit.[58]

The Plaza announcement dramatically appreciated the currency. One month after the Plaza meeting, with the yen at 216, Prime Minister Nakasone said that "the efforts to see the yen appreciate will continue."[59] Shortly thereafter BOJ Governor Sumita called for a further appreciation of the yen, which then rose to 202 in early November—its highest level since January 1981.[60] Japanese authorities followed through on the Plaza meeting with considerably greater enthusiasm and determination than their German counterparts.

Strong conflicts emerged nonetheless between BOJ and MOF over the *endaka* policy. In sum, BOJ preferred a stronger yen than did the government and was more willing to tighten monetary policy to support it. In late October, BOJ Governor Sumita used the occasion of a temporary stabilization of exchange rates, and the expressed desire of Japanese politicians to see a still higher yen, to tighten monetary conditions. On 24 October, he declared his desire to see interest rates rise, and BOJ tightened monetary conditions in its daily money market operations.

However, this move, which was not subject to MOF approval, touched off a sharp domestic and international dispute. Rather than taking the view that higher Japanese interest rates would bolster the yen, consistent with declared government policy, Paul Volcker, the chairman of the US Federal Reserve Board of Governors, sharply criticized the move as risking a precipitous depreciation of the dollar. The US Treasury and MOF were concerned that the move would slow Japanese and world growth, and thus slow the adjustment process that was so important to containing protectionist sentiment on Capitol Hill. These critical reactions compelled BOJ to reverse its policy course only a few weeks later, in December. Notwithstanding this about-face, foreign officials and MOF intensified pressure on BOJ at a meeting of the G-5 finance ministers and central bank governors in London in mid-January 1986. The exchange rate, furthermore, crossed the 200 mark during the week after the London meeting. Despite an earlier declaration by Governor Sumita that BOJ would not further reduce interest rates unilaterally, it did precisely that at the end of the month.

Finance Minister Takeshita had said that market conditions would

---

58. US Treasury Department, "Announcement of the Ministers of Finance and Central Bank Governors of France, Germany, Japan, the United Kingdom, and the United States," press release, Washington, 22 September 1985.

59. *Washington Post*, 23 October 1985.

60. *JEI Report*, 15 November 1985, pp. 3–4.

support a rise to the 190 level and that Japanese industry could live with that rate.[61] By 10 February the rate had surpassed that level and MOF switched to a hands-off policy. Governor Sumita, while still favorably disposed to further appreciation, expressed his concern that the yen was rising too rapidly. Takeshita and Sumita publicly differed over the desirability of another reduction in the discount rate to stem the rise of the currency and sustain domestic growth.[62] By 19 February, however, the yen had broken through the 180 barrier, below which Sumita expressed his hope that exchange rates would stabilize. Under strong pressure from Japanese industry, Takeshita, too, said that Japan would take a "wait-and-see attitude for some time" with regard to the yen.[63]

Thus ended official Japanese support for yen appreciation. This unprecedented policy was brief, lasting from summer 1985 through February 1986, and corresponded to a 25 percent rise in the yen's value. The *endaka* policy faded into a stabilization policy, however, despite the collapse in the price of oil in early 1986 that would greatly benefit Japan's trade balance. The Japanese government also shifted to yen stabilization long before the political problem of trade protectionism in the United States was solved. With the benefit of hindsight, it is clear that the exchange rate of 180 was nowhere close to the figure required either to bring sufficient adjustment or to defuse US-Japanese trade conflict. The shift in policy put the Japanese government in direct conflict with US exchange rate policy. At the same levels at which Japanese officials called for stability, US Treasury Secretary Baker declared openly that the administration "would not be displeased to see a further, orderly, gradual decline of the dollar."[64]

Phase 3: Yen Stabilization, 1986–88

Japan's resistance to the appreciation of the yen, beginning in March 1986, was unilateral. The United States did not intervene with Japanese authorities, nor did the Fed hold interest rates high to defend the dollar. In February 1987, at the Louvre, the Reagan administration agreed to try to place a floor under the dollar in cooperation with Japan and the G-7 partners, initiating a second subphase. Although multilateral, this effort

---

61. *JEI Report*, 31 January 1986, p. 3.

62. *Wall Street Journal*, 14 February 1986.

63. Arguing that an exchange rate of 160 would be catastrophic, Japanese industry criticized the policy that Takeshita had followed. Industry representatives told him that if he wanted to get votes, he should go to Narita airport, because only Japanese returning from abroad would benefit from the higher yen. Interviews, Tokyo, January–February 1991. See, as well, *Washington Post*, 2 March 1986.

64. *JEI Report*, 28 February 1986, p. 1.

was ineffective because of the half-hearted commitment on the part of the United States and disagreement over monetary coordination. January 1988 marks the beginning of successful multilateral cooperation to support the dollar and restrain the yen, then in the 120s.

Unilateral Efforts, March 1986–February 1987

The yen set a new postwar record by surpassing the October 1978 high of 175.5 in mid-March 1986. Expressing a governmentwide view, Prime Minister Nakasone then told the Diet that the level of the yen was "excessive." Sumita expressed concern about the possibility of a dollar "crash." At this time, BOJ yielded to MOF pressure to intervene to restrain, rather than to promote, the yen's rise.[65] The unenviable task of halting the yen's appreciation in the face of blatant conflict with the US Treasury fell to Finance Minister Takeshita. He suggested that the United States and Japan had agreed on the need for stability in the yen-dollar rate—a statement that US Treasury Secretary Baker angrily denied.[66]

Once the exchange rate fell to record lows, the fear of American protectionism was replaced with the fear of real harm to Japanese industry and traded goods producers generally. Commentators raised the specter of the "hollowing out" of the Japanese economy. A stream of private interests pleaded and pressured Liberal Democratic Party (LDP) politicians to halt the yen appreciation and to relieve some of the pain of adjustment to the new rates.

This lobbying drive was similar to that of US industry during the previous period of dollar strength.[67] But in Japan, the reaction to the strong yen was more immediate, widely shared, and effective than the pressure that American business applied to the US government. The Japanese government placed the halting of the runaway yen at the top of its economic policy agenda. And Japanese authorities deployed a wide array of policy measures to that end and to compensate the particularly vulnerable firms and sectors for the costs of adjustment.

During the five months April–August 1986, BOJ purchased roughly $12.4 billion to halt the yen's rise—the first such sustained effort since the second yen realignment in the late 1970s. Japanese authorities acted alone in buying billions of dollars to support the currency, however, and therefore less effectively than had intervention been concerted with the other advanced industrial countries.

Japanese monetary policy was eased to dampen the upward pressure on the yen and to help to offset the contractionary impulse of the revaluation that had already occurred. On 7 March, BOJ reduced the discount

---

65. *Wall Street Journal*, 20 March 1986.

66. *Financial Times*, 14 April 1986.

67. See Destler and Henning, *Dollar Politics*, chapter 7.

rate for the second time in five weeks in a concerted easing with the Federal Reserve and the Bundesbank. In the third week of April, the BOJ reduced the discount rate by one-half point, again with the Federal Reserve. With world interest rates falling, Japan had little choice but to reduce rates in tandem if it was to avoid even more rapid appreciation of the yen. Short-term market interest rates fell from about 6.5 to 4.5 percent between mid-1985 and spring 1986, not counting the peak of 8 percent in autumn 1985. During the first four months of 1986, BOJ reduced the discount rate from 5.0 to the previous postwar low, set in the early 1970s, of 3.5 percent.

Nakasone and Takeshita hoped to use the G-7 economic summit meeting to be held in Tokyo in early May 1986 to secure international endorsement for exchange rate stabilization. Nakasone, the host, would show statesmanship by offering a large package of domestic and external adjustment measures in exchange for the participation of others in settling the exchange markets. Nakasone commissioned a report from an advisory group chaired by Maekawa, who had retired from BOJ in December 1984, to present a set of proposals in advance of the summit.

The report urged the government to adopt a new and explicit policy of transforming the Japanese economy from export-led to domestic demand–led growth, and offered a substantial list of qualitatively specific measures that the group argued would further international adjustment.[68] But the key ministries had pressed successfully for the elimination of quantitatively specific proposals, such as setting a fixed date for the elimination of the current account surplus, from the final version.[69] The report was not adopted by the cabinet as official government policy, nor by the Diet, nor even fully by Nakasone himself. The domestic standing of the report was therefore dubious from the outset.

The Tokyo summit was a success from the standpoint of creating an institutional mechanism for macroeconomic policy coordination among the G-7 and a list of indicators to facilitate that task.[70] But it was a severe domestic political embarrassment for the host, who failed to secure his main objective—unequivocal endorsement of exchange rate stability from President Reagan. As the yen rose above the 170 level in June, Nakasone directed the vice minister of finance for international affairs, Toyoo Gyohten, to restore it to that level before the elections in July.[71] But,

---

68. "The Report of the Advisory Group on Economic Structural Adjustment for International Harmony," submitted to Prime Minister Yasuhiro Nakasone, 7 April 1986.

69. *Japan Times*, 8 April 1986, cited by Kent Calder, "Japanese Foreign Economic Policy Formation: Explaining the Reactive State," *World Politics* 40 (July 1988): 526, 529.

70. For an analysis of this achievement, see Wendy Dobson, *Economic Policy Coordination: Requiem or Prologue?* POLICY ANALYSES IN INTERNATIONAL ECONOMICS 30 (Washington: Institute for International Economics, April 1991).

71. Volcker and Gyohten, *Changing Fortunes*, p. 257.

while MOF intervened, the yen continued to rise and reached 158 in mid-July.

The failure to get agreement on stabilization did not actually harm the prime minister politically. The economic uncertainty surrounding the yen appreciation and weakness of the economy predisposed the Japanese electorate against taking political risks with the opposition. In an election in early July, the LDP won a resounding victory in the Diet, by the largest majority in the party's history. Nakasone successfully leveraged that victory into an unprecedented fifth year as prime minister.

In the new Nakasone cabinet, Kiichi Miyazawa replaced Takeshita as finance minister. Miyazawa was an LDP faction leader, a former bureaucrat at MOF, and a speaker of English with international connections. With the yen at 155 to the dollar and business confidence flagging, Miyazawa's first task was to convince Baker that a stabilization of the yen was necessary. He met with Baker for the first time as finance minister in San Francisco in early September. There, Baker asked for stronger domestic demand in Japan through a supplemental budget and interest rate cuts. Miyazawa argued that stabilizing the yen was necessary for sustaining domestic demand. They arrived at a bargain in principle at the joint meetings of the World Bank and International Monetary Fund in Washington at the end of September and directed their deputies to negotiate a package.

Miyazawa, a strong advocate of expansionary fiscal policy before he became finance minister, had already initiated the development of a supplemental budget. Unusually large at ¥3.6 trillion ($23.2 billion at then prevailing exchange rates), the supplemental budget was passed by the cabinet in September. Miyazawa also pressed BOJ to lower the discount rate from 3.5 to 3.0 percent, a move that was announced at the same time the "Baker-Miyazawa accord" was made public, at the end of October. As a quid pro quo for domestic stimulus, Baker agreed that the exchange rate, 153 on the day of the agreement but 163 on the day of the announcement, was "broadly consistent with the present underlying fundamentals."[72] This was the first of four agreements that attempted to halt the appreciation of the yen against the dollar, only the last of which succeeded on a lasting basis.

Officials at BOJ decided in summer 1986 that they did not want to ease monetary policy further. They argued firmly to MOF that monetary ease was the wrong prescription for demand expansion. Fiscal expansion was the more desirable means to stimulate domestic demand. But the new bilateral accord gave Miyazawa strong leverage with the central bank. BOJ officials took comfort in the fact that the government had

---

72. For an in-depth examination of the negotiation of this agreement, and the inside controversy surround the depreciation of the yen between the time of the agreement and the announcement, see Funabashi, *Managing the Dollar*, pp. 156–63.

expressed coresponsibility for buoying demand. But the "real money" embodied in the supplemental budget later proved to be much smaller than originally advertised. Furthermore, under MOF's guidance the government approved the smallest budget increase in postwar history for fiscal 1987.

International conflict over growth policy continued after the turn of the year. US Treasury Deputy Secretary Richard G. Darman gave a background interview in which he criticized the demand policies of the surplus countries. As the yen shot toward 150, the Japanese business community deluged the government with strong objections. Purely for exchange rate reasons, Miyazawa and Sumita decided to lower the discount rate again, a move that was delayed.[73] Second, Miyazawa traveled to the United States to seek Baker's cooperation. Surprising his hosts and securing no prior assurances of the US commitment to stabilization, he took a substantial risk in making the trip. His willingness to take that risk is a measure of strength of outcry from the business community for Miyazawa to act. Baker made no commitment to currency stability, disappointing his Japanese counterpart. The Treasury nonetheless intervened in the markets, selling a token $50 million for yen, as the exchange rate neared the 150 level in late January.[74]

Unsuccessful Multilateral Resistance

The US Treasury finally decided to call a halt to the depreciation of the dollar in February 1987 and enlisted the help of its G-5 partners including Japan.[75] At the meeting at the Louvre in Paris over the weekend of 21–22 February, Baker agreed to state in the communiqué that the United States endorsed exchange rate stability "at around current levels," and to participate in concerted intervention to support the dollar. In exchange, the surplus countries were to expand domestic demand further.

For its part, Japan had announced prior to the Louvre meeting another half-point reduction in the discount rate, to 2.5 percent, effective just after the meeting. The BOJ staff resisted this move. But international political pressure and the strength of the yen again bolstered Miyazawa's position vis-à-vis his central bank. Miyazawa had also agreed to another supplemental budget, which BOJ thought was desirable. So, against the advice of some BOJ staff, Sumita went along with the record-setting rate cut.

Some officials at MOF were inclined to reject the US bargain, now

---

73. Funabashi, *Managing the Dollar*, p. 58.

74. *Wall Street Journal*, 21 January 1987; *Washington Post*, 22 January 1987; Federal Reserve Board data.

75. For reviews of US decision making prior to the Louvre, see Funabashi, *Managing the Dollar*; Destler and Henning, *Dollar Politics*.

that the potential for a free fall of the dollar compelled the Treasury to take action. The large supplemental budget was not welcomed by the Budget Bureau. The International Finance Bureau remembered, furthermore, that Baker and his colleagues had not cooperated when the Japanese side had sought as *demandeur* measures to stabilize the currencies. But the pressure from private groups and politicians, principally the Office of the Prime Minister, on the International Finance Bureau to stabilize the yen was intense. The reaction of private interests and their influence on exchange rate policy through politicians did not permit MOF officials to stare down US officials over the exchange rate.

At the Louvre, as Yoichi Funabashi reports, the finance ministers and central bank governors agreed upon secret target ranges for the yen and the D-mark. The central rate for the yen was set at 153.5 to the dollar; 5 percent margins created a band roughly between 146 and 161 yen. Miyazawa tried to raise the band above the politically important 150 level. His interlocutors objected to skewing the range for the yen, however, and Miyazawa had weakened his bargaining stance by announcing the discount rate cut before the meeting. His attempt was thus frustrated, and Miyazawa left the meeting quite unhappy.

Although there was a consensus at the Louvre to intervene to maintain the target ranges, the Japanese agenda was to prevent the rise of the yen, not to support it from falling.[76] The Louvre Accord proved to be of little assistance in meeting Japanese objectives in the short term, despite the multilateral character of the stabilization effort. The exchange rate moved to the bottom of the 5 percent margin by the end of March, defying record amounts of intervention.[77] At the following G-7 meeting of ministers and governors, Baker proposed that the central rate for the yen range be reset at 146 to the dollar. Miyazawa reluctantly accepted that proposal, creating a new target range of about 139–153.5.

The yen nonetheless continued to fall, to just above 137 at the end of April—a new postwar high in "violation" of the new limit. Prime Minister Nakasone raised the exchange rate problem with President Reagan in a meeting in Washington at the end of April. But Baker, included in the gathering, argued against stronger American participation in currency operations.[78] In May, Makoto Utsumi, director general of the International Finance Bureau, took the additional step of asking Japanese financial institutions to stop speculating against the dollar.[79]

---

76. Volcker and Gyohten, *Changing Fortunes*, p. 268.

77. The Japanese side alone bought over $6 billion in March and almost $10 billion in April—in addition to the roughly $9 billion prior to the Louvre Accord in January.

78. Funabashi, *Managing the Dollar*, p. 191.

79. MOF reinforced this guidance by requiring daily reports of the dollar transactions of the main institutions. *Euromoney*, September 1989, pp. 108–09.

In the spring, Miyazawa fulfilled the fiscal promise which he had made at the Louvre. He and other LDP politicians overcame opposition within both the party and the MOF bureaucracy to the supplemental budget and pushed it through the Diet. Assembled at the Policy Affairs Research Council of the LDP, outside the usual MOF channels, the supplemental budget proved to be the largest in Japan's postwar history, amounting to ¥6 trillion.[80] Foreign pressure was fundamental to the politicians' overcoming MOF on the supplemental budget. Without *gaiatsu*—the Japanese phrase for this external pressure—there would have been no such package.

The remainder of the spring, summer, and early autumn of 1987 was a respite for MOF as far as the exchange rate was concerned. With the help of extensive intervention in the spring and renewed private capital flows to the United States, the yen rebounded and kept to the desired target range. The coordinated effort seemed to be working. Governor Sumita welcomed the renewed weakness of the yen as it reached 150 in July.[81] As the yen rose above 143, Miyazawa expressed complacency for the prospects for the Japanese economy; Sumita said that he expected the yen to trade within this range in the near future.[82]

But stability within the new range was short-lived, lasting only as long as the fragile G-3 consensus on monetary policy. BOJ, having been strong-armed by Miyazawa and MOF into easing monetary policy, became increasingly concerned in mid-1987 about the surge in real estate prices and strengthening of growth prospects. BOJ issued window guidance to the banks to limit the volume of credits, for land purchases in particular. At this signal, interest rates rose in both the money and bond markets, a development that BOJ did not offset.[83] Officials at BOJ hoped to raise the discount rate by the end of the year. The Japanese central bank thus welcomed the Federal Reserve's raising of the American discount rate in early September, shortly after Alan Greenspan replaced Paul Volcker as chairman, as an opportunity to turn the corner toward tightening in Japan without putting renewed upward pressure on the yen.

But US Treasury Secretary Baker strongly objected to the worldwide trend toward tightening when the Bundesbank also allowed interest rates

---

80. Over $40 billion at then-prevailing exchange rates. As the budget was being assembled, MOF did not disclose new projections that increased estimated tax revenues for the year. Yukio Noguchi, "Japan's Fiscal Policy and External Balance," manuscript, September 1989, pp. 3–4.

81. *JEI Report*, 10 July 1987, pp. 1–3.

82. *JEI Report*, 28 August 1987, p. 9; 21 August 1987, pp. 2–3.

83. *JEI Report*, 10 July, 7 August, and 2 and 30 October 1987.

to rise.[84] The October 1987 world stock market crash ensued. Extreme volatility on the Tokyo Stock Exchange forced BOJ to inject liquidity. However, responding to the crash in New York, American monetary policy eased substantially more than Japanese monetary policy, and by the end of October the yen had soared to a new postwar record of 137.55.[85]

The yen's appreciation above the adjusted Louvre range brought loud objections from Japanese business leaders.[86] At the end of October, Miyazawa reiterated Japan's commitment to the Louvre arrangements and opposed yet another downward revision of the target range for the yen-dollar rate. Miyazawa also emphatically warned that Japan would intervene to keep the exchange rate above 140 and MOF and BOJ followed up with heavy intervention.[87] These operations brought total intervention for the year 1987 to roughly $35 billion—equal to more than 1 percent of GNP—a record for annual dollar purchases by a single central bank.

During the remainder of autumn 1987, the G-7 finance ministries and central banks argued over how to repair the damage to international coordination. Japan was less the focus of Baker's invective than was Germany. But that did not prevent the yen, as well as the D-mark, from resuming its upward climb against the dollar as US interest rates fell. The yen pierced not only the line in the sand at 140 but, in early December, the 130 level as well. BOJ's attempt to tighten monetary policy without destabilizing currency markets, in sum, had clearly failed. The Japanese central bank would not escape the situation of extremely low interest rates for another 18 months.

Successful Multilateral Stabilization

At the time of the 22 December "telephone accord," which renewed the call for exchange rate stability, the yen stood at about 126 to the dollar. In spite of the new declaration, made possible by a new US budget accord, the dollar continued to slide through the Christmas–New Year's

---

84. Baker had argued to Greenspan that the Fed chairman should secure assurances from Japan and Germany that they would not ratchet interest rates upward with the Fed move, but Greenspan rejected this advice. See Destler and Henning, *Dollar Politics*, pp. 62–66.

85. During the week of the stock market crash, the yen-dollar rate remained remarkably steady, actually rising from 141 to 144.

86. The heads of Toyota, Hitachi, *Keidanren*, and *Keizai Doyukai* implored the government to cap the yen and to call an emergency meeting of the G-7. *JEI Report*, 6 November 1987, p. 5.

87. BOJ reportedly bought $1 billion during October 26–30 alone. *Financial Times*, 30 October 1987; *JEI Report*, 6 November 1987, p. 4.

holiday period. The yen registered a new record of 120.25 at the beginning of the first trading day of 1988. At that point—delayed for several days after the new accord but timed for high impact—the G-7 mounted a massive and concerted dollar-support operation. That successful "bear trap" effectively established a lower boundary for the exchange rate and returned the yen-dollar rate to the high 120s.

Noboru Takeshita, who had replaced Nakasone as prime minister, met with President Reagan in Washington in mid-January 1988. There they reinforced the dollar-support operation with a statement that Japan would make yen available to the Fed (in exchange for Special Drawing Rights), BOJ would accommodate lower interest rates, and a further decline of the dollar would be "counterproductive."[88] Treasury reinforced this policy stance with state-ments by Baker during the following weeks.

The success of the dollar support policy set the stage for the rebound of the currency that occurred in the middle of the year. Driven by the renewed tightening of American monetary policy and favorable trade numbers, the appreciation of the dollar sparked speculation in the United States of an election-year conspiracy among the finance ministries and central banks to promote the election of George Bush as president.[89]

For reasons of trade and security policy, many Japanese officials perceived an interest in Republican control of the US presidency. Some form of trade legislation had been assured of passage through the Congress when the Senate switched to Democratic control in 1987.[90] The feared Gephardt amendment had lost favor after the stock market crash. But the final contents of the trade act remained unresolved. The US 1988 elections provided a strong incentive to keep interest rates low and capital flowing eastward across the Pacific.

Japan continued to support the dollar and capital flow to the United States with monetary policy and intervention, as it had in 1987. BOJ bought about $10 billion over the course of the year. Relative stability of

---

88. *Wall Street Journal*, 14 January 1988.

89. David Hale, "US Economic Outlook and Monetary Policy," testimony before the Senate Committee on Banking, Housing, and Urban Affairs, *Federal Reserve's Second Monetary Policy Report for 1988*, 12 and 13 July 1988; Jeffrey E. Garten, "How Bonn, Tokyo Slyly Help Bush," *New York Times*, 21 July 1988; *Washington Post*, 22 July 1988; Irwin M. Stelzer, "The Election Dollar," *The American Spectator*, September 1988, pp. 28–33. In responding to question posed at the above hearings of the Senate Banking Committee, Alan Greenspan denied knowledge of any conspiracy.

90. Trade conflict did not decline with the yen-dollar exchange rate. Measured in real terms, as a percentage of GNP, the Japanese trade and current account surplus peaked in 1986 and declined for four years steadily thereafter. But measured in US dollars—which, though declining in value, were the standard of measurement of the congressional authors of trade legislation—the Japanese global surplus peaked in 1987 and only barely declined in 1988.

the yen-dollar rate favored Republican government in the United States, as it calmed nervous financial markets.

But, as sympathetic as Japan might have been to Republican control of the White House, Japanese policy manifestly did not engineer an increase in the dollar's rate against the yen by anything like the dollar's rise against the D-mark. The dollar peaked at about 135, only 7 percent above its level at the time of the telephone accord of December 1987, and well within the trading range over the previous year. Moreover, to the extent that currency stability was fostered by MOF and BOJ, policy responded to the economic and political interests of Japan, not the United States.

The relative stability of the exchange rate in 1988 was actually something of a disappointment to BOJ officials, who hoped that a weakening of the currency might afford another opportunity to tighten monetary policy. The Bundesbank successfully turned the corner on monetary policy with the benefit of just such a depreciation of the D-mark. A rise in the exchange rate would have enabled BOJ to argue more convincingly to MOF for a discount rate increase. Those hopes were dashed when the yen again appreciated toward its late-1987 highs in autumn 1988. The markets were influenced by open speculation by American economists such as Martin Feldstein that the rate would eventually go to 110 or even 100 (levels not reached until five years later). Despite interest rate increases in the United States and Europe, therefore, both Miyazawa and Sumita ruled out increases in the Japanese discount rate in mid-1988.[91]

American pressure for monetary ease had ceased by this time. The perception is now commonplace in Japan that interest rates were kept at all-time lows throughout 1988 out of deference to the Reagan administration and international cooperation.[92] Secretary Baker's sharp reaction to the slight tightening before the October 1987 crash gives this perception superficial plausibility. But there is no evidence of either overt or covert American pressure on Japan to keep interest rates low once the Fed began raising its own rates in spring 1988. The strength of the dollar against the D-mark and Baker's departure from the Treasury Department at mid-year resolved American concerns about Japanese monetary tightening.

Domestic political events in Japan, by contrast, did reinforce the exchange rate constraint on monetary tightening. Revelations of illegal stock trading began to embroil senior politicians and their aides, Miyazawa

---

91. *JEI Report*, 16 September 1989, p. 4.

92. See, for example, Ryuichiro Tachi et al., *The Mechanism and Economic Effects of Asset Price Fluctuations* (Tokyo: Ministry of Finance, Institute for Fiscal and Monetary Policy, April 1993), pp. 64–65.

Table 4.2   Japan: government budget balances

Year	Central government[a]		General government	
	Trillion yen	Percent GNP	Trillion yen	Percent GNP
1980	−14.5	−6.0	−10.6	−4.4
1981	−13.0	−5.0	−9.5	−3.7
1982	−13.8	−5.1	−9.5	−3.5
1983	−13.8	−4.9	−8.5	−3.0
1984	−13.3	−4.4	−6.6	−2.2
1985	−11.7	−3.6	−2.6	−0.8
1986	−10.9	−3.3	−3.7	−1.1
1987	−9.2	−2.6	−0.7	−0.2
1988	−8.3	−2.2	5.6	1.5
1989	−7.7	−1.9	9.6	2.4
1990	−8.5	−2.0	11.5	2.7
1991	−6.2	−1.4	11.8	2.6
1992	−5.6	−1.2	11.7	2.5

a. Central government refers to the general account budget and includes the Fiscal Investment and Loan Program (FILP); general government includes budget balances for the central and local governments, and social security fund.

Sources: OECD, *OECD Economic Surveys*; *Japan,* various issues.

first among them. Because the finance minister and other senior politicians were distracted, BOJ could not initiate the *nemawashi* (consensus building) required to push through an increase of the discount rate. Without help from external quarters, BOJ was left to fret over the effects of continued monetary ease on asset prices.

It was becoming clear in the meantime that the Japanese economy would weather the effects of yen appreciation, trade adjustment, and stock market crash. The economic contraction that had characterized the first quarter of 1986 proved to be the exception rather than a harbinger of things to come. Domestic demand rose impressively, by 5 and 7.5 percent in 1987 and 1988, offsetting the contractionary effect of the decline in the surplus, to yield GNP growth of 4.2 and 5.7 percent.

The special adjustment measures and supplemental budgets notwithstanding, the fiscal deficit of the central government continued to fall (table 4.2). At 3.6 percent of GNP in 1985, the deficit fell to 2.2 percent in 1988. The general government budget balance shifted from a deficit of 0.8 percent of GNP to a *surplus* of 1.5 percent in those same years. Monetary policy thus offset the fiscal contraction and sustained domestic demand.

Summary

Private-sector opposition to the strong yen drove the Japanese authorities to resist currency appreciation. Private pressure on the political system was so powerful that MOF was compelled to try to limit the yen's rise unilaterally, before the ministry had secured American cooperation.

Owing to financial market liberalization, Japanese authorities placed less emphasis on capital controls and more emphasis on adjustments in domestic monetary policy as an instrument to try to achieve their exchange rate objectives.

Japan responded to the yen appreciation with a mix of loose monetary and tight fiscal policy, exactly the opposite of the mix pursued by the first Reagan administration. American officials pressed LDP politicians and MOF for expansionary domestic demand. Japanese officials responded with supplemental budgets that contained far less real stimulus than advertised. The dominant trend in Japanese fiscal policy was contractionary. In other words, MOF successfully deflected the pressure for extra demand onto BOJ and monetary policy.

The Japanese policy mix had two important consequences that concern this analysis. First, tight fiscal and easy monetary policy provided a favorable macroeconomic environment for corporate adaptation to the high yen. Low interest rates facilitated industrial investment, which surged in the late 1980s and provided another round of productivity increases that would manifest in renewed growth in the trade surplus in the early 1990s.

Second, the policy mix produced a dramatic surge in the price of financial and real estate assets in Japan. The Nikkei 225 Stock Average rose from 13,113 at the end of 1985 to 26,000 just before the crash of October 1987. The Nikkei broke the 30,000 level by the end of 1988 and would reach 38,915 at the end of 1989. Commercial real estate prices in the Tokyo metropolitan area would rise to 2.7 times their 1985 levels in 1990. Residential housing prices would rise to 2.3 times their 1985 level. At the end of 1990, real estate assets in Japan would be valued at four times the value of all of the land assets in the United States![93] The asset price bubble would have profound effects on the Japanese economy, Japan's foreign economic relations, and the management of the exchange rate.

Phase 4: Yen Defense, 1989–90

During 1989 and 1990, the external monetary problem confronting Japan reversed itself dramatically. Japanese authorities grappled with the problem of yen weakness, a relatively rare occurrence, rather than currency strength. Their response revealed a fundamental adjustment of exchange rate preferences.

Prelude: 1989

The international and domestic environments of Japan's exchange rate policy changed in important ways at the end of the 1980s. First, with the

---

93. Tachi et al., *The Mechanism and Economic Effects of Asset Price Fluctuations*, pp. 1–2.

advent of the Bush administration in the United States, Treasury Secretary Nicholas F. Brady appeared to be uninterested in currency management. The markets questioned the American commitment to currency stability just as the Federal Reserve raised US interest rates further to stem inflation. Further impetus for dollar appreciation was provided by signs of definite improvement in the US trade deficit with Japan.

Second, the government of Prime Minister Takeshita was rocked by the Recruit Cosmos scandal. When it was revealed that a former aide had profited illegally from trading in shares of that company, Miyazawa was forced to resign as finance minister in early December 1988. The revelations expanded throughout the winter and spring of 1989, touching virtually all the senior figures in the LDP, as well as other political parties. Finally, in April, Takeshita himself resigned to take responsibility for widespread loss of confidence in the Japanese political system, his popularity at a record low for a sitting Japanese prime minister. (This was only the beginning of a series of nonstop political money scandals that created widespread disillusionment with the Japanese political system, a strong movement for political reform, and a reorganization of political parties beginning in 1993.)

In an election in mid-July 1989, the party lost its majority in the upper house, the House of Councillors, for the first time since the creation of the LDP in the mid-1950s. Sosuke Uno, Takeshita's successor as prime minister, was forced to resign after less than two months in office. He was followed by Toshiki Kaifu, a one-time education minister, member of the small Komoto faction, and virtually unknown abroad. Prime Minister Kaifu was not expected to last in office beyond the selection of a new party president in the autumn. Disarray among the political parties and disillusionment of the public at large was compounded by the death of Emperor Hirohito in January 1989.

These economic and political events placed downward pressure on the yen, a tendency exacerbated by the lack of insulation of monetary policy from political influence. Beginning the year in the low 120s, at which MOF and BOJ intervened again, the yen fell to 152 by mid-June. For the first time since the beginning of the yen stabilization policy in early 1986, weakness rather than strength was the problem confronting Japanese exchange rate policy.

American trade pressure continued even after the passage of the 1988 trade act. The US Trade Representative designated Japan as a "priority foreign country" under Super 301 in 1989, which led indirectly to a series of negotiations under the title Structural Impediments Initiative (SII), concluded in mid-1990. During 1989, the Japanese external accounts showed substantial improvements in dollar terms. In real terms, the improvement was particularly impressive, with the current account and trade surpluses falling to about 2 and 3 percent of GNP, respectively. But, though members of Congress were temporarily at bay on the trade issue, and the Bush administration did not want trade conflict, Japan did not want a weakening of the yen that could spoil the improvement. MITI was thus more worried about restimulating foreign recrimination over trade than it was about the immediate competitiveness of Japanese companies, which had begun to adjust to the high yen, and urged MOF to defend the currency in the 140s.[94]

Growth and corporate profits were strong, despite the depressive effects of the previous yen appreciation. Japanese GNP, after having grown by 5.7 percent in 1988, was growing 4.9 percent in 1989. Rather than stimulating growth, arguably, the priority target for policy was restraining inflation. Incipient price pressures were emerging in 1989: oil prices were firming, wage increases were expected to be 2 percent above those in 1988, and the 3 percent consumption tax began its phased implementation in April.[95] The prices of financial and real estate assets continued to skyrocket upward. On the international side, Japan had benefited from the appreciation of the yen through lower import prices for several years. But the weakness of the yen in 1989 threatened to reverse this effect and to compound domestic price pressures.

MOF and BOJ therefore fought with determined intervention to halt the depreciation of the yen. Immediately after the G-7 meeting in early April, at which the yen stood at 132–133, well within the post–stock market crash trading range, they *sold* large amounts of dollars in a concerted action with other central banks.[96] For the first time since autumn 1985, therefore, Japan intervened against the dollar.[97] Japanese authorities' conversion to the new exchange rate levels had been swift and complete. MOF and BOJ now sold dollars to keep the yen from moving below levels that Miyazawa had fought so hard to keep the yen from appreciating above as recently as November and December 1987!

As the yen depreciated further, in spring 1989, Japanese authorities continued to sell large quantities of dollars in May and again in June. In June, MOF applied administrative guidance to insurance companies, pension funds, and commercial banks to stop speculation against the yen.[98]

---

94. Jiji Press Service, 16 May 1989.

95. *JEI Report*, 10 March 1989.

96. *New York Times*, 3 April 1989; *JEI Report*, 7 April 1989, p. 2. Up until this point, Japanese authorities had continued to buy substantial amounts of dollars, raising international reserves to over $100 billion in April 1989.

97. At this point, the nominal effective exchange rate the yen was about 50 percent above its average 1985 level and the real effective exchange rate was more than 30 percent above its average 1985 level.

98. *Euromoney*, September 1989, pp. 108–09; *JEI Report*, 23 June 1989, p. 2, and 6 October 1989, p. 4; Kyodo News Service, 14 and 15 June 1989.

Upon taking office, Prime Minister Uno instructed MOF to take steps to stabilize the yen. Finance Minister Tatsuo Murayama, renewing his pledge to act resolutely to support the Japanese currency, warned speculators that they might regret buying dollars.[99]

The Bank of Japan, still searching for a way out of the extremely easy monetary stance, became acutely concerned about inflation prospects. Early in the year, therefore, it restarted its behind-the-scenes campaign to raise interest rates. MOF and the other ministries resisted tightening, arguing that inflation had not actually materialized. This time, however, external factors worked in favor of the Japanese central bank. A depreciation of the yen, spawned in part by the tightening of monetary policy in the United States, gave BOJ an important lever in its bargaining with the government over the direction of monetary policy.

In contrast to their reassurances in 1988 that no changes in monetary policy were being contemplated, in 1989 Bank of Japan Governor Sumita and Deputy Governor Mieno repeatedly warned about inflationary tendencies in the economy.[100] The central bank nudged the call rate upward, from its low of about 3.25 percent in June 1988 to over 4.0 in spring 1989. BOJ also sought international endorsement of G-7 meetings for placing inflation fighting at the top of the policy agenda. Sumita hinted that the February G-7 meeting had given tacit approval to an increase in the Japanese discount rate.[101] He headed the Japanese delegation to the G-7 meeting in early April in Washington—which the Recruit scandal prevented Murayama from attending—where he stressed the Japanese commitment to the fight against inflation.[102]

MOF and BOJ offered public interpretations of exchange rate developments to suit their preferences on domestic monetary policy. Although the mid-130s was a mere 8 percent above the telephone-accord level, BOJ characterized these exchange rates as undesirable, not justified by the economic fundamentals, and requiring a discount rate increase should the yen depreciate further. Most MOF officials resisted an increase in the discount rate. They suggested that the yen at this level was in fact acceptable, not an excessive depreciation, and did not warrant an interest rate increase.[103] BOJ was also opposed by MITI and EPA on the question of the discount rate increase.[104]

---

99. Kyodo News Service, 15 June 1989; *New York Times*, 19 May 1989.

100. *JEI Report*, 10 March 1989, pp. 2–3; Kyodo News Service, 20 and 25 April and 1 May 1989.

101. *JEI Report*, 10 March 1989.

102. IMF, press review, 3 April 1989.

103. Kyodo News Service, 8, 9, 10, 12, 17, 18, 19, and 25 May 1989.

104. Asahi News Service, 31 March 1989; *Financial Times*, 24 May 1989.

But, rather than taking a unified stand on monetary policy, the MOF bureaus were split. The Banking Bureau favored the BOJ argument that monetary policy had been too lax, while the International Finance Bureau opposed an increase as internationally uncooperative. The balance of view within MOF shifted, moreover, as officials there also became increasingly concerned about the domestic inflation statistics and the weakness of the yen.[105]

Finally, as the yen fell to 144, its lowest level since the stock market crash, MOF relented. Sumita announced a discount rate increase of 75 basis points, to 3.25 percent—the first increase since March 1980. Thus began a series of interest rate increases in Japan, which continued until the end of 1990. BOJ had waited a long time for reinforcement from the exchange rate in its domestic struggle over monetary policy, but now finally succeeded in turning the corner toward a tighter stance, one year later than did the Bundesbank.

But the continuing strength of the dollar necessitated further intervention. When the G-7 met in Washington in late September 1989, on the fourth anniversary of the Plaza Agreement, the yen was at 145. In a major, concerted effort to cap the dollar at this point, central banks, including BOJ, intervened after the meeting.[106] When the Bundesbank announced another interest rate increase, consistent with the effort, the new finance minister, Ryutaro Hashimoto, said that Japan would not follow and that no change in Japanese monetary policy was being contemplated for the near future.[107]

BOJ continued to push market rates upward independently in the meantime, however. The call rate, 4.1 percent at the time of the May discount rate increase, was 5.6 percent at the end of September, a large 2.35 percent spread above the discount rate. MOF also initiated negotiations with the Ministry of Post and Telecommunications over an (0.37 percent) increase in fixed-term postal savings deposit rates (which necessitated adjustment with discount rate increases to prevent flight to alternative accounts). In mid-October, Sumita announced another increase in the discount rate, to 3.75 percent, citing the weakness of the yen, at 145, and an increase in domestic prices as the reasons for the move.[108]

---

105. Wholesale prices in May were 3.4 percent over a year earlier. Import prices in May were 10.6 percent above a year earlier and 3.5 percent above those of April. *JEI Report*, 23 June 1989, p. 2.

106. Between April and October Japan sold roughly $20 billion.

107. *JEI Report*, 20 October 1989, p. 1.

108. *New York Times*, 12 October 1989. Hashimoto declared the yen appreciation that followed to be "not bad" for the Japanese economy. Kyodo News Service, 16 October 1989.

Yen Plunge: 1990

The tightening of Japanese monetary policy might have revived confidence in the yen. However, the Liberal Democratic Party appeared to be weak during the approach to the lower house elections. The prospect of the LDP losing control of both houses of the Diet to a coalition headed by the Japan Socialist Party, coupled with the turn in monetary policy, undermined the confidence of the Japanese stock market. Rather than bolstering the yen, therefore, monetary tightening in 1989 was viewed as too little, too late. A public dispute between the Ministry of Finance and BOJ over monetary policy compounded the general lack of confidence. Electoral politics, bureaucratic conflict, falling confidence, and capital outflow conspired to reverse, temporarily, the appreciation of the yen that had occurred since the Plaza.

Yasushi Mieno replaced Sumita as BOJ governor in mid-December 1989 and pressed for an increase in the discount rate with determination of which Haruo Maekawa would have been proud. A consensus on the rate increase had been nearly achieved in mid-December, when the move was leaked to the press. Hashimoto, who reportedly had not yet personally approved the measure, was angry at what he thought was a BOJ attempt at a fait accompli.[109] The finance minister called a press conference to emphatically reject the need for such an increase.[110]

The public conflict was widely viewed as a contest of wills between Hashimoto and the new career BOJ governor, and a test of the independence of the central bank. BOJ prevailed in this round and announced a discount rate increase from 3.75 to 4.25 percent on 25 December. In the process, though, the angry Hashimoto openly questioned BOJ's and Mieno's institutional authority on the matter of discount rate decisions, baldly flouting the public fiction that such matters were the province of BOJ alone. The dispute required the intercession of Miyazawa and Takeshita, Hashimoto's faction leader, on Mieno's behalf.[111] The open conflict undermined the beneficial effect of the interest rate increase on the exchange market's confidence.

---

109. MOF and BOJ had reportedly agreed not to leak agreements on the discount rate. Foreign officials had complained of the standard procedure by which a few Tokyo bankers were permitted to trade on what amounted to inside information on tips of discount rate changes. The ban, second, represented a truce between the two bureaucracies, as leaks had become part of their bargaining strategy over rate changes. It is unclear which bureaucracy was responsible for the December leaks. See Bill Chapman, "Tokyo: Is Monetary Policy Out of Sync at the Top?" *The International Economy*, June/July 1990, pp. 64–66.

110. Kyodo News Service, 19 and 20 December 1989.

111. Henny Sender, "A Prince Comes of Age at the BOJ," *Institutional Investor*, April 1990.

Not to be dissuaded, Mieno inveighed against the asset-price inflation during early 1990. BOJ warned against insidious inflationary pressures in the Japanese economy, and it continued to raise the call rate.[112] Rumors circulated that the Bank of Japan was laying the groundwork for another rate increase. MOF officials and others continued, therefore, to roundly criticize the BOJ governor—to the point where his tenure in office became the subject of open speculation. Weakness in the financial markets spurred capital outflow, weighed on the yen in January and February, and therefore stimulated the concern of the International Finance Bureau. Makoto Utsumi, now vice minister for international affairs, sharply criticized Mieno and BOJ for risking further destabilization of the markets.[113]

Hashimoto and officials at MOF held BOJ at bay through the election for the lower house in late February. Hashimoto was not eager to aggravate financial instability during the run-up to the election. Key MOF officials were genuinely unpersuaded of the need for further tightening on inflation grounds and were concerned that a discount rate increase would create problems for the financial institutions they regulated. But BOJ's suspicions about incipient inflation were supported by the emerging statistics.[114] Therefore, a full 1 percent increase was announced on 20 March, to 5.25 percent, after the yen had again fallen back through the 150 level.

As in the previous December, the move failed to impress the currency market, which had substantially discounted the news. News of the rate increase knocked shares on the Tokyo stock exchange down below 30,000 on the Nikkei average, a loss of 23 percent from the beginning of the year to the third week in March. (This was only the beginning of what would prove to be a long process of asset-price deflation.)

The LDP had managed to cling to its lower house majority in the parliamentary elections in mid-February, but the yen had not rallied to this news, either. As in 1989, MOF and BOJ together waged a verbal war against the low yen.[115] They sold an estimated $12.5 billion from January through April to support the yen, moreover, in addition to tightening monetary conditions. MOF directed life insurance companies to stop

---

112. *Financial Times*, 2 February 1990.

113. Sender, "A Prince Comes of Age at the BOJ"; *Financial Times*, 9 March 1990.

114. Consumer and wholesale prices in the first quarter of 1990 were 3.4 and 3.7 percent above their year-earlier levels, the largest increases in several years. And the money supply (M2+CDs) continued to grow at almost 12 percent.

115. At the 146 level, Hashimoto pledged to do his utmost to defend the currency. Mieno said that the currency's undervaluation should be corrected. Kyodo News Service, 16 January, and 1 and 5 February 1989, respectively.

dumping yen for dollars. The yen nonetheless fell to 160 at the end of March 1990 with the fall in equity prices.

Rattled by the sharp fall of the stock market, their unilateral yen-support measures having failed, Hashimoto and MOF sought help from the US Treasury and the G-7. Given their record of dollar support, by far the strongest among the G-7, Japanese officials had reason to expect sympathy from the US Treasury. The harm that yen depreciation would inflict on US competitiveness reinforced this expectation. But exchange rate management was not a priority for Secretary Brady, who was widely perceived at that time to be disengaged from international issues in general. Treasury furthermore was in the process of bargaining with MOF over financial liberalization in the SII talks. MOF was thus told that the stock market plunge and yen depreciation was a Japanese, not a bilateral, problem.[116]

Utsumi asked for greater cooperation at a G-7 deputies meeting in London at the end of February.[117] As the Nikkei fell below 30,000 in late March, Hashimoto met with Brady to ask for his help. At a meeting of the G-7 ministers and governors in early April in Paris, focused primarily on Japanese financial market instability, the Japanese delegation proposed a coordinated interest rate move to stabilize the currencies.[118]

The US side, though it intervened in the foreign exchange market, withheld unequivocal support for the yen. Rather than endorsing Hashimoto's statement that the yen was undervalued against the dollar, Brady stressed the need for action on SII.[119] Brady in fact positively denied that the yen was too weak, at almost 160, in testimony before Congress.[120] Hashimoto and Utsumi tried to make the most of the tepid communiqués, arguing to the Japanese press that the yen had been "singled out" for support and that the G-7 agreed that this level was a problem.[121] But

116. *New York Times*, 25 March 1990.

117. *International Herald Tribune*, 1 March 1990.

118. *Wall Street Journal*, 9 April 1990. Japanese officials warned, at a second G-7 meeting in Washington in early May, that further increases in the Japanese discount rate could spark a competitive spiral of monetary tightening.

119. Kyodo News Service, 26 March 1990.

120. IMF, press review, 18 April 1990. Undersecretary Mulford and Assistant Secretary for International Affairs Charles Dallara expressed more concern about the exchange rate. See *Washington Post*, 20 April 1990.

121. The May communiqué read: "The Ministers and Governors . . . noted the yen had stabilized since their meeting in Paris, but remained of the view that the present level may have undesirable consequences for the global adjustment process." US Treasury Department, press release, Washington, 6 May 1990. The communiqué notably omitted any reference to measures to raise the yen.

Treasury Undersecretary David Mulford openly contradicted the Japanese interpretation of the May communiqué, saying that the G-7 stance had not in fact changed since the Paris meeting.[122]

A multilateral or bilateral effort would arguably have prevented this depreciation of the yen, generally regarded as undesirable from a policy standpoint. Japan's policy of unilateral support was manifestly insufficient to prevent it. The yen's lowest value in nominal terms was comparable to that at the time of the autumn 1986 Baker-Miyazawa accord. Owing to the fall of the Berlin Wall and speculation over the future unification of Germany, furthermore, the yen had fallen substantially against the D-mark as well. And it had fallen against the Asian currencies too. In real effective terms, therefore, the yen had temporarily nearly fallen back to its level prior to the Plaza Agreement![123] In light of the renewed expansion of the Japanese trade surplus that would ensue in the following years (discussed below), the failure to support the yen represents an unfortunate missed opportunity for monetary cooperation.

Meanwhile, BOJ officials continued their campaign for tighter monetary policy, spurred on by double-digit growth of the broad money supply that continued into the summer. At the end of August, the discount rate was raised for the fifth time in 15 months, to 6.0 percent.[124] MOF approved this move despite the further fall in the Nikkei average to below 24,000 in the third week of August. BOJ also directed the 12 city banks to reduce the volume of lending. The Iraqi invasion of Kuwait had occurred in early August and the resulting increase in oil prices amplified concerns about domestic inflation and the relative weakness of the yen as rationales for further tightening.

Whereas American monetary policy began to ease immediately after the Iraqi invasion of Kuwait in August 1990, Japanese monetary policy remained tight throughout 1990 and into 1991. Divergent monetary trends in the United States and Japan produced a fundamental change in the interest rate differential. Before BOJ began to tighten in 1989, the differential had favored dollar-denominated assets throughout the 1980s. But by autumn 1990 the differential in real interest rates favored Japanese government bonds by as much as 3 percent.[125] From April through Sep-

---

122. Yomiuri News Service, 10 May 1990.

123. During the month of May the yen averaged only 6.2 percent above the 1985 annual average. International Monetary Fund, *International Financial Statistics*, August 1990, p. 309.

124. BOJ and MOF reportedly agreed on yet another ODR increase in early August. When Iraq invaded Kuwait, that move was postponed. BOJ instead began to raise market rates again. News services, 30 August 1990.

125. *Financial Times*, 19 October 1990; *Wall Street Journal*, 2 November 1990.

tember, accordingly, Japan's capital outflow fell to $26 billion, from $47.3 billion during the previous six months.[126]

The yen responded accordingly, putting a definitive end to the period of weakness and the need for support. From mid-August through mid-October, the yen rose from 150 to 124.50, near its previous record high, and remained in the vicinity of 130. Neither Japanese nor US authorities intervened during the rise. The strength of the yen relieved concerns by BOJ and others about oil price–induced inflation.

Within merely a few months, yen strength, weak stock markets, and expectations of reduced growth induced the other bureaucracies to press BOJ to reverse its monetary tightening. When the Nikkei average fell to nearly 20,000 at the beginning of October, Hashimoto called on the central bank to ease monetary policy as part of a package of stock market–support measures.[127] The director general of the Economic Planning Agency, Hideyuki Aizawa, criticized the tight monetary policy and called for a discount rate cut.[128]

Having fought so hard to tighten policy, however, BOJ refused to yield to these pressures.[129] When the Federal Reserve reduced the US discount rate in mid-December, BOJ officials said Japan would not follow.[130] The Japanese central bank maintained this stance through several additional Fed rate cuts and well into 1991.

Summary

The yen defense episode reveals, first, the extraordinary transformation of exchange rate preferences in Japan during the second half of the 1980s. The first and second major appreciations of the yen, in the early and late 1970s, were fully reversed in real terms by a combination of productivity increases and reversals of the nominal exchange rate. But the reversal of the third realignment of the yen was firmly resisted by Japanese authorities. This reflected a greater ability to contend with the higher yen, to be sure, through increased domestic investment and productivity, foreign direct investment, and offshore sourcing. But, during 1991–92, the yen remained 20 to 30 percent above the pre-Plaza level in

---

126. *Financial Times*, 3–4 November 1990.

127. *Washington Post*, 2 October 1990.

128. Kyodo News Service, 11 and 14 December, 1990.

129. Kyodo News Service, 15 October and 28 November 1990. Mieno said that the economy, which had grown at an annualized 4.1 percent in the third quarter, was growing slightly too fast for price stability, and that a mild slowdown, which the bank did not forecast, would not induce BOJ to cut rates without an easing of inflationary pressures. Associated Press, 18 December 1990.

130. Associated Press, 19 December 1990.

real effective terms, at which Japanese industry, politicians, and bureaucrats were quite content.

Second, the acceptance of the high yen was not accompanied by an acceptance of high fluctuations or a passive posture on the part of Japanese authorities. Senior Japanese officials continued to be highly engaged on exchange rate policy, as during earlier years, and used the full panoply of instruments. They issued statements that indicated that MOF and BOJ had clear views about the appropriate level for the yen and indicated what levels they intended to support and defend. More important, Japanese authorities also used generous amounts of intervention, and used changes in monetary policy to support the exchange rate objectives.

Administrative guidance, third, continued to number among those instruments. MOF had given general guidance in previous years on the desirability of investing in US Treasury securities at the quarterly bond auction in New York, for example. In spring 1989 and summer 1990, MOF gave crisis-specific guidance to dampen speculation against the yen, just as it had in 1987 to dampen speculation in favor of the yen.

The 1989–90 episode, fourth, illustrates the scope and limits of BOJ's autonomy on domestic monetary policy. BOJ's successful tightening of monetary policy hinged on two things. First, it hinged on persuading officials in MOF that a tightening of monetary policy was indeed necessary. Second, BOJ required support from foreign exchange markets to tighten. Before the yen weakened, the Japanese central bank had been unsuccessful in persuading MOF to tighten monetary policy. The fall of the yen was important in persuading MOF of the necessity for discount rate increases.

Phase 5: Yen Strength Restored, 1991–92

With the yen's strength restored, exchange rate matters were not a particularly pressing issue for Japan during 1991–92. The dollar breached previous record lows against the D-mark in early 1991, at the beginning of the Persian Gulf War, prompting a round of G-7 intervention to support it. But the yen at that time remained comfortably in the 120s and Japanese authorities therefore remained on the sidelines. The 1991–92 period is most revealing for the politics of domestic monetary policy.

During this period the Japanese domestic economy slowed dramatically. The asset-price bubble had been definitively pricked. The problem confronting policymakers was now the reverse: preventing the asset-price deflation from going too far. With real estate and stock prices tumbling, much of the collateral on which financial institutions made loans during the late 1980s disappeared. The restructuring of balance sheets on the part of Japanese corporations and financial institutions exacerbated the weakness of financial markets. The Nikkei resumed its downward slide, bottoming out below 15,000 in autumn 1992. Japan's adherence to the Basel Accord on capital adequacy reinforced the downward spiral: falling stock prices reduced the capital of Japanese banks under the accord's accounting convention and constrained their lending activities.

The fall in the stock market and the weakness of domestic demand created strong and continuing pressures on BOJ to ease monetary policy and, once BOJ began to ease in July 1991, to ease faster. Pressure for interest rate cuts came from all directions: politicians, businessmen, and bankers. In April 1992, LDP kingpin Shin Kanemaru said that interest rates should be reduced even if it required removing the BOJ governor.[131]

Governor Mieno publicly and vociferously defied these pressures. He solemnly declared at several points during the process of reducing rates, such as in November 1991, that BOJ would cut interests rates no further. But Mieno nevertheless recanted in the face of widely expressed discontent. From July 1991 to July 1992, BOJ reduced the discount rate five times, from 6.0 to 3.25 percent. The central bank reduced the call rate from a peak of above 8.0 percent in early 1991 to about 4.0 percent in late 1992 (figure 4.4).

The slowing of the Japanese economy combined with the lagged effects of the weakness of the yen during 1989–90 to cause a renewed increase in the external surplus (figure 4.1). The fiscal 1992 trade surplus, over $111 billion, became the largest surplus ever registered by any country in dollar terms. As the only major, industrialized surplus country in the world, and the country with the biggest nominal imbalance, Japan was truly exceptional.

Japan became the target of American pressures on trade policy once again as a result of this surplus and the persistence of the bilateral imbalance. President Bush, in an effort to demonstrate that his foreign policy prowess could yield benefits for American jobs as his reelection campaign approached, traveled to Tokyo in January 1992 to press for greater access to Japanese markets in particular sectors. The president brought American automobile executives with him to underscore his priorities. Prime Minister Kiichi Miyazawa, who had assumed office in November 1991, and his government considered their response to American pressure on the eve of Bush's arrival.

With Japan's global surplus soaring, a yen appreciation was arguably the correct solution, and indeed the least costly solution for Japan. The future Clinton administration would successfully encourage an appreciation of the yen during the first half of 1993. Had Miyazawa and Bush agreed to promote an appreciation of the yen in early 1992, the two countries might well have avoided, and would have certainly forestalled

---

131. *Nikkei Weekly*, 11 April 1992.

or moderated, the conflict that plagued the US-Japan relationship in 1993 and 1994. But Miyazawa and Finance Minister Tsutomu Hata did not offer a joint statement on yen appreciation as a substitute for trade concessions during the Bush trip. Instead, the Japanese side agreed to purchases in the automobile and other sectors, the compliance with which would become a bone of contention with the Clinton administration.

The Miyazawa cabinet sought to boost growth with a large supplemental budget during 1992. Advertised as 10.7 trillion yen, the package would have amounted to 2.3 percent of GNP. But, as with the supplemental budgets of 1986 and 1987, there was less stimulus in this budget than met the eye. Though the real stimulus was substantial indeed, it remained small in the broad scheme of restrictive Japanese fiscal policy. The central government in Japan ran a deficit of 1.4 percent in 1991 and almost 1.2 percent in 1992. But the general government, including the social security account, ran surpluses of 2.6 percent in 1991 and 2.5 percent in 1992 (table 4.2).

Japanese growth, a healthy 4.5 percent in 1991, slumped to 1.5 percent in 1992. Forecasts for even slower growth continued into 1993, notwithstanding another supplemental budget.[132] The renewed appreciation of the yen in the first half of 1993, spawned in part by statements of the new Clinton administration, thus came when the Japanese economy was in the trough of the business cycle. Remarkably, Japanese authorities nonetheless accepted the appreciation of the yen into record territory of 110–120. Above the 110 level, MOF and BOJ intervened to try to prevent the yen from rising further. Once that attempt proved to be unsuccessful, however, Japanese authorities did not seek to drive the currency back down and the exchange rate rested between 100 and 110 for much of the remainder of the year.

Conclusions

The organization of the private sector and the structure of government institutions in Japan rendered external monetary policy responsive (or susceptible) to societal pressures. Private actors pressed the government very strongly to oppose the appreciation of the yen during the realignments of the early 1970s, late 1970s, and mid-1980s. During most of the postwar era, as well, politicians and Ministry of Finance bureaucrats dominated the Bank of Japan not only on exchange rate policy but also on domestic monetary policy. The institutional subordination of BOJ provided a powerful channel through which private-sector preferences

---

132. For a useful discussion of the supplemental budgets of fiscal 1992 and 1993, see Jan VanDenBerg, "Japanese Stimulus: Truth and Advertising," *International Economic Insights*, July/August 1993, pp. 2–4.

regarding the exchange rate were transmitted into policy outcomes. Politicians and MOF responded with the full panoply of instruments at their disposal. Some of these tools had only transitional or fading impact; others, such as easing monetary policy, had a more lasting effect on the exchange rate.

During the 1950s and 1960s, exchange rate policy was an integral part of a national strategy of export-stimulated industrial development and economic growth. When balance-of-payments surpluses emerged, the Japanese government clung tenaciously to the 360 yen-for-dollar parity. Not only did Japan refuse to alter the exchange rate under the Bretton Woods regime—in contrast, as we shall see, to Germany's two revaluations of the Deutsche mark—but the government maintained the 360 rate for several trading days even after the parity was clearly defunct.

During the 20 years since the breakdown of the Bretton Woods regime, the Japanese government has sought stability in the nominal exchange rate.[133] MOF and BOJ were not always successful in limiting fluctuations of the yen. But the *objective* of policy was clear—stability—and Japanese authorities pursued that goal with much greater intensity than did American authorities. Because the dominant trend in the value of the yen since the early 1970s has been upward, the pursuit of stability generally, though not always, entailed resistance to appreciation.

The period surrounding the Plaza Agreement is a brief exception to this pattern of seeking stability. Faced with unprecedented protectionist pressure in the US Congress, Japanese policy actively sought an upward realignment of the yen. Notably, however, Japanese preferences for maintaining a strong export position did not change. Rather, the Japanese calculus as to how to limit the damage to their global market position simply shifted. Cooperation with the second Reagan administration to raise the yen was the least undesirable solution to the political problem on trade policy within the United States at that time. Had the Japanese government pursued an appreciation even after the United States was satisfied, we might have had to conclude that the basic competitiveness orientation of Japanese exchange rate preferences had fundamentally changed as early as 1985. To the contrary, though, after only a moderate appreciation and long before trade protectionism in the US Congress was defanged, the Japanese government reverted to resisting yen appreciation in March 1986 out of traditional concerns for competitiveness.

In their effort to maintain exchange rate stability, MOF and BOJ em-

---

133. In addition to the policy history in the previous section, see David J. Green, "Exchange Rate Policy and Intervention in Japan," *Keizai-Shirin* (The Hosei University Economic Review) 57 (1989): 129–67; Henrik Schmiegelow, "Japan's Exchange Rate Policy: Policy Targets, Nonpolicy Variables, and Discretionary Adjustment," in *Japan's Response to Crisis and Change in the World Economy*, Michele Schmiegelow, ed. (Armonk, NY: M.E. Sharpe, 1986), and works cited therein, n. 25.

ployed the full range of direct policy instruments: declarations, intervention, capital controls, and administrative guidance. As capital controls were eased, MOF and BOJ sought to stabilize the exchange rate increasingly through changes in domestic monetary policy. Indeed, Japanese monetary policy coincides closely with exchange rate developments over the last 25 years.[134] As figure 4.6 shows, the four troughs in the official discount rate, during 1972–73, 1978–79, 1987–89 and 1992–93, occurred during the four major appreciations of the yen.

Fundamentally, Japanese pursuit of exchange rate stability in nominal terms implied a deliberate policy of depreciating the currency in real terms. The hallmark of the Japanese postwar economy is its high rate of national savings and investment, characteristics that were positively encouraged by government policy. Because productivity in traded goods rose spectacularly, as a result the yen's real rate declined during the fixed-rate regime. Moreover, despite large fluctuations after the switch to floating rates, the long-term competitiveness of Japanese industry was sustained. The real value of the yen in summer 1985 was almost exactly that at the advent of flexible rates![135]

In the late 1980s, though, Japanese exchange rate preferences and policy changed remarkably. Currency rates that had been firmly resisted as the yen was appreciating in 1986 and 1987 were firmly, and in time successfully, defended as the yen depreciated in 1989 and 1990. Along with acceptance of and support for the higher yen, MOF and BOJ moderated their objections to the international use of the yen. This shift in preferences was confirmed by Japanese authorities' acceptance of the appreciation of the yen into the 110–120 range, record levels in real effective as well as in nominal bilateral terms. Once the yen appreciated into the 100–110 range despite intervention in 1993, Japanese officials did not actively seek a depreciation. The causes of this departure from the general postwar pattern of policy outcomes, which are related to changes within the private sector, are discussed in chapter 7.

This discussion of Japan will close by considering the pattern of monetary and fiscal policymaking and its relationship to the subordination of the central bank. When pressured from abroad to stimulate domestic demand in the second half of the 1980s, Japan loosened monetary policy while continuing to tighten fiscal policy. The government adopted several supplemental budgets with the aim of stimulating the economy. But the stimulus that was provided by one hand was removed by another,

---

134. Ralph C. Bryant calculates that the exchange rate has been more important than domestic output and one-third as important as domestic inflation in the reaction function of BOJ. See "Model Representations of Japanese Monetary Policy," *Monetary and Economic Studies* 9 (September 1991): 11–62, especially p. 51.

135. See, for example, International Monetary Fund, *World Economic Outlook* (1983), p. 125; May 1990, p. 20.

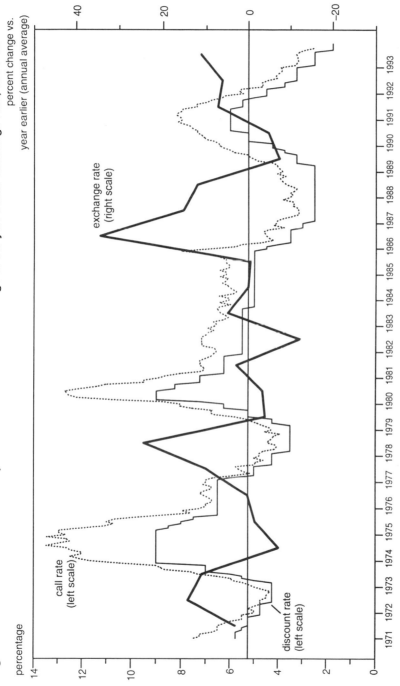

Figure 4.6   Correlation between Japanese interest rates and change in the yen-dollar exchange rate, 1971–93

percentage

percent change vs.
year earlier (annual average)

call rate
(left scale)

discount rate
(left scale)

exchange rate
(right scale)

Source: International Monetary Fund, *International Financial Statistics.*

173

via tight regular budgets and fiscal drag orchestrated by MOF. Contrary to expectations, Prime Minister Nakasone's objective of eliminating issuance of deficit bonds was met on time in fiscal 1990. During the 1980s, in other words, MOF successfully re-immobilized fiscal policy as a tool of international adjustment or countercyclical management. Japan thus returned to the pre-Tanaka (before mid-1970s) period of fiscal rigidity.[136]

Monetary policy, in the final analysis, carried the burden of offsetting the simultaneous contraction of the budget deficit and fall in the current account surplus in the late 1980s. Given the choice between deferring fiscal consolidation or easing monetary policy, MOF officials greatly preferred the latter. Because BOJ was not independent, easing monetary policy was the path of least resistance for LDP politicians. In this sense, MOF's Budget Bureau had greater autonomy from political demands than BOJ. As one inside observer comments, "MOF never compromises to foreigners on fiscal policy, only on monetary policy."

An observation of Shijuro Ogata, the deputy governor of the Bank of Japan until 1986, applies particularly well to Japan's experience in the 1980s:

> If monetary policy alone is excessively and almost exclusively relied upon, . . . too low interest rates with too much liquidity in the face of stagnation and/or currency appreciation may undermine domestic price stability. Nevertheless, because of institutional and political inflexibility of other policies, other more appropriate actions tend to be delayed or insufficient. As a result, monetary policy measures are too often called upon, despite their limited effectiveness and even adverse impact.[137]

Indeed, the expansionary monetary policy of the second half of the 1980s produced an explosion of financial and real estate asset prices in Japan. Japan will be grappling with the consequences of this policy error throughout most of the 1990s.

The asset-price inflation is symptomatic of a historical pattern of Japanese macroeconomic policymaking that stems jointly from the immobilization of fiscal policy and persistent upward pressure on the yen. In response to the first yen realignment, Japanese authorities maintained excessively low interest rates that produced a domestic inflation of goods and asset prices. Notably, because fiscal policy carried a larger share of the burden of stimulating the economy in the late 1970s, monetary policy was not as easy and inflation was more moderate after the second yen realignment.

---

136. Gardner Ackley and Hiromitsu Ishi, "Fiscal, Monetary, and Related Policies," in *Asia's New Giant: How The Japanese Economy Works*, Hugh Patrick and Henry Rosovsky, eds. (Washington: Brookings Institution, 1976), pp. 153–247.

137. Shijuro Ogata, "Central Banking: A Japanese Perspective," in *Industrial Finance and Financial Policy*, Hans R. Stoll, ed. (New York: Quorum Books, 1990) p. 121.

The liberalization of capital controls in the 1980s gave new meaning to the macroeconomic policy mix. The combination of tight fiscal policy and easy monetary policy suppressed the appreciation of the yen during 1986–88.[138] A fiscal expansion, on the other hand, would have reduced capital outflow and put *upward* pressure on the yen. But the monetary expansion placed *downward* pressure on the yen, in addition to safeguarding, indeed advancing, the objective of reducing the budget deficit. The external ramifications of the domestic policy mix therefore strongly influenced the macroeconomic policy preferences of ministries, politicians, and private interests.

External capital liberalization transformed the private-interest politics of fiscal and monetary policy between the 1970s and 1980s. During the second yen realignment in the late 1970s, Japanese business and MITI clamored for a fiscal stimulus. However, because such a stimulus would result in a strengthening of the yen, with the greater capital mobility which prevailed in the 1980s, Japanese business had much less incentive to look to the government budget for stimulus. Notably, *Keidanren* (the Federation of Economic Organizations) was not at the forefront of the campaign for a large supplemental budget in 1987, as it was in 1978.[139] In 1993 and early 1994, Japanese business pressed for fiscal stimulus, but only after interest rates had already been brought to record lows and the country continued to confront a profound domestic recession. Even then the business organizations acquiesced in limitations that MOF placed on stimulus measures.

External financial liberalization added exchange rate and competitiveness considerations to the list of domestic reasons for Japanese business to lobby politicians and the bureaucracy for monetary expansion. Monetary ease, furthermore, facilitated adjustment to the higher yen through investment, whereas fiscal stimulus would deprive the private sector of funds. These incentives, plus the susceptibility of BOJ to outside pressures, made influence attempts on the part of business irresistible.

---

138. Financial liberalization also diverted the inflationary consequences of monetary expansion away from the goods market and toward the asset market.

139. If the objective of reducing the budget deficit could be taken as given, furthermore, the downward pressure on the yen created an additional incentive for Japanese business to encourage capital liberalization.

5

Monetary and Exchange Rate Policymaking in Germany

The Federal Republic of Germany has pursued domestic and external monetary policies under both the fixed and flexible exchange rate regimes that contrast greatly to those of the United States and Japan. German policy was formed in a regional context quite different from that of the other two countries. At the heart of Europe, Germany was a divided country for most of the postwar period, and the Federal Republic was increasingly integrated with its partners within the European Community.

These differences in Germany's regional environment did not preordain the differences in policy outcomes, however. The division of Germany and links to Europe created a unique set of challenges to German policymakers—spillover effects of the macroeconomic policies of Germany's neighbors, regional exchange rate stabilization, and national unification. But this context of policy challenges did not determine the substance of the German policy response. The content of policy was determined largely by the nature of German institutions, specifically the structure of private sector preference formation on exchange rate issues and the independence of the Bundesbank. Each set of challenges produced struggles, sometimes fierce, over policy among the central bank, federal government, ministries, and private actors. The outcomes of these struggles were determined largely by the institutional prerogatives of the protagonists.

As described in chapter 3, the federal government has defined the parameters within which the Bundesbank has operated, domestically and internationally. Over the postwar decades, the federal government established and changed the international monetary regimes to which the central bank was obliged to adhere. At times, such as the creation of the European Monetary System (EMS), the establishment of G-7 cooperation and the negotiations over Economic and Monetary Union (EMU), the Bundesbank resisted international obligations and fought to dissuade the government. But, when it prevailed in these conflicts, be it European monetary integration or German monetary unification, the federal government surrendered the management of currency operations to the Bundesbank, ensuring that the central bank's preferences would be applied.

While negotiating between themselves over external monetary policy, the Bundesbank and the government responded to societal preferences. The German public, as is well known, is inflation averse. German business also strongly prefers exchange rate stability over instability. The organization of the private sector, the relationship between banking and industry, has conditioned German preferences for external monetary stability (discussed in chapter 2). German societal preferences thus held both objectives, domestic price stability and exchange rate stability, with high intensity. It was the unenviable task of the government and Bundesbank to reconcile these preferences when the goals conflicted with one another, as they frequently have over the postwar period.

Some accounts of German policymaking have stressed the unique dedication of Germany to the objective of domestic price stability. This interpretation contains a core of truth; but it would be too simple to argue that the national preference for low inflation determined German exchange rate policy. In its quest to minimize price inflation, Germany has not encouraged or accepted a highly valued D-mark irrespective of competitiveness considerations. Rather, the German preferences for external monetary stability and competitive valuation of the D-mark have competed strongly with the preference for domestic price stability for dominance over exchange rate policy. Of the two objectives, external and internal monetary stability, domestic price stability was generally the higher priority. But exchange rate stability was a very close second priority, and for limited periods of time it occasionally trumped the domestic objective.

Therefore, Germany pursued exchange rate stabilization, insofar as it was practical given the international regime or lack of it, with vigor equal to the pursuit of internal price stability. If economic conditions made the two goals irreconcilable, then German authorities would eventually revalue the Deutsche mark or let it float upward. When monetary policy was targeted toward stabilizing the exchange rate, and internal price stability was jeopardized, Germany would retarget monetary policy toward domestic prices earlier than would Japan, for example, when confronting a similar situation.

Germany accepted an appreciation only as a last resort, however, after great effort to reconcile the two objectives and avoid the dilemma altogether. To stabilize European exchange rates after the end of Bretton

Woods, Germany intervened in foreign exchange markets and encouraged other governments to pursue stability policies. During the same period, at crucial points, Germany applied domestic monetary policy to suppress an appreciation of the D-mark. Germany's use of monetary policy to manage the exchange rate has been less extensive than Japan's but substantially greater than that of the United States.

Germany's external monetary policy has been extraordinarily successful in advancing the nation's economic interests. Owing in large part to that success, manifest in extraordinary trade surpluses at the end of the 1980s, the Federal Republic was able to unify Germany without undermining its international economic position. The division of responsibility between the Bundesbank and the government also served Germany well in international negotiations. German institutions, as discussed below, contributed to the evolution of the EMS as a zone of monetary stability, until the early 1990s, that was effectively anchored by the D-mark. German policymaking structures also helped to deflect, for good or for ill, US pressure for policy adjustments.

The five sections following this introduction present a history of monetary and exchange rate policymaking in Germany. Each section discusses the processes and institutions by which policy is made as well as policy outcomes. The first section treats policymaking under the Bretton Woods regime. The second examines policy under the flexible exchange rate regime, when Germany began to pursue a two-track policy of flexibility with respect to the dollar and stabilization with respect to the European currencies. The third, fourth, and fifth sections review policy during, respectively, German unification, the negotiations over European monetary integration, and the crises in the Exchange Rate Mechanism of the EMS during 1992–93. The final section concluding the chapter summarizes German policy outcomes and the role of institutions and societal organization in producing that pattern.

In October 1993, Germany officially ratified the Treaty on European Union that had been initialed at the Maastricht meeting of the European Council in December 1991. The treaty, which entered into force at the beginning of November 1993, commits the members of the Union (except Britain and, in the case of rejection by referendum, Denmark) to create an EMU including a common currency. The treaty provides a fixed timetable by which monetary union would be achieved, although countries not meeting specified criteria for economic convergence would receive a derogation. As the Maastricht Treaty was being ratified, however, successive crises of currency speculation forced a near unraveling of the Exchange Rate Mechanism of the EMS, calling into question the ability of European governments to abide by the treaty commitments. If the treaty were in fact fully implemented, the currency and institutions of the new European monetary union would supersede and eclipse a German monetary policy.

Figure 5.1   Germany: trade and current account balances, 1950–93

billions of D-marks

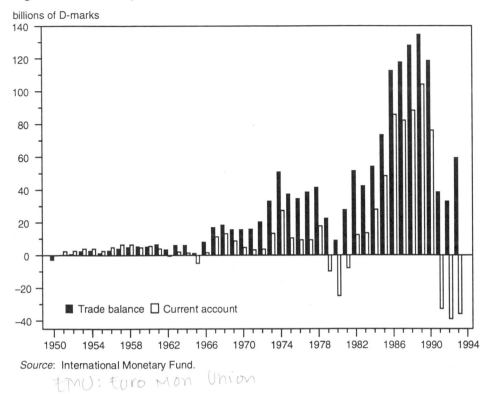

Source: International Monetary Fund.

EMU: Euro Mon Union

By studying German policymaking and EMU in the meantime, we can anticipate some of the problems that could arise in transition to monetary union in Europe. Moreover, because the institutions for the EMU are modeled on German institutions and policy processes, we might also anticipate the future policy behavior of the European monetary union, external as well as internal, by analyzing German institutions in the past.

The Bretton Woods Regime

No period better illustrates Germany's recurring dilemma between internal and external balance than that under the Bretton Woods international monetary regime of par value exchange rates. The solidarity of the bank-industry alliance was at its peak during the early decades of the postwar period, as was its influence in German politics. Also during the 1950s and 1960s, the predominance of the government over exchange rate policy was supreme.

A historical latecomer to industrialization, and defeated in World War II, Germany vigorously rebuilt its export markets. Through investment,

Figure 5.2 Germany: trade and current account balances, 1950–93

percentage of GDP

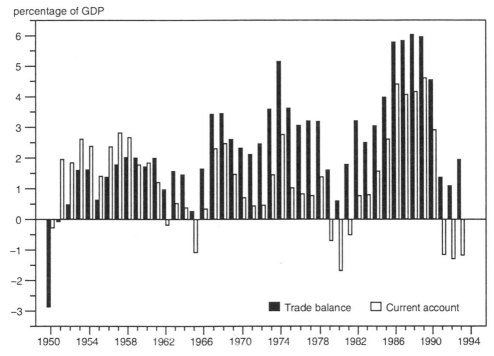

Source: International Monetary Fund.

industrial productivity rose impressively during the 1950s and 1960s. German macroeconomic policies, based on domestic price stability and restrictive government finance, proved to be, in the words of one seasoned analyst, "extremely potent promoters of exports."[1]

The export strategy succeeded in creating persistent trade surpluses beginning in the 1950s (figures 5.1 and 5.2). These, coupled with partial liberalization of capital controls, placed persistent upward pressure on the D-mark. Under the rules of the fixed-rate regime, the Bundesbank was obliged to counter the strength of the D-mark with foreign exchange intervention and, ultimately, an expansionary monetary policy. Otmar Emminger, a high official in the Bundesbank and its future president, lamented the chronic conflict between internal and external monetary stability. Writing in the mid-1970s, he observed:[2]

1. Henry Wallich, *Mainsprings of the German Revival* (New Haven: Yale University Press, 1955). The quotation appears on p. 244.

2. Otmar Emminger, *The D-mark in the Conflict between Internal and External Equilibrium, 1948-75*, Essays in International Finance 122 (Princeton: Princeton University, International Finance Section, June 1977), pp. 42–43.

Looking back over the past twenty-five years, it is striking that there were only rare periods in which German stabilization policy did not have to wrestle with the repercussions of major external disequilibria or was not impeded and constrained by having to pay attention to external equilibrium and especially to interest-rate and liquidity differentials with respect to foreign countries.

The German government, by decisions of the cabinet, revalued the D-mark twice under the par value regime, in 1961 and 1969, floated the currency in May 1971, and then refixed it at a substantially higher rate in December of that year as part of the Smithsonian agreement. Each revaluation was a divisive decision fraught with great political risks for the government. The senior economic officials in the trade unions, political parties, and research institutes supported revaluations as soon as large surpluses emerged. German banking and industry, by contrast, opposed revaluations, and proposed substitute remedies for the surpluses. The chairman of the powerful Deutsche Bank, Hermann Josef Abs, personified this approach. A leader of German industry, Fritz Berg, once warned that a D-mark revaluation would result in a "catastrophe for the entire economy."[3] The political class was divided. Some politicians, notably the minister of economics, Ludwig Erhard, favored prompt revaluation. But the chancellor and his ministers usually deferred to the powerful forces of banking and industry.[4] Private-sector political pressure for low valuation could not block the international economic tide pushing the D-mark upward, but it successfully delayed and limited the size of the revaluations.[5] As a result, in spite of the revaluations, the D-mark remained dynamically undervalued throughout the fixed-rate period.[6]

During these debates, the Bundesbank did not press consistently for revaluations of the D-mark. Strong preferences for exchange rate stability on the part of crucial constituencies for central bank independence, industry and banking in particular, meant that the Bundesbank could

3. Hugo M. Kaufmann, "A Debate over Germany's Revaluation, 1961: A Chapter in Political Economy," *Weltwirtschaftliches Archiv* 103 (1969): 205.

4. Michael Kreile, "West Germany: The Dynamics of Expansion," in *Between Power and Plenty*, P. Katzenstein, ed., pp. 213–16; Helmut Schlesinger and Horst Bockelman, "Monetary Policy in the Federal Republic of Germany," in *Monetary Policy in Twelve Industrial Countries*, Karel Holbik, ed. (Boston: Federal Reserve Bank of Boston, 1973), pp. 237–38; Kaufmann, "A Debate over Germany's Revaluation, 1961," pp. 181–209, especially pp. 202–8; P. Hall, *Governing the Economy*, pp. 237–38; Otmar Emminger, *D-Mark, Dollar, Währungskrisen* (Stuttgart: Deutsche-Verlags Anstalt, 1986), chapters 2–5.

5. Emminger, disappointed at the size of the 1961 revaluation, derided it as "a compromise between those in favor of the measure and those against it." Martin Mayer, *The Fate of the Dollar* (New York: Times Books, 1980), p. 92.

6. W. P. Wadbrook, *West Germany's Balance of Payments Policy* (New York: Praeger, 1972); Wilhelm Hankel, "Germany: Economic Nationalism in the International Economy," in *West Germany: A European and Global Power*, Wilfrid Kohl and Giorgio Basevi, eds. (Lexington, MA: Lexington Books, 1980), pp. 22–30.

Table 5.1   Chancellors and coalition governments under the Federal Republic of Germany

Chancellor	Coalition	Beginning of term
Konrad Adenauer	CDU/CSU	15 September 1949
Ludwig Erhard	CDU/CSU/FDP	15 October 1963
Kurt-Georg Kiesinger	CDU/CSU/SPD	1 December 1966
Willy Brandt	SPD/FDP	21 October 1969
Helmut Schmidt	SPD/FDP	16 May 1974
Helmut Kohl	CDU/CSU/FDP	1 October 1982
Helmut Kohl (United Germany)	CDU/CSU/FDP	3 October 1990

not ignore this objective without jeopardizing its free status.[7] The central bank thus defined its mission as pursuing both domestic price stability *and* the par value, until the conflict between the two objectives became clearly irreconcilable. The Central Bank Council was internally split between the faction that insisted on the fixed parity, which initially held the majority, and the faction that favored revaluations for the sake of domestic price stability. As the dilemma became more intractable through the 1960s and early 1970s, the latter faction gained influence.[8]

The dramatic revaluation of 1969 differed from the usual pattern of policymaking in two particular respects. First, in this instance the Central Bank Council was united in proposing the revaluation of the D-mark. The Grand Coalition government of Chancellor Keisinger opposed the revaluation, with the Christian Democratic Union/Christian Social Union (CDU/CSU) members of the cabinet such as Franz-Josef Strauss leading the opposition[9] (see table 5.1 for a chronology of governments). Second, on this occasion exchange rate policymaking extended beyond the government, Bundesbank, and private interest groups to encompass the electorate at large. In the election of September 1969, the Social Democratic Party (SPD) campaigned on a platform including a revaluation. Led by Economics Minister Karl Schiller, the SPD effectively sided with the Bundesbank, arguing that a revaluation would favor workers and consumers. The CDU/CSU, closer to banking and industry, continued to oppose the revaluation. The formation of the SPD-FDP (Free Democratic Party) coalition after the election decided the issue in October. The influence of electoral politics on exchange rate policy formation, however, is the exception rather than the rule.

---

7. John B. Goodman, "The Politics of Central Bank Independence," *Comparative Politics* 23 (April 1991), pp. 329–49.

8. Emminger, *D-mark, Dollar, Währungskrisen.*

9. Emminger, *D-mark, Dollar, Währungskrisen,* chapter 5; Kreile, "West Germany," pp. 215–16.

When upward pressure on the D-mark continued in the early 1970s, a bitter political struggle over the application of capital controls ensued. In mid-1972, the Bundesbank, led by Karl Klasen, who had previously led the Deutsche Bank, supported the use of capital controls to stem destabilizing inflows. Schiller, minister for finance and economics under the social-liberal coalition, recommended that the D-mark be floated along with other European currencies against the dollar. When a majority of the cabinet rejected his proposal in favor of capital controls, Schiller resigned over the matter. That the Bundesbank would favor imposition of capital controls indicates the intensity of its continuing aversion to D-mark revaluation.[10] These controls nonetheless proved to be futile in early 1973, when foreign exchange speculation forced the Bundesbank to purchase unprecedented quantities of US dollars to maintain the parity. Then the federal government and Bundesbank finally agreed to allow the D-mark to float flexibly in the foreign exchange markets for the second time. By default, the governments of the advanced industrial countries, exhausted from international negotiations over regime reform, and weary of mediating among the conflicting domestic constituencies on currency questions, ushered in the new regime of flexible exchange rates.

The Bundesbank took immediate advantage of the switch to floating exchange rates. The downfall of the Bretton Woods regime enabled the Bundesbank to formulate a "new assignment" for monetary policy. It could now focus more intently on domestic price stability.[11] The Central Bank Council tightened monetary policy throughout 1973, to reverse the liquidity expansion in the dying days of the fixed-rate regime, and it instituted money supply growth targets during the following year, effective 1975, that have continued to the present day. As we shall see, the Bundesbank would maintain a keen interest in the external value of the D-mark, notwithstanding the new regime. With the change in the international regime, in addition, the locus of policy authority, particularly with respect to the dollar, shifted decisively from the government toward the Bundesbank. Curiously, this shift occurred with very little public debate or discussion, much less a deliberate decision by political authorities.

---

10. Schiller later complained that "Klasen had the *Weltanschauung* of the Deutsche Bank. . . . It was the mentality of Hermann Josef Abs." David Marsh, *The Bundesbank: The Bank that Rules Europe* (London: Heinemann, 1992), p. 191.

11. Fritz W. Scharpf, *Crisis and Choice in European Social Democracy*, translated by Ruth Crowley and Fred Thompson (Ithaca, NY: Cornell University Press, 1991), chapter 7; Jeremiah M. Riemer, "Crisis and Intervention in the West German Economy: A Political Analysis of Changes in the Policy Machinery during the 1960s and 1970s" (Ph.D. diss., Cornell University, 1983), pp. 199–284.

The Two-Track Policy of Flexibility and Stabilization in the 1970s and 1980s

Germany consolidated its strategy for the post–Bretton Woods period by the end of the 1970s. German officials concluded that the United States was unreliable, from their experience with the American monetary expansion in the early 1970s and the dispute over the locomotive strategy during 1977–78. Their conclusion would later be reinforced by the Reagan-era US budget deficits. Based on this calculation, Germany eschewed agreements with the United States that might require expansionary macroeconomic policies.

Europe, however, was a different matter. Though some European governments were even more unreliable than the American government, in this view, Germany's economic and political destiny was tied to them fundamentally by virtue of geography and economic integration. Within Europe, furthermore, Germany could hope to exercise real influence over macroeconomic policies that could not be exercised over the United States; and Germany was in a stronger political position to resist pressures for expansion of demand from other European governments than from the United States. Therefore, Germany continued to stabilize European currencies through the "snake," after the end of the Bretton Woods parity system.[12] With the creation of the EMS in the late 1970s, Germany committed itself to a two-track strategy of European monetary cooperation coupled with global flexibility.

The discussion below will alternate between German policy with respect to Europe and with respect to the US dollar and global macroeconomic cooperation.

Creation of the EMS

Chancellor Helmut Schmidt and French President Valéry Giscard d'Estaing, in 1978, breathed political life into proposals to create an EMS. Chancellor Schmidt was frustrated in his altercation with the Carter administration over the locomotive strategy, and vulnerable to the ensuing appreciation of the D-mark.[13] Because the D-mark had developed as a main alternative to the dollar in private and official reserves—playing a "counter-

---

12. Norbert Kloten, "Germany's Monetary and Financial Policy and the European Community," in *West Germany*, Kohl and Basevi, eds., pp. 177–99.

13. For a full discussion of the locomotive controversy between the Carter administration and the Schmidt government during 1977–78, and the Bundesbank's reaction to the D-mark appreciation, see Robert D. Putnam and C. Randall Henning, "The Bonn Summit of 1978: A Case Study in Coordination," in *Can Nations Agree? Issues in International Economic Cooperation*, Richard N. Cooper, Barry Eichengreen, Gerald Holtham, Putnam and Henning (Washington: Brookings Institution, 1989), pp. 12–140.

pole" role—weakness of the dollar tended to put upward pressure on the D-mark against the other European currencies as well. Stabilizing the D-mark against the French franc, Belgian franc, Italian lira, and so forth would spread the pressure for appreciation across a larger monetary area, sheltering the German economy.[14]

The German and French leaders developed their initiative in secret, concealed from their own government ministries and central banks, as well as from the European Commission. This secrecy was necessary, in their judgment, to prevent the proposal from being stillborn. From the German economics ministry had come, in Schmidt's view, "hardly any fruitful European initiative," and Schmidt expected no help on this proposal either. He feared instead that the economics ministry would delay, criticize, and marshal parliamentary and journalistic opposition to the initiative. For that reason, Schmidt was glad that he had moved the Department of Money and Credit to the finance ministry, an SPD portfolio, where the finance minister, his friend Hans Matthöfer, could keep the bureaucracy in the dark until the appropriate moment. From the Bundesbank, Schmidt has written, "One could expect not only criticism but carefully orchestrated resistance."[15]

Once Schmidt and Giscard received the endorsement of the other heads of government at the European Council meeting of July 1978, they opened the matter to the ministries and central banks, while still keeping tight rein on the international negotiations over the system. Members of the Central Bank Council were furious at having been effectively blindsided by the chancellor. In a controversy that left a bitter aftermath, the Bundesbank raised several key objections to the breadth, pace, and extent of the proposed exchange rate arrangements. In particular, the Bundesbank objected to the obligation to intervene and to extend D-mark loans to other central banks with which to defend their currencies at the margins—both of which would affect the Bundesbank's capacity to control the domestic money supply.[16]

---

14. The authoritative account of the establishment of the EMS is Peter Ludlow, *The Creation of the European Monetary System* (London: Butterworth Scientific, 1982). On the trans-Atlantic dispute as a motive for Schmidt, see chapter 3. On sustaining export-led growth as a motive, see Hankel, "Germany," p. 30; Kloten, "Germany's Monetary and Financial Policy," pp. 194–95. On Schmidt's belief that the EMS would help to disperse the pressure for appreciation over a larger monetary area, see Deutsche Bundesbank, *Auszüge aus Presseartikeln*, no. 87 (1978): 8–9, cited by Kloten, p. 194, n. 24.

15. Excerpts from the memoirs of Helmut Schmidt, published in *Die Zeit*, 24 August 1990.

16. Emminger, *D-mark, Dollar, Währungskrisen*, chapter 12; Ludlow, *The Creation of the European Monetary System*, pp. 196–98.

Schmidt reports that, to persuade the Bundesbank to agree to the EMS, he subtly threatened to change the Bundesbank law.[17] In fact, Schmidt's coalition partner, the Free Democratic Party, and the minister of economics, Otto Lambsdorff, would not have agreed to this tactic. But Schmidt's threat underscored the depth of the chancellor's personal commitment to the EMS—politically significant in its own right—and foreshadowed the tenacity with which future governments would pursue monetary integration.

A domestic political consensus, in any case, supported Schmidt's basic objective. European monetary integration had been endorsed in principle since the Werner Report of 1970.[18] There had been broad support for the European snake, from which the French had dropped out twice. Key groups and bureaucracies deferred to the chancellor in his effort to try to "bring the French back in."

None of the nationally organized private-sector groups, called "peak associations" in Germany, were politically active in opposition to the EMS proposal. The German Federation of Savings Associations and the German Chamber of Commerce and Industry were concerned about the plan. The German Federation of Industry, while warning that all countries in the EMS should pursue price stability, expressed support for Schmidt's initiative. The banking sector was divided on the issue. But Schmidt had the confidence of the heads of the big three private banks, one of whom, Wilfried Guth, the head of Deutsche Bank, would soon be invited by Schmidt to succeed Emminger as president of the Bundesbank (Guth declined the invitation).

The Bundesbank could not ignore public support for regional exchange rate stability. The central bank's latitude on the issue, after all, ultimately rested on a simple majority in the Bundestag, as Schmidt's threat to change the law served to remind Bundesbank officials. Although privately hostile, in public the Bundesbank did not reject the system outright. Cautioning about the risks, the Central Bank Council chose to work with Schmidt and the government on the design of the system and the important technical agreements necessary to operate it.[19] The fact that the chancellor wanted the Bundesbank's support for his initia-

---

17. Marsh, *The Bundesbank*, pp. 194–95; Kennedy, *The Bundesbank*, p. 81, n. 6. Schmidt's account has not been corroborated by others involved in the episode.

18. This report, presented by a group chaired by the prime minister of Luxembourg, Pierre Werner, presented a blueprint to achieve full monetary integration within the Community over the following decade. Pierre Werner et al., "Report to the Council and the Commission on the Realisation by Stages of Economic and Monetary Union in the Community," Supplement to Bulletin II-1970 of the European Communities, Brussels.

19. Officials within the Finance Ministry also objected to the plan, but faithfully executed the directives of the minister, to Matthöfer's relief and satisfaction.

tive gave the central bank some bargaining leverage. And the Bundesbank used it to extract important concessions from the government in the design of the system—concessions that fundamentally altered how the EMS would operate over the coming years.

First, the Bundesbank argued that the European Currency Unit (ECU) should not be placed at the center of the system, and that each central bank's intervention obligation should be defined in terms of bilateral exchange rates.[20] This would effectively place the D-mark at the center of the system and would prevent Germany from being singled out for intervention or easing of monetary policy.

Second, the Bundesbank sought to minimize its obligation to lend D-marks to the other participating central banks with which to intervene in the defense of their currencies. The Bundesbank successfully convinced Schmidt and his aides to take these positions in negotiations with the French government.

Third, the chancellor attended a meeting of the Central Bank Council in Frankfurt on 30 November 1978, the first such meeting since Chancellor Konrad Adenauer visited the Bank deutscher Länder in 1950, to persuade the members to support the new arrangements as they had been negotiated. Schmidt insisted that the question of German participation in the EMS was a political decision reserved for the government. That decision, he continued, was wrapped in high politics: Germany's broader role in Europe, the legacy of World War II and the Holocaust, and the threat of Eurocommunism.[21]

But the chancellor also pledged that the Bundesbank would not be forced into an overexpansionary domestic monetary policy for the sake of the system. The government would not maintain unrealistic central rates, and if it was unable to reach an accord with the European partners on a realignment, the Bundesbank would retain the right to "opt out" of the system if domestic monetary stability were threatened. This promise was echoed in a speech to the Bundestag by Lambsdorff in early December.[22]

---

20. The divergence indicator is based on the European Currency Unit, a basket currency broadly similar to the Special Drawing Rights (SDR) issued by the IMF. As a basket currency, its value reflects a weighted average of European currencies (including Community currencies outside the Exchange Rate Mechanism [ERM])—those with high as well as low inflation rates. Using the divergence indicator to establish the intervention and adjustment obligations of the member states would have instilled within the ERM a tendency for countries to converge to the average, rather than the lowest, inflation rate. The Bundesbank, backed by the German government, therefore insisted that the divergence indicator be marginalized in favor of the parity grid of bilateral rates. With the parity grid at the center, the system would tend toward the lowest inflation rate, which historically had been that of Germany.

21. Marsh, The Bundesbank, p. 194.

22. Deutscher Bundestag, Stenographischer Bericht, 122 Sitzung, 6 December 1978, pp. 948 ff., cited by Ludlow, The Creation of the European Monetary System, p. 284, n. 90.

It was formalized in an exchange of letters between Finance Minister Matthöfer and Bundesbank President Emminger which, while often cited by inside officials, remain unpublished. Crucially, however, the government reserved for itself, not the central bank, the authority to determine whether such stability-threatening circumstances obtained.

The chancellor's desire for the Bundesbank's accession to the EMS, and his willingness to bargain with Frankfurt for it, stemmed from important institutional differences between the former Bretton Woods regime and the European system. Because the Common Market had been formed under the fixed exchange rate regime governed by the Bretton Woods agreements, the Treaty of Rome provided no legal basis for the Franco-German monetary initiative. The treaty merely stated that exchange rates were to be treated as a matter of "common concern" among the Community members. Schmidt and his counterparts were not willing to conduct a cumbersome amendment to the Treaty of Rome to enact the EMS. The chancellor wanted to save his political capital to alter the treaty later to accommodate a second agreement, which he was already planning, including a European fund to finance intervention and payments imbalances.

The new exchange rate system, therefore, would have to be managed by central banks without formal legislative directive, that is, voluntarily. Indeed, the key operational founding document of the EMS is an agreement among central banks.[23] Once the EMS was in place, the German government left the day-to-day operation of the system almost entirely up to the Bundesbank. However, when the central parities were in question, any realignment could be determined only by unanimous agreement of the finance ministers.

The amendments to the basic design of the EMS and the operational control of the Bundesbank made a tremendous difference to the system. During the 1980s, the European countries' economic policies converged toward the German price-stability orientation. Numerous examples attest to the importance of the EMS in implementing more disciplined monetary policies among the European partners. Owing to the structure of the system, the others adjusted to German monetary policies far more often than Germany adjusted to theirs.

Deficit-Recession Trauma: 1979–82

Germany entered the 1980s with shaken self-confidence. The second oil price shock in spring 1979 caught the economy in an exposed position.

---

23. See "Agreement between the Central Banks of the Member States of the European Economic Community Laying Down the Operating Procedures for the European Monetary System," issued at Basel, Switzerland, 13 March 1979, reproduced in Jacques van Ypersele and Jean-Claude Koeune, *The European Monetary System: Origins, Operation, and Outlook* (Luxemburg: Office for Official Publications of the European Communities, 1985), pp. 129–33.

After the first oil shock, Germany had had surplus capacity with which to export, the Bundesbank having tightened monetary policy in early 1973. At the time of the second oil price shock, by contrast, both monetary and fiscal policy were stimulative and export potential was diminished. Thus, in 1979, rather than continuing to run large surpluses, as after the first oil shock, Germany ran its first deficits since 1965 (figures 5.1 and 5.2). These developments traumatized German policymakers, politicians, and businessmen.[24]

The fiscal measures agreed upon at the Bonn summit in 1978 contributed to strong growth of 4.5 percent in 1979. However, the pace of expansion slowed dramatically, to 1.8 percent, in 1980 with the shrinkage of the trade surplus. More worrying, the rate of consumer price inflation was accelerating, from 2.6 percent in 1978 to 4.1 percent in 1979, 5.5 percent in 1980, and would register 6.4 percent in 1981[25] (table 5.2). Conflict within the SPD-FDP coalition, returned to government in the election in 1980, aggravated economic uncertainty. In early 1980, for the first time since the transition to flexible exchange rates at the global level, the D-mark entered a period of sustained weakness.

The Carter administration had actively lobbied the Schmidt government for expansionary fiscal policies through the Bonn Summit of 1978.[26] Since then, however, American macroeconomic policy had taken a drastic change of course. First, the Federal Reserve initiated its famous policy reversal in October 1979. Helmut Schmidt and Otmar Emminger, among other German officials, had strongly urged Fed Chairman Paul Volcker to undertake this restrictive turnaround to put an end to the weakness of the dollar.[27] Unaware of the degree of monetary tightening that was to come, they interpreted the US policy change as a great victory and welcomed it wholeheartedly. Second, the Reagan administration, entering office in January 1981, promptly sponsored a drastic increase in the federal budget deficit and suspended American intervention in the foreign exchange markets.

---

24. The Bundesbank commented: "There is no doubt that, to the extent of the current account deficit, Germany is living beyond its means—a situation that can be tolerated for a short while but would pose serious problems in the longer run." Deutsche Bundesbank, *Report for the Year 1980*, p. 18.

25. For an analysis of the contribution of the Bonn summit measures to this predicament, see Gerald Holtham, "German Macroeconomic Policy and the 1978 Bonn Summit," in Cooper et al., *Can Nations Agree?*, pp. 141–77. Holtham largely exonerates the summit of blame, contrary to the widespread and persistent perception in Germany.

26. Putnam and Henning, "The Bonn Summit of 1978," pp. 141–77.

27. Volcker and Gyohten, *Changing Fortunes*, p. 145; Emminger, *D-Mark, Dollar, Währungskrisen*, pp. 390–98.

Table 5.2 Germany: inflation, 1970–93 (percentages)

Year	Consumer prices	Wholesale prices
1970	3.51	2.85
1971	5.18	2.77
1972	5.49	3.46
1973	7.00	9.85
1974	7.05	13.03
1975	5.96	3.44
1976	4.44	5.79
1977	3.82	1.78
1978	2.59	−0.81
1979	4.12	6.91
1980	5.49	7.86
1981	6.42	7.76
1982	5.23	5.45
1983	3.24	0.10
1984	2.51	2.79
1985	2.20	0.50
1986	−0.25	−7.40
1987	0.20	−3.78
1988	1.20	1.01
1989	2.76	5.11
1990	2.69	0.63
1991	3.46	1.58
1992	3.97	0.10
1993	4.17	−1.14

Source: OECD, Main Economic Indicators, various issues.

Domestic Monetary Policy

Rather than emulate the US policy of monetary tightening, the Bundesbank might have targeted the domestic economy, which experienced recession in 1981, sluggish growth thereafter, and rates of unemployment not seen since the 1950s. The D-mark was weak, however, and easing monetary policy to fight the recession would have required countenancing a downward overshooting of the German currency against the dollar. Several prominent groups and individuals advocated this strategy, including the five economic research institutes, a minority of the *Sachverständigenrat* (Council of Economic Experts), and some export firms.[28] Some even advocated a devaluation of the D-mark within the EMS.[29]

---

28. Mitglieder der Arbeitsgemeinschaft deutscher wirtschaftswissenschaftlicher Forschungsinstitute e.V., Essen, *Die Lage der Weltwirtschaft und der westdeutschen Wirtschaft im Fruhjajr 1980*, Berlin, 28 April 1980, and the autumn report issued on 24 October 1980, cited by John B. Goodman, *Monetary Sovereignty*, p. 92; Fritz Scharpf, *Crisis and Choice in European Social Democracy* (Ithaca, NY: Cornell University Press, 1991), p. 151; Hugo M. Kaufmann, *Germany's International Monetary Policy and the European Monetary System* (New York: Columbia University Press, 1985), p. 97. These groups reasoned that a depreciation would lead to expectations of subsequent appreciation that would help to sustain capital inflow, implicitly applying the Dornbusch model of exchange rate overshooting.

29. Kaufmann, *Germany's International Monetary Policy*, p. 97.

Figure 5.3 Germany: monthly exchange rates, 1975–93

1985 average = 100, logarithmic scale

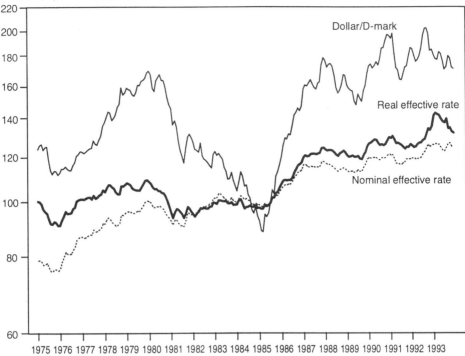

Source: International Monetary Fund, *International Financial Statistics*.

The Bundesbank accepted a certain amount of D-mark depreciation during 1980 and recognized that improving the competitiveness of German industry was the key to eliminating the current account deficit.[30] The central bank therefore tightened monetary policy only gradually while intervening in the foreign exchange market to prevent a further slide in the D-mark. With large interest rate differentials in favor of the dollar—rising to more than a full 10 percent at the end of 1980—central bank officials expected that intervention could accomplish little more than simply finance the external deficit.

But by February 1981 the D-mark had depreciated by 26 percent against the dollar and 15.6 percent on a real, effective basis from its peak in early 1980 (figure 5.3). Further depreciation was unnecessary for restoring the competitiveness of German industry and could aggravate inflation, which remained a problem through 1981. Official reserves, moreover, were being depleted rapidly by intervention to support the D-mark.

The Bundesbank decided that it was time to halt the depreciation and

---

30. Deutsche Bundesbank, *Annual Report for the Year 1980*, p. 22.

Figure 5.4 Germany: monthly interest rates, 1980–93

percentage

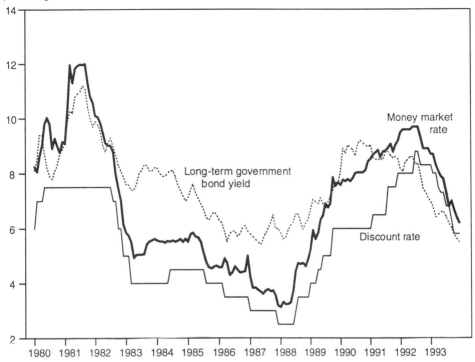

Source: International Monetary Fund.

to finance external deficits with private capital inflows rather than official reserves. It tightened monetary policy dramatically, by suspending the regular Lombard facility and replacing it temporarily with a special Lombard facility at 12.0 percent—an unprecedented 3 percentage point increase to an unprecedented level (figure 5.4). The Bundesbank was clear as to its motive: to halt the slide of the D-mark.[31]

External Monetary Policy

The D-mark continued to weaken, in spite of the extraordinary tightening, until August 1981, when the exchange rate averaged more than 2.50

31. Deutsche Bundesbank, *Annual Report for the Year 1980*, p. 3. "Towards the middle of February 1981 the situation in the foreign exchange markets deteriorated to such an extent that the Bundesbank thought it advisable to stabilise confidence in the Deutsche Mark by considerably raising the German interest rate level, thus countering the danger of a growing importation of inflation at the same time. . . . The expectations that the Bundesbank had attached to this forceful use of its monetary policy instruments—namely that the exchange rate of the Deutsche Mark would be stabilised—were fulfilled in the first few weeks of March."

to the dollar. The Bundesbank supplemented high interest rates with large interventions in the foreign exchange market. German intervention was supplemented by D-mark purchases by the Federal Reserve, toward the end of the Carter administration, and by other European central banks when the German currency dropped to its floor within the EMS in 1980 (late March and late October) and 1981 (February). The net external asset position of the Bundesbank declined DM25.7 billion in 1980 alone—more than financing the current account deficit for the year. In 1981, DM21.5 billion in dollar sales by the Bundesbank were almost fully offset by purchases under the EMS to leave the net external position down only DM3.2 billion.

The German government also used capital controls and capital import programs to support the D-mark and manage the balance of payments. In step with the tightening of monetary policy in early 1981, the Bundesbank eliminated the remaining controls on capital inflows, permitting short-dated bonds and money market instruments to be sold to nonresidents. (Long-term instruments had been liberalized previously.) The finance ministry, meanwhile, issued government notes abroad, mainly to Saudi Arabia, in both 1980 and 1981, to finance the government budget deficit and, indirectly, the current account deficit.[32]

Government-Bundesbank Conflict

In tightening monetary policy, the Bundesbank provoked a serious conflict with the government. High interest rates produced a domestic recession in Germany during 1981 and limited growth to 1 percent in 1982. For the first time since the early postwar period, Germany experienced large-scale unemployment, crossing the two million mark at the beginning of 1982. Contention within the social-liberal coalition over how to respond to these problems eventually led, in September 1982, to the coalition's demise.[33]

The Schmidt government had criticized the tightening of monetary policy from the very beginning, the initial change in late 1978. As interest rates rose, so did Schmidt's objections. However, with inflation high and the D-mark weak, Schmidt himself did not criticize the Bundesbank directly in public. Sensitive to criticisms that he might be soft on inflation, Schmidt let surrogates publicly criticize the popular central bank. But Schmidt suspected that the Central Bank Council was trying to undermine his coalition and criticized it privately. And once American interest rates began to fall in mid-1982, Schmidt repeatedly asked the

---

32. Deutsche Bundesbank, *Report for the Year 1980*, pp. 16 and 26, n. 1.

33. For a description of the strains within the coalition that led to its downfall, see Scharpf, *Crisis and Choice in European Social Democracy*, pp. 150–57.

president of the Bundesbank, Karl Otto Pöhl, to cut German interest rates faster.[34]

Schmidt also struck out at the Reagan administration, complaining that its policy mix had produced real interest rates within Germany higher than at any time "since the birth of Christ." Economics Minister Lambsdorff said that, while the fight against inflation was laudable, Reagan had chosen the wrong means in that battle. American fiscal policy should be tightened and monetary policy loosened.[35]

Bundesbank President Pöhl rebuked his government for these criticisms and defended US monetary policy. Bonn should spend less time criticizing the United States and more time putting its "own house in order," by reducing German budget deficits, he said.[36] Bundesbank officials argued that by doing so Germany might decouple its interest rates from American rates.

The conservative-liberal coalition of the CDU/CSU/FDP replaced the social-liberal coalition in October 1982 and Helmut Kohl became chancellor. The Bundesbank began to reduce interest rates aggressively. It was assisted in this maneuver by falling American interest rates, an improvement in Germany's external accounts, and a resurgence in the D-mark. Members of the Central Bank Council, in addition, were far more secure with the conservative economic agenda of the new coalition and the confidence of the markets that the new government inspired. Despite some concern that it might appear to be partisan during the weeks approaching the March 1983 election, the Bundesbank decided that it was safe to ease monetary policy rapidly. Political pressure on the Bundesbank fell accordingly.[37]

Policy in the Young EMS

The Bundesbank remained deeply suspicious of the EMS and wary of encroachment of the system on the bank's independence. Vice President Helmut Schlesinger, in particular, warned that participation in the system could cause a dangerous expansion of liquidity. At several points, indeed, German intervention to restrain the D-mark within its EMS margins raised liquidity substantially.

---

34. Goodman, *Monetary Sovereignty*, pp. 95–96.

35. *New York Times*, 21 and 22 July 1981.

36. *New York Times*, 4 August 1981. See as well Deutsche Bundesbank, *Report for the Year 1980*, pp. 45–46—issued in May 1981—which argued, "Owing to the importance of the United States in the world economy, the resolute anti-inflationary monetary policy being pursued there is in the best interest of all countries, even if last year this policy led to the exceptionally high levels of interest rates and marked shifts in exchange rates with which we still have to live today."

37. Goodman, *Monetary Sovereignty*, pp. 97–98.

International economic turmoil during the early years of the EMS might have prompted the most hostile opponents within the Bundesbank to try to break free of the system that had been imposed upon them. The second oil shock, high inflation, record interest rates in the United States, and, finally, the election of the Socialists in France together formed a powerful argument that the circumstances in which the EMS had been created, and the assumptions on which it was based, had fundamentally changed. Despite hostility within the Central Bank Council toward the EMS, however, there was no Bundesbank attempt to opt out. Neither the government, business, nor banking sectors would have lent significant support for such a move, and their support would have been necessary to sustain an opting out.

German trade competitiveness benefited substantially from membership in the system. Because German inflation was lower than that of its European partners, nominal exchange rate stability created gradual depreciation of the currency in real terms. This helped Germany to recover from its current account deficits of 1979–81 and to reestablish surpluses thereafter until national unification in 1990. In the absence of a demonstrable, unavoidable threat to internal monetary stability—and none existed—the private sector supported Germany's participation in the system.

The danger that the EMS would cause liquidity expansion in Germany was reduced by the flexible administration of the central parities. Not only had the German government ceded operational control over the system to the Bundesbank and its fellow central banks, but it kept its promise to approve realignments when necessary to avoid large disequilibria. The European governments approved four realignments during the first four years of the EMS—in September 1979, October 1981, June 1982, and March 1983—typically after a bout of intervention to restrain the D-mark. The realignment of October 1981 illustrates the cooperative working relationship between the government and the Bundesbank. When the Belgian finance minister resisted a large devaluation of the Belgian franc, proposing a smaller one instead, German Finance Minister Matthöfer threatened to authorize the Bundesbank to stop intervening to support the currency. In the face of this threat, the Belgian government capitulated to the larger devaluation.

Moreover, the Bundesbank itself found the EMS useful on several counts. Exchange rate stabilization was a clear benefit as long as it did not impinge upon monetary autonomy. The system did help to create greater monetary stability in Europe during a period of great volatility globally. Most important, the D-mark was exceptionally weak, owing partly to the strength of the dollar, and the Bundesbank actually benefited from Europewide support for the currency within the system.[38] Con-

---

38. Deutsche Bundesbank, *Report for the Year 1981*, pp. 78–81. The Bundesbank remained, however, critical of further development of the EMS.

Table 5.3 Germany: money growth, 1975–93
(percentages, annual rates)

Year	Target	Definition	Outcome
1975	8.0	CBM; year on year	9.8
1976	8.0	CBM; annual average	8.3
1977	8.0	CBM; annual average	10.0
1978	8.0	CBM; annual average	11.8
1979	6.0–9.0	CBM; year on year	5.3
1980	5.0–8.0	CBM; year on year	5.5
1981	4.0–7.0	CBM; year on year	3.2
1982	4.0–7.0	CBM; year on year	6.0
1983	4.0–7.0	CBM; year on year	6.8
1984	4.0–6.0	CBM; year on year	4.7
1985	3.0–5.0	CBM; year on year	5.2
1986	3.5–5.5	CBM; year on year	7.2
1987	3.0–6.0	CBM; year on year	6.5
1988	3.0–6.0	M3; year on year	6.9
1989	5.0	M3; year on year	4.5
1990	4.0–6.0	M3; year on year	5.5
1991	3.0–5.0	M3; year on year	6.2
1992	3.5–5.5	M3; year on year	8.4
1993	4.5–6.5	M3; year on year	8.8

CBM = Central Bank Money.

Source: Deutsche Bundesbank, monthly and annual reports.

trary to expectations that EMS participation would hinder its ability to control the money supply, the Bundesbank actually undershot its monetary growth targets in 1979 and 1981 (table 5.3).

The realignment of March 1983 was the most critical moment for finance ministry–Bundesbank cooperation and a crucially defining event in the evolution of the EMS. The French Socialist economic program of growth through fiscal and monetary expansion had produced two substantial devaluations in the EMS but a continuing stream of trade deficits and capital outflow from France, motivated by double-digit inflation and expectations of further devaluations.[39] Since the creation of the EMS, the cumulative revaluation of the D-mark against the franc amounted to roughly 18 percent. But the cumulative consumer price inflation differential amounted to about 28 percent, handicapping French competitiveness by the 10 percent gap. By early 1983, the French government faced a choice between invoking restrictive policies, with a devaluation, or leaving the EMS altogether and erecting higher barriers to capital and trade flows.

Chancellor Schmidt had communicated his disapproval of the Socialist

---

39. The French government had proposed reinforcing the EMS to insulate Europe from high interest rates in the United States, but Bonn and Frankfurt, suspecting this to be a ploy to win German acquiescence to inflationary French policies, rejected the plan.

program from the outset. But the change in government in Germany brought the unsustainability of French economic policies to a head. The downfall of the German social-liberal coalition not only called into question the use of expansionary fiscal policy as a political strategy, to say the least, but installed a conservative-liberal government dedicated to fiscal consolidation. Chancellor Kohl's government was strengthened in that objective by national elections in early March; conversely, the Socialist government in France was weakened in regional elections shortly thereafter.

German finance ministry officials held tough negotiations with the Elysée and French finance ministry. Their discussions were multilateralized in the Ecofin Council. The outcome, delayed by intense bargaining during which central banks were permitted to let exchange rates transgress the EMS limits, was announced on 21 March: a revaluation of the D-mark by 5.5 percent and a devaluation of the franc by 2.5 percent, in addition to changes among the other currencies. French President François Mitterrand and his government had decided to stay in the system and tighten monetary and fiscal policies dramatically, reversing the course of economic policy set since the advent of the Socialist government in 1981.

Mitterrand's abrupt change of course to maintain a fixed rate with the D-mark signaled the consolidation of German dominance of the EMS. The Bundesbank had succeeded in promoting the parity grid over the divergence indicator as the arbiter of adjustment obligations within the ERM and thus deemphasized the role of the ECU in favor of the D-mark as the stability anchor. The March 1983 negotiations demonstrated that, when tensions arose between low-inflation Germany and high-inflation partners, it would be the partners, not Germany, that would amend their policies.[40]

By the time the conservative-liberal coalition came to power in Germany, the EMS had become so generally accepted that the new government did not seriously question Germany's participation. There was no serious opposition to it in the country. Hans-Dietrich Genscher, foreign minister and chairman of the FDP, the junior coalition party within both governments, saw the EMS as cement for the special relationship with France and a building block for further European integration.

German policy within the EMS, and thus its character as a D-mark zone, was determined by close cooperation between the Bundesbank and the government on EMS policy. Though the EMS might have offered him a mechanism with which to extract an expansionary monetary policy from the central bank, Schmidt did not try to use it for that pur-

---

40. For a discussion of the dominance of Germany and the D-mark within the EMS, see Francesco Giavazzi and Alberto Giovannini, *Limiting Exchange Rate Flexibility: The European Monetary System* (Cambridge: MIT Press, 1989), esp. chapters 4 and 5.

pose, despite his bitter criticism of the central bank's restrictive monetary policy. And the conservative-liberal coalition eased political pressure on the central bank altogether. In the triangular bargaining among the Bundesbank, German government, and other European governments, there would be times when Bonn would side with foreign capitals against Frankfurt in the management of the EMS. But the first phase of the system, 1979–83, was a period of close government-Bundesbank cooperation on European monetary affairs.

Further D-mark Depreciation: 1983–85

The German economy responded to the decline in interest rates with renewed growth in 1983. The rate of inflation fell to 3.2 percent from 5.2 percent in the preceding year. Germany had reestablished its traditional external surplus during 1982. The new government was committed to a gradual reduction in fiscal deficits. Assured that the German economic fundamentals were in good order—with the exception of a persistently high rate of unemployment[41]—the Bundesbank perceived no need to tighten domestic monetary policy to prevent a depreciation of the D-mark, until the dollar entered the stratosphere in early 1985.

Between the March 1983 realignment of the EMS and the dollar peak in February 1985, domestic German monetary policy was steady.[42] The interest differential with the United States continued to favor the dollar. Downward pressure on the D-mark persisted, therefore, even after the restoration of growth and external surpluses for Germany. Furthermore, the strength of the dollar, stimulated by the American policy mix and abetted by the nonintervention stance of the US Treasury, was not justified by a comparison of cost competitiveness in the two countries.[43]

The Bundesbank participated in preparation of the Jurgensen Report of the G-5, and was content with its conclusion, released at the Williamsburg summit in 1983, that foreign exchange intervention was not likely to be effective if in conflict with the "fundamentals."[44] Bundesbank Pres-

---

41. Affirming the policy assignment effective since the mid-1970s (described by Scharpf, *Choice and Crisis in European Social Democracy*), the president of the Bundesbank declared flatly, "It's not our job to guarantee full employment; we're concerned with stability and price levels." *Euromoney*, October 1983, p. 201.

42. There were small exceptions. The Bundesbank raised market interest rates in September 1983 from 5.0 to 5.5 percent to offset what was regarded as an overeasing the previous March in the failed attempt to avoid a realignment within the EMS. (Interview with Karl Otto Pöhl, *Euromoney*, October 1983, p. 202.) It matched that increase with a hike in the official discount rate in early 1984.

43. Deutsche Bundesbank, *Report for the Year 1984*, p. 62.

44. Deutsche Bundesbank, *Report for the Year 1983*, pp. 70–74.

ident Pöhl publicly expressed his skepticism of the effectiveness of large-scale interventions in principle.[45]

However, the fundamental cost trends favored the falling D-mark, not the rising dollar. The Bundesbank therefore determined that foreign exchange intervention could indeed be useful and intervened frequently in the markets to suppress the rise of the US currency and support the D-mark. After the short-term interest rate differential rose from 4.1 to 6.3 percent between February and August 1984, in particular, the Bundesbank entered the markets. It amplified its foreign exchange operations during the first months of 1985, when the dollar peaked against the D-mark at 3.47 in February. During 1983, 1984, and the first three months of 1985, the Bundesbank bought roughly 51.3 billion of its own currency in exchange for dollars (figure 5.5).

The Williamsburg declaration on exchange rate policy also recognized that intervention could be more effective when coordinated among several countries and emphasized governments' readiness to act jointly when to do so would be helpful. Drawing on this statement, German authorities asked the US Treasury and Japanese finance ministry to join in concerted dollar-selling operations. The United States and Japan ostensibly agreed to do so at the January 1985 meeting of the G-5 in Washington. But the Treasury abided by this agreement by intervening only with modest sums, amounting to less than $600 million, and the Japanese not at all. Officials at the Bundesbank resented the lack of participation from the United States and Japan. They would recall this episode later in the year when American and Japanese officials came around to the German view that the dollar had been overvalued. ,

Without strong international backing for capping the dollar, the German central bank increased market rates of interest by about one-quarter point at the beginning of February 1985. The strength of the dollar had once again placed the Bundesbank in a dilemma. Though the domestic economic situation did not warrant a tightening, a persistent weakening of the D-mark might rekindle inflation, which had been successfully reduced to between 2.0 and 2.5 percent.[46] In consequence, the Bundesbank was pleased when the combined effects of monetary tightening and intervention appeared for the moment to reverse the sinking D-mark.

The contractionary effects of monetary tightening on the German economy were substantially offset by the export boom associated with the overstrong dollar. External demand also enabled the government to consoli-

---

45. "I think we should not exclude occasional intervention to avoid erratic fluctuations, but I am no fan of large-scale intervention. It can't change the fundamentals, as recent experience shows, and we ourselves have never urged the United States to intervene." *Fortune*, 5 September 1983, p. 46.

46. Deutsche Bundesbank, *Report for the Year 1984*, p. 2.

Figure 5.5 **Bundesbank operations in the dollar/D-mark market, 1983–94** (monthly)[a]

billions of D-marks

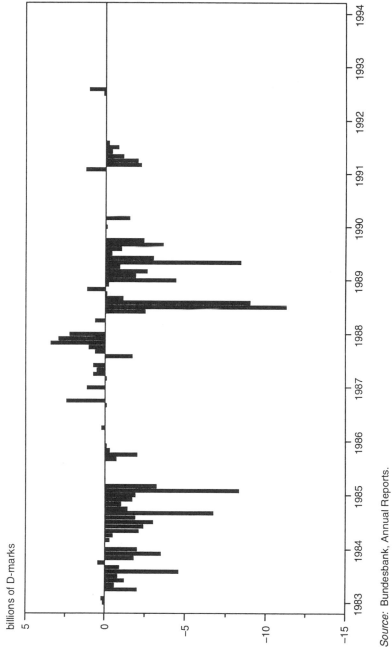

Source: Bundesbank, Annual Reports.

a. Includes operations by other central banks where they affect the external position of the Bundesbank..

date the fiscal deficit without further raising unemployment. During the period 1983–85, the average annual growth of the German economy was 2.3 percent. Remarkably, a full 1.8 percent of this was supplied by expansion of the trade surplus, and a mere 0.5 percent from domestic demand.

Though there was some discontent with the slow pace of economic recovery in Germany, neither the government nor private groups expressed discontent with the Bundesbank's exchange rate policy toward the dollar. The export solution helped to alleviate internal conflicts over both external and internal economic policies. However, American trade politics, and protectionist pressure in the US Congress in particular, disrupted the consensus on German exchange rate and monetary politics.

The Plaza Agreement

When mounting protectionism in the US Congress forced the Reagan administration to try to realign exchange rates, Treasury Secretary James Baker first approached Japanese officials. Only after the bilateral American-Japanese negotiations were well along, within one month of the Plaza meeting, were the Europeans consulted. Despite their view that the dollar exchange rate had been excessive, German officials had several reservations about agreeing to a dollar realignment.

First, Reagan administration and Fed officials had pressed Germany and the other surplus countries for expansionary demand policies.[47] Second, dollar depreciation threatened to get out of control and rupture the EMS. Third, Germany had already made a substantial contribution to dollar realignment, with the interventions it had conducted without substantial American and Japanese assistance during February and March.

During the negotiations leading up to the Plaza announcement, German officials consistently bargained for a much looser, nonbinding agreement than the one favored by their American and Japanese counterparts. That included the matters of the quantities of dollars to be sold, the new exchange rate levels sought, and the general political commitment to reduce imbalances. Bundesbank President Pöhl, Finance Minister Gerhard Stoltenberg, and the state secretary at the Ministry of Finance, Hans Tietmeyer, met with their French and British counterparts in Luxembourg to coordinate intra-European policy. The German side argued to the Americans and Japanese that the EMS countries should be considered as a group when calculating intervention obligations.[48] Most

---

47. For the development and rationale of the US position, see I. M. Destler and C. Randall Henning, *Dollar Politics: Exchange Rate Policymaking in the United States* (Washington: Institute for International Economics, 1989), chapter 4.

48. Yoichi Funabashi, *Managing the Dollar: From the Plaza to the Louvre* (Washington: Institute for International Economics, 1988), chapter 1. Funabashi discusses Germany in his chapter 5.

important, the German side firmly and successfully resisted American pressure to stimulate domestic demand.[49]

The markets responded dramatically to the Plaza communiqué and concerted intervention to depress the dollar. On the first trading day after the announcement, the D-mark (as well as the yen) registered its largest one-day rise against the dollar during the floating-rate period, moving from 2.84 to 2.69 to the dollar.[50] Consistent with Germany's position during the preparation of the agreement, however, German support for dollar depreciation proved to be substantially more limited than that of the other Plaza participants.

At 2.65 marks to the dollar, little more than 7 percent above the Plaza level, Pöhl declared that the exchange rate had reached a point "that is acceptable to us," hoping to stabilize it.[51] The assistant secretary of the treasury for international affairs, David Mulford, retorted that Germany had been the "least responsive" of the five represented at the Plaza and had "not satisfied" the administration.[52] Pöhl responded that too much had been interpreted into the agreement, which, he said, in no way endorsed movement to a target zone system. He added that "there is no economic justification for a more expansive fiscal policy" in Germany.[53] Thus began a two-year conflict between the German government and the Reagan administration over macroeconomic and exchange rate policy.

Resisting Appreciation: 1986–87

In late 1985 and the beginning of 1986, German exchange rate policy shifted from limiting the depreciation of the D-mark against the dollar to limiting its appreciation. The currency realignment, one year under way, would continue for two more years—though nobody at the Bundesbank or finance ministry could know in January 1986 how far the D-mark would eventually rise. The depressive effects on the German economy were already becoming apparent in early 1986. Yet Secretary Baker ignored German pleas to stop "talking down" the dollar.

---

49. The Plaza communiqué announced no significant policy changes for Germany . The government would, among other things, use fiscal policy to "encourage private initiative and productive investments and maintain price stability," "reduce progressively the share of the public sector in the economy through maintaining firm expenditure control," and adhere to the earlier-established schedule for tax cuts in 1986 and 1988. The Bundesbank would "continue to ensure a stable environment conducive to the expansion of domestic demand on a durable basis."

50. *New York Times*, 24 September 1985.

51. *Wall Street Journal*, 8 and 9 October 1985.

52. *Washington Post*, 20 November 1985.

53. *Washington Post*, 20 November 1985; *Wall Street Journal*, 12 December 1985.

German officials also were subject to continuing American pressure to expand domestic demand. Baker's demands for expansionary macroeconomic policy were backed by congressional threats to the international trading system should the US current account deficit persist. These formidable political pressures and D-mark appreciation placed great strain on the cooperation between the government and Bundesbank. At first, Bonn and Frankfurt presented a united front on exchange rate and macroeconomic policy; later, under strains of the ever stronger D-mark, the government would press the Bundesbank for monetary ease.

When the dollar fell below DM2.36, Finance Minister Stoltenberg declared that Germany "ha[d] no interest in further declines" of the currency.[54] He and Pöhl repeated the statement at a similar exchange rate level in mid-April.[55] They did not intervene in the foreign exchange market, though, until the exchange rate crossed the DM2.00 threshold in mid-September, for the first time in five years.[56]

The appreciation of the D-mark against the dollar provided a strong incentive to expand domestic demand in Germany to replace foreign demand. When confronted with interest rate reductions in the United States as well, the Bundesbank had little choice but to reduce interest rates in Germany too. The alternative was to countenance even greater appreciation of the D-mark, and thus an even greater slowing of the German economy—or a fiscal expansion, to which the federal government was implacably opposed.

But the Bundesbank, with the government's support, strongly resisted foreign pressure for interest rate reductions and reform of the international monetary system through 1986.[57] Germany refused the bargain that Japan accepted in the form of the Baker-Miyazawa accord of October: domestic demand stimulus in exchange for Baker's public and material support for currency stability. In early 1987, however, that bargain became increasingly attractive for several reasons.

First, the dollar fell precipitously by mid-January, to 1.83 D-mark, a level Stoltenberg described as exaggerated ("*überzeichnet*") and Pöhl described as having "gone far enough." The German Federation of Industry (BDI) expressed alarm at these new lows for the dollar and warned that export and domestic growth would be difficult to sustain. The Ger-

---

54. *Wall Street Journal*, 14 February 1986.

55. *New York Times*, 10 April 1986.

56. *Financial Times*, 19 September 1986.

57. European finance ministers and central bankers—illustrating the progress toward European monetary solidarity achieved since the locomotive dispute of the 1970s—refused to break ranks with the Bundesbank and criticized Baker for trying to use the "dollar weapon" to extract a demand stimulus in Germany. See *Financial Times*, 22 September 1986; *Wall Street Journal*, 23 September 1986.

man Association of Industry and Trade (DIHT) accused the United States of "currency dumping" and warned that the D-mark could rise against the EMS currencies as a result, a recent realignment notwithstanding.[58]

Second, in direct conflict with the G-7's stated need to reduce current account imbalances, the German current account surplus for 1986 had soared from DM48.4 billion in 1985 to DM85.1 billion. The new levels, 4.4 percent of German GNP, were far higher than those of any other large industrial country, including Japan.

Third, the national elections in January 1987 returned the governing conservative-liberal coalition to power. During the campaign, the liberal FDP proposed that the 1988 tax cuts should be advanced to 1987. The coalition thus agreed to reduce taxes by DM8.5 billion in January 1988 and DM25.0 billion, on a net basis, in January 1990. The election also precipitated realignment within the EMS, but that failed to calm the currencies in the system. Both currency instability and the medium-term fiscal stimulus reduced the political opportunity cost of a bargain with Baker.

The Louvre Accord

In response to these changed circumstances, the Bundesbank agreed to reduce the discount rate to 3.0 percent. At that time, Pöhl endorsed the proposal to advance the tax cuts, saying that the Bundesbank had "delivered" as far as monetary ease was concerned. Frankfurt later also would play down the overshooting of the money supply targets, saying that it would be inappropriate to tighten money with an appreciating D-mark.[59]

Next, the government and the Bundesbank accepted the stimulus-for-stability bargain offered by Baker at the Louvre meeting on 22 February. At that meeting, Baker agreed to stop talking down the dollar, and the ministers and governors established 5 percent target ranges for currency fluctuation. With the D-mark/dollar rate at 1.825 just prior to the meeting, the target range was DM1.738 to DM1.926.[60] On the fiscal front, Stoltenberg agreed to bring forward an unspecified amount of the planned 1990 cuts (later set at DM5.2 billion) to 1988.

The D-mark stayed within the target range during the following several months. The Bundesbank intervened in token amounts to limit the dollar's rise in March, and then in moderate amounts to limit its fall. The Bundesbank managed to avoid a substantial share of the burden of financing the US current account deficit in 1987, carried by other central banks. Nevertheless, both Stoltenberg and Pöhl argued strongly that the

---

58. *Neue Zürcher Zeitung*, 17 January 1987.

59. *Financial Times*, 2 April 1987.

60. Funabashi, *Managing the Dollar*, chapter 8.

United States should take responsibility for financing its own deficits, implying that American interest rates should be raised if necessary to do so.[61]

The Bundesbank was acutely aware that the Louvre Accord and the system of secret target ranges established there jeopardized its independence vis-à-vis its government, through the finance ministry's prerogatives over parity setting. It was for this reason the central bank had long since railed against precisely this sort of innovation in the international monetary system.[62]

The acid test of the Bundesbank's independence under the Louvre Accord came when the Central Bank Council decided, in September 1987, to tighten monetary policy. Officials in Frankfurt had been uneasy with low interest rates, approved under the duress of the pre-Louvre depreciation of the dollar. For the third year in a row, money supply growth was overshooting the target range, which the Bundesbank had widened from 3.5 to 5.5 percent to 3.0 to 6.0 percent (table 5.3). Though some overshooting could be tolerated temporarily, particularly when dollar weakness lowered import prices, the central bank perceived inflationary risks in letting it continue.

When the new Federal Reserve chairman, Alan Greenspan, raised the discount rate at the beginning of September, therefore, the Bundesbank saw this occasion as an opportunity to raise German interest rates. In late September, the Central Bank Council, led by Schlesinger, voted to raise the repurchase ("repo") rate by 10 basis points, effective in early October. Karl Otto Pöhl, who opposed the increase and was outvoted, flew to Washington later that same day to attend the annual meetings of the IMF and World Bank. There he broke the unwelcome news to

---

61. Karl Otto Pöhl, "Are We Moving Towards a More Stable International Monetary Order?" speech at the American Institute for Contemporary German Studies, Washington, 7 April 1987; Gerhard Stoltenberg, "The United States and Europe: Main Objectives for Economic Policies and International Cooperation," speech at Georgetown University, Washington, 10 April 1987.

62. To quote from its *Report for the Year 1985* (p. 86): "On the basis of all experience, ideas that are tantamount to introducing formal exchange rate regulations overestimate the disciplinary effect they can have on the economic and monetary policies of the countries concerned. Above all, however, the experience is ignored that under the present conditions of large-scale international capital transactions satisfactory possibilities hardly exist of shielding national monetary policy from disturbing foreign exchange movements in the absence of floating exchange rates among the major currencies. At all events, the Bundesbank was put in a position to pursue a monetary policy geared to stability on a lasting basis despite repeated massive inflows of capital only by floating the Deutsche Mark against the dollar. From the point of view of monetary policy, even relatively wide target zones for the exchange rates between the major currencies would, in the final analysis, not be any different from a system of fixed exchange rates; if target zones are to fulfil their purpose they would also need to be defended—with all the consequences to which this can give rise for monetary stability." See also p. 57.

Stoltenberg, who asked Pöhl not to discuss it at the Fund/Bank meetings. Within days, though, the Bundesbank's change of direction became clear, as the repurchase rate rose from its previous, steady level of 3.50 percent by not only 10 but 35 basis points in mid-October.[63]

As is now well-known, this decision and Secretary Baker's aggressive response sparked conflict that culminated in the worldwide stock market crash of 19 October. Baker met with Stoltenberg and Pöhl on the day of the crash in an effort to repair the damage. They agreed on a "flexible application" of the Louvre Accord to stabilize currencies, which were calm during the stock market crisis. They privately sanctioned a lowering of the dollar against the D-mark, a slight reduction in the Bundesbank's repurchase rate, in exchange for the Treasury's defending the lower dollar.[64] After a council meeting on 5 November attended by Stoltenberg, the Bundesbank announced a half-point Lombard rate cut to 4.0 percent and a return of the repurchase rate to the precrash 3.50 percent.

Stoltenberg was careful not to criticize the Bundesbank by name publicly, as he criticized the US Treasury secretary.[65] But it was clear that he and the finance ministry held views different from the Bundesbank about the desirability of maintaining the Louvre Accord. Stoltenberg and the federal government were sensitive to the political context of the stabilization effort. The depreciation of the dollar would eliminate some of the advantages of German producers over American competitors. Equally important, the tightening of monetary policy would be perceived as uncooperative at a time when the moment of truth for the US Congress on trade policy was approaching. Stoltenberg was therefore a tough inside advocate for monetary ease.[66]

In early November, the dollar fell to its previous all-time low against the D-mark of 1.70. At this rate, Stoltenberg declared that the D-mark had appreciated as much as it should.[67] In the face of policy disarray in Washington, however, the dollar slid to successive new lows against the German currency. The Bundesbank purchased substantial quantities of dollars on the foreign exchange markets. Intervention being insufficient

---

63. Bundesbank officials argued that this tightening was consistent with the Louvre Accord. See Hermann-Josef Dudler, "Monetary Policy and Exchange Market Management in Germany," in *Exchange Market Intervention and Monetary Policy* (Bank for International Settlements, Monetary and Economic Department: Basel, March 1988), p. 88.

64. *Wall Street Journal*, 21 October 1987.

65. Stoltenberg said that, although a fall in the dollar was preferable to slowing growth, Baker made a "mistake" but that "others also made mistakes." *Financial Times*, 5 November 1987.

66. See, for example, Samuel Brittan, "From Locomotive to Slowcoach," *Financial Times*, 22 February 1988.

67. *Washington Post*, 5 November 1987.

to stem the slide, however, Chancellor Kohl telephoned Pöhl to ask for an easing of monetary policy.[68] The Central Bank Council granted this request in early December by reducing the discount rate to 2.5 percent, the lowest level in the history of German central banking.[69]

A round of concerted foreign exchange intervention by the G-7 finally halted the three-year depreciation of the dollar at the beginning of 1988. At its low on 4 January, the dollar registered DM1.563. The dollar stabilization plus the easing of German monetary policy ended the US-German currency conflict of the 1980s. But G-7 cooperation proved to seriously constrain the freedom of maneuver of the Bundesbank.

Because the United States was impervious to foreign pressure to reduce the budget deficit, the G-7 coordination process was far more difficult than the EMS to steer toward Bundesbank preferences. To make matters worse for the German central bank, Stoltenberg affirmed the importance of G-7 exchange rate cooperation and dollar stabilization on several occasions in 1988.[70] He specifically endorsed DM1.70, the rate in early February, as an appropriate rate under the circumstances.[71]

Stoltenberg was a popular finance minister and at the peak of his political influence in early 1988.[72] His success at fiscal consolidation earned him great credibility and a strong reputation. Stoltenberg was considered the most likely successor to Chancellor Kohl, and his position on exchange rate management resonated with industry's desire to avoid further appreciation of the currency.

Coming from a popular, respected, and credible politician, with broad societal backing, visible support for G-7 cooperation constrained the Bundesbank. Stoltenberg's proclamations of support created a context of market expectations in which it was difficult for the Bundesbank to act independently without again provoking financial instability. Frankfurt therefore avoided tightening monetary policy before the Federal Reserve raised American interest rates.

Strengthening the EMS

The tension that D-mark/dollar movements created within the EMS was an additional, compelling reason for Germany to resist the depreciation

---

68. *Financial Times*, 14 September 1992.

69. In addition, Stoltenberg proposed that Germany conclude a firm agreement with the US Treasury to intervene in support of the dollar, which the Bundesbank opposed. Marsh, *The Bundesbank*, p. 40, n. 27.

70. Reported, for example, by *Die Welt*, 13 January 1988; *Reuters* and *DPA*, 4 February 1988.

71. *Associated Press–Dow Jones*, 8 February 1988.

72. Political scandals in his home state of Schleswig-Holstein would undermine his political status within the federal government only later.

of the dollar. The conventional wisdom had been that, because the D-mark played the role of "counterpole" to the dollar, the EMS would be strained during periods of dollar weakness and supported during periods of dollar strength.[73] The EMS had never been tested by a period of sustained dollar weakness until after the Plaza accord. The appreciation of the D-mark against the dollar produced EMS realignments in spring 1986 and winter 1987.

The realignment negotiations generated great bitterness on the part of Germany's partners, the French in particular. Within the Committee of Central Bank Governors, meeting at Basel, they wrested substantial concessions from the Germans on the operation and use of the very-short-term financing facility provided under the EMS. Announced at an Ecofin meeting at Nybourg in September 1987, this agreement (1) enlarged and extended this facility, (2) permitted funds raised thereby to be used for optional, *intramarginal* interventions (which the Bundesbank had discouraged), and (3) made debts partly repayable in ECU rather than entirely in the currency of the lender (i.e., D-marks). In exchange, the European partners agreed to permit exchange rates to fluctuate more freely within the margins.[74]

The Bundesbank and federal government were concerned about the liquidity effects within Germany of extending D-mark financing for intramarginal EMS interventions.[75] But the macroeconomic conflict with the United States, while contributing to EMS instability, had made the alternatives to European monetary integration unattractive. Global monetary relations were hardly hospitable for Germany on its own, as the United States was refusing to take responsibility for the financing of its 1987 current account deficit. Bundesbank officials, moreover, were aware that the transatlantic conflict would probably intensify when they raised their interest rates, as they planned to do. They therefore acceded to the Basel-Nybourg agreement, just in time for a new bout of instability in the wake of the autumn 1987 conflict.

Tightening EMS, Unraveling Target Ranges: 1988–89

During the late 1980s, the Bundesbank's independence was threatened from several quarters. Not only did the Louvre Accord and G-7 cooperation threaten the ability of the Bundesbank to tighten monetary policy, but the change in EMS operating rules concluded at Basel-Nybourg was

---

73. Giavazzi and Giovannini, *Limiting Exchange Rate Flexibility*, chapter 6.

74. Deutsche Bundesbank, *Report for the Year 1987*, pp. 64–70.

75. Intramarginal interventions had indirectly caused large increases in German liquidity prior to the 1986 realignment, for example. Dudler, "Monetary Policy and Exchange Market Management in Germany," pp. 83–85.

followed by an ambitious push from Bonn to strengthen European monetary cooperation.[76] Under a siege mentality, the Bundesbank rejected opportunities for exchange rate stabilization, even when the D-mark was weak. The German economy nonetheless performed extraordinarily well by international standards.

European Initiatives

European politics presented an even greater potential threat to Bundesbank independence in early 1988 than the Louvre Accord and G-7 cooperation. In January, on the 25th anniversary of the Franco-German Treaty of 1963, the German and French governments agreed to create a defense council to coordinate security policy and an "economic and financial council." Comprising the economic and finance ministers and the central bank governors of the two countries, the Franco-German council would meet four times each year. It was entrusted with the task of "maximum possible coordination" of economic policies, international and European, of the two countries. Originally conceived as a symbolic statement to commemorate the 1963 treaty, this governmental agreement was upgraded at the last minute to the status of a formal treaty protocol.[77] It would have the force of law in Germany, and as such countermand the Bundesbank Act of 1957. The draft amendment made no provision for central bank independence.[78]

The Bundesbank objected strenuously to the proposal when it was made public. Frankfurt had not been consulted during the preparation of the draft protocol. Central bank officials were deeply suspicious that this was yet another French maneuver to replace the D-mark with the ECU at the heart of the EMS, and thus undermine the anchor role performed by the Bundesbank. The public charge by French Prime Minister Jacques Chirac that the Bundesbank had been insufficiently supportive of the EMS, and Chirac's proposal that the system should be either reformed or abolished, gave these suspicions credibility.[79] The Central Bank Council demanded that the accord specifically protect the independence of the Bundesbank, and this provision was included in the final version of the treaty passed by the Bundestag.[80]

---

76. The *Economist* declared that these pressures constituted the biggest challenge to the central bank's independence in its history. *The Economist*, 13 February 1988, pp. 76–79.

77. *Economist*, 13 February 1988.

78. Kennedy, *The Bundesbank*, pp. 94–97.

79. *AP-DJ* and *DPA*, 7 January 1988. Chirac was critical of the Bundesbank's policy of intervening only in US dollars, rather than other European currencies such as the French franc. Pöhl rebutted these accusations after a Central Bank Council meeting in early February. *Financial Times*, 22 January 1988.

80. Kennedy, *The Bundesbank*, pp. 94–97.

A second European challenge to the Bundesbank's status proved to be far more durable. At the same time that Prime Minister Chirac criticized German policy within the EMS, French Finance Minister Edouard Balladur proposed the "rapid pursuit of the monetary construction of Europe" in a memorandum to the Ecofin Council. German Foreign Minister Genscher responded favorably with a memorandum of his own that proposed the creation of a European central bank, independent from national governments, and a common currency. Genscher argued that the European central bank and common currency were necessary to the completion of the single market and proposed early consideration of monetary union by a committee of experts to be appointed by the European Council.[81]

Bundesbank officials were furious with Genscher for his agreement in essence with the French position. President Pöhl publicly denied that he opposed a European central bank in principle. But he strongly discouraged the movement by arguing that the political basis for monetary union was dubious. He explained that the D-mark, not the ECU, had become the stability anchor of the EMS, and added, "It would be disastrous if one tried to loosen this anchor."[82] Calculating that the finance minister would counterbalance the foreign minister, Bundesbank officials urged Stoltenberg to weigh in on these negotiations.[83]

Finance Minister Stoltenberg, who chaired the Ecofin Council during the first half of 1988, was indeed more cautious than Genscher. However, Stoltenberg's priority was to secure full and irrevocable liberalization of financial controls and capital flows within the single market. Financial liberalization was a long-standing demand of both the German Finance Ministry and the Bundesbank. In a memorandum of his own, Stoltenberg stressed that any European central bank would have to be completely independent and possess a mandate to pursue price stability. But, far from ruling out progress toward monetary union, he agreed to consider it provided other governments dropped their objections to financial liberalization.[84] When, at an Ecofin meeting in June 1988, the other governments approved a plan to end all capital controls among the Community countries, the coast was clear for a meaningful discussion of monetary union.[85]

The Bundesbank had favored the abolition of capital controls, among other reasons, because it calculated that without them France and Italy

81. Daniel Gros and Niels Thygesen, *European Monetary Integration: From the European Monetary System to European Monetary Union* (London: Longman, 1992), pp. 311–17.

82. *Financial Times*, 3 March 1988.

83. *Frankfurter Allgemeine Zeitung*, 1 and 2 March 1988.

84. Gros and Thygesen, *European Monetary Integration*, pp. 311–17.

85. *New York Times*, 14 June 1988.

would have to implement tougher anti-inflation policies to sustain their currencies within the EMS. But, in addition to insulating the French and Italian economies, French and Italian capital controls had also protected the Bundesbank from having to undertake intervention that threatened domestic stability. The decision to remove this protection—coming as it did after the German concessions in Basel-Nybourg—provided an additional incentive for the German central bank to explore whether EMU could be advanced on the Bundesbank's own terms.

Meeting at Hanover, shortly after the Ecofin meeting, the European Council, the heads of state and government of the 12 EC countries, adopted Genscher's proposal to establish a special committee to prepare a comprehensive study on how EMU might be developed. Commission President Jacques Delors, a former French finance minister, was appointed to chair the Committee for the Study of Economic and Monetary Union. The committee, given one year to prepare a report, was dominated by the central bankers of the Community, Pöhl most senior among them.

The decisions taken at the Ecofin Council and European Council meetings prodded the Bundesbank to seize the initiative and attempt to regain some control over the monetary integration negotiations. Pöhl advised the Delors Committee that economic convergence would have to precede monetary union, rather than vice versa, and that convergence would "probably not exist for the foreseeable future." In the meantime occasional realignments would be necessary within the ERM. To the extent that competence in the monetary field was transferred to the Community, the Committee of Central Bank Governors, which Pöhl chaired, would be the appropriate body to receive it.[86]

The German government and Bundesbank also tried to persuade the British to take a more active role. Both Stoltenberg and Pöhl encouraged Prime Minister Margaret Thatcher and Chancellor Nigel Lawson to bring the pound sterling into the Exchange Rate Mechanism of the EMS.[87] The German finance ministry's aim in doing so was to balance the weight of France in the integration process. The Bundesbank wanted to counter French influence and slow the momentum that the monetary negotiations had suddenly gained.

---

86. Karl Otto Pöhl, "The Further Development of the European Monetary System," in *Report on Economic and Monetary Union*, Committee for the Study of Economic and Monetary Union (Luxembourg: Office for Official Publications of the European Communities, 1989), pp. 129–55. His paper also argued that broader economic and political integration would have to parallel monetary union and that, for political reasons, no monetary union should be formed from a subgroup of the Community membership.

87. *AP-DJ*, 28 March 1988; *The Economist*, 13 February 1988.

Monetary Policy

In 1988, German domestic demand was slowing from its rate of 3.4 percent in 1986 and 2.7 percent in 1987. Even before the stock market crash, growth was weak, only 1.7 percent in 1987; forecasts anticipated no upturn. Unemployment appeared to be stuck at about 9 percent. Economists pondered the German economy's failure to respond to the stimulative monetary policy.[88] Conscious that interest rates were at all-time lows, the Bundesbank argued that any additional stimulus to domestic demand should come from the fiscal side.[89] Despite weak domestic demand, surprisingly, Secretary Baker and the Reagan administration desisted in their efforts to prod Bonn to stimulate.

With inflation low and growth weak, the Bundesbank had no immediate desire to tighten its super-easy monetary policy. It waited until the US Federal Reserve raised American interest rates in spring and summer 1988 and the dollar strengthened. But money supply growth had overshot the Bundesbank's targets for three years in a row and was in the process of doing so in 1988 as well (table 5.3). The anti-inflation hawks on the Central Bank Council argued that the overshooting placed Germany in an exposed position, wherein a weak D-mark would quickly feed inflation. Beginning in early summer, therefore, the Bundesbank began to raise interest rates.[90] This time there was no adverse reaction in the world stock markets. The Bundesbank successfully turned the corner, one year earlier than the Bank of Japan.

A Missed Opportunity

The Bundesbank also intervened to defend its currency during the dollar rally of 1988. Intervention began at the 1.72 level in early June and continued until after the dollar peaked at 1.92 in mid-August. Between June and September, the net external asset position of the Bundesbank owing to dollar interventions fell DM23.9 billion[91]—the largest interventions in defense of the D-mark since early 1985 (figure 5.5). Partly at

---

88. New explanations for the sluggishness of the German economy focused on microeconomic constraints. Leslie Lipschitz, Jeroen Kremers, Thomas Mayer, and Donogh McDonald, *The Federal Republic of Germany: Adjustment in a Surplus Country*, IMF Occasional Paper 64 (Washington: International Monetary Fund, January 1989).

89. The Bundesbank was repeating its advice to the government during the locomotive controversy in 1978.

90. Hermann-Josef Dudler, "Monetary Control and Exchange Market Management: German Policy Experience from the 1985 Plaza Agreement to the 1989 Summit of the Arch," paper presented to the Bank of Israel and David Horowitz Institute Conference on Aspects of Central Bank Policymaking, Tel-Aviv, 3–5 January 1990, pp. 13–15.

91. Including roughly $2.5 billion of US operations.

the request of the Bundesbank, US authorities joined these intervention operations.

The Bundesbank's response was very different during the dollar rally of 1989, the second in as many years.[92] Pöhl declared in January of 1989 that his priority was to fight inflation, by supporting the D-mark and tightening credit, even at the expense of growth.[93] The Bundesbank participated in joint intervention operations at the beginning of the year.

But the German central bank discontinued dollar interventions in the spring. At one point, the Central Bank Council discussed interventions and decided to suspend them, on the grounds that they would be ineffective under the prevailing conditions. The Land central bank presidents probably overrode a majority of the Directorate on this matter. Representing the views of the council as a whole nonetheless, Pöhl's public comments on the strong dollar were conspicuously complacent.

The Bundesbank's reluctance to participate in concerted intervention drew criticism from its G-7 partners.[94] The German finance ministry was not happy. With the markets suspecting that the Bundesbank had foresworn defense of the D-mark, the dollar surpassed its August 1988 highs in May and kept going to DM2.05, which it reached in early June.[95]

The events of mid-1989 constitute a missed opportunity to support exchange rate stability with domestic monetary policy in a nondilemma situation. American interest rates had peaked, but German interest rates had still to be raised further. Between the middle of 1988 and the end of 1989, the Bundesbank raised the discount rate six times, from 2.5 percent to 5.5 percent. The Bundesbank might have increased interest rates more aggressively in spring 1989 to dampen the depreciation of the D-mark and support the target ranges informally operated by the G-7. Instead, the Central Bank Council waited until the end of June to raise the discount and Lombard rates another one-half point, and then until early October to raise them again. The increases were clearly not timed to foster exchange rate stability. The Central Bank Council, besieged by threats to its independence, resisted giving any impression that domestic monetary policy would be used to stabilize currencies.

---

92. The slide of the D-mark in 1989 was fueled by the imposition of a withholding tax on interest income of foreign holders of German bonds, designed to block tax evasion. Under a firestorm of protest, the tax was later revoked.

93. *Wall Street Journal*, 27 January 1989.

94. *Wall Street Journal*, 19 May 1989.

95. Wendy Dobson, *Economic Policy Coordination: Requiem or Prologue?* POLICY ANALYSES IN INTERNATIONAL ECONOMICS 30 (Washington: Institute for International Economics, April 1991), pp. 110–15.

The Would-Be EMS Realignment

The Bundesbank's October tightening, in fact, appeared to be specifically designed to force the European governments to realign the EMS. As early as the end of 1988, Bundesbank officials had come to the conclusion that another general realignment was desirable owing to accumulated inflation differentials. In June 1989, the Spanish government brought the peseta, another high-inflation currency, into the ERM. By October 1989, more than two and a half years had passed since the realignment of January 1987, the longest period without an adjustment of the central rates since the founding of the EMS.

A realignment of the EMS was firmly resisted by the governments, however. During discussions within the Ecofin Council about whether to realign in early autumn 1989, French Prime Minister Rocard telephoned Chancellor Kohl to say that under no circumstances would he permit a devaluation of the French franc against the D-mark. Kohl backed the French government, and told the Bundesbank in no uncertain terms that Bonn would not agree to a realignment—a clear illustration of the ultimate authority of the government in EMS realignment decisions.

In January 1990, the Italian government devalued the central rate for the lira modestly while bringing the currency into the narrow 2.25 percent bands of the ERM. The Bundesbank tried to use this occasion to secure a broader realignment involving other currencies, but was again thwarted.[96] Distinguishing his views from those of the French and German governments, Karl Otto Pöhl declared, "A realignment of the EMS is not on the agenda because the major players in that system do not want it."[97] This was the last active attempt by the German central bank to achieve a realignment before German unification, which would dramatically strengthen the economic case for a revaluation.

The decision taken at the Hanover summit by the German and other European governments to fully liberalize capital movements by July 1990 marked the beginning of a new period in the history of the EMS. This new, fourth phase of the system, which lasted about three years, was intended to serve as the transition to monetary union. It was characterized by (1) high capital mobility among all member countries, (2) relatively stable prices within the core group, (3) a commitment to limit the use of realignments to exceptional circumstances, (4) movement of the Italian lira from broad to narrow bands, and, with the eventual inclusion of Britain (October 1990) and Portugal (April 1992) in the ERM, (5) a

---

96. *Financial Times*, 10 January 1990.

97. When asked if Germany was asking for a D-mark revaluation, Pöhl said, "I don't think you can say that. The German position is more differentiated. . . . That is a very delicate subject." *Financial Times*, 10 January 1990.

Table 5.4 Germany: government budget balances, 1980–93

Year	Central government[a]		General government	
	Billion DM	Percent GNP	Billion DM	Percent GNP
1980	−27.6	−1.9	−53.7	−3.6
1981	−38.0	−2.5	−70.2	−4.6
1982	−37.7	−2.4	−65.2	−4.1
1983	−31.9	−1.9	−56.4	−3.4
1984	−28.6	−1.6	−49.2	−2.8
1985	−22.7	−1.3	−37.4	−2.1
1986	−23.3	−1.2	−36.0	−1.9
1987	−27.9	−1.4	−47.6	−2.4
1988	−36.0	−1.7	−54.8	−2.6
1989	−15.0	−0.7	−9.0	−0.4
1990	−21.0	−0.9	−30.5	−1.3
1991	−52.0	−2.0	−109.5	−4.2
1992	−30.0	−1.0	−111.1	−3.7
1993	−68.0	−2.2	−140.0	−4.5

Source: Deutsche Bundesbank, annual and monthly reports, various issues. Data for 1993 are preliminary. Data pertain to unified Germany, beginning in 1991.

wider membership.[98] The presumption against realignments within the new EMS proved to be premature, under the circumstances that faced Germany and its European partners in the early 1990s.

Overview

The international controversy over macroeconomic policy coordination during the second half of the 1980s had centered on stimulating demand in surplus countries. But for all the G-7 talk about stimulative packages, it is clear in retrospect that fiscal policy played no sustained role in stimulating German demand. Under the conservative-liberal coalition, between 1983 and 1989, the German federal budget deficit fluctuated between 1 and 2 percent of GNP (table 5.4). Measures of the stimulative impulse show that German fiscal policy was slightly contractionary in 1985, neutral in 1986 and 1987, slightly expansionary in 1988, and contractionary in 1989. When changes in state and local budgets are considered, German fiscal policy was roughly neutral during the 1986–89 period as a whole. By comparison, in Japan, where monetary expansion created greater latitude for fiscal consolidation, the contractionary fiscal impulse amounted to 2.7 percent of GNP.[99]

Germany had many reasons to be pleased with its macroeconomic performance at the end of the 1980s. There had been weak spots in

---

98. Gros and Thygesen, *European Monetary Integration*, chapter 5.

99. IMF, *World Economic Outlook*, May 1991, tables A16 and A17, pp. 147–48.

economic performance over the course of the decade. Unemployment, although falling, had remained above 2 million people since 1982. Growth was below the OECD average for the decade as a whole. German investment and productivity growth also ranked low among the other main industrial countries over the decade. Nonetheless, at the end of the decade, the economy appeared to be in very good condition. During 1988 and 1989, private demand proved to be unexpectedly robust. The trade surplus broadened, pushing German economic growth to a very respectable 3.7 and 3.8 percent in those years. Unemployment declined to 7 percent and consumer price inflation, nearly snuffed out during 1986–88, remained below 3 percent.

Germany's external performance was remarkable. From 1986 through 1989, the current account ran an unprecedented string of surpluses substantially above 4 percent of GNP in each year. The trade surplus registered 6 percent of GNP during these years, propelling Germany temporarily to the status of the world's greatest exporter. Relative to the size of the economy, these surpluses surpassed by far the surplus of Japan.

While the D-mark had appreciated greatly against the dollar, it had been stabilized against the European currencies. Thus, after the 20 percent appreciation between 1985 and 1987, the nominal effective exchange rate confronted by German industry remained quite stable (figure 5.3). Comparatively low inflation conferred additional competitive advantages on Germany within the EMS area as well as outside it.[100] While the trade surplus with the United States shrank between 1985 and 1989, the surplus vis-à-vis the Community countries expanded from DM32 billion to DM94 billion! The surplus also increased against the other countries that had pegged their currencies to the D-mark: Austria and Switzerland.[101] By supporting external surpluses while at the same time restraining domestic inflation, domestic and external monetary policy had served Germany very well.

The timing of this macroeconomic success was fortunate. When the decline of communism in the Soviet Union sparked a popular political revolution in the German Democratic Republic (GDR) in 1989, the Federal Republic was well positioned to absorb the costs of German unification.

German unification is an exceptional but revealing case of policymaking and is treated in the next section. Unification fundamentally changed

---

100. Gros and Thygesen, *European Monetary Integration*, chapter 5. The real depreciation of the D-mark within the EMS is greater when calculated on the basis of consumer price inflation rather than unit labor cost, and particularly pronounced against the Italian lira and Spanish peseta.

101. *Monthly Report of Deutsche Bundesbank*, various issues, table IX.2. The balance with the United States fell from a DM23 billion surplus in 1985 to a DM8 billion surplus in 1989 and to a small deficit in 1991.

the politics of the European integration, the subject of the second following section.

German Unification

The unification of the country presented enormous challenges to the Federal Republic, a task made especially difficult by the rapidity of the political disintegration of the GDR. The absorption of the East by the West, which formally occurred on 3 October 1990, marked the end of the Cold War and the beginning of a new era of European and world politics. The process of unification, in its political and economic aspects, has been examined in depth elsewhere.[102] The focus of the present study is the management of monetary and exchange rate policy by the Bundesbank and government during unification, and the ramifications of their decisions for European integration and international monetary cooperation.[103]

The Bundesbank, this study has argued, is the most independent of the world's leading central banks. Yet, during the process of unification, the government dominated several key monetary policy decisions. Because unification internalized what had been a part of external monetary policy—the relationship between the D-mark and the East German mark—decisions of the government struck at the heart of the Bundesbank's exclusive monetary authority. These events illustrate that even independent central banks, which are delegated monetary authority within, not outside, a state governmental structure, are dependent on changes in their political environment.

German Monetary Union

Once the Berlin Wall was breached on 9 November 1989, the two German governments began to negotiate the terms of political unification. East German citizens were now free to settle in the West—and in fact had been doing so in large numbers since Hungary permitted free emigration for them in spring 1989. The influx presented an economic and social problem of major proportions in the West.

---

102. See, for example, Catherine McArdle Kelleher, "The New Germany: An Overview," and Michael Kreile, "The Political Economy of the New Germany," in *The New Germany and the New Europe*, Paul B. Stares, ed. (Washington: Brookings Institution, 1992), pp. 11–54, 55–92; W. R. Smyser, *The Economy of United Germany: Colossus at the Crossroads* (New York: St. Martin's Press, 1992); Paul J. J. Welfens, ed., *Economic Aspects of German Unification* (Berlin: Springer-Verlag, 1992); Leslie Lipschitz and Donogh McDonald, eds., *German Unification: Economic Issues*, Occasional Paper 75 (Washington: International Monetary Fund, December 1990).

103. See as well Marsh, *The Bundesbank*, chapter 8, pp. 196–227.

Chancellor Kohl, also concerned that unification depended on the precarious political position of Soviet leader Mikhail Gorbachev, therefore decided to aggressively pursue political unification and offered a 10-point plan to achieve it.[104] At the beginning of February 1990, the Chancellor proposed an early union of the two countries in economic, monetary, and social matters to serve until such time as full political unification could be secured. In this way, Kohl and his government sought to reassure East German citizens and stem migration across the inter-German border.

In a stunning display of the primacy of political power over monetary management, Chancellor Kohl dominated, almost humiliated, the Bundesbank during negotiations over German monetary union. On 6 February, completely unaware of Kohl's decision, Pöhl met with his East German counterpart and declared that an early move to German monetary union was "a fantasy."[105] Helmut Schlesinger described the idea as "very unrealistic."[106] Applying the logic of the long-standing German argument vis-à-vis the European partners, the East German economy, whose structure and productivity was so different from that of a Western capitalist country, had to converge toward that of the West before monetary union could be seriously contemplated.[107]

Only hours after Pöhl's statement to the press, the chancellor announced that his government was launching negotiations immediately with the East German government over currency union. To underscore his commitment to the decision, Kohl added, "I consider this step necessary," citing a "severe psychological deterioration" in the East. The president of the Bundesbank made an unusual appearance at the cabinet meeting convened the next day to formally endorse the decision. Constrained by the political imperative of unification, however, Pöhl voiced no objection.[108] Despite his and the Bundesbank's well-known reservations, Pöhl declared that the central bank would "loyally support" the decision of the government.[109]

---

104. For the evolution of the strategy of the Chancellor's Office, see the account by Kohl's controversial foreign policy advisor, Horst Teltschik, *329 Tage: Innenansichten der Einigung* (Berlin: Siedler Verlag, 1991).

105. "We both believe it would be premature to already consider such a far-reaching step at this stage," he elaborated. *Wall Street Journal*, 7 February 1990.

106. *Financial Times*, 7 February 1990.

107. For a comparison of the East and West German economies at the time of unification, see Deutsche Bank, Economics Department, *German Economic and Monetary Union* (Frankfurt: Deutsche Bank, June 1990); Lipschitz and McDonald, eds., *German Unification*.

108. Teltschik, *329 Tage*, pp. 130–32.

109. *Wall Street Journal*, 8 February 1990.

The chancellor had made currency union with East Germany part of the "general economic policy of the Government," in the words of the Bundesbank law, which the Bundesbank was obliged to support. German unification was the supreme political goal of the Federal Republic, one espoused continuously by the political parties and institutions (even if they never dreamed it could be realized), and incorporated into the constitution. Short of a demonstrable threat to the German economy and financial system, the Bundesbank had no political standing to oppose a government decision to use currency union to achieve unification.

Having been abjectly defeated on the timing of monetary union, the Bundesbank scrambled to ensure that the terms of the union protected monetary stability and the central bank's bureaucratic prerogatives. Frankfurt promulgated three far-reaching conditions for monetary union: that the GDR fundamentally reform its economic system, a condition tantamount to accepting virtually the entire set of West German laws and institutions; that the East German banking system be reconstructed along Western lines; and that East Germany surrender control over monetary policy to the Bundesbank. These conditions were essentially endorsed and applied by the Bonn government.

Weakened by the desire of its now assertive populace for unification, the outgoing GDR government conceded almost all of the West German demands in the negotiations during winter and spring 1990. The D-mark would become the currency of the united Germany. The Bundesbank would have sole authority to manage the currency. The Bundesbank would effectively colonize the monetary and banking system of the GDR until such time as the GDR was absorbed by the Federal Republic. Bundesbank officers would be authorized to carry firearms, if needed, to provide security during the changeover to the D-mark.

The Bundesbank did not have its way, however, on one important substantive issue of monetary policy: the conversion rate between D-marks and the East German marks. The currency conversion directly affected the size of the money supply in the new monetary union. The conversion decision also directly determined the wealth of East German citizens and thus, potentially, the results of the upcoming series of elections in the GDR, in which the SPD was favored. Shortly before the GDR national elections in mid-March, therefore, Kohl announced that the conversion rate would be one-to-one for an unspecified amount of savings.[110] For many reasons, of which this was an important one, the CDU and FDP won the election in the East.

The Bundesbank issued a counterproposal within weeks that would have converted East German savings at two-for-one beyond the first

---

110. *New York Times*, 14 March 1990. Kohl made this announcement in a campaign speech for conservative political parties in the East German town of Cottbus.

2,000 East German marks, which could be converted at parity.[111] Because purchasing-power-parity comparisons suggested a conversion rate of something closer to 4.4 East German marks per D-mark, Frankfurt argued that even two-for-one was generous.[112] The Bundesbank put its reputation on the line, dispersing senior officials to television talk shows to argue the case for the less favorable rate.[113] Vice President Schlesinger and other Bundesbank officials threatened to tighten monetary policy if the government granted the generous conversion rate.[114] The Bundesbank expected popular political backing: an overwhelming majority of West German citizens opposed the one-for-one conversion rate.[115]

But Kohl's preelection pledge, ambiguous though it was, proved to be politically irreversible. East Germans demonstrated in large numbers for the favorable conversion rate. In the face of this popular outcry, no senior politician in Bonn was willing to back the Bundesbank's proposal. The governing coalition therefore decided to convert up to 4,000 East German marks at parity for most adults.[116] Importantly, wages, salaries and pensions were also to be converted at parity. The state treaty ratified by the two governments established 1 July 1990 as the date of economic, monetary, and social union.[117] On that day, East Germans exchanged their marks, physically resembling play money, and bank balances for D-marks in festive celebration. Again on an important matter of monetary policy, the Bundesbank was overruled.

Members of the Central Bank Council sharply criticized the Bonn government for its failure to consult them on a range of issues. Not only had Kohl circumvented the Bundesbank on German monetary union, he did not consult the central bank on the establishment of a German Unity Fund—for which the Bundesbank was responsible for issuing government debt—or for an April initiative on European monetary union (discussed below). Wilhelm Nölling, president of the Land Central Bank in Hamburg and regarded as less hard-line on monetary questions, said,

---

111. *Monthly Report of the Deutsche Bundesbank*, July 1990, pp. 14–16.

112. Deutsche Bank, *German Economic and Monetary Union*, p. 23.

113. *Washington Post*, 24 April 1990.

114. *Financial Times*, 6 and 24 April 1990, and 24 May 1990.

115. One poll indicated that 86 percent of West Germans opposed the one-for-one conversion rate.

116. Children were allowed to convert 2,000 marks, and adults over 59 years of age 6,000 marks, at parity. Savings beyond these levels, and all other claims and liabilities, were converted at two-for-one. See "Terms of the Currency Conversion in the German Democratic Republic on 1 July 1990," *Monthly Report of the Deutsche Bundesbank*, June 1990, pp. 40–45.

117. For an analysis of the State Treaty, see Deutsche Bank, *German Economic and Monetary Union*.

"The government has to finally stop acting as if the autonomy of the Bundesbank has been put aside for the process of reunification."[118] Pöhl himself seriously considered resigning at this point, in protest of the government's treatment of the central bank, and later acknowledged that he probably should have done so.[119]

The unification experience demonstrates that broad societal and political support is necessary for the Bundesbank to prevail in conflicts with the government. The division of the country had caused anguish and frustration for its citizens, on both sides of the divide. Consequently, one objective that could successfully compete with price stability among Germans was national unification. German monetary unification, more precisely, illustrated that the Bundesbank's popular support depends primarily on its defense of price stability and that the German public views central bank independence to be a means to that objective, rather than an end in itself.

German institutions and the public at large were concerned about inflation and the financial costs of unification. But the immediate threat to domestic price stability and the economy that might arise from a generous conversion rate was in fact quite dubious. In the absence of a demonstrable, sure threat, the private banks and the peak associations were not willing to back the Bundesbank in its conflict with the government on issues that the government judged to be decisive in unification. For example, rather than supporting the Bundesbank, Helmut Geiger, the president of the German Savings Bank Association, the most conservative of all the German peak associations, said that the Central Bank Council's conversion proposal was not politically realistic.[120]

The conversion rate decision has since been criticized as the source of Germany's subsequent economic troubles and the ultimate cause of the severe tightening of monetary policy on the part of the Bundesbank in 1991 and 1992.[121] But the decision on the conversion rate should be placed in perspective, relative to the numerous other economic policy decisions that attended German unification.

---

118. Wilhelm Nölling, *Geld und die deutsche Vereinigung* [Money and German Unification], Hamburger Beiträge zur Wirtschafts- und Währungspolitik in Europa, Heft 8 (Hamburg, July 1991), pp. 67–71. Nölling was joined in this criticism by Helmut Hesse, the president of the Land Central Bank in Lower Saxony.

119. Dieter Balkhausen, *Gutes Geld und Schlechte Politik: Der Report über die Bundesbank* [Good Money and Bad Politics: A Report on the Bundesbank] (Düsseldorf: Econ Verlag, 1992); *Financial Times*, 15 May 1992. Pöhl nonetheless criticized Nölling and Hesse at the time for making their criticism of the federal government public. See Nölling, *Geld und die deutsche Vereinigung*, pp. 67–71; Marsh, *The Bundesbank*, pp. 217–21.

120. Despite his warning that unification would be expensive. *New York Times*, 8 February 1990; *Financial Times*, 6 April 1990.

121. See, for example, Wilhelm Nölling, *Geld und die deutsche Vereinigung*, pp. 21–26.

The conversion rate was generous indeed, and was clearly based on political rather than economic considerations. The one-shot increase in the money supply that the conversion entailed rendered the control of the monetary aggregates and inflation on the part of the Bundesbank more difficult. However, because several different conversion rates were in fact used, the average conversion rate was not one-for-one but 1.8 East German marks for one D-mark, which compared favorably to the Central Bank Council's recommendation of a two-for-one conversion. The generous conversion contributed only a few percentage points to the money supply in excess of the requirements for noninflationary growth.[122] The monetary overhang that resulted, while posing a problem for the Bundesbank, could be managed by liquidity operations and adjustments in money supply growth targets without enormous difficulty. The Bundesbank itself acknowledged this reality at the time, and indeed emphasized it, as it sought to reassure the financial markets that it would nonetheless be able to maintain its stable course.[123]

Compared with other economic policy decisions made in the wake of German unification, therefore, the impact of the conversion rate was relatively modest. The slow pace of privatization and investment in the five new Länder, public transfer payments to the former East Germans, fiscal policy, and wage agreements—not the conversion rate—were the primary cause of Germany's economic tribulations after unification.

---

122. The increase in the D-mark money supply owing to the conversion would ideally have been proportionate to the productive capacity of the East German economy relative to the West German economy, with an allowance for what was expected to be a greater preference for East Germans to hold money (as opposed to higher-yielding investment assets). But the size of the East German economy and the liquidity preference of East Germans were two key uncertainties facing West German policymakers. The conversion in fact added 15 percent (DM180 billion) to the D-mark money supply, compared to what was expected to be a 10 percent increment in productive capacity.

After unification, it became clear that the productive capacity of the five new Länder had been overestimated, and was in actuality closer to 7 percent of the productive output of the former West Germany rather than 10 percent. At the same time, however, the holdings of M3 on the part of East Germans fell dramatically during the first year after German monetary union, as people switched unexpectedly quickly into higher-yielding assets. By the middle of 1991, M3 holdings in the former East Germany had fallen to perhaps 11.5 percent of the preunification D-mark money supply. This decline was reflected in slow growth in all-German M3 during the first half of 1991. In recognition of this slowdown, the Bundesbank lowered its growth targets for all-German M3 in July 1991 from 4–6 percent to 3–5 percent. Thus, the overhang produced by the generous conversion was no more than 4 or 5 percent of the money supply at the most.

See "Review of the 1991 Monetary Target," *Monthly Report of the Deutsche Bundesbank*, July 1991, pp. 14–18; Deutsche Bundesbank, *Report for the Year 1990*, pp. 46–51; Deutsche Bundesbank, *Report for the Year 1991*, pp. 45–48.

123. "The Monetary Union with the German Democratic Republic," *Monthly Report of the Deutsche Bundesbank*, July 1990, p. 19. See also "One Year of German Economic, Monetary, and Social Union," *Monthly Report of the Deutsche Bundesbank*, July 1991, pp. 19–20.

Fiscal and Wage Environment

Whereas the Bundesbank successfully met the monetary challenge of unification, the fiscal and labor market conditions proved to be far more constraining. Kohl's strategy of rapid unification entailed enormous costs, which were only gradually realized. Other Eastern European countries could retain international competitiveness through the depreciation of their currencies. The five new Länder constituting the former East Germany, by contrast, no longer had an exchange rate vis-à-vis the Federal Republic, and its new exchange rate vis-à-vis the rest of the world forced them to compete on Western terms. The federal government had to shield the people from the resulting collapse of industrial production through fiscal transfers that would amount to DM140 billion, over two-thirds of total Eastern GNP, in 1991.[124] (The annual fiscal transfer is thus roughly the same order of magnitude as the one-shot monetary transfer that was effected through the July 1990 currency conversion, but continues year after year.)

In the spring of 1990, however, during the negotiations over the State Treaty, the governing coalition promised West Germans that it would not raise their taxes to cover the cost of unification.[125] Already in autumn 1990 the transfer payments to the former East Germany—effected through the federal budget, a special Fund for German Unity, and the social insurance and unemployment compensation programs, among other channels—began to mount. It had become clear that the public-sector deficits of the united Germany, including the budgets for the Bundespost, Bundesbahn, and Treuhandanstalt, would be on the order of 5 or 6 percent of GNP.

The Bundesbank bitterly criticized the government's no-tax-increase pledge. The central bank also warned the federal, Land, and local governments to limit spending, or interest rates would have to be raised. With the national election on 2 December safely behind him, and the conservative-liberal coalition returned to power, Kohl reversed his posi-

---

124. The original government estimates, calculated in early 1990, claimed that the economic costs of German unification would amount to only 1 or 2 percent of West German GNP per year. Even the opposition SPD, which argued that the government was minimizing these estimates, did not foresee the enormity of the cost overrun. The former state secretary of the Ministry of Economics, Otto Schlecht, reflects on these estimates: "We deceived ourselves about the size and depth of the restructuring crisis. We gave prominence to the positive elements [about East German economic prospects] and forced the negative ones into the background. This was because we wanted people to take heart—and because there was an election campaign." Quoted in Marsh, *The Bundesbank*, p. 213.

125. Finance Minister Theo Waigel said, "We would be taking leave of our senses if we crippled a well-functioning [West German] economy with tax increases." *Wall Street Journal*, 21 May 1990.

tion on taxes in early 1991. The government produced a deficit-reduction package that included a personal and corporate income tax surcharge of 7.5 percent to last one year beginning 1 July 1991. But the package only dented the dramatic increase in the public-sector deficit, which, not including the side budgets of state agencies, amounted to DM120 billion. Total government borrowing on German capital markets amounted to DM141 billion in 1991, about 5.5 percent of GNP.

On the wage front, trade unions in the new Länder pressed for an accelerated equalization of wage levels to those in the West. In the West, workers and unions sought to protect disposable incomes from higher taxes and inflation. The wage round of spring 1992 was particularly hard-fought, with widespread strikes by the public-sector union, the first in many years. The Bundesbank, as it usually does, attempted to intervene in favor of lower wage settlements, by stressing the inflationary consequences and the tightening of monetary policy that might be necessary to squelch them. The settlements in 1991 and 1992 were somewhat more than 6 percent.

Anticipating growing budget deficits, rising wages, and consumer price inflation above 4 percent, the Bundesbank resumed the tightening of monetary policy at the end of 1990. Between the end of 1990 and mid-1992, Frankfurt raised the discount rate from 6.0 to 8.75 percent, the highest level of the postwar period. Market interest rates were raised from just below 8.0 to about 9.6 percent. Ironically, the German policy mix now resembled that under the first Reagan administration one decade earlier.

The federal government had virtually ignored the Bundesbank when making post-unification fiscal decisions. Unable to persuade the federal government to address the fiscal deficit, Pöhl finally decided to resign as Bundesbank president.[126] To dispel suspicions that the government had tried to undercut the stability policy of the central bank, the conservative-liberal coalition appointed the Bundesbank's vice president, Helmut Schlesinger, whose inflation-fighting credentials were impeccable, to replace Pöhl as of August 1991. Hans Tietmeyer, now a member of the Bundesbank's Directorate and an adviser to Kohl on unification, was promoted to vice president.

External Dimension

On the foreign exchange markets, the D-mark weakened at first with the growing awareness of the economic terms of unification. The Bundesbank demonstrated its preferences for a strong D-mark by a surprise

---

126. "I had been talking myself blue in the face for 18 months," Pöhl later declared. "Everything I said was ignored. . . . If I had had the feeling that I could have prevented [the deterioration of the budgetary position], I would not have quit." Marsh, *The Bundesbank*, p. 41.

intervention at the 1.73 level in early January 1990 to defend the currency, the highest level ever of support intervention. During the spring of 1990, when the terms of monetary union were most uncertain, Bundesbank officials affirmed that the D-mark would continue to play an anchor role in the EMS and international monetary system.

Officials at the Bundesbank, from the beginning of German unification, worried about the possibility of a loss of market confidence in the German currency. Over the subsequent years this concern, shared by officials within the government, became an overarching feature of external monetary policy. Officials feared, in particular, that a weakening of the D-mark—in combination with large domestic fiscal deficits, high wage settlements, rising inflation, a deteriorating current account position, and an abundance of D-mark assets held abroad—could trigger a more general crisis of confidence. Bundesbank officials wanted to avoid, at all costs, a repeat of the 1980–81 experience of current account deficits accompanied by private capital outflows. This consideration provided an additional incentive to raise interest rates and maintain tight monetary policy over the years following unification.

Once the markets became convinced that the Bundesbank would indeed tighten monetary policy despite the political constraints, however, the D-mark appreciated against the dollar. The German currency was buoyed by long-term interest rates, which rose above US long-term interest rates for the first time in more than a decade, and set a new high of 1.44 in January 1991.[127] The Bundesbank participated in concerted intervention to limit this rise, under pressure from the Finance Ministry, as it would again when these levels were breached in mid-1992.

The strength of the currency and of internal demand in the wake of unification completely eliminated the extraordinary external surplus. The trade surplus plunged from DM135 billion in 1989 to DM21 billion in 1991. The current account balance plummeted from a DM108 billion surplus in 1989 to a DM34 billion deficit in 1991. The surplus starting position, in Hans Tietmeyer's words, constituted a "war chest" for German unification. Germany could provide for extraordinary internal demand by running down its surplus. Had Germany started from rough balance, external finance could well have constrained unification. The large external surplus at the outset, by contrast, protected Germany's international position.

Judging from previous transatlantic conflicts over macroeconomic policy, one might have expected the Bush administration to have welcomed Germany's stimulus to domestic demand as a contribution to the reduction of international payments imbalances. Instead, the Bush administration sharply criticized the German policy mix. American officials argued

---

127. Export industries objected to the record high D-mark. See *Wall Street Journal*, 13 December 1990.

that high German interest rates reduced growth not only in Germany but in Europe as a whole, owing to the EMS, and the world. In spring 1991, US Treasury Secretary Nicholas F. Brady directly assaulted the restrictive policy of the Bundesbank. In April, on the occasion of a G-7 meeting in Washington, President Bush appealed to Germany to reduce interest rates.[128] These appeals were rejected by the Bundesbank. The German government's response to pleas to reduce fiscal deficits was noncommittal.

German unification was precisely the sort of country-specific real shock for which a revaluation within the ERM would have been in order.[129] The Bundesbank had pressed for a realignment within the ERM even before unification and continued to favor one. The German government, however, rejected this option. Bonn argued at the time that the other European governments would not agree to it, which was true. But the German government itself was not anxious to add the competitive strains of a revaluation to the burden already placed on the economy by unification. The first round effects of German unification on the other European countries were positive, notwithstanding the decision to maintain the D-mark parity unchanged, as German imports soared. But the second round effects, dominated by rising German interest rates, proved to be sharply negative.

Reorganization of the Bundesbank

German unification required an amendment to the Bundesbank law, which had designated Frankfurt as the provisional seat of the bank only so long as Germany was divided. The amendment provided an opportunity to those within the central bank and the government who wanted to consolidate the size of the Central Bank Council. The Land central bank presidents, who dominated the Central Bank Council numerically, had been criticized abroad for parochialism in setting monetary policy. On questions such as monetary coordination among the central banks participating in the EMS, for example, many Land central bank presidents had sided with conservative members of the Directorate and against Pöhl, particularly during the late 1980s. Pöhl and others argued that increasing the number of people on the council by five, one Land central bank president for each of the new Länder, would accentuate this tendency, render the body unmanageable, and raise administrative costs unnecessarily.

---

128. Robert D. Hormats, "Patterns of Competition," in *From Occupation to Cooperation: The United States and United Germany in a Changing World Order*, Steven Muller and Gebhard Schweigler, eds. (New York: W. W. Norton, 1992), pp. 178–79.

129. John Williamson has argued this position since 1990.

Before resigning from the Bundesbank presidency, Pöhl proposed reducing the number of Land central banks to eight, one for each pair of Länder. The plan particularly threatened the small Länder that would lose their banks, not to mention their presidents, and divided the Central Bank Council. The council nonetheless mustered a simple majority in favor of the proposal and passed the recommendation on to the federal government.

The ensuing dispute, which lasted until mid-1992, raised central issues of German federalism. Several of the Land governments argued that having their own banks was a prerogative under the federalist structure of the Basic Law. They argued, further, that the federal structure of the Central Bank Council fundamentally protected the independence of the Bundesbank. The Land government of Rhineland-Palatinate formally proposed that all 16 Länder have regional banks and representation on the Central Bank Council, a proposal approved by the Bundesrat. Reimut Jochimsen, the president of the Land Central Bank in North Rhine–Westphalia, offered a compromise proposal whereby 12 banks would represent the 16 Länder.

But the federal government, which favored a smaller council, had certain tactical and procedural advantages. First, deadlock over reorganization would prevent any of the new Länder from establishing banks and representation. The governments of the new Länder thus had an incentive to compromise. Second, the Bundesrat could reject the government's bill, passed in the Bundestag, only by a two-thirds majority. Finance Minister Waigel's decision to reduce the number of Land central banks to nine, rather than eight, and to have two of the new Länder, Saxony and Thuringia, establish a bank between themselves, prevented a two-thirds coalition in opposition within the Bundesrat. The final agreement adhered closely to the government's original proposal. (The newly constituted regional districts and Central Bank Council are presented in table 5.5.)

European Economic and Monetary Union

Germany confronted several related challenges at the beginning of the decade of the 1990s: political and economic instability in Eastern Europe and the imminent disintegration of the Soviet Union; liberalization and renewal of the economy of the former East Germany; and anxieties among western partners over Germany's commitment to the European Community. The German government responded by emphatically reaffirming its commitment to European integration, which, though potentially compounding the burdens of unification, offered a way out of multiple political dilemmas.

Chancellor Kohl and Foreign Minister Genscher made Economic and

Table 5.5 Members of the Central Bank Council of the Deutsche Bundesbank, 1994

President	Hans Tietmeyer	
Vice president	Johann Wilhelm Gaddum	
Members of the Directorate	Wendelin Hartmann	
	Gerd Häusler	
	Otmar Issing	
	Edgar Meister	
	Helmut Schieber	
	Günter Storch	
Presidents of the Land central banks	**President**	**Länder**
	Guntram Palm	Baden-Württemberg
	Lothar Müller	Bavaria
	Dieter Hiss	Berlin and Brandenburg
	Helmut Hesse	Bremen, Lower Saxony, and Saxony-Anhalt
	Hans-Jurgen Krupp	Hamburg, Mecklenburg–Western Pomerania, and Schleswig-Holstein
	Horst Schulmann	Hesse
	Reimut Jochimsen	North Rhine–Westphalia
	Hans-Jürgen Koebnick	Rhineland-Palatinate and Saarland
	Olaf Sievert	Saxony and Thuringia

Source: Deutsche Bundesbank.

Monetary Union a central element of that commitment. Initiated at the Hanover summit of June 1988, the EMU process received further impetus through the publication of the Delors Report, which articulated a three-stage path to monetary union.[130] The European Council, meeting at Madrid in June 1989, accepted the report and decided to begin the first stage on 1 July 1990—at which point governments would remove all remaining capital controls, or schedule their removal, and commit to bringing their currencies, including the pound sterling, into the Exchange Rate Mechanism of the EMS.

In December 1989, shortly after the Berlin Wall fell, Chancellor Kohl agreed with his European counterparts at Strasbourg to convene an Intergovernmental Conference (IGC) to negotiate an amendment to the Treaty of Rome to establish monetary union. With President Mitterrand, during the following January, the German chancellor declared that the "political construction" of the Community should be "accelerated," Ger-

---

130. Committee for the Study of Economic and Monetary Union, *Report on Economic and Monetary Union in the European Community* (Luxembourg: Office of the Official Publications of the European Communities, 1989). For a summary of the main meetings and documents leading to the Maastricht Treaty, see Peter B. Kenen, *EMU after Maastricht* (Washington: Group of Thirty, 1992), chapter 1.

man unification notwithstanding, and proposed an IGC on political union as well.[131] The Dublin European summit in April 1990 took that decision. In political as well as monetary union, French-German cooperation was the kernel of European integration. Indeed, in winter 1990, Kohl and Mitterrand floated briefly, if somewhat fancifully, the notion of economic and political union as early as 1993.

Negotiations over EMU fused external and domestic monetary considerations. As a foreign policy initiative, it was a matter that involved the foreign ministry and the government. As a foreign economic initiative, EMU involved the finance ministry and economics ministry. As a matter that touched the heart of monetary policy, it was also in part the province of the Bundesbank. The intense bargaining among these institutions within Germany, as well as between Germany and the partner European governments, reveals a great deal about them, their preferences, and how Bundesbank officials themselves understand their role in German politics and economics.

The Bundesbank's original approach to EMU was publicly cool and privately hostile.[132] The project would, if carried to its ultimate end, fully replace the power and dominance of the Bundesbank and the D-mark within the EMS with a European monetary institution and currency that the Bundesbank would have only a small and indirect role in managing. Frankfurt recognized from the outset, however, that EMU was first and foremost a political decision for the government. Bundesbank officials warned and argued about the timing, terms, and conditions, but did not publicly criticize the government for committing itself to the final objective of monetary union.

Further, the Bundesbank's views on EMU, as on the EMS, evolved substantially. Karl Otto Pöhl's initial strategy was to stress the high degree of political commitment that monetary union entailed and recommend that the governments proceed only very gradually. In July 1989, after the Delors Report and Hanover summit, he said, "The Bundesbank can live very well with the status quo."

By the end of the year, however, circumstances had changed a great deal. First, the political decision to proceed with the IGC had been taken at the Strasbourg summit. Second, the Bundesbank had fought for a realignment of the EMS in October and lost. The German government had surrendered the exchange rate instrument as a means of adjustment within Europe. The Bundesbank faced a choice. It could resist the government's decision against realignments and obstruct the path the gov-

---

131. The two leaders stated in a later communiqué, "We think that the moment has come to transform the relations among the member states into a European Union. . . ." Agence France Presse, "Texte du Message de MM. Mitterrand et Kohl sur la Construction Politique de L'Europe des Douze," Paris, 19 April 1990 (Author's translation).

132. See as well Marsh, *The Bundesbank*, chapter 9, pp. 228–55.

ernment had chosen to negotiate European monetary union, and run great political risks in doing so. Or the German central bank could enter the fray, present the (stringent) conditions under which monetary union would be acceptable, and try to secure it on Bundesbank terms.

Pöhl chose to put forward his own position on monetary union and challenge the European governments to accept the conditions. A speech in Paris in January 1990 revealed a subtle but important turning point in his position. There, he reviewed the valuable role as nominal anchor played by the D-mark and stressed that it should not be lightly sacrificed. He went on to elaborate, though, on the conditions under which a European monetary union would become at least equally desirable as a D-mark-dominated EMS. The conditions were demanding, but Pöhl professed a sincere willingness to support EMU if they were satisfied.[133]

Some other senior Bundesbank officials were implacably opposed to EMU and regarded Pöhl as being far too willing to accommodate the German and European governments. Pöhl had been, after all, a member of the committee that issued the Delors Report and supported its basic conclusions. Vice President Schlesinger in particular fundamentally distrusted the EMU project and the willingness and capacity of foreign governments, such as in Italy, to agree to and abide by German stability terms.

Many Bundesbank officials would have been pleased if the tough conditions they had set forth were rejected by the European partners. But, to the surprise of EMU skeptics and supporters alike, the other European capitals, Paris in particular, began to show unexpected willingness to consider German terms. In addition, the Länder of Hesse and North Rhine–Westphalia appointed new presidents to their Land central banks, Karl Thomas and Reimut Jochimsen. Their appointments shifted the balance on the Central Bank Council away from Schlesinger's and toward Pöhl's position on EMU.

The Central Bank Council in September 1990 issued a statement on EMU publicizing the position that it urged the government to take in its negotiations in the upcoming IGC.[134] Unanimously endorsing the state-

---

133. Karl Otto Pöhl, "Basic Features of a European Monetary Order," lecture organized by *Le Monde*, Paris, 16 January 1990. He concluded by saying, "There is no way back. The task before us is to set the points correctly so that the European train reaches the destination we all want to arrive at." For an analysis, see "Mapping EMU," *International Economic Insights*, July–August 1990, pp. 7–8.

134. See *Monthly Report of the Deutsche Bundesbank*, October 1990, pp. 40–44. Monetary policy would have to be formulated uniformly at the European level by a European System of Central Banks (ESCB) dedicated by statute to the objective of price stability above all other goals. Member states and national central banks would have to be bound by the decisions of the ESCB. The ESCB would have to be endowed with "durably guaranteed independence in institutional, functional and personal terms." The

ment, drafted by Hans Tietmeyer, the Central Bank Council strongly discouraged an early move to irrevocably fixed exchange rates. The lack of convergence among national economies would "pose a considerable threat to monetary stability," especially for Germany. It listed the convergence criteria that could make monetary union safe for stability: low inflation, low government deficits, similar long-term interest rates, and a lasting period of exchange rate stability within the EMS. Most important, the transition to monetary union should be undertaken only if the criteria were fulfilled, not according to fixed deadlines irrespective of convergence.[135]

The Bundesbank recommended not simply itself as a model for the European Central Bank—frequent references to the "EuroFed" notwithstanding—but its own legal structure plus the amendments that it would have made to its own law. The Bundesbank sought to spare the European central bank the battles which it had had to fight in Germany. Those included battles over the interpretation of the main objective of the Bundesbank, currency stability versus supporting the general economic policy of the government; authority to deal in all financial instruments to assert monetary control; and, above all, external monetary policy. The Bundesbank was concerned, rightly, that given the very different political environment in Europe as a whole, the ESCB would not emerge as victorious in these battles of the future as the Bundesbank had been in the past.

Bundesbank officials also were acutely aware, from their own policy-

---

central banks of member states would also have to be made independent, if they were to participate in a truly independent ESCB.

The ESCB should have full control over monetary instruments. It must not be required to fund government budget deficits. Importantly, the ESCB's internal monetary policy should not be hampered by external monetary policy. To prevent this, the ESCB should have sole responsibility for foreign exchange intervention and should be involved in and coresponsible for all other external monetary policy decisions.

Greater economic convergence would have to be achieved among the countries. In particular, that meant that (1) inflation should be "very largely stamped out in all the countries," and price differences "virtually eliminated"; (2) budget deficits should be reduced to low levels; (3) convergence should be reflected in the markets, as evidenced by a "virtual harmonisation of capital market rates"; and (4) countries should have participated in the Exchange Rate Mechanism without capital controls.

Fundamentally, the statement argued that inflation in a monetary union "will depend crucially on economic and fiscal policy and on the stance of management and labour in *all* member states. They will have to satisfy in full the requirements of an Economic and Monetary Union." "In the final analysis, a Monetary Union is thus an irrevocable joint and several community which, in the light of past experience, requires a more far-reaching association, in the form of a comprehensive political union, if it is to prove durable."

135. See also Deutsche Bundesbank, *Report for the Year 1990*, p. 10. "Fixed timetables may increase the pressures fostering convergence, but cannot by any means be a substitute for it. At all events, the creation of a sound economic basis for the economic and monetary union must be given precedence over the desire to establish a European central bank system as soon as possible and thus create an institutional *fait accompli*."

making history, of the constraints that the fiscal and wage environment place on the autonomous operation of monetary policy.[136] Their convergence criteria sought to spare the ESCB from these constraints, or at least to minimize them. Bundesbank officials expected that the fiscal and wage-setting conditions in Europe as a whole would be considerably less favorable than in Germany alone. They also expected that central bank independence would be a less popular principle in Europe as a whole than in Germany. Central bank sympathizers therefore sought to compensate for the environmental disadvantages, as they saw them, by strengthening the legal elements of central bank independence at the European level *beyond* what the Bundesbank enjoys at the national level. They succeeded in one dramatic and fundamental respect: as part of the subsequent Maastricht agreement, the statutes of the ESCB providing independence were to be "constitutionally" enshrined in the European treaties.

Because of the importance attached to fiscal, wage, and political constraints on central bank autonomy, the Bundesbank favored a so-called two-speed monetary union. The 12 current members of the Community should not establish the union all at once. Rather, if there were to be monetary union at all, only those countries that fully satisfy the convergence criteria should participate. Initially, this would be a relatively small group of countries clustered around Germany and France. Later, countries such as Italy, Spain, Greece, Portugal, and the United Kingdom might qualify. The United Kingdom insisted on the special right to opt out of the union. But the governments of the southern tier, which had relied greatly on the promise of benefits from EMS membership and monetary union to justify tightening macroeconomic policies, strongly opposed the concept of two-speed union. On the question of country participation, indeed, the government of Italy and the Bundesbank were diametrically opposed.

The Bundesbank influenced the European debate over EMU through its leadership position within the Committee of Central Bank Governors. That committee drafted the statute for the ESCB to be negotiated and ratified as part of the treaty itself. The draft statute, completed in November 1990, shortly before the beginning of the IGC, sought to establish the legal obligation of the ESCB to defend price stability and the independence of the bank. Though many of them were under the political control of their governments, the other central bank governors had accepted the Bundesbank's position on these basic principles.[137]

---

136. Deutsche Bundesbank, "Interview mit Bundesbankpräsident Karl Otto Pöhl," *Auszüge aus Presseartikeln*, Frankfurt, 19 July 1991, p. 4.

137. Several issues nonetheless remained unresolved in the draft statutes, including the division of responsibilities between the central council and the executive board of the bank, external monetary policy, the bank's capital, and its role in banking supervision. *Financial Times*, 14 and 15 November 1990.

Ultimately, however, the Bundesbank was dependent on the German finance ministry's willingness to put forward its position in the intergovernmental conference that negotiated the treaty amendment. The German government accepted the basic principles of stability and central bank independence. Germany had benefited from them and so would Europe; nothing less could be ratified by the Bundestag and Bundesrat. Moreover, with unification firmly secured, Germany could afford to risk alienating the European partners by asserting its preferences more strongly in the IGC.

The German government position nonetheless differed with the Bundesbank on several other substantial points. At the Maastricht summit, Chancellor Kohl agreed to establish fixed dates for monetary union. On the crucial question of participation in monetary union, Bonn deferred to other governments in refusing to press for the two-speed concept in formal terms, though the door was left wide open to multiple speeds as a practical matter. The German government agreed to a decision-making process that would not exclude the possibility that convergence failure could be overridden by political decision. Bonn also agreed to a convergence criterion that the Central Bank Council had not endorsed, the ratio of government debt to GNP.

What was at stake was not simply the final design of the monetary union but also the political strategy for persuading other governments to make the difficult decisions to prepare their economies for entry. The German government decided to offer greater certainty that monetary union would be created, by establishing fixed dates to induce other governments to adopt restrictive measures. The Bundesbank, on the other hand, worried that any ambiguity about the violability of the convergence criteria would be exploited. It was concerned that, by leaving the door open for a political rather than a purely technical decision on country inclusion, the German government, rather than the Italian government, for example, would be the one to concede.

In addition, the government and Bundesbank disagreed over external monetary policy for the monetary union. Government control over exchange rate policy could be used as a back door to political influence over domestic monetary policy. This long-standing argument within Germany between the government and the central bank was now replayed in Europe over the question of EMU. Karl Otto Pöhl proposed that the ESCB have complete authority over external monetary policy of the monetary union. He was unable to persuade the Committee of Central Bank Governors to adopt this proposal, however. The German finance ministry wanted to retain a clear role for political authorities in exchange rate policy and, in particular, as is the case within Germany, over formal exchange rate regimes and changes in central parities.

The external monetary policymaking process in the prospective monetary union was one of the last issues to be resolved in the IGC. The governments agreed that international reserves would be owned by the ESCB and that the ESCB would be solely responsible for foreign exchange operations. The agreement explicitly distinguished between exchange rate policies within and outside formal exchange rate regimes. In a formal arrangement, the Council of Ministers would make exchange rate decisions by unanimity after consulting with the ESCB. Outside formal arrangements, the Council of Ministers was limited to issuing "general orientations" for the ESCB.[138] In both cases, price stability was not to be jeopardized. The final formulation thus strengthened the ESCB vis-à-vis the Council of Ministers relative to the Bundesbank's position vis-à-vis the federal government.

At Maastricht, the Netherlands, in December 1991, the European Council sealed the final bargain on the treaty amendment.[139] The Maastricht Treaty provided for a European Union with a three-pillar structure, of which Economic and Monetary Union is to be one pillar. The heads of state and government agreed to establish monetary union perhaps as early as 1997 but in any case no later than 1 January 1999. In 1996, though, another intergovernmental conference will be convened to complete the elements of political union left undone at Maastricht.

The concessions made by the other European governments in the design of monetary union leading to Maastricht were extraordinary. The French government in particular proved to be flexible, for example, in accepting unconditional central bank independence, underscoring the depth of historical change in French political economy. The German government and Bundesbank received virtually every important negotiating item for which they had asked in the monetary area.

The Bundesbank, however, felt betrayed by Chancellor Kohl's commitment to proceed to monetary union along a fixed timetable, a commitment that had not been reviewed by the Bundesbank before the Maastricht summit. Within days after the European Council meeting, Reimut Jochimsen, the president of the Land central bank in North Rhine–Westphalia, charged that the fixed timetable, combined with the irreversibility of the third stage, represented a breach of the broad understanding developed in Germany in 1990 and 1991 on the terms of monetary union.[140] The Central Bank Council, in a formal statement, argued

---

138. Ambiguous as it is, Article 109 of the Maastricht treaty is nonetheless more specific and detailed than is the corresponding legislation in the largest countries with independent central banks, the United States and Germany.

139. Commission and Council of the European Communities, *Treaty on European Union* (Luxemburg: Office of the Official Publications of the European Communities, 1992). The best analysis of the EMU agreement is Kenen, *EMU after Maastricht.*

140. Reimut Jochimsen, "The European System of Central Banks and the Role of National Central Banks in the Economic and Monetary Union," presentation to the seminar on Economic and Monetary Union, European Institute of Public Administration, Maastricht, Netherlands, 16 December 1991.

that, because of the importance of the fiscal and wage environment in which the future central bank would operate, the successful implementation of the Maastricht plan for monetary union would depend on forming a more comprehensive political union.[141] To stiffen the resolve of the German government at that crucial point later in the decade when country participation would be decided, the statement stressed that the decision should be "geared solely to the stability-policy performance."

The Central Bank Council was careful to observe the line between its authority and that of the government, and specifically stated that EMU was first and foremost a political decision to be taken by the latter.[142] In fact, during the debate over treaty ratification, neither the Central Bank Council nor the senior officers of the Bundesbank directly stated whether Germany should or should not ratify it. Many of them were nonetheless deeply hostile to the Maastricht formula.[143]

The Bundesbank's policy actions following Maastricht amplified its muted, formal objections to the treaty. The German central bank remained manifestly unwilling to give the benefit of the doubt to growth objectives when setting monetary policy, despite the fact that a slowing of growth could jeopardize ratification of the Maastricht Treaty. Immediately after the Maastricht summit, the Bundesbank raised the discount rate one-half point to 8.0 percent. In the Central Bank Council debate, Schlesinger and Tietmeyer were overruled in their wish to limit the increase to one-quarter point.[144] The Land central bank presidents anticipated a hard-fought round of wage negotiations in winter and spring 1992 and wanted to moderate wage settlements with higher interest rates. The discount rate now stood at the highest level of the postwar period. By summer 1992, the wage negotiations were over. The result was an increase in the neighborhood of 6 percent, too high by the Bundesbank's preferences but less than the increase in 1991. Consumer price increases were forecast to decline in the coming months. More important still, Denmark rejected the Maastricht Treaty in a referendum in early June. Because the treaty required ratification by all 12 member states, the Danish rejection threw the Community into a political crisis over how to resolve the impasse. Currencies and long-term interest rates within the EMS began to diverge.

---

141. "The Maastricht decisions do not yet reveal an agreement on the future structure of the envisaged political union and on the required parallelism with monetary union. Future developments in the field of the political union will be of key importance for the permanent success of the monetary union." *Monthly Report of the Deutsche Bundesbank*, February 1992, p. 51.

142. *Monthly Report of the Deutsche Bundesbank*, February 1992, p. 51.

143. For the critical view of one Central Bank Council member who has since retired, see Wilhelm Nölling, *Monetary Policy in Europe after Maastricht* (New York: St. Martin's Press, 1993).

144. Marsh, *The Bundesbank*, p. 248–49.

These considerations notwithstanding, the Bundesbank raised the discount rate yet again, by 0.75 percent, in July. The move unleashed a deluge of criticism: Chancellor Kohl privately opposed the increase; Finance Minister Theo Waigel tried to prevent it; the German Institute for Economic Research (DIW) in Berlin criticized it; the leader of the metalworkers union, Franz Steinkühler, advocated restraints on the "uncontrolled power" of the central bank.[145] The discount rate increase recalled the Bundesbank's effort to force a realignment within the EMS in October 1989. Whether some members of the Central Bank Council deliberately sought a realignment when taking the decision to increase interest rates in July 1992 cannot be known with certainty. The German central bank nonetheless appeared to be kicking the EMS and the Maastricht Treaty when they were most vulnerable.[146]

The ERM Crises of 1992–93

The intractable conflict between German monetary policy and the domestic needs of the non-German participants in the ERM produced a nearly continuous series of currency crises between mid-1992 and mid-1993. The crises were brought to an end in early August 1993 only by the nearly complete unraveling of the margins of fluctuation of the currencies within the system. Occurring ironically only shortly before full ratification of the Maastricht Treaty, this unraveling clouded the future of European monetary union. The bargaining between the federal government and the Bundesbank during these crises demonstrates the continuing relevance and durability of their agreement struck at the creation of the EMS.

Autumn 1992 Crisis

Chancellor Kohl and Finance Minister Waigel had not proposed a revaluation of the D-mark within the EMS to the European partners at the time of German unification. The combined effects of German unification, depreciation of the US dollar, and growing uncertainty about French ratification of the Maastricht Treaty, however, conspired to force, in the most disruptive way, just such a revaluation in autumn 1992.[147] Beginning in the

---

145. *Financial Times*, 30 July, 1–2 August, and 11 August 1992.

146. Helmut Schlesinger denied any hostility toward the EMS in general or neglect of economic conditions in partner countries. Deutsche Bundesbank, *Auszüge aus Presseartikeln*, 4 August 1992, pp. 1–2.

147. For a discussion of the fundamental and proximate causes of the crisis, see Richard Portes, "EMS and EMU after the Fall," *The World Economy*, January 1993; and reply by John Williamson, "The Fall of the Hard EMS," manuscript, 25 February 1993; Barry Eichengreen and Charles Wyplosy, "The Unstable EMS," *Brookings Papers on Economic Activity*, 1993: 1, pp. 51–143.

first week of September, several waves of speculation sparked the worst crisis in the European currency markets since March 1973. German decision making during this crisis in particular illustrates the prerogatives of the government on setting the central parities and the limits of that authority when it conflicts with domestic monetary stability.

The currencies of the high-inflation countries had become substantially overvalued against the D-mark since the last realignment in 1987. The pound sterling had entered the ERM at an overvalued central parity in October 1990. In early September 1992, the US dollar depreciated to record lows against the European currencies as American interest rates were reduced, placing additional strains on the ERM.[148] At the same time, British interest rates also were reduced, and the Italian budget deficit continued to spin out of control. To top it off, public opinion polls showed the margin in favor of the Maastricht Treaty in the approaching French referendum of 20 September to be declining.

The Ecofin Council met at Bath, England, over the weekend of 5–6 September in an ill-fated attempt to head off the crisis—the most acrimonious such meeting Ecofin participants can recall. British Chancellor of the Exchequer Norman Lamont repeatedly pressed Helmut Schlesinger to agree to reduce German interest rates. Schlesinger replied that making such a commitment was impossible. When Lamont asked him for the fourth time, the exasperated and embittered Schlesinger stood to leave the meeting. He was restrained by Waigel, who sided firmly with the Bundesbank president in the debate. In the end, the Ecofin Council released a communiqué reiterating the intent of the ministers and governors to intervene, and saying that the Bundesbank "in present circumstance [had] no intention to increase interest rates" further.[149] When Lamont purveyed the impression that the Bundesbank would be more forthcoming on domestic monetary policy, Schlesinger observed that this communiqué contained no new information about Bundesbank intentions. Fundamentally, Schlesinger and others on the Central Bank Council had long believed that the appropriate remedy for strains within the ERM was not a reduction in German interest rates but a realignment.

Massive speculation against the Italian lira during the week following the Bath Ecofin meeting forced the Bundesbank into currency operations amounting to DM24 billion, an unprecedented quantity, mostly in the form of D-mark credits to the Bank of Italy (figure 5.6). On Friday, 11 September, Kohl, Waigel, and State Secretary Horst Köhler met with Schlesinger and Tietmeyer in the Bundesbank president's office in Frankfurt

---

148. In late August, Finance Minister Waigel proposed to US Treasury Secretary Brady that they act jointly to halt the slide of the dollar by announcing that US and German interest rates would converge. Secretary Brady, who wanted the Federal Reserve to lower interest rates further, rejected the offer.

149. *Financial Times*, 7 September 1992.

Figure 5.6 Bundesbank operations in the European Monetary System, 1983–94 [a]
(monthly)

billions of D-marks

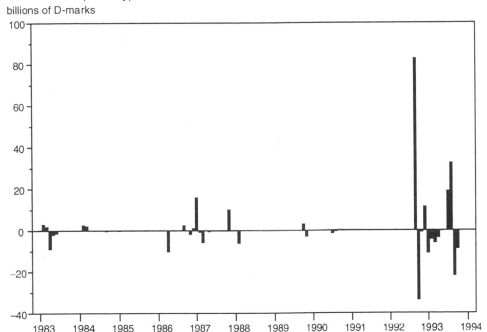

Source: Bundesbank, Annual Reports.

a. Includes operations by other central banks where they affect the external position of the Bundesbank and debt settlement.

to assess the damage.[150] Schlesinger and Tietmeyer argued persuasively that this liquidity creation constituted precisely the circumstance under which the Bundesbank-government EMS agreement of 1978 provided for either a realignment or opting out of the system. Schlesinger asked Kohl to approve negotiations with partner governments for a realignment, to which the chancellor agreed. Schlesinger and Tietmeyer specifically asked for a broad realignment including the Italian lira, Spanish peseta, and British pound. In exchange, the two top officials of the Bundesbank agreed to recommend a reduction in interest rates to the Central Bank Council. The amount of the interest rate reduction would depend, they stipulated, on the number of currencies participating in the realignment and the extent of their devaluation.

The agreement with the Italians, negotiated over the weekend by Köhler and coordinated in the Monetary Committee of the EC, was a 7 percent

---

150. Peter Norman, "The Day Germany Planted a Currency Time Bomb," *Financial Times*, 13 December 1992.

devaluation of the lira. The Bundesbank's Central Bank Council agreed to reduce the discount rate by one-half point to 8.25 percent and the Lombard rate by one-quarter point to 9.5 percent. In the course of the negotiations, however, Tietmeyer and Köhler let it be known that Germany desired a broader realignment than against the Italian lira alone, but had been thwarted.[151] When Schlesinger's remarks to this effect to a German journalist were reported by the wire services on Tuesday, 15 September, an avalanche of speculation fell upon the pound and the lira. In a bitter defeat for Lamont and Major, the pound was driven from the ERM on 16 September, accompanied by the lira. These currencies would fluctuate freely against the D-mark until further notice. The Spanish peseta was devalued by 5.0 percent on the same day. During the months that followed, the Portuguese escudo, Irish punt, and Nordic currencies technically outside the ERM also fell prey to speculation, as did the Spanish peseta a second time. By the end of the year, the pound and lira stood at levels roughly 30 percent below their previous central parities against the D-mark.[152]

The center of the ERM, the central rate between the French franc and the D-mark, continued to hold firm at the beginning of 1993, however. The French referendum of 20 September produced only a very slim majority in favor of the Maastricht Treaty, a *"petit oui,"* and thus raised further doubts about France's commitment to the treaty as a whole and the central rate in particular. In the face of speculation against the franc—by contrast to their position on other currencies—the German government and Bundesbank expressed complete solidarity with the French government in its tenacious determination to maintain the parity. That solidarity was sealed in two bilateral official statements in December 1992 and January 1993. France, after all, had lower inflation and much lower budget deficits than Germany, and it had raised interest rates to defend the parity, something the British had done only at the last minute.

The floating of the pound provoked months of British-German recrimination in which Lamont accused the Bundesbank of intentionally undermining the British currency. The German solidarity with the French further inflamed the sentiments of the British government, which charged the Bundesbank with selective adherence to the rules of the ERM. Bundesbank officials did not deny that they differentiated among the European currencies in terms of the merits of their central parities, but argued that they adhered strictly to their formal obligations under the EMS agreements.

---

151. Peter Norman and Lionel Barber, "The Monetary Tragedy of Errors That Led to Currency Chaos," *Financial Times*, 11 December 1992.

152. For a chronology of the crisis, see IMF, *World Economic Outlook: Interim Assessment* (Washington: IMF, January 1993), pp. 1–5, 19–30. For the Bundesbank's account, see *Monthly Report of the Deutsche Bundesbank*, October 1992, pp. 14–16.

Indeed, Bundesbank intervention in defense of each of the major currencies was massive. During the month of September alone, it amounted to an incredible DM92.7 billion, a doubling of the Bundesbank's international reserves. This included support operations of DM36 billion on the day the pound and lira exited the ERM, an all-time world record on a daily basis. These operations mostly took the form of D-mark credits to the Bank of Italy, Bank of England, and Bank of France. The Bundesbank also purchased these currencies on its own account for the first time in significant quantities. These operations, if not sterilized, would have ended the Bundesbank's tight domestic monetary policy. But Frankfurt successfully absorbed most of this liquidity.[153] Meanwhile, on the domestic side, the Bundesbank's tight monetary policy drove Germany into a recession in the third quarter of 1992. The cyclical downturn produced two important benefits for the German central bank. First, the recession moderated wage claims and settlements, a trend visible by early 1993. Second, the recession forced the federal government, Länder governments, opposition parties, and social partners to negotiate a Solidarity Pact in 1993. The pact was not likely to reduce the overall public-sector borrowing requirement, but it did restrain future growth in the deficit.

July 1993 Crisis

Given the domestic recession and the slowing of growth across Europe, the Bundesbank's reduction in interest rates after September 1992 was agonizingly slow. Rather than acting decisively when the moment for easing monetary policy arrived, as in past recessions, the Bundesbank reduced interest rates tentatively and in small decrements. The Bundesbank was widely criticized for this hesitancy, by Köhler of the finance ministry, among others.[154]

Meanwhile, in France, the Socialist government was soundly defeated in elections in March 1993 and a conservative government, headed by Edouard Balladur, installed. Eager to address the recession and rising unemployment in France, the new conservative government proceeded to reduce interest rates without parallel reductions by the Bundesbank. France, followed by a few other low-inflation European countries, succeeded in reducing short-term interest rates below German rates while (temporarily) maintaining the strength of the French franc relative to the D-mark. Emboldened by these developments, French officials even suggested that the franc might actually replace the D-mark as the anchor of the ERM.[155]

---

153. "The Impact of External Transactions on Bank Liquidity, the Money Stock, and Bank Lending," *Monthly Report of the Deutsche Bundesbank*, January 1993, pp. 19–34.

154. *Financial Times*, 14 January 1993.

155. *Economist*, 29 May 1993, pp. 78–79; 26 June 1993, pp. 7, 82–83; 10 July 1993, p. 76.

These French statements proved to be a serious error, as they accentuated German fears about D-mark vulnerability and profoundly alienated German economic officials. French Finance Minister Edmond Alphandéry fatally compounded this error by stating in late June that a meeting of the Franco-German Economic Council would consider a joint reduction in interest rates. Whereas the German government had sided with the French government in the past, in light of the actions and declarations of the new French government, the German government now sided firmly with the Bundesbank and canceled the Economic Council meeting.[156]

When, within a matter of weeks, the Bundesbank disappointed widespread expectations of a substantial further reduction in interest rates, the French franc came under heavy selling pressure in the foreign exchange markets. Expectations that the French government would eventually have to respond to rising unemployment by reducing interest rates further, particularly in light of the presidential elections scheduled for April 1995, weighed heavily on the franc. At the end of July, speculation against the franc reached a magnitude similar to that against the pound and lira in September 1992, supplemented by speculation against the Danish krone. During the month of July, the Bundesbank acquired the foreign exchange equivalent of DM60 billion, mainly in support of the franc, DM30 billion of which poured into the Bundesbank during 30 July alone.[157]

At this point, the Bundesbank again approached the German government to negotiate either a realignment within the ERM or a widening of the bands of fluctuation. During a weekend meeting of the Ecofin Council, German finance ministry officials negotiated intensively with their counterparts. The French government proposed that the D-mark be floated out of the ERM, but was blocked by the smaller countries, the Netherlands in particular, that insisted on maintaining a close link to the D-mark. The agreed solution, announced on 2 August, was a widening of the margins of fluctuation from 2.25 percent, or 6 percent for the escudo and peseta, to 15 percent. The D-mark and Dutch guilder remained tied within the old, narrow bands. Because the wide bands permit fluctuations of as much as 30 percent, they are nearly tantamount to floating exchange rates.

The shift to wide bands within the ERM was not a complete disaster. The ERM survived, after all, and technically was spared a formal realignment of the central parities. The French government did not exploit the width of the bands by further reducing interest rates without corresponding reductions in German interest rates, and the franc thus depre-

---

156. *Wall Street Journal*, 25 June 1993.

157. *Monthly Report of the Deutsche Bundesbank*, August 1993, p. 24.

ciated only moderately. Importantly, the long-term interest rates of Germany, France, the Netherlands, Belgium, Luxembourg, and Denmark, as well as Austria, Norway, and Britain, remain tightly bunched, suggesting that markets expect convergence in monetary policies and inflation rates.[158] A solid core of countries might well be able to move to monetary union directly from wide bands.[159] Nonetheless, the shift to wide bands represented a spectacular defeat for the European governments, seriously jeopardized the objective of monetary union, and threatened Franco-German relations more generally.

Once the July crisis had passed, the Bundesbank continued to reduce interest rates. The Central Bank Council lowered the discount and Lombard rates by 0.5 percent in September, and, under the leadership of a new president, Hans Tietmeyer, in October. Between July 1992 and October 1993, the discount rate had been lowered by 3.0 percent to 5.75 percent and the Lombard rate by an equivalent amount. Each downward step, however, proved to be too late to prevent the successive currency crises and to save the narrow bands of the ERM.

By raising interest rates, keeping them high for a prolonged period, and easing only gradually, the Bundesbank, with the help of the markets, scored a spectacular victory in the crises of 1992–93. Although the switch to wide bands was not necessarily the outcome the Bundesbank preferred, the German central bank nonetheless secured several important external objectives simultaneously.

First, by breaking the taboo against realignments in principle that had rigidified the parity grid in September 1992, the Bundesbank reclaimed the exchange rate instrument that had earlier been effectively surrendered.[160] The shift to wide bands in August 1993, moreover, greatly reduced the likelihood that the Bundesbank would be called upon to intervene at the margin. Second, the succession of realignments and the shift to wide bands effectively stripped away the higher inflation countries from the low-inflation core group, driving the final nail in the coffin of the one-speed monetary union. Third, the 1992–93 crises signaled a return to the so-called economist approach to European monetary integration that the Bundesbank favored. Governments dedicated themselves

---

158. IMF, "Recent Changes in the European Exchange Rate Mechanism," *World Economic Outlook* (Washington: IMF, October 1993), pp. 29–47. This article also contains a useful chronology of the 1993 crisis.

159. See Niels Thygesen, "Monetary Arrangements," comments by Peter B. Kenen, Massimo Russo, and Wolfgang Rieke, *Reviving the European Union*, C. Randall Henning, Eduard Hochreiter, and Gary Clyde Hufbauer, eds. (Washington: Institute for International Economics, 1994), pp. 43–80.

160. At that time, Finance Minister Waigel conceded that the system had operated too inflexibly and should in the future be fixed but adjustable. Theo Waigel, speech to the Hanns Seidel Foundation, Washington, 21 September 1992.

to convergence of inflation rates and overall economic conditions as a prerequisite for the restabilization of European exchange rates, rather than to an attempt to achieve convergence through exchange rate stabilization. Fourth, the fixed timetable for monetary union, the provision of the Maastricht Treaty to which the Bundesbank most strongly objected, was rendered not credible. European monetary union, if it were achieved at all, was now more likely to take place on the Bundesbank's terms.

Most important, the Kohl government observed the terms of the Bundesbank-government understanding established at the time of the creation of the EMS throughout the turmoil of 1992-93. The near unraveling of the ERM was a severe setback for Kohl's objectives for the European Union. The domestic recession jeopardized political support for the conservative-liberal coalition during the federal elections in 1994, as well as support for the CDU/CSU in elections within each of the Länder. The government criticized the agonizing slowness with which the Bundesbank eased monetary policy after July 1992, and had widespread support from the private sector and the economic research institutes in this criticism. Nonetheless, when tight monetary policy caused enormous speculative inflows, the government cleaved to the Bundesbank. Neither Kohl nor the finance ministry attempted on these occasions to use their authority over realignments to extract a more expansionary domestic monetary policy from the German central bank. In autumn 1993, Bundesbank officials were quite content with the cooperation they had received from the government throughout the crises.

Treaty Ratification

In December 1992, the coalition government secured ratification of the Maastricht Treaty, notwithstanding the ongoing crises within the ERM. Had the issue been subjected to a popular vote by referendum, as in Denmark, Ireland, and France, the treaty might well have been defeated. But the German Basic Law contains no provision for referendums and the treaty was ratified instead by the Bundesrat and Bundestag, under the control of the coalition parties and the SPD.

During the ratification debate, popular concern about surrendering the D-mark was reinforced by critical statements of academic economists. Treaty opponents cited statements by French President Mitterrand that the Council of Ministers rather than the ESCB would have ultimate control over monetary policy.[161] But the private-sector peak associations were

---

161. Mitterrand's statement was publicized by the Bundesbank. Deutsche Bundesbank, "Déclarations de Monsieur François Mitterrand, Président de la République," *Auszüge aus Presseartikeln*, Frankfurt, 9 September 1992, pp. 1–2; Helmut Hesse, "ECU Now and Later, Some Considerations after Maastricht," in Deutsche Bundesbank, *Auszüge aus Presseartikeln*, 30 October 1992, p. 7.

favorably disposed to the treaty, provided the key stipulations were met.[162] The chief economists of the three large German banks, furthermore, vigorously defended the treaty from their academic counterparts.[163] The political parties and politicians were predominantly persuaded of the necessity of the treaty. Ratification was wrapped in an issue more profound than the D-mark alone: Germany's commitment to European economic and political integration in general.

Ratification was purchased with two major concessions by the federal government. First, the Länder were given a major role in the setting of German policy in the Council of Ministers. Second, and more important for the future of monetary union, the party factions in the Bundestag and Bundesrat secured a critical agreement from the government, ancillary to the ratification legislation, to allow a so-called second vote on monetary union. Prior to entry into the third stage of EMU—assuming that the Maastricht Treaty is fully ratified—the Bundestag will hold a second vote on the question of whether the other member states of the European Union have satisfied the convergence criteria laid out in the treaty. This mechanism is designed to ensure that the federal government at that time does not issue a political waiver to countries, such as Italy, that have not in fact satisfied these criteria. This procedure would be outside the framework of the Maastricht Treaty, but would in practice be politically binding upon the government.[164] The German Constitutional Court strongly reinforced the convergence criteria by arguing, in a crucial decision on the Maastricht Treaty in October 1993, that it would be unconstitutional for the government to dismiss them.[165]

---

162. See, for example, Federation of German Industries, "Opinion on European Economic and Monetary Union," presented to hearings before the Finance Committee of the Bundestag, Cologne, 18 September 1991; Hans Peter Stihl, president of the Federation for Industry and Commerce, "Remarks to the Association for European Monetary Union," Frankfurt, 26 May 1992, reprinted in Deutsche Bundesbank, *Auszüge aus Presseartikeln*, Frankfurt, 2 June 1992, pp. 6–7.

163. Ernst Moritz Lipp, Ulrich Ramm, and Norbert Walter, "Reply to the Manifesto of Sixty Professors Regarding the Maastricht Resolutions," Frankfurt, 15 June 1992.

164. Deutscher Bundestag, "Beschlussempfehlung und Bericht des Sonderausschusses Europäische Union '(Vertrag von Maastricht)' [Recommendation and Report of the Special Committee on European Union (Treaty of Maastricht)]," Drucksache 12/3895; Deutscher Bundestag, "Entschliessungsantrag der Fraktionen der CDU/CSU, SPD und F.D.P. zu dem Gesetzentwurf der Bundesregierung zum Vertrag vom 7. Februar 1992 über die Europäische Union [Determination of the Fractions of the CDU/CSU, SPD and FDP. Regarding the Draft Law of the Federal Government on the Treaty of 7 February 1992 on the European Union]," Drucksache 12/3906. See as well Nölling, *Monetary Policy in Europe after Maastricht*, pp. 140–41.

165. "Germany: Federal Constitutional Court Decision Concerning the Maastricht Treaty," *International Legal Materials* 33 (March 1994): 388–444.

Once the Constitutional Court approved the Maastricht Treaty, the federal president signed the document for Germany, the last country to ratify. The Maastricht Treaty therefore entered into force at the beginning of November 1993. Although the crises of 1992–93 cast doubt on the timetable, and while Germany has deferred crucial decisions on the particular partners with which it would agree to a monetary merger, the entry into force of the Maastricht Treaty marked a solemn commitment in principle by Germany and its European partners to create a monetary union. The second stage of monetary union, characterized principally by the creation of the European Monetary Institute (EMI), began as scheduled in January 1994. The European Council, at a special meeting to mark the entry into force of the treaty, decided to locate the EMI and the European Central Bank in Frankfurt. Taken at the behest of Chancellor Kohl, this decision should bolster popular German confidence in the stability orientation of the European Central Bank and a future common currency. Germany has therefore maximized the probability that European monetary union, whenever it might happen, will abide by German preferences.

Summary and Conclusions

Germany is distinct from the United States and Japan in having both an independent central bank and a centrally structured system of private-sector organization and representation solidified by close connections between banks and industry. Because the Bundesbank is more independent than the Bank of Japan, German authorities have targeted domestic monetary policy toward the exchange rate somewhat less often than have Japanese authorities over the postwar period. Because banking is closer to industry in Germany than in the United States, German external monetary policy has been more oriented to stability, more conscious of competitiveness, and more consistent over time than American policy.

Close ties between banking and industry, simply put, have instilled strong preferences for exchange rate stability in the German private sector. Stakes in industry—through shareholdings, long-term debt holdings, and management responsibility—have instilled in German banks a positive interest in the international competitiveness of German industry. (These stakes are reviewed in greater detail in chapter 2.) The solidarity of interests among German banks and industry in a competitive, stable currency greatly influenced the debates that preceded the revaluations of the D-mark in 1961 and 1969. Those revaluations were delayed, therefore, and the D-mark remained "dynamically undervalued" under the Bretton Woods regime.

These societal preferences continued to influence external and domestic monetary policy after the transition to flexible exchange rates and into the 1970s and 1980s. These preferences also lay behind the drive for European monetary integration. Germany's private banks, while skeptical of the EMS at the outset, did not actively oppose its creation and did not actively support the Bundesbank in its fight over the EMS with the government. The leaders of the powerful Deutsche Bank in particular consistently and enthusiastically supported European monetary integration.[166] Once implemented, the EMS proved to be an advantage for German exporters, given the inflation differentials with European countries. Political activity by private interest groups declined substantially during the 1980s. That decline was not because the private sector lost interest in exchange rate developments, but rather because German producers became extraordinarily successful under the German policy regime.

German exchange rate policy tolerated far more flexibility toward the US dollar during the 1970s and 1980s than toward the European currencies. The differentiation between the European currencies and the dollar did not stem from differentiated preferences on the part of the private sector. German producers valued D-mark stability against both the dollar and European currencies. Rather, the two-track exchange rate policy stemmed from Germany's greater influence over European capitals than over the US government in macroeconomic matters. Even vis-à-vis the dollar, though, German policy was active, invoking not only foreign exchange intervention but alterations in domestic monetary policy to defend and support desired levels for the D-mark/dollar exchange rate.

German officials never accepted the laissez-faire policy espoused periodically by American policymakers over the years. The Bundesbank and finance and economics ministries acknowledged that sometimes the foreign exchange markets became detached from fundamental considerations of comparative cost. By the Bundesbank's own description,[167]

> [E]xperience has shown that the possibility cannot be ruled out that for considerable periods the exchange rate as determined by the market does not accurately reflect major economic fundamentals, such as inflation differentials vis-à-vis other countries or the current account position. Hence a tendency towards excessive appreciation or depreciation of the Deutsche Mark may emerge at times in the exchange market, and monetary policy cannot disregard this.

German authorities have historically intervened more frequently and in greater amounts than American monetary authorities. The Bundesbank also adjusted domestic monetary policy with reference to exchange rate

---

166. See, for example, Wilfried Guth, "The Prospects in the European Community for Closer Monetary Cooperation and the Establishment of a Central Bank," in *Weltwirtschaft und Währung: Aufsätze und Vorträge, 1967–1989* (Mainz: v. Hase & Koehler, 1989, pp. 345–70. See also Lipp, Ramm, and Walter, "Reply to the Manifesto of Sixty Professors Regarding the Maastricht Resolutions."

167. Deutsche Bundesbank, *The Deutsche Bundesbank*, pp. 13–14.

targets more frequently (chapter 7). The central bank was not required to do so under flexible exchange rates, as it was under the fixed rate regime, but nonetheless chose to do so. During the locomotive dispute of 1977–78 and during the mid-1980s, the Bundesbank substantially overshot its money supply growth targets to prevent a further appreciation of the D-mark. During 1981, the Bundesbank raised interest rates to prevent a further depreciation of the currency.[168]

The German government and the Bundesbank, which perceived their mission to be the maintenance of stable macroeconomic conditions conducive to export-dependent growth and economic advancement, particularly in the early postwar years, generally accommodated societal preferences for external as well as internal stability. But the policymaking institutions did not passively transmit preferences for exchange rate stability into policy outcomes. When exchange rate stability came into conflict with domestic price stability—a conflict that arose more frequently under the Bretton Woods system than under flexible exchange rates— the independence of the Bundesbank became a distinguishing feature of German policymaking.

When choosing between external and internal stability became unavoidable, the Bundesbank targeted domestic monetary policy toward limiting inflation. Compare Germany's experience to Japan's. Under the Bretton Woods regime, Germany revalued the D-mark twice, in 1961 and 1969, while Japan maintained its early postwar parity through August 1971. In 1981, faced with rising American interest rates, the Bundesbank raised interest rates dramatically while the Bank of Japan eased monetary policy. In the late 1980s, after having lowered interest rates to limit the appreciation of the currency, the Bundesbank tightened monetary policy more than a year earlier than the Bank of Japan and avoided the asset-price inflation that later plagued Japan.

The intensity of the German aversion to inflation, though, highlights the importance that Germany also attached to exchange rate stability. Inflation could have been avoided by timely revaluations under fixed rates, and by unimpeded appreciation under floating. Instead, the government and the Bundesbank tried to pursue both internal *and* external monetary stability. German policy deployed an array of instruments to delay and resist the upward valuation of the currency when its rise was not justified by comparative costs. When explaining the reasons for the

---

168. Dudler, "Monetary Policy and Exchange Rate Management in Germany." See as well Ben Bernanke and Frederic Mishkin, "Central Bank Behavior and the Strategy of Monetary Policy: Observations from Six Industrialized Countries," *NBER Macroeconomics Annual 1992*, Olivier Jean Blanchard and Stanley Fischer, eds. (Cambridge: MIT Press, 1992), p. 202. Bernanke and Mishkin conclude, "Over the past two decades, the principal object of short-term discretionary policy by the Bundesbank has been the exchange rate."

increasing influence of external considerations on monetary policymaking in the 1980s, the member of the Bundesbank's Directorate who was least likely to compromise internal for external stability cited "a constant necessity to keep an eye on the competitiveness of German industry."[169]

German policy never actively promoted a "competitive devaluation" or "competitive depreciation" of the D-mark in nominal terms. The German strategy was more subtle and effective than these beggar-thy-neighbor tactics. Rather, Germany sought to harvest the rewards of low domestic inflation for international competitiveness by stabilizing the D-mark in nominal terms against the other European currencies. Given lower inflation in Germany than abroad, German producers thereby benefited from a depreciation of the D-mark in real terms. This strategy entailed the "import" of inflation from partner countries. But, to the extent that some inflation was acceptable, German producers' competitiveness benefited from inflation being imported rather than domestically produced.

Many German economic policymakers lamented the persistent conflict between internal and external monetary stability over the postwar period caused by inflows of capital. But the international demand for assets denominated in D-marks was only half the source of the German dilemma. German preferences for *both* external and internal stability were also to blame. Without a strong attachment to exchange rate stability, upward pressure on the D-mark would not have presented a dilemma to Germany.

The choice of domestic price stability over exchange rate stabilization, therefore, was made only as a last resort. The Bundesbank and government's first preference, by far, was to avoid the dilemma altogether. In an attempt to drive a wedge, so to speak, between exchange rates and stability-oriented domestic policy, Germany deployed an array of policy instruments. Those instruments included active use of public declarations, foreign exchange intervention, German capital controls, foreign capital controls, and changes in foreign macroeconomic policies, especially monetary policy, as well as selective compensation for firms, such as the manufacturers of Airbus, harmed by appreciation. The strategy of dilemma avoidance included, above all, strongly discouraging the international use of the D-mark. The Bundesbank acquiesced to greater D-mark holdings among European central banks in the 1980s, to support the

---

169. "Prof. Schlesinger Examines the Interplay between Domestic and External Constraints in Monetary Policy," address by the vice president of the Deutsche Bundesbank, Dortmund, West Germany, 10 November 1988, translated by the Bank for International Settlements. Schlesinger's advice to the GDR on the eve of unification is also exceptionally revealing: "The Federal Republic's own experience (of introducing the D-mark after the Second World War) taught us that it is better, at the beginning, to go in the direction of under- rather than overvaluation." *Financial Times*, 7 February 1990.

stabilization regime, only subject to Bundesbank approval over their disposition.[170]

German external policy served German international interests very well during the 1980s, without sacrificing domestic monetary stability. This study has not examined the relationship between external monetary policy and the market behavior of exchange rates, nor has it argued that there is a consistent, direct relationship between the two. But exchange rate data clearly show (figure 5.3) that in real, effective terms the D-mark has been quite stable indeed. The unprecedented current account surpluses testified to the adroit management of policy and left Germany well-prepared, fortuitously, for unification.

German policymakers continued to attach great importance to the exchange rate after unification. The Bundesbank in particular feared that weakness in the D-mark, coupled with the domestic fiscal deficits and inflation, would undermine market confidence. Conscious of the need for private capital inflows to finance current account deficits and rebuild the economies of the five new Länder, the Bundesbank maintained a tighter domestic monetary policy than otherwise would have been the case. For this reason, the postunification emphasis on the exchange rate did not imply a commitment to use monetary policy to defend the ERM. The competitiveness of German industry received less consideration, on the margin, among the broadened list of competing economic problems after unification. Unification was a unique historical event, however, and policymaking under these unusual circumstances should not be taken as the historical norm. German policymaking, moreover, is likely to revert to historical patterns after the economic consequences of unification are resolved.

German policymaking institutions also have been effective in advancing German interests in international bargaining in the monetary field. The independence of the Bundesbank and the division of responsibility between it and the government on exchange rate policy enabled Germany to face down challenges from the other European countries and the United States over adjustment. Because the government had agreed with the Bundesbank not to permit participation in the EMS to produce excessive liquidity expansion, the threat that Germany could opt out of the system bolstered German insistence that others institute restrictive macroeconomic policies. At the same time, the orientation of its domestic and external monetary policy toward stability, and the high consistency in its policy approaches over time, enabled Germany to offer a reliable bargain to the European partners that were willing to accept the anti-inflation terms. For these reasons, the ERM attracted a greater number

---

170. On the evolving role of the D-mark, see George S. Tavlas, *On the International Use of Currencies: The Case of the Deutsche Mark*, Essays in International Finance 181 (Princeton: International Finance Section, Princeton University, March 1991).

of currencies over the 1980s and early 1990s while at the same time becoming effectively a D-mark zone.

The United States, in contrast to the European countries, was unwilling to adjust domestic macroeconomic policy for the sake of exchange rate stability. The independence of the Bundesbank, with the government's support, dictated that Germany pursue a policy of flexibility rather than stabilization toward the dollar. The Bundesbank was the institutional flashpoint when adjustment obligations within the G-7 became contentious. The relationship between national institutions and international cooperation will be discussed in the final chapter.

6

Monetary and Exchange Rate Policymaking in the United States

The external monetary policy of the United States during the postwar period contrasts markedly with that of Germany and Japan. American policy evolved through cycles of neglect to activism and back to neglect over the decades. US policymakers periodically countenanced large and sustained overvaluations of the dollar. When dollar overvaluations became too burdensome on the trade balance or economic growth, American monetary authorities switched abruptly to an activist policy stance. Once they became actively engaged, administration officials' first response to these problems was typically to favor a substantially lower dollar through unilateral measures. At several points, they used dollar depreciation as a lever with which to extract expansionary macroeconomic policies from foreign governments. In general, compared with German and Japanese policy, American policy has thus been less consistent over time, less oriented to exchange rate stability, and less conscious of the competitiveness ramifications of currency valuation.

The organization of the private sector, government institutions, and policy processes has produced this distinctive pattern of American policy outcomes. The unique role of the United States in the international monetary system and the relative closure of the American economy, as argued in chapter 1, contribute to but fail to provide a fully satisfactory explanation for this pattern. In the United States, the private sector is fractionalized by distant relations between banks and industry, which divide and obscure societal preferences with respect to external monetary policy. The Treasury Department effectively shares authority and influence over exchange rate policy with the Federal Reserve, which is of course relatively independent in setting domestic monetary policy, although the division of labor between them is ambiguous in some key respects. Institutional divisions within the private and public sectors leave decision makers with little guidance and much autonomy and leave policy without a clear direction for long periods.

More has been written (in all languages) on the political economy of international monetary policy of the United States than on that of Germany and Japan. The first wave of literature, published in the 1970s and early 1980s, treated the US policy experience under the Bretton Woods regime, its breakdown, and the transition to floating exchange rates.[1] These studies stressed the importance of hegemonic decline, the primacy attached to monetary autonomy, and the strength and role of central executive decision makers as fundamental determinants of, for example, the American decision to jettison the fixed-rate regime.[2] This rich body of work was successful as far as it went, and is cited favorably in the account that follows, but has two limitations for the purposes of the present study.

First, these explanations tended to dismiss the role of private-sector organization and societal preferences on exchange rate policy. Because exchange rates were generally not the focus of domestic political activity during the 1960s and 1970s, this first wave of literature tended to overlook the potentially important role of private-sector interest groups, the Congress, the linkages to American trade politics, and international trade relations. Collectively, these authors produced a formidable list of reasons as to why international monetary policy was very *unlikely* to become the focus of domestic political activity. As a result, this literature

---

1. The literature on US policy under the Bretton Woods regime is extensive. See Robert V. Roosa, *Monetary Reform for the World Economy* (New York: Harper & Row, 1965) and *The Dollar and World Liquidity* (New York: Random House, 1967); C. Fred Bergsten, *The Dilemmas of the Dollar: The Economics and Politics of United States International Economic Policy* (New York: New York University Press, 1975); Charles A. Coombs, *The Arena of International Finance* (New York: John Wiley & Sons, 1976); Benjamin J. Cohen, *Organizing the World's Money: The Political Economy of International Monetary Relations* (New York: Basic Books, 1977); Stephen D. Krasner, "United States Commercial and Monetary Policy: Unravelling the Paradox of External Strength and Internal Weakness," in *Between Power and Plenty: Foreign Economic Policies of Advanced Industrial States*, ed. Peter J. Katzenstein (Ithaca, NY: Cornell University Press, 1978), pp. 51–87; Richard N. Gardner, *Sterling-Dollar Diplomacy in Current Perspective: The Origins and the Prospects of Our International Economic Order*, rev. ed. (New York: Columbia University Press, 1980); Martin Mayer, *The Fate of the Dollar* (New York: Times Books, 1980); John S. Odell, *U.S. International Monetary Policy: Markets, Power, and Ideas as Sources of Change* (Princeton: Princeton University Press, 1982); Robert Solomon, *The International Monetary System, 1945–1981*, rev. ed. (New York: Harper & Row, 1982); Joanne Gowa, *Closing the Gold Window: Domestic Politics and the End of Bretton Woods* (Ithaca, NY: Cornell University Press, 1983).

2. See, for example, Krasner, "United States Commercial and Monetary Policy"; Odell, *U.S. International Monetary Policy*; Gowa, *Closing the Gold Window*.

did not extend well into the period of the 1980s. Under the first Reagan administration, driven by the highly skewed macroeconomic policy mix, the dollar became a major focus of industry lobbying and congressional discontent—giving rise to a second wave of literature on the subject.[3] Although this period was exceptional in US exchange rate policymaking, it demonstrates that private preferences, or the absence of coherently expressed preferences, are fundamental.

Second, the literature on the political economy of US exchange rate policy is not well adapted to the comparative purposes of the present study.[4] Comparisons to policymaking in other issue areas, such as trade, have taken precedence over comparisons to other countries' external monetary policymaking. The present study cannot merely rely on the body of previous work, therefore, and requires a review of US international monetary policymaking across the decades configured for comparative purposes.

This chapter, like the preceding chapters on Germany and Japan, proceeds chronologically through the case history of US external and domestic monetary policymaking. The first section discusses policy evolution under the Bretton Woods international monetary regime. The second section describes American policy at the transition to and during the first years of the flexible-rate regime. The third section addresses the tumultuous, and in many ways unique, period of exchange rate policymaking during the first and second Reagan administrations. Here, I borrow liberally from my earlier book with I. M. Destler on US exchange rate policy during the 1980s.[5] The fourth section describes the erosion of international monetary cooperation under the Bush administration. The final section summarizes and concludes the chapter.

---

3. These works include C. Randall Henning, *Macroeconomic Diplomacy in the 1980s: Domestic Politics and International Conflict among the United States, Japan, and Europe*, Atlantic Paper 65 (London: Croom Helm, for the Atlantic Institute for International Affairs, 1987); Yoichi Funabashi, *Managing the Dollar: From the Plaza to the Louvre* (Washington: Institute for International Economics, 1988); Stephen D. Cohen, *The Making of United States International Economic Policy: Principles, Problems, and Proposals for Reform*, 3rd ed. (New York: Praeger, 1988), chapter 10, pp. 205–19; C. Randall Henning and I. M. Destler, "From Neglect to Activism: American Politics and the 1985 Plaza Accord," *Journal of Public Policy* 8 (July–December 1988): 317-34; I. M. Destler and C. Randall Henning, *Dollar Politics: Exchange Rate Policymaking in the United States* (Washington: Institute for International Economics, 1989); Jeffrey A. Frankel, "The Making of Exchange Rate Policy in the 1980s," in *American Economic Policy in the 1980s*, Martin Feldstein, ed. (Chicago: University of Chicago Press for NBER, 1994), pp. 293–341.

4. The previous work on US policymaking in this area has sprung from the subfields of american politics, foreign policymaking, and international political economy rather than comparative political economy.

5. Destler and Henning, *Dollar Politics*.

Presiding over the Bretton Woods Regime

Role of the United States

Under the Bretton Woods regime of fixed exchange rates that prevailed for two and a half decades after World War II, the United States played a unique role at the center of the system. The United States, after all, possessed by far the most powerful economy; American goods were valued and American investment was courted abroad; the US dollar became almost universally accepted as a reserve and transactions currency, and the United States therefore became the main source of liquidity for international payments. The United States originally adopted a passive attitude with respect to the balance of payments, letting it be set essentially by the total of its partners' payments objectives. By adopting this so-called Nth country role, the United States removed any conflict over balance of payments objectives among countries within the system. The United States at the same time became passive with respect to the progressive overvaluation of the dollar in real terms.

These roles were not imposed by the regime; they were the product of the US government's own policy choices and its response to the balance of payments and exchange rate policies of its partners. The regime constructed at Bretton Woods, New Hampshire, in 1944, under the sponsorship of the United States, had not foreseen the development of a dollar-based system that relied on the United States running deficits to supply liquidity. Nor did it provide contingencies for the loss of confidence in the key currency when dollar holdings became large—a basic contradiction in the construction of the regime first described by economist Robert Triffin, thus labeled the "Triffin dilemma."

These roles evolved as they did because the United States determined its domestic macroeconomic policies in isolation from balance-of-payments and dollar problems, more or less, and because the United States did not have a strong sense of what exchange rate for the dollar would be appropriate for the American economy. Thus, when the economies of Europe and Japan recovered from postwar devastation, and their productivity in traded goods increased dramatically, the United States held a complacent view with respect to the progressive overvaluation of the dollar in real terms.

Defending the Dollar

Adopting the Nth-country role did not consign the United States to passivity in international monetary policy generally. To the contrary, in the 1960s American authorities worked actively to defend the dollar and to sustain the international monetary regime their predecessors had created. That activism, though, was limited to ad hoc balance of payments

Table 6.1 Postwar administrations in the United States

President	Party	Date of inauguration
Harry S Truman	Democrat	12 April 1945
Dwight D. Eisenhower	Republican	20 January 1953
John F. Kennedy	Democrat	20 January 1961
Lyndon B. Johnson	Democrat	22 November 1963
Richard M. Nixon	Republican	20 January 1969
Gerald R. Ford	Republican	9 August 1974
Jimmy Carter	Democrat	20 January 1977
Ronald Reagan	Republican	20 January 1981
George Bush	Republican	20 January 1989
Bill Clinton	Democrat	20 January 1993

programs, capital controls, and foreign exchange intervention—devices employed to drive a wedge between domestic macroeconomic policies and international confidence in the dollar. The Eisenhower, Kennedy, and Johnson administrations studiously avoided confronting the emerging central conflict between dollar valuation and domestic economic growth (see table 6.1 for a chronology of administrations). The activist measures that American officials did employ, second, were directed toward sustaining a progressively *overvalued* US dollar.

After World War II, the United States first confronted the problem of a dollar shortage abroad. But as foreign economies recovered and American deficits arose, the dollar shortage turned into an oversupply. John F. Kennedy was the first American president to confront the dollar glut. Fearful that foreign governments and central banks might exchange their dollars for US gold, as was their right under the Bretton Woods regime, President Kennedy reportedly worried about the balance of payments almost as much as he did about nuclear war. President Kennedy repeatedly affirmed the sanctity of the gold parity of the dollar.[6] The United States began intervention in the foreign exchange market in March 1961 shortly after his inauguration. To ensure that foreign exchange would be available for dollar defense, the United States led the creation of the Group of 10, issued foreign currency–denominated bonds, and opened swap agreements with foreign central banks. US officials sought to stimulate the economy by reducing long-term interest rates through debt management while at the same time supporting short-term interest rates in order to maintain confidence in the dollar, a strategy called "Operation Twist." In July 1963, Kennedy and his advisers invoked capital controls in the form of the Interest Equalization

6. For the Kennedy administration's approach to international monetary policy, see Theodore C. Sorensen, *Kennedy* (New York: Harper & Row, 1965), pp. 405–12; Roosa, *The Dollar and World Liquidity*; Solomon, *The International Monetary System*, chapter 3, pp. 34–62.

Tax.[7] The Kennedy administration's domestic economic program, however, remained essentially untouched by troubles with the dollar.

American policy continued to take a series of rearguard actions in defense of the dollar under President Lyndon B. Johnson. Capital controls were expanded to a voluntary program applied to bank lending. To relieve some of the dollar's burden of acting as an international currency, the Treasury acceded to the creation of Special Drawing Rights (SDRs) at the International Monetary Fund.[8] The United States entered a series of agreements on gold with its allies, with the central object of sustaining confidence in the gold convertibility of the dollar while also dissuading holders of dollars from actually converting them into gold. The Treasury and the Federal Reserve actively supported the British pound prior to its 1967 devaluation, out of fear that the weakness of the pound could be contagious for the dollar. And they exploited the swap network to intervene in defense of the dollar in substantial quantities.[9] Nonetheless, again, the dollar problem had little impact on Johnson's macroeconomic programs, particularly decisions regarding the financing of the Vietnam War.[10]

The US trade balance remained in surplus throughout the 1960s. But, as war and social expenditures, the budget deficit, and inflation rose during the second half of the decade, capital outflow and the balance of payments deficit increased as well, jeopardizing confidence in the dollar. While refusing to adjust domestic macroeconomic policies, however, senior officials also refused to consider a dollar devaluation. Any talk of a devaluation, however discreet and confidential, was at times specifically forbidden.[11] By the beginning of the 1970s, by the Treasury's own estimates, the overvaluation of the dollar had grown to 10–15 percent.[12]

Finally, the tension between domestic macroeconomic priorities and maintaining the international status of the dollar became unavoidable

---

7. The IET was a tax of 1 percent on all foreign securities sold in the United States. Canada and Japan were exempted. See John A. C. Conybeare, *United States Foreign Economic Policy and the International Capital Markets: The Case of Capital Export Controls, 1963–1974* (New York: Garland, 1988).

8. Odell, *U.S. International Monetary Policy*, chapter 3, pp. 79–164.

9. See, for example, Coombs, *Arena of International Finance*, pp. 188–203.

10. Though concern about the dollar might have been a factor persuading Congress to pass a tax increase in 1968.

11. A central conflict under the gold-exchange standard constrained serious discussion of certain options within American administrations. Any discussion of a devaluation against gold, not to mention a suspension of convertibility, threatened to become self-fulfilling almost instantaneously. Holders of dollars would have a powerful interest in converting their holdings before the devaluation took place.

12. Treasury Department, Office of Financial Analysis, "The U.S. International Competitive Position and the Potential Role of Exchange Rates in the Adjustment Process," confidential report to Undersecretary Paul A. Volcker, Washington, 28 May 1971, cited by Odell, *U.S. International Monetary Policy*, p. 252.

Figure 6.1 United States: trade and current account balances, 1953–93

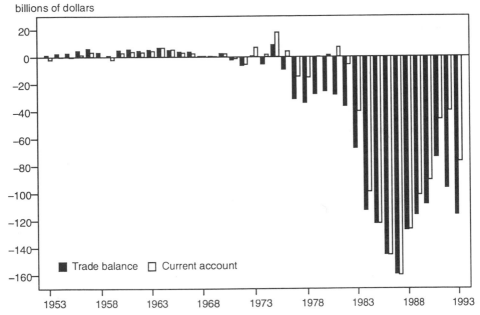

billions of dollars

Sources: International Monetary Fund, *International Financial Statistics*, and US Department of Commerce.

under the presidency of Richard M. Nixon. In 1968 and 1969 the trade surplus had been almost eliminated. After a brief respite owing to a recession in 1970, the United States ran its first trade deficit in the post-war period—and indeed its first deficit of the century—in 1971 (figures 6.1 and 6.2). US monetary policy began to ease in 1970, contributing to the tendency of capital to flow out of dollar assets. At the same time, though inflation had not been conquered, President Nixon wished to stimulate economic growth.

Jettisoning the Gold Standard

Against this backdrop, Nixon convened his senior economic and political advisers for a meeting at Camp David on 13 August 1971 that decisively changed the course of American economic policy, and with it international monetary policy.[13] Two days later, Nixon announced a "New Eco-

---

13. For thorough analyses of this decision, see Odell, *U.S. International Monetary Policy*; Gowa, *Closing the Gold Window*. For accounts of the participants, see Volcker and Gyohten, *Changing Fortunes*, chapter 3, pp. 59–100; William Safire, *Before the Fall: An Inside View of the Pre-Watergate White House* (Garden City, NY: Doubleday, 1975), pp. 509–28; James Reston, Jr., *The Lone Star: The Life of John Connally* (New York: Harper & Row, 1989), pp. 402–32.

Figure 6.2 United States: trade and current account balances, 1953–93

percentage of GDP

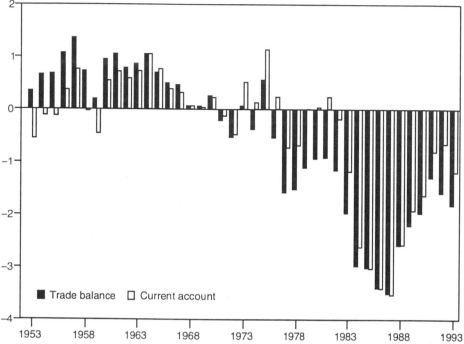

Sources: International Monetary Fund, *International Financial Statistics* and US Department of Commerce.

nomic Policy" that for the domestic economy instituted a comprehensive set of wage and price controls and cut taxes. On the international side, Nixon shocked foreign governments with two bombshells. In one fell swoop, Nixon ended the gold-drain problem by unilaterally suspending gold convertibility of the dollar, taking the country off the gold standard. Second, Nixon unilaterally imposed a temporary surcharge of 10 percent on all goods imported from abroad.

The suspension of gold convertibility and the import surcharge were aggressively pursued by the new Treasury Secretary and former Texas Democrat John B. Connally, whom Nixon had inducted into his administration as a replacement for David Kennedy. Federal Reserve Chairman Arthur Burns, former chairman of the Council of Economic Advisers (CEA) under Eisenhower and a longtime Nixon adviser, argued with Connally to maintain gold convertibility at the Camp David meeting. Orchestrating the devaluation of the dollar, which would require multilateral negotiations, would be nearly inconceivable without effectively suspending gold convertibility, however. The Treasury and the Fed would have to expect a huge volume of requests for gold conversion, far greater than could be satisfied, by holders of soon-to-be-devalued dollars.[14]

Nixon's August 1971 decision represented a clear choice that domestic macroeconomic performance was not to be subordinated to the former goal of maintaining a stable, and overvalued, dollar. The dollar devaluation did not necessarily require an abandonment of the fixed exchange rate regime. But the suspension of gold convertibility did constitute regime transformation. And though the G-10 governments agreed on a realignment of exchange rates in the Smithsonian agreement during the following December, that agreement completely unraveled by March 1973. The August 1971 decision thus marks the beginning of the end of the Bretton Woods regime.

The Federal Reserve during this period did not play the role of an independent central bank yearning to break free of the shackles of the gold standard or fixed exchange rate regime. To the contrary, the Federal Reserve was the strongest supporter of the regime within the American government. Chairman Burns supported a devaluation but also held profound antipathy for flexible exchange rates and argued strenuously for maintaining the dollar standard and fixed-rate regime at the Camp David meeting. Concerns about payments deficits, gold outflow, and confidence in the dollar argued in favor of more restrictive monetary policy, thus reinforcing the Fed's predilection on domestic grounds to fight rising inflation, of which Burns had already been critical.

The Treasury on the other hand ultimately withdrew its support for the regime precisely to avoid constraints on the easing of monetary policy. Treasury had organized programs of support for the US balance of payments and the regime, but ultimately withdrew into the Nixon policy of benign neglect of the exchange rate, revoking authorization for extended foreign exchange intervention. Ultimately, it was Connally, at Volcker's active urging, and with Nixon's consent, who ended gold convertibility.[15]

The role of the Congress was ambivalent and sometimes contradictory. On the one hand, members of Congress expressed strong support for maintenance of the gold parity of the dollar. On the other hand, they wanted to avoid restrictive measures to achieve this goal. The Congress provided a forum in which alternative solutions to the balance of payments problem were discussed. In early August 1971, Representative Henry Reuss, a subcommittee chairman particularly active on the issue, introduced a "sense of the Congress" resolution calling for the devaluation of the dollar. But the Congress at this time was far more of a sideshow than a central player on international monetary policy.

---

14. Volcker and Gyohten, *Changing Fortunes*, chapter 3.

15. Odell, *U.S. International Monetary Policy*, pp. 247–66.

The defense and foreign policy complex sought to ensure that economic disputes did not adversely affect alliance cohesion. As long as the Treasury and the Federal Reserve defended the Bretton Woods regime, they were generally content. Once that policy shifted in 1971, however, they became very concerned. When international monetary negotiations showed little sign of progress and threatened political relations with Europe, the national security adviser, Henry A. Kissinger, intervened with President Nixon to persuade Secretary Connally to soften his position on dollar devaluation.[16]

The United States supported the Bretton Woods regime, therefore, only so long as the costs of doing so remained fairly small in terms of domestic priorities. During the first half of the postwar era, the United States did not change domestic monetary policy for the sake of maintaining the Bretton Woods parity. That responsibility rested with foreign governments and central banks, which intervened to maintain the parities. The limits to the asymmetrical operation of the fixed-rate regime were reached when American monetary policy became highly expansionary during the Vietnam War. When the rules of the regime threatened to constrain American monetary policy, the United States jettisoned the regime.[17]

The break with gold and the first dollar devaluation were the product of a policymaking system, centered around the Treasury and Federal Reserve, very much autonomous from particularistic societal pressures. Some bankers and businessmen opposed capital controls that constrained their international financial operations. But no private sector coalition promoted or opposed the devaluation of the dollar or the dollar's link to gold.[18] Nothing like the coalitions that were mobilized in the debates over currency revaluation in Japan and Germany existed in the United States at that time. Interest group activity and congressional agitation

---

16. Henry A. Kissinger, *The White House Years* (Boston: Little, Brown, 1979), pp. 949–62.

17. Joanne Gowa sums up this period:

> [D]omestic economic policy was considered virtually sacrosanct, very largely immune from the conduct of US balance-of-payments or international monetary policy. The latter was, instead, the residue of domestic economic policy, reflecting the primacy of national policy over the demands of the international monetary regime. That the two did not collide irreconcilably before 1971 was the result partly of the noninflationary course of US domestic macroeconomic policy adhered to until the mid-1960s, partly of the vigorous demand for US dollars abroad in the early years of the Bretton Woods system and partly of the more recent series of ad hoc arrangements concluded between the United States and other governments to insulate the monetary system from the effects of a long series of US payments deficits.

See Gowa, *Closing the Gold Window*, p. 25.

18. Odell, *U.S. International Monetary Policy*, pp. 42–44, 236–39, 346–48.

therefore played little or no direct role in the key American decisions in the early 1970s. The Treasury and Federal Reserve instead responded to the political desire to preserve maximum flexibility for the instruments of domestic macroeconomic management.

The period from the late 1950s through the confrontation over dollar devaluation, ending with the realignment agreement at the end of 1971, represents the first cycle of neglect to activism in US international monetary policy. That cycle would repeat itself in the 1970s and 1980s.[19]

The New Floating Exchange Rate Regime

Transition to Floating Rates and Early Policy

After the Smithsonian agreement, the fixed exchange rate regime continued to hemorrhage badly. Faced with a growing payments deficit, American officials concluded within months of that realignment that a second devaluation was needed.[20] Under the direction of a new Treasury secretary, George P. Shultz, Paul Volcker negotiated a second devaluation, announced in mid-February 1973. But that too failed to stem the tide of speculation against the dollar. By the beginning of March, the dollar was floating freely against all major currencies. The Nixon administration was fundamentally unwilling to bear the costs of maintaining the regime.

During this period, the Treasury restrained the Federal Reserve from intervening in the foreign exchange market to defend, first, the Smithsonian parities, second, the realignment agreed in February 1973, and, third, the depreciating dollar after the unraveling of the February accord at the beginning of March.[21] As under the Bretton Woods system, by far the largest share of intervention to defend the new parities was conducted by central banks other than the Fed. Though it had achieved large devaluations of the dollar, the US Treasury would not accept greater intervention responsibility to defend these exchange rates. At the time of

---

19. Cycles of neglect to activism in US international monetary policy are identified and explained in C. Fred Bergsten, "America's Unilateralism," in Bergsten, Etienne Davignon, and Isamu Miyazaki, *Conditions for Partnership in International Economic Management*, Report to the Trilateral Commission 32 (New York: Trilateral Commission, 1986), pp. 3–14; Henning, *Macroeconomic Diplomacy in the 1980s*, pp. 50–52; Benjamin J. Cohen, "An Explosion in the Kitchen? Economic Relations with Other Advanced Industrial States," in Kenneth A. Oye, Robert J. Lieber, and Donald Rothchild, eds., *Eagle Defiant: United States Foreign Policy in the 1980s* (Boston: Little, Brown, 1983), pp. 105–30.

20. Before the first devaluation, Treasury officials concluded that a devaluation of 10–15 percent was required to restore balance to US payments. The Smithsonian agreement provided for only an 8 percent devaluation, on a trade-weighted basis including the Canadian dollar against which no devaluation took place.

21. Coombs, *Arena of International Finance*, pp. 204–39.

Figure 6.3 Dollar/D-mark exchange rates, 1970–93

logarithmic scale, monthly average

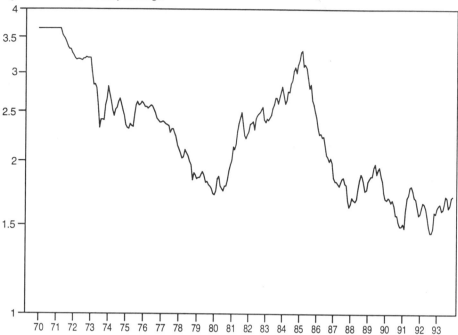

Source: International Monetary Fund.

the second devaluation, Treasury Secretary Shultz emphasized that the United States had not agreed to intervene in foreign exchange markets to defend the new parity. Shultz also announced the phased abolition of capital controls, completed in January 1974.[22]

After the switch, by default, to floating exchange rates, the dollar gyrated wildly for two years. By July 1973, the dollar had plummeted 30 percent below the exchange rate set for the D-mark in February and about 20 percent below the levels set for the other European currencies. At that point, the Treasury acceded to pleas from the Federal Reserve Bank of New York to intervene, though it authorized operations only in modest quantities.[23] The intervention, and later the Arab oil embargo in October, succeeded in halting the depreciation and almost fully reversing the previous drop by the beginning of 1974 (figures 6.3 and 6.4).

Although maintaining the fixed-rate regime was consistent with the Fed's predilection to fight inflation, Fed officials were unwilling to use

---

22. Odell, *U.S. International Monetary Policy*, p. 317.

23. Coombs, *Arena of International Finance*, p. 232.

Figure 6.4 Dollar-yen exchange rates, 1971–93

logarithmic scale, monthly average

Source: International Monetary Fund.

the international argument as a rationale for tightening monetary policy. The Fed was under strong pressure from the Congress and administration to keep the domestic economy buoyant under Nixon's wage and price controls. Rather than tightening monetary policy to defend the dollar, therefore, the Fed eased further in early 1972 to stimulate the domestic economy.[24] By early 1973, inflation had risen and both domestic and international factors argued for monetary tightening. But even Chairman Burns, who very much disliked floating rates, was unwilling to countenance the political reaction to the increase in interest rates necessary to lend credibility to the February 1973 parities. When the US and European finance ministers and central bank governors agreed on the joint European float against the dollar in early March, Burns vociferously dissociated monetary policy from the agreement.[25] Though the Fed

24. Woolley, *Monetary Politics*, chapter 8, pp. 154–80.

25. Speaking in Paris after negotiating the second dollar devaluation, Shultz and Burns were asked about the ramifications for monetary policy. Burns took the microphone and exclaimed, "American monetary policy is not made in Paris, it is made in Washington." Volcker and Gyohten, *Changing Fortunes*, p. 113.

would tighten monetary policy within weeks, as Volcker retrospectively observes, this move came too late to save the dollar, the fixed rate parities, and price stability.[26]

The argument that there was an intractable conflict between the fixed-rate regime and American monetary autonomy, and that the Nixon administration opted for the latter, greatly overstates the opportunity cost of maintaining the regime. The monetary flexibility that the United States insisted upon preserving was a false sovereignty. Maintaining the fixed-rate system demanded not that the United States tighten monetary policy as opposed to keeping it lax, but that the Fed raise interest rates earlier, beginning in 1972, rather than waiting until 1973 to make the decisive shift. The United States exploited the flexibility preserved at the cost of the fixed-rate regime not to sustain the health of the American economy but to commit a gross error of monetary overexpansion. That mistake fueled US and world inflation that required a severe recession to correct.

Negotiating International Monetary Reform

Against the backdrop of the breakdown of fixed exchange rates, the first oil shock, and the world recession, the United States negotiated with its partners to reform the international monetary system. The forum for these important discussions was the Committee of Twenty (C-20), the finance ministers from the industrial and developing countries representing the membership of the International Monetary Fund (which later became the Interim Committee of the Fund).[27]

The primary American objective in these negotiations was to rectify the adjustment asymmetry embodied in the Bretton Woods regime. Deficit countries had been subjected to stronger pressures for adjustment and US officials sought to redistribute this burden onto the surplus countries as well. Volcker designed and Shultz proposed an "indicators approach" to assigning the burden of adjustment to deficit and surplus countries. Treasury at the same time also proposed a scheme for limited asset settlement, fixing exchange rates within wider bands, and temporary floating when necessary. (No other country proposed a similarly comprehensive reform plan.)

The European countries sought above all to restrict the ability of the United States to finance external deficits with dollar liabilities and there-

---

26. Volcker and Gyohten, *Changing Fortunes*, p. 114.

27. These negotiations are chronicled and analyzed in Solomon, *International Monetary System, 1945–1981*; Volcker and Gyohten, *Changing Fortunes*, pp. 114–35; Odell, *U.S. International Monetary Policy*, pp. 292–323; B. J. Cohen, *Organizing the World's Money*, pp. 108–152; John Williamson, *The Failure of World Monetary Reform, 1971–1974* (New York: New York University Press, 1977).

by avoid any external constraint on domestic macroeconomic policy. The United States might have accepted some restraints, but not in the absence of more symmetrical pressures for adjustment. Two years of negotiations, buffeted by surging inflation, the first oil shock, and a worldwide recession, failed to produce agreement. The shift to the floating exchange rate regime was codified by an agreement, primarily between the United States and France, at the first meeting of the heads of state and government at Rambouillet in 1975.

Meanwhile, as the dollar fell and rose again over the course of 1974, foreign exchange interventions were limited to smoothing operations under both the late Nixon and early Ford administrations. When the dollar fell again at the beginning of 1975, Burns secured the approval of the new Treasury secretary, William Simon, to increase intervention and concluded a cooperative accord with the German Bundesbank and Swiss National Bank.[28] Once the dollar strengthened, intervention remained small for the remainder of the Ford administration.

During 1975 and 1976, the world was mired in the deepest recession of the postwar period, reeling from the first oil shock. As American recovery began and the external balance was (temporarily) rectified, however, the Ford administration took a laissez-faire attitude with respect to the dollar and foreign demand. In 1976, administration officials argued that the recovery was sufficiently quick and sustainable and rejected suggestions for domestic and foreign stimulus.[29]

Carter Administration and Locomotive Dispute

Jimmy Carter sought to stimulate the US economy immediately upon assuming the presidency in January 1977. Macroeconomic conditions had favored his candidacy over Gerald Ford's reelection; American inflation was around 6 percent, unemployment around 7.5 percent and growth 3.0 percent. His economic advisers concluded that a stimulus was important to assuring that the economy did not relapse into recession. The heart of Carter's program was a $31 billion tax cut spread over 1977 and 1978.

The Carter team argued that it was necessary for Germany and Japan, both surplus countries, to stimulate their economies as well.[30] Within

---

28. Coombs, *Arena of International Finance*, pp. 236–37.

29. See, for example, the statements of CEA Chairman Alan Greenspan and colleagues in Council of Economic Advisers, *Annual Report for 1977*, pp. 118 and 124.

30. Putnam and Henning, "The Bonn Summit of 1978: A Case Study in Coordination."

days of the inauguration, Vice President Mondale traveled to Europe and Japan. Undersecretary of State for Economic Affairs Richard N. Cooper and Assistant Secretary of the Treasury for International Affairs C. Fred Bergsten, among others, traveled with him. They took this message to the German and Japanese governments. The administration's program was not contingent upon Germany and Japan following suit. If Bonn and Tokyo declined to administer stimulus, however, they should expect a depreciation of the dollar against their currencies.

The German and Japanese governments resisted, predictably, the American advice. And, when Treasury Secretary Michael Blumenthal indicated that a rise of their currencies against the dollar was in order, the dollar began a slide that was to last a year and a half. All the while, the United States refused to take strong action in the foreign exchange market. First, the US trade deficit was deteriorating again. Second, the depreciation of the dollar was putting pressure on foreign governments to expand domestic demand to offset the restriction on imports imposed by the appreciation of their currencies.

At Carter's first economic summit meeting in London in May 1977, the partner countries agreed to substantial economic growth targets. As the year wore on, however, it became clear that the United States would be the only country to meet its target. Under these circumstances, the Treasury was not inclined to surrender the "dollar weapon" by taking strong measures to support its value. When Germany and Japan implored the United States to support its currency, the Carter administration responded only symbolically and with half measures.

The arguments over the "locomotive theory," as the administration's proposals for surplus countries to stimulate their economies came to be called, were replayed at the G-7 summit meeting in Bonn in July 1978. This meeting, by contrast, produced a genuine and substantial agreement on macroeconomic policy coordination. German Chancellor Helmut Schmidt and Japanese Prime Minister Takeo Fukuda agreed to administer fiscal stimulus to their economies. President Jimmy Carter agreed, in exchange, to lift controls on US oil prices, which would dampen American demand and imports, widely perceived to be threatening the world economy.

Exchange rates were largely neglected as a topic of conversation at the summit itself. The Bonn meeting represents something of a missed opportunity for other governments to press the United States for tighter monetary policy. Such a policy shift would have been justified not only by the depreciation of the dollar but by the upward creep of American inflation. Carter's response to the inflation problem was a half-hearted, voluntary program, announced in late October, which deeply disappointed the financial markets. Within a few days, the dollar plummeted to new record lows of 1.71 against the D-mark and 171 against the yen. Against the D-mark, these levels were 20 percent below those of early August.

Finally, to prevent the exchange rate from further exacerbating American inflation, the Carter administration suddenly switched to supporting the dollar on 1 November 1978.[31] Blumenthal and Solomon announced to the press that a foreign-currency war chest of unprecedented size, $30 billion, had been assembled to defend the dollar from existing reserves, swap agreements, and IMF drawings. The Treasury also agreed, for the first time since the early 1960s, to issue bonds denominated in foreign currencies, so-called Carter bonds, to complete the foreign exchange war chest. (Carter bonds were issued in D-marks and Swiss francs. Japanese petitions to issue them in yen as well were politely rebuffed.) The administration also announced that the Federal Reserve would raise the discount rate one full point, to 9.5 percent, and impose a supplementary reserve requirement. This was the first time that a discount rate change was announced by the president rather than the Fed.[32]

These actions effectively placed a floor beneath the dollar during the following months. For the remainder of the Carter administration, the Treasury maintained an active stance in the foreign exchange market. Treasury officials sought to build foreign exchange reserves as a war chest for intervention, if needed, and to repay the foreign currency borrowed with the Carter bonds.

US international monetary policy had completed its second full cycle in as many decades. The late Nixon and Ford administrations had been content with floating exchange rates, and willing to let the effort to reform the international monetary system in the C-20 negotiations lapse inconclusively. The Carter administration was aggressively active, pressing others for faster growth and refusing to undertake adjustment or substantial intervention on its part. By late 1978, US authorities were cooperating with foreign central banks and governments and accepting part of the burden of coordination. That cooperation ended with the departure of the Carter administration from government at the beginning of 1981.

After the switch to more active management of the exchange rate, the Carter administration negotiated with its counterparts over the creation of a so-called Substitution Account. As proposed, the account would be a receptacle into which to retire the "dollar overhang" in the portfolios of foreign central banks without putting further downward pressure on its value vis-à-vis foreign currencies on the open market. Carter administra-

---

31. Putnam and Henning, "The Bonn Summit of 1978," pp. 84–87; Stephen D. Cohen and Ronald I. Meltzer, *United States International Economic Policy in Action* (New York: Praeger, 1982), chapter 2; Herman Nickel, "The Inside Story of the Dollar Rescue," *Fortune*, 4 December 1978, pp. 40–44; Alan R. Holmes and Scott E. Pardee, "Treasury and Federal Reserve Foreign Exchange Operations," *Federal Reserve Bank of New York Quarterly Review* 4 (spring 1979): 67–87.

32. Mayer, *Fate of the Dollar*, p. 295.

tion officials and the Congress were unwilling to accept significant costs associated with the account, however, and thus reached no agreement with foreign counterparts.[33]

The switch to an active intervention policy preceded the decisive change to tight money by almost one year. Because monetary tightening after October 1978 lagged rather than led the increase in inflation, it did not produce a sustained rise in the dollar's value. But the coming transformation in Fed monetary policy, in October 1979, would begin to shift the long-term trend in the dollar upward.

In early August 1979, G. William Miller replaced Blumenthal as Treasury secretary and Volcker replaced Miller as Federal Reserve chairman. Volcker, who had served as president of the Federal Reserve Bank of New York since 1974, was increasingly alarmed by the steady rise of inflation and the negligible impact of monetary tightening on market expectations. Price increases announced by the Organization of Petroleum Exporting Countries (OPEC) in March aggravated the inflation problem. Determined to get ahead of the curve, Volcker planned a bold move.

On their way to the 1979 joint meeting of the IMF and World Bank in Belgrade, Yugoslavia, Volcker, Miller, and Shultz met with Schmidt and Emminger in Hamburg. The Germans complained bitterly about the dollar and American monetary policy. Volcker suggests that the force of the German message moderated Miller and Shultz's objections to the Fed chairman's chosen course of action.[34]

Volcker convened a special meeting of the Federal Open Market Committee (FOMC) on Saturday, 6 October, that launched the new policy regime. Thereafter, the Fed would focus mainly on moderating the growth of the money supply, allowing interest rates to rise or fall as much as necessary to achieve that result. Under this cloak of monetarism, Volcker and the Fed initiated a sustained tightening of monetary conditions.[35]

---

33. Joanne Gowa, "Hegemons, IOs, and Markets: The Case of the Substitution Account," *International Organization* 38 (autumn 1984): 661–83.

34. Volcker and Gyohten, *Changing Fortunes*, pp. 166–69.

35. With the focus on the money supply, the Fed appeared to take on distinctly monetarist stripes. Volcker found monetarism—defined as strict adherence to the constant money growth rule—to be useful under circumstances of high inflation. But the Fed chairman was wary of the extreme claims of the school and never characterized himself as a monetarist. Henry Wallich, a Fed governor who favored tight money in 1979, characterized Volcker's shift to money supply targeting as a "pact with the devil." See Volcker and Gyohten, *Changing Fortunes*, pp. 166–68; Greider, *Secrets of the Temple*, p. 105. Milton Friedman later criticized the Fed for using the language and symbols of monetarism opportunistically to justify a tightening of monetary policy, all the while guarding its bureaucratic prerogative to manage monetary policy flexibly. See Milton Friedman, "A Memorandum to the Fed," *Wall Street Journal*, 30 January 1981; "The Federal Reserve and Monetary Instability," *Wall Street Journal*, 1 February 1982; *Wall Street Journal*, 3 June 1980.

Table 6.2 United States: federal budget deficits, 1980–93
(dollars in billions)

Fiscal year	Amount
1980	73.8
1981	79.0
1982	128.0
1983	207.8
1984	185.4
1985	212.3
1986	221.2
1987	149.8
1988	155.2
1989	152.5
1990	221.4
1991	269.5
1992	290.2
1993	327.3

Source: Council of Economic Advisers, *Economic Report of the President*, February 1994, table B-77.

The Reagan Era

The tightening of American monetary policy did not produce a sustained upswing of the dollar immediately. Foreign central banks were, after all, tightening in tandem with the Federal Reserve in 1979 and 1980. Ronald Reagan's accession to the presidency in January 1981, with his domestic economic program, profoundly changed the course of the dollar and US international monetary policy.[36] President Reagan and his senior officials ushered in another period of laissez-faire neglect of the dollar.

The economic program that Reagan announced was virtually completely domestic in focus. International considerations were an afterthought for the supply-siders, monetarists, and orthodox fiscal conservatives who vied to dominate administration policy. The president's Program for Economic Recovery sought to reduce taxes, control federal spending on domestic and social programs, eliminate regulation, and reduce inflation through tight monetary policy. This program, supplemented by huge increases in defense spending, produced unprecedented federal budget deficits in the first Reagan administration—a structural fiscal problem that would hound each succeeding administration (table 6.2).

These budget deficits collided with the tight monetary policy of the Federal Reserve to produce record high interest rates (figure 6.5). Nominal interest rates had peaked before Reagan entered office. But, pro-

36. For a full discussion, see Destler and Henning, *Dollar Politics*; Henning, *Macroeconomic Diplomacy*; B. J. Cohen, "An Explosion in the Kitchen?"

Figure 6.5 United States: interest rates, 1980–93

percentage

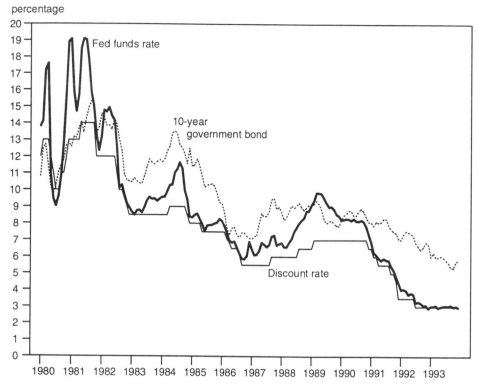

Source: International Monetary Fund, *International Financial Statistics*.

pelled by government demands on the capital markets, current and expected, real interest rates rose through 1981 to 9 percent by early 1982 and remained above 7 percent throughout the first Reagan administration. These interest rates were a magnet for internationally mobile capital, which flowed to the US in record quantities. These inflows, as is now well known, propelled the dollar dramatically upward and the US position in international trade downward.

The Treasury Department, under the leadership of Secretary Donald T. Regan, decided not to resist the appreciation of the dollar. In April 1981, when the dollar was just beginning to rise, Undersecretary for Monetary Affairs Beryl W. Sprinkel announced that Treasury would halt all intervention in the foreign exchange market.[37] Only under very extraordinary circumstances, such as the shooting of the president in March, would Treasury permit these operations. Regan and Sprinkel also re-

---

37. *New York Times*, 17 April 1981; US Congress, Joint Economic Committee, *International Economic Policy*, hearings, 97th Cong., 1st sess., 4 May 1981, pp. 27–28.

nounced the other instruments of exchange rate management: declaratory policy, capital controls, and changes in monetary and fiscal policy with the intent of affecting the dollar. They would accept completely the market's verdict on the appropriate exchange rate. Treasury would not even develop an internal view of what level of the dollar might be justified by the economic fundamentals.

President Reagan and Secretary Regan not only refused to cap the dollar's rise, they actively cheered the currency upward! In 1984, the dollar continued to rise above 2.60 D-marks and remained in the range of 220–260 yen. But the higher the dollar rose, the more they cheered. Regan extolled the benefits of the strength of the currency, reducing US inflation and expanding growth abroad, and observed with complacency that it might not fall for three more years.[38] In his 1985 State of the Union address, President Reagan called for making the United States the "investment capital of the world."[39] The president and the Treasury secretary continued to argue through the summer of 1985 that the strong dollar was good for the US economy and that the trade deficit was not harmful.[40]

The administration had one compelling incentive to show optimism for the dollar's strength. In 1983, the US budget deficit grew to $207.8 billion and the current account deficit set a new record of $43.6 billion and was headed toward $98.8 billion in 1984. Sustaining the recovery from the economic recession of 1982 depended vitally on capital inflows to finance these "twin deficits." Secretary Regan in particular was conscious of the need to finance the burgeoning budget deficit.

In 1984, therefore, Regan, Sprinkel, and Assistant Secretary for International Affairs David C. Mulford moved enthusiastically to expand the pool of international savings on which the United States could draw. They negotiated an agreement on capital market liberalization with the Japanese Ministry of Finance.[41] In the 1984 tax bill, Treasury persuaded the Congress to eliminate a 30 percent withholding tax on interest payments to foreign holders of US and corporate bonds.[42] Treasury also granted permission to corporations to issue bearer bonds to foreigners.

---

38. *New York Times*, 1 and 23 February, 5 June 1984.

39. "State of the Union," Address Delivered Before a Joint Session of the Congress, February 1985, reprinted in *Weekly Compilation of Presidential Documents* 21 (6), p. 140.

40. See White House, "News Conference by the President," press release, Washington, 17 September 1985.

41. See Jeffrey A. Frankel, *The Yen-Dollar Agreement: Liberalizing Japanese Capital Markets*, POLICY ANALYSES IN INTERNATIONAL ECONOMICS 9 (Washington: Institute for International Economics, February 1984).

42. US Congress, Joint Committee on Taxation, *General Explanation of the Revenue Provisions of the Deficit Reduction Act of 1984*, 98th Cong., 2nd sess., 31 December 1984, pp. 387–98.

Treasury designed a new issue of government bonds for foreign purchasers and Mulford traveled to Europe and Sprinkel to Japan to market them. The net effect of these measures was to mobilize large sums of foreign savings for American use.

During the period of the strong dollar, the Treasury and the Fed were privately at odds over intervention policy. Volcker and Anthony Solomon, now president of the Federal Reserve Bank of New York, urged Treasury to authorize substantial intervention during periods of exchange market instability. Fed officials welcomed the dampening of inflation provided by the strong dollar but feared that the overvaluation of the currency would lead to a sudden fall.[43] Volcker and Solomon's petitions coincided with pleas from the European and Japanese government for greater American activism. When Regan and Sprinkel rebuffed these proposals, Volcker considered flouting Treasury's prohibition against intervention but rejected this option. Taking that defiant course of action would have provoked a political donnybrook that might have jeopardized support for the Fed's domestic policy of inflation fighting and that certainly would have undermined the effectiveness of the foreign exchange operation.[44]

Volcker also considered and rejected easing monetary policy to restrain the dollar. Without a reduction in the budget deficit, however, an easing of monetary policy would constitute an abandonment of the primary objective of fighting inflation. The soaring dollar of late 1984 and early 1985 seemed to Volcker to be completely detached from fundamentals such as monetary policy in any case. The Fed itself was not under attack directly for the strong dollar. It would leave the management of the dollar problem to the political authorities.[45]

Volcker and the Fed also resisted any bargains, explicit or implied, linking interest rate cuts to reductions in the budget deficit, though such a deal would have helped to restrain the dollar. The Fed chairman rightly feared that, with the Congress and the executive in a standoff over fiscal policy, the central bank would be the only party to deliver on its side of the bargain. Volcker instead stated that he expected interest rates to decline if the budget deficit were substantially reduced.[46]

---

43. Volcker was advised on this matter by Sam Y. Cross, executive vice president for foreign exchange operations of the New York Fed, and Edwin Truman, director of the international finance division of the Board of Governors staff. Volcker and Gyohten, *Changing Fortunes*, pp. 238–39.

44. Volcker and Gyohten, *Changing Fortunes*, pp. 180–81.

45. Volcker and Gyohten, *Changing Fortunes*, p. 181.

46. Destler and Henning, *Dollar Politics*, pp. 30–31; Volcker and Gyohten, *Changing Fortunes*, pp. 181–82. Currency strength therefore affected the respective relationships between fiscal and monetary policy very differently in the United States and in Japan. When the yen rose in the second half of the 1980s, rather than staying the course the Bank of Japan eased monetary policy, which enabled the Ministry of Finance to reduce the deficit further.

Figure 6.6 United States: effective exchange rates, 1975–93

monthly average; 1985 = 100, logarithmic scale

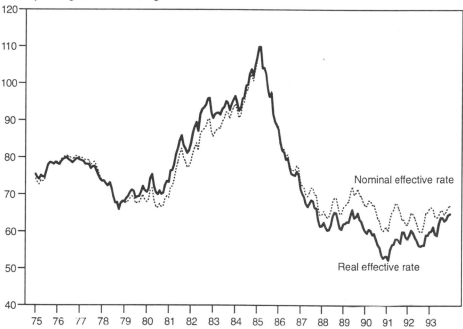

Source: International Monetary Fund.

Domestic Political Reaction

In early 1985 the dollar reached levels unprecedented in the floating rate period, 67 percent above its 1980 average on a trade-weighted basis (figure 6.6). These exchange rates provided a windfall to foreign producers competing against US companies; they brought unbearable pressures on US producers, in both home and foreign markets. As a result, these interests made the strong dollar a domestic political issue as never before in modern American history. They brought political pressure to bear on the administration, directly and through the Congress, to jettison the laissez-faire policy toward the dollar and adopt activism. Destler and I have recounted this unique and fascinating episode elsewhere in detail.[47] The account presented here focuses on the essential elements of the story.

---

47. Henning and Destler, "From Neglect to Activism"; Destler and Henning, *Dollar Politics*.

Table 6.3   United States: merchandise trade, 1970–91

	Billions of current dollars			Billions of 1982 dollars		
Year	Imports	Exports	Balance	Imports	Exports	Balance
1970	40.9	44.5	3.6	146.5	123.8	−22.7
1971	46.6	45.6	−1.0	160.9	122.7	−38.2
1972	56.9	51.8	−5.1	183.0	134.9	−48.0
1973	71.8	73.9	2.1	200.7	165.0	−35.7
1974	104.5	101.0	−3.5	195.1	181.3	−13.8
1975	99.0	109.6	10.6	168.3	176.5	8.1
1976	124.6	117.8	−6.8	206.6	181.8	−24.8
1977	152.6	123.7	−28.9	230.3	181.8	−48.5
1978	177.4	145.4	−32.0	252.8	200.7	−52.1
1979	212.8	184.2	−28.6	256.4	223.1	−33.3
1980	248.6	226.0	−22.6	242.9	245.3	2.5
1981	267.7	239.3	−28.4	253.7	241.2	−12.5
1982	250.6	215.2	−35.4	250.6	215.2	−35.4
1983	272.7	207.5	−65.2	285.0	205.9	−79.1
1984	336.3	225.8	−110.5	356.8	218.8	−138.0
1985	343.3	222.4	−120.9	377.8	222.2	−155.6
1986	370.0	226.2	−143.8	410.3	231.6	−178.7
1987	414.8	257.7	−157.1	427.6	254.7	−172.9
1988	452.1	325.8	−126.3	444.6	303.9	−140.7
1989	484.6	371.4	−113.2	464.3	339.9	−124.4
1990	507.4	396.2	−109.2	472.6	365.2	−107.5
1991	499.4	428.1	−71.3	472.9	393.7	−79.1

Sources: *Economic Report of the President*, February 1992; *Survey of Current Business*, various issues.

Hardship Wrought by Overvaluation

The unprecedented rise of the dollar produced massive dislocation in the US economy, particularly in trade-exposed industries. The deep recession of 1981–82, which dampened imports, delayed the adverse effects on the trade account. But once the economic recovery of 1983–84 gathered steam, the costs of the strong dollar became more visible, as the United States began in 1984 to run a four-year string of world-record-setting, 12-digit trade deficits: from $35.4 billion in 1982 to $110.5 billion in 1984, and $120.9 billion in 1985, with further increases in store for 1986 and 1987.

US exports stagnated while imports rose at a furious pace during the recovery. US imports shot up from $250.6 billion in 1982 to $336.3 billion in 1984 and $343.3 billion in 1985. But these nominal figures understate the pain to American producers and workers and the drag on US economic growth. Because the prices of imported goods were on average declining, the volume of imports was rising even more quickly. Measured in 1982 dollars, real imports rose to $356.8 billion in 1984 and $377.8 billion in 1985. The real trade deficit, measured similarly, registered $138.0 and $155.6 billion in 1984 and 1985, respectively (table 6.3).

Import penetration therefore damaged sectors of the economy in spite of the beneficial effects of the domestic recovery. The ratio of merchandise imports to total US goods production, in real terms, which had stayed flat at about 19 percent in 1980–82, jumped to 21 percent in 1983, 23 percent in 1984, 24 percent in 1985, and 26 percent in 1986.

The manufacturing sector suffered disproportionately. Manufacturing imports as a share of real manufacturing output rose from 19.7 percent in 1980 to 32.0 percent in 1985, while the comparable ratio for manufactured exports declined from 25.5 percent to 17.7 percent during those five years. The import ratio for manufactures was headed toward 34.1 percent for 1986, while that for exports was down again to 17.2 percent.[48] These real import ratios were much higher than any in US postwar experience, and the rate of change was unprecedented. Import penetration affected the overall position of US companies, depressing the rate of capacity utilization and the growth of unfilled orders.[49]

The manufacturing workforce never experienced the economic recovery of the mid-1980s; employment virtually stagnated at the lows reached in the trough of the 1982 recession.[50] Similarly, the agricultural sector remained in recession through most of the decade, not only because of weak commodity prices and discriminatory foreign import and export practices but as a result of the strong dollar as well.[51]

Not all sectors lost from the strong dollar. As the exchange rate represents the relative price of traded and nontraded goods, the loss to traded-goods producers was theoretically equaled by gains in the nontraded-goods sector. Consumers, in addition, benefited from cheaper imports. But those sectors and companies that benefited from the strong dollar did not lobby the Reagan administration to continue the nonintervention policy. Those who were hurt by the strong dollar, by contrast, launched a formidable campaign to overturn the administration's hands-off stance.

Private-Sector Pressure

The excruciating pain that weak exports and booming imports caused US producers drove them into the political arena as never before.[52] Despite the formidable barriers to private-sector lobbying activity on exchange rate matters, both business and labor sought a reversal of administration policy. The strong dollar was not the only source of pain for

48. Destler and Henning, *Dollar Politics*, tables 7.1 and 7.2.

49. Destler and Henning, *Dollar Politics*, figures 3.1 and 3.2, pp. 35–36.

50. *Economic Report of the President*, January 1989, table B-43, pp. 356–57.

51. *Economic Report of the President*, January 1989, tables B-8 and B-9, pp. 318–19.

52. For a detailed account of interest group lobbying on the exchange rate issue in the mid-1980s, see Destler and Henning, *Dollar Politics*, chapter 7.

the industrial sector, but it was widely, and accurately, perceived to be a primary if not the leading cause.[53]

Petitioners did not by any means restrict their lobbying efforts to exchange rate matters alone. Those hurt by the flood of imports mounted a broadscale attack on international economic policy, including the administration's policy of open trade. Many appealed to the Congress to provide relief in the form of trade barriers. Because Congress does not legislate exchange rate policy as it does trade policy, in fact, the threat of trade protectionism was the most potent and credible weapon at its disposal in this conflict with the Reagan administration.

The effort to overturn the nonintervention decision of Regan and Sprinkel began with rumblings of discontent from heavy industry as early as 1982. In the autumn of that year, Lee L. Morgan, chairman of Caterpillar Inc., a company highly dependent on foreign export markets, called the yen-dollar rate, which then peaked at 278, "the single most important trade issue facing the United States." With the support of the Business Roundtable Task Force on International Trade and Investment, which he chaired, Morgan initiated a sustained lobbying campaign to persuade both the Congress and administration to get the dollar down.

As the dollar continued to rise against the European currencies and American trade competitiveness declined further, the business coalition for policy change grew. It was reinforced by labor. Driven by declining membership in its industrial unions, the AFL-CIO took a serious interest in the exchange rate for the first time. Though it concentrated its political resources on trade and industrial policy remedies, the AFL-CIO was solidly in the exchange rate activist camp.[54]

The chorus of objections to Treasury's laissez-faire policy rose to a crescendo in 1984 and 1985, peaking decisively in the late summer of 1985. Morgan and the Business Roundtable were joined by the National Association of Manufacturers, the Advisory Committee on Trade Negotiations, and the US Council for International Business.[55] The activity of these trade

---

53. For studies linking the strong dollar, trade competitiveness, and the condition of the manufacturing sector, see, among others, Paul R. Krugman and George Hatsopoulos, "The Problem of U.S. Competitiveness in Manufacturing," *New England Economic Review*, January–February 1987, pp. 18–29; William H. Branson and James P. Love, "US Manufacturing and the Real Exchange Rate," in Richard C. Marston, ed., *Misalignment of Exchange Rates: Effects on Trade and Industry* (Chicago: University of Chicago Press, 1988), pp. 241–74.

54. See, for example, US House of Representatives, Committee on Ways and Means, Subcommittee on International Trade, *U.S. Trade Deficit*, hearings, 98th Cong., 2nd sess., 28 and 29 March, 10, 12, 15, and 25 April 1984, pp. 366–77; AFL-CIO, "Statement by the AFL-CIO Executive Council on Trade," Washington, 8 May 1985.

55. For examples, see Advisory Committee on Trade Negotiations, *Chairmen's Report on a New Round of Multilateral Trade Negotiations*, 15 May 1985; National Association of Manufacturers, "The U.S. Dollar Exchange Rate Problem: NAM Position Paper," Washington,

associations was supported and supplemented by the CEOs of large and powerful companies. In mid-1985, Lee Iacocca of Chrysler, Colby Chandler of Kodak, and Roger Smith of General Motors, the world's largest company, joined the crowd arguing for dollar depreciation.

Most of these executives had been hesitant to raise this problem with the Reagan administration. The president had been sympathetic to their concerns as businessmen and shared their preference for market-oriented solutions. They also generally regarded the dollar, correctly, as a symptom of the skewed macroeconomic policy mix. Their first preference was to correct the problem at its source.

But as the dollar soared and the costs to industry multiplied, a growing number of private voices argued that no potential remedy should be spurned. Even if the Reagan administration was unwilling to adopt "first-best" policies, it should still, they argued, reverse the Regan-Sprinkel nonintervention decision. Most companies, moreover, regarded any "second-best" policy of dollar depreciation to be vastly preferable to trade protectionism.

In the absence of action on the macroeconomic or exchange rate front, however, many American companies were willing to entertain support for protectionist trade policy, and threatened to desert the administration's free-trade coalition. The Advisory Committee on Trade Negotiations, appointed by the administration itself to advise on the launching of a new trade round, argued that multilateral trade negotiations should not proceed until the exchange rate problem was resolved.[56]

Industry lobbyists and company executives took their case directly to the administration. Regan and Sprinkel, however, flatly rejected these petitions. Even as the dollar peaked in late February 1985 at 3.47 D-marks and 265 yen, the Treasury permitted foreign exchange operations in only small quantities. When corporations took their case to the Federal Reserve, Volcker and his colleagues told them that there was nothing that they could do, without a change of fiscal policy or the Treasury's intervention policy, that would not jeopardize the goal of reducing inflation. Private-sector pressures were therefore deflected to the Congress.

Congress responded with a two-pronged approach.[57] The first tactic

---

16 July 1985; Business Roundtable, "The Trade Deficit—Its Causes, Consequences, and Cures," January 1985; US Council for International Business, "Statement on a New Round of Multilateral Trade Negotiations: Recommended US Business Objectives," Washington, 18 April 1985, pp. 1–2, and *Annual Report 1985*, p. 4.

56. Advisory Committee on Trade Negotiations, *Chairmen's Report on a New Round of Multilateral Trade Negotiations*, submitted to the United States Trade Representative, 15 May 1985.

57. Destler and Henning, *Dollar Politics*, pp. 38–40; I. M. Destler, *American Trade Politics*, 2nd ed. (Washington: Institute for International Economics; New York: Twentieth Century Fund, 1992), pp. 77–91.

was an attempt to require in law that the administration conduct foreign exchange intervention. The second strategy was a legislative attack on the administration's trade policy. The administration had been so neglectful of the trade concerns of the Congress, by the summer of 1985, that it almost lost control of trade policy completely. The Congress would hold the open trade policy hostage, in effect, to a change in the administration's international monetary policy.

The groundswell of private activism on the exchange rate and trade policy during 1982–85 and the response of the Congress is exceptional in the history of US international monetary policy. The episode illustrates that the absence in the United States of private-sector organization as seen in other countries does not prevent lobbying by business groups on exchange rate issues. As the coming policy reversal shows, furthermore, this lobbying can be episodically effective. But subsequent policy developments will also suggest that the fractionalized US private sector cannot sustain government engagement in exchange rate policy indefinitely. In the absence of close ties between finance and industry, episodes of activist exchange rate policy on the part of the United States tend to be short-lived.

Policy Reversal, 1985

In the second Reagan administration, Reagan's former Chief of Staff James A. Baker III assumed responsibility for the Treasury Department as secretary. After switching jobs with Donald Regan in January 1985, Baker faced formidable political problems in foreign economic policy: burgeoning trade protectionism on Capitol Hill, the threat of further desertions from the open-trade coalition, and a direct legislative attack on the Treasury's prerogatives on exchange rate policy. From his vantage point at Treasury, Baker could not influence the macroeconomic policy mix directly, as both fiscal and monetary policy were outside his control. He could act, though, on exchange rate policy, and he thus initiated a secret review of his predecessor's nonintervention decision. He was assisted in this reassessment by Deputy Secretary Richard G. Darman and Assistant Secretary Mulford.

The now-famous Plaza Agreement, the result of that review and of the Treasury team's negotiations with its partners in the Group of Five (G-5), was announced in New York City on 22 September.[58] The finance ministers and central bank governors of the five countries observed that

---

58. On the genesis of the Plaza accord, see Henning and Destler, "From Neglect to Activism"; pp. 317–33, Destler and Henning, *Dollar Politics*, chapter 3; Funabashi, *Managing the Dollar*.

the convergence of their rates of economic growth "have not been reflected fully in exchange markets." They agreed, in the operative sentence of the communiqué, that "some further orderly appreciation of the main nondollar currencies against the dollar is desirable." In the Plaza communiqué they also intimated that they might intervene to encourage dollar depreciation, and in fact sold tens of billions of dollars collectively in concerted intervention during the following several weeks.[59]

The exchange markets responded dramatically. The dollar dropped 4.3 percent on an effective basis on the Monday following the announcement and continued to drop over the following several days. The success of the announcement exposed the accord's limitations when the Germans balked at prospects of further depreciation. No clear exchange rate goal had been set for the operations. More fundamentally, no clear commitments of monetary and fiscal policy changes backed up the new goal. Baker, Darman, and Mulford had sought demand stimulus from Germany and Japan, but no such commitments were visible in the Plaza communiqué and several principals denied having agreed to such changes.[60]

The Plaza decision nonetheless marks a key turning point in US international monetary policy. As they had during previous policy cycles, American officials underwent a fundamental transition from neglect to activism. First, the Treasury was now willing to take a stand on what exchange rate levels would be desirable. Second, American officials were now willing to use declarations and foreign exchange operations to bring them about.

The new activism was not unadulterated cooperation. Beyond the first few weeks, when the G-5 shared the goal of dollar depreciation, the new activism quickly became aggressive. When first the Germans, and then the Japanese, began to resist the appreciation of their currencies, Secretary Baker refused to lend his support to their efforts. He withheld his support for currency stabilization for German and Japanese promises to stimulate their economies. At times he went further and subtly, even blatantly, undermined their efforts to limit D-mark and yen appreciation. The Plaza meeting thus initiated a two-year period of macroeconomic conflict during which Baker would exploit this "dollar weapon." The 1985–87 period in this respect reenacted the 1971–73 and 1977–78 periods of aggressive unilateralism. Though the new strategy made Baker unpopular abroad in some quarters, it served his main political objective: it dampened the burgeoning trade protectionism in the Congress, something foreign governments also wanted very much to avoid.

---

59. Department of Treasury, press release, Washington, 22 September 1985. American intervention amounted to $3.08 billion between 23 September and 7 November 1985.

60. See, for example, *Wall Street Journal*, 24 September 1985.

Figure 6.7   United States: foreign exchange intervention, daily operations in dollar/D-mark market, 1985–92

millions of dollars

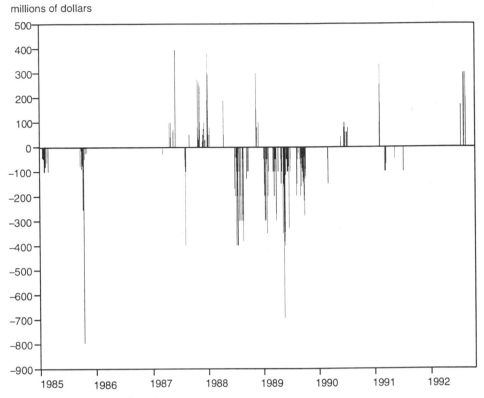

Source: Federal Reserve Board.

Treasury's commitment to activism therefore was limited to realigning, not stabilizing, the dollar's external value. Treasury remained unwilling to commit large sums to intervention operations. Even when trying to drive the dollar down, immediately after the Plaza, the Treasury and Fed sold only modest sums compared with their G-5 counterparts. From the beginning of November 1985 through the end of January 1987, a period when Germany and Japan were trying to cap their currencies, American authorities engaged in not a single instance of intervention (figures 6.7 and 6.8). The main burden of intervention, again, rested with the Europeans and Japanese.

Baker's strategy of talking down the dollar depended crucially, however, on the domestic monetary policies of the Federal Reserve. Baker had consulted with Volcker about his plans for the Plaza meeting in August. In the meeting he asked whether his plan to realign the dollar was likely to be undercut by a tightening of monetary policy. Volcker

Figure 6.8 United States: foreign exchange intervention, daily operations in dollar-yen market, 1985–92

millions of dollars

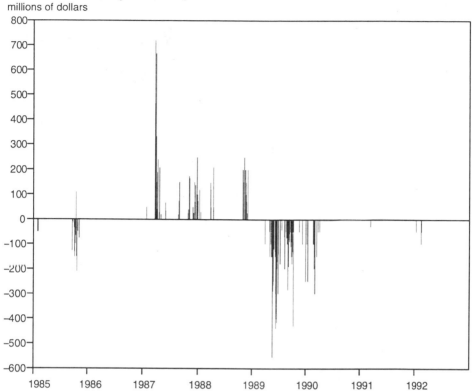

Source: Federal Reserve Board.

made no promises but did convey the distinct impression that, with the economy slowing and inflation declining, there was no serious risk of a tightening. But the Fed chairman warned the Treasury secretary about provoking a precipitous decline of the dollar. Volcker was worried, in particular, that a sharp drop of the dollar would damage confidence, stimulate capital outflow, and compel the Fed to tighten monetary policy—a hypothetical sequence of events known as the "hard landing scenario."[61]

The Fed had raised interest rates in spring 1984 and lowered them again in the autumn and early 1985. Within five months after the Plaza Agreement, the Fed began another round of monetary loosening. The economic argument for these cuts was the weakness in growth and in-

---

61. Volcker and Gyohten, *Changing Fortunes*, pp. 243–44. For an explication of the hard landing scenario, see Marris, *Deficits and the Dollar*.

flation, reinforced by a large decline in oil prices. In easing monetary policy, the Fed was not contributing to the administration's effort to depreciate the dollar. To the contrary, Volcker's concern was exactly the opposite and was reflected in a refusal to ease in late 1985.[62]

By February 1986, however, President Reagan had selected a majority of the Board of Governors with the addition of two new appointees. Those appointees were eager to cut the discount rate, primarily on domestic grounds. Volcker, concerned about a possible run on the currency, insisted that any reduction be coordinated internationally. In an inside drama known as the "palace coup," the details of which are still sketchy, the Reagan appointees overruled the chairman and voted a discount rate cut in early February. Volcker reacted sharply to this loss of control within the board and threatened to resign. A compromise was agreed that same day whereby the cut was deferred to give Volcker time to negotiate a coordinated reduction with the Bundesbank and Bank of Japan, which he did. The story illustrates the priority given within the Fed to the domestic factors at that time and the special role of the chairman in articulating the international considerations.

Between March and August the Fed reduced the discount rate four times, from 7.5 to 5.5 percent, the last two unilaterally. Further interest rate reductions were becoming increasingly unlikely, and Fed officials would soon begin to question whether they had gone one discount rate cut too far. By September 1986, the sliding dollar was approaching the 150 yen level and surpassed the 2.00 D-mark level. These rates compare to 240 yen and 2.84 D-marks at the time of the Plaza Agreement. Volcker again warned Baker against talking down the dollar and making deliberately vague statements with that intent.

Switch to Stabilization, 1986–87

Baker therefore abandoned his strategy of talking down the dollar in favor of currency stabilization. The transition was a gradual one to be sure. For one thing, the US trade deficit had shown no definite signs of improvement in 1986. For another, Baker could not be confident that any attempt to stabilize the dollar could yet succeed; and he was adept at dissociating himself from political failures. But the risk that the US economy would overheat was rising. And Baker knew that one thing had not changed since the Plaza: talking down the dollar was fundamentally inconsistent with rising interest rates.

Baker therefore embarked on a series of four deals that exchanged verbal or material support for dollar stabilization, his concession, for

---

62. Paul A. Volcker, "Comment," in *American Economic Policy in the 1980s*, Feldstein, ed., pp. 150–51; Volcker and Gyohten, *Changing Fortunes*, pp. 246–47.

promises to stimulate foreign growth, the German and Japanese quid pro quo. He began with a bilateral agreement with Japanese Finance Minister Kiichi Miyazawa, who was eager to avoid the 150 yen/dollar rate, in October 1986. After an intervening dispute with the Germans, Baker then multilateralized the agreement in the form of the Louvre Accord in late February 1987. The yen continued to rise in March and early April, however, and Baker thus renegotiated the level of dollar support against that currency. Finally, following the bitter exchange between him and the Germans that involved the stock market crash in October, Baker negotiated the telephone accord of December.[63]

In shifting his strategy, Baker was responding in part to the views of the financial community, which had previously been silent on exchange rate issues, relative to the "real" sector. Many private American financial institutions had perceived an interest in the strong dollar because it seemed to create and reflect confidence, a strategic asset for financiers. In addition, some private bankers had been frustrated that the corporate sector had failed to control costs in the late 1970s and early 1980s and viewed the strong dollar, with some at the Federal Reserve, to be an "incomes policy." Despite these sympathies, the most influential commercial and investment bankers had not lobbied for the strong dollar policy of the first Reagan administration. By the same token, though, they had not supported those corporate officials from the real sector who lobbied against the strong dollar during 1982–85.

The passivity of the financial community changed in early 1987. When in December and January Baker and Darman's tactic of talking down the dollar seemed to threaten a hard landing, many bankers privately voiced strong opposition. They, like the Federal Reserve, were concerned that persistent depreciation would repel internationally mobile capital and that interest rates would rise. They also feared that, at a time American monetary policy was particularly lax, the depreciation of the dollar would reignite inflation. Because of the influence of these fears on the financial markets, Baker could not ignore these warnings. At the same time, however, the trade problem remained unresolved, and Baker struggled to find a balance between the two threats over the course of the year.

When Baker agreed to the Louvre Accord, US international monetary policy crossed an extraordinary threshold. As has been documented by Funabashi, the G-5 plus Canada agreed there on a secret system of target ranges for the dollar/yen and dollar/D-mark exchange rates of plus and minus 5 percent.[64] The US commitment to these ranges was partial

---

63. See Funabashi, *Managing the Dollar*; Destler and Henning, *Dollar Politics*; Dobson, *Economic Policy Coordination*, chapter 5.

64. Funabashi, *From the Plaza to the Louvre*, pp. 177–210.

and halting. But—though the ranges would never be publicly acknowledged, they would be rebased several times, and their outer margins would become tattered—the concept of a target range remained an element of US policy for several years thereafter. Not since the final days of the Bretton Woods regime had the United States entertained such a strict notion of desirable limits to exchange rate fluctuation.

After the Louvre Accord, the Treasury also authorized foreign exchange intervention in the largest quantities since the Carter administration. Between 24 March and 4 May the Fed bought almost $4.0 billion against yen in an effort to stem the decline. These quantities were nonetheless small in comparison to the dollar purchases of European and Japanese central banks. During the year 1987, foreign central banks financed roughly two-thirds of the record $163.5 billion current account deficit.[65] (During most of the year, private capital ceased to flow to the United States on a net basis, as Volcker and private financiers had feared.) The US government, by contrast, financed only about $8.5 billion through sales of foreign exchange.[66]

The new external monetary policy faced its most severe test in the autumn of 1987. Baker sharply criticized foreign interest rate increases in September and October 1987, which reveals the multiple pressures he confronted at the time. The trade bill, which had been working its way through the Congress, had not yet been defanged of the most egregiously protectionist provisions. Baker had managed to contain congressional protectionism by showing real benefits to US producers from the international macroeconomic policy coordination. Foreign interest rate increases, even if only matching Fed increases, threatened to reverse this political process, with disastrous consequences for the administration's trade strategy.

Secretary Baker had a second important reason to be concerned about monetary tightening in autumn 1987 aside from the consequences for trade policy—the 1988 presidential election. The Federal Reserve, after all, had tightened monetary policy in October 1979, in response to rising inflation, rising interest rates abroad, and a weak dollar, with disastrous consequences for the Carter administration.

Shortly after Alan Greenspan replaced Volcker as chairman, the Fed raised interest rates. Baker advised Greenspan to first seek the assurances of the Bank of Japan and the Bundesbank that they would not follow suit, but Greenspan rejected this advice. When the Bank of Japan and the Bundesbank raised interest rates slightly, Baker bitterly criticized the

---

65. Bank for International Settlements, *Fifty-Eighth Annual Report* (Basel: Bank for International Settlements, 1988), pp. 188–89.

66. See "Treasury and Federal Reserve Foreign Exchange Operations," *Federal Reserve Bank of New York Quarterly Review* 12, nos. 1, 3, 4 (spring, autumn, winter 1987): 57–70; 49–54; 48–59.

action as a violation of the spirit of their cooperation and said that the Louvre Accord did not require the United States to ratchet interest rates upward if that were required to prevent a depreciation of the dollar. As the subsequent October stock market crash revealed, Baker had underestimated the importance that the markets attached to G-7 cooperation. That debacle was Baker's greatest mistake as Treasury secretary. The incident shows, though, that the administration was not willing to jeopardize domestic growth for the new exchange rate policy of stabilization.

After the stock market crash, some members of the financial community leveled their sights on the Louvre effort to stabilize exchange rates, aiming at the regime of coordination rather than the level of the dollar per se. The Economic Advisory Committee of the American Bankers Association declared the Louvre Accord a "mistake" and opposed any development of a target range regime.[67] The founder and chairman of the Chicago Mercantile Exchange, on which the trading of futures and options on foreign currencies had been growing rapidly, formed a group labeled the American Coalition for Flexible Exchange Rates. The coalition funneled literature extolling the virtues of flexible exchange rates to the public and its members met with administration officials and members of Congress.[68] But it was short-lived, never met as a full group, and, notably, the CEOs of the large, New York banks never joined.

Opposition came from academic economists as well. The monetarist Shadow Open Market Committee, the inspiration for Sprinkel's nonintervention stance, sharply criticized the shift toward activism under Baker and warned against any targeting of monetary policy on the exchange rate.[69] Opposition to dollar stabilization came from nonmonetarists as well, including Martin Feldstein and Herbert Stein, former chairmen of the Council of Economic Advisers.[70]

---

67. Exchange rate stabilization had contributed to interest rate increases and threatened the independence of the Federal Reserve, the group argued. See American Bankers Association, press release, Washington, 4 February 1988; ABA press release, Napa, CA, 1 July 1988; and the testimony of Milton W. Hudson in US House of Representatives, Committee on Banking, Subcommittee on Domestic Monetary Policy, *Hearings on Conduct of Monetary Policy in 1987*, 100th Cong., 2nd sess., 17 and 24 March 1988, pp. 12, 79–93.

68. Leo Melamed, ed., *The Merits of Flexible Exchange Rates: An Anthology* (Fairfax, VA: George Mason University Press, 1988).

69. See Shadow Open Market Committee, "Policy Statement," New York, 25 March 1985; "An Open Letter to Alan Greenspan: Policy Statement," New York, 14 September 1987; "Policy Statement," New York, 19 September 1988.

70. US House of Representatives, Committee on Banking, *Impact of the Stock Market Drop and Related Economic Developments on Interest Rates, Banking, Monetary Policy, and Economic Stability*, hearings, 100th Cong., 1st sess., 29 October 1987. See as well William A. Niskanen, "A Lower Dollar vs. Recession," *New York Times*, 27 October 1987, p. A35.

In contrast to the influence of the financial markets on Treasury thinking, there is no evidence that the statements of financial groups on behalf of exchange rate flexibility influenced Baker on exchange rate policy or caused an abandonment of the target range system, which was maintained throughout his tenure ending in August 1988. But this lobbying effort illustrates the intensity of the preferences of one segment of the financial sector, and some economists, in favor of exchange rate flexibility. Any Treasury secretary seeking to systematically limit currency flexibility would require a political counterweight to this small but potentially influential constituency.

Bear Trap and Dollar Rally of 1988

The financial panic of October 1987 affected stock markets worldwide. Central bankers suspected that the sudden elimination of huge amounts of paper wealth would cause a recession and they thus temporarily eased monetary policy. Baker, German Finance Minister Stoltenberg, and Bundesbank President Karl Otto Pöhl met immediately after the crash and agreed to let the dollar fall somewhat further against the D-mark, which it did steadily through the end of the year. The attention of the financial markets was focused on intense budget negotiations between the administration and the Congress. Once they agreed on modest reductions compared to baseline projections, the United States and G-7 on 22 December reaffirmed their commitment to the Louvre strategy of policy coordination and reiterated their common interests in exchange rate stability.[71]

At 1.63 D-mark and 126 yen at the time of the announcement, the dollar slid to 1.56 D-mark and 120 yen at the end of the year. At those new lows, however, the Treasury finally called a halt to the depreciation by leading a round of concerted intervention. That "bear trap," which caught the market by surprise on the first trading day of the new year, signaled a determined effort to place a firm floor under the dollar. The operation was an impressive display of the effectiveness of well-executed concerted intervention. Once the dollar rebounded, Baker followed up with statements signaling that any renewed decline would be viewed as "counterproductive."[72]

By early 1988, the second Reagan administration completed its transition from confrontational to cooperative activism in international monetary policy. Thereafter the administration would intervene in unprecedented quantities and relax pressure on foreign governments to reflate their economies. This less confrontational stance was made possible by

---

71. US Department of the Treasury, press release, Washington, 22 December 1987.

72. *Financial Times*, 2 March 1988.

the elimination of the notorious Gephardt amendment from the trade bill in late 1987, the pickup in US export growth, and confident predictions of reductions in the trade deficit for 1988. Most of all, fears that the stock market crash would produce a recession subsided and the Federal Reserve steadily increased interest rates throughout the year.

The markets responded by bidding up the dollar. The dollar rise was more dramatic against the D-mark than against the yen, piercing the 1.92 D-mark level in August shortly after the second increase in the discount rate since mid-1987. Though this rate was the upper level of the range agreed upon at the Louvre, that range had been lowered after the crash to the vicinity of 1.60–1.80. Between 27 June and 23 August, therefore, American authorities sold $4.7 billion for D-marks, the largest purchase of foreign currency ever on the open markets by the United States. Because the dollar remained below 140 yen, though, there were no interventions in the yen market. After the Bundesbank raised interest rates further, the upward pressure on the dollar subsided.

Baker's declaratory policy, however, did not reinforce these foreign exchange operations to cap the dollar. To the contrary, his silence in the face of dollar appreciation gave rise to the theory that he engineered the upswing for the electoral convenience of his friend and Republican candidate for president, George Bush.[73] The temporary rise in the dollar was a symbolic benefit, and helped to restore American economic confidence and avoid a disastrous repetition of the October crash. Thus, while Baker denied these charges, Treasury did not discourage the widespread impression in the financial markets that the G-7 would support the dollar through the election.

Baker's skillful political management of the exchange rate policy had addressed only an intermediate cause and not the fundamental source of the external imbalance. As the Reagan era drew to a close, the underlying fiscal problem persisted; the autumn 1987 budget agreement had deferred the tough political fiscal choices, not resolved them. The early and mid-1980s revealed an American political-economic system that was manifestly not self-equilibrating. The Reagan budget deficits had produced high interest rates, capital inflows, and a soaring dollar. But the resulting trade deficit did not stimulate political pressure to redress the original source of the problem. American business in particular was too divided on the question of taxation and public spending to underpin a societal consensus on budget deficit reduction. Instead, political pressure, stimulated by import penetration, was directed to an intermediate cause rather than the basic cause of the pain, trade and exchange rate policy.

---

73. See, for example, Jeffrey E. Garten, "How Bonn, Tokyo Slyly Help Bush," *New York Times*, 21 July 1988; *Washington Post*, 22 July 1988; Irwin M. Stelzer, "The Election Dollar," *The American Spectator*, September 1988, pp. 28–33.

The Bush Administration

Ronald Reagan and his lieutenants had been masterful at sliding the political costs of his economic policies into the future. George Bush inherited an American economy whose current success masked simmering long-term structural problems—the savings and loan banking collapse, the overhang of private debt, exploding cost of health care and health-care entitlements, the stagnation of productivity and real wages—in addition to the immediate problem of rising inflation. The new president might have sounded a call to economic arms to confront these structural problems squarely early in his administration. But he had hamstrung himself severely in promising "no new taxes."[74] Though Bush described the budget deficit as "a matter of grave urgency," it would in fact rise considerably during his tenure.

President Bush and his Treasury secretary, Nicholas F. Brady, were predisposed against attending personally to exchange rate matters. When asked, immediately after his election, about the recent fall of the dollar and market anxieties over future economic policies, Bush's first reaction was complacent: "Once in a while I think about those things, but not much." When the dollar dropped further, he sought to reassure the markets, reaffirming his commitment to the existing framework "built around policy coordination and exchange rate stability," though he would not go so far as "to peg the dollar to any existing currency."[75] But, as the dollar fell to 121–123 yen and 1.73–1.75 D-mark, Secretary Brady echoed Bush's original sentiment, saying, "I don't really worry about it very much."[76]

Target Ranges Unravel, 1989–90

Indeed, under the Bush administration, the problem posed by the exchange rate had changed greatly from that at the outset of the second Reagan administration. Not only had the large realignment been accomplished, but the trade deficit had declined substantially (figures 6.1 and 6.2). On the other hand, inflation, which had been roughly 4.5 percent since 1987, was rising. Fearing an overheating of the economy without help from the fiscal side, the Federal Reserve continued to tighten monetary policy during the first several months of 1989, as it had throughout 1988.

In response to rising interest rates, the dollar staged a second major rally in as many years. In contrast to the rally of 1988, though, in 1989

---

74. For an illuminating discussion of the origin of Bush's "Read my lips, no new taxes" pledge, see Bob Woodward, "Origin of the Tax Pledge," *Washington Post*, 4 October 1992.

75. *Washington Post*, 15 November 1988.

76. *Wall Street Journal*, 21 November 1988.

the dollar shattered the upper bounds of the G-7 target ranges. The US currency soared above 2.04 marks and 150 yen in May, and remained high throughout the summer.

The administration's response was ambiguous and somewhat contradictory. In public declarations, the secretary of the Treasury was complacent. Two meetings of the G-7 had been held in Washington during the winter and spring. The first focused mainly on the international debt problem and released no communiqué, at Brady's insistence. The second gently intimated that an orderly depreciation of the dollar was called for by adding the qualifier to previous language that an *excessive* slide would be counterproductive.[77] The dollar was not discussed at the July G-7 summit meeting in Paris. Despite projections by private economists and international agencies that the high dollar would cause a renewed deterioration of the US current account deficit, and that tight US monetary policy would cause a recession, the heads of state focused only on the favorable economic conditions prevailing among the G-7 at the moment. Feeling no need for better policy coordination, and apparently content with US efforts to meet the Gramm-Rudman targets for budget deficit reduction, Secretary Brady rhetorically asked, "Why change the throttle settings?"[78]

In foreign exchange operations, by contrast, the Treasury and Fed intervened in record quantities to rein in the runaway dollar. During May and June, they sold more than $7.0 billion against Japanese yen and $4.7 billion against D-mark—larger dollar sales than in any previous two-month period. The intervention operations in the early summer were not internationally concerted. The lack of international cooperation in exchange markets, and the absence of reinforcing declarations, undercut the effectiveness of intervention. The G-7 finally pulled together, in late September, declaring that the rise of the dollar was "inconsistent" with continued reduction in current account imbalances.[79] The Treasury and Fed supported this concerted stance by injecting another $5.8 billion into the markets between mid-August and mid-October.[80]

---

77. Statement of the Group of Seven, press release, Washington, 2 April 1989.

78. McNeil-Lehrer News Hour, PBS broadcast, 17 July 1989.

79. Statement of the Group of Seven, press release, Washington, 23 September 1989. The communique declared: "The Ministers and Governors considered the rise in recent months of the dollar inconsistent with longer run economic fundamentals. They agreed that a rise of the dollar above current levels or an excessive decline could adversely affect prospects for the world economy. In this context, they agreed to cooperate closely in exchange markets."

80. Calculated from intervention statistics provided by the Federal Reserve Board of Governors, Washington. See also "Treasury and Federal Reserve Foreign Exchange Operations," *Federal Reserve Bank of New York Quarterly Review*, autumn 1989, pp. 61–66, and winter 1990, pp. 54–60.

Those foreign exchange operations exposed, in an unusually public way, a broadening rift between the Treasury and the Federal Reserve over intervention policy. Because the operations were so large as to consume the resources of the Exchange Stabilization Fund (ESF), the Treasury requested access to its foreign exchange warehousing facility at the Fed. The Federal Open Market Committee granted these requests. Vice Chairman Manuel Johnson, however, opposed interventions, on the grounds that a higher dollar would help fight inflation. He therefore voted against the warehousing authorization and, with Governor Wayne Angell, against raising the Fed's ceiling on holdings of foreign exchange on its own account.[81]

Equally importantly, the Fed undertook no effort to coordinate interest rate movements with other G-7 central banks to move the dollar gently lower. Beginning in the spring, the Fed began easing monetary policy while the Bank of Japan and Bundesbank had tightened, which normally puts downward pressure on the dollar. The credibility in the markets of G-7 cooperation might have been preserved or enhanced had those moves been coordinated and jointly announced. However, in contrast to Baker in 1986, Secretary Brady did not promote a packaging of monetary policy trends in this way. The September G-7 communiqué failed to persuade the independent central banks to engage in a publicly cooperative effort.

The Fed in fact considered easing monetary policy to reduce upward pressure on the dollar. But, meeting just days after the G-7 communiqué, the FOMC instead decided to leave monetary policy unchanged. Indeed, the FOMC actually emphasized its *un*willingness to use, or even be believed to be using, domestic monetary policy to restrain the dollar. The minutes of the meeting stated that members "were concerned that an easing of policy so soon after the G-7 meeting would be misinterpreted as an attempt to use monetary policy to force the dollar lower."[82] So

---

81. "Record of Policy Actions of the Federal Open Market Committee: Meeting Held on August 22, 1989," Federal Reserve, press release, Washington, 6 October 1989, p. 18. See as well *Washington Post*, 8 October 1989, H1; *Wall Street Journal*, 16 January 1990, p. A1.

82. The FOMC minutes continue:

> While the dollar was an important factor influencing the course of the US economy and prices, monetary policy should not be used, in the judgment of the Committee, to attain particular levels for the foreign exchange value of the dollar that could conflict with domestic policy objectives. In current circumstances, an easing might well provoke an undesirable sharp decline in the external value of the dollar. The members also discussed the recent substantial intervention by G-7 and other nations against the dollar. Some members expressed concern that if this intervention resulted in a sizable depreciation of the dollar, the inflationary consequences could be viewed as inconsistent with the Committee's long-run policy of achieving price stability.

See "Record of Policy Actions of the Federal Open Market Committee Meeting Held on October 3, 1989," Federal Reserve, press release, Washington, 17 November 1989, p. 10–11.

sensitive had Fed officials become to threats to their independence in domestic monetary policymaking that they sought specifically to dispel any perception that monetary policy might be diverted to reducing the value of the dollar.

The threats to the Fed's independence on the domestic side were real, not imaginary. President Bush, from the very beginning of his administration, warned the Fed not to overreact in the fight against inflation and said that monetary policy should not be tightened.[83] Richard Darman, now director of the Office of Management and Budget, criticized the Fed for keeping interest rates too high.[84] Brady was unwilling to organize a G-7 effort to limit the dollar's appreciation in the late spring; but he nonetheless used the dollar's strength as a rationale to press the Fed to reduce interest rates.[85] Members of Congress submitted bills to restrict the Fed's independence, a standard tactic to demonstrate congressional displeasure with tight monetary policy.[86] Though such bills rarely become law, Fed officials cannot dismiss out of hand the possibility that they might. Congressional proposals become a threat particularly when the administration endorses a review of Fed structures, as Brady later did in August 1992.[87]

In November 1989, the Treasury presented its second annual report on exchange rate and international economic policy to the Congress. The statement, mandated by the Omnibus Trade and Competitiveness Act of 1988, brushed over the Treasury-Fed conflict.[88] As has become typical in these reports, Treasury emphasized exchange rate and financial relationships with the East Asian countries. Korea, Taiwan, and the People's Republic of China, in particular, have each been cited therein for manipulating their currencies to maintain unfair trading advantages. Treasury officials have praised the reporting procedure as helpful in their negotiations with the governments of these coun-

---

83. *New York Times*, 26 January 1989; *Wall Street Journal*, 22 March 1989.

84. Reuters News Service, 14 August 1989.

85. *Washington Post, Wall Street Journal*, 2 June 1989.

86. Representatives Lee Hamilton (D-IN) and Byron Dorgan (D-ND), for example, proposed a bill that would have placed the secretary of the Treasury on the FOMC, changed the terms of the chairman and vice chairman to coincide with presidential terms, and forced same-day disclosure of monetary policy decisions, among other changes. See *H.R. 2795*, 101st Cong., 1st sess., 29 June 1989.

87. Then, Secretary Brady announced that the administration "could undertake some useful exploration" of proposals to reorganize the Fed, including specifically that of Rep. Lee Hamilton that would eliminate the FOMC voting rights of Federal Reserve bank presidents. See *Wall Street Journal*, 5 August 1992.

88. Department of the Treasury, "Report to the Congress on International Economic and Exchange Rate Policy," Washington, October 1989.

tries.[89] But the Treasury has generally avoided sensitive issues relating to the G-7 currencies in these reports.

The Congress might have used the reporting procedure to arbitrate the dispute between the Treasury and Fed over the priority to be attached to trade adjustment versus inflation control in exchange rate policy. After the 1989 report, members of the banking committees questioned Mulford and Johnson closely on their disagreements over intervention and the Fed's unwillingness to advance the timing of the easing of monetary policy to support the Treasury's exchange rate policy.[90] But, because trade legislation had recently been enacted and the trade and current account deficits were declining, the trade issue was not the congressional priority that it had been in 1985–87. Congress was not complacent about inflation, moreover, and thus faced the same dilemma as the administration. Congressional oversight in this case, therefore, conveyed the desire to avoid any renewed deterioration in the overall trade account and to achieve progress in talks with Korea and Taiwan. But the Congress would not arbitrate the Fed-Treasury split and could not render clear guidance on the appropriate tradeoff between fighting inflation and adjustment.

The dollar declined below the 1.70 D-mark level by the end of 1989, as German interest rates rose. Over the course of the year the US currency had pierced the upper boundary of the imputed target range against the German currency and then fallen back through the lower boundary. Against the Japanese yen, in contrast, it remained basically unchanged from the highs reached in the summer at around 145, significantly above the upper boundary of the 120–140 yen range.

American exchange rate policy at the end of the decade had thus come full circle and now resembled, in some respects, the policy of the late Carter administration 10 years earlier. The target ranges adopted in 1987 had unraveled, but the United States still acted to limit exchange rate flexibility at the extremes. The Bush administration took a view as to the appropriate direction in which the exchange rate should move, and used foreign exchange intervention and occasional declarations by the G-7 to help achieve that objective. Macroeconomic coordination was

---

89. Members of Congress would regularly press the Treasury to show positive results in negotiations with the newly industrializing economies during hearings on the reports, pressure that was not lost on Seoul and Taipei. Secretary Brady described the process as "an enormously useful vehicle" during testimony in spring 1989.

90. US House of Representatives, Committee on Banking, Subcommittee on International Development, Finance, Trade and Monetary Policy, *Exchange Rates*, hearings, 101st Cong., 1st sess., 31 October and 16 November 1989; Senate Committee on Banking, Subcommittee on International Finance and Monetary Policy, *Review of the Department of the Treasury's Second Annual Report on International Economic and Exchange Rate Policy*, hearings, 101st Cong., 1st sess., 16 November 1989.

no longer practiced with enthusiasm, but it was not the dirty word it had been during the early 1980s, and the rhetoric of cooperation was used at times to calm the markets.

In keeping with the cyclical pattern of policy, US international monetary policy also began to revert toward exchange rate neglect. As in previous periods of declining trade deficits, exchange rate matters seemed to become less compelling for senior policymakers. Indeed, Secretary Brady's interest in stabilizing the dollar's value seemed to decline as time went by. Nonetheless, US policy could not return to the laissez-faire neglect of the Ford administration or first Reagan administration, for several reasons.

The experience of the 1980s had shifted the American political economy on international monetary matters. At the beginning of the decade, Ronald Reagan had denied that trade deficits were harmful and had positively encouraged capital inflow. At the end of the decade, by contrast, the trade imbalance was generally viewed as a major problem, which, though declining impressively from its peak in 1987, remained large. Foreign ownership of US assets was viewed as a mixed blessing, at best, and the buildup of foreign debt a continuing drain on American savings and standards of living. Private groups remained active on trade policy, with the Uruguay Round far from completion. US companies had in general lost interest in exchange rate policy per se. But a flicker of interest among them in late 1989 demonstrated that, having been activated in the mid-1980s, they might be more easily reactivated in the future.[91]

The Congress, moreover, had enhanced its own role in both trade and exchange rate matters through legislation. The exchange rate reporting requirement of the 1988 trade act had established an ongoing consultative process on international economic policy between the Treasury and the banking committees. That process mandated testimony by the secretary himself, when asked, on the substance of the report. Since the inauguration of the report in October 1988, the banking committees have not sought to use this procedure to alter the exchange rate policy of the Treasury. Rather, they actively reinforced the Treasury in seeking revaluations of the Korean won, New Taiwan dollar, and Chinese yuan, and kept competitiveness considerations before the department. In the event of renewed misalignment of the dollar, moreover, the reporting process remains a potential avenue for congressional pressure.[92] For the Bush administration, therefore, there was no going back to complete laissez-faire—at least not yet.

---

91. "Conference on US Competitiveness and the Dollar," Institute for International Economics, Washington, 4 December 1989.

92. Acknowledged by David Mulford, for example, in Competitiveness Policy Council, Trade Policy Subcouncil, transcript of meeting, Washington, 10 June 1992, pp. 179–80.

The fundamental transformation of world affairs that confronted the Bush administration in its second year altered the environment not only for foreign policy but for exchange rate and monetary policy as well. The end of the Cold War brought German unification, a German economic boom and, with a delay, rising German interest rates—with attendant consequences for European integration, growth, and currency stability.

Meanwhile, the Japanese asset bubble began to burst, the ever-growing Japanese economy began to falter, and the yen began to fall. Between 23 February and 20 March, the Treasury and Fed spent $1.68 billion trying, with Japanese authorities, to support it. These operations were mild compared with US intervention in the summer and autumn of 1989. They nonetheless provoked yet another dispute between the Fed and Treasury over intervention policy. Governors Angell and John LaWare and Cleveland Federal Reserve Bank President Lee Hoskins not only voted against the warehousing and foreign currency authorizations, but they openly challenged the legal basis for these facilities, although the facilities had been in operation for nearly three decades. In the public FOMC record, they stated that warehousing "could be viewed as avoiding the congressional appropriations process called for under the Constitution."[93] The dispute caught the attention of House Banking Committee Chairman Henry B. Gonzalez (D-TX), who convened a set of hearings on the subject.[94]

The Fed's resistance to purchasing foreign exchange contributed to the immobilization of US policy at a time when the Japanese yen nearly returned, in May 1990, to its pre-Plaza level on a real effective basis. Treasury Undersecretary David Mulford and Assistant Secretary Charles Dallara expressed their concern publicly. Brady, however, overruled them, stating that the weakness of the yen was no cause for concern.[95] Treasury officials were engaged in parallel negotiations with Japan on financial market liberalization. Brady was unwilling to consider a bargain whereby the United States supported the yen in exchange for liberalization concessions. The failure to stem the fall of the yen set the stage for the resurgence of the Japanese trade surplus in 1991 and 1992.

In contrast, the D-mark, after holding near the 1.70 level during the first half of the year, rose against the dollar after German monetary union on 1 July. US authorities signaled their approval by participating in concerted intervention to prevent the German currency from falling below that level.

---

93. "Record of Policy Actions of the Federal Open Market Committee Meeting Held on March 27, 1990," Federal Reserve, press release, Washington, 18 May 1990, p. 20.

94. US House of Representatives, Committee on Banking, Finance, and Urban Affairs, *Review of Treasury Department's Conduct of International Financial Policy*, hearings, 101st Cong., 2nd sess., 14 August 1990.

95. *Washington Post*, 20 April 1990.

The easing of US monetary policy ceased in 1990. The Fed maintained the federal funds rate around 8.25 throughout the first nine months of the year. Because consumer price inflation rose to 6.1 percent and was shadowed by long-term interest rates, some Fed officials suggested that the next monetary policy move might have to be a tightening rather than a loosening. But by mid-1990 it had become clear that the tight money stance had had its intended effect of slowing the economy. The longest peacetime expansion in US history ended in the third quarter of the year. The recession, aided by the disruptive effects of the Iraqi invasion of Kuwait and the UN coalition intervention, would last through the first quarter of 1991.

As US economic activity dropped, the Congress and administration began what had become a regular ritual of readjusting the Gramm-Rudman fiscal deficit targets. This negotiation proved tougher than previous negotiations. President Bush swallowed his "read my lips" pledge not to raise taxes, an act that he would later argue was forced upon him by the Democratcontrolled Congress.[96] The 1990 budget agreement proved to be little better than previous fixes of the fiscal problem. Fed Chairman Greenspan nonetheless gave his blessing to the agreement and began again to reduce interest rates. Thus began a series of interest rate cuts that would last through 1991 and most of 1992, bringing nominal rates to their lowest levels since the early 1960s.

In the fourth quarter of 1990, the dollar therefore broke through its previous record low against the D-mark and past the 1.50 level. In contrast to the previous encounter with these levels, immediately before the Louvre Accord, the administration and Fed were complacent. Secretary Brady's aversion to foreign exchange operations again prevailed over the advice of his senior officials to act. Brady announced that, because the decline had been orderly, he was not overly concerned about it. As it broke into record territory, American authorities undertook no intervention to halt it. The economy, fundamentally, was in recession and inflation was a diminishing threat. In an illustration of the primacy of domestic concerns over exchange rate considerations, the Fed cut interest rates further at the end of the year despite record lows of the dollar against the D-mark.

Economic Stagnation, 1991–92

The Gulf War victory in February 1991 catapulted President Bush's approval ratings to the highest ever for a sitting president. President Bush might have used his political capital to address difficult domestic issues,

---

96. See Bob Woodward, "Primary Heat Turned Deal Into a 'Mistake,' " *Washington Post*, 6 October 1992.

including budget deficit reduction. But in his triumphant 1991 State of the Union message before the Congress he declined to ask for the sacrifices that would allow him to address this long-term issue. Instead, with the 1992 general election campaign beginning within one year's time, the administration pressured the Federal Reserve and foreign central banks for an easing of monetary policy to initiate a sustainable recovery.

The improvement in the trade balance was a singular bright spot on the administration's economic record. By 1990, it had become clear that the realignment of the dollar during 1985–87 had worked as most economists had predicted.[97] Since 1987, US exports had grown at double-digit percentage rates. The trade deficit fell from $157 billion at its peak in that year to $109 billion in 1990. The recession ensured that the trade deficit would continue to decline in 1991, which it did to $71 billion (table 6.3). Trade politics had cooled on Capitol Hill since the passage of the 1988 trade act, but the Bush administration was anxious to preserve these improvements. First, the administration wanted to secure from the Congress extension of fast-track negotiating authority for the North American Free Trade Agreement (NAFTA) and the slow-moving Uruguay Round. Second, the trade improvement was one of the few economic successes to which it could point.

The Federal Reserve aggressively cut interest rates at the beginning of 1991, so much so that a serious split developed within the FOMC about the wisdom of further cuts.[98] The administration tried to tilt the internal Fed debate in its favor by continuing to press for rate reductions, on the grounds that the banking system had been so traumatized that even creditworthy borrowers were being denied funds. To underscore its dissatisfaction with the apparent halt to the rate reductions at midyear, the administration delayed the appointment of two governors and the announcement that Chairman Greenspan would be reappointed.[99] Substantial cuts resumed after August.

The Treasury and Federal Reserve participated in two significant foreign exchange operations in 1991. The first, in January 1991, placed a floor under the dollar at about 1.45 D-mark. For the first time since September 1989, the G-7 took determined concerted action in the foreign exchange market. Once US interest rates stopped falling in April, the dollar rebounded sharply and by summer became too strong, threaten-

---

97. Paul R. Krugman, *Has the Adjustment Process Worked?* POLICY ANALYSES IN INTERNATIONAL ECONOMICS 34 (Washington: Institute for International Economics, October 1991); C. Fred Bergsten, ed., *International Adjustment and Financing: The Lessons of 1985–1991* (Washington: Institute for International Economics, 1991).

98. *Washington Post*, 5 April 1991; *New York Times*, 8 April 1998; Alan Murray, "The New Fed," *Wall Street Journal*, 5 April 1991, p. 1.

99. *Los Angeles Times*, 23 September 1992.

ing to halt the good recent performance of exports. The G-7 again led a series of concerted interventions designed to cap the dollar at around 1.80 D-mark and 140 yen.

Both sets of concerted operations were successful. They did not, however, represent a resurrection of the target range concept, though these ceilings represented the upper limits of the now-defunct ranges. The Brady Treasury continued to pursue its ad hoc approach to limiting exchange rate fluctuations. Because the administration wanted the Fed to cut interest rates further, Brady resisted any G-7 agreements that might constrain monetary loosening. In addition to stimulating the domestic economy, monetary ease would have the benefit of sustaining export growth through a low dollar, which Treasury did nothing to discourage as long as the US currency behaved calmly.

In spring 1991 the administration launched a campaign, led by Brady, for interest rate reductions around the world. Brady pressed the issue on foreign governments at the OECD and in the G-7.[100] President Bush himself appealed to the G-7 ministers and central bank governors to reduce interest rates in a meeting at the White House at the time of the April Interim Committee meeting.[101] The prescription was appropriate for Japan. It would have been appropriate also for some European countries, had they not been joined to Germany in the Exchange Rate Mechanism (ERM). But the European countries were tightening their commitment to monetary cooperation, despite German unification and the skewed policy mix that resulted. In the absence of a fiscal correction by Bonn, the Bundesbank was determined to fight the rising rate of inflation with tight monetary policy.

In a sense, the tables had turned on the United States: the Bush administration confronted in Germany the same policy mix to which the first Reagan administration had subjected Europe. Just as the Fed had refused to ease monetary policy in the absence of a large cut in the budget deficit, the Bundesbank also was steadfast. Brady, with his own budget deficit soaring, was in no position morally to press fiscal restriction on the Kohl government. Moreover, Brady's pressure on Germany had virtually no important resonance within Germany itself. It only embittered US-German relations at a delicate moment and, when the Bundesbank tightened rather than eased monetary policy, revealed the absence of any semblance of policy coordination within the G-7.

At the turn of the year, the White House and Treasury became deeply worried that they would have to fight the 1992 presidential election campaign handicapped by a stagnating economy. Technically, the second quarter of 1991 marked the end of the recession. But the rebound was so tepid that it failed to halt the rise in unemployment, which would

---

100. *New York Times, Wall Street Journal*, 16 April 1991.

101. *New York Times, Wall Street Journal*, 29 April 1991.

not peak, at 7.6 percent, until the summer of 1992. Some forecasters predicted a "double dip" recession. Criticism mounted that President Bush, a formidable operator on the international scene, was neglecting the domestic economy.

Bush's problem was not so much the disorganization of his administration on domestic economic policy—it was disorganized—but the exhaustion of the standard tools of macroeconomic stimulus. Fiscal policy had been immobilized by the deficits. The benefits of the dramatic reduction in interest rates had been attenuated and delayed by the restructuring of the banking system and the consolidation of private debt. George Bush was now paying the price for Ronald Reagan's success.

With its domestic options exhausted, therefore, the administration focused on external solutions to US economic stagnation in 1992. First, it willfully countenanced the depreciation of the dollar; second, it redoubled its offensive to secure a multilateral commitment to global growth within the G-7. In an ill-fated, ill-conceived trip that would haunt the administration for its remaining year, President Bush traveled to Tokyo to demonstrate that his international prowess could be harnessed to the defense and creation of American jobs.

The bilateral trade imbalance in Japan's favor had bottomed out at $41.8 billion in 1990. Though the bilateral deficit had grown only slightly in 1991, Japanese imports of American goods had begun to fall, and Japan's global trade surplus surged. A large Japanese fiscal stimulus and yen appreciation could have helped to reverse this trend.[102] Bush, however, failed to press an appreciation of the yen on the Japanese government during his trip and accepted a fiscal stimulus that was insufficient to meet the 3.5 percent growth target Japanese officials privately conveyed.[103] Instead, Bush pushed for preferential treatment of American auto and autoparts producers, whose CEOs traveled with him, to which Japan was far less receptive.

Bush's meetings with Japanese Prime Minister Kiichi Miyazawa produced a so-called strategy for world growth, which was extended to the G-7 at a meeting of the finance ministers and central bank governors at

---

102. See, for example, C. Fred Bergsten, "Taming Japan's Trade Surplus," *New York Times*, 28 December 1991.

103. President Bush and Prime Minister Miyazawa declared only that "recent exchange rate movements were consistent with current economic developments." But Secretary Brady acknowledged that there had been "no particular commitment with regard to exchange rates." White House, "Statement by President Bush and Prime Minister Miyazawa on a Strategy for World Growth," press release, Washington, 8 January 1992.

The Federal Reserve and the Bank of Japan nonetheless intervened jointly a few days later to prevent the dollar from rising above 130 yen, and again, with less success, in mid-February. This suggests that the Treasury would probably have accepted a dollar-yen rate in record territory, around 115, but was not willing at that time to push actively for it.

the Holiday Inn near John F. Kennedy International Airport two weeks later. But that plan was transparently devoid of policy measures that could provide the promised stimulus. In the event, both the European and Japanese economies were beginning to stagnate, and the impressive performance of the American export sector was coming to a halt in 1992. (The merchandise trade deficit would increase to $101 billion in 1992 from $73.4 billion in 1991.)

The administration tried again at the Munich G-7 summit meeting in July. But, again, this was very much an exercise in symbolic politics. Secretary Brady declared after the summit that all of the seven countries were committed to raising growth. Days later, the Bundesbank increased interest rates yet again. In response, the dollar sank to a record low against the German currency of DM1.44. At that level, the Fed and Treasury intervened in concert with others. The differential between American and German short-term interest rates was roughly 6.5 percent, however. To make matters worse for the dollar, President Bush declared in his acceptance speech at the Republican National Convention that he had been wrong to repudiate his no-tax pledge and that he would not do it again if reelected. On that news, the dollar dropped sharply and concerted intervention failed to brake the fall.

The Federal Reserve, for its part, continued to ignore the weakness of the dollar and focused on the domestic economy when setting monetary policy. This became an acute problem for the Europeans in the summer of 1992, after the first referendum in Denmark rejected the Maastricht Treaty. At that point, dollar depreciation drove a wedge between the D-mark and the weaker currencies of the ERM, such as the British pound and Italian lira. Wanting above all a reduction in American interest rates, Brady rejected a proposal of the German Finance Ministry in August to agree to a floor under the bilateral exchange rate and to announce, with the central banks, that their interest rate differential would diverge no further. Instead, the Fed reduced interest rates to lows not seen since the early 1960s—2.5 percent on the discount rate—and the dollar continued its slide, albeit a gradual one. The new record lows, set in early September, were 1.3865 D-mark and 118.60 yen.

Treasury Secretary Brady was virtually silent on yet another fundamental issue. In Europe, the intergovernmental conference (IGC) on Economic and Monetary Union (EMU) met throughout the year 1991. These European negotiations settled on a far-reaching plan, embodied in the Maastricht Treaty concluded at the December 1991 meeting of the European Council, to create a common currency and central bank. These agreements have fundamental long-term consequences for the United States, the role of the dollar, the future of the international monetary system, international macroeconomic policy coordination, and US-European monetary relations. The Departments of State and Defense took an active interest in the treatment of the security issues in the parallel IGC on political union—the Western European Union, the Franco-German corps, and their relationship to NATO. The Treasury Department, by contrast, watched intently but did not act on US interests in EMU, the architecture of its institutions, the process by which Europe would determine the exchange rate policy for the future common currency and thus its relationship to G-7 cooperation. Assistant Secretary Dallara voiced his concern that Europe would be inward looking during any transition to monetary union.[104] Mulford argued privately that European countries and Germany in particular were "schizophrenic" in their differentiation between exchange rate and macroeconomic cooperation within Europe and externally.[105] But the matter was hardly mentioned in Treasury's reports to the Congress on exchange rate and international economic policy. Treasury's only engagement seemed to be with the short-term cyclical consequences of the convergence criteria embodied in the Maastricht Treaty. With justification, Secretary Brady became concerned that they would create a zone of deflation in Europe that would have an adverse impact on the world economy. The beginning of 1992, however, was at least one year too late to affect European decision making on these convergence rules.

When waves of speculation struck the ERM in September 1992, forcing the British pound and Italian lira out of the system, the Bush administration sought to demonstrate leadership from the sidelines. The president convened the members of the Interim Committee in the East Room of the White House to tell them that multilateral macroeconomic cooperation should be improved.[106] Bush suggested that the commodity-price index, including gold, which is already a part of the G-7 multilateral surveillance exercise, should be given particular attention—an election-year tip of the hat to Republican gold bugs bearing the unmistakable imprint of Secretary of State (and former Treasury Secretary) James Baker. Beyond this, however, the president offered no new suggestions for reinforcing coordination. Secretary Brady proposed that the G-10 conduct a study on international capital mobility and its effect on currency management.[107]

---

104. US Department of the Treasury, "Remarks by the Honorable Charles H. Dallara to the US-German Economic Policy Group at the Institute for International Economics," press release, Washington, 7 March 1991.

105. Competitiveness Policy Council, Trade Policy Subcouncil, transcript of meeting, Washington, 10 June 1992.

106. White House, "Remarks by the President in Address to Finance Ministers and Central Bank Governors," press release, Washington, 20 September 1992.

107. Brady had led the commission that investigated the 1987 stock market crash and recommended that circuit breakers be applied to the markets. That experience inspired his proposal to study the autumn 1992 currency turmoil. See US Treasury, "Remarks of Secretary Nicholas F. Brady to the Kennedy School of Government, Harvard University," press release, Washington, 17 December 1992.

These supportive statements notwithstanding, in the final year of the Bush administration it became apparent that the G-7 process of macro-economic policy coordination and exchange rate stabilization had completely broken down. The American recovery was very weak, Europe and Japan were headed for recessions, and the G-7 had enacted only token measures and symbolic statements in an insufficient effort to restore confidence. The disintegration of G-7 cooperation was not entirely the fault of the United States, of course; the German policy mix, exchange rate inflexibility between Germany and its European partners, and the restrictiveness of Japanese fiscal policy all played important roles.

But the G-7 coordination process received only weak support from the secretary of the Treasury, the president, and the rest of the administration. Mulford and Dallara at Treasury were virtually the only officials in the US government who sought actively to preserve the framework of the cooperative exercise and nurture the limping credibility of the wounded target-range concept. The Federal Reserve would not rise in defense of G-7 cooperation. Secretary Brady was only intermittently amenable to suggestions from his staff for activism in the exchange rate arena.

Therefore, the exchange rate for the dollar fluctuated within wide margins of 119–163 against the yen and 1.39–2.05 against the D-mark over the term of the Bush administration. The United States intervened at the extremes, heavily during 1989, which helped to keep the rate for the most part with ranges that were considerably narrower.[108] But in the light of renewed growth in external imbalances, the need for realignment of exchange rate ranges, particularly against the yen, and economic stagnation in the OECD countries, this was a modest achievement. Greater achievements required the active involvement of the most senior administration officials.

The Early Clinton Administration

The administration of President Bill Clinton inherited an American economy with serious long-term structural problems in the midst of a gradually accelerating cyclical recovery. That recovery coincided with deepening recessions in Europe and Japan, which further raised the US trade and current account deficits in 1993. The cyclical positions of these economies were broadly reminiscent of those at the advent of the last Democratic administration in 1977. The Clinton administration, however, did not propose a global action program within the G-7 as sweeping or

---

108. Mulford defends G-7 exchange rate cooperation as practiced through mid-1992. See Competitiveness Policy Council, Trade Policy Subcouncil, transcript of meeting, Washington, 10 June 1992, pp. 151–52.

strident as the locomotive approach of the Carter administration. In fiscal 1993, the US federal budget deficit declined substantially, which the new administration justifiably cited as a demonstration of the American commitment to international cooperation. The Clinton team called, in turn, for fiscal stimuli in Japan, whose surpluses increased with the recession-mired European Union as well as with the United States, and a reduction in interest rates in Europe. The administration pressed for these measures at, in addition to the G-7 and bilateral forums, a special "jobs summit" in Detroit in March 1994. The Clinton international economic team did not go so far as to spark sharp conflicts over macroeconomic policy, though, and instead vowed to take a more diplomatic approach. A looming question for the US economy was when the Fed would begin to tighten monetary policy, a question answered when interest rates were raised in February 1994.

During his first year in office, President Clinton directed the energies of his administration in the foreign economic arena mainly toward trade liberalization, which he argued would contribute to economic recovery. His administration completed the unfinished trade agreements of his predecessor by securing congressional ratification of NAFTA and negotiating a conclusion to the Uruguay Round—two cliffhangers that were resolved only in the closing hours of bargaining. Clinton also hosted in Seattle the first summit meeting of the countries of the Asia Pacific Economic Cooperation forum, which pledged to continue to pursue regional economic liberalization.

Beyond these multilateral and regional trade matters, the Japan problem absorbed most of the Clinton administration's remaining energy. Anxious to avoid the pitfalls of previous US-Japan trade agreements, the administration sought verifiable commitments on access to the Japanese market. Appreciation of the yen represented another avenue for addressing the bilateral imbalance as well Japan's global trade position and its impact on growth and employment abroad. The Japan problem therefore also dominated exchange rate policy during 1993.

In February 1993, within weeks of his Senate confirmation, Treasury Secretary Lloyd Bentsen signaled the desirability of yen appreciation. In mid-April, meeting with Prime Minister Kiichi Miyazawa in Washington, Clinton observed that if few results could be expected in the trade negotiations, a yen appreciation would reduce the Japanese trade surplus. These remarks helped to drive the yen upward, past the 110 level to the 100 level in August—the fourth realignment of the Japanese currency since the switch to floating exchange rates. The Treasury and Fed intervened to support the dollar against the yen on two occasions: before a meeting of the G-7 in late April, to mollify the Japanese government, and once the exchange rate neared 100 in mid-August.

Several Clinton administration officials believed that the 100–110 range was generally appropriate for the yen/dollar rate. If this range reduced growth prospects for the Japanese economy, they calculated, all the more reason the Japanese government should administer a fiscal stimulus. These policy moves were not tantamount to a bilateral regime of exchange rate management, however. To the contrary, senior Treasury officials avoided any public discussion of what range might be desirable for the yen and said on more than one occasion that "manipulation" of exchange rates was inappropriate.[109]

In contrast to its movements against the Japanese yen, the dollar rose gently against the European currencies on the whole over 1993, owing to a gradual lowering of European interest rates. The administration and Fed stood on the sidelines as the European governments introduced wide bands in the ERM and shortly thereafter initiated stage two of monetary union by creating the European Monetary Institute. The rise of the dollar against the European currencies, and the Canadian dollar as well, offset its decline against the yen; the effective exchange rate for the United States actually rose during 1993.[110]

By the end of its first year, in sum, the Clinton administration had employed the exchange rate as an instrument of international economic policy but had not explicitly pursued a target-range strategy. Administration officials had used the G-7 summit and ministerial meetings to discuss growth and employment issues, but had not reformed or enhanced these meetings for international economic activism. It remained unclear what the Clinton administration would choose to do with the G-7 process, which had suffered neglect but was not beyond rehabilitation.

Review and Conclusion

Official and private sector institutions have strongly influenced the evolution of American external monetary policy over the postwar period. The US private sector, as discussed earlier, is fractionalized and therefore expresses preferences regarding the exchange rate for the dollar which are generally diffuse and vague. The Treasury Department and the Federal Reserve effectively share authority over exchange rate policy even though the terms of their cooperation are sometimes ambiguous. The institutional underpinnings of American exchange rate policy are thus distinct from those of Japan and Germany (with which a full comparison is conducted in chapter 7).

If the US private sector could articulate coherent preferences on currency valuation and stability, such a consensus could anchor policy and

---

109. US Department of the Treasury, "Report to the Congress on International Economic and Exchange Rate Policy," Washington, May 1993 and November 1993.

110. Council of Economic Advisers, *Annual Report 1994*, pp. 205–48.

lend it continuity over time, as it does in Germany and Japan. Without such an anchor a number of factors that would otherwise be secondary are able to influence policy. Those factors include partisan party politics, bureaucratic politics, political and economic ideology, and transient economic considerations. Among the economic considerations are desire for maximum flexibility in formulating domestic monetary policy, the effect of the exchange rate on domestic inflation, and the trade balance. These additional influences tend to be variable and conflicting, and thus, as each waxes and wanes, produce the cyclical pattern of policy outcomes.

The absence of a societal anchor, importantly, renders international monetary policy vulnerable to institutional conflicts within the US government. The Treasury and Federal Reserve frequently differ over the priority to be given to exchange rate valuation, or stability, and the appropriate tradeoff between trade adjustment and price stability. When such conflicts arise, no private sector consensus exists that can help to arbitrate the opposing bureaucratic views.

This chapter demonstrates that the cyclical pattern of American policy behavior has been well entrenched over the postwar period. The cycles exhibit three stages. US administrations have preferred to be unencumbered by external monetary constraints. Thus, in the first instance, they treated the exchange rate (or the balance of payments) as the residual of domestic macroeconomic policies. The late Eisenhower administration, the second Nixon administration and Ford administration, the first Reagan administration, and the Bush administration represented periods of relative neglect of external monetary affairs. Such neglect inevitably led to exchange rate misalignments or payments imbalances with deleterious domestic consequences. American officials initially responded to the external problems by seeking adjustment on the part of foreign governments, typically through expansionary macroeconomic policy, a strategy that usually proved to be internationally confrontational. The first Nixon administration, early Carter administration, early second Reagan administration, and Clinton administration (in the case of Japan) represented this second stage in the policy cycle. When the limits of that strategy were reached, the US administration would settle with its foreign counterparts on multilateral cooperative arrangements on payments and exchange rates. The Smithsonian agreement of 1971, the Bonn summit and dollar rescue of 1978, and the shift to defense of the dollar over the course of 1987 represented turning points to the third, cooperative stage of the cycle. Senior US officials gave priority to international monetary matters, however, only so long as those issues were proximate constraints on the achievement of basic economic objectives. Once external threats abated, the administration and Federal Reserve would become uninterested in external monetary policy again, beginning the cycle anew.

The transition from neglect to activism in the mid-1980s, while following the general cyclical pattern of policy, was an exception to the general rule that private actors have not been mobilized on exchange rate policy in the United States. At that time corporations, trade associations, and labor unions, responding to the evaporation of export markets and unprecedented import penetration, appealed first to the administration and Federal Reserve. When blocked, they appealed to the Congress, which exercised leverage over the administration primarily via its control of trade legislation. Although this effort forced the second Reagan administration to realign the dollar, it did not include the financial community. Because a broad societal consensus was lacking, the activist policy was not sustained over the subsequent period when external constraints were not binding. The mid-1980s are thus an exception that demonstrates the rule.

The politics and institutions of US international monetary policy, finally, have evolved over time. Changes in exchange rate policymaking procedures and prerogatives render the issue more prone to domestic politicization in the event that a sustained overvaluation should reemerge. Private interest groups remain activated on trade policy issues, and once mobilized on exchange rate issues could be more easily remobilized in the future. The biannual reports by the Treasury to the Congress offer an additional venue for the Banking Committees to weigh in on exchange rate policy. Therefore, while the Treasury and Federal Reserve will continue to dominate this policy preserve, they will have to be more attentive to the possibility of internal politicization in periods of exchange rate fluctuation and growing trade deficits. The question arises as to whether these changes are fundamental enough to produce a lasting, basic policy reorientation toward consistency, competitiveness and exchange rate stability.

My tentative answer is that American exchange rate politics have not been fundamentally transformed. These alterations are primarily changes on the margin. Sensitivity to the exchange rate and international competitiveness under the early Clinton administration is not a product of institutional change or an abandonment of the cyclical pattern of policy necessarily. Rather, consistent with the evolution of policy cycles in the past, it is owing to the persistence and renewed growth of the US trade deficit. In periods of declining deficits (beyond the immediate future) and reasonably valued exchange rates, the American tendency to neglect the external monetary dimension will probably reassert itself. In the absence of institutional change, the politics of exchange rate policymaking over the remainder of the 1990s and into the 21st century are less likely to resemble those of the extraordinary period of the mid-1980s than those of earlier decades.

Institutional reform, therefore, will probably be required to permanently extinguish the cycles of neglect to activism. This analysis has highlighted two arenas in which change might bring about this result—public and private institutions.

First, because the American private sector is divided, the political mobilization of private actors is a slow process and the degree of economic
disruption and dislocation must be correspondingly large to produce a
unified lobbying effort and overcome the skepticism, if not outright resistance, on the part of the banking and financial community to exchange rate activism.

Second, the separation of the policy authority in the Treasury and
Federal Reserve is another distinguishing institutional feature of US
policymaking. These two bureaucracies have disagreed frequently, clash-
ing sharply over intervention policy at the end of the Bretton Woods
regime, shortly after the switch to floating, under the first Reagan administration, and during 1989–90. Basic agreement between the two is a
necessary condition for foreign exchange operations to be effective. The
sharing of this policy authority, therefore, instills a clear bias toward
inaction in the foreign exchange markets.

7

Comparing and Explaining
Policy Outcomes

The three preceding chapters presented case histories of domestic and external monetary policymaking in Japan, Germany, and the United States. The first section of the present chapter compares the information on policy outcomes—the dependent variable in this study—gathered in those chapters. The second section then develops a more complete explanation for the differences in policy outcomes among these countries.

The argument presented below is that the way the private sector is organized through the financial system determines the solidarity and coherence of societal preferences regarding exchange rates. How the government is organized, mainly the degree of central bank independence, determines the degree to which private preferences are translated into policy outcomes. In countries where private banks are close to industrial firms, societal preferences favor low valuation of the currency but independent central banks can check the influence of these preferences on policy.

Comparing Policy Outcomes

During most of the postwar period, Japan and Germany adopted external monetary policies that were sensitive to the competitiveness of national industry. They not only maintained a competitively valued currency through the use of foreign exchange intervention and changes in domestic monetary policy but also used capital controls and discouraged the international use of the currency to dampen capital inflows.[1] The United States, on the other hand, often neglected the impact of exchange rates on the competitiveness of traded-goods sectors altogether. During this period, American authorities used foreign exchange intervention less often than their main partners, and adjusted domestic monetary policy only when trying to support, not depress, the dollar. With only ineffective exceptions, the United States took a laissez-faire attitude toward capital movements, and US authorities held an ambivalently positive attitude toward the international role of the dollar.

This study seeks to explain the behavior of governments in the external monetary field. It does not explain the behavior of exchange rates per se or even the relationship between exchange rate policy and exchange market outcomes—that is, the effectiveness of government action. That is the subject of other studies.

Nevertheless, the postwar pattern of currency valuation broadly coincides with national external monetary policies in some significant respects. Both the D-mark and the yen were periodically substantially undervalued, as measured by the emergence of chronic trade and current account surpluses for both countries, under both the Bretton Woods and flexible-rate regimes. Periods of overvaluation of these currencies, if any, have been brief. By contrast, the United States experienced a substantially overvalued dollar for prolonged periods in both the 1960s and 1980s. The dollar has not been either substantially or moderately undervalued for a significant duration.

Structured Comparison

This study uses five criteria to assess the external monetary policy outcomes of the three countries: extent of foreign exchange intervention, extent of capital controls and selective liberalization, degree to which an international role of the currency is encouraged, extent of the application of domestic monetary policy to exchange rate targets, and policy consistency over time. Because these instruments are close substitutes, as discussed in chapter 1, they must be considered together.

The overall picture that emerges is one of substantially differentiated policy outcomes among the United States, Germany, and Japan. Table 7.1 summarizes the pattern of policy outcomes presented below. The table describes generalizations for the postwar period as a whole. Changes in policy orientation, which have been considerable, and recent trends are treated in a separate section below.

---

1. A policy oriented toward competitiveness, by the definition used in this study, seeks an exchange rate consistent with expanding or maintaining market share in tradeable goods. The term does not mean competitive devaluation and is consistent with either a depreciating or stable currency.

Table 7.1 External monetary policy outcomes[a]

	Japan	Germany	United States
Foreign exchange intervention	High	Moderate	Low
Capital controls and policies	High	Moderate	Low
International role of the currency	Discouraged	Discouraged	Ambivalently positive
Domestic monetary policy	High	Moderate	Low
Policy consistency	Moderate	High	Low

a. Government use of these policy instruments to manage the balance of payments and external value of the currency over the postwar period.

Foreign Exchange Intervention

For almost the entire postwar period, American intervention has been smaller in volume than European and Japanese intervention in the dollar market and often nonexistent. Because of American reluctance to intervene, the European countries and Japan held de facto responsibility for foreign exchange intervention under the Bretton Woods regime. A system of swap arrangements established reciprocal access to central bank credit to supply US authorities with funds for foreign exchange operations, part of the strategy to protect the American gold stock. Even under this system, though, the heaviest burden of active intervention by far fell on Europe and Japan.

The pattern of American passivity and European and Japanese activism regarding intervention was related, to be sure, to the requirements of the Bretton Woods regime. The roles these countries adopted, however, were not preordained by the agreements at Bretton Woods. These roles represented explicit policy choices on the part of the United States and its partners and consequently determined the path along which the international monetary regime evolved.

Accordingly, that pattern persisted into the 1970s, well after the demise of the fixed-rate regime. Japan and Germany continued to intervene despite the shift to flexible rates and despite the maintenance of capital and exchange controls. Japan not only intervened, moreover, but was also accused of ignoring the reemergence of its trade surplus and actively intervening to prevent the yen from rising. Germany was not accused of any such suspect intervention. Generally, the Bundesbank tried to avoid operations in the dollar market. Appreciation of the D-mark during 1977–78 nonetheless forced Germany to limit the rise of the German currency by buying dollars on the foreign exchange markets.

American authorities intervened episodically. Although they resurrected intervention operations in 1961, they intervened heavily for the first time only in the late 1960s, in an effort to forestall the demise of the Bretton Woods regime. The United States intervened heavily again during 1978–79, to the tune of $25 billion. American activism, however, was relatively limited in duration. Furthermore, the US authorities intervened primarily in D-marks and avoided yen operations for the most part. In addition, foreign central banks financed the bulk of American external deficits through their own foreign exchange operations. The Bundesbank and the Japanese governments were particularly critical of American passivity in the face of dollar depreciation in 1977–78.

For the 1980s, one crude measure, the average monthly absolute change in foreign exchange reserves, suggests that Japan intervened most frequently, Germany less frequently and the United States least frequently.[2] This general pattern is confirmed by more precise measurements of intervention per se. According to Catte, Galli, and Rebecchini, Japan intervened somewhat more frequently and in much larger quantities than Germany and the United States in the dollar market during the second half of the decade.[3] Dominguez and Frankel show that Germany intervened more frequently than the United States during 1982–88.[4] Late in the 1980s, American authorities intervened on roughly the same scale as foreign authorities. But, whether the recent change is lasting or ephemeral, American intervention during both the fixed- and flexible-rate periods as a whole has been smaller in scale than that of most of the foreign partners.[5]

The imbalance of intervention effort among the three countries is accentuated when considered relative to trade volumes, economic size, and the international use of the currency. Total output in the United States is now roughly two-thirds larger than the GNP of Japan and roughly three times larger than the GNP of Germany. For most of the postwar period the differences have been much greater. Despite being briefly eclipsed

---

2. The average change was over $1,040 million for Japan, $908 million for Germany, and under $790 million for the United States during 1980–90. During 1980–87, before the United States began to intervene more heavily, the average monthly change was $894 million for Japan, $871 million for Germany, and $535 million for the United States. Calculated by the author from Bank of Japan, *Economic Statistics Annual*; Deutsche Bundesbank, *Monthly Report*; Federal Reserve, *Federal Reserve Bulletin*: various issues. The measure is crude because these changes include receipts and payments for purposes other than foreign exchange intervention, such as interest and transactions in support of US military forces abroad.

3. Catte, Galli, and Rebecchini, "Concerted Interventions and the Dollar," table 2, p. 5.

4. Dominguez and Frankel, *Does Foreign Exchange Intervention Work?*, table 5.1, p. 75.

5. This comparison of the volumes of intervention is not meant to be a normative assessment of the wisdom of these policies. In fact, the smaller the volume of intervention necessary to reach exchange rate objectives, the better. The comparison, rather, is simply meant to rank the degree of government activism.

by Germany in the mid-1980s, the United States remains the world's largest exporter. Finally, the international use of the dollar remains far greater than the use of the D-mark or Japanese yen, and the foreign exchange markets are correspondingly larger as well. (See the section below on national policies toward the international role of the currency.) Thus, Japanese and German interventions appear to be even more active when compared with American intervention in relative terms than when compared in absolute terms.

The frequency of unilateral intervention is another meaningful indicator. Concerted intervention is generally acknowledged to be more effective in the foreign exchange market than unilateral intervention. Thus, the number of unilateral interventions reflects the willingness to undertake costly intervention with substantially less assurance of success. Both Japan and Germany were more likely to intervene unilaterally in the dollar market than the United States, which rarely intervened alone.[6]

Moreover, intervention in the dollar market is only a portion of Bundesbank "intervention," when we count the German participation in the Exchange Rate Mechanism (ERM) of the European Monetary System (EMS). The operations on the part of the Bundesbank within the ERM are of three types. First, during intramarginal operations, the Bundesbank intervenes in dollars, selling (or buying) them in exchange for the currency of the European partner. Second, when intervening at the margin, the Bundesbank is formally obligated to buy (or sell) other European currencies in exchange for the D-mark. During the ERM crises of 1992–93, the Bundesbank purchased large quantities of other European currencies directly. Generally, however, the Bundesbank shuns other European currencies in favor of the dollar in its foreign exchange reserve holdings. Thus, third, when interventions at the margin are required, the Bundesbank prefers to extend D-mark credits to central banks within the ERM. Those central banks in turn sell the German currency to defend their own. As figure 5.6 illustrates, those credits have been of considerable size, and during autumn 1992 and summer 1993 they were enormous. Japan participated in no similar regional exchange rate stabilization arrangement and thus neither engaged in nor financed substantial intervention outside the dollar market. The United States, naturally, intervened only in the dollar market.

---

6. For the 1985–91 period, Catte, Galli, and Rebecchini display roughly ten unilateral interventions by Germany, seven by Japan, and one very minor intervention by the United States. "Concerted Intervention and the Dollar," figure 3. For the 1974–88 period, Iida calculates a substantially higher rate of coordinated intervention for the U.S. than for Japan. See Keisuke Iida, "The Political Economy of International Economic Cooperation," manuscript, Princeton University, July 1991, tables 1 and 2, pp. 24–25.

Capital Controls

Among the three countries considered here, Japan has made the greatest use of capital and exchange controls in managing the exchange rate and international payments. Through the Foreign Exchange and Trade Control Law of 1949, in particular, the Japanese government strictly controlled inflows and outflows of capital. These controls were formal prohibitions on capital transactions and restrictive licensing for financial institutions engaged in international business. There were also informal controls, such as administrative guidance of the foreign exchange positions of Japanese banks.

Capital and exchange controls helped Japan to resist upward (and downward) pressures on the yen not only under the Bretton Woods regime but after the switch to flexible exchange rates as well. The Ministry of Finance (MOF) selectively liberalized financial transactions during both the first and second oil shocks to limit depreciations and appreciations of the yen and manage the balance of payments.[7] The Japanese government retained capital controls until well into the 1980s and surrendered these instruments only under combined American and private Japanese political pressure.[8] Even so, the Japanese government retains a greater capacity than either of the other two countries to exercise suasion over private financial institutions and to invoke formal controls in an emergency.

German policymakers, while opposed to capital controls in principle, also resorted to them in practice. After eliminating controls on capital movements in 1958, the finance ministry reestablished controls on inflows in 1960 and continued to apply them until the second revaluation of the D-mark in 1969. Controls were reimposed during the exchange crisis in 1971 and, because capital flows proved to be volatile under the flexible-rate regime, were retained into the early 1980s.[9] The German government, like the Japanese government, selectively liberalized capital controls to manage international payments and actively promoted capital inflows during 1980–81. Germany benefited from the controls on outflows imposed by its partners in the EMS, principally France and Italy,

---

7. Edward J. Lincoln, "Japanese Bond and Stock Markets," in *Inside the Japanese System*, Daniel I. Okimoto and Thomas P. Rohlen, eds. (Stanford: Stanford University Press, 1988), pp. 63–64; Fukao, "Liberalization of Japan's Foreign Exchange Controls"; Otani, "Exchange Rate Instability and Capital Controls."

8. Louis W. Pauly, *Opening Financial Markets: Banking Politics on the Pacific Rim* (Ithaca, NY: Cornell University Press, 1988); Frances McCall Rosenbluth, *Financial Politics in Contemporary Japan* (Ithaca, NY: Cornell University Press, 1989).

9. George S. Tavlas, *On the International Use of Currencies: The Case of the Deutsche Mark*, Essays in International Finance 181 (Princeton: International Finance Section, Princeton University, March 1991), pp. 36–37. On Germany and Japan, see John B. Goodman and Louis W. Pauly, "The Obsolescence of Capital Controls? Economic Management in an Age of Global Markets," *World Politics* 46, no. 1 (October 1993), pp. 60–70.

whose investors would otherwise have invested in German markets and thereby placed upward pressure on the D-mark. Bonn and Frankfurt urged the removal of French and Italian controls only after a certain degree of inflation convergence had been achieved and German dominance of the EMS had been established.

The United States resorted to capital controls in the 1960s and early 1970s.[10] These controls, however, were half-hearted and porous in comparison to the capital controls of Germany and Japan. The restrictions on bank lending, for example, were formally voluntary. American authorities accepted the development of the international bond market in London, stimulated by the Interest Equalization Tax (IET). American acceptance of these offshore markets contrasted sharply with the hostility of German and Japanese authorities to the development of such markets outside their jurisdictions. And American restrictions were dismantled earlier than Japanese and German restrictions.

In the first half of the 1980s, under the first Reagan administration, the US Treasury pursued a deliberate strategy of promoting capital inflow. This strategy had four elements: the elimination of withholding tax on interest payments to foreign holders of US government and corporate bonds, the issuance of foreign-targeted bonds, pressure on Japan to liberalize its capital controls, and talking up the United States as a destination for investment.

The Reagan administration strategy of international borrowing, however, stands in marked contrast to the policies pursued by German and Japanese authorities to manage capital flows. First, the latter selectively liberalized to dampen payments imbalances (usually surpluses) and exchange rate swings. By contrast, the American authorities sought to finance domestic capital requirements, thus putting *upward* pressure on an already strong dollar and increasing the trade deficit rather than simply financing a pre-existing shortfall in external payments. The Reagan policies thus aggravated, rather than dampened, the current account deficit and currency volatility.

Second, the US controls on capital outflows in the 1960s and the promotion of capital inflows in the 1980s contributed to the overvaluation of the dollar during those periods. American policies, particularly the controls on outflows during the 1960s, recall the use of capital controls by Britain, which tried to sustain an overvaluation of the pound. German and Japanese controls, which mainly restrained capital inflows, generally suppressed the appreciation of undervalued currencies.

---

10. John A. C. Conybeare, *United States Foreign Economic Policy and the International Capital Markets: The Case of Capital Export Controls, 1963–1974* (New York: Garland, 1988); Samuel Pisar, "Capital Restraint Programs," in *United States International Economic Policy in an Interdependent World*, papers submitted to the Commission on International Trade and Investment (Williams Commission) (Washington: GPO, July 1971), pp. 87–112.

A government's use of capital controls was also related to the degree to which that government's policy promoted the use of its own financial center as the leading international financial center. The American government was mildly supportive of the New York–based financial institutions in their collective role as an international financial center. The IET showed the limits, though, of Washington's willingness to sustain American financial institutions in this role. The Japanese government discouraged Tokyo's role as an international financial center, by contrast, until large volumes of borrowing by Japanese corporations from Japanese investors began to take place abroad, outside the Ministry of Finance's jurisdiction. At that point, MOF grudgingly acquiesced to pressures for liberalization.

The German Bundesbank and the finance ministry had little interest in developing an international financial center in Germany during most of the postwar period. They began, however, an important round of liberalization in 1985, which has continued to the present. The loss of financial business to London and Paris provided the initial impetus for liberalization. The volume of financial transactions was expanding dramatically and was expected to further increase with the single European market in financial services. The German government launched *Finanzplatz Deutschland* to reclaim some of this business for Frankfurt. With the movement toward Economic and Monetary Union accelerating at a dizzying pace at that time, Frankfurt's status as an international financial center had the additional benefit of strengthening the city's candidacy to become the seat of the European Central Bank.

International Role of the Currency

Of the three currencies considered here, the dollar plays by far the greatest international role as a unit of account and a currency for official reserves, private investment portfolios, and transactions. In official reserves, the D-mark plays the second most important role, and the Japanese yen the third most important (table 7.2). This ranking is replicated in the currency shares of private external assets, although the pound sterling occasionally outranks either the D-mark or the yen (table 7.3).

Compared with the role of each of these three countries in international investment and international trade, the American currency plays a greater than proportionate role, the D-mark a roughly proportionate role, and the yen a substantially less than proportionate role.[11] As an invoicing currency in each country's own imports and exports, the dollar and D-mark play greater roles in American and German trade, respectively, than does the yen in Japanese trade, which ranks even behind France

---

11. For a concurring view, see Commission of the European Communities, *European Economy* 44 (October 1990), special issue entitled "One Market, One Money," p. 187.

Table 7.2 Currency shares of official foreign exchange holdings, 1980–92 (percentages)

Currency	1980	1982	1984	1986	1988	1990	1991	1992
Dollar	68.6	70.5	69.4	66.0	64.7	56.4	56.2	62.9
Deutsche mark	14.9	12.3	12.3	14.9	15.7	19.7	17.3	13.1
Yen	4.3	4.7	5.7	7.6	7.7	9.1	9.9	8.5
Pound sterling	2.9	2.5	3.0	2.8	2.8	3.2	3.8	3.7
French franc	1.7	1.2	1.1	1.2	1.0	2.1	3.6	2.4
Swiss franc	3.2	2.8	2.1	1.9	1.9	1.5	1.4	1.3
Netherlands guilder	1.3	1.1	0.8	1.1	1.1	1.2	1.2	0.8
Unspecified	3.1	5.0	5.8	4.5	5.1	6.8	6.7	7.3

Source: IMF *Annual Report,* various issues, table 1.2.

and Italy.[12] On a regional basis, the role of the yen in East Asia remains significantly smaller than that of the D-mark in Europe.[13]

The main point here is that this pattern is not simply the result of historical practices in the private markets but also a function of deliberate government policy toward the role of the currency. Both Germany and Japan vigorously and systematically resisted the international use of their currencies—particularly as a currency for private assets and official reserves—during most of the postwar period. In particular, the two governments limited borrowing by foreign residents in their domestic capital markets in D-mark or yen. Both governments were acutely aware of, and wanted to avoid, the conflict between the provision of liquidity and the preservation of confidence in the key currency that had plagued the dollar and, in a different sense, the pound sterling.[14] Because the Bundesbank and Bank of Japan might have to adjust monetary policy in re-

12. George S. Tavlas and Yuzuru Ozeki, *The Internationalization of Currencies: An Appraisal of the Japanese Yen* (Washington: International Monetary Fund, January 1992), table 17, p. 32.

13. Tavlas and Ozeki, *The Internationalization of Currencies*, tables 30 and 31, p. 49. In both official reserves and trade invoicing, the D-mark was used more in Europe than the yen was used in East Asia at the end of the 1980s. See also Jeffrey A. Frankel, "Is a Yen Bloc Forming in Pacific Asia?" *Finance and International Economy*, vol. 5 (Oxford: Oxford University Press, 1992), pp. 5–20; Yasuhiro Maehara, "The Internationalization of the Yen and Its Role as a Key Currency," *Journal of Asian Studies* 4 (1993): 153–70.

14. This problem was known as the Triffin Dilemma, after the international economist who described it, Robert Triffin. See, for example, Toyoo Gyohten, "Internationalization of the Yen: Its Implication for US-Japan Relations," in *Japan and the United States Today*, Hugh T. Patrick and Ryuichiro Tachi, eds. (New York: Center on Japanese Economy and Business, Columbia University, 1989), pp. 84–89; Yoshio Suzuki, *Japan's Economic Performance and International Role* (Tokyo: University of Tokyo Press, 1989), pp. 117–19, 130–35.

Table 7.3 Currency shares of private external assets, 1982–92 (percentages)[a]

Asset type and currency	1982	1983	1984	1985	1986	1987	1988	1989	1990	1991	1992
Shares of external bank loans											
Dollar	82.0	73.1	65.9	57.4	61.5	59.8	64.2	77.0	58.9	84.5	75.4
Japanese yen	5.3	10.6	17.4	20.2	17.5	11.7	6.1	5.3	1.7	1.1	1.4
Pound sterling	1.1	1.7	2.0	4.2	7.9	18.1	17.4	6.4	17.5	4.2	1.9
Deutsche mark	2.0	2.0	2.9	2.7	3.8	3.1	2.8	3.2	6.7	2.1	1.8
ECU	0.4	1.2	3.9	8.4	2.6	2.8	3.3	4.6	8.7	3.9	15.0
Swiss franc	0.1	0.7	1.8	3.0	2.1	0.7	0.3	0.4	0.1	0.6	0.3
Other	4.2	7.3	5.7	3.9	3.7	4.5	5.9	3.1	6.4	3.6	4.2
Denominations of external bond issues											
Dollar	51.5	45.4	49.2	46.4	46.3	33.3	35.4	51.9	33.3	28.5	36.9
Japanese yen	7.5	7.4	7.4	9.5	10.8	14.2	8.7	8.3	13.5	12.9	11.2
Pound sterling	2.3	3.9	5.6	4.6	5.3	9.0	10.8	6.8	9.5	9.1	7.6
Deutsche mark	9.4	11.7	9.0	9.8	9.2	9.2	11.6	6.4	8.3	7.1	10.4
ECU	1.0	3.5	3.6	5.7	3.7	4.4	5.4	5.2	8.1	11.1	6.8
Swiss franc	19.2	22.8	16.4	12.7	12.0	14.4	12.4	7.5	10.5	7.3	5.8
Other	5.0	5.0	5.2	8.3	9.4	15.5	15.6	13.9	16.8	24.0	21.3
Denominations of eurocurrency deposits[b]											
Dollar				67.9	63.5	58.2	60.0	59.7	51.9	50.5	46.3
Japanese yen				3.4	4.5	5.8	5.5	5.5	5.0	4.9	4.6
Pound sterling				2.0	2.1	2.8	3.4	3.1	4.2	3.8	4.0
Deutsche mark				11.4	12.8	14.2	13.3	13.9	16.2	15.7	16.5
ECU				2.6	2.6	2.8	3.0	3.2	4.5	5.5	5.8
Swiss franc				6.4	7.2	7.7	5.4	4.9	5.6	5.1	5.4
Other				6.2	7.2	8.4	9.4	9.7	12.6	14.6	17.1

a. Percentage calculated at 1990 exchange rates.
b. Data for 1992 are through September.

Sources: OECD, *Financial Market Trends*, Nos. 24, 28, 33, 38, 42, 45, 53, 54; Bank for International Settlements, *International Banking and Financial Markets*, February 1993; George S. Tavlas, *On the International Use of Currencies: The Case of the Deutsche Mark*, Essays in International Finance, No. 181 (Princeton: Princeton University, March 1991), table 13, p. 32.

sponse to capital movements, monetary control would be impaired under both fixed and flexible exchange rate regimes.

The policy of discouraging international use of the currency persisted into the period of floating exchange rates. Even among the members of the European "snake" and the EMS in its early years, Germany firmly resisted the use of the D-mark as a reserve currency.[15] As German confidence in the EMS rose, and the European partners reduced inflation, the Bundesbank gradually accepted greater use of the D-mark in the international reserves of the other ERM countries for intervention within the system. By 1989, the D-mark constituted roughly 23.4 percent of the foreign exchange reserves of Community countries.[16] An important reason for German acquiescence in greater official D-mark holdings was that their disposition was subject to Bundesbank influence through central bank cooperation in the ERM.

The Bundesbank also eased objections to the private use of the D-mark in international assets and liabilities in the second half of the 1980s. Greater private use of the currency in portfolios and transactions promoted *Finanzplatz Deutschland*. Unlike the case with official reserves, however, no agreements govern the disposition of privately held D-marks abroad. The Bundesbank remains acutely concerned that the volume of outstanding foreign D-mark assets and liabilities could destabilize exchange markets.[17] The ERM crises of 1992–93 dramatically confirmed those fears. Accordingly, Germany has only gradually eased restrictions related to D-mark usage, for example restrictions on foreign institutions' participation in and management of foreign D-mark bond issues. Owing to these restrictions, private use of the D-mark, as a currency of denomination of external loans, bond issues, and Eurocurrency deposits, has lagged behind use of the D-mark in official reserves.[18]

The yen-dollar agreement of 1984 ostensibly sought to increase the international role of the Japanese yen.[19] A few years later, after the dollar had depreciated, MOF officials proposed that the United States issue government bonds denominated in yen in an effort to support the US currency. (They were rebuffed by the US Treasury.) The proportion of

---

15. The German central bank concedes, "The Deutsche Mark has acquired this international status somewhat against the will of the Bundesbank, for the role of being a second reserve currency may well pose considerable problems for a country." *Monthly Report of the Deutsche Bundesbank,* May 1988, p. 22.

16. Tavlas, *On the International Use of Currencies,* table 14, p. 33.

17. See *Monthly Report of the Deutsche Bundesbank,* May 1987, pp. 34–42; January 1990, pp. 33-43; May 1991, pp. 23–31; and November 1991, pp. 40–44.

18. Tavlas, *On the International Use of Currencies,* table 13, p. 32.

19. Frankel, *The Yen-Dollar Agreement.*

international reserves held in yen has risen modestly from 4.4 percent in 1980 to 9.9 percent in 1991.

However, raising yen usage has clearly not been a significant thrust of policy on the part of the Japanese government or central bank. This "is not an urgent priority," says one former senior MOF official.[20] Japanese officials entered the 1984 yen-dollar agreement with the expectation that its immediate effect would be to increase capital outflows more than inflows, thereby reducing the value of the yen in the short term rather than increasing it. Since then, they have taken in public a decidedly neutral stance on the role of the currency. MOF, moreover, has resisted domestic financial liberalization, in the bankers' acceptance market in particular, which could have increased the yen's external role. Japanese institutional investors, who suffered large losses on dollar portfolios in the 1980s, could avoid exchange rate risk if foreign borrowers issued yen-denominated securities. In this light, MOF's reluctance to facilitate a greater international role for the yen suggests continuing underlying concern about monetary and exchange rate control.

In contrast, while the United States did not seek a dominant role for the dollar under the Bretton Woods regime, American officials accepted its reserve currency role with equanimity. The United States at times toyed with schemes to relieve the dollar and American monetary policy of this burden, but stopped short of encouraging a decline in the role of the currency.[21] Special Drawing Rights (SDRs), created in the 1960s, were not allowed to supplant the dollar. The US Treasury agreed to the creation of SDRs only in a form more substitutable for gold than dollars, and even then did not authorize the IMF to make large distributions.[22] Negotiations over the substitution account in the late 1970s foundered on American unwillingness to accept part of the potential costs of guaranteeing the dollar balances of foreign central banks.[23] The first Reagan administration (1981–85) encouraged Japanese financial market liberalization and persuaded the Congress to agree to it as likely to increase the international role of the yen and thereby its value against the dollar. But the real, not-so-hidden agenda of Treasury Secretary Donald Regan was to secure American access to Japanese savings and access by American financial institutions to the less-developed Japanese market in financial services.[24]

---

20. Interviews, Tokyo, January–February 1991.

21. For a thorough discussion, see Bergsten, *Dilemmas of the Dollar*.

22. On US policy regarding the creation of the SDR and the initial allocations, see Odell, *U.S. International Monetary Policy*, chapter 3.

23. Joanne Gowa, "Hegemons, IOs, and Markets: The Case of the Substitution Account," *International Organization* 38, no. 4 (autumn 1984): 661–83.

24. See the discussion in chapter 6.

Although the role of the dollar has been declining, American policy has not substantially encouraged this trend. The dollar remains the dominant currency for both official and private uses. The comparable treatment of the dollar for official and private purposes—in contrast to differentiated usage of the D-mark and yen—reflects the ambivalent stance of American policy on this issue.

Domestic Monetary Policy

When declarations, intervention, and capital controls failed to drive a wedge between exchange rates and domestic monetary policy, authorities also modified domestic monetary policy to attain exchange rate and international payments objectives. Adjustments in domestic monetary policy could be made in a straightforward fashion by changing interest rates or bank reserves. Alternatively, domestic monetary policy could be altered indirectly, by leaving the effects of foreign exchange intervention on domestic liquidity unsterilized.[25]

Again, though, the Bank of Japan, Bundesbank, and Federal Reserve incorporated external considerations into domestic monetary policy to greatly varying degrees. Japan altered domestic monetary policy more frequently and more extensively than did Germany. Germany, in turn, did so more often than did the United States. American authorities rarely adjusted domestic monetary policy for the sake of external goals. In those cases where US external monetary policy was activist, American officials relied on the direct instruments of exchange rate policy, such as declarations and intervention, much more heavily than on changes in interest rates and money growth.

During the first half of the postwar era, with the brief exception of Operation Twist, the United States did not change domestic monetary policy for the sake of maintaining the Bretton Woods parity. Indeed, the United States jettisoned the regime when its rules threatened to constrain American monetary policy.[26] By contrast, Germany and Japan frequently subjected monetary policy to the imperatives of the exchange rate parity and the balance of payments. These national differences were in part the consequence of the postwar regime and US hegemony. Some officials within the Bundesbank argued for breaking free from these inflation-imposing constraints, and the D-mark was floated briefly before

---

25. This study has differentiated between sterilized and unsterilized intervention, the latter being tantamount to a change in domestic monetary policy. Most intervention is now routinely sterilized in the three countries studied here. But that has not always been the case. In earlier decades, owing to the limitations of national financial markets, Japan and Germany were sometimes unable to sterilize all their foreign currency operations. As a result, they adjusted domestic monetary policy more frequently than did the United States.

26. See, for example, Gowa, *Closing the Gold Window.*

the revaluation of 1969 and then again in May 1971. But ultimately it was the American administration that dealt the *coup de grace* to the Bretton Woods regime.

Even under floating exchange rates, however, Germany and Japan continued to give far greater weight to exchange rates when setting monetary policy than did the United States. Monetary expansion in both countries in the early 1970s limited the appreciation of their currencies against the dollar under the new regime. The Bundesbank distinguished itself from the Bank of Japan by tightening monetary policy earlier after the switch to floating rates and by establishing growth targets for domestic monetary aggregates beginning in 1975. Nonetheless, during the locomotive controversy of 1977–78, the Bundesbank countenanced substantial overshooting of its newly instituted domestic targets, and the Bank of Japan eased interest rates to stem appreciation of their respective currencies.

The Federal Reserve was concerned mainly about domestically generated inflation when it embarked on its new, strict monetary policy in October 1979, though support for the dollar was regarded as an additional benefit of the tightening. The Fed had raised interest rates during the dollar rescue of November 1978, which succeeded in stabilizing the currency, albeit at a low rate. By autumn 1979, though, inflation had increased while credit continued to expand rapidly, prompting Volcker to tighten sharply.[27]

Germany and Japan were thrust into a broadly similar situation by the new restrictive course of American monetary policy. Both the D-mark and yen weakened substantially. Moreover, in 1979 and 1980, the oil price increases reduced the trade surpluses of both countries drastically and pushed them into current account deficit. These were the first significant current account deficits for each country since the mid-1960s, with the exception of Japan's one-year deficit in 1974. Consumer price inflation was comparably high in both countries. Growth slowed in both countries as well. Initially, both countries responded similarly by letting their currencies depreciate somewhat while at the same time tightening monetary policy.

But in 1981 the monetary policy reaction of Germany and Japan diverged markedly. The different responses, in the face of generally similar circumstances, place the differences between the two countries in stark relief and thus deserve attention here. In February 1981, the Bundesbank raised interest rates to all-time highs, even in the face of high

---

27. German authorities had pressed American officials to tighten monetary policy. But those demands underscored the importance of limiting inflation per se rather than dollar depreciation and had a greater impact on the thinking of the administration than of the Federal Reserve, according to Volcker. See Volcker and Gyohten, *Changing Fortunes*, pp. 167–69.

unemployment, specifically to defend the value of the D-mark. The Bank of Japan, in contrast, continued to loosen monetary policy and countenanced a yen depreciation. Japan eased monetary policy sooner than Germany despite higher growth prospects and far lower unemployment. Japanese consumer price inflation in 1980 was considerably higher than German inflation; it remained above 5.0 percent in 1981 and fell only slightly faster than German inflation thereafter.

Differences in domestic economic conditions, therefore, do not explain the differences in domestic monetary policies at this revealing juncture. Instead, differences in the priority attached to defending the currency explain the course taken by monetary authorities in both countries. When faced with the choice between supporting domestic demand and risking inflation, on the one hand, or supporting the external value of the currency, on the other, Japan opted for the former and Germany opted for the latter in 1981. In making this choice, Japan attached even greater importance to external competitiveness, relative to price stability, than did Germany. Owing to these monetary policy choices, Germany experienced a severe recession, which Japan completely avoided. As the next section argues, the greater independence of the Bundesbank compared with the Bank of Japan was crucial in producing this result.

The 1980–81 period is unusual in that Germany and Japan were confronted with weakness in their currencies rather than strength. The more usual pattern, in which Germany and Japan eased monetary policy to limit currency appreciation, reasserted itself by the mid-1980s. During 1986–89, the US Federal Reserve eased monetary policy and then tightened it again. During both phases, the Fed was cognizant of the policy effects on the dollar, and the exchange rate influenced the timing of policy change in early 1987. But American monetary policy was principally determined by domestic imperatives.

German and Japanese authorities, by contrast, eased monetary policy to forestall and limit appreciation of their currencies. Both reduced the discount rate to record lows in tandem with the Federal Reserve. Both central banks again countenanced substantial overshooting of their domestic money supply growth targets. Both waited until their currencies weakened again before tightening monetary policy.

But again, as in 1981, Germany pursued a tougher monetary line than Japan. Whereas the Bank of Japan participated in two joint discount rate decreases with the Federal Reserve in 1986, for example, the Bundesbank participated in only one. The Bundesbank, not the Bank of Japan, triggered the October 1987 conflict with the US administration and the stock market crash when Frankfurt tried to shadow increases in American interest rates. The Bundesbank successfully turned the corner on tightening monetary policy, without a market crash, in 1988, one year before the Bank of Japan. The Bundesbank's tightening helped Germany to avoid the inflation that subsequently plagued Japan in the asset market.

In the early 1990s, the three countries continued to differ as to the importance attached to exchange rate stabilization in setting domestic monetary policies. The Federal Reserve lowered interest rates to boost the domestic economy with little regard for the record lows being registered against the D-mark and yen. The Bank of Japan lowered interest rates as well. During 1991–92, the Bank of Japan did so primarily to fight off recession and bankruptcy of Japanese financial institutions. During 1993, the appreciation of the yen had once again become an important consideration, and the Bank of Japan reduced interest rates to record lows. The Bundesbank, consumed in its fight against inflationary consequences of German unification, was unwilling to reduce interest rates quickly enough to avoid either a severe recession or the unraveling of the ERM during 1992–93. With the experience of 1980–81 uppermost in their minds, Bundesbank officials eased monetary policy painstakingly gradually to maintain international confidence in the D-mark and try to prevent a depreciation against the dollar.

In conclusion, to generalize for the postwar period as a whole, Japan has targeted domestic monetary policy toward the exchange rate more often and more extensively than the other two countries. Indeed, the troughs in Japanese interest rates coincide almost exactly with the three major yen realignments in 1971–73, 1976–78, and 1985–87, as well as the fourth realignment in 1993 (figure 4.6). When faced with an appreciating currency, the Bank of Japan eased monetary policy more, held interest rates lower longer, or retightened monetary policy later than did the Bundesbank. Germany nonetheless also incorporated exchange rate considerations into domestic monetary policy, in 1977–78, 1981, and 1986–88, far more frequently and extensively than did the United States.

Policy Consistency

Among the three countries considered here, the United States pursued the least consistent policy over the decades reviewed in the previous chapters. German and Japanese external monetary policies were both far more consistent than American policy, with Germany's being the most consistent of all. The changeability of policy over time differs from the use of the four instruments discussed above as a measure of policy outcomes, but is nonetheless equally important.

Since the 1960s, American external monetary policy has evolved through cycles of neglect and activism. These cycles were closely associated with changes in administration and in most cases with a change in party control.[28] The cycle of the 1980s began with the laissez-faire policy of the

---

28. C. Fred Bergsten, "America's Unilateralism," in Bergsten, Etienne Davignon, and Isamu Miyazaki, *Conditions for Partnership in International Economic Management*, Report to the Trilateral Commission 32 (New York: Trilateral Commission, 1986), pp. 3–14;

first Reagan administration, turned into active conflict with the Europeans and Japanese over who should adjust macroeconomic policies under the second Reagan administration, and then evolved into a more balanced policy of G-7 cooperation. Policy reverted toward neglect under the Bush administration, though not to the same degree as in previous cycles. The early Clinton administration adopted a relaxed stance toward the European currencies but a more active stance toward the Japanese yen. This shift of policy regarding the yen was reminiscent of the Ford-Carter transition.

German external monetary policy, by contrast, took its cue from the relationship between foreign and domestic costs of production, which instilled consistency over these decades. The Ministry of Finance and the Bundesbank pursued a two-track policy of flexibility against the dollar and stabilization against the European currencies. The terms of German participation in European exchange rate stabilization arrangements have been constant. The steadiness of the German terms of the European monetary bargain—stressing price stability—was an important source of the success and growth in membership of the ERM over the 1980s and through 1991.

Germany has been less consistent in its policy toward the US dollar. German institutions and private actors prefer stability in the dollar/D-mark rate, and Germany's substantial intervention in 1977–78, 1980–81, 1984–85, and the late 1980s reflects this. But Germany has exhibited less willingness at other times to bear the costs of currency operations to promote dollar/D-mark stability. Public statements have varied regarding desirable currency rates and the utility of foreign exchange intervention and international cooperation to achieve them.

Japanese policy, like German policy, does not move in the extended cycles that have characterized American policy. But Japanese policy has been less consistent, on balance, than German policy. Endeavoring to keep the yen competitively valued, the Japanese government has been forced by the markets and by foreign governments into reassessments of its view of the desirable level of the yen.[29] Such reevaluations, lurching and episodic, have coincided with the four major yen appreciations since

---

C. Randall Henning, *Macroeconomic Diplomacy in the 1980s*, pp. 50–52; Benjamin J. Cohen, "An Explosion in the Kitchen? Economic Relations with Other Advanced Industrial States," in Kenneth A. Oye, Robert J. Lieber, and Donald Rothchild, eds., *Eagle Defiant: United States Foreign Policy in the 1980s* (Boston: Little, Brown, 1983), pp. 105–30.

29. We would expect that a currency valued close to its equilibrium exchange rate should exhibit more long-term stability than a currency that becomes severely misaligned from time to time. A currency misaligned for a prolonged period would tend to compensate in the opposite direction in the next period. To the extent that monetary authorities struggle against market forces to keep a currency undervalued or overvalued, moreover, the exchange rate could be expected to exhibit greater volatility in the short term as well.

the breakdown of Bretton Woods. The Japanese government, for example, strongly resisted the appreciation of the yen above 150 in early 1987, and then in 1989 it strongly resisted depreciation below these levels. These adjustments in policy goals have been reactive rather than self-initiated. German adjustments of desirable exchange rates have been more incremental, grounded in a continuous reassessment of comparative cost.

Japan responded to the first and second major appreciations by allowing the yen to fall thereafter, thus offsetting the loss of competitiveness. This strong revealed preference for low valuation was one important reason Japan received so little cooperation from the Americans and Europeans when market forces placed strong upward pressure on the yen. Exchange rate outcomes reflect the lower stability of policy. The D-mark and yen followed similar long-term trends in nominal and real effective terms since the early 1970s. But, owing to the Japanese government's willingness to allow the yen to slide to compensate for previous spurts of appreciation, the yen experienced short- and medium-term exchange rate volatility twice that of the D-mark.[30]

In the policies that Germany and Japan pursued with respect to the dollar, their governments and central banks followed in large measure the policy evolution of the American administration. When the United States pursued a policy of neglect, foreign governments intervened less frequently in the market. This was not because these governments did not prefer exchange rate stability; they did. German and Japanese authorities cut back on intervention because they recognized that it would be less effective when undertaken without the participation of US authorities.

Review

A couple of revealing comparisons capture the fundamental differences among the United States, Germany, and Japan in external monetary policymaking. The effectiveness of private-sector coalitions pleading for a limitation of currency appreciation differed markedly between Germany and Japan, on the one hand, and the United States, on the other. During 1977 and 1986, German and Japanese producers complained to their respective governments after moderate appreciations of their currencies against the dollar, and they amplified their complaints as their

---

30. The standard deviation of the monthly exchange rate from the one- and two-year moving averages has been more than twice as large for Japan as for Germany. Calculated by the author from nominal effective exchange rate statistics (MERM) provided by the International Monetary Fund, *International Financial Statistics*. For a comparison of the monthly percentage change of the MERM rate for Germany and Japan, see Tavlas, *On the International Use of Currencies*, table 2, p. 16.

currencies rose further over 1978 and 1987. Government policy in both countries responded to the competitiveness problem by trying to limit the appreciation. During the only episode of comparable appreciation of the dollar, 1981–85, American producers also complained to the Reagan administration. Before 1985, the administration virtually ignored their plea, in marked contrast to the governmental response to the private sector in Japan and Germany. One important reason for the difference, as the following section argues, lies in the breadth of the private-sector coalition. American producer interests eventually succeeded by appealing to the Congress, which in turn threatened to torpedo the administration's open trade policy. That confrontational recourse was not necessary in Germany and Japan.

The Reagan administration's initial response to the pain of traded goods producers was cavalier. Faced in 1984 with an unprecedented fiscal deficit and a growing trade deficit, the Regan Treasury embarked on a campaign to finance these deficits rather than to adjust. President Reagan denied that the unprecedented pressure on traded goods producers and the trade deficit was a problem. In his 1985 State of the Union speech, delivered when the dollar neared a two-decade high, he called for making the United States the "investment capital of the world." This episode is not representative; it was unusual, even for American policy. The key point is that this would never happen in Germany and Japan. Even the most aberrant of policy outcomes in these two countries are far more favorable to the competitiveness needs of traded-goods producers.

This section has provided a comparison of the pattern of policy outcomes for the postwar period as a whole. There have been, of course, considerable changes over time in the external monetary behavior of each of these countries. The change has arguably been greatest for Japan. Those changes are discussed and explained at the end of the following section.

Explaining Policy Outcomes

We now complete the explanation for the differences in policy among the three countries considered in this study. The previous section described the historical pattern of policy outcomes—the dependent variable of the study—for the United States, Germany, and Japan. This section links those outcomes to the discussion of bank-industry relations discussed in chapter 2 and central bank independence and institutional arrangements discussed in chapter 3. The institutional organization of the private and public sectors, the reader will recall, jointly determines policy outcomes. These are not the only relevant variables. But they are the variables, this study argues, that provide the most complete interpretation of the differences in policy outcomes among these countries.

Figure 7.1 Countries and independent variables

Central bank status

	Subordinate	Independent
Weak	(Britain)	United States
Strong	Japan (France)	Germany

Connection between banks and industry (left axis label, rows Weak / Strong)

Britain and France are listed here for comparative purposes, although they are not the subject of case studies in this book. Reforms in early 1994 granted a degree of independence to the Bank of France, and this could change the classification of France in the future.

The Main Argument

The three countries considered here have three different combinations of the independent variables, as described in the matrix in chapter 1, reproduced here as figure 7.1. Each combination has produced a different pattern of policy outcomes. Those connections are reviewed here for each country; the specific roles of the independent variables are then discussed.

Japan has had strong ties between private banks and industry and a central bank that is subordinate to the Ministry of Finance. Private Japanese preferences favored a low-valued yen during most of the postwar period. The collective dominance of bureaucrats in the Ministry of Finance and the politicians of the Liberal Democratic Party (which dominated most of the postwar governments) over the Bank of Japan provided an efficient conduit through which those preferences were relatively faithfully transmitted into policy. At several key junctures, the Bank of Japan was unable to resist pressure from the ministry and from politicians to ease monetary policy to moderate the appreciation of the yen.

In Germany, close ties between banking and industry underpinned a consensus in favor of a competitive and stable external valuation of the D-mark. The government and the Bundesbank did their best to serve this consensus, and tried to reconcile conflicts between exchange rate stability and domestic monetary stability. But when that conflict became irreconcilable and unavoidable, the independence of the Bundesbank asserted itself over private preferences for competitiveness. Thus, domestic monetary policy was targeted toward the exchange rate less frequently in Germany than in Japan.

US external monetary policy, in contrast with German and Japanese policy, had no firm anchor in private preferences. Without strong ties between banks and industry, the private sector sent weak, discordant, and conflicting signals to government policymakers regarding its exchange rate preferences, though the mid-1980s represented a notable exception. The Treasury and Federal Reserve thus were relatively autonomous and unconstrained by private pressures during most of the postwar period. The exchange rate was treated as the residual of domestic macroeconomic policies until it created severe problems for the balance of payments and trade policy. State autonomy also rendered exchange rate policy vulnerable to capture by ideological political appointees. These tendencies created a cyclical pattern of neglect and activism in policy outcomes.

Role of Private Preferences

This study argues that societal preferences, and the private-sector institutions through which they are formed, are fundamental to understanding external monetary policy outcomes. Agencies of the government act and react to developments in exchange markets with these private-sector preferences in mind, particularly when those preferences are clearly articulated. Government institutions do not by any means automatically satisfy private preferences. They have their own set of preferences that are partly independent from societal interests. But, especially in the absence of countervailing considerations, government ministries and central banks serve their private sectors and ignore or oppose societal preferences at risk to their autonomy.

The structure of the national financial system—and in particular the relationship between banks and industry that derives from financial structure—strongly conditions the external monetary preferences of the private sector. Within the credit-based systems of Germany and Japan, banks have large portfolios of loans to industrial firms, equity stakes in many firms, and substantial participation in corporate management. As a result, German and Japanese banking institutions historically have been vitally interested in the international competitiveness and success of their corporate clients, to a degree far beyond American banks. Bank-industry ties reinforced interest aggregation and enhanced access to policymaking on the part of producer interests in Germany and Japan.

German and Japanese external monetary policy has therefore been solidly grounded in private-sector preferences. The private consensus on the need for a competitively valued currency was clearly communicated to policymakers in both countries. That voice was not unanimous in either Germany or Japan; but a clear majority of the private sector underpinned a national consensus favoring a competitive and stable external valuation of the currency.

The communication between private banks and governments on sensitive financial matters such as foreign exchange is generally highly confidential and closely guarded. As a result, access to direct evidence of the influence of banks over governments in this secretive policy domain is restricted. There is nonetheless a significant body of accumulated evidence that suggests that bank-industry relations, bank preferences, and bank influence have affected policy outcomes importantly.

The role of banks in domestic opposition to revaluations was especially prominent in Germany and Japan under, and during the demise of, the Bretton Woods regime. Owing to their stakes in industrial exports, banks opposed the pro-revaluation movements that were formed, primarily by academic and official economists, in both countries. The intensity of the banks' opposition subsided under the flexible exchange rate regime as their interests became more complex over time. German and Japanese banks nonetheless continued to form part of the pro-producer coalition on exchange rates when the D-mark and yen rose sharply against the dollar during the late 1970s and mid-1980s.

The German banking community did not oppose the creation of the European Monetary System. Some influential Frankfurt bankers, in fact, endorsed the EMS and the drive for Economic and Monetary Union with enthusiasm. European currency stabilization, among other reasons, had produced a depreciation of the D-mark in real terms over the 1980s and thus important competitiveness improvements for German industry. In the debate within Germany over EMU, the views of the major German banks conflicted sharply with those of a number of German academic economists opposed to the Maastricht Treaty.

In the United States, by contrast, the banking community's interest in corporate competitiveness was, though present, considerably smaller. Within the capital market–based system of industrial finance, the US banks developed a much more attenuated relationship with corporations. American banks were typically not allies of industry in seeking low or stable currency valuation. In the relatively rare cases in which they became strongly engaged on this policy question, American banks pressed for government intervention to support a precipitously dropping dollar. As a result, the American private sector had much more complex, pluralistic, and varied preferences with respect to the exchange rate than did the private sectors in Germany and Japan.

American policymakers, therefore, tended to receive conflicting guidance of relatively low intensity from different quarters of the private sector—if they received any guidance at all. With one notable exception, the private sector was of little constraint—or usefulness—to American officials in making exchange rate policy. Whereas German and Japanese authorities pursued a more competitiveness-conscious, stability-oriented set of policies, American authorities neglected competitiveness considerations far more often when formulating policy.

The episode of the 1980s is the exception to this general pattern, and one that demonstrates the rule. With many American banks unsympathetic to industry's problems, the financial sector did not participate in the political movement to limit the appreciation of the dollar during the first Reagan administration. With far less leverage over the management of industrial enterprises than their foreign counterparts, some bank CEOs hoped that the appreciation of the dollar would force rationalization and cost saving upon what they then perceived to be a spendthrift and undisciplined industrial sector. With only one or two exceptions, no strong advocates emerged in the financial community for foreign exchange intervention or an easing of monetary policy to stem the dollar's rise. Most influential commercial and investment bankers neither actively opposed nor actively supported those corporate officials from the real sector who called for a depreciation of the dollar in 1982–85. American bankers sent strong warnings to the Treasury on exchange rate policy only when the dollar dropped precipitously and threatened to destabilize the other financial markets during the first weeks of 1987.

The US experience of the 1980s shows that close bank-industry relations are not strictly necessary for private preferences to exert themselves strongly over officials responsible for exchange rate policy. Under conditions of rapidly increasing import penetration and trade deficits, producer interests secured a more competitiveness-conscious policy without the active support of private bankers. Extreme conditions were required to produce this policy change, however, and the reversion toward neglect under the Bush administration shows that a competitiveness orientation is difficult to sustain in the absence of supporting private preferences that are broadly organized.

Aside from their effect on bank-industry relations within each country, national financial systems affected exchange rate policy through a second channel. In particular, financial structures affected exchange rate policy also through market constraints imposed by the international role of the currency. Japan and Germany, with traditionally bank-intermediated financial systems, were slow to liberalize financial markets; this in turn constrained financial liquidity and diversity and limited the international attractiveness of their currencies. The United States, on the other hand, has prided itself on its broad and deep financial markets. American authorities have granted liberal access to those financial markets for the multifaceted purposes, including foreign exchange hedging and speculation, of private and official international actors. (The IET is an exception to this rule.) The US financial markets and the access to them enjoyed by financial institutions worldwide have buoyed the international popularity of the dollar for both portfolio and vehicle purposes.

The popularity of the dollar has enabled American borrowers to avoid exchange rate risk. Moreover, on the margin, the dollar's role has facilitated the financing of American current account deficits (though the value of this seigniorage is often greatly exaggerated). The international role of the currency has also entailed great costs for the United States, however. Large foreign holdings of dollars constrained US authorities from devaluing the dollar under Bretton Woods. Preserving the dollar's role and preventing panic flight away from the US currency acted as one incentive, among others, to tighten monetary policy to prevent a precipitous depreciation in autumn 1978 and early 1987. Large international holdings of the currency made the US dollar more vulnerable to speculation, particularly during crises. These holdings contributed to a US policy that countenanced excessive valuation and fluctuation of the currency. Japanese and German authorities effectively avoided this complication, on anything like the American scale, during most of the postwar period.

Role of Central Bank Independence

Government institutions, as stated above, do not passively translate private preferences directly into policy in unadulterated form. Like a prism, the political and policy process refracts private preferences in the process of translating them into policy outcomes. How private preferences are transmitted into policy depends on the organization of the institutions of government, specifically the status of the central bank and the arrangements for external monetary policymaking.

A comparison of Japan and Germany puts the importance of central bank independence into stark relief. The banking community had a similar interest in industrial competitiveness in each of the two countries, but differences in central bank independence produced differences in policy outcomes. In the United States, the absence of any private sector consensus on currency matters left the independent Federal Reserve without societal opposition or guidance.

In Japan, the central bank was subordinate to the Ministry of Finance, which gave the prime minister, finance minister, and the cabinet direct influence over Japanese exchange rate policy. The bureaucrats in the Ministry of Finance could often successfully shield their core priorities, such as fiscal deficit reduction, from the political pressures coming from the Liberal Democratic Party. But frequently, this shield did not also protect lesser priorities of the ministry, such as exchange rate policy, or protect the Bank of Japan. Accordingly, private preferences and pressures were transmitted through the ministry and central bank into exter-

nal and domestic monetary policy. Government institutions in Japan refracted private preferences less than did government institutions in Germany. As the previous section demonstrated, Japanese authorities were
most likely to intervene in the foreign exchange market, employ capital
controls to manage the exchange rate and balance of payments, and
adjust domestic monetary policy for exchange rate objectives.

In Germany, by contrast, private preferences were not translated into
policy outcomes as directly. At key points, the Bundesbank was able to
block the transmission of these preferences into policy outcomes. When
low valuation of the D-mark unavoidably conflicted with fighting inflation, the Bundesbank would accept appreciation. There were times when
the Bundesbank acquiesced up to a point in an undervalued D-mark out
of fear for its independence in the face of an angry bank-industry coalition.[31] But the German central bank nonetheless overruled export (and
import-competing) interests more frequently than did the Bank of Japan.

The difference in the domestic status of the Bank of Japan and Bundesbank revealed itself in policy outcomes in several instances. Whereas
Japan accepted no revaluation under the Bretton Woods regime and clung
tenaciously to the 360 parity for two weeks even after the first Nixon shock
of August 1971, Germany countenanced two revaluations, in 1961 and
1969, and floated the D-mark in May 1971. While Japan used the switch
to floating exchange rates as an opportunity to inject a burst of monetary
growth, Germany used it as an opportunity to tighten monetary policy.
When the yen and D-mark were weak at the beginning of the 1980s, the
Bank of Japan eased domestic monetary policy while the Bundesbank
tightened policy. After the reemergence of macroeconomic policy coordination in the mid-1980s, Japanese monetary authorities advertised a willingness to cooperate on monetary policy that the Bundesbank did not.
Though both central banks eased monetary policy to stem upward pressure on their currencies during 1986–87, the Bank of Japan kept policy
relaxed for more than a year after the Bundesbank retightened policy.

Relatively weak, confused, and conflicting signals from the American
private sector rarely offered reliable guidance for the US government.
By the same token, though, this fact ensured that American governing
institutions were autonomous and unconstrained by private pressures.[32]
For most of the postwar period, private preferences on exchange rates

---

31. John B. Goodman, "The Politics of Central Bank Independence," *Comparative Politics*
23 (April 1991): 329–49.

32. This was the conventional interpretation of US exchange rate policymaking during
the 1960s and 1970s. See Stephen D. Krasner, "United States Commercial and Monetary
Policy," in *Between Power and Plenty*, Katzenstein, ed.; Odell, *U.S. International Monetary
Policy*; Gowa, *Closing the Gold Window*. The 1980s showed that the observed autonomy
of the state had been due to the absence of private political activity as much as to state
strength per se.

rarely presented a threat to the inflation-fighting efforts of the Federal Reserve. Until the mid-1980s, the Treasury was similarly unconstrained by the private sector.

The key questions of American external monetary policy were governed through the uneasy modus vivendi struck between the Treasury and Federal Reserve, which left the policy process more segmented than in the other two countries. The Fed and Treasury often agreed on basic matters of exchange rate policy, of course. Nonetheless, conflicts between them rendered intervention policy episodic. Divisions among government institutions and the short attention span of senior politicians on currency matters contributed to periodicity in policy activism. No societal consensus on external monetary objectives adjudicated conflicts politically between the two bureaucracies or otherwise compelled them to cooperate. Because these institutions were not grounded in a solid private-sector consensus, policy countenanced large overvaluations for sustained periods under trade deficits, in sharp contrast to German and Japanese policy.

The domestic politics of exchange rate policy changed greatly in the United States during the 1980s, as reviewed in chapter 6. The strong dollar and resulting import penetration drove traded-goods producers into the political arena with unprecedented vigor. Their effort succeeded in inducing the second Reagan administration to jettison its hands-off attitude toward the dollar and to seek a depreciation and then stabilization. The shift was accomplished, without the active support of banks, through the Congress, which used its powers of legislation in both trade and exchange rate areas. Treasury's policy shift was limited, however, by the stance of the Federal Reserve, which, concerned about inflation, tightened monetary policy in 1987. This prompted Secretary Baker to agree to stabilize exchange rates prematurely at the Louvre. Once the dollar reached a competitive range, in late 1987 and early 1988, maintaining that range during the Bush administration foundered, in the absence of a supportive private consensus, on the Fed's tightening of monetary policy to control inflation and the Fed's resistance to foreign exchange operations that would limit renewed appreciation.

Central Bank–Ministry Arrangements Regarding Intervention

The nature of the division of responsibility for external monetary policy between the central bank and finance ministry (reviewed in chapter 3) supplements the other two independent variables. The tendency for US policy to lapse into periodic neglect was accentuated by the fact that the Treasury and the Fed effectively share authority over foreign exchange intervention. A former chairman of the Federal Reserve Board, Paul A. Volcker, writes:[33]

---

33. Volcker and Gyohten, *Changing Fortunes*, p. 235.

[The distribution of authority between the Treasury and the Fed] often leads, I must confess, to rather inefficient stop-and-start operations. . . . [D]uring operations, an inordinate amount of time is taken to reconcile differences. The bureaucratic problems are not unique to the United States government and are apt to arise in any country where the authority to act is shared. But this is one of those areas where our system of checks and balances often works against effective results. The people actually doing the intervention need enough authority and flexibility to react to market conditions as they occur, not after an ad hoc conference in Washington.

Unit-veto decision making on foreign exchange intervention thus creates a bias toward inaction when such operations would otherwise be desirable.[34]

Because the Bank of Japan is subordinate to the Ministry of Finance, intervention authority is not similarly divided in Japan. Because there is a more clearly articulated agreement between the Bundesbank and the Bonn government on intervention responsibilities, particularly regarding the EMS currencies, divided authority does not create this same bias toward inaction in Germany either. Central bank–ministry coordination poses a lesser challenge to a currency policy oriented toward a competitive and stable external valuation in Japan and Germany.

Aside from contributing to the differences in policy outcomes among the three countries, these interbureaucratic arrangements for external monetary policymaking also contribute to differences in the efficacy of foreign exchange intervention among them. There are three reasons why institutional arrangements and the efficiency of unilateral intervention are connected. First, foreign exchange intervention usually bets the resources of the central bank. Finance ministries are less likely to be cautious and parsimonious in the use of central banks' funds than are the central banks themselves.[35] Second, when the central bank operates alone, the timing and strategy is best-suited to its objectives in exchange rate management. When the central bank must negotiate with the finance ministry over the terms, conditions, and timing of intervention, by contrast, its operational flexibility is restricted and its actions are more likely to be less than optimal. As the former deputy governor of the Bank of Japan, Shijuro Ogata, writes, "[E]xchange market intervention can be useful, but in a number of countries the too tight control over intervention policy by their treasuries tends to make exchange market intervention inflexible and ineffective."[36] Third, foreign exchange interventions

---

34. Volcker observes that the Treasury has typically been the more reluctant of the two bureaucracies to intervene. Volcker and Gyohten, *Changing Fortunes*, p. 234.

35. In US intervention over the decades, the instances in which only Treasury funds are used are rare.

36. Shijuro Ogata, "Central Banking: A Japanese Perspective," in *International Finance and Financial Policy*, Hans R. Stoll, ed. (New York: Quorum Books, 1990), pp. 117–21. The quotation appears on p. 121.

that are conducted at the discretion of the central bank might be perceived by the markets as signals about the future direction of domestic monetary policy.[37] Foreign exchange intervention conducted by the finance ministry would not provide signals about monetary policy when the central bank is independent.

Intervention efficiency among these countries is inversely related to the degree of involvement of the finance ministry in foreign exchange operations. When engaging in operations in the dollar market that are not concerted among the three central banks, the Bundesbank and Federal Reserve are widely acknowledged as getting more short-term bang for the intervention buck than is the Bank of Japan. Of the two most effective central banks, the Bundesbank is reputed to get marginally better returns per dollar of intervention than does the Fed.[38] Private speculators in the foreign exchange markets for the dollar fear the Bundesbank, respect the Federal Reserve, and at times discount the Bank of Japan.[39]

However, the Bundesbank appears to have maintained its reputation for effectiveness in part by withdrawing from the dollar market when market forces were strong, specifically to preserve its credibility. The Bundesbank's intervention reputation in the markets for the European currencies, moreover, suffered from the 1992–93 crises in the ERM along with those of the other European central banks. Thus, the reputation for being an effective intervenor corresponds with the size of foreign currency operations, which, in turn, is also a function of institutional arrangements.[40]

Extending the Argument to Britain and France

The argument developed here also applies to the cases of Britain and France. These two remaining members of the Group of Five (G-5) have

---

37. For a discussion of the effects of intervention through this signaling channel, see Dominguez and Frankel, *Does Foreign Exchange Intervention Work?*, pp. 58–60.

38. The former head of foreign exchange operations for the Bundesbank, Franz Scholl, once complained about the intervention tactics of the Federal Reserve Bank of New York. He said that the Fed's actions reminded him of his cat. "You never hear it. You never know when it's operating. And you never know if it's caught anything." Quoted in Marsh, *The Bundesbank*, p. 85.

39. No study of which this author is aware quantifies the relative effectiveness of intervention by different central banks. This ranking is based on private assessments on the part of market participants, officials, and observers interviewed by the author. Although these assessments are informal, the consensus on this ranking is quite broad.

40. Getting the most bang for the buck should not be the highest priority of external monetary policy, of course. Pursuing appropriate exchange rate goals is far more important than maintaining maximum credibility in intervention operations. This analysis illustrates, rather, the relevance of arrangements between the central bank and government to exchange rate management.

not been the focus of this study, principally because they have been treated in considerable depth elsewhere.[41] Possessing subordinated central banks during the period under review, these two countries would appear in the two left-hand quadrants of the matrix in figure 7.1. (In early 1994, the Bank of France was granted a significant degree of independence in determining domestic monetary policy.) Differences between them in bank-industry relations, however, produced striking differences in historical policy outcomes. For most of the postwar period, France had a highly intermediated financial system that compares with the credit-based systems of Germany and particularly Japan. Britain had a capital market–based system that compares with that of the United States.[42]

In its attentiveness to competitiveness, as the argument presented here would suggest, French policy was similar to that of Germany and Japan. Both France and Britain experienced substantial domestic inflation during the postwar period. Rather than countenance an appreciation of the French franc in real terms, the French government frequently devalued and depreciated the currency. The real value of the franc has been remarkably stable as a result. Like Japan, France readily resorted to capital controls to protect the currency and balance of payments, and thereby discouraged the international use of the franc. Depreciations notwithstanding, the French government has characteristically been the most conscious of exchange rate stability among the G-5. At the regional level, France, with Germany, created the EMS.

Rather than sympathize with industry, by contrast, the British banking community was firmly wedded to the international financial status of the City of London. Under fixed exchange rates, the city perceived a high and stable valuation of the pound sterling to be very much in its interest as a financial center. The city exerted its preferences on treasury's external monetary policy through the Bank of England.[43] The Bank of England, lacking independence on domestic monetary policy, welcomed the fixing of the parity as a counterweight to political pressure to reduce interest rates.

As a result, Britain repeatedly experienced overvaluation of the pound sterling dating back to the interwar period. Winston Churchill's fateful decision as chancellor of the exchequer to repeg the pound to its pre–

---

41. For the comparison between France and Britain, see Hall, *Governing the Economy*, especially pp. 244–45, 250–51; Katzenstein, ed., *Between Power and Plenty*.

42. Zysman, *Governments, Markets, and Growth*; Cox, *State, Finance, and Industry*; Geoffrey Ingham, *Capitalism Divided? The City and Industry in British Social Development* (New York: Schocken Books, 1984), pp. 62–78.

43. See, for example, Stephen Blank, "Britain," in *Between Power and Plenty*, P. Katzenstein, ed., pp. 89–138; Frank Longstreth, "The City, Industry, and the State," in *State and Economy in Contemporary Capitalism*, Colin Crouch, ed. (New York: St. Martin's Press, 1979), pp. 157–190.

World War I parity in 1925 is arguably the most notorious error in international monetary history. Under the Bretton Woods regime, rather than devalue the pound, Britain interrupted expansionary policies when inflation worsened and the balance of payments deficit rose to a level that could not be financed. The one exception, the devaluation of 1967, was too small and delayed to rescue British competitiveness.

Under floating exchange rates, Britain was complacent in the face of extreme swings in the value of its currency. The pound appreciated a stunning 87 percent in real terms between the end of 1976 and beginning of 1981, with the blessing of the Callaghan and Thatcher governments. None of the other four currencies within the G-5 ever displayed as sharp a movement at any time over the postwar period.

At the European level, in contrast to France, the Callaghan government refused to participate in the EMS when it was created. The Thatcher governments steadfastly refused to join the system throughout the 1980s. Moreover, when Britain finally entered the ERM in autumn 1990, John Major as chancellor of the exchequer established a substantially overvalued central rate for the pound! This decision, reminiscent of Churchill's mistake in 1925, met a calamitous conclusion in the European currency crisis of September 1992.[44] During the two-year debate in Britain over the central rate for the pound, remarkably, industry came to favor a devaluation while the City of London remained implacably opposed.

The British pattern of policy outcomes compares to US policy in its tolerance of overvaluation, flexibility, and misalignments. The comparison between Britain and the United States, as between Britain and France, reinforces the conclusion that private preferences are fundamental. Britain and the United States exhibit similar policy outcomes regardless of the independence of the central bank in the US case. Only when private preferences favor a low-valued currency does central bank independence become especially meaningful for external monetary policy. Uniting policy authority through central bank subordination can be no substitute for anchoring public institutions in a broad private-sector consensus.

Distance between banks and industry creates choices among their varied preferences over which politicians, parties, and ministries' bureaucracies contend. Capital market–based financial systems, in other words, open the space for political conflict over exchange rate policy. Credit-based financial systems narrow the range of policy choices that will be tolerated by the private sector. Close relations between banks and industry offer less scope for, and even penalize, contentious, distributive, partisan politics over external monetary policy. Accordingly, the exchange rate has been used for partisan economic purposes in the United States

---

44. For a comparison of French and British policies during the crises within the ERM, see David R. Cameron, "British Exit, German Voice, French Loyalty: Defection, Domination, and Cooperation in the 1992–93 ERM Crisis," manuscript, Yale University, 1993.

and Britain, whereas this has been rare or impossible in Germany, Japan, and France.

The comparison between Britain and the United States also demonstrates that the openness of the economy, as measured by trade flows relative to domestic output, does not alone underpin policies that are conscious of exchange rate stability and oriented toward competitiveness. Openness instead accentuates opportunities for governments to use the external sector for their economic purposes, even if those purposes are narrow or partisan. Governments are more likely to use the external sector to impose cost discipline on the domestic economy, as both the Thatcher and Reagan governments did, at the expense of international competitiveness when banks are distant from industry and private preferences for competitiveness are weak and feebly articulated.

Change and Continuity

The preceding argument explains the difference in policy outcomes for the postwar period as a whole. Does the argument, though, explain the trends and changes in external monetary policy exhibited by the three countries since the late 1980s? Central bank independence has been relatively constant over the last decade; thus it can explain continuity but not change in policy outcomes. Bank-industry relations, by contrast, have changed substantially. As the argument advanced above would suggest, moreover, the country whose domestic financial system and bank-industry relations changed the most, Japan, also experienced the greatest change in external monetary policy.

Recall from chapter 2 that, of the three countries considered here, the German financial system has changed the least, the American financial system has changed somewhat, and the Japanese financial system has changed the most. In particular, Japanese bank financing of manufacturing corporations, as measured by bank loans to this sector as a percentage of total bank loans, declined markedly during the 1980s (table 2.5). Bank ownership of corporate equity and involvement in corporate management were relatively constant. Banks remain much closer to industry in Japan than they are in the United States, for example. Nonetheless, the fall in bank exposure to the manufacturing sector through the loan portfolio represents a significant change within Japan over time.

Japanese external monetary policy has changed accordingly since the mid-1980s. Whereas the Japanese government countenanced a reversal of the first and second realignments of the yen—particularly in real terms— it opposed the reversal of the third realignment of 1985–87. The Ministry of Finance and Bank of Japan intervened vigorously to try to prevent the third realignment as it was occurring. But, once the realignment had taken place, the Japanese ministries did not seek a reversal. Although the markets eventually drove the yen down to 160 to the dollar in spring 1990, the Ministry of Finance and Bank of Japan intervened to prevent the exchange rate from moving above the 132 level in spring 1989 and intensified their intervention in 1990. This signaled a sharp break from the exchange rate preferences revealed by Japanese authorities' intervention behavior in the past.

The Japanese trade and current account surpluses facilitated the shift, naturally. Notably, however, this policy shift occurred when the external surplus was declining and *before* the surge in the surplus of 1992–93 had begun. In 1993, Japanese authorities accepted the rise of the yen to the 110–120 range and, after unsuccessfully resisting further appreciation, did not actively seek to drive the currency below the 100–110 range. Japanese authorities thus accepted the yen's appreciation to record levels not only in nominal bilateral terms but in real effective terms as well.

In Germany, the change in bank-industry relations has been relatively small and gradual, in spite of the unification of the country. Accordingly, the private sector preferences for German external monetary policy have remained very stable. The new developments in German policy—principally the commitment to Economic and Monetary Union under the Maastricht Treaty—reflect long-held private-sector preferences for exchange rate stability. Private-sector preferences are not the only impetus for German pursuit of EMU. Monetary integration is wrapped in a much larger set of issues relating to Germany's commitment to the European Union. Nonetheless, the political decision to proceed with EMU, qualified though it may be, is consistent with German private-sector preferences.

In the United States, as recounted in chapter 2, the banks experienced increased disintermediation during the 1980s. US exchange rate policy was quite competitiveness-oriented during the second half of the decade, a shift seemingly at odds with the trend toward disintermediation. Does this contradict the argument linking bank-industry relations to external monetary preferences? The answer is no, for several reasons.

Separate the long-term trend in the pattern of American policy outcomes from changes over the course of the policy cycle. With a large and growing trade deficit, American exchange rate policy was likely to become more competitiveness-oriented in the mid-1980s, as it did in 1971 and 1977. The influence of the trade balance has always been present in the American syndrome of policy cycles. The argument here is not that bank-industry relations are the sole determinant of policy, simply that they are fundamental. The persistence of the US trade deficit through the 1980s and first half of the 1990s has prolonged the trade-sensitive phase but has not ended the cyclical pattern of American policy. It would be premature to describe US policy as having undergone a permanent shift in the direction of greater sensitivity to the competitiveness of industry. The test of this contention will come when the United States returns to rough balance in the trade account. The Treasury's retreat from an activist policy under Secretary Brady—exemplified in part by the decision not to support the Japanese yen in 1990—at a time when the trade deficit was declining but far from extinguished lends credence to the prediction that policy cycles are likely to recur.

The disintermediation of American banks in the 1980s made it all the less likely that banks would ally with industry to cap the strong dollar in the mid-1980s and thus provide a solid political foundation preventing a retreat under Secretary Brady from the Baker policies. Continued disintermediation works against the emergence of an American private-sector consensus that could underpin policy consistency and put a permanent end to the cyclical pattern of policy change at that point in the indefinite future when the trade account returns to balance.

8

Lessons, Observations, and Recommendations

The review of policymaking in this book has identified and analyzed three factors fundamental to the conduct of external monetary policy in the United States, Germany, and Japan: the preferences of private actors, the status of the central bank (independent or subordinate), and the arrangements between central banks and governments regarding external monetary policy. In this chapter, we examine the ramifications of these findings to identify the institutional framework and policymaking processes that best facilitate successful policy outcomes and international cooperation.

The analysis that follows changes the course set in the previous chapters in two respects. First, the previous chapters conducted a positive analysis, examining the causal links among private preferences, public institutions, and policy outcomes. This chapter is normative, or prescriptive, and thus issues recommendations for changes in institutions and policy processes in the United States, Japan, Germany, and the European Union. Second, while earlier chapters examined the domestic sources of external monetary policy outcomes, this chapter extends that analysis to the effects on international cooperation. The proposals made in this chapter have the dual purpose of improving policy outcomes for each country and improving international macroeconomic cooperation.

The first section reviews the lessons drawn from the positive analysis that bear on the architecture of national institutions and the design of policy processes. The second section addresses the relationship between domestic institutions and policymaking, on the one hand, and international cooperation on the other. The third section offers a set of institutional recommendations, in some cases far-reaching, for the United States, Japan, Germany, and the European Union.

Lessons

The first lesson of this analysis is that private-sector preferences, and how they are aggregated and expressed, are central to explaining the differences in policy outcomes among countries and basic to generating policies that serve the exchange rate needs of producers exposed to international competition. Close relations between banks and industry, in particular, help to solidify a private-sector consensus in favor of a policy that is oriented to a competitive and stable external value for the national currency. These ties help to anchor the governmental institutions with a sense of broad, national purpose and objectives when making policy. Clear societal preferences give guidance for resolving conflicts among public institutions and government agencies. Without clearly articulated private preferences, which are less likely to form when banks and industry are distant, policy is more likely to become detached from the interests of sectors engaged in international competition.

A second lesson of this analysis is that the status of the central bank—independent or subordinate—determines the extent to which private preferences for a low-valued currency are translated into policy. Central banks and other government institutions, in the absence of countervailing considerations, are predisposed to serve their private sectors. But, when domestic inflation is high, central bank independence serves as an important check on the demands of traded-goods producers for a low-valued currency. The independence of central banks, where it exists, limits the extent to which domestic monetary policy will be targeted toward external objectives. By contrast, central banks that are subordinate to the government offer relatively weak resistance to pressures to ease monetary policy to maintain low valuation of the currency.

A third major lesson is that the relationship between the central bank and government—the finance ministry in particular—on external monetary issues is an important, secondary determinant of the quality of policy outputs. In countries where the central bank is independent, the central bank's preference for domestic price stability inevitably will collide with the preferences of other government ministries to serve competitiveness. The designated division of labor between the central bank and finance ministry, the clarity of their understanding (regarding intervention responsibilities, for example), and the extent to which the arrangement receives endorsement in the broader political sphere, including the other government ministries, the national legislature, political parties, and private actors, will determine whether and how those conflicts are resolved.

Establishing the institutional prerogatives of the two bureaucracies, including the conduct of negotiations with foreign governments over the pegging of the currency, renegotiations over parities, and intervention in the foreign exchange markets, among other institutional authorities, is a contentious process. Central banks and finance ministries thus avoid clearly specifying which institution will exercise these prerogatives unless they are forced to do so by actual participation in an exchange rate stabilization mechanism or an unavoidable realignment of currency values. And, of course, the absence of a clear agreement between them can cause central banks and finance ministries to miss opportunities for exchange rate stabilization and international cooperation.

Of the three countries considered here, Germany's private-sector organization and public institutions historically have served the country's interests in external monetary policy best. The Bundesbank is independent and has a relatively well-articulated agreement with the government in Bonn governing Germany's participation in the European Monetary System (EMS). German policymaking, of course, did not always proceeded smoothly over the decades. The Bundesbank and government ministries, in fact, fought bitterly over external monetary policy at times. But, even when sharp conflicts arose, the Bundesbank and government were compelled to resolve their differences by a private-sector consensus that valued external stability of the D-mark at exchange rates consistent with basic cost comparisons with foreign partners.

German policy outcomes, described in chapter 5, have thus served Germany very well in the postwar period. Although German policy has committed errors, external monetary policy generally was oriented to external stability and competitiveness and was consistent in these respects over time. The German government maintained the conditions in which German industry could flourish in European and world markets. Germany racked up enormous trade surpluses and a large net creditor position. The large trade surpluses of the late 1980s were not themselves necessarily welfare-enhancing, but they placed the Federal Republic in an advantageous position to absorb East Germany in 1990 without falling prey to a balance-of-payments or foreign exchange crisis. Further, Germany accomplished these external goals without, as was often feared, fundamentally undermining domestic price stability.

German institutions and policy consistency provided a durable basis for the development of the EMS and the expansion of its membership through 1990. The private consensus favoring external stability for the D-mark underpinned Germany's commitment to European monetary integration. The independence of the Bundesbank secured the commitment to price stability as the fundamental objective toward which Germany would lead the EMS. The institutional agreement between the government and the Bundesbank provided a framework in which the conflict that arose periodically for Germany from EMS participation, between exchange rate stability on the one hand and domestic price stability on the other, could be mediated. When resolving that conflict depended on securing the agreement of other European countries to pursue monetary restraint, German internal institutional arrangements became a source of bargaining leverage. Because the Bundesbank and the objective of domestic price stability held privileged status in Germany, reflected in the terms of the Bundesbank-government bargain over EMS participation, the high-inflation European countries were confronted with the choice between monetary restraint and leaving the system. As a result, the EMS evolved and prospered on German, not French or Italian, terms. The German position would have been far less dominant within the EMS had the German government, under the terms of its EMS arrangement with the Bundesbank, been able to extract an expansionary domestic monetary policy.

The institutional strength of the Bundesbank is often blamed for the unraveling of the ERM during the crises of 1992 and 1993. But the main culprit in the ERM fiasco was the conflict between the fiscal policy pursued by the German federal government in the wake of unification and the resistance on the part of other European governments, in which the German government acquiesced, to a devaluation of their currencies against the D-mark. Given the decision to countenance huge public-sector budget deficits, the appropriate exchange rate policy was to allow the D-mark to appreciate substantially against the currencies of the European partners beginning as early as 1990 or 1991. That Bonn deferred to French opposition on this matter, rather than confronted Paris directly, represents a failure of policy. The institutional arrangement between the government and the Bundesbank on European currency matters is not the chief source of this policy error. German unification, furthermore, is a highly exceptional political event and by no means nullifies the achievements of German policy over the postwar period.

German policymaking institutions have not served German interests perfectly, however. Although not the main culprit of the 1992–93 Exchange Rate Mechanism (ERM) debacle, the Bundesbank raised interest rates higher and lowered them more slowly than was probably necessary to combat domestic inflation. Rather than ease more quickly, and thereby forestall or avoid the splintering of the ERM, the Bundesbank chose to squelch any suspicion that its determination to fight inflation might be flagging. In Group of Seven (G-7) matters, similarly, the Bundesbank guarded its independence so jealously that it spurned opportunities for exchange rate stabilization even in cases, as in 1989, when stabilizing the D-mark against the dollar called for raising, not lowering, German interest rates. Thus, despite good policy performance over the decade, there remains room for improvement in German policymaking institutions.

Japanese policymaking institutions also served that country's international competitiveness, with a private consensus underpinned by close bank-industry relations. As reviewed in chapter 4, when confronted with demands from the United States and other foreign governments to stimulate its domestic economy in the mid-1980s, Japan responded with monetary rather than fiscal stimulus. The Ministry of Finance (MOF) succeeded in completely eliminating the fiscal deficits over the decade. This record stands in marked contrast to the experience of the German government, which was equally determined, before unification, to reduce budget deficits but was not assisted by control over monetary policy.

Japanese policy outputs, therefore, erred on the side of yen undervaluation, overexpansionary monetary policy and, in the 1980s and early 1990s, a skewed mix of monetary and fiscal policies. As a result, Japan experienced high inflation in the 1970s, asset-price inflation in the second half of the 1980s, and a series of trade conflicts and the threat of trade protection from major partners, specifically the United States, with debilitating consequences for foreign relations overall. Contributing importantly to these errors was the lack of independence of the Bank of Japan compared to that of the Bundesbank and Federal Reserve.

Compared with German and Japanese policies, US external monetary policy has not served national interests in competitiveness and exchange rate stability as well. US policy, as discussed above, has countenanced sustained overvaluations of the dollar, has been quite inconsistent over time, and has often treated the exchange rate as the mere residual of monetary and fiscal policy. The United States has an independent central bank, which is certainly desirable, but lacks an institutional mechanism for aggregating private preferences and bringing them to bear on policymaking. Second, the arrangement between the Federal Reserve and the Treasury regarding intervention responsibilities and the proper relationship between domestic monetary policy and exchange rates is ambiguous, to say the least. Conflicts between these proud bureaucracies are rarely resolved in the context of a private or political consensus that extends beyond the two agencies and encompasses other executive agencies, the Congress, and affected interests.

External monetary policy has not been the only source of economic difficulty for the United States, of course. The chief failure of American economic policy has been the excessive and continuing fiscal deficits of the federal government. This error is magnified by the very low rate of private savings in the United States compared with countries such as Germany and Japan. American domestic politics is the fundamental cause of this imbalance and the source of its potential solution. However, the creation of government institutions and processes that could give expression to private preferences for exchange rate stability and competitive valuation would serve to highlight the deleterious external consequences of failing to correct the internal deficit. Improving interbureaucratic communication and cooperation on exchange rate policy would help to focus decision making on the root causes of external imbalances as well.

The following sections offer recommendations for rectifying some of the shortcomings and inefficiencies in policymaking within each country. These proposals will also help to strengthen and improve international macroeconomic and exchange rate cooperation both bilaterally and within the G-7, where trilateral monetary relations are discussed. Before proceeding to a discussion of country-specific recommendations, therefore, we briefly consider the recent history of G-7 monetary coordination and the domestic institutional requirements of international cooperation.

Domestic Institutions and International Cooperation

This study has examined the domestic institutional sources of external monetary policy. The institutions and policy process at the national level affect not only national policy outcomes but also, by extension, the conduct of exchange rate and macroeconomic policy coordination at the international level. National institutions have frequently constrained international cooperation in, for example, the meetings of the G-7 finance ministers and central bank governors. Owing to failures to reconcile conflicts at the national level, principally between governments and central banks over domestic and external monetary policy, opportunities for G-7 cooperation have been missed. In the absence of international cooperation to limit extreme fluctuations, exchange rates have been more volatile as a result.

Consider macroeconomic and exchange rate policy coordination as practiced within the G-7 during the 1980s, which suffered from several shortcomings.[1] First, the governments within the G-7 greatly overemphasized the use of domestic monetary policy to resolve international economic conflicts.[2] Rather than undertake politically difficult adjustments of policies under their direct control, such as fiscal policy, governments in several cases promoted adjustment of interest rates. Changes in monetary policy, however, cannot substantially change current account imbalances over the long term.[3] Second, the Japanese, American, and German governments sometimes used the G-7 process as a lever to extract more expansionary domestic monetary policies from their central banks. Governments used international cooperation as a back door, in other words, for political influence over domestic monetary policy.

---

1. Japanese, German, and American policies within the G-7 framework are discussed, respectively, in chapters 4, 5, and 6.

2. See Funabashi, *Managing the Dollar*; Destler and Henning, *Dollar Politics*; Dobson, *Economic Policy Coordination*.

3. An expansionary monetary policy will reduce the external value of the currency and shift the current account balance toward surplus in the short to medium term. However, the increase in domestic prices resulting from monetary ease will gradually raise the external value of the currency in real terms, eroding competitiveness over time. Ultimately, only changes in the savings-investment balance, which can be achieved through changes in fiscal policy, can produce lasting changes in the external balance.

The Bank of Japan, Bundesbank, and Federal Reserve therefore understandably developed a deep distrust of the G-7 process. The three central banks rebelled once the current account imbalances fell, the threat of protectionism in the United States abated, and James Baker resigned as US Treasury secretary. This distrust was so deep that central banks refused to use domestic monetary policy to stabilize exchange rates even in circumstances when doing so would have *supported* the domestic objectives of all of them. For example, an agreement in mid-1989 that the Federal Reserve would not raise interest rates further and that the Bank of Japan and Bundesbank would advance the timing of interest rate increases with the aim of stabilizing exchange rates would probably have prevented the appreciation of the dollar at that time. These interest rate adjustments would have been consistent with the domestic needs of all three countries.[4] As a result of the tension between governments and central banks over the use and misuse of international cooperation, the G-7 process has fallen into disrepair.

The experience of the G-7 in the 1980s, and the policymaking experience of the three countries over the earlier decades, yields several important conclusions regarding the institutional basis of international cooperation. The coercion of independent central banks, first of all, is not a durable basis around which to build international cooperation. Unless central bank independence were to be eliminated—which this author would emphatically oppose—the G-7 must accept it as a reality of the cooperation process. Central banks must be assured that, in stabilizing exchange rates, monetary policy coordination will not be used as a substitute for changes in other government policies, such as fiscal policies, when those are the fundamental cause of international economic problems. Central banks should be fully included in G-7 deliberations leading to any stabilization agreement.[5] Central banks should be entrusted with the operational management of regimes designed to stabilize exchange rates.

At the same time, however, central banks cannot be left to operate in a political vacuum when managing exchange rates. Exchange rate stabilization and central bank cooperation must occur within the context of international agreements among governments, which provide political backing and accountability. The governments must also take responsibility for negotiating any necessary realignments of the central parities or target ranges that define the system. The broader political commitment

---

4. In fact, with hindsight, we can say that these domestic policy adjustments would have been superior to the paths that monetary policy actually followed in all three countries on domestic grounds alone, irrespective of the benefits of exchange rate stabilization.

5. Dobson, *Economic Policy Coordination*, pp. 137–40.

to exchange rate stabilization and cooperation, in turn, must be grounded in the societal preferences of each country. If, for example, the Bundesbank had been left unconstrained in the late 1970s, the EMS would not have been created, although German central bankers later found the system very useful.

The broad economic and political responsibilities of governments and the domestic monetary responsibility of central banks, particularly independent ones, create a pervasive bureaucratic tension over the stabilization of exchange rates. Owing to the functional link between domestic monetary policy and the exchange rate, conflicts between governments and central banks inevitably arise. Often, it is easier for governments and central banks to let the exchange rate fluctuate than to try to resolve this intractable bureaucratic conflict. Flexible exchange rates, in other words, can be the default outcome when central banks and governments fail to overcome their differences over the terms of exchange rate stabilization. This conflict can never be fully reconciled, but it can be managed so as not to interfere with exchange rate stabilization. Ambiguities in the domestic bargains that define the rights and obligations of central banks and their finance ministries in external monetary policymaking therefore were an additional factor that contributed to the breakdown of G-7 cooperation.

Recall, from chapter 3, the arrangement between the German Bundesbank and finance ministry regarding EMS matters. The government is responsible for negotiating the central parities of the ERM and realignments. The Bundesbank owns international reserves and has full operational discretion in intervention operations, within the constraints imposed by the exchange rate commitments. Under circumstances where domestic monetary stability is threatened by participation in the system, however, the government agrees with the Bundesbank to negotiate a realignment or to allow the Bundesbank to opt out of the system. But, although they consult intensively, it is the government rather than the Bundesbank that ultimately decides whether domestic monetary stability is actually threatened. This bargain, moreover, rests on a foundation broader than simply the two agencies themselves. The bargain has been discussed publicly, endorsed by key politicians, and presented to international bodies. This formula has reassured the Bundesbank and thus underpinned German participation in the EMS. The internal institutional arrangements for G-7 cooperation in all three countries should be informed by this example.

When the division of labor between finance ministries and central banks can be specified in the field of external monetary policy, the interests of these bureaucracies suggests that an agreement to limit currency fluctuations is quite natural. As was also discussed in chapter 3, central banks give a relatively high priority to fighting inflation and, for that reason, object to a very low valuation of the currency. Finance ministries, while also typically concerned about inflation, give a higher priority than do central banks to international competitiveness and economic growth, as does the rest of the government, and thus oppose a very high valuation of the currency. The two bureaucracies can typically benefit, therefore, from a bargain in which the finance ministry agrees to act to support the currency from becoming weak while the central bank, in exchange, agrees to act to prevent the currency from becoming extremely strong. Such a bargain would protect each agency from the exchange market outcome that would harm the objective it holds relatively intensively.[6]

The best way to resurrect and advance the G-7 process of exchange rate and macroeconomic coordination, therefore, would be to explicitly adopt a framework of principles that embody these lessons. Such a framework, to summarize the preceding discussion, would consist of four essential components: (1) central bank independence and operational management of exchange rate stabilization, (2) international agreements among governments on the exchange rate system and government decisions on realignments of parities or adjustments of bands, (3) domestic decision-making processes that keep government policy grounded in societal interests, and (4) well-articulated domestic-level bargains between central banks and finance ministries governing their prerogatives in external monetary policymaking. This framework for cooperation would parallel, internationally, the institutional architecture of the EMS, which has worked well, notwithstanding the recent speculative crises and widening of the margins. At the domestic level, the proposed framework parallels the understanding between the German government and Bundesbank governing German participation in the EMS.

This four-part G-7 framework would have its limitations. The guarantees to central banks that participation would not be allowed to undermine price stability limit the domain of conditions under which exchange rate stabilization could be conducted. In particular, the framework could

---

6. One reason that these agreements are not concluded more frequently is the intertemporal nature of this bargain. While the agreement would be in the interest of both parties, at any one time only one agency is served by invoking the bargain. For example, when the dollar is high and rising, the Treasury is concerned and the Federal Reserve is complacent. In this instance, only the Treasury's priority would be served by official intervention against the US currency. The Federal Reserve might agree to this bargain because it would secure Treasury support to defend the currency once it fell too low at some indefinite point in the future. But of course the Fed would fear that the Treasury would not live up to the bargain when time came to repay the favor. Such a bargain thus hinges on establishing credibility that the finance ministry will act in the interest of the central bank, and vice versa, when the trend in currency valuation reverses in the future. The credibility problem is aggravated by uncertainty about changing economic conditions and the appropriate central rate over the medium and long term. The credibility of the partners is enhanced, however, when the two bureaucracies are enveloped in a societal or political consensus in favor of exchange rate stability.

not be applied when fiscal policy is sharply at odds with the goal of exchange rate stabilization. Had it been in place during the early 1980s, the Reagan budget deficits might well have undermined exchange rate stabilization. The network of institutions within Germany and among the European partners in the EMS was demonstrably not sufficient to preserve exchange rate stability in Europe in the wake of the postunification fiscal deficits in Germany. Clearly, governments must secure economic conditions that free central banks to cooperate in the stabilization of exchange rates. External and domestic monetary policies cannot substitute for tackling politically sensitive domestic economic and financial problems.

Despite its shortcomings, however, such a framework would be an improvement over the status quo and would be less likely than present G-7 arrangements to miss opportunities for cooperation. Like the EMS in its early years, a loose global monetary system could operate even with relatively frequent realignments and yet still stabilize market expectations and modulate extreme currency fluctuations. Furthermore, this institutional framework could accommodate a variety of alternative proposals to stabilize exchange rates. These proposals include, but are not limited to, broad target zones and the Williamson-Miller blueprint.[7]

The country-specific recommendations that appear in the following section would help to make national policymaking institutions "safe" for this conception of G-7 cooperation. I emphasize that, while these recommendations would support international cooperation, they are also desirable on purely national grounds. The following recommendations should therefore be considered within each country irrespective of agreement with foreign partners on the framework outlined above or other mechanisms for international monetary cooperation.

Recommendations

The institutional configuration of policymaking in each country, this study has argued, can be assessed with reference to central bank status, central bank–government agreements, and the aggregation of private-sector preferences, the three factors that determine differences in policy outcomes. Central bank independence helps to protect domestic price stability. Solid agreements between central banks and governments, finance ministries in particular, help to manage and restrain interbureaucratic conflicts over the direction of external monetary policy. Private preferences, when organized and articulated, can anchor these institutions of government

---

7. John Williamson and Marcus H. Miller, *Targets and Indicators: A Blueprint for the International Coordination of Economic Policy*, POLICY ANALYSES IN INTERNATIONAL ECONOMICS 22 (Washington: Institute for International Economics, September 1987).

in a broader sense of national economic interest. With these findings in mind, proposals for reform of institutions and policy processes are proposed below for the United States, Japan, Germany, and the European Union.

United States

American policymaking suffers from a division of the private sector in formulating private preferences and a division of the state in formulating policy. The comparative analysis in this book places in a new light previous proposals to institutionalize the input of the private sector in the process of exchange rate policymaking. This study has argued that private-sector preferences are fundamental to exchange rate policymaking. Private interests have usually been one step, if not several steps, removed from exchange rate policymaking in the United States over the decades, the mid-1980s being the great exception that proves the rule. Their exclusion from the policymaking arena contributed to periodic neglect of the exchange rate by decision makers, neglect that was particularly egregious in comparative perspective.

Furthermore, the comparison with Britain suggests that the United States is not likely to become more competitiveness conscious, stability oriented, or consistent in exchange rate policy as the US economy becomes more open. The United States, like Britain, exhibits wide dispersion of external monetary preferences among private groups, a function of the relatively distant relationship between banks and industry, which in turn creates latitude for partisan politics over the exchange rate that does not exist in Germany and Japan. Thus, the British example suggests instead that, as trade grows relative to the size of the American economy, the temptation of the US administration to exploit the exchange rate opportunistically for partisan purposes will increase, in the absence of private-sector institutions capable of organizing preferences broadly. This has already occurred, during the first Reagan administration, and could easily recur, particularly if the US trade account were to return to near balance.

Therefore, when considering institutional reform in this policy area, it is not sufficient to focus on the apparatus of government institutions. The basic importance of private interests and private consensus building must be acknowledged as well. Previously, I. M. Destler and I recommended that the input of private interests be institutionalized in the policy process in the United States through the formation of a private-sector Advisory Group on Exchange Rates akin to those that advise the US Trade Representative on trade policy. The members of this small group would be appointed by the president on a recommendation of the secretary of the Treasury and would reflect the overall composition of the American economy. The group would meet with cabinet-level economic and trade officials at least twice each year and issue periodic reports to the administration and Congress. Destler and I also recommended a role for the US Congress in establishing guidelines and broad objectives for exchange rate policy, into which private interests might have input. With the administration, the Congress could formulate a current account target as a priority international economic goal, consistent with long-term US savings and investment needs, and oversee exchange rate policy with this guideline in mind.[8]

These proposals appear to be all the more compelling in light of the international comparison conducted in this study. An advisory group would not provide the same consensus-building functions supplied by close bank-industry relations in Germany and Japan. Until American banking law and practices are changed to permit closer relationships between banks and industry—a long-term prospect if it happens at all— the formation of private preferences will be handicapped by the divide separating these two parts of the private sector. However, institutionalized private-sector input could nonetheless partially compensate for the deficiency in "natural" private-sector organization and thus help to offset the fractionalization of private groups endemic to the US external monetary policymaking. A private advisory process could achieve this by opening channels of access to policymakers, thereby stimulating private advocacy when the costs of organization otherwise would discourage representation, and facilitating consensus building among private actors.

This study would not, of course, advocate the "democratization" of exchange rate policymaking. Interest groups should not make policy, obviously, and the Congress should not legislate directly on intervention or otherwise interfere in foreign exchange operations. The role of private groups should be advisory, and appointments to this panel should be broadly and carefully selected. The role of the Congress should clearly be limited to setting broad goals, in cooperation with the executive, within which the Federal Reserve and Treasury should act. This would replicate the division of labor between the two branches of government in trade policy and such vital and secretive areas of foreign policy as intelligence and military engagement. By formulating, with the administration, a current account target, the Congress can contribute to exchange rate goal setting in a way that is meaningful but not meddlesome.

Some observers fear the involvement of private interests and the Congress in the setting of goals for exchange rate policy.[9] It is true that isolated members of Congress have sometimes challenged the Treasury and Fed's exchange rate policies in unconstructive ways. But the actions

---

8. For the details of these proposals, see Destler and Henning, *Dollar Politics*, pp. 155–61.

9. Dominguez and Frankel, *Does Foreign Exchange Intervention Work?*, pp. 52–53, 138.

of Congress as a whole in this area—such as the Exchange Rates and International Economic Policy Coordination Act of 1988, embodied in the 1988 trade act, have been moderate and responsible. Senior Treasury officials resisted Congress's assertion of exchange rate policy oversight authority during the drafting of this legislation. Once the Treasury actually began sending biannual reports to Congress on exchange rates and international economic policy, however, senior officials praised the banking committees of both houses for the constructive role they played—a conversion similar to that undergone by the Federal Reserve in reporting monetary growth targets under the Humphrey-Hawkins Act of 1978.

Under all foreseeable circumstances, American exchange rate policy is safe from "capture" by special interests and a hypothetical Congress hellbent on competitive depreciation of the dollar. The analysis in this study suggests that the danger to American policy is quite the opposite: that it becomes completely unhinged at times from the stability needs of US producers and neglectful of the impact of the exchange rate on the economy. This happened not only in the mid-1980s, although that was the most dramatic example of neglect, but under the Bretton Woods regime, during the mid-1970s, and during 1989–90 as well. Given this policy history, and the continued fragmentation of the private sector and public institutions, it is highly unlikely that broadening the policymaking process would produce an error in the opposite direction; that is, too much attention to the exchange rate, overemphasis on currency stability, or beggar-thy-neighbor depreciation.

As the comparison to Germany and Japan suggests, private groups have a vital role to play in the exchange rate arena, albeit removed from the direct management and execution of policy. They can contribute to the establishment of broad objectives for policy and can help to specify how tradeoffs among objectives should be made. Importantly, the consensus they might facilitate could indirectly adjudicate conflicts between government agencies, such as the Treasury and Federal Reserve, and thereby unblock bureaucratic deadlock. In this way, private preferences can provide an anchor for government institutions and policy and contribute to policy consistency and exchange rate stability.

The effects of the fractionalization of the private sector on policymaking in the United States are compounded by the division of authority between the Treasury and the Federal Reserve. Both bureaucracies must necessarily be involved intimately in international monetary policymaking. But effective joint responsibility over intervention operations creates a unit-veto system biased toward inaction.[10] There are two solutions to the fractionalization of the American state: create a regularized interagency process to clarify government objectives in exchange rate policy and

---

10. Volcker and Gyohten, *Changing Fortunes*, pp. 234–35; Destler and Henning, *Dollar Politics*, pp. 88–90.

identify the relationship between those objectives and fiscal, monetary, and trade policy; and strengthen the relationship between the Treasury and Federal Reserve on international monetary policy specifically.

Destler and I earlier also recommended the creation of an executive branch review of exchange rate policy that could inform Treasury's biannual reports to Congress and the president's annual economic report. We argued that this interagency review would be greatly aided by the creation of a cabinet-level economic policy group with a staff based in the White House. The cabinet-level group, having jurisdiction over domestic and international economic policy, could make the crucial connections and trade-offs among fiscal, trade, and exchange rate policies.

President Clinton has established just such a cabinet-level body, the National Economic Council (NEC). The NEC, or a subgroup designated by the president, is the appropriate forum to discuss external monetary policy and its relationship to the budget, taxes, and trade policy. The Treasury secretary should lead a review of exchange rate policy and solicit input from the other members of this forum at least twice each year. Ideally, this review would be conducted before the spring and fall meetings of the G-7 finance ministers and central bank governors. The NEC, or again an appropriate subgroup, should also address exchange rate matters when preparing the president, with the designated "sherpas," for the annual G-7 economic summit meetings.

The purpose of this proposal is not to remove the authority for exchange rate policymaking from the Treasury. To the contrary, owing to its responsibilities for financial markets, financial regulation, and government finance, among other things, the Treasury is the agency in which this competence naturally resides. The point is to place the Treasury at the center of a broad policy review within the executive that can bring the full range of appropriate considerations to bear.

When exchange rate matters are discussed in the NEC, the chairman of the Federal Reserve Board should be invited to attend. The Federal Reserve would not be required to participate in NEC meetings if it thought that its independence on domestic monetary policy might be compromised. But, because the viability of exchange rate policy depends on domestic monetary policy, the views of the Fed are important and should be sought. The Fed could use this forum as an opportunity to offer its advice on the link between exchange rates and, for example, fiscal policy.

This proposal borrows a procedure used in Germany, where the Bundesbank has the right to participate in meetings of the cabinet when issues within its competence are raised. The German chancellor, his ministers, and their deputies are admitted to meetings of the Central Bank Council as well, though they of course cannot vote. Although participation of the chancellor in meetings of the Central Bank Council is rare, cross-participation at the ministerial and subcabinet levels has been rather frequent and has been useful to both the government and central bank. The practice has certainly not damaged the independence of the Bundesbank, and there is little reason to believe that it would damage the independence of the Federal Reserve.

The division of labor and the understanding between the Federal Reserve and Treasury on external monetary policy can be improved in a couple of respects. Chapter 3 described the division of responsibilities between these bureaucracies. Both organizations own foreign reserves but all operations must be approved by the Treasury. The Fed, however, controls many of the resources potentially available for intervention, has the larger share of swap agreements with foreign central banks, and must therefore be heeded by the Treasury. This entangled relationship produces inefficiencies and conflicts, the resolution of which, at the operational level, must be brokered by the executive vice president of the New York Fed in charge of the foreign exchange desk.

The bias toward inaction in the foreign exchange markets could be corrected by untangling this relationship. The authority of the Fed to conduct foreign exchange operations, which now rests on interpretation of the statutes, should be stated explicitly in the law to put to rest questions on this score that are raised periodically by individual members of Congress and others seeking to block intervention. The Fed also should be given much greater leeway to intervene at its discretion in the foreign exchange markets without constantly having to seek the permission of the Treasury.[11] At the same time, the Treasury should retain the authority it currently possesses to establish, in agreements with foreign governments, formal and informal target ranges for the exchange rates between the dollar and other currencies. The Fed's obligation to defend those ranges would not need to be clarified, if the ranges were embodied in the law as were the Bretton Woods arrangements. But the Fed's obligation to defend informal targets or ranges that are not explicitly adopted by the Congress should also be clearly established in law. In particular, the Fed should have an obligation to defend exchange rate targets that are the subject of executive agreements among governments and have broad support within the United States.

The Fed should be guaranteed that, in the event that defending target ranges endangers domestic monetary stability, the Treasury will negotiate a realignment or the Fed will be relieved of the obligation to intervene. As is the case in Germany, though, it must ultimately be the administration's decision whether domestic monetary stability is threatened

---

11. One benefit to granting greater discretion to the Fed on foreign currency operations could well be an improvement in the effectiveness of intervention. To the extent that intervention is perceived by the markets to embody more "inside information" about the future course of domestic monetary policy, as discussed in chapter 7, such operations should be more effective.

by maintenance of the parity. This type of agreement would provide a domestic legal and institutional foundation for the United States to participate in any G-7 mechanism for currency stabilization that was successfully reinvigorated and reinstituted.

Japan

Japan possesses the least independent central bank of the three countries considered here. The subordination of the Bank of Japan to the Ministry of Finance has gradually lost its rationale over the postwar period. During postwar reconstruction and economic revitalization, Ministry of Finance control over the central bank made sense from the standpoint of supporting government industrial priorities and balance-of-payments objectives under the Bretton Woods regime. Economic maturation and financial liberalization over the decades, however, have rendered these rationales obsolete. Cognizant of those changing circumstances, Liberal Democratic Party (LDP) politicians and ministerial bureaucrats eased their grip on monetary policy over the course of the 1970s.

The Ministry of Finance retains substantial influence and potential control over the Bank of Japan even today, however. Continued ministry powers over the central bank have led to a substitution of monetary for fiscal stimulus during periods of yen strength, slow growth, and recession. The dominance of the Ministry of Finance also subjected the Bank of Japan to the variable relations between the ministry's bureaucrats and the LDP politicians who constituted the government. Political stability in Japan, marked by the dominance of the Liberal Democratic Party from 1955 to 1993, spared the Japanese central bank from changes in party control of the government. Subordination of the Bank of Japan perpetuates lingering suspicion in the financial markets and foreign governments— even when restrictive monetary policy is invoked—that Japanese domestic monetary policy could at some point be manipulated opportunistically for short-term or narrow, self-interested purposes by future governments.

The time has come for the Japanese government to grant full independence to the Bank of Japan. The benefits for Japan of having a subordinated central bank, such as they were, have declined while the costs continue to rise. With greater international economic interdependence, the costs for Japan's foreign partners of this anachronistic institutional arrangement are rising as well. The skewed macroeconomic policy mix and the perpetuation of huge trade surpluses is a salient example of these costs. Three developments in particular argue for liberating the Bank of Japan, operationally and institutionally, at this time.

The first, paramount consideration is the transformation of the Japanese political party system and the possibility of alternation in party control of the government. Disillusionment on the part of the Japanese public with the political process, the splintering of the LDP over the

issue of political reform, and the lower house election of July 1993 eject-
ed the LDP from government for the first time since the formation of
the party in the mid-1950s. A seven-party coalition led by the popular
Prime Minister Morihiro Hosokawa assumed power in August 1993. This
coalition was succeeded by a minority government headed by Tsutomu
Hata in April 1994 and then an LDP-Socialist government headed by
Tomiichi Murayama at the end of June. Changes in party control have
now become a reality in Japan, and changes in the party composition of
the governing coalition are a certainty in the future. The new fluidity of
Japanese party politics has produced strong incentives to use domestic
monetary policy for political ends that did not exist during the extraordinary period of LDP dominance of 1955–93.

The present coalition government is in a precarious political position.
The threat of further disillusionment on the part of the electorate, the
possibility of defections from the ruling coalition, and a failure to administer a decisive fiscal stimulus to the economy have tempted the present
government to pressure the Bank of Japan to reduce interest rates. In
the future, successive rounds of expansionary monetary policy, stimulated by alternation in party control of the government, would damage
confidence in financial markets and harm the interests of all political
parties. Thus, both the present ruling parties and the opposition could
benefit by tying the hands of future governments to an orthodox monetary policy by freeing the Bank of Japan now. Central bank independence would contribute to financial and economic stability at a time of
political transition and perhaps instability.[12]

Japan's current position in the prolonged business cycle is the second
reason to grant the Bank of Japan independence. A necessary restructuring of the balance sheets of Japanese banks has been largely accomplished
and the economic recession in Japan appears to be now bottoming out.
The liberation of the central bank could go hand in hand with the long-
awaited reforms in the banking system that will be possible once that
restructuring is completed. In addition, freeing the Bank of Japan would
help to prevent delays in the tightening of monetary policy from the
current unprecedently low interest rates once a full recovery takes place.

The personnel appointment cycle at the central bank is the third reason to act on the bank's status now. The present governor, Yasushi Mieno,
will complete his term of office in December 1994. The selection of his

---

12. Tying the hands of future governments has been an important incentive to liberate
central banks in a number of other countries. For the cases of European countries, see
Goodman, "The Politics of Central Bank Independence." For the cases of New Zealand
and Chile, see John Williamson, ed., *The Political Economy of Policy Reform* (Washington:
Institute for International Economics, 1994), pp. 73–101; 225–32. In early 1994, moreover,
the conservative government of France granted substantially greater independence to
the Bank of France to underscore its commitment to noninflationary monetary policy
and to maintain the confidence of financial markets.

predecessor through the conventions followed in recent decades would place a retired official of the Ministry of Finance at the helm of the Bank of Japan. Placing a MOF man at the head of the central bank, as now appears likely in the absence of a change in bank status, would strengthen the possibility that the ministry will continue to succeed in substituting monetary for fiscal stimulus, as occurred during Satoshi Sumita's term as governor during the second half of the 1980s. That substitution, as argued above, contributed to asset-price inflation and limited the correction of the current account surplus in the past.

Several institutional and legal changes would have to be introduced to provide the needed level of independence for the Bank of Japan. First, the dismissal authority of the minister of finance and the cabinet over senior bank officers would have to be revoked. Second, the Ministry of Finance's authority over the central bank's budget and the ministry's ability to audit the central bank would be withdrawn. Third, the basic objectives of the Bank of Japan as set down in the law should be rebalanced in favor of monetary and financial stability at the expense of supporting the general economic policy of the government. Fourth, the legal provisions that allow central bank financing for government deficits should be abandoned (although they are less important at present in light of the current fiscal stringency). These changes would require that the law governing the Bank of Japan be fundamentally rewritten and passed by the Diet.

Greater independence would also entail revamping the internal structure of the Bank of Japan. Several models would be applicable. One possibility could be to abolish the Policy Board and elevate the positions of the governor, vice governor, and executive directors of the bank to formal policymaking status. They would take all the decisions pertinent to monetary policy and manage the specialized departments, as do the members of the Bundesbank's Directorate. This new body, which could be named the Executive Council, would be a formalization of the informal roundtable process that already exists.

Elevating the *marutaku* (roundtable) has the advantage of building on existing institutions, as well as the proven and established networks of interaction within the bank, and would therefore be preferable to trying to reinvigorate the withering Policy Board. Grafted onto the Bank of Japan structure, the Policy Board has never become the locus of real authority on monetary policy. The legally enshrined convention of reserved representation on the board for particular economic sectors is an anachronism. The appointments to the new Executive Council should be people of the highest professional standing, and of independent stature, from business, finance, academe, and government.

Granting genuine independence to the Bank of Japan would naturally require a new agreement with the government on external monetary policymaking. Resolving the conflict between exchange rate stabilization and domestic monetary stability would be of particular importance. The new arrangement could apply the tested and successful formula in Germany and vest authority for formal and informal parity setting with the Ministry of Finance; grant the Bank of Japan full authority over intervention operations; stipulate that parities will not be maintained if they create domestic monetary instability, particularly inflation; and establish that the Bank of Japan advises on this matter but the government, ultimately, determines whether internal stability is endangered.

This package of institutional reforms would have several benefits for Japan in the international context. First, in the process of formulating external monetary policy, freeing the Bank of Japan could help to correct for the overemphasis on industrial competitiveness at the expense of consumers that has characterized Japanese policy in the past. The weakening of the lending relationship between banks and industry has contributed to private-sector acceptance of the appreciation of the yen, as argued in the previous chapter. But lending is only one of several bank-industry connections; equity holdings and management participation remain high, suggesting that a private-sector consensus favoring strong competitiveness might linger. Central bank independence in Japan could perform the same role it has occasionally performed in Germany: blocking low currency valuation in times of domestic inflation.

Second, freeing the Bank of Japan would help to correct the skewed mixture that Japan has had of tight fiscal and easy monetary policy. At the end of 1993, the general government fiscal deficit in Japan amounted to about 1 percent of GNP, owing to the deep recession, which represented a surplus of roughly equal size on a cyclically adjusted basis. Japan as a consequence runs a large current account surplus. Three supplemental budgets, in August 1992, April 1993, and September 1993, failed to prevent the economy from sliding into recession. Although these special budgets provided some economic stimulus, the amount of "new money" in them, as in the supplemental budgets of 1986 and 1987, was far less than advertised. Nor are the fiscal measures that were proposed in February 1994 likely to change fundamentally the government's overall fiscal position over the long term. Correcting the chronic fiscal-monetary mismatch in Japan, therefore, appears to require institutional change.

The historical pattern of substituting monetary for fiscal stimulus prompts the question whether institutional reforms should go beyond the monetary sphere to encompass fiscal policymaking as well. Such reforms naturally would focus on the Ministry of Finance and its relationship to the other ministries and the Diet. The concentration of budget, tax, and financial authority in the Ministry of Finance is extraordinary. The Ministry of Finance is quite independent from politicians, political parties, and the Diet. The cabinet and the legislature possess only a modest capacity to prepare, evaluate, or legislate fiscal proposals without the ministry's cooperation. This study has analyzed monetary and exchange rate policy, and would not offer specific proposals on the fiscal side. The analysis presented here, though, tends to support those in Japan who advocate a reevaluation of the concentration of authority in the ministry and its relationship to the other organs of Japanese government. Granting full independence to the Bank of Japan would be one way, of course, to clip the extraordinary powers of the ministry.

Defenders of the dominance of the Ministry of Finance over the Bank of Japan might argue that central bank independence could make Japan a less cooperative partner in the G-7. The fundamental flaw in macroeconomic policy coordination as practiced within the G-7 during the second half of the 1980s, however, was precisely that it focused too heavily on monetary policy. Granting independence to the Bank of Japan would help to correct that problem.

Consider for a moment the likely outcome of Japanese macroeconomic policymaking during the 1980s, on the assumption that the Bank of Japan had been as independent as, for example, the Bundesbank. The outcome of this counterfactual scenario cannot be known with certainty, of course. The case history in chapter 4 nonetheless suggests that monetary policy in Japan would have eased more slowly in 1986, would have been tighter during 1987 and 1988, and would have begun to tighten earlier than spring 1989. Monetary policy would still have eased on account of the strong yen, just as German monetary policy eased on account of the strong D-mark. But an independent Bank of Japan would have eased less and would have been able to deflect some of the pressure for policy adjustment onto the government budget, as was also true in Germany. A tighter monetary stance would have helped to prevent or at least moderate the weakness of the yen in 1989 and 1990, a principal cause of the renewed increase in Japan's chronic surplus that currently plagues US-Japan relations and the world trading system.

The challenges that presently test the capacity of the United States, Japan, and the rest of the world to cooperate to reduce severe current account imbalances and stimulate the world economy make the lessons of this counterfactual reasoning all the more important. As governments confront this task, in an economic situation that bears some important similarities to the mid-1980s, the government of Japan would do well to ease its institutional hold over the Bank of Japan. Doing so could contribute to a result more satisfying and more permanent than that of the previous round of intensive macroeconomic diplomacy.

Germany and the European Union

The mistakes in German external monetary policymaking have been in the direction of overzealousness in the defense of Bundesbank independence and domestic price stability. Because the Bundesbank feared the erosion of its independence under the guise of G-7 cooperation, the German central bank shunned exchange rate stabilization even in some cases, such as in 1989, when it did not actually threaten domestic price stability. The strong aversion to any obligation to stabilize the D-mark/dollar rate—in contrast to the qualified acceptance of exchange rate stabilization vis-à-vis the European currencies during 1979–93—has contributed to missed opportunities for G-7 cooperation.

In the past, the Bundesbank had greater reason to fear the G-7's encroachment upon its independence because of the political weight of the United States and the importance of American foreign policy to divided Germany. The Bundesbank and the German government were potentially vulnerable to American entreaties on monetary policy, in contrast to their monetary dominance over the other countries in Europe. Former Finance Minister Gerhard Stoltenberg's pressure on the Bundesbank during the operation of the target ranges established under the Louvre Accord confirmed these fears. That experience raised the specter of a return to something like the Bretton Woods regime, under which the Bundesbank was compelled to run an overexpansionary monetary policy while the United States refused to tighten fiscal or monetary policy.

Notably, the Bundesbank-government agreement that defines the parties' rights and obligations in the EMS context does not apply in the G-7 context. The appropriate remedy for the tendency to miss opportunities for G-7 cooperation, therefore, is to extend the agreement between the Bundesbank and the government regarding the EMS to global currency stabilization. The government would assert its authority to commit Germany to exchange rate stabilization, of course, and to conduct international negotiations over realignments. At the same time, the Bundesbank would be assured that currency stabilization beyond Europe, as within the EMS, would not be allowed to undermine domestic monetary stability. This is a guarantee that the Bundesbank did not have under the Bretton Woods regime, and would reassure Frankfurt that stabilization of the D-mark/dollar rate would not be tantamount to a return to the 1960s.

If the European Union is eventually able to overcome the formidable obstacles to Economic and Monetary Union, the German institutions will be replaced by the institutions of the European currency union as the European leg of transatlantic and global monetary cooperation. The widening of the bands of fluctuation within the ERM certainly clouds the prospects for the monetary union. Nonetheless, the ratification of the Maastricht Treaty and the creation of the European Monetary Institute, seated in Frankfurt, establish essential prerequisites for forward movement of monetary integration. Although a one-speed monetary union is clearly not possible within this decade, a multispeed union, in which a hard core of northern European countries, including states not yet members of the European Union, proceed first, remains a distinct possibility.[13]

---

13. See, for example, Thygesen, "Deepening the European Union: Monetary Arrangements."

The prospect of Economic and Monetary Union (EMU) in the long term raises the question, what would be the external monetary behavior of the new union and its posture toward international monetary cooperation? This study has identified the key characteristics to which we should refer when answering that question: private-sector organization and central bank independence.

The character of the European financial system, specifically the relationship between banks and industry, will affect the formation of private-sector preferences. At this time, however, the future of the single market in financial services is unclear. Whether the European financial market follows the model of the German financial system, dominated by universal banks, or of the British financial system, with segmented banking sectors and greater emphasis on direct finance, remains to be seen.[14] The transition to the single market is producing a great deal of restructuring in financial services and might, but will not necessarily, lead to greater disintermediation of banks.

We know a good deal more, by contrast, about the future policymaking institutions of the prospective European monetary union. These are laid down in the Maastricht Treaty and the Protocol on the Statute of the European System of Central Banks (ESCB).[15] First, the degree of legally sanctioned independence of the ESCB would be extraordinary by international standards. Each of the national central banks that constitute the system must be made independent. The officers of the bank are specifically forbidden to solicit or accept instructions from governments regarding monetary policy. Domestic price stability is the legally enshrined priority for the ESCB when carrying out its responsibilities. Add to these guarantees the fact that the ESCB's status, unlike the Bundesbank's freedoms, will be effectively constitutionally enshrined in the European treaties, which can be amended only unanimously. In the first few years of the monetary union, the new central bank would probably act in earnest to demonstrate its independence to establish its credibility in the marketplace. The ESCB's desire to do so would be accentuated by speculation, in transition to the monetary union, that its policies could not be as stability oriented as those of the Bundesbank because of the less hospitable political and economic environment in which it is embedded.

Second, Article 109 of the Maastricht Treaty lays down the legal relationship between the ESCB and the Council of Ministers on exchange rate policy. Representatives of the Council of Ministers would hold the authority to negotiate formal and informal exchange rate agreements with for-

---

14. A question raised in, for example, Ethan B. Kapstein, *Governing the Global Economy: International Finance and the State* (Cambridge, MA: Harvard University Press, 1994), chapter 6.

15. Council and Commission of the European Communities, *Treaty on European Union* (Luxembourg: Office of the Official Publications of the European Communities, 1992).

eign governments. But the ESCB would retain the right to be consulted in the process of making formal and informal exchange rate commitments. The council could, by a qualified majority vote, formulate "general orientations" for exchange rate policy in the absence of an "exchange rate system." Those broad guidelines would be "without prejudice to the primary objective of the ESCB to maintain price stability." Formal agreements that peg the ECU to the dollar or yen, however, would require a *unanimous* vote within the council after consulting the European Central Bank (ECB), the commission, and the European Parliament. This is an onerous requirement, particularly after the enlargement of the European Union.

These institutional arrangements, very simply, are a recipe for a policy of exchange rate flexibility with respect to currencies outside the European region. The predisposition toward flexibility would be further reinforced by structural changes in the monetary union's relationship to the United States that would render the union less vulnerable to fluctuations in the ECU/dollar exchange rate. Had the Bundesbank possessed veto power within Germany over the EMS, the system would probably never have been created. Instead, the Bundesbank was effectively maneuvered by Chancellor Schmidt into accepting the system. There would be no "government" of the European Union to shepherd the ESCB toward exchange rate stabilization vis-à-vis the dollar, however. Even if movement toward political union strengthens and unifies the governing institutions of the European Union, furthermore, the European central bank would have a stronger hand in exchange rate policy than the Bundesbank has in Germany. My reluctant conclusion is that the new monetary union would probably be a difficult partner in global monetary cooperation and exchange rate stabilization.

There are two constructive responses to this probable state of affairs. First, Article 109 of the Maastricht Treaty should be substantially revised to remove the probable bias toward exchange rate flexibility. The procedures for negotiating formal exchange rate stabilization agreements should be streamlined. Council decisions should be subject to qualified majority voting. The balance between exchange rate stability and internal price stability should not be prejudged. At a minimum, that balance should be tilted away from exchange rate stability no more than are current arrangements within Germany. An intergovernmental conference is scheduled to be convened in 1996 on the subject of institutional reform, including the issue of moving toward greater reliance on qualified majority voting. This intergovernmental conference presents an opportunity to amend the exchange rate provisions of the Maastricht Treaty.

The second constructive response would be to reinvigorate macroeconomic cooperation within the G-7 now, during the transitional and formative years of the prospective European monetary union. By nurturing multilateral cooperation, the G-7 can create a benign monetary environment into which EMU could be born. If the benefits of cooperation are demonstrated to the people who will govern the ESCB and other European institutions, multilateral cooperation might be grandfathered, so to speak, by the monetary union. If instead the G-7 governments attempt to deflect the responsibility for macroeconomic policy adjustments onto one another, the new European monetary authorities will be more likely to take a dim, narrow view of international cooperation. If, for example, exchange rate stabilization within broad-banded target ranges, as employed in the late 1980s, were to become the explicit policy of the G-7 member governments before the time of the creation of the new monetary union, the chances that the ESCB and Council of Ministers would continue this policy would be greatly improved.

There are two reasons to believe that this might be a reasonably robust reed on which to rest hope for international monetary cooperation. The first is a reason Europe could accept G-7 cooperation now; the second a reason G-7 cooperation could positively affect post-monetary-union European exchange rate policy. First, fluctuations against the dollar drive wedges between the European currencies, as demonstrated before the autumn 1992 currency crisis. This wedging effect afflicts the relationship between the D-mark and the high-inflation currencies especially acutely. Therefore, global exchange rate stabilization would facilitate the achievement of European monetary union and might be necessary for achieving a monetary union that is any more ambitious in geographic scope than the northern, low-inflation core group of countries.

Second, when the common market was created in the 1950s and 1960s, the existence of the Organization for European Economic Cooperation and the General Agreement on Tariffs and Trade helped to ensure that it would not succumb to pressures for protectionism and closure. G-7 cooperation could provide a similar context of multilateralism and cooperation for European monetary unification. In addition to promoting growth, employment, and financial stability worldwide, therefore, the prospect of European monetary union provides a strong reason for the governments and central banks of the G-7 to reinvigorate international economic cooperation now.

This chapter offers, on the basis of the preceding analysis of the book, recommendations for changes in institutions and policy processes to improve policy outcomes and international monetary cooperation. Taken together, these recommendations lay the domestic institutional foundations for a cooperative international monetary regime. Under this regime, as envisioned in the set of principles described earlier, independent central banks could cooperate operationally to coordinate monetary policy and stabilize currencies. The central banks would act within a political framework agreement, as they do within the Exchange Rate Mechanism, that would be negotiated among the governments of the United States, Japan, and Germany or, perhaps at some point in the future, the European Union. Naturally, the recommendations made here are not the only potentially useful reforms. Changes in international institutions also would be constructive, and governments must not abuse the process of monetary cooperation with, for example, maladjusted fiscal policies. These other areas, however, are not the focus of this analysis.

In analyzing domestic and external monetary policy in the United States, Germany, and Japan, this book has examined institutional determinants in the government and private sectors. As the book acknowledged at the outset, however, institutions do not alone determine policy outcomes. Although they are not necessary or sufficient for explaining the differences in policy outcomes among countries, other factors come into play. There is a limit to what can be achieved through institutional change, in other words, and institutional change cannot alone guarantee optimal policy outcomes and international cooperation. No particular set of institutional arrangements is completely foolproof.

However, some institutional arrangements and policy processes are clearly better than others in, for example, using a societal consensus to anchor policymakers, using central bank independence to pursue price stability, and reconciling conflicts between governments and central banks over exchange rate policy. Injecting broader considerations into US policymaking, granting full independence to the Bank of Japan, and concluding a bargain between the German government and Bundesbank regarding G-7 cooperation would beneficially alter the balance of influences over policy outcomes within each country. The changes in institutions and policy processes recommended here could substantially improve the odds of avoiding policy mistakes of the past without also committing new ones. By contributing to stability-oriented exchange rate policies and policy consistency, they could equip governments and central banks to seize future opportunities for international cooperation.

References

General

Alesina, Alberto. 1988. "Macroeconomics and Politics." In Stanley Fischer, ed., *NBER Macroeconomics Annual 1988*. Cambridge: MIT Press, pp. 13–69.

Alesina, Alberto. 1989. "Politics and Business Cycles in Industrial Democracies." *Economic Policy* (April): 57–98.

Alesina, Alberto, and Lawrence H. Summers. 1990. *Central Bank Independence and Macroeconomic Performance: Some Comparative Evidence*. Harvard International Economic Research Discussion Paper 1496 (May).

Alesina, Alberto, and Guido Tabellini. 1988. "Credibility and Politics." *European Economic Review* 32: 542–50.

Allen, Christopher S. 1990. *Democratic Politics and Private Investment: Financial Regulation in the Federal Republic of Germany and the United States*. Research Report 2. Washington: American Institute for Contemporary German Studies (November).

Aufricht, Hans. 1961. *Central Banking Legislation: A Collection of Central Bank, Monetary and Banking Laws*. Vol. 1 and 2. Washington: International Monetary Fund.

Bade, Robin, and Michael Parkin. 1985. "Central Bank Laws and Monetary Policy." Manuscript, University of Western Ontario.

Bank of Japan. 1991. *Economic Statistics Monthly* (August): table 82.

Bank for International Settlements. 1988. *Fifty-Eighth Annual Report*. Basel: Bank for International Settlements.

Bank for International Settlements. 1991. *International Banking and Financial Market Developments* (May).

Barro, Robert J., and David B. Gordon. 1983. "Rules, Discretion, and Reputation in a Model of Monetary Policy." *Journal of Monetary Economics* 12 (July): 101–21.

Bergsten, C. Fred, ed. 1991. *International Adjustment and Financing: The Lessons of 1985-1991*. Washington: Institute for International Economics.

Bernanke, Ben, and Frederic Mishkin. 1992. "Central Bank Behavior and the Strategy of Monetary Policy: Observations from Six Industrialized Countries." In Olivier Jean Blanchard and Stanley Fischer, eds., *NBER Macroeconomics Annual 1992*. Cambridge: MIT Press.

Binaian, King, Leroy O. Laney, and Thomas D. Willett. 1986. "Central Bank Independence: An International Comparison." In E.F. Toma and M. Toma, eds., *Central Bankers, Bureaucratic Incentives, and Monetary Policy*. Dordrecht/Boston: Kluwer, pp. 199–218.

Bisignano, Joseph R. 1990. "Structures of Financial Intermediation, Corporate Finance, and Central Banking." Basel: Bank for International Settlements. Manuscript (December).

Bisignano, Joseph R. 1992. "Corporate Control and Financial Information." In Richard O'Brien, ed., *Finance and International Economy*. Vol. 5. Oxford: Oxford University Press, pp. 107–21.

Blank, Stephen. 1978. "Britain." In P. Katzenstein, ed., *Between Power and Plenty*. Madison: University of Wisconsin Press, pp. 89–138.

Borio, C. E. V. 1990. *Leverage and Financing of Non-Financial Companies: An International Perspective*. Basel: Bank for International Settlements (May).

Bouvier, Jean. 1988. "The Banque de France and the State from 1850 to the Present Day." In Gianni Toniolo, ed., *Central Banks' Independence in Historical Perspective*. Berlin/New York: de Gruyter, pp. 73–104.

Cairncross, Alec. 1988. "The Bank of England: Relationships with the Government, the Civil Service, and Parliament." In Gianni Toniolo, ed., Central Banks' Independence in Historical Perspective. Berlin/New York: de Gruyter, pp. 39–72, 73–104.

Cargill, Thomas F., and Michael M. Hutchinson. 1990. "Monetary Policy and Political Economy: The Federal Reserve and Bank of Japan." In Thomas Mayer, ed., *Political Economy of American Monetary Policy*. Cambridge/New York: Cambridge University Press, pp. 165–80.

Cooper, Richard N., Barry Eichengreen, Gerald Holtham, Robert D. Putnam, and C. Randall Henning. 1989. *Can Nations Agree? Issues in International Economic Cooperation*. Washington: Brookings Institution.

Cox, Andrew, ed. 1986. *State, Finance, and Industry: A Comparative Analysis of Post-War Trends in Six Advanced Industrial Economies*. New York: St. Martin's Press.

Cukierman, Alex. 1992. *Central Bank Strategy, Credibility, and Independence: Theory and Evidence*. Cambridge/London: The MIT Press.

Cukierman, Alex, Steven B. Webb, and Filin Neyapti. 1992. "Measuring the Independence of Central Banks and Its Effect on Policy Outcomes." *The World Bank Economic Review* 6 (September): 353–98.

Dam, Kenneth W. 1982. *The Rules of the Game: Reform and Evolution in the International Monetary System*. Chicago: University of Chicago Press.

DeLong, J. Bradford, and Lawrence H. Summers. 1993. "Macroeconomic Policy and Long-Run Growth." In *Policies for Long-Run Economic Growth*. Kansas City, MO: Federal Reserve Bank of Kansas City, pp. 93–128.

Dobson, Wendy. 1991. *Economic Policy Coordination: Requiem or Prologue?* POLICY ANALYSES IN INTERNATIONAL ECONOMICS 30. Washington: Institute for International Economics.

Dominguez, Kathryn, and Jeffrey Frankel. 1993. *Does Foreign Exchange Intervention Work?* Washington: Institute for International Economics.

Eckstein, Harry. 1975. "Case Study and Theory in Political Science." In Fred Greenstein and Nelson Polsby, eds., *Handbook of Political Science*. Vol. 7. Reading, MA: Addison-Wesley, pp. 79–137.

Edison, Hali J. 1990. "Foreign Currency Operations: An Annotated Bibliography." International Finance Discussion Papers 380. Washington: Federal Reserve Board of Governors (May).

Edison, Hali J. 1993. *The Effectiveness of Central Bank Intervention: A Survey of the Post-1982 Literature*. Princeton Studies in International Finance, Special Paper 18. Princeton: Princeton University Press.

Edwards, Franklin R., and Robert A. Eisenbeis. 1991. "Financial Institutions and Corporate Investment Horizons: An International Perspective." Harvard Business School and Council on Competitiveness. Manuscript (9 April).

Eijffinger, Sylvester, and Eric Schaling. 1993. "Central Bank Independence: Searching for

Eijffinger, Sylvester, and Eric Schaling. 1993. "Central Bank Independence: Searching for the Philosophers' Stone." In Donald E. Fair and Robert J. Raymond, eds., *The New Europe: Evolving Economic and Financial Systems in East and West*. Dordrecht/Boston: Kluwer.

Federal Reserve Bulletin. Various issues.

Financial Times. Various issues.

Fleming, J. M. 1962. "Domestic Financial Policies under Fixed and under Floating Exchange Rates." *IMF Staff Papers* 9 (November): 369–79. Frankel, Allen B., and John D. Montgomery. 1991. "Financial Structure: An International Perspective." *Brookings Papers on Economic Activity*. Washington: Brookings Institution.

Frieden, Jeffry A. 1991. "Invested Interests: The Politics of National Economic Policies in a World of Global Finance." International Organization 45 (autumn).

Funabashi, Yoichi. 1988. *Managing the Dollar: From the Plaza to the Louvre*. Washington: Institute for International Economics.

George, Alexander L. 1979. "Case Studies and Theory Development: The Method of Structured, Focused Comparison." In Paul Lauren, ed., *Diplomacy*. New York: Free Press, pp. 43–68.

Gerschenkron, Alexander. 1962. *Economic Backwardness in Historical Perspective: A Book of Essays*, Cambridge, MA: Harvard University Press.

Giovannini, Alberto. 1993. "Exploring the Political Dimension of Optimum Currency Areas." In *The Monetary Future of Europe*. London: Centre for Economic Policy Research.

Goldsheid, Rudolph. 1958. "A Sociological Approach to Problems of Public Finance." In Richard A. Musgrave and Alan Peacock, eds., *Classics in the Theory of Public Finance*. New York: Macmillan.

Goodman, John B. 1991. "The Politics of Central Bank Independence." *Comparative Politics* 23 (April): 329–49.

Goodman, John B. 1991. *Central Bank–Government Relations in Major OECD Countries*. Prepared for the US Congress, Joint Economic Committee, 102nd Cong., 1st sess. Washington: GPO.

Goodman, John B. 1992. *Monetary Sovereignty: The Politics of Central Banking in Western Europe*. Ithaca, NY: Cornell University Press.

Goodman, John B., and Louis W. Pauly. 1993. "The Obsolescence of Capital Controls? Economic Management in an Age of Global Markets." *World Politics* 46 (October): 50–82.

Gourevitch, Peter. 1986. *Politics in Hard Times: Comparative Responses to International Economic Crises*. Ithaca, NY: Cornell University Press.

Grilli, Vittorio, Donato Masciandaro, and Guido Tabellini. 1991. "Political and Monetary Institutions and Public Financial Policies in the Industrial Countries." *Economic Policy* 13 (October): 342–92.

Group of Ten. 1993. "International Capital Movements and Foreign Exchange Markets." A Report to the Ministers and Governors by the Group of Deputies (April).

Hall, Peter. 1986. *Governing the Economy: The Politics of State Intervention in Britain and France*. New York: Oxford University Press.

Hayes, Samuel L., ed. 1993. *Financial Services: Perspectives and Challenges*. Boston: Harvard Business School Press.

Hayes, Samuel L., and Philip M. Hubbard. 1990. *Investment Banking: A Tale of Three Cities*. Boston: Harvard Business School Press.

Henning, C. Randall. 1987. *Macroeconomic Diplomacy in the 1980s: Domestic Politics and International Conflict among the United States, Japan, and Europe*. Atlantic Paper 65. London: Croom Helm, for the Atlantic Institute for International Affairs.

Henning, C. Randall, Gary Clyde Hufbauer, and Eduard Hochreiter, eds. 1994. *Reviving the European Union*. Washington: Institute for International Economics.

Hodgman, Donald R. 1974. *National Monetary Policies and International Monetary Cooperation*. Boston: Little, Brown and Company.

Hubbard, R. Glenn. 1990. *Asymmetric Information, Corporate Finance, and Investment.* Chicago: University of Chicago Press, for NBER.

Iida, Keisuke. 1991. "The Political Economy of International Economic Cooperation." Manuscript (July).

Ingham, Geoffrey. 1984. *Capitalism Divided? The City and Industry in British Social Development.* New York: Schocken Books, pp. 62–78.

Issing, Otmar. 1992. "Policies for Long-Run Economic Growth—The Contribution of Monetary Policy." In Deutsche Bundesbank, *Auszüge aus Presseartikeln* (31 August): 3.

Johnson, Chalmers. 1982. *MITI and the Japanese Miracle: The Growth of Industrial Policy, 1925–1975.* Stanford: University Press.

Kapstein, Ethan B. 1994. *Governing the Global Economy: International Finance and the State.* Cambridge, MA: Harvard University Press.

Katzenstein, Peter J., ed. 1978. *Between Power and Plenty: Foreign Economic Policies of Advanced Industrial States.* Madison: University of Wisconsin Press.

Kenen, Peter B. 1988. *Managing Exchange Rates.* London: Royal Institute for International Affairs.

Kydland, Finn E., and Edward C. Prescott. 1977. "Rules Rather Than Discretion: The Inconsistency of Optimal Plans." *Journal of Political Economy* 85 (June): 473–91.

Levi, Margaret. 1988. *Of Rule and Revenue.* Berkeley: University of California Press.

Lindberg, Leon N., and Charles S. Maier, eds. 1985. *The Politics of Inflation and Economic Stagnation.* Washington: Brookings Institution.

Lohmann, Susanne. 1992. "Optimal Commitment in Monetary Policy: Credibility versus Flexibility." *American Economic Review* 82 (March): 273–86.

Lombra, Raymond E., and Willard E. Witte, eds. 1982. *Political Economy of International and Domestic Monetary Relations.* Ames, IA: Iowa State University Press.

Longstreth, Frank. 1979. "The City, Industry, and the State." In Colin Crouch, ed., *State and Economy in Contemporary Capitalism.* New York: St. Martin's Press, pp. 157–90.

Lorsch, Jay W., and Elizabeth A. MacIver. 1991. "Corporate Governance and Investment Time Horizons." Harvard Business School and Council on Competitiveness. Manuscript (May).

March, James G., and Johan P. Olsen. 1989. *Rediscovering Institutions: The Organizational Basis of Politics.* New York: Free Press.

Marris, Stephen N. 1985. *Deficits and the Dollar: The World Economy at Risk.* Washington: Institute for International Economics (December).

Marshall, Alfred. 1919. *Industry and Trade.* London: Macmillan.

Maxfield, Sylvia. 1990. *Governing Capital: International Finance and Mexican Politics.* Ithaca, NY: Cornell University Press.

Moggridge, D.E. 1969. *The Return to Gold 1925: The Formulation of Economic Policy and Its Critics.* London: Cambridge University Press.

Moran, Michael. 1984. "Politics, Banks, and Markets: An Anglo-American Comparison." *Political Studies* 32: 173–89.

Morgan, Stanley. 1990. *Capital International Perspective* (September). New York.

Mundell, Robert. 1963. "Capital Mobility and Stabilization Policy under Fixed and Flexible Exchange Rates." *Canadian Journal of Economics and Political Science* (November): 117–97.

Nölling, Wilhelm. 1993. *Monetary Policy Europe after Maastricht.* New York: St. Martin's Press.

North, Douglass C. 1990. *Institutions, Institutional Change, and Economic Performance.* Cambridge, UK: Cambridge University Press.

Parkin, Michael. 1986. "Domestic Monetary Institutions and Deficits." In James M. Buchanan, Charles K. Rowley, Robert D. Tollison, eds., *Deficits.* New York: Blackwell, pp. 310–37.

Pauly, Louis W. 1988. *Opening Financial Markets: Banking Politics on the Pacific Rim.* Ithaca, NY/London: Cornell University Press.

Posen, Adam S. 1993. "Why Central Bank Independence Does Not Cause Low Inflation: There Is No Institutional Fix for Politics." In Richard O'Brien, ed., *Finance and the International Economy: 7.* Oxford: Oxford University Press, pp. 40–65.

Putnam, Robert D., and C. Randall Henning. 1989. "The Bonn Summit of 1978: A Case Study in Coordination." In Richard N. Cooper, et al., *Can Nations Agree? Issues in International Economic Cooperation.* Washington: Brookings Institution.

Ramseyer, J. Mark. 1993. "Columbia Cartel Launches Bid for Japanese Firms." *The Yale Law Journal* 102, no. 8 (June).

Roe, Mark J. 1993. "Some Differences in Corporate Structure in Germany, Japan, and the United States." *The Yale Law Journal* 102, no. 8 (June).

Romano, Roberta. 1993. "A Cautionary Note on Drawing Lessons from Comparative Corporate Law." *The Yale Law Journal* 102, no. 8 (June).

Salomon Brothers. 1992. *How Big Is the World Bond Market?—1992 Update.* New York (October).

Shonfield, Andrew. 1969. *Modern Capitalism: The Changing Balance of Public and Private Power.* London: Oxford University Press.

Spindler, J. Andrew. 1984. *The Politics of International Credit: Private Finance and Foreign Policy in Germany and Japan.* Washington: Brookings Institution.

Steinherr, Alfred, and Christian Huveneers. 1989. *Universal Banks: The Prototype of Successful Banks in the Integrated European Market?* Brussels: Centre for European Policy Studies.

Stokman, Frans N., Rolf Ziegler, and John Scott, eds. 1985. *Networks of Corporate Power: A Comparative Analysis of Ten Countries.* Oxford: Polity Press.

Suzuki, Yoshio. 1990. "Autonomy and Coordination of Monetary Policy in a Global Economic Order." *CATO Journal* 10, no. 2 (fall).

Taylor, Dean. 1982. "The Mismanaged Float: Official Intervention by the Industrialized Countries." In Michael B. Connolly, ed., *The International Monetary System: Choices for the Future.* New York: Praeger, pp. 49–84.

Toniolo, Gianni, ed. 1988. *Central Banks' Independence in Historical Perspective.* Berlin/New York: de Gruyter.

US General Accounting Office. 1993. *Competitiveness Issues: The Business Environment in the United States, Japan, and Germany.* Washington: GAO (August).

US Treasury. 1985. "Announcement of the Ministers of Finance and Central Bank Governors of France, Germany, Japan, the United Kingdom, and the United States." Press Release, 22 September. Washington.

Vittas, Dimitri, ed. 1978. *Banking Systems Abroad.* London: Inter-Bank Research Organisation.

Volcker, Paul A., and Toyoo Gyohten. 1992. *Changing Fortunes: The World's Money and the Threat to American Leadership.* New York: Times Books.

Williamson, John, ed. 1993. *The Political Economy of Policy Reform.* Washington: Institute for International Economics.

Woolley, John T. 1985. "Central Banks and Inflation." In Leon N. Lindberg and Charles S. Maier, eds., *The Politics of Inflation and Economic Stagnation.* Washington: Brookings Institution, pp. 318–48.

Zysman, John. 1983. *Governments, Markets, and Growth: Financial Systems and the Politics of Industrial Change.* Ithaca, NY: Cornell University Press.

Japan

Ackley, Gardner, and Hiromitsu Ishi. 1976. "Fiscal, Monetary, and Related Policies." In Hugh Patrick and Henry Rosovsky, eds., *Asia's New Giant: How The Japanese Economy Works.* Washington: Brookings Institution, pp. 153–247.

Advisory Group on Economic Structural Adjustment for International Harmony.

1986. "The Report of the Advisory Group on Economic Structural Adjustment for International Harmony." Submitted to Prime Minister Yasuhiro Nakasone, 7 April.

Angel, Robert C. 1991. *Explaining Economic Failure: Japan in the 1969–1971 International Monetary Crisis.* New York: Columbia University Press.

Aoki, Masahiko, and Hugh Patrick. 1992. "The Japanese Main Bank System: An Introductory Overview." Papers presented to the EDI/World Bank Workshop on the Japanese Main Bank System, 29 July–1 August, Washington.

Aoki, Masahiko. 1984. "Aspects of the Japanese Firm." In Aoki, ed., *The Economic Analysis of the Japanese Firm.* New York/Amsterdam: North-Holland.

Balassa, Bela, and Marcus Noland. 1988. *Japan and the World Economy.* Washington: Institute for International Economics.

Bank of Japan. 1984. *Nihonginko Hyakunenshi.* Tokyo: The Bank of Japan.

Bank of Japan. 1990. "Japan's Short-term Money Market and Its Issues." Summary of the Money Market Study Group's Report. Tokyo (8 June).

Bank of Japan, Research and Statistics Department. 1986. "The Recent Development of the Japanese Economy and Macroeconomic Policy Objectives." Tokyo (March).

Bergsten, C. Fred. 1977. Testimony to US Congress, House of Representatives Banking Committee. In *Managing International Economic Interdependence: Selected Papers of C. Fred Bergsten, 1975–1976.* Lexington, MA: D. C. Heath & Co.

Bergsten, C. Fred, and Marcus Noland. 1993. *Reconcilable Differences? United States–Japan Economic Conflict.* Washington: Institute for International Economics.

Boltho, Andrea. 1975. *Japan: Economic Survey, 1953–1973.* London: Oxford University Press, p. 120.

Bryant, Ralph C. 1991. "Model Representations of Japanese Monetary Policy." *Monetary and Economic Studies* (9 September): 20.

Calder, Kent E. 1988. "Japanese Foreign Economic Policy Formation: Explaining the Reactive State." *World Politics* (July): 518–41.

Calder, Kent E. 1988. *Crisis and Compensation: Public Policy and Political Stability in Japan, 1949–1986.* Princeton: Princeton University Press.

Calder, Kent E. 1989. "Elites in an Equalizing Role? Ex-Bureaucrats as Coordinators and Intermediaries in the Japanese Government-Business Relationship." *Comparative Politics* (July): 379–403.

Calder, Kent E. 1990. "Linking Welfare and the Developmental State: Postal Savings in Japan." *Journal of Japanese Studies* 16 (winter): 31–59.

Calder, Kent E. 1993. *Strategic Capitalism: Private Business and Public Purpose in Japanese Industrial Finance.* Princeton, NJ: Princeton University Press.

Campbell, John Y., and Yasushi Hamao. 1992. "Changing Patterns of Corporate Financing and the Main Bank System." Papers presented to the EDI/World Bank Workshop on the Japanese Main Bank System, 29 July–1 August, Washington.

Caves, Richard E., Jeffrey A. Frankel, and Ronald W. Jones. 1990. *World Trade and Payments: An Introduction.* 5th ed. Glenview, IL: Scott Foresman.

Caves, Richard E., and Masu Uekusa. 1976. *Industrial Organization in Japan.* Washington: Brookings Institution.

Cohen, Jerome B. 1950. *Japan's Economy in War and Reconstruction.* New York: Columbia University Press.

Curtis, Gerald L. 1988. The Japanese Way of Politics. New York: Columbia University Press.

Destler, I. M., and Hisao Mitsuyu. 1982. "Locomotives on Different Tracks: Macroeconomic Diplomacy, 1977–1979." *Coping with U.S.-Japanese Economic Conflicts.* Lexington, MA: D. C. Heath, pp. 243–70.

Dodwell Marketing Consultants. 1982. *Industrial Groupings in Japan.* Tokyo.

Eccleston, Bernard. 1986. "The State, Finance and Industry in Japan." In Andrew Cox, ed. *State, Finance, and Industry.* New York: St. Martin's Press, pp. 6–79.

Feldman, Robert A. 1986. *Japanese Financial Markets: Deficits, Dilemmas, and Deregulation.* Cambridge: MIT Press.

Flaherty, M. Therese, and Itami Hiroyuki. 1988. "The Banking-Industrial Complex." In Daniel I. Okimoto and Thomas P. Rohlen, eds., *Inside the Japanese System: Readings on Contemporary Society and Political Economy.* Stanford: Stanford University Press, pp. 54–63.

Foreign Exchange Fund and Special Account Law (Law 56, 30 March 1951). *EHS Law Bulletin Series: Series of Japanese Laws in English Version.* Tokyo: Eibun-Horei-sha, Inc.

Frankel, Jeffrey A. 1991. "Japanese Finance in the 1980s: A Survey." In Paul Krugman, ed., *Trade With Japan: Has the Door Opened Wider?* Chicago: University of Chicago Press, pp. 48–49.

Frankel, Jeffrey A. 1992. "Is a Yen Bloc Forming in Pacific Asia?" In Richard O'Brien, ed., *Finance and International Economy.* Vol. 5. Oxford: Oxford University Press, pp. 5–20.

Fukao, Mitsuhiro. 1990. "Liberalization of Japan's Foreign Exchange Controls and Structural Changes in the Balance of Payments." *Monetary and Economic Studies* (8 September).

Fukui, Haruo, Peter H. Merkl, Hubertus Müller-Groeling, and Akio Watanabe, eds. 1993. *The Politics of Economic Change in Postwar Japan and West Germany.* New York: St. Martin's Press.

Garten, Jeffrey E. 1988. "How Bonn, Tokyo Slyly Help Bush." *New York Times* (21 July).

Gerlach, Michael L. 1989. "*Keiretsu* Organization in the Japanese Economy: Analysis and Trade Implications." In Johnson, Tyson, Zysman, eds., *Politics and Productivity: The Real Story of Why Japan Works.* Cambridge, MA: Balinger, pp. 141–74.

Gerlach, Michael L. 1992. *Alliance Capitalism: The Social Organization of Japanese Business.* Berkeley: University of California Press, pp. 118–25.

Gyohten, Toyoo. 1989. "Internationalization of the Yen: Its Implication for U.S.-Japan Relations." In Hugh T. Patrick and Toyoo Gyohten, eds., *Japan and the United States Today.* New York: Columbia University, pp. 84–89.

Green, David Jay. 1989. "Exchange Rate Policy and Intervention in Japan." *Keizai-Shirin* 135.

Hale, David D. 1990. "Economic Consequences of the Tokyo Stock Market Crash." Paper prepared for the U.S.-Japan Consultative Group on Monetary Policy, Washington (23–24 July).

Hale, David. 1988. "U.S. Economic Outlook and Monetary Policy." Testimony before the US Senate Committee on Banking, Housing, and Urban Affairs. *Federal Reserve's Second Monetary Policy Report for 1988* (12 and 13 July).

Hayama, Masaru. 1982. Kaizu Naki Kokai: Hendo Sobasei Ju-nen. Tokyo: Toyo Keizai Shimposha, pp. 189–90.

Haynes, Stephen E., Michael M. Hutchinson, and Raymond F. Mikesell. 1986. *Japanese Financial Policies and the U.S. Trade Deficit.* Essays in International Finance 162. International Finance Section, Princeton University (April).

Hollerman, Leon. 1979. "International Economic Controls in Occupied Japan." *Journal of Asian Studies* 38 (August): 719.

Hollerman, Leon. 1988. *Japan, Disincorporated: The Economic Liberalization Process.* Stanford: Hoover Institution Press.

Horiuchi, Akiyoshi. 1989. "Informational Properties of the Japanese Financial System." *Japan and the World Economy* 1, (no. 3).

Horiuchi, Akiyoshi. 1993. "Monetary Policies: Japan." In Haruo Fukui, et al., eds., *The Politics of Economic Changes in Postwar Japan and West Germany.*

Hoshi, Takeo, Anil Kashyap, and David Scharfstein. 1990. "Bank Monitoring and Investment: Evidence from the Changing Structure of Japanese Corporate Banking Relationships." In R. Glenn Hubbard, ed., *Asymmetric Information, Corporate Finance, and Investment.* Chicago: Chicago University Press.

Iida, Keisuke. 1990. *The Theory and Practice of International Economic Policy Coordination.* Ph.D. dissertation. Harvard University (May).

"International Economic Controls in Occupied Japan." 1979. *Journal of Asian Studies* (August): 719.

International Monetary Fund. 1989. "Capital Account Developments in Japan and the Federal Republic of Germany: Institutional Influences and Structural Changes." *World Economic Outlook* (April): 84–89.

Ishii, Naoko, Warwick McKibbin, and Jeffrey Sachs. "The Economic Policy Mix, Policy Cooperation, and Protectionism: Some Aspects of Macroeconomic Interdependence among the United States, Japan, and Other OECD Countries." *Journal of Policy Modelling* 7, no. 4: 533–72.

Ito, Takatoshi. 1992. *The Japanese Economy.* Cambridge, MA: MIT Press.

Ito, Takatoshi. 1994. "U. S.-Japan Macroeconomic Policy Coordination: Agenda for the 1990s and Beyond." In Yoichi Funabashi, ed. *Japan's International Agenda.* New York: New York University Press, pp. 81–110.

Iwata, Kazumasa. 1989. "Political Process of Monetary Policy Making in Japan." Working Paper 13, Department of Social and International Relations, University of Tokyo (October).

Johnson, Chalmers. 1982. *MITI and the Japanese Miracle.* Stanford: Stanford University Press.

Johnson, Chalmers, Laura D'Andrea Tyson, John Zysman, eds. 1989. *Politics and Productivity: The Real Story of Why Japan Works.* Cambridge, MA: Ballinger.

Kinoshita, Tomohiro. 1990. "The Federal Reserve System and the Bank of Japan." Manuscript (May).

Komiya, Ryutaro, and Motoshige Itoh. 1988. "Japan's International Trade and Trade Policy." In Takashi Inoguchi and Daniel Okimoto, eds., *The Political Economy of Japan: Volume 2, The Changing International Context.* Stanford: Stanford University Press, pp. 173–224.

Komiya, Ryutaro, and Miyako Suda. 1983. *Japan's Foreign Exchange Policy: 1971–82.* Tokyo: Nihon Keizai Shinbunsha. Canberra, Australia: Australian National University.

Kosai, Yutaka. 1993. "Anti-inflation Policy: Japan." In Haruo Fukui, et al., eds., *The Politics of Economic Changes in Postwar Japan and West Germany.* New York: St. Martin's Press.

Langdon, Frank C. 1961. "Big Business Lobbying in Japan: The Case of Central Bank Reform." *American Political Science Review* 55 (September).

Lincoln, Edward J. 1988. *Japan: Facing Economic Maturity.* Washington: Brookings Institution.

Lincoln, Edward J. 1988. "Japanese Bond and Stock Markets." In Daniel I. Okimoto and Thomas P. Rohlen, eds., *Inside the Japanese System: Readings on Contemporary Society and Political Economy.* Stanford: Stanford University Press, pp. 54–63.

Maehara, Yasuhiro. 1993. "The Internationalization of the Yen and Its Role as a Key Currency." *Journal of Asian Studies* 4: 153–70.

McDonald, Jack. 1989. "The Mochiai Effect: Japanese Corporate Cross-Holdings." The Journal of Portfolio Management (fall).

McKenzie, Colin, and Michael Stutchbury. 1992. *Japanese Financial Markets and the Role of the Yen.* North Sydney: Allen & Unwin.

Ministry of Finance. 1960. *Chuo Ginko Seido: Kinyu Seido Chosakai Toshin Narabi Kankei Shiryo.* Tokyo (December).

Nakagawa, Koji. 1981. *Taikenteki Kinyu-seisaku-ron: Nichigin no mado kara [Personal Experiences in Financial Policy: From the Window of the Bank of Japan].* Tokyo: Nihon Keizai Shimbun-sha.

Nakao, Masaaki, and Akinari Horii. 1991. *The Process of Decision-Making and Implementation of Monetary Policy in Japan.* Bank of Japan Special Paper 198. Tokyo (March): 31.

Nakatani, Iwao. 1984. "The Economic Role of Financial Corporate Grouping." In Masahiko Aoki, ed., *The Economic Analysis of the Japanese Firm.* New York/Amsterdam: North-Holland.

Noguchi, Yukio. 1989. "Japan's Fiscal Policy and External Balance." Manuscript (September).

Ogata, Shijuro. 1990. "Central Banking: A Japanese Perspective." In Hans R. Stoll, ed., *International Finance and Financial Policy.* New York: Quorum Books.

Okimoto, Daniel I., and Thomas P. Rohlen, eds. 1988. *Inside the Japanese System: Readings on Contemporary Society and Political Economy.* Stanford: Stanford University Press, pp. 54–63.

Otani, Ichiro. 1983. "Exchange Rate Instability and Capital Controls: The Japanese Experience, 1978–1981." In David Bigman and Teizo Taya, eds., *Exchange Rate and Trade Instability: Causes, Consequences, and Remedies.* Cambridge, UK: Ballinger, pp. 331–33.

Patrick, Hugh T. 1962. *Monetary Policy and Central Banking in Contemporary Japan.* Bombay: Bombay University Press, pp. 34–35.

Patrick, Hugh, and Henry Rosovsky. 1976. *Asia's New Giant: How the Japanese Economy Works.* Washington: Brookings Institution.

Pauly, Louis W. 1988. *Opening Financial Markets: Banking Politics on the Pacific Rim.* Ithaca, NY: Cornell University Press.

Pempel, T. J. 1973. "Japanese Foreign Economic Policy: The Domestic Bases for International Behavior." *Between Power and Plenty: Foreign Economic Policies of Advanced Industrial States.* Madison: University of Wisconsin Press, pp. 152.

Pempel, T. J. 1982. *Policy and Politics in Japan: Creative Conservatism.* Philadelphia: Temple University Press.

Roosa, Robert V. 1986. *The United States and Japan in the International Monetary System 1946–1985.* New York: Group of Thirty.

Rosenbluth, Frances McCall. 1989. *Financial Politics in Contemporary Japan.* Ithaca, NY: Cornell University Press.

Samuels, Richard J. 1987. *The Business of the Japanese State: Energy Markets in Comparative and Historical Perspective.* Ithaca, NY: Cornell University Press.

Sakakibara, Eisuke. 1993. *Beyond Capitalism: The Japanese Model of Market Economics.* Lanham/New York/London: Economic Strategy Institute.

Sakakibara, Eisuke, and Yukio Noguchi. 1977. "Dissecting the Finance Ministry-Bank of Japan Dynasty: End of the Wartime System for Total Economic Mobilization." *Japan Echo* 4 (autumn).

Schmiegelow, Henrik. 1986. "Japan's Exchange Rate Policy: Policy Targets, Nonpolicy Variables, and Discretionary Adjustment." *Japan's Response to Crisis and Change in the World Economy.* Armonk, NY: M.E. Sharpe.

Sender, Henny. 1988. "The Bank of Japan under Siege." *Institutional Investor* (November): 59.

Sender, Henry. 1990. "A Prince Comes of Age at the BOJ." *Institutional Investor* (April).

Sheard, Paul. 1985. *Main Banks and Structural Adjustment in Japan.* Australia-Japan Research Centre, Research Paper 129 (December): 57.

Sheard, Paul. 1992. "The Role of the Main Bank When Borrowing Firms Are in Financial Distress." Paper presented to the EDI/World Bank Workshop on the Japanese Main Bank System, 29 July–1 August, Washington.

Shiraishi, Takashi. 1989. *Japan's Trade Policies: 1945 to the Present Day.* London and Atlantic Highlands, NJ: Athlone Press, pp. 37–41, 68–9.

Singleton, Kenneth J., ed. 1993. *Japanese Monetary Policy.* Chicago: University of Chicago Press, for NBER.

Smith, Allan D. 1984. "The Japanese Foreign Exchange and Foreign Trade Control Law and Administrative Guidance: The Labyrinth and the Castle." *Law and Policy in International Business*: pp. 417–76.

Suzuki, Yoshio. 1985. "Japan's Monetary Policy over the Past 10 Years." *Bank of Japan Monetary and Economic Studies* 3, no. 2 (September): 8.

Suzuki, Yoshio. 1989. *Japan's Economic Performance and International Role.* Tokyo: University of Tokyo Press.

Suzuki, Yoshio, ed. 1987. *The Japanese Financial System.* Oxford: Clarendon Press, pp. 314–15.

Tachi, Ryuichiro, et al. 1993. *The Mechanism and Economic Effects of Asset Price Fluctuations.* Tokyo: Ministry of Finance, Institute for Fiscal and Monetary Policy (April).

Tavlas, George S., and Yuzuru Ozeki. 1992. *The Internationalization of Currencies: An Appraisal of the Japanese Yen.* International Monetary Fund Occasional Paper 90. Washington: International Monetary Fund (January).

VanDenBerg, Jan. 1993. "Japanese Stimulus: Truth and Advertising." *International Economic Insights* (July/August): 2–4.

Westney, D. Eleanor. 1987. *Imitation and Innovation: The Transfer of Western Organizational Patterns to Meiji Japan.* Cambridge, MA: Harvard University Press.

Wood, Christopher. 1992. *The Bubble Economy: Japan's Extraordinary Speculative Boom of the '80s and the Dramatic Bust of the '90s.* New York: Atlantic Monthly Press.

Yamamura, Kozo, ed. 1990. *Japan's Economic Structure: Should It Change?* Seattle: Society for Japanese Studies.

Yamamura, Kozo, and Yasukichi Yasuba, eds. 1987. *The Political Economy of Japan. Vol. 1: The Domestic Transformation.* Stanford, CA: Stanford University Press.

Yoshino, Toshihiko. 1977. "The Creation of the Bank of Japan: Its Western Origin and Adaptation." *The Developing Economies* (22 December).

Zielinski, Robert, and Nigel Holloway. 1991. *Unequal Equities: Power and Risk in Japan's Stock Market.* Japan: Kodansha International Ltd.

Germany and Europe

Agence France Presse. 1990. "Texte du Message de MM. Mitterrand et Kohl sur la Construction Politique de L'Europe des Douze." Paris (19 April).

Balkhausen, Dieter. 1992. *Gutes Geld & schlechte Politik: Der Report über die Bundesbank.* Düsseldorf: Econ Verlag.

Bank for International Settlements. 1988. "Prof. Schlesinger Examines the Interplay between Domestic and External Constraints in Monetary Policy." Address by the Vice President of the Deutsche Bundesbank, Dortmund, West Germany (10 November).

Cameron, David. 1993. "British Exit, German Voice, French Loyalty: Defection, Domination, and Cooperation in the 1992–93 ERM Crisis." Manuscript, Yale University.

Catte, Pietro, Giampaolo Galli, and Salvatore Rebecchini. 1992. "Concerted Interventions and the Dollar: An Analysis of Daily Data." Paper prepared for the Ossola Memorial Conference, Perugia (July).

Commission and Council of the European Communities. 1992. *Treaty on European Union.* Luxembourg: Office of the Official Publications of the European Communities.

Commission of the European Communities. 1990. "One Market, One Money." *European Economy* 44 (October): 187.

Committee for the Study of Economic and Monetary Union. 1989. *Report on Economic and Monetary Union in the European Community.* Luxembourg: Office of the Official Publications of the European Communities.

Cooper, Wendy. 1992. "The Finanzplatz Fairy Tale." *Institutional Investor* (May): 29–36.

Deeg, Richard E. 1992. "The State, Banks, and Economic Governance in Germany." Paper presented to the American Political Science Association annual meeting, Chicago (3–6 September).

De Grauwe, Paul, and Lucas Papademos. 1990. *The European Monetary System in the 1990s.* London/New York: Longman.

Deutsche Bank. 1990. *German Economic and Monetary Union.* Frankfurt: Deutsche Bank (June).

Deutsche Bank. 1990. *Deutsche Bank Bulletin* (April).

Deutsche Bundesbank. 1988. *30 Jahre Deutsche Bundesbank: Die Entstehung des Bundesbankgesetzes vom 26. Juli 1957.* Frankfurt: Deutsche Bundesbank.

Deutsche Bundesbank. 1989. *The Deutsche Bundesbank: Its Monetary Policy Instruments and Functions.* Special Series 7, 3rd ed. Frankfurt: Deutsche Bundesbank.

Deutsche Bundesbank. 1992. "Déclarations de Monsieur François Mitterrand, Président de la République." *Auszüge aus Presseartikeln.* Frankfurt (9 September): 1–2.

Deutscher Bundestag. 1978. *Stenographischer Bericht.* 122 Sitzung (6 December).

Deutscher Bundestag. 1993. "Beschlussempfehlung und Bericht des Sonderausschusses Europäische Union '(Vertag von Maastricht)' [Recommendation and Report of the Special Committee on European Union (Treaty of Maastricht)]. Drucksache 12/3895.

Deutscher Bundestag. 1993. "Entschliessungsantrag der Fraktionen der CDU/CSU, SPD und F. D. P. zu dem Gesetzentwurf der Bundesregierung zum Vertag vom 7 February 1992 über die Europäische Union [Determination of the Fractions of the CDU/CSU, SPD and F.D. P. Regarding the Draft Law of the Federal Government on the Treaty of 7 February 1992 on the European Union]. Drucksache 12/3906.

Dudler, Hermann-Josef. 1988. "Monetary Policy and Exchange Market Management in Germany." In *Exchange Market Intervention and Monetary Policy,* 65–96. Bank for International Settlements, Monetary and Economic Department, Basel (March).

Dudler, Hermann-Josef. 1990. "Monetary Control and Exchange Market Management: German Policy Experience from the 1985 Plaza Agreement to the 1989 Summit of the Arch." Paper presented to the Bank of Israel and David Horowitz Institute Conference on Aspects of Central Bank Policymaking, Tel-Aviv (3–5 January): 13–15.

Dyson, Kenneth. 1986. "The State, Banks, and Industry: the West German Case." In Cox, ed., *State, Finance, and Industry,* pp. 118–41.

Dziobek, Claudia. 1992. "The German Banking System and Financial Market Reforms." Manuscript presented at Brookings Institution. Washington: (18 November).

Edwards, J. S. S., and Klaus Fischer. N.d. "An Overview of the German Financial System." Paper prepared for the Centre for Economic Policy Research, London.

Edwards, J. S. S., and Klaus Fischer. 1991. *Banks, Finance and Investment in West Germany since 1970.* Discussion Paper 497. London: Centre for Economic Policy Research (January).

Ehrenberg, Herbert. 1976. *Zwischen Marx und Markt: Konturen einer infrastrukturorientierten und verteilungswirksamen Wirtschaftspolitik.* Munich: Deutscher Taschenbuch Verlag.

Eichengreen, Barry, and Charles Wyplosz. 1993. "The Unstable EMS." *Brookings Papers on Economic Activity* 1, pp. 51–143.

Emminger, Otmar. 1977. *The D-mark in the Conflict between Internal and External Equilibrium.* Essays in International Finance 122. Princeton: Princeton University, International Finance Section (June).

Emminger, Otmar. 1986. *D-Mark, Dollar, Währungskrisen.* Stuttgart: Deutsche-Verlags Anstalt.

Esser, Josef. 1990. "Bank Power in West Germany Revised." *West European Politics* 13.

Federation of German Industries. 1991. "Opinion on European Economic and Monetary Union." Statement to the Finance Committee of the Deutsche Bundestag. Cologne (18 September).

Federation of German Stock Exchanges. 1992. *Annual Report 1991.* Frankfurt.

"Gesetz zur Änderung des Grundgesetzes." 1992. *Bundesgesetzblatt* 58 (24 December): 2087.

Franks, Julian, and Colin Mayer. 1990. "Capital Markets and Corporate Control: A Study of France, Germany, and the UK." *Economic Policy* 11: 191–231.

"Germany: Federal Constitutional Court Decision Concerning the Maastricht Treaty." *International Legal Materials* 33 (March 1994): 388–444.

Giavazzi, Francesco, and Alberto Giovannini. 1989. *Limiting Exchange Rate Flexibility: The European Monetary System.* Cambridge, MA: MIT Press.

Giavazzi, Francesco, Stefano Micossi, and Marcus Miller. 1988. The *European Monetary System.* Cambridge, UK: Cambridge University Press.

Gottschelk, Arno. 1988. "Stimmrechtseinfluss der Banken in den Aktionärversammlungen von Grossunternehmen." *WSI Mitteilungen* (May).

Gros, Daniel, and Niels Thygesen. 1988. The *EMS: Achievements, Current Issues, and Directions for the Future.* Paper 35. Brussels: Centre for European Policy Studies.

Gros, Daniel, and Niels Thygesen. 1992. *European Monetary Integration: From the European Monetary System to European Monetary Union.* London: Longman.

Guerrieri, Paolo, and Pier Carlo Padoan. 1989. The *Political Economy of European Integration: States, Markets, and Institutions.* Savage, MD: Barnes & Noble Books.

Guth, Wilfried. 1989. "The Prospects in the European Community for Closer Monetary Cooperation and the Establishment of a Central Bank." In *Weltwirtschaft und Währung: Aufsätze und Vorträge, 1967–1989.* Mainz: v. Hase und Koehler Verlag: 345–70.

Hankel, Wilhelm. 1976. "Monetary Stability and the Welfare State." *German Tribune* (6 June): 6–7. Reproduced in Katzenstein, *Politics in West Germany.* Philadelphia: Temple University Press.

Hankel, Wilhelm. 1980. "Germany: Economic Nationalism in the International Economy." In Wilfrid Kohl and Giorgio Basevi, eds., *West Germany: A European and Global Power.* Lexington, MA: Lexington Books, pp. 22–30.

Hanrieder, Wolfram, ed. 1982. *Helmut Schmidt: Perspectives on Politics.* Boulder: Westview.

Harm, Christian. 1992. "The Relationship between German Banks and Large German Firms." World Bank, Country Economics Department, Working Papers (May).

Henning, C. Randall. 1991. "Europäische Währungsunion und die Vereinigten Staaten." In Manfred Weber, ed., *Europa auf dem Weg zur Währungsunion.* Darmstadt, Germany: Wissenschaftliche Buchgesellschaft, pp. 317–40.

Henning, C. Randall. 1992. "Management of Economic Policy in the European Community." In *Europe and the United States: Competition and Cooperation in the 1990s.* Committee on Foreign Affairs, US House of Representatives. Washington: GPO.

Hesse, Helmut. 1992. "ECU Now and Later, Some Considerations after Maastricht." In Deutsche Bundesbank, *Auszüge aus Presseartikeln* (30 October): 7.

Holtfrerich, Carl-Ludwig. 1986. The *German Inflation 1914-1923: Causes and Effects in International Perspective.* Berlin/New York: de Gruyter.

Holtfrerich, Carl-Ludwig. 1988. "Relations between Monetary Authorities and Governmental Institutions: The Case of Germany from the 19th Century to the Present." In G. Toniolo, ed., *Central Banks' Independence in Historical Perspective.* Berlin/New York: de Gruyter, pp. 91–167.

Holtham, Gerald. 1989. "German Macroeconomic Policy and the 1978 Bonn Summit." In Richard N. Cooper, Barry Eichengreen, Gerald Holtham, Robert D. Putnam, and C. Randall Henning, *Can Nations Agree? Issues in International Economic Cooperation* (Washington: Brookings Institution) 141–77.

Hormats, Robert D. 1992. "Patterns of Competition." In Steven Mullen and Gebhard Schweigler, eds., *From Occupation to Cooperation: The United States and United Germany in a Changing World Order.* New York: W. W. Norton, 178–79.

Johnson, Peter A. 1991. *Unpopular Measures: Translating Monetarism into Monetary Policy in Germany and the United States.* Ph.D. diss., Cornell University.

Johnson, Peter A. 1992. "Constraints on the Role of Ideas in Economic Policymaking in Germany and the United States." Paper presented to the American Political Science Association, Chicago (3–6 September).

Jochimsen, Reimut. 1991. "European Economic and Monetary Union." Speech at the University of Dortmund, Dortmund (10 July).

Jochimsen, Reimut. 1991. "The European System of Central Banks and the Role of National Central Banks in the Economic and Monetary Union." Presentation to the seminar on Economic and Monetary Union, European Institute of Public Administration, Maastricht, The Netherlands (16 December).

Katzenstein, Peter J. 1987. *Policy and Politics in West Germany: The Growth of a Semisovereign State*. Philadelphia: Temple University Press.

Katzenstein, Peter J. 1989. *Industry and Politics in West Germany: Toward the Third Republic*. Ithaca, NY/London: Cornell University Press.

Kaufmann, Hugo M. 1969. "A Debate over Germany's Revaluation, 1961: A Chapter in Political Economy." *Weltwirtschaftliches Archiv*, 103.

Kaufmann, Hugo M. 1985. *Germany's International Monetary Policy and the European Monetary System*. New York: Columbia University Press, 97.

Kelleher, Catherine McArdle. 1992. "The New Germany: An Overview." In Paul B. Stares, ed., *The New Germany and the New Europe*. Washington: Brookings Institution, pp. 11–54, 55–92.

Kenen, Peter B. 1992. *EMU After Maastricht*. Washington: Group of Thirty.

Kennedy, Ellen. 1991. *The Bundesbank: Germany's Central Bank in the International Monetary System*. London: Royal Institute for International Affairs.

Kloten, Norbert. 1980. "Germany's Monetary and Financial Policy and the European Community." In Kohl and Basevi, eds., *West Germany*, pp. 177–99.

Kloten, Norbert. 1989. "The Delors Report." *The World Today* (August–September).

Kloten, Norbert, Karl-Heinz Ketterer, and Rainer Vollmer. 1985. "West Germany's Stabilization Performance." In Leon N. Lindberg and Charles S. Maier, eds., *The Politics of Inflation and Economic Stagnation*. Washington: Brookings Institution, pp. 353–402.

Kohl, Wilfrid L., and Giorgio Basevi, eds. 1980. *West Germany: A European and Global Power*. Lexington, MA: Lexington Books.

Kreile, Michael. 1992. "The Political Economy of the New Germany." In Paul B. Stares, ed., *The New Germany and the New Europe*. Washington: Brookings Institution.

Kreile, Michael. 1978. "West Germany: The Dynamics of Expansion." In P. Katzenstein, ed., *Between Power and Plenty*.

Lipp, Ernst Moritz, Ulrich Ramm, and Norbert Walter. 1992. "Reply to the Manifesto of Sixty Professors Regarding the Maastricht Resolutions" (15 June).

Lipschitz, Leslie, Jeroen Kremers, Thomas Mayer, and Donogh McDonald. 1989. *The Federal Republic of Germany: Adjustment in a Surplus Country*. IMF Occasional Paper 64. Washington: International Monetary Fund (January).

Lipschitz, Leslie, and Donogh McDonald, eds. 1990. *German Unification: Economic Issues*. Occasional Paper 75. Washington: International Monetary Fund (December).

Ludlow, Peter. 1982. *The Creation of the European Monetary System*. London: Butterworth Scientific.

Markovits, Andrei S. 1982. *The Political Economy of West Germany: Modell Deutschland*. New York: Praeger.

Marsh, David. 1989. *The Germans: A People at the Crossroads*. New York: St. Martin's Press.

Marsh, David. 1992. *The Bundesbank: The Bank That Rules Europe*. London: Heinemann.

Mitglieder der Arbeitsgemeinschaft deutscher wirtschaftswissenschaftlicher Forschungsinstitute e.V., Essen. 1980. *Die Lage der Weltwirtschaft und der westdeutschen Wirtschaft im Fruhjajr*. Berlin (28 April).

Nölling, Wilhelm. 1991. "Geld und die deutsche Vereinigung." *Hamburger Beiträge zur Wirtschafts- und Währungspolitik in Europa*. Hamburg (15 July).

Nölling, Wilhelm. 1992. "Good-by to the Deutsche Mark?" *Hamburger Beiträge zur Wirsthafts- und Währungspolitik in Europa*. Hamburg (1 April).

Nölling, Wilhelm. 1993. *Monetary Policy in Europe after Maastricht*. New York: St. Martin's Press.

Norman, Peter. 1992. "The Day Germany Planted a Currency Time Bomb." *Financial Times* (13 December).
Norman, Peter, and Lionel Barber. 1992. "The Monetary Tragedy of Errors That Led to Currency Chaos." *Financial Times* (11 December).
Oberbeck, Herbert, and Martin Baethge. 1989. "Computer and Pinstripes: Financial Institutions." *Industry and Politics in West Germany: Toward the Third Republic*. Ithaca, NY: Cornell University Press, pp. 275–306.
Pauly, Louis W. 1992. "The Politics of Monetary Union: National Strategies, International Implications." *International Journal* 47 (winter): 93–111.
Pöhl, Karl Otto. 1987. "Are We Moving Towards a More Stable International Monetary Order?" Speech to the American Institute for Contemporary German Studies. Washington (7 April).
Pöhl, Karl Otto. 1990. "Basic Features of a European Monetary Order." *Le Monde* (16 January).
Pöhl, Karl Otto. 1992. "A New Monetary Order for Europe." The 1992 Per Jacobsson Lecture. Washington: Per Jacobsson Foundation (20 September).
Portes, Richard. 1993. "EMS and EMU after the Fall." *The World Economy* (January).
Riemer, Jeremiah M. 1982. "Alterations in the Design of Model Germany." In Andrei S. Markovits, ed., *The Political Economy of West Germany*. New York: Praeger, pp. 53–89.
Riemer, Jeremiah M. 1982. "West German Crisis Management: Stability and Change in the Post-Keynesian Age." In Norman J. Vig and Steven E. Schier, eds., *Political Economy in Western Democracies*. New York: Holmes and Meier, pp. 229–54.
Riemer, Jeremiah M. 1983. *Crisis and Intervention in the West German Economy: A Political Analysis of Changes in the Policy Machinery during the 1960s and 1970s*. Ph.D. diss., Cornell University.
Scharpf, Fritz. 1991. *Crisis and Choice in European Social Democracy*. Ithaca, NY: Cornell University Press.
Scharrer, Hans-Eckart. 1993. "West Germany." In Haruo Fukui, et al., eds., *Politics of Economic Change in Postwar Japan and West Germany*. New York: St. Martin's Press, pp. 115–44.
Scharrer, Hans-Eckart. 1989. "Germany between Internal and External Balance." Manuscript. Hamburg, Germany.
Schlesinger, Helmut, and Horst Bockelman. 1973. "Monetary Policy in the Federal Republic of Germany." *Monetary Policy in Twelve Industrial Countries*. Boston: Federal Reserve Bank of Boston.
Schmidt, Helmut. 1985. *A Grand Strategy for the West*. New Haven: Yale.
Schmidt, Helmut. 1989. *Men and Powers: A Political Retrospective*. New York: Random House, pp. 266.
Sherman, Heidemarie C. 1990. "Central Banking in Germany and the Process of European Monetary Integration." *Tokyo Club Papers* 3. Tokyo: Tokyo Club Foundation for Global Studies, pp. 147–78.
Smyser, W.R. 1992. *The Economy of United Germany: Colossus at the Crossroads*. New York: St. Martin's Press.
Stihl, Hans Peter. 1992. "Remarks to the Association for European Monetary Union." Frankfurt, 26 May. Reprinted in Deutsche Bundesbank, *Auszüge aus Presseartikeln*. Frankfurt (2 June): 6–7.
Stokman, Frans N., Rolf Ziegler, and John Scott, eds. 1985. *Networks of Corporate Power: A Comparative Analysis of Ten Countries*. Oxford: Polity Press.
Stoltenberg, Gerhard. 1987. "The United States and Europe: Main Objectives for Economic Policies and International Cooperation." Speech at Georgetown University, Washington (10 April).
Tavlas, George S. 1991. *On the International Use of Currencies: The Case of the Deutsche Mark*. Essays in International Finance 181. Princeton: Princeton University (March).
Teltschik, Horst. 1991. *329 Tage: Innenansichten der Einigung*. Berlin: Siedler Verlag.

Thygesen, Niels. 1994. "Deepening the European Union: Monetary Arrangements." In Henning, Hufbauer, and Hochreiter, eds., *Reviving the European Union*, pp. 43–66.

Vig, J. Norman, and Steven E. Schier, eds., 1982. "West German Crisis Management: Stability and Change in the Post-Keynesian Age." *Political Economy in Western Democracies*. New York: Holmes and Meier.

Wadbrook, W. P. 1972. *West Germany's Balance of Payments Policy*. New York: Praeger.

Waigel, Theo. 1992. Speech to the Hanns Seidel Foundation. Washington (21 September).

Wallich, Henry. 1955. *Mainsprings of the German Revival*. New Haven: Yale University Press.

Welfens, Paul J. J., ed. 1992. *Economic Aspects of German Unification*. Berlin: Springer-Verlag.

Werner, Pierre, et al. 1970. "Report to the Council and the Commission on the Realisation by Stages of Economic and Monetary Union in the Community." Supplement to Bulletin II-1970 of the European Communities, Brussels.

Williamson, John. 1993. "The Fall of the Hard EMS." Manuscript (25 February).

Williamson, John, and Marcus H. Miller. 1987. *Targets and Indicators: A Blueprint for the International Coordination of Economic Policy*. POLICY ANALYSES IN INTERNATIONAL ECONOMICS 22. Washington: Institute for International Economics (September).

van Ypersele, Jacques, and Jean-Claude Koeune. 1985. *The European Monetary System: Origins, Operation and Outlook*. Luxembourg: Office of the Official Publications of the European Communities.

van Ypersele, Jacques. 1985. *The European Monetary System: Origins, Operation, and Outlook*. Luxembourg: Office of the Official Publications of the European Communities.

Ziegler, Rolf. 1985. "Conclusion." In Frans N. Stokman, Rolf Ziegler, and John Scott, eds., *Networks of Corporate Power: A Comparative Analysis of Ten Countries*. Oxford: Polity Press, pp. 267–87.

Ziegler, Rolf, Donald Bender, and Hermann Biehler. 1985. "Industry and Banking in the German Corporate Network." In Frans N. Stokman, Rolf Ziegler and John Scott, eds., *Networks of Corporate Power: A Comparative Analysis of Ten Countries*. Oxford: Polity Press, 92–111.

United States

Advisory Committee on Trade Negotiations. 1985. *Chairman's Report on a New Round of Multilateral Trade Negotiations* (15 May).

AFL-CIO. 1985. "Statement by the AFL-CIO Executive Council on Trade." Washington (8 May).

American Bankers Association. 1988. Press release. Washington (4 February).

American Bankers Association. 1988. Press release. Napa, CA (1 July).

American Bankers Association. 1991. *International Banking and Financial Market Developments*. May.

Beck, Nathaniel. 1984. "Domestic Political Sources of American Monetary Policy: 1955–82." *Journal of Politics* 46.

Bergsten, C. Fred. 1975. *The Dilemmas of the Dollar: The Economics and Politics of United States International Economic Policy*. New York: New York University Press.

Bergsten, C. Fred. 1986. "America's Unilateralism." In Bergsten, Etienne Davignon, and Isamu Miyazaki, *Conditions for Partnership in International Economic Management*. Report to the Trilateral Commission 32. New York: Trilateral Commission.

Bergsten, C. Fred. 1991. "Taming Japan's Trade Surplus." *New York Times* (28 December).

Board of Governors of the Federal Reserve System. 1984. *The Federal Reserve System: Purposes and Functions*. Washington: Board of Governors.

Board of Governors of the Federal Reserve System. 1990. *Federal Reserve Act and Other Statutory Provisions Affecting the Federal Reserve System.* Washington: Board of Governors.

Branson, William H., and James P. Love. 1988. "US Manufacturing and the Real Exchange Rate." In Richard C. Marston, ed., *Misalignment of Exchange Rates: Effects on Trade and Industry*, pp. 241–74. Chicago: University of Chicago Press,

Business Roundtable. 1985. "The Trade Deficit—Its Causes, Consequences, and Cures" (January).

Cantor, Richard. "The Institutionalization of Wealth Management and Competition in Wholesale Investor Services." *International Competitiveness of U.S. Financial Firms.* Federal Reserve Bank of New York: 116–36.

Cohen, Benjamin J. 1977. *Organizing the World's Money: The Political Economy of International Monetary Relations.* New York: Basic Books.

Cohen, Benjamin J. 1983. "An Explosion in the Kitchen? Economic Relations with Other Advanced Industrial States." In Kenneth A. Oye, Robert J. Lieber, and Donald Rothchild, eds., *Eagle Defiant: United States Foreign Policy in the 1980s*, pp. 105–30. Boston: Little, Brown.

Cohen, Stephen D. 1988. *The Making of United States International Economic Policy: Principles, Problems, and Proposals for Reform.* 3rd ed. New York: Praeger.

Cohen, Stephen D., and Ronald I. Meltzer. 1982. *United States International Economic Policy in Action.* New York: Praeger.

Competitiveness Policy Council, Trade Policy Subcouncil. 1992. Transcript of meeting. Washington (10 June).

Conybeare, John A. C. 1988. *United States Foreign Economic Policy and the International Capital Markets: The Case of Capital Export Controls, 1963–1974.* New York: Garland.

Coombs, Charles A. 1976. *The Arena of International Finance.* New York: John Wiley & Sons.

Cumming, Christine M., Bonnie E. Loopesko, and Charles M. Lucas. 1992. "The U.S. Financial System at the Crossroads: Financial Stability and Financial Reform." *International Competitiveness of U.S. Financial Firms.* Federal Reserve Bank of New York: 1–36.

Destler, I. M. 1992. *American Trade Politics.* 2nd ed. Washington: Institute for International Economics, and New York: Twentieth Century Fund.

Destler, I. M., and C. Randall Henning. 1989. *Dollar Politics: Exchange Rate Policymaking in the United States.* Washington: Institute for International Economics.

Estrella, Arturo. 1986. "Domestic Banks and Their Competitors in the Prime Commercial Loan Market." In *Recent Trends in Commercial Bank Profitability.* Federal Reserve Bank of New York (September).

Federal Reserve Bank of New York. 1991. *The International Competitiveness of U.S. Financial Firms: Products, Markets, and Conventional Performance Measures.*

Federal Reserve Bank of New York. 1992. *The International Competitiveness of U.S. Financial Firms: The Dynamics of Financial Industry Change.*

Feldstein, Martin, ed. 1994. *American Economic Policy in the 1980s.* Chicago: University of Chicago Press.

Frankel, Jeffrey A. 1984. *The Yen-Dollar Agreement: Liberalizing Japanese Capital Markets.* POLICY ANALYSES IN INTERNATIONAL ECONOMICS 9. Washington: Institute for International Economics (February).

Frankel, Jeffrey A. 1994. "The Making of Exchange Rate Policy in the 1980s." In Martin Feldstein, ed., *American Economic Policy in the 1980s.* Chicago: University of Chicago Press.

Friedman, Milton. 1981. "A Memorandum to the Fed." *Wall Street Journal*, 30 January.

Friedman, Milton. 1982. "The Federal Reserve and Monetary Instability." *Wall Street Journal*, 1 February.

Friedman, Milton, and Anna J. Schwartz. 1963. *A Monetary History of the United States, 1867–1960.* Princeton: Princeton University Press.

Gardner, Richard N. 1980. *Sterling-Dollar Diplomacy in Current Perspective: The Origins and the Prospects of Our International Economic Order*. Rev. ed. New York: Columbia University Press.

Gonzalez, Henry B. 1993. "The Federal Reserve System Accountability Act." *Congressional Record* (5 January): H64–68.

Gowa, Joanne. 1983. *Closing the Gold Window: Domestic Politics and the End of Bretton Woods*. Ithaca, NY: Cornell University Press.

Gowa, Joanne. 1984. "Hegemons, IOs, and Markets: The Case of the Substitution Account." In *International Organization* 38 (autumn): 661–83.

Gowa, Joanne. 1988. "Public Goods and Political Institutions: Trade and Monetary Policy Processes in the United States." *International Organization* 42 (winter): 15–32.

Greider, William. 1987. *Secrets of the Temple: How the Federal Reserve Runs the Country*. New York, London, Toronto, Sydney, Tokyo: Simon and Schuster.

Hackley, Howard H. 1961. "Memorandum to the Federal Open Market Committee on Legal Aspects of Proposed Plan for Federal Reserve Operations in Foreign Currencies." 22 November.

Hale, David D. 1991. "Will the Weakness of the U.S. Financial System Prevent an Economic Recovery in 1991?" Paper prepared for the US-Japan Economic Policy Group, Tokyo (April).

Hamilton, Lee H. 1989. Statement before the Subcommittee on Domestic Monetary Policy, Committee on Banking, Housing, and Urban Affairs, US Senate (9 November).

Haraf, William S., and Rose Marie Kushmeider, eds. 1988. *Restructuring Banking and Financial Services in America*. Washington: American Enterprise Institute.

Havrilesky, Thomas. 1993. *The Pressures on American Monetary Policy*. Boston, Dordrecht: Kluwer.

Henning, C. Randall, and I. M. Destler. 1988. "From Neglect to Activism: American Politics and the 1985 Plaza Accord." *Journal of Public Policy* 8 (July–December): 317–33.

Holmes, Alan R., and Scott E. Pardee. 1979. "Treasury and Federal Reserve Foreign Exchange Operations." *Federal Reserve Bank of New York Quarterly Review* 4 (spring): 67–87.

Johnson, Manuel. 1990. "Monetary Policy Outlook." Speech sponsored by Washington Analysis Corporation, Washington, 24 October.

Kane, Edward J. 1982. "External Pressure and the Operations of the Fed." In Raymond E. Lombra and Willard E. Witte, eds., *Political Economy of International and Domestic Monetary Relations*. Ames, Iowa: Iowa State University Press, pp. 211–32.

Kettl, Donald F. 1986. *Leadership at the Fed*. New Haven: Yale University Press.

Kissinger, Henry A. 1979. *The White House Years*. Boston: Little, Brown.

Knight, Robert H. 1962. "Memorandum to the Secretary of the Treasury." Reproduced in US Congress, House, Committee on Banking, *Report on the General Agreements to Borrow*. 87th Cong., 2nd sess., 6 January.

Kolko, Gabriel. 1963. *The Triumph of Conservatism: A Reinterpretation of American History, 1900–16*. New York: Macmillan.

Krasner, Stephen D. 1978. "United States Commercial and Monetary Policy: Unraveling the Paradox of External Strength and Internal Weakness." In Katzenstein, ed., *Between Power and Plenty: Foreign Economic Policies of Advanced Industrial States*. Madison: University of Wisconsin Press, pp. 51–87.

Krugman, Paul R. 1991. *Has the Adjustment Process Worked?* POLICY ANALYSES IN INTERNATIONAL ECONOMICS 34. Washington: Institute for International Economics, October.

Krugman, Paul R., and George Hatsopoulos. 1987. "The Problem of U.S. Competitiveness in Manufacturing." In *New England Economic Review* (January/February): 18–29.

Livingston, James. 1986. *Origins of the Federal Reserve System: Money, Class, and Corporate Capitalism, 1890–1913*. Ithaca, NY/ London: Cornell University Press.

Mayer, Martin. 1980. *The Fate of the Dollar*. New York: Times Books.

Mayer, Thomas, ed. 1990. *The Political Economy of American Monetary Policy.* Cambridge, UK/New York: Cambridge University Press.

Melamed, Leo, ed. 1988. *The Merits of Flexible Exchange Rates: An Anthology.* Fairfax, VA: George Mason University Press.

Melton, William C. 1985. Inside the Fed: Making Monetary Policy. Homewood, IL: Dow Jones–Irwin.

Mintz, Beth, and Michael Schwartz. 1985. The Power Structure of American Business. Chicago: University of Chicago Press.

Mulford, Daniel C. 1990. "Statement before the Committee on Banking, Finance and Urban Affairs, US House of Representatives." Washington: US Department of the Treasury (14 August).

Munger, Michael C., and Brian E. Roberts. 1990. "The Federal Reserve and Its Institutional Environment: A Review." In Thomas Mayer, ed., *The Political Economy of American Monetary Policy.* Cambridge, UK/New York: Cambridge University Press, pp. 83–98.

National Association of Manufacturers. 1985. "The US Dollar Exchange Rate Problem: NAM Position Paper." Washington (16 July).

Nickel, Herman. 1978. "The Inside Story of the Dollar Rescue." *Fortune* (4 December): 40–44.

Niskanen, William A. 1987. "A Lower Dollar vs. Recession." *New York Times* (27 October): A35.

Odell, John S. 1982. *U.S. International Monetary Policy: Markets, Power, and Ideas as Sources of Change.* Princeton: Princeton University Press.

Owens, John E. "The State Regulation and Deregulation of Financial Institutions and Services in the United States." In Cox, ed., *State, Finance, and Industry.* New York: St. Martin's Press, 172–230.

Pauls, B. Dianne. 1990. "U.S. Exchange Rate Policy: Bretton Woods to Present." *Federal Reserve Bulletin* 76 (November): 891–908.

Pisar, Samuel. 1971. "Capital Restraint Programs." In *United States International Economic Policy in an Interdependent World.* Washington: GPO.

Porter, Michael E. 1992. *Capital Choices: Changing the Way America Invests in Industry.* A research report presented to the Council on Competitiveness, Washington.

Reagan, Ronald. 1985. "State of the Union." Address Delivered before a Joint Session of the Congress, February, reprinted in *Weekly Compilation of Presidential Documents* 21 (6): 140.

Reston, James, Jr. 1989. *The Lone Star: The Life of John Connally.* New York: Harper and Row.

Roosa, Robert V. 1965. *Monetary Reform for the World Economy.* New York: Harper and Row.

Roosa, Robert V. 1967. *The Dollar and World Liquidity.* New York: Random House.

Safire, William. 1975. *Before the Fall: An Inside View of the Pre-Watergate White House.* Garden City, NJ: Doubleday.

Shadow Open Market Committee. 1985. "Policy Statement." New York (25 March).

Shadow Open Market Committee. 1987. "An Open Letter to Alan Greenspan: Policy Statement." New York (14 September).

Shadow Open Market Committee. 1988. "Policy Statement." New York (19 September).

Solomon, Robert. 1982. *The International Monetary System, 1945–1981.* Rev. ed. New York: Harper & Row.

Sorensen, Theodore C. 1965. *Kennedy.* New York: Harper & Row.

Spero, Joan. 1980. *The Failure of the Franklin National Bank: Challenge to the International Banking System.* New York: Columbia University Press.

Starobin, Paul. 1991. "Bypassing Banks." *National Journal* (9 March).

Stelzer, Irwin M. 1988. "The Election Dollar." *The American Spectator* (September): 28–33.

Sweet, Lawrence M. 1992. "Competition in Wholesale Credit Services." In Federal Reserve Bank of New York, *The International Competitiveness of U.S. Financial Firms: the Dynamics of Financial Industry Change.* New York, pp. 95–111.

Sylla, Richard. 1988. "The Autonomy of Monetary Authorities: The Case of the US Federal Reserve System." In Gianni Toniolo, ed., *Central Banks' Independence in Historical Perspective.* Berlin/New York: de Gruyter, pp. 17–38.

Timberlake, Richard H. 1978. *The Origins of Central Banking in the United States.* Cambridge, MA: Harvard University Press.

Todd, Walker F. 1992. "Disorderly Markets: The Law, History, and Economics of the Exchange Stabilization Fund and U.S. Foreign Exchange Market Intervention." In George Kaufman, ed., Research in Financial Markets: Private and Public Policy. Vol. 4. Greenwich, CT: JAI Press.

US Congress, Joint Economic Committee. 1981. *International Economic Policy.* Hearings, 97th Cong., 1st sess. (4 May).

US Congress, Joint Committee on Taxation. 1984. *General Explanation of the Revenue Provisions of the Deficit Reduction Act of 1984,* joint committee print, 98th Cong., 2nd sess. (31 December).

US Council for International Business. 1985. "Statement on a New Round of Multilateral Trade Negotiations: Recommended US Business Objectives." Washington (18 April).

US Council for International Business. 1985. *Annual Report 1985:* 4.

US House of Representatives. 1989. *H.R. 2795.* 101st Cong., 1st sess, 29 June.

US House of Representatives. 1989. *H.R. 3512 and H.R. 3066.* Hearing, 101st Cong., 1st sess. (9 November).

US House of Representatives, Committee on Banking, Finance, and Urban Affairs. 1988. *Impact of the Stock Market Drop and Related Economic Developments on Interest Rates, Banking, Monetary Policy, and Economic Stability.* Hearings, 100th Cong., 1st sess. (29 October 1987).

US House of Representatives, Committee on Banking, Finance, and Urban Affairs. 1990. *A Racial, Gender, and Background Profile of the Directors of the Federal Reserve Banks and Branches.* Staff report (August), 101st Cong., 2nd sess.

US House of Representatives, Committee on Banking, Finance, and Urban Affairs. 1990. *Review of Treasury Department's Conduct of International Financial Policy.* Hearing, 101st Cong., 2nd sess. (14 August).

US House of Representatives, Committee on Banking, Finance, and Urban Affairs. 1992. *The Monetary Policy Reform Act of 1991.* Hearing, 102nd Cong., 1st sess. (13 November 1991).

US House of Representatives, Committee on Banking, Finance, and Urban Affairs, Subcommittee on Domestic Monetary Policy. 1988. *Conduct of Monetary Policy in 1987.* Hearings, 100th Cong., 2nd sess. (17 and 24 March).

US House of Representatives, Committee on Banking, Finance, and Urban Affairs, Subcommittee on Domestic Monetary Policy. 1989. Zero Inflation. Hearing on *H. J. Res. 409,* Part 1, 25 October 1989, 101st Cong., 1st sess.

US House of Representatives, Committee on Banking, Finance, and Urban Affairs, Subcommittee on Domestic Monetary Policy. 1990. *Zero Inflation.* Hearing on H.J. Res. 409, Part 2, 6 February 1990, 101st Cong., 2nd sess.

US House of Representatives, Committee on Banking, Finance, and Urban Affairs, Subcommittee on International Development, Finance, Trade and Monetary Policy. 1990. *Exchange Rates.* Hearings, 101st Cong., 1st sess. (31 October and 16 November 1989).

US House of Representatives, Committee on Ways and Means, Subcommittee on International Trade. 1984. *US Trade Deficit.* Hearings, 98th Cong., 2nd sess. (28 and 29 March, 10, 12, 15, and 25 April).

US Senate, Committee on Governmental Affairs. 1978. *Voting Rights in Major Corporations.* Washington: GPO.

US Senate, Committee on Banking, Subcommittee on International Finance and Monetary Policy. 1989. *Review of the Department of the Treasury's Second Annual Report on*

International Economic and Exchange Rates Policy. Hearing, 101st Cong., 1st sess. (16 November).

US Treasury Department, Office of Financial Analysis. 1971. "The U.S. International Competitive Position and the Potential Role of Exchange Rates in the Adjustment Process." Confidential report to Undersecretary Paul A. Volcker. Washington (28 May).

US Treasury Department, press release. 1987. Washington (22 December).

US Treasury Department. 1988–92. "Report to the Congress on International Economic and Exchange Rate Policy." Washington.

US Treasury Department. 1991. "Remarks by the Honorable Charles H. Dallara to the US-German Economic Policy Group at the Institute for International Economics." Press release. Washington (7 March).

US Treasury Department. 1992. *Exchange Stabilization Fund Annual Report, 1991* (October).

US Treasury Department. 1992. "Remarks of Secretary Nicholas F. Brady to the Kennedy School of Government, Harvard University." Press Release. Washington (17 December).

Volcker, Paul A. 1994. "Comment." In Martin Feldstein, ed., *American Economic Policy in the 1980s.* Chicago: University of Chicago Press.

Wagner, Richard E. 1986. "Central Banking at the Fed: A Public Choice Perspective." *The Cato Journal* 6 (Fall).

White House. 1985. "News Conference by the President." Press Release. Washington (17 September).

White House. 1992. "Statement by President Bush and Prime Minister Miyazawa on Strategy for World Growth." Press Release. Washington (8 January).

White House. 1992. "Remarks by the President in Address to Finance Ministers and Central Bank Governors." Press release. Washington (20 September).

Widman, F. Lisle. 1982. *Making International Monetary Policy.* Washington: The International Law Institute, Georgetown University Law Center.

Williamson, John. 1977. *The Failure of World Monetary Reform, 1971-1974.* New York: New York University Press.

Woodward, Bob. 1992. "Origin of the Tax Pledge." *Washington Post* (4 October).

Woodward, Bob. 1992. "Primary Heat Turned Deal Into a 'Mistake'." *Washington Post* (6 October).

Woolley, John T. 1984. *Monetary Politics: The Federal Reserve and the Politics of Monetary Policy.* Cambridge: Cambridge University Press.

Woolley, John T. 1988. "Partisan Manipulation of the Economy." *Journal of Politics* 50, no. 2: 355–60.

Index

Bank of Japan (*Continued*)
coalition building, 30
comparison of, 328*f*, 328–29
and external monetary policy, 28–31, 327, 338–39
French, 12–13, 13*f*, 328*f*, 337
German, 12, 13*f*, 44, 246, 328*f*, 328–29, 339–40
Japanese, 12, 13*f*, 43–44, 57, 328*f*, 328–29, 339, 346, 361
and national financial system, 58–59
policy recommendations, 344
US, 12, 13*f*, 328*f*, 328–29, 339, 353–54
Banking Act of 1933 (Glass-Steagall Act), 40, 45, 45*n*
Banking Act of 1935, 45*n*
Banking Bureau (Japan), 76
Banking system. *See* Financial systems
Bank of England, 67–68, 114–15, 115*t*, 241, 328*f*, 337
Bank of France, 114–15, 115*t*, 241, 328*f*, 337, 359*n*
Bank of Italy, 11, 238, 241
Bank of Japan, 15, 39, 44, 63
administrative guidance, 82–84, 133, 160, 168, 172
appointments, 73, 115, 359–60
authority over monetary instruments, 72–73, 115
domestic monetary policy, 67–80, 168, 321–24, 359
exchange rate policy, 80–84, 117–19, 118*t*, 121
Executive Council, 360
Foreign Department, 82
foreign exchange intervention, 81–82, 117–19, 133–34, 137, 146, 172, 335–36, 339–40, 361. *See also* Yen, realignment
government financing, 74–75, 116, 116*n*, 360
government relations, 70–71, 75–80, 119, 121, 136*n*, 328, 335–36, 359–62
governors, 73–74, 74*t*, 360. *See also specific governor*
independence, 66*n*, 66–84, 71*n*, 119, 347, 359–62, 367
versus other central banks, 114–17, 115*t*, 246, 328*f*, 332–34
and international cooperation, 349
and international role of currency, 317
Ministry of Finance relations, 70–71, 75–77, 119, 136*n*, 328, 332, 335–36, 358, 360, 362
organization, 69–70, 116–17, 360
oversight, budget, and audit, 75, 116
Policy Board, 67, 69–70, 70*n*, 73*n*, 73, 360
Economic Planning Agency, 69–70, 72, 80, 161
price stability objective, 73
status, 77–80

subordination, 70–75, 170–74, 326, 332, 335, 358
Trust Fund Bureau, 81
Bank of Japan Act, 67
Bank of Japan Law, 73–74
Bankruptcy laws, 39, 46
Basel Accord, 42, 169, 209
Basel-Nybourg agreement, 209, 212
Basket currency, 188*n*
BDI. *See* German Federation of Industry
BdL. *See* Bank deutscher Länder
Bear trap, 155, 288–89
Belgian franc, 186, 196
Belgium, interest rates, 243
Bentsen, Lloyd, 304
Berg, Fritz, 182
Bergsten, C. Fred, 126, 126*n*, 268, 324*n*
Berlin Wall, fall of, 166, 218, 229
BIS. *See* Bank for International Settlements
Blessing, Karl, 92*t*
Blumenthal, Michael, 268–70
Bo, Hideo, 128
BOJ. *See* Bank of Japan
Bond markets, 21–22, 50–51, 51*t*
Bonn summit of 1978, 128–29, 190, 190*n*, 268, 306
Brady, Nicholas F., 159, 165, 227, 238*n*, 290–93, 293*n*–294*n*, 295–96, 299, 300*n*, 301–2, 302*n*, 303, 341
Brandt, Willy, 183*t*
Bretton Woods regime, 3–4, 14–16, 310–11, 314, 321. *See also* Fixed exchange rates
collapse, 77, 96, 99, 122, 137, 178–79, 184, 261, 266, 308, 312, 322, 326, 330. *See also* Flexible exchange rates
versus European Monetary System, 189
foreign constituencies under, 32
German policy under, 95, 99, 179–84, 246, 248, 363
Japanese policy under, 77, 81, 122–34, 171, 358
US policy under, 110–11, 254*n*, 254–63, 266, 320, 332, 355, 357
Britain, 336–39
bank-industry relations, 12–13, 13*f*, 328*f*, 353
capital controls, 315
central bank. *See* Bank of England
economy, openness of, 4*n*
EMS participation, 212, 215, 233, 238, 337, 338*n*
exchange rate policy, 24*n*, 337–38
external monetary policy, 4*n*, 7, 117–19, 118*t*
financial system, 337
inflation, 337
interest rates, 238, 243
policy outcomes, 337
policy recommendations, 353
private preferences, 337
British Commonwealth, 32

German preference for, 178, 196, 214, 246, 248–50
global, 366
two-track strategy for, 16
Exchange Rate Mechanism, 188n, 366
bands, 25, 97, 242–43, 305, 363
British participation, 212, 229
creation, 96
crises (1992-93), 11, 179, 237–46, 302, 313, 319, 324, 336, 338n, 338, 346
German participation, 227, 242, 313, 325
and US policy, 299, 301, 305
wide bands, 242-43
withdrawal of pound and lira, 240-41
Exchange rate policy
bank preferences, 22–26, 40
democratization, 354
German, 177–251
Bretton Woods regime, 95, 99, 179–84, 246, 248, 363
flexible exchange rates, 99, 179, 183–84, 246–48, 322, 333
and unification, 166, 179, 215, 217–18, 225–27, 237, 250
Japanese, 121–75, 273
Bretton Woods regime, 77, 81, 122–34, 171, 358
flexible exchange rates, 133–34, 137, 143, 322
and national financial systems, 331–32
and political environment. See Political environment, and exchange rate policy
US, 149, 253–307, 333–34, 340, 354–56
Bretton Woods regime, 110–11, 254n, 254–63, 266, 320, 332, 355, 357
flexible exchange rates, 254–55, 261, 263–70, 322
Exchange Rates and International Economic Policy Coordination Act of 1988, 355
Exchange Stabilization Fund, 108n, 111–13, 112n, 292
Executive committee. See marutaku
Explanations for policy outcomes, 2-8, 327-41
Export competitiveness, 5, 35
German, 5, 181, 200–202
Japanese, 5, 135–44
External monetary policy, 8–12. See also Exchange rate policy
and bank-industry relations, 28–31, 327, 338–39
banking preferences on, 22–26, 40
British, 4n, 7, 117–19, 118t
central bank, 6–8, 60–62, 65–66
and central bank independence, 24, 327
changes, 339–41
comparison, 2–5, 117–19, 118t
competitiveness-oriented, 10, 310n
definition, 8
versus domestic monetary policy, 65

elements, 9t, 9–10
European Monetary Union, 195–99, 234–35
finance ministry role, 6–7, 60, 62
French, 4n, 7
German, 1, 14–16, 85, 94–101, 117–19, 118t, 193–94, 246
versus Japan and US, 309–27, 311t
governmental role, 6–7, 62, 65–66, 309
industry preferences, 22–23, 27–28
Japanese, 1, 14–15, 80–84, 117–19, 118t, 121–75
changes, 339–40
versus Germany and US, 121, 309–27, 311t
legal framework, 66
legislative role, 62–64
outcomes, comparison, 309–27, 311t
private-sector preferences, 6–8, 19–60, 309, 326–27
framework for analysis, 20–31
stability-oriented, 10
US, 1, 14, 16, 101, 109–14, 117–19, 118t, 121
versus Japan and Germany, 121, 309–27, 311t

FDP. See Free Democratic Party
FECL. See Foreign Exchange and Foreign Trade Control Law of 1949
Federal Court of Audit (German), 93
Federal deposit insurance, 45n
Federal Open Market Committee, 103–6, 108–9, 111, 113, 270, 292, 296, 298
Federal Republic of Germany. See Germany
Federal Reserve Act of 1913, 102, 104n–105n, 105
Federal Reserve Bank(s), 102–5
audits and reviews, 109
presidents, 104–5, 105n, 107–8, 108n
Federal Reserve Bank of New York, 23n, 104–5, 111–13, 264, 270, 274, 336n, 357
Federal Reserve System, 15, 63, 67
appointments, 107–8, 115–16
authority over monetary instruments, 106, 115
Board of Governors, 102–4, 106–8, 116, 284
chairman, 103–4, 107t, 107–10, 356. See also specific c hairman
domestic monetary policy, 69, 101–7, 132, 153, 159, 167, 213, 253–54, 269, 282–84, 290, 298, 301, 321–24
exchange rate policy, 149, 253–54, 286, 305–7, 334, 354–56
external monetary policy, 101, 109–14, 117–19, 118t
foreign exchange intervention, 109–14, 111n–112n, 117–19, 119n, 129, 151, 256–59, 264–65, 274, 282, 291–92, 296, 298–99, 304, 334–36, 357n, 357–58
and German exchange rate policy, 194
gold agreements, 258, 260–61

Foreign exchange reserves
  German, 313
  Japanese, 137, 138f
France, 336–39
  bank-industry relations, 12–13, 13f, 328f, 337
  capital controls, 211–12, 314–15, 337
  central bank. See Bank of France
  competitiveness issues, 337
  economic policy, 197n, 197–98
  economy, openness, 4n
  EMS participation, 233, 235, 337, 338n, 346
  external monetary policy, 4n, 7
  financial system, 337
  inflation, 337
  interest rates, 241–43
  Maastricht Treaty referendum, 237–38, 240, 244
Franco-German corps, 302
Franco-German Economic Council, 210, 242
Franco-German monetary initiative, 188–89
Franco-German Treaty of 1963, 210
Franco-Prussian War of 1870–71, 86
Frankel, Jeffrey, 11–12, 12n, 312
Frankfurt, as financial center, 316
Free Democratic Party, 93n, 100–101, 101n, 183, 187, 190, 195, 198, 205
French franc, 97, 186, 197–98, 215, 240–42, 337
French Socialist Party, 196–97, 241
Friedman, Milton, 270n
Fujii, Hirohisa, 79t
Fukuda, Takeo, 80, 128–29, 268
Full Employment and Balanced Growth Act of 1978, 106, 108
Funabashi, Yoichi, 145, 152, 285, 285n

G-3. See Group of Three
G-5. See Group of Five
G-7. See Group of Seven
Gaddum, Johann Wilhelm, 92t, 93, 229t
gaiatsu, 153
Galli, Giampaolo, 312, 313n
GDR. See German Democratic Republic
Geiger, Helmut, 222
General Accounting Office (GAO), 109
General Agreement on Tariffs and Trade, 366
gensaki bills, 40
Genscher, Hans-Dietrich, 100, 198, 211–12, 228
Gephardt amendment, 155, 289
German Association of Industry and Trade, 205
German Basic Law, 90–91, 95, 228, 244
German Chamber of Commerce and Industry, 187
German Constitutional Court, 245–46
German Democratic Republic, 217. See also German unification
German Federation of Industry, 187, 204
German Federation of Savings Associations, 187

German Institute for Economic Research, 237
German Savings Bank Association, 222
German unification, 177, 218–28, 296, 299, 345–46
  banking system changes, 56, 85, 87–89, 227–28
  budget deficits, 94, 196
  currency conversion, 220–23, 221n, 223n
  economic issues, 16, 219n, 222–23, 223n–224n, 224–25, 250, 296, 324
  European effects, 227
  and exchange rate policy, 166, 179, 215, 217–18, 225–27, 237, 250
  monetary, 178, 218–23
  public-sector deficit, 224–25
  transfer payments, 224
German Unity Fund, 221
Germany
  bank holdings of corporate securities, 37–38, 39n, 48, 49f
  bank-industry relations, 12, 13f, 44, 246, 328f, 328–29, 339–40
  bond market, 50–51, 51t
  budget deficits, 94, 195–96, 199, 216t, 216, 322, 347, 352
  capital controls, 184, 194, 211–12, 311t, 314–16
  capital liberalization, 181, 184, 215
  capital markets, 48–50, 50t
  central bank, 85n, 85–86. See also Deutsche Bundesbank; Land central banks
  chancellors, 100, 183t, 183–84, 356
  coalition governments, 183t, 183–84, 190, 194–95, 198–99, 205, 216, 224, 244
  currency. See D-mark
  currency conflict with US, 199–208
  current account balances, 180f–181f, 181, 250
  deficit-recession trauma (1979-82), 189–99
  discount rate, 90, 205–6, 208, 214, 236–37, 240, 243, 323
  domestic monetary policy, 69, 85, 91, 162, 181, 191–93, 200–202, 213n, 213, 246–48, 299, 321–24
    versus Japan and United States, 311t, 321–24
  domestic price stability preference, 178, 183–84, 189, 248–50, 345, 362
  economic/industrial development, 19, 51–52, 53t, 199, 202, 217, 224
  economics ministry, 186
  economy, 4, 21
  EMS participation, 96–99, 117–19, 118n, 178–79, 185, 187–89, 195–99, 208–12, 217, 230–31, 233, 236, 238, 239f, 240–41, 250–51, 314–15, 325, 330, 335, 345–46, 350–52, 363, 365
  EC commitment, 228–37
  exchange rate policy, 177–251
    Bretton Woods regime, 95, 99, 179–84, 246, 248, 363

Germany (*Continued*)
  flexible exchange rates, 99, 179, 183–84,
    246–48, 322, 333
  and Group of Seven, 178, 205, 208–10, 214,
    216, 227, 251, 346, 362–63, 367
  export competitiveness, 5, 181, 200–202
  external monetary policy, 1, 14–16, 85, 94–
    101, 117–19, 118*t*, 193–94, 246
    versus Japan and US, 309–27, 311*t*
  finance ministry
    central bank relations, 98–99, 197–98
    exchange rate policy, 186, 214, 226, 234,
      325
    external monetary policy, 100–101
  financial disclosure requirements, 38–39
  financial system
    changes, 55–56, 58, 85, 87–89, 227–28, 339
    structure, 36–39
  foreign exchange intervention, 94–100, 117–
    19, 156, 179, 181, 186, 194, 200, 201*f*,
    225–27, 335–36
    versus US and Japan, 310–13, 311*t*
  foreign exchange reserves, 313
  foreign ministry, external monetary policy,
    100–101
  IMF involvement, 88, 93, 95, 99–100, 206–7
  industrial competitiveness, 192, 196, 330, 345
  inflation, 190, 191*t*, 192, 194, 196–97, 199,
    213–14, 217, 222, 248–49, 322–23, 333
  interest rates, 162, 193, 193*f*, 194–95, 204,
    206, 213–14, 225–27, 238–39, 241–43,
    248, 289, 294, 296, 301, 346, 349
  intermediation, 48, 54*t*, 54–55
  and international role of currency, 317, 319,
    331
  macroeconomic policy, 181, 185, 216–17,
    226–27, 247, 251, 333
  monetary policy, 177–251
  money growth, 197, 197*t*
  policy consistency, versus Japan and US,
    311*t*, 324–26
  policy outcomes, 345–46
    explanation, 327–41
    versus Japan and US, 309–27, 311*t*
  policy recommendations, 362–67
  political environment, and exchange rate
    policy, 188, 204, 207
  post–World War II occupation, 36*n*, 36, 86
  private preferences, 178, 187, 224–25, 246–48,
    326–27, 329, 340
    versus US and Japan, 329–32
  reaction to oil shocks, 189–90, 196
  recession, 194, 241, 244, 303, 323–24
  regional environment, 177
  securities market, 37
  selective liberalization, 211, 314, 331
  trade surpluses, 180*f*–181*f*, 181, 217, 226, 345
  two-track policy of flexibility and
    stabilization, 185–218, 247, 325
  unemployment, 194, 213, 217

World Bank involvement, 93, 95, 99–100,
  206–7
Gerschenkron, Alexander, 7, 7*n*
Giscard d'Estaing, Valéry, 101*n*, 185–86
Glass-Steagall Act (Banking Act of 1933), 40,
  45, 45*n*
Gold-exchange standard, 257, 258*n*
  jettison, 12, 259–63
Gold Reserve Act of 1934, 111
Gonzalez, Henry B., 108*n*, 296
Gorbachev, Mikhail, 219
Gourevitch, Peter, 7, 7*n*
Government. *See also specific government*
  action, versus exchange market outcomes, 8
  central bank financing, 64, 116, 116*n*
  central bank relations, 56, 61, 63, 65–66, 71,
    119, 334–36, 343–45, 350–67
    policy recommendations, 344–45, 352–67
  competitiveness concerns, 65, 327, 330
  external monetary policy, 6–7, 62, 65–66,
    309
  and international role of currency, 317
Government bonds, for foreign purchasers,
  273–74
Gramm-Rudman budget deficit reduction
  targets, 291, 297
Grand Coalition government, 183
Great Britain. *See* Britain
Great Depression, 45
Greece, EMU participation, 233
Greenspan, Alan, 104, 107*t*, 107, 153, 154*n*,
  206, 286, 297
Group of Three, 153
Group of Five, 4*n*, 151, 200, 280–82, 285, 336–
  38
Jurgensen Report, 199
Group of Seven, 1, 99, 104, 114, 118, 325, 348
  breakdown, 349–50
  and German exchange rate policy, 178, 205,
    208–10, 214, 216, 227, 251, 346, 362–63,
    367
  and Japanese exchange rate policy, 129, 135,
    147, 149, 152, 154–55, 160–62, 165, 165*n*,
    166, 168
  macroeconomic cooperation within, 365–66
  policy framework, 351–52
  reference ranges, 25
  and US exchange rate policy, 268, 287, 289,
    291, 291*n*, 292, 298–305, 356
Group of Ten, 116, 257, 261, 302
Guth, Wilfried, 187
Gyohten, Toyoo, 149

Hall, Peter, 7, 7*n*
Hanover summit, 215, 229–30
Hard landing scenario, 283
Hartmann, Wendelin, 229*t*
Hashimoto, Ryutaro, 72, 79*t*, 162–63, 164*n*,
  164–65

Monetary Control Act of 1980, 108n
Monetary instruments, authority over, 64, 72–
    73, 90–91, 106, 115
Monetary policy
    counterfactual, 11
    domestic. See Domestic monetary policy
    expansionary, 348n
    external. See External monetary policy
    German, 177–251
    Japanese, 121–75
    measurement of, 9
    US, 253–308
Morgan, Lee L., 278
Morinaga, Teiichiro, 74t, 78, 132
Morita, Akio, 28n
MOSS talks. See Market-Oriented Sector
    Specific talks
Mulford, David, 165n, 166, 203, 273–74, 280–
    81, 294, 296, 302, 303n, 303
Müller, Lothar, 229t
Multinational corporations, 27
Mundell, Robert, 141–42, 141n–142n
Mundell-Fleming model, 141-42
Munich summit, 301
Murayama, Tatsuo, 79t, 161
Mutual funds, 46–47, 51

NAFTA. See North American Free Trade
    Agreement
Nakasone, Yasuhiro, 71, 79t, 80, 135–36, 136n,
    139, 144–46, 148–50, 152, 155, 174
National Association of Manufacturers, 278
National Bank of Belgium, 67
National debt. See Budget deficits
National Economic Council, 356
National Socialist Party, 86
NATO, 302
Nazi Reichsbank, 67
NEC. See National Economic Council
nemawashi, 71, 157
Netherlands
    EMS participation, 242
    interest rates, 243
New Deal reforms, 102
New Economic Policy, 259–60
New institutionalism, 7, 7n
Newly industrializing economies (NIEs), 113,
    294n
New Taiwan dollar, 295
New York, as financial center, 316
New York Federal Reserve Bank. See Federal
    Reserve Bank of New York
Nikkei Stock Average, 158, 164–69
Nixon administration, 123, 125, 133, 257t, 259–
    62, 265–67, 269, 306, 333
Nölling, Wilhelm, 221
Nominal effective exchange rate statistics, 326n
Nontradeable sector, exchange rate
    preferences, 33

Nordic currencies, 240
North American Free Trade Agreement, 298,
    304
Norway, interest rates, 243
Nth country role, 256

OECD, 299, 303
Official discount rate (ODR), 76, 115, 139, 156,
    162–63
Offshore markets, 315
Ogata, Shijuro, 174, 335
Ohira, Masayoshi, 78, 79t, 80
Oil embargo, 264
Oil shocks
    German reaction, 189–90, 196
    Japanese reaction, 78, 125, 131, 135, 143, 314
    US reaction, 264, 266–68
Omnibus Trade and Competitiveness Act of
    1988, 113, 113n, 293
Open market operations (OMOs), 79, 115
Operation Twist, 257, 321
Organization for European Economic
    Cooperation, 366
Organization of Petroleum and Exporting
    Countries (OPEC), 270
Overborrowing, 39
Overloan, 39

Palace Coup, 284
Palm, Guntram, 229t
Paris, as financial center, 316
Peak associations, 187
Pension funds, 46n, 46–47, 51, 84, 160
Persian Gulf War, 168, 297
Plaza Agreement, 12, 134, 144n, 145–47, 162,
    166, 171, 202–3, 203n, 209, 280n, 280–84
Pöhl, Karl Otto, 92t, 93, 93n, 195, 200, 202–6,
    206n, 207–8, 210n, 211, 212n, 212, 214–15,
    215n, 219, 222, 225n, 225, 227–28, 230–31,
    231n, 234, 288
Policy. See also specific policy
    and exchange rates, 11–12
    explanations, 2–5
    stance, determination, 8–9
Policy consistency, 10, 310
    comparison, 311t, 324–26
Policymakers, channels of access to, 6, 29–31,
    354
Policymaking
    national, 62
    and international monetary regime, 14–15
    public institutions, comparison, 114–19
Policy outcomes
    comparison, 309–27, 311t, 338
    versus exchange market outcomes, 8
    explanation, 327–41
    successful, processes that facilitate, 343–67
Policy recommendations, 352–67

Service sector, exchange rate preferences, 33
Shadow Open Market Committee, 287
Shibusawa, Keizo, 74t
Shonfield, Andrew, 7, 7n
Shultz, George, 111, 118n, 263–64, 265n, 266, 270
Sievert, Olaf, 229t
SII. See Structural Impediments Initiative
Simon, William, 267
Sleeping board, 69
Smithsonian exchange agreements, 125–26, 182, 261, 263, 263n, 306
Snake. See European Narrower Margins Arrangement ("snake")
Social Democratic Party, 93, 93n, 100, 101n, 183, 190, 220, 244
Societal preferences. See Private preferences
Solidarity Pact of 1993, 241
Solomon, Anthony, 269, 274
Soviet Union, 217, 228
Spain, EMS participation, 233
Spanish peseta, 96, 215, 239–40
SPD. See Social Democratic Party
Special Drawing Rights, 112n, 188n, 258, 320
Special Lombard facility, 193
Sprinkel, Beryl W., 136–37, 140, 272, 274, 278–79, 287
Stability, policy oriented toward, 10
State
    developmental role, 3, 5, 59, 69
    in Japan, 44n, 68n
    domestic position, 3
    external monetary policy role, 5
    financial system and economic policy roles, 59–60
State banks, 37, 37n
State Treaty, 221, 224
Stein, Herbert, 287
Steinkühler, Franz, 237
Stimulus-for-stability bargain, 205
Stock markets, 21. See also specific exchange
    crisis/crash, 154, 154n, 165, 169, 207, 213, 285, 287–89, 302n, 323
    German, 37
    Japanese, 40–41, 41n
    size, 48–50, 50t
Stock trading, illegal, in Japan, 156–57
Stoltenberg, Gerhard, 202, 204–5, 207, 207n, 208, 211–12, 288, 363
Storch, Günter, 93n, 229t
Strasbourg summit, 230
Strauss, Franz-Josef, 93n, 183
Structural Impediments Initiative, 159
Structural realism, 2–4
Substitution Account, 269–70, 320
Sumita, Satoshi, 71, 74, 74t, 145–48, 151, 153, 161–63, 360
Supreme Commander for the Allied Powers, 70n
Suzuki, Yoshio, 142

Suzuki, Zenko, 79t, 135
Swap facilities, 112, 257–58, 269, 311
Swiss National Bank, 267
System Open Market Account, 104

Taiwan, 293–95
Takeshita, Noboru, 71, 78, 79t, 131n, 140, 144–46, 147n, 147–50, 155, 159, 163
Tanaka, Kakuei, 71, 77–78, 125
Target ranges, dollar exchange rates, 285–88, 290–97, 299, 304–5
Tariffs, 9
Technological advance, financial services provision, 52, 58
Telephone accord, 154, 285
Thatcher, Margaret, 212, 338
Thomas, Karl, 231
Tietmeyer, Hans, 92t, 93, 202, 225–26, 229t, 232, 236, 238–40, 243
Time inconsistency, 62–63
Tokyo, as financial center, 316
Tokyo Stock Exchange, 154, 164
Tokyo summit of 1986, 149
Trade
    international, currency, 9
    volume, and foreign exchange intervention, 312
Tradeable sector, exchange rate preferences, 33–34
Trade balances, US, 258–59, 259f, 268, 273, 276t, 276–77, 284, 289–90, 298, 303, 307, 327, 334, 340–41
Trade imbalances, US-Japan, 135, 144, 155n, 159–60, 171, 296, 300, 304
Trade policy
    measurement, 8–9
    US, 134, 144, 148, 159–60, 171, 202, 207, 278–81, 286, 298, 307, 327, 347, 349
Trade protectionism, 34
Trade surpluses
    German, 180f–181f, 181, 217, 226, 345
    Japanese, 340, 358, 362
Trade unions
    after German unification, 225
    exchange rate preferences, 34
Treasury Department, US, 101
    capital controls, 315
    domestic monetary policy, 253–54
    and European monetary union, 302
    exchange rate policy, 136–37, 165, 253–54, 266, 268, 272, 278–79, 305–6, 331, 334, 354–56
    external monetary policy, 109–14, 117–19, 118t
    Federal Reserve relations, 101, 110n, 294, 329, 334, 347, 351n, 357
    foreign exchange intervention, 109–14, 117–19, 119n, 129, 151, 256–59, 264, 269, 272–74, 282, 291–92, 296, 298–99, 304, 357–58

United States (*Continued*)
  Treasury Department. *See* Treasury
    Department, US
  unemployment, 267, 277, 299–300
  World Bank involvement, 104, 270
Universal banks, 36, 56
Uno, Sosuke, 79*t*, 159, 161
Uruguay Round, 295, 298, 304
Usami, Makoto, 74*t*
Utsumi, Makoto, 152, 164–65

Vietnam War, 258, 262
Volcker, Paul A., 107*t*, 113*n*, 146, 153, 190, 261,
  263, 266, 270, 270*n*, 274*n*, 274, 279, 282–
  84, 286, 322, 334, 335*n*

Wage stagnation, 290
Waigel, Theo, 224*n*, 228, 237–38, 238*n*, 243*n*
Wallich, Henry, 270*n*
Warehousing, 108*n*, 112, 112*n*, 292, 296
Watanabe, Michio, 79*t*, 136*n*, 137, 139
Wealth, institutionalization, 52, 58
Weimar Republic, 86
Werner Report of 1970, 187, 187*n*
Western European Union, 302
West Germany. *See* Germany
Williamsburg summit, 199–200
Williamson, John, 352, 352*n*
World Bank
  German involvement, 93, 95, 99–100, 206–7
  Japanese involvement, 150
  US involvement, 104, 270
World War I, 86
World War II, 67–68, 86, 101

yakuin shuukai. See marutaku
Yamagiwa, Masamichi, 74*t*
Yen
  appreciation, 122, 128–30, 134, 144–47, 158,
    167, 169–70, 304, 310, 324, 326, 340, 361
  defense (1989–90), 158, 167
  depreciation, 134, 160, 165–66, 310, 323, 326
  exchange rates, 122–23, 125, 127*f*, 130, 130*f*,
    172, 173*f*, 264, 265*f*, 303
  international role, 134, 146, 172, 331
    versus other currencies, 311*t*, 316–21, 317*t*–
      318*t*
  plunge (1990), 163–67
  realignment, 15, 122, 122*n*, 124, 324–25
    first (1971-73), 122–27, 339
    second (1977-78), 122, 127–30, 133, 175, 339
    third, 122, 167
    fourth, 122
  regional role, 317, 317*n*
  restraint (1986-1987)
    multilateral, 151–54
    unilateral, 148–51
  retreat (1979-80), 129–33
  stabilization, 147–58, 161, 171
    multilateral, 154–57
  strength (1991-92), 168–70
  weakness (1981-85), 135–44
Yen-Dollar Agreement, 140–41, 319–20
Yen-dollar exchange rate, target ranges, 285–
  86, 304–5
Yen-dollar market, US intervention, 282, 283*f*
Yuki, Toyotaro, 73, 73*n*

zaibatsu, 39, 41
zenginkyo, 83
Zentralbankrat. See Central Bank Council
Zysman, John, 7, 7*n*

Other Publications from the
Institute for International Economics

POLICY ANALYSES IN INTERNATIONAL ECONOMICS Series

1 The Lending Policies of the International Monetary Fund
John Williamson/*August 1982*
ISBN paper 0-88132-000-5   72 pp.

2 "Reciprocity": A New Approach to World Trade Policy?
William R. Cline/*September 1982*
ISBN paper 0-88132-001-3   41 pp.

3 Trade Policy in the 1980s
C. Fred Bergsten and William R. Cline/*November 1982*
(out of print)   ISBN paper 0-88132-002-1   84 pp.
Partially reproduced in the book *Trade Policy in the 1980s.*

4 International Debt and the Stability of the World Economy
William R. Cline/*September 1983*
ISBN paper 0-88132-010-2   134 pp.

5 The Exchange Rate System, Second Edition
John Williamson/*September 1983, rev. June 1985*
(out of print)   ISBN paper 0-88132-034-X   61 pp.

6 Economic Sanctions in Support of Foreign Policy Goals
Gary Clyde Hufbauer and Jeffrey J. Schott/*October 1983*
ISBN paper 0-88132-014-5   109 pp.

7 A New SDR Allocation?
John Williamson/*March 1984*
ISBN paper 0-88132-028-5   61 pp.

8 An International Standard for Monetary Stabilization
Ronald I. McKinnon/*March 1984*
ISBN paper 0-88132-018-8   108 pp.

9 The Yen/Dollar Agreement: Liberalizing Japanese Capital Markets
Jeffrey A. Frankel/*December 1984*
ISBN paper 0-88132-035-8   86 pp.

10 Bank Lending to Developing Countries: The Policy Alternatives
C. Fred Bergsten, William R. Cline, and John Williamson/*April 1985*
ISBN paper 0-88132-032-3   221 pp.

11 Trading for Growth: The Next Round of Trade Negotiations
Gary Clyde Hufbauer and Jeffrey J. Schott/*September 1985*
ISBN paper 0-88132-033-1   109 pp.

12 Financial Intermediation Beyond the Debt Crisis
Donald R. Lessard and John Williamson/*September 1985*
ISBN paper 0-88132-021-8   130 pp.

13 The United States-Japan Economic Problem
C. Fred Bergsten and William R. Cline/*October 1985, 2d ed. January 1987*
(out of print)   ISBN paper 0-88132-060-9   180 pp.

Economic Sanctions Reconsidered (in two volumes)
  Economic Sanctions Reconsidered: Supplemental Case Histories
  Gary Clyde Hufbauer, Jeffrey J. Schott, and Kimberly Ann Elliott/*1985, 2d ed.*
    December 1990

ISBN cloth 0-88132-115-X	928 pp.
ISBN paper 0-88132-105-2	928 pp.

  Economic Sanctions Reconsidered: History and Current Policy
  Gary Clyde Hufbauer, Jeffrey J. Schott, and Kimberly Ann Elliott/*December 1990*

ISBN cloth 0-88132-136-2	288 pp.
ISBN paper 0-88132-140-0	288 pp.

Pacific Basin Developing Countries: Prospects for the Future
Marcus Noland/*January 1991*

ISBN cloth 0-88132-141-9	250 pp.
ISBN paper 0-88132-081-1	250 pp.

Currency Convertibility in Eastern Europe
John Williamson, editor/*October 1991*

ISBN cloth 0-88132-144-3	396 pp.
ISBN paper 0-88132-128-1	396 pp.

Foreign Direct Investment in the United States
Edward M. Graham and Paul R. Krugman/*1989, 2d ed. October 1991*

ISBN paper 0-88132-139-7	200 pp.

International Adjustment and Financing: The Lessons of 1985-1991
C. Fred Bergsten, editor/*January 1992*

ISBN paper 0-88132-112-5	336 pp.

North American Free Trade: Issues and Recommendations
Gary Clyde Hufbauer and Jeffrey J. Schott/*April 1992*

ISBN cloth 0-88132-145-1	392 pp.
ISBN paper 0-88132-120-6	392 pp.

American Trade Politics
I. M. Destler/*1986, 2d ed. June 1992*

ISBN cloth 0-88132-164-8	400 pp.
ISBN paper 0-88132-188-5	400 pp.

Narrowing the U.S. Current Account Deficit
Allen J. Lenz/*June 1992*

ISBN cloth 0-88132-148-6	640 pp.
ISBN paper 0-88132-103-6	640 pp.

The Economics of Global Warming
William R. Cline/*June 1992*

ISBN cloth 0-88132-150-8	416 pp.
ISBN paper 0-88132-132-X	416 pp.

U.S. Taxation of International Income: Blueprint for Reform
Gary Clyde Hufbauer, assisted by Joanna M. van Rooij/*October 1992*

ISBN cloth 0-88132-178-8	304 pp.
ISBN paper 0-88132-134-6	304 pp.

Who's Bashing Whom? Trade Conflict in High-Technology Industries
Laura D'Andrea Tyson/*November 1992*

ISBN cloth 0-88132-151-6	352 pp.
ISBN paper 0-88132-106-0	352 pp.

SPECIAL REPORTS

FORTHCOMING

Foreign Direct Investment in the United States, Third Edition
Edward M. Graham and Paul R. Krugman

Global Competition Policy
Edward M. Graham and J. David Richardson

Toward a Pacific Economic Community?
Gary Clyde Hufbauer and Jeffrey J. Schott

Managing the World Economy: Fifty Years After Bretton Woods
Peter B. Kenen, editor

Measuring the Costs of Protection in Japan
Yoko Sazanami, Shujiro Urata, and Hiroki Kawai

The Uruguay Round: An Assessment
Jeffrey J. Schott

The Case for Trade: A Modern Reconsideration
J. David Richardson

The Future of the World Trading System
John Whalley, in collaboration with Colleen Hamilton

Estimating Equilibrium Exchange Rates
John Williamson, editor

For orders outside the US and Canada please contact:

Longman Group UK Ltd.
PO Box 88
Harlow, Essex CM 19 5SR
UK

Telephone Orders: 0279 623923
Fax: 0279 414130
Telex: 81259

Canadian customers can order from the Institute or from either:

RENOUF BOOKSTORE
1294 Algoma Road
Ottawa, Ontario K1B 3W8
Telephone: (613) 741-4333
Fax: (613) 741-5439

LA LIBERTÉ
3020 chemin Sainte-Foy
Quebec G1X 3V6
Telephone: (418) 658-3763
Fax: (800) 567-5449